A GUIDE TO MANUSCRIPTS RELATING TO AMERICA IN GREAT BRITAIN AND IRELAND

A GUIDE TO MANUSCRIPTS RELATING TO AMERICA IN GREAT BRITAIN AND IRELAND

Edited by

B. R. CRICK
B.Sc. (Econ.), Ph.D.

and

MIRIAM ALMAN
B.A., B.Com., F.S.A.L.A.

under the general supervision of

H. L. BEALES
M.A.

PUBLISHED FOR THE
BRITISH ASSOCIATION FOR AMERICAN STUDIES
BY THE OXFORD UNIVERSITY PRESS
1961

Oxford University Press, Amen House, London E.C.4

GLASGOW NEW YORK TORONTO MELBOURNE WELLINGTON
BOMBAY CALCUTTA MADRAS KARACHI KUALA LUMPUR
CAPE TOWN IBADAN NAIROBI ACCRA

PRINTED IN GREAT BRITAIN

I confess to you that I doubt the policy of giving such unrestricted access to American writers to our State Papers. . . . I can readily believe that it might serve powerfully to confirm an anti-English feeling even in the present day. Is it fair towards the descendants of those who favoured the mother country—and adhered to her cause—to disclose the communications which they have had with the British government? . . . Huskisson when he was Secretary of State gave facilities to another American writer to inspect the correspondence in the State Paper Office of which he soon found reason to repent.

PEEL TO ABERDEEN, *14 December 1829*
British Museum, Add. MSS. 40312, ff. 81–82

PREFACE

THE expansion of the teaching of American history and literature in British Universities since the Second World War, and the continued growth of interest by American scholars in the British antecedents of American civilization, have made some attempt to describe source materials timely and appropriate. A generous grant from the United States Information Service in Great Britain enabled the British Association for American Studies to launch a Survey of Sources for American Studies in Great Britain and Ireland, with the immediate purpose of doing what usefully could be done in a two-year period towards revealing the range and location of sources now available for the study of American history and literature.

The definition of the scope of the work and the control of expenditure were left entirely in the Association's hands, and the Association delegated to the Survey the carrying out of its bibliographical function. It was decided to pursue two objects, and no more. Firstly, to survey the adequacy of printed resources in British university and other great libraries to support the teaching of American history and literature; secondly, to publish a guide to historical manuscripts, in the widest sense—all those, as is explained in the Introduction, not covered by the guides which the Carnegie Institution, as a former patron of historical scholarship, had sponsored before the First World War. The first object was fulfilled by the publication of an almost unique national stocktaking, entitled 'A Survey of Library Resources in the United Kingdom for the Teaching of American History and Literature in the Universities', in the *Journal of Documentation*, vol. xiv, pp. 103–18, 1958. Members of the staff of the Survey also produced a 'Union List of American Newspapers in Great Britain and Ireland', which was issued in October 1958 as a special supplement to the *Bulletin of the British Association for American Studies*.

This present *Guide* to manuscripts is the fruit of two years' work of a research team that began as two people and ended with five working full time. The Survey has covered a great deal of ground and asked or searched in all the obvious quarters,

and many far from obvious. But the members of the Survey
would be the last to deny that much potentially interesting
Americana may yet come to light. It seems to be necessary to
point out that those who have worked on the compiling of this
list of manuscripts make no claim to finality or completeness.
Their aim has been severely pragmatic, and the whole work of
the Survey is, in a sense, something of a protest against that
perfectionist attitude to the listing of records that seemingly
never reaches a time when it is ripe to publish its results. The
Survey offers this *Guide* as likely to be of immediate utility to
a large number of scholars, and it looks to them for the information which will enable it to extend its utility by making
further locations of source materials known to it.

The working staff of the Survey were: Mr. B. R. Crick,
who was in general charge of the organization and administration of research and investigation; Mrs. Miriam Alman,
who joined the Survey when some of the field work was
completed to undertake the formidable task of compiling,
checking, and indexing; Mrs. Naomi Connelly, who undertook
from Manchester the heavy responsibility of the field work and
investigation in the north of England, and then assisted in the
editing; Mr. Dennis Porter, now of the Department of Western
Manuscripts at the Bodleian Library, who did much field work
in the south, including the bulk of the work in the British
Museum and the Bodleian Library; Mrs. Anne Daltrop, who
did most of the other bibliographical work on printed books
and newspapers, but who also worked on manuscripts in London,
Cambridge, and the West Country; and right from the
beginning of the Survey, Mrs. Anna Hackel was its administrative secretary, with special charge of the vital early stages of
circularizing for information. Also Mrs. Eilis Ellis of Dublin
worked for the Survey a month, completing work begun in
Dublin by Mr. Crick.

Such a work is necessarily the work of a team and, furthermore,
of a team which has spent at least a large part of its energies in
extracting reports from other people—scholars with first-hand
knowledge of a particular collection or, more often by far, the
librarian or archivist in whose custody the papers in question
are found. We are in the debt of an exceptionally large number
of people. Space does not allow us even to mention all those

perhaps who should be thanked, and permits us only to thank
in general terms some whose exceptional help must be recorded.

Firstly, and above all, must be mentioned the Registrar of
the National Register of Archives, Miss W. D. Coates: there
can be but few historical research workers in the country who
are not, in some way, indebted to her very great knowledge and
helpfulness. And in the same breath should be mentioned the
Secretary of the Historical Manuscripts Commission itself,
Mr. R. H. Ellis. The Librarian of H.M. Customs and Excise,
Mr. R. C. Jarvis, submitted an original and important report
on the entire body of Custom House Records. Mr. George
Reese, who was in charge of research in Great Britain for the
Virginia Colonial Records Project, generously and helpfully
exchanged information with us at every stage. It would be
invidious to single out names, but many officials of the British
Museum, the Public Record Office, the House of Lords Record
Office, the National Library of Wales, the National Library of
Scotland, the Public Record Office of Northern Ireland, the
Public Record Office and also the State Paper Office in Dublin,
and in particular the National Library of Ireland, gave us great
help. Dr. E. McLysaght, the Chairman of the Irish Manuscripts Commission, was an invaluable informant amid the
world of Dublin records.

Extracts from the Public Record Office Search Room Lists
and Indexes, in which Crown Copyright is reserved, are printed
by permission of the Controller of Her Majesty's Stationery
Office.

Additionally, we owe a considerable debt to the following
scholars: Mr. George Shepperson of the University of Edinburgh
who, together with Mr. A. C. Grant, a graduate student of his,
was mainly responsible for supervising the work in Scotland;
Dr. Peter Marshall of the University of Bristol who, together
with Mr. L. Billington, a graduate student of his, did much
work in Bristol and its neighbourhood; Mr. W. E. Minchinton
of the University College of Swansea contributed greatly by
his large knowledge of the ramifications of Bristol trade in the
eighteenth century; Professor Arthur Bestor of the University
of Illinois, when Harmsworth Visiting Professor of American
History at Oxford, gave invaluable advice in the early stages
of the Survey; Mr. Geoffrey Seed of the University of St.

Andrews submitted reports on local records, as did Mr. J. D. Hargreaves of the University of Aberdeen; Dr. J. R. Pole of University College London worked on the House of Lords Record Office; Professor W. Turrentine Jackson of the University of California gave us much information about sources of Scottish capital investment in the American West; Dr. J. A. Woods helped greatly with papers relating to Edmund Burke and furnished us with many clues about eighteenth-century papers generally; and also we thank, for a variety of help and advice that sometimes defies brief description: Dr. Dorothy Adler, Dr. Kenneth Bourne of the London School of Economics, Dr. W. H. Chaloner of the University of Manchester, Professor L'Abbé Chapeau of the University of Angers (for help with the papers of Cardinal Manning), Dr. Charlotte Erickson of the London School of Economics, Mr. P. d'A. Jones (for a report on the papers of Robert Owen), Professor Aubrey Land of the University of Nebraska, Mr. V. A. McClelland, Mr. Michael Millgate of the University of Leeds, Mr. C. Priestley of the University of Nottingham (for a report on the Newcastle Papers), Mr. Vivian Vale of the University of Southampton, Dr. Joseph Wall of Grinnell College, Iowa (for help with papers concerning Andrew Carnegie), and to Professor Esmond Wright of the University of Glasgow. Dr. E. R. R. Green of the University of Manchester gave great help in connexion with our Irish reports, particularly on Fenian papers.

But perhaps our greatest debt is to the archivists and custodians of papers, notably the county archivists, too numerous to mention all by name, without whose help and interest this work would have been impossible. Archivists, in whose archives the staff of the Survey worked, invariably went to great pains in suggesting material and subsequently checking and often expanding our reports; so our specific thanks to just those archivists who were able themselves to submit (quite beyond the call of duty) full reports of materials in their custody should simply stand as representative of our thanks to the whole profession: Mr. E. J. Davis (the County Archivist of Buckinghamshire), Miss Mary Finch (the Archivist of the Corporation of Chester), Miss Joan Sinar (the County Archivist of Devon), Miss Margaret Holmes (the County Archivist of Dorset), Mr. John S. Swan (formerly Borough Librarian of South Shields),

Mr. J. S. Dearden (of Bembridge School, Isle of Wight), Dr. Felix Hull (the County Archivist of Kent), Mrs. J. Varley (the Archivist to the Lincolnshire Archives office), the Secretary of Barclays Bank Ltd., Mr. R. Brooke-Caws (the Keeper of the Archives at Messrs. Coutts and Co.), Miss E. D. Mercer (the County Archivist of Middlesex), the Rev. W. B. H. Chandler and the Rev. H. G. B. Folland (of the Norwich Diocesan Committee for the Care of Books and Documents), Miss Mary C. Hill (the County Archivist of Shropshire), Mr. L. H. Barber (the Archivist of C. & J. Clark Ltd., Street, Somerset), Mr. M. P. Statham (the Archivist of the Bury St. Edmunds and West Suffolk Record Office), Mr. D. Charman (the Archivist of the Ipswich and East Suffolk Record Office, Mr. Francis W. Steer (the Archivist of the East Sussex Record Office), Mr. V. H. Woods (the City Librarian of Birmingham), Mr. M. G. Rathbone (the County Archivist of Wiltshire), and Mr. G. Slevin (the Chief Herald of Ireland).

But we must be forgiven for also mentioning by name some archivists in whose archives we found it convenient to compile our own reports, but whose knowledge and suggestions of what to look for extended far beyond their own papers: Mr. F. G. Emmison (the County Archivist of Essex), Dr. W. O. Hassall (of the Department of Western Manuscripts of the Bodleian Library), Mr. R. Sharpe France (the County Archivist of Lancashire), Mr. P. L. Hull (the County Archivist of Cornwall), Mr. Ivor P. Collis (the County Archivist of Somerset), Miss Joyce Godber (the County Archivist of Bedfordshire), Miss K. Lindsay-Macdougall (formerly of the National Maritime Museum, Greenwich), Mr. P. Hepworth (the City Librarian of Norwich), and Mrs. Georgiana Blois (formerly archivist to the late Countess Mountbatten of Burma).

The editors are, of course, solely responsible for the final form of each entry; none of our helpers or informants can be held to blame for the use made of their information. The goodwill of private owners in allowing us to work on and publish reports about their papers was heartening; we render specific acknowledgements in the text.

We should also thank the Committee of the British Association for American Studies, particularly Mr. Frank Thistlethwaite, then Chairman, who undertook the labour of reading the final

manuscript; the secretary, Professor Marcus Cunliffe, to whom
the scheme owes much of its conception; and the treasurer,
Dr. Dennis Welland. And also our gratitude is very great,
even on this purely manuscript side of the Survey, to our
advisory committee of University Librarians, Mr. K. W.
Humphreys (Birmingham), Mr. B. S. Page (Leeds), Mr. J. W.
Scott (University College, London), and Mr. G. Woledge
(British Library of Political and Economic Science). Lastly, we
must thank with great warmness Miss Margaret Haferd, the
Librarian of the American Library in London, who has helped
us constantly, ungrudgingly and enthusiastically; and also the
several incumbents of the post of U.S. Cultural Attaché in Great
Britain during the compiling and printing of this *Guide*.

Finally, the general Director of the Survey asks leave to make
a personal acknowledgement. Illness prevented him from giving
more than a fraction of the attention to the making of the *Guide*
that he had hoped to give. Inevitably a very heavy burden fell
on the shoulders of Mr. Crick, and Mrs. Hackel most ably
helped him to carry it. Mr. Crick's energy and devotion have
been the inspiring force in giving the *Guide* its wide coverage
and its practical value.

H. L. BEALES

CONTENTS

WALES AND MONMOUTHSHIRE

SCOTLAND

CONTENTS xxiii

INTRODUCTION

The Scope of the Work

THIS *Guide* seeks to draw attention to the location and to give a brief description of all manuscripts in Great Britain and Ireland relating to the history and literature of the American colonies and the United States which did not fall within the scope of the following volumes published by the Carnegie Institution of Washington, D.C.:[1]

Charles M. Andrews, *Guide to the Materials for American History, to 1783, in the Public Record Office of Great Britain*, 2 vols. (Washington, D.C., 1912, 1914).

Charles M. Andrews and Frances G. Davenport, *Guide to the Manuscript Materials for the History of the United States to 1783, in the British Museum, in Minor London Archives, and in the Libraries of Oxford and Cambridge* (Washington, D.C., 1908).

Charles O. Paullin and Frederic L. Paxson, *Guide to the Materials in London Archives for the History of the United States since 1783* (Washington, D.C., 1914).

'History' and 'literature' have both been construed in the widest possible sense to include all materials that could possibly be of significance to political, economic, social, and intellectual history, whether concerning American domestic and international affairs, or direct American influences in the British Isles.

Material *exclusively* West Indian has not been included.[2] However, Canadian material of even marginal relevance to the American colonies or the United States has generally been included down to the British North America Act of 1867.[3]

Relation to the Earlier Works

Early in the life of this Survey, when it was not clear how

[1] These are out of print but microfilms are obtainable from the Carnegie Institution of Washington, or replicas in xerography from Micro Methods Ltd., East Ardsley, Wakefield, Yorkshire.

[2] But see Herbert C. Bell, David W. Parker, and others, *Guide to British West Indian Archive Materials, in London and in the Islands, for the History of the United States* (Washington, D.C., 1926).

[3] Cutting off Canadian material at 1867 does not mean that, for example, Foreign Office and private papers relating to the subsequent Alaska Boundary question and the Newfoundland Fisheries disputes have been ignored; they have been included as part of British-American relations.

much ground we could cover within our resources, we decided
to begin work upon those archives and libraries untouched by
the above Guides, and also to search for material in private or
commercial hands. This last task was an entirely new departure.
It was not possible (except in the special case of Custom House
papers) to check systematically either the accuracy of or
omission from the earlier Guides. It did, however, prove
possible to include archives and libraries already covered by
these Guides and to report accessions subsequent to their
publication. Whether a revision of these earlier Guides (as
distinct from a reissue of them, for they have long been out of
print and are all but unobtainable) would be worth while is a
moot point. Certainly Andrews, Davenport, Paullin, and
Paxson may sometimes be found gliding too lightly for contemporary needs over records relating to economic and social
history; but there is no doubt that the broad basis of their
achievement is admirably sound. The scope and method of this
Guide imply more a compliment than a criticism of them: for
they gave so much detail that they found it impossible to
progress beyond the obvious major archives of London, Oxford,
and Cambridge.

It may be helpful at this point to name those archives and
libraries in which we have taken the work of Andrews, Andrews
and Davenport, and Paullin and Paxson as read and have
simply reported subsequent accessions:

BODLEIAN LIBRARY

BRITISH MUSEUM

CONGREGATIONAL LIBRARY

DR. WILLIAMS'S LIBRARY

ENGLISH PROVINCE ARCHIVES, SOCIETY OF JESUS[1]

LIBRARY OF THE SOCIETY OF FRIENDS

FULHAM PALACE (now transferred to Lambeth Palace)

HOUSE OF LORDS RECORD OFFICE

GUILDHALL (now part of the Corporation of London Records Office)

LAMBETH PALACE

MAGDALENE COLLEGE, CAMBRIDGE (Bibliotheca Pepysiana)

PUBLIC RECORD OFFICE

ROYAL SOCIETY

TRINITY HOUSE (but practically completely destroyed during the Second
World War)

[1] It has not been possible, in this case, due to the absence from England of the
archivist concerned, to establish whether or not there have been any available
accessions.

Some smaller London archives which do not appear in the above table, but which were included in the earlier Guides, are the subject of *complete* reports in this present volume (even though greater detail may sometimes be found in the earlier works and where this is so, we so state). These few exceptions are simply for the dogged reader's convenience: to cut down as far as possible the need to use two separate books to attack one archive.

Source and Style of Reports

Reports have been compiled from five sources:

(i) Professional archivists concerning materials in their custody.

(ii) The staff of the Survey and members of the British Association for American Studies.

(iii) Reports filed with the National Register of Archives. (When any entry in this *Guide* ends with the letters 'N.R.A.', it means that it is taken from such a report.)

(iv) The published reports of the Historical Manuscripts Commission. (Since many of the Historical Manuscripts Commission reports are now over fifty years old, we checked with the Secretary of the Commission to see whether the material still rested in the same place, or had been dispersed or deposited; but such papers were not normally directly examined by us.[1])

(v) Private individuals in response to appeals in the national and local press and in the publications or news-letters of local history societies, trade associations, and so forth. In this way we were able to collect and to photostat original emigrant letters, a collection which has been deposited in the British Library of Political and Economic Science, London School of Economics.

The present style of reporting has been, with a few exceptions, far less detailed than that of Andrews, since we deliberately set out to cover far more ground than he. Our field workers and informants were asked to give enough information for a scholar

[1] The American references up to the Ninth Appendix to the 15th Report of the Historical Manuscripts Commission were drawn together in the 'Guide to the Items Relating to American History in the Reports of the English Historical Manuscripts Commission and their Appendices', *Annual Report of the American Historical Association* for 1898, pp. 611–700 (Government Printing Office, Washington, D.C., 1899). We have included references to all these items and also to those in subsequent H.M.C. volumes.

to see whether or not papers relating to his special interest occurred in a collection, but not to try to do his work for him—either by assessing their significance or, still worse, by transcribing parts of them. Any form of listing is a calculation of what can be most usefully done for contemporary and conceivable future interests within the limits of time and money available. Therefore, individual papers within a collection have rarely been itemized; more often we have simply given general descriptions of the principal topics referred to in whole collections, or in groups of papers within collections. This, of course, has led to some unavoidable lack of balance; a closely related and highly important collection of fifty or sixty letters could be described in the same space as it takes to describe three trivial, separate, and unconnected letters found in one place; but the decision whether or not to include certain detail has always been taken in the form of considering whether it is worth indexing; this test has immediately cut out repetition of even important subject matters within the same section of the same report.

Further, there are inconsistencies in the level of detail given and in the criteria of selection adopted, simply because the reports have been compiled by many hands; but we have thought it more helpful to allow some unevenness, rather than strive for an identical final style which would inevitably have been at the expense of the more detailed reports. For example, certain classes of dormant printed materials have occasionally been included; while maps were not sought after, such rare maps as have crept in have been left; strictly genealogical materials, however, have been resolutely excluded.

However, the most obvious and important unevenness is to be found in our treatment of the Public Record Office. This has been necessarily superficial—in the quite literal sense that only very rarely did we go beneath the surface of the large number of departmental lists and calendars down to the papers themselves. To have done so would have been an enterprise probably as large as this again in time and pages—as it were, Burke's 'great Serbonian bog into which whole armies have sunk'. Our original objective and priority of work was, firstly, the largely uncharted field outside London; and only secondly London outside the Public Record Office, but including the British Museum. Our treating of the Public Record Office at all must be regarded as somewhat of an act of supererogation —though doubtless a limited commission is more useful than outright omission. Indeed, throughout *we have striven, in emulation of the best of archivists, to put contemporary helpfulness before the chimeras of the complete description and of an absolute consistency.* But if funds were ever available, a revised edition of the Carnegie Guides to the Americana in the Public Record Office, brought up to date with their level of detail, would certainly be a very great boon to scholars.

It is not always easy to state precisely in each very different case how much reliance has been placed on existing catalogues and lists, and how much on actual examination of the papers; but where existing catalogues and lists have been published, the reference has been given; and where, in the case of a very large collection without any reliable catalogue or list, a mere sample was made of the papers, we have always said so. Wherever possible, material has been arranged in chronological order; but in the larger archives we have followed the arrangement of the archives' own finding lists. All dates have been rendered in the style of the document or list from which they were taken. All place names have been indexed, as have all proper names, except those of emigrants and transported felons or indentured apprentices. And outside the great and more obvious archives, we have tried to cite all published articles or books that have made substantial use of a particular collection, though it would be misleading to view this form of annotation as definitive. Similarly, for the convenience of American scholars, we have tried to state whether items have been microfilmed for an American library; but precise information on this topic is often surprisingly difficult to discover.[1]

[1] Relatively few British archives have, in fact, been in the habit of keeping a readily available list showing which of their papers have been reproduced, for whom, and where they are. We felt it too large a task to try to gain this information from the larger American libraries. However, though somewhat out of date, it is worth mentioning Grace Gardner Griffin's *Guide to Manuscripts Relating to American History in British Depositories Reproduced for the Division of Manuscripts of the Library of Congress* (Washington, D.C., Library of Congress, 1946); also Lester K. Born, compiler, *British Manuscripts Project: a Checklist of the Microfilms Prepared in England and Wales for the American Council of Learned Societies, 1941–1945* (Washington, D.C., Library of Congress, Photoduplication Service, 1955). Scholars will of course note the 'Guide to Photographed Historical Material in Canada and the United States' being prepared by Richard W. Hale, Jr., for the Committee on Documentary Reproduction of the American Historical Association.

We did not feel able to ascertain whether individual items in private possession, but relating to affairs of State, were unique or copies of, or copied in, official papers in the Public Record Office. To have been able to say confidently whether copies exist in the Public Record Office or elsewhere would have been a task so large as to render impossible, within the resources available, the comprehensive scope and range of this volume. However, in a few cases where papers have not been used before for scholarly purposes, or used very little, and where access to them is not likely to be easy, we have given more detail than usual, so that a specialist may readily check for himself their relation to papers in the Public Record Office or elsewhere.

Reports supplied by professional archivists, or compiled by the Survey itself from an archive where there is an official archivist or custodian, were in all cases submitted to that official for correction before the final manuscript of this report was prepared in 1958, and again in proof in 1960 (when certain corrections and changes of location were made, though it was not possible to incorporate addenda).

Custom House Papers

There is one important exception to the general rule that we complement and do not incorporate the earlier work of the Carnegie Guides, namely, Custom House Papers. This is also an exception to the otherwise entirely geographical arrangement of this *Guide*.

It is particularly to be noted, with reference to the Public Records Act (1958) secc. 3 & 4, that the place of final deposit of some of these records has not, at the time of writing, yet been decided. Some of the papers are physically located in customs offices in ports throughout the United Kingdom; some are in the Public Record Office, and some are in the Library of H.M. Customs and Excise, but it seemed most helpful for ease of comprehension to treat these papers as if they were in the last-named Library (see pp. 188–207)—and this is consistent with the fact that Customs papers, whether held in the Customs headquarters or in the outports, although legally in the custody of the Lord Chancellor, are at present administratively the responsibility of the Librarian of the Board of Customs and Excise.

Andrews also treated them as one entry, but as part of the Public Record Office; and he did not make clear that many of the papers he described were in fact located elsewhere. However, in view of the fact that even Andrews appears at times to have lost his way amid the famously complicated paths of these records, we were very fortunate that the Librarian of H.M. Customs consented to rewrite completely Andrews's introduction, and to revise thoroughly his detailed entries. The present report, then, incorporates, corrects, and adds to Andrews's account of Custom House Papers, and thus stands complete in itself.

Parish, Poor Law, and Quarter Sessions Records

Before the Poor Law of 1834, and in some districts for some years afterwards, parish records may contain references to assisted emigration. The minutes of the Boards of Guardians of the Poor Law Unions after 1834 will also contain occasional references, many of which are simply copies of correspondence conducted with the Poor Law Commissioners at Somerset House, now in the Public Record Office (see p. 281).

These references are so repetitious in character and few and scattered in extent that it was not thought worth while to search systematically parish records even in likely areas, let alone to search all records known. As the index will reveal, some examples have been included by our staff (notably in Norfolk); and where county archivists or others have included them as part of a longer report, we have not excluded them.

Quarter Sessions records have been treated in the same manner.[1] Until 1776 they contain occasional references to sentences of transportation to the colonies, and more rarely the correspondence between the officers of the court and a merchant or factor concerning the transportation bonds. Many Quarter Sessions records are in print.[2]

[1] The exceptionally detailed report for the Middlesex County Record Office (pp. 346–9) is a good example of these two huge classes of records.

[2] For the general scope of English local records, on the above points and generally, see especially: A. Hamilton Thompson, *Parish History and Records*, 1926, and *A Short Bibliography of Local History*, 1928 (Historical Association Leaflets Nos. 66 and 72); F. G. Emmison and I. Gray, *County Records*, 1948 (Historical Association Pamphlet No. S. 3); W. E. Tate, *The Parish Chest: a Study of the Records of Parochial Administration in England*, 2nd ed. (Cambridge, 1951); and L. J. Redstone and F. W. Steer, eds., *Local Records: Their Nature and Care* (London, 1953).

Business Records

Though we have appealed in trade papers and made a great many varied approaches to firms, banks, and investment trusts, the number of new finds, though including some interesting items, is disappointing. Business records contributed heavily to the war-time salvage drive; there was much quite indiscriminate pulping; and actual war damage, particularly in Liverpool, took a heavy toll. In the best of times, some business firms tend to destroy their old records far too casually. Some archivists and historians have in the past neglected economic records; and the consequences of past neglect take even longer to repair in an archive than in a library. Many firms, especially banks, appear to have feared the inconvenience and publicity which might have arisen from answering an inquiry as general as we had to make. We know of some banks, for instance, who are willing to help specific inquirers about specific subjects, but who cannot open whole classes of their records to inspection nor, in several cases, even allow the fact that they possess records at all to be mentioned here. A major obstacle is often a purely physical one: business firms have no accommodation for the scholarly reader. The situation regarding business records may improve in the coming years through the activities of the Business Archives Council (see below); and there are signs that the once common assumption that records less than a hundred years old are not 'history' is rapidly giving way to growing interest among local and amateur historians in the local effects of Victorian industrialism. The growing use of microfilm also holds out hope of more economical retention and storage of business records.

Access to Records

The mention of papers in this volume does not necessarily imply that they are available for inspection. It must be emphasized that papers in private possession are private property. Most owners are amazingly co-operative considering the inconvenience that permission for a scholarly visitation can put them to; from our experience their continued helpfulness depends upon scholars approaching owners without appearing to assume a right to see papers, explaining to them precisely why their papers may be relevant, asking permission before quoting from the papers in print (even apart from the legal implications), and informing the owners when and where such published work occurs: this last point helps to make private individuals informed custodians of their own records

A smaller practical adage, which experience has impressed upon us, is the advisability of writing well in advance to the archivist when wanting to inspect papers in almost all local record offices. Record officers will often, when circumstances permit, go to great pains to search out and prepare papers for a wandering scholar when given good warning. They are among the most conscientious and hard-worked of public servants, and among the most helpful—when approached with a proper regard for the difficulties of their high vocation.

Record Organizations

It may be helpful to visiting scholars to say something about official and unofficial record bodies and what these can do to help them.

The HISTORICAL MANUSCRIPTS COMMISSION has published, since 1869, several hundred printed reports on manuscript collections in Great Britain, mostly of the eighteenth century or earlier.[1] Scholars wishing to consult the original documents, many of which have been moved from their original homes, should apply to the Secretary, Historical Manuscripts Commission, Quality House, Quality Court, Chancery Lane, London, W.C.2.

The NATIONAL REGISTER OF ARCHIVES, founded in 1945 as a branch of the Historical Manuscripts Commission and also located at the same address, maintains a large and increasing collection of typescript reports on privately owned manuscript collections all over the country. The National Register of Archives advises on the care, preservation, and deposit of manuscripts in danger of destruction, and does some original reporting itself, and through its voluntary county committees. The reports are covered by full indexes of personal names, place names, and owners of manuscripts, and a subject index is also being compiled. These indexes and reports may be inspected on application to the Registrar, National Register of Archives, who

[1] *Reports of the Royal Commission on Historical Manuscripts, Revised to 31 August 1956* (London, H.M.S.O., 1956). (Government publications sectional list no. 17.)

welcomes serious scholars and can often direct them to the sources they seek. As already stated, all our entries which end 'N.R.A.' originate from reports in the office of the National Register; to view such materials, when they are in private hands, application should always be made through the Registrar, *never* direct to the owners. Since 1955 the National Register has issued yearly a *List of Accessions to Repositories*, and also, since 1948, a *Bulletin* describing important manuscript collections already deposited.[1]

The BRITISH RECORDS ASSOCIATION, the Charterhouse, London, E.C.1, is an unofficial but influential body, membership of which is open to all persons and institutions interested in the preservation and use of archive material. The journal *Archives* is published twice yearly and contains *inter alia* articles on newly discovered collections, and a very useful continuing series on 'Local Archives of Great Britain'. Some of the occasional publications are very useful to historical scholars, for instance the *Handlist of Record Publications* (1951) and the *List of Record Repositories in Great Britain* (1956) (the latter gives information about times of opening, facilities, &c.). The British Records Association has an active Records Preservation Section which at present is giving particular attention to London solicitors' offices.

The SOCIETY OF ARCHIVISTS is a professional body whose membership is confined to practising archivists. Historical scholars will, however, find in its *Journal* (published twice yearly) useful articles upon particular manuscript collections.

The BUSINESS ARCHIVES COUNCIL, 9 King's Bench Walk, London, E.C.4, has a national central committee of archivists, scholars, and business men, and is building up a system of regional committees. It aims to discover business records, arrange for their preservation, and eventually to establish a register of them. A bibliography of business histories has been published by the Council.[2] The Council has recently begun to work in close conjunction with the British Records Association and the National Register of Archives.

The NATIONAL REGISTER OF ARCHIVES (SCOTLAND), H.M.

---

[1] *Bulletin*, No. 7, pp. 3–8, Winter 1955, includes an informative account of the scope and progress of the N.R.A. and its county committees.

[2] See Business Archives Council, *Ninth Report of the Committee*, pp. 7–17 (London, 1954). These histories are, however, of varying utility.

General Register House, Edinburgh 2, fulfils a similar function to that of its namesake in London. Reports of the inspections it initiates and some photostat copies of inventories are preserved in the Scottish Record Office. Brief copies of these reports are sent to the National Register of Archives in London and also to the Library of Congress. There is, as yet, no index to the collections in the Scottish Register.

The PUBLIC RECORD OFFICE OF NORTHERN IRELAND, Law Courts Buildings, May Street, Belfast, as well as being a repository of State Papers, also searches for, acquires or copies, and lists historical manuscripts in private hands.

The IRISH MANUSCRIPTS COMMISSION, 73 Merrion Square, Dublin, will help scholars trying to find particular manuscripts of Irish interest not in the National Library of Ireland, as well as fulfilling its main function of publishing Irish historical and literary records.[1] It has an Inspector of Manuscripts whose duty is to acquire or to copy manuscripts in private hands for the National Library of Ireland, Dublin. The National Library itself pursues a vigorous acquisition policy respecting manuscripts and is currently engaged on a huge undertaking to index all materials, printed and manuscript, in Ireland or elsewhere, relating to Irish history.

Though the INSTITUTE OF HISTORICAL RESEARCH, Malet Street, London, W.C.1, is not a record office, visiting scholars will find that it possesses on open shelves, thus far more conveniently than the British Museum, a very good collection of published catalogues, lists, and guides to British records, and many unpublished lists. It also contains the best collection of printed American historical documents and similar source books in Britain and, in the American Bibliography Room, most American archive publications.

It might also be helpful to add a word about the VIRGINIA COLONIAL RECORDS PROJECT since our two tasks have overlapped. Their work in British archives has naturally been far more detailed than ours; indeed, it can be assumed, since we have regularly exchanged information with each other, that colonial Virginian references in all large collections have been not merely listed in detail by them, but have also been microfilmed.

---

[1] See Irish Manuscripts Commission, *Catalogue of Publications Issued and in Preparation, 1928–1957* (Dublin, Stationery Office, 1957).

We do, however, so state each time this helpful duplication occurs. Their reports act as an index to the microfilms being placed in the Virginia State Library, Richmond, Va.[1]

As the Preface has already made clear, we claim no more for this work than that it may be of some substantial use in opening up the vast range of papers outside the major archives, as well as completing earlier work in these great archives. Much important material is still to be found; if in some areas or topics we have only been able to uncover enough to reveal larger possibilities beyond, we are well satisfied for the needs of the present to have done just that. We hope that scholars, custodians, and owners will continue to send corrections, additions, and notes on new discoveries to the editors, care of the British Association for American Studies, 13 Endsleigh Street, London, W.C.1. It would be rash to anticipate a second edition but, if interest warrants, some arrangement at least will be made for issuing occasional lists of addenda in the *Bulletin* of the Association.

B. R. C.

[1] For an account of the project see J. P. Boyd, 'A New Guide to the Indispensable Sources of Virginia History', *William and Mary Quarterly*, 3rd series, vol. xv, pp. 3–13, 1958. Copies of the reports, it is hoped, will be available in major British libraries.

London School of Economics and Political Science

July 1959

ENGLAND

BEDFORDSHIRE

Bedfordshire Record Office,[1] Shire Hall, BEDFORD

STUART PAPERS. Pennsylvania papers. *c.* 200 documents, 2 volumes and 2 maps. 1673–1787.

The Stuarts are descended from the Earls of Bute, and are connected by marriage with the descendants of William Penn.

Pennsylvania material includes: Maps of 'Neobelgium', *c.* 1673 (printed); and Maryland, 1742. Grants of land by William Penn, 1681–1708 (127 documents). Six miscellaneous deeds, 1692–1786. Legal code, 1704–5; and Charter of Liberties, a 1717 copy of the Charter of 1701 (1 volume). Mortgages on province, 1708–41 (17 documents). Two Acts of Assembly, 1717–18, 1759. Papers on boundary disputes with Maryland, 1732–80; and unlawful settlement in Pennsylvania by men of Connecticut, 1754–74 (14 documents). Depositions as to interference in trade by Virginians, 1774. Minutes of Assembly, 1787 (printed volume). List of American manuscripts, 1674–1737, in this collection, made *c.* 1740.

CARTERET PAPERS. 1 document. 1690.

Release of 1690 includes a copy of the will of Sir George Carteret (d. 1680), who bequeathed plantations in New Jersey.

LUCAS PAPERS (Deeds of Manor of Staysmore). 3 documents. 1773–86.

Relate to the disposal of property at Carlton, Beds., by Thomas Palmer, who emigrated and became a merchant in Philadelphia.

ARPIN, EDWARD. Diary (23 pages), 1800–30.

Parish clerk of Felmersham, Beds. Mentions the departure of thirty-nine men, women, and children of the parish for Boston in 1829.

WHITBREAD PAPERS. *c.* 70 letters, 9 printed items. 1810–14.

One file only, inscribed 'American affairs', was available for inspection. (The remainder of this large collection has since been deposited in the Record Office.) It contains letters and printed items addressed to Samuel Whitbread (1764–1815), M.P. Correspondents include:

Barclay, George. Four letters, 6–12 Feb. 1812, concerned with the capture of an American frigate the *Dolly* by the French.

Denham, J. D. Hull, 9 Feb. 1813. Recently in New York, discusses, *inter*

---

[1] *Guide to the Bedfordshire Record Office* (Bedford, 1957).

alia, distress of British merchants, impressment, British sailors willingly serving in United States ships; character of Madison and of Clinton.

Dickins, Asbury. American Consular Office, London, 8 Aug. 1812, sending a copy of a message from his kinsman, Willis Alston, United States Congressman for North Carolina, relating to encouragement of Indians by British agents.

Macdonald, Thomas. 1 May 1811, describing the difficulties of his task as First Commissioner for American Claims, and enclosing printed orders of the Board, &c.

Mullett, Thomas. Eighteen letters, London, June 1810–May 1813. Arranges introductions between Whitbread and Americans in London, including William Pinkney; gives advice and encouragement to Whitbread's attacks on government policy towards America, sending him newspapers, letters, and abstracts, which he has received from America, for Whitbread's use in the House of Commons.

White, Campbell P. Belfast, 3 Dec. 1812, sending a document showing the number of American vessels captured by Britain and France.

Wilberforce, W. 29 Feb. 1812, discussing speeches on American affairs.

Witz, T. L. New York, 22 June 1811, opposing proposals for peace with France.

Other correspondents to submit opinions on American disputes, 1812–14, include:

Britannicus, J. Brown, J. Grubb, Jorgen Jorgensen, J. M., Ab. Mann, John Mansfield, Lord Milton, Peter Payne, George Ponsonby, Thos. Potts, William Roscoe, Ralph Stevenson, Thomas Thornely.

Also printed pamphlets and press cuttings relating to American affairs.

PARISH RECORDS.

(*a*) Hockliffe. Overseers' accounts, 1828–38, include an item of £10 for payment of the passage of an emigrant to America in 1833.

(*b*) Oakley. Miscellaneous papers, 1819–44, include accounts of expenses for parishioners who emigrated to America in 1831, with names of emigrants and shippers' receipts.

QUARTER SESSIONS RECORDS.

Include transportation bonds of criminals to America, 1731, 1734.

Duke of Bedford, WOBURN ABBEY

BEDFORD PAPERS. 1593–1765.

(*a*) 'An abstract of the lawes of Newe England', n.d. [Imperfect].[1]

(*b*) 'A discourse upon our forraigne plantations . . . and the grounds of erecting a West India company', n.d.[2]

[1] H.M.C. ii, p. 3 [250].   [2] Ibid., p. 4 [264].

(c) 'Travills, adventures, and observations of Captaine John Smith, in Europe, Asia, Africa, and America, 1593–1629, etc.'[1]

(d) Letter, 6 Feb. 1734, from Thos. E—, of W—, includes 'considerations relating to the present condition of the colonies'.[2]

(e) 'Some observations on the right of the Crown of Great Britain to the North-west continent of America, with copies of Mons. Geraldine's letter, 1736, to the trustees for Georgia, and the answer of the Indian nations in Georgia in alliance with Great Britain (in Mr. Martyn's of Apr. 7, 1748).'[3]

(f) 'Peace of 1763. Vol. 1 (March 1761–August 1762). [Copied by Mr. Wiffen?] Peace of Paris. (March 1761–June 1763.) (Copies.) 2 vols.'[4]

(g) List of papers, 1764–5, relating to the affairs of the North American colonies; in the handwriting of John, 4th Duke of Bedford.[5]

BERKSHIRE

A. Godsal, Esq., Estate Office, HAINES HILL, Twyford

GARTH, CHARLES (c. 1734–84). Letter-books (copies). 1762–74.

Charles Garth, M.P. for Devizes; agent for South Carolina in Great Britain 1762–75, and for a short time also for Georgia and Maryland. A long article[6] by Sir Lewis Namier describes these letter-books and his career.

Berkshire Record Office,[7] Shire Hall, READING

DOWNSHIRE PAPERS. 1609–1773.

Largely the papers of William Trumbull (d. 1635), British Minister at Brussels 1609–25; and his grandson, Sir William Trumbull (1639–1716), M.P., diplomat, and Secretary of State. (Letters unless otherwise stated.)

[1] Ibid., p. 4 [259].
[2] Ibid., p. 3 [207].
[3] Ibid., p. 3 [208].
[4] Ibid., p. 2 [80] and [81].
[5] Ibid., p. 2 [84].
[6] 'Charles Garth and his Connexions' and 'Charles Garth, Agent for South Carolina', English Historical Review, vol. liv, pp. 443–70, and 632–52, 1939.
[7] Guide to the Berkshire Record Office (Reading, 1952).

(*a*) 9 Nov. 1609, from John More to William Trumbull, mentions the scattering of Sir Thomas Gates's ships sailing for Virginia.[1]

(*b*) 30 Nov. 1609, from J. Beaulieu to Trumbull, states that all by Gates's vessel have arrived safely, and adds that there is dissension among the settlers 'by reason of their minister being somewhat of a Puritan' and antagonizing the High Church party.[2]

(*c*) 1611–13, to Trumbull, on conditions in Virginia, the lottery, and Spanish opposition to English settlement there. Correspondents include Thomas Albery; Jean Beaulieu; Samuel Calvert; Francis Cottington, agent in Spain; Sir John Digby, Ambassador to Spain; Sir Thomas Edmondes, Ambassador to France; Maurice, Landgrave of Hesse Cassel; John More; John Wither; and John Woodall.

(*d*) Eight letters, 1615–24, to Trumbull, about the Virginia settlement, the attacks upon it by the savages, and its products.

(*e*) Agreement, 9 Apr. 1622, between Sir William Alexander, Sir Robert Mackeleaneane and John Mason of London, and Thomas Hopkins of Rotherhithe, mariner, that the last-named shall take a ship to Virginia or the northern parts of New England in return for a certain sum.

(*f*) Petition, *c.* 1630, of George Rookes, a London merchant, and John Barnabee, a Virginia planter, to trade, and to plant certain commodities and to transport these to His Majesty's dominions. Letter, 30 Sept. 1630, from the Privy Council to the Council and Governor of Virginia, ordering them to allow this. Corn, woad, rapeseed, flax, and hemp are specifically mentioned as allowed to be planted, and tobacco forbidden.

(*g*) Deed of sale, 19 Feb. 1663, of a moiety in Maryland and New England by Henry Alexander, 4th Earl of Stirling, to Lord Berkeley.

(*h*) 12 June 1686, from Don Pedro Ronquillo, Spanish Ambassador in London, to Sir William Trumbull, asking for information about an alleged treaty of commerce between France and the North American colonies.[3]

(*i*) Newsletter, 15 May 1688, to Messrs. Goodman & Martin states, 'A patent is past the seals and a great stock raised for carrying on the copper mines in New England, which are better than those of Denmark or Sweden.'[4]

(*j*) Manuscript newsletter, 1 Aug. 1695, about the arrival of ships from Virginia.

(*k*) 'A short account of the English plantations in America' (endorsed by Sir William Trumbull, *c.* 1695) (volume of 19 pages). Deals with situation, government and trade of Massachusetts Bay, New York, New Hampshire, Virginia, Maryland, New Jersey, Pennsylvania, Delaware, and Carolina.

---

[1] Transcript, H.M.C. Downshire MSS. ii [75], p. 126. (Listed as held by the Marquess of Downshire, Easthampstead Park, Berkshire.) All Virginia material has been microfilmed by the Virginia Colonial Records Project.

[2] Transcript, ibid. ii, p. 195.   [3] Transcript, ibid. i (i), pp. 181–2.

[4] Transcript, ibid., p. 292.

(*l*) 17 Feb. 1696, from Peter Coode, William Glynn, and Thomas Malby, to Sir William Trumbull, mentions Americans indulging in piracy on the coast of Arabia.[1]

(*m*) Grant of an annuity, 19 Dec. 1696, to Henry Alexander, 5th Earl of Stirling, in return for his relinquishing to the Crown his rights in New York 'and any part thereof in America'.

(*n*) Warminghurst, 4–11 Jan. 1697, from William Penn to Sir William Trumbull, complaining of the usurpation of jurisdiction in the colonies by the Court of Admiralty.[2]

(*o*) 13 June 1709, from John Bartlett to Sir William Trumbull, describing preparations for an expedition against Canada, and the willingness of the New Englanders and Indians to take part.[3]

(*p*) Petition, n.d., of Edward, Lord Cornbury, to be granted a patent of the monopoly of coining pence and groats in the American colonies.

(*q*) 'Present state of the British colonies in America', 1773 (large volume). Contains reports from the governors of some of the colonies—Massachusetts Bay, New Hampshire, Connecticut, New York, New Jersey, Pennsylvania, Virginia, Georgia, and West Florida—in reply to questions put by Lord Dartmouth, Secretary of State for the Colonies. The replies deal with such matters as situation, size, rivers, harbours, constitution, trade, manufactures, smuggling, produce, mines, inhabitants, militia, forts, Indians, revenue, expenses, establishments, and valuation.

HARTLEY RUSSELL PAPERS. 1689–*c*. 1785.

(*a*) Copy of Virginia petition, 20 May 1689, complaining of the 'oppression practiced by the late Governor'.

(*b*) Papers connected with David Hartley, the younger (1732–1813), M.P., and relating especially to peace negotiations with the Americans, 1777–83. These include draft propositions for averting war, and for making peace after the war had broken out; drafts of the preliminaries of peace, 1782; and instructions to the Commissioners. There are a number of unsigned, undated notes by Hartley, one of which argues the American case against Britain (as does a draft speech, ? for delivery in the House of Commons), and another which describes the benefit to both countries of maintaining the connexion between them. There is also an unaddressed, unsigned copy letter, 11 Aug. 1778, from Hartley to Franklin, about an exchange of prisoners at Calais, and the rejection by Congress of the peace feelers of 1777. (A copy of Congress's resolution of rejection is among the papers.) The subject of American prisoners of war is frequently referred to in these papers. There are several supporting documents on American affairs, mostly copies of letters or of well-known State Papers, some dating back to the Stamp Act controversy.

[1] Transcript, ibid. i(ii), p. 622.   [2] Transcript, ibid., pp. 727–8.
[3] Transcript, ibid., p. 877.

(c) Pamphlets, printed speeches, and resolutions about events just before, during, and immediately after the War of Independence, including 'Committee upon the American Trade Bill', 1783, and the 'Case of the American Loyalists', n.d.

BELSON PAPERS. 1 document. 1789.

Address, 1789, from the Philadelphia Yearly Meeting of Friends to George Washington, extending good wishes for the success of his administration and his personal happiness, with his reply.[1]

READING AND WITNEY MONTHLY MEETINGS OF THE SOCIETY OF FRIENDS.

The minutes of these Monthly Meetings and their constituent earlier meetings include references to Quaker emigrants from the later part of the seventeenth century.

PARISH RECORDS.

(a) Aston Tirrold. Vestry Minutes (1 volume). Resolution of 1852 directs the churchwardens and overseers to borrow £55 for defraying the emigration expenses of poor persons.

(b) Moulsford. Register of baptisms and burials, 1772–1812 (1 volume), contains only 19 pages of entries; the rest of the volume consisting of a diary, 1846–1909, kept by successive incumbents and referring to events of local and national interest. The entry for 24 Apr. 1859 mentions two labourers, John Ring and David Horne, as having sailed for New York. A note is added later, 'N.B., they came back at Christmas greatly disgusted.'

(c) Reading, St. Mary. Vestry Minutes, 1829–68 (1 volume). Resolution of 1832 that 'the question of advancing money to persons emigrating to America be left to the discretion of the parish officers'.

(d) Warfield. Churchwardens' accounts, 1586–1840 (2 volumes). An entry for 1617 'layd out of the churchboxe, for Virginia the XIIth January 5 shills.'.

The Royal Archives, Round Tower, WINDSOR CASTLE, Windsor

The Royal Archives contain the personal papers of the Royal Family. They are not open for inspection. The chief papers concerning North America have, however, been published in the following works:

S. M. Pargellis, ed., *Military Affairs in Northern America, 1748–1765. Selected Documents from the Cumberland Papers in Windsor Castle* (London and New York, 1936).

[1] See *Writings of George Washington*, ed. by John C. Fitzpatrick, vol. xxx, p. 416 (Washington, D.C., 1939).

Sir John Fortescue, ed., *The Correspondence of King George the Third from 1760 to December 1783*, 6 vols. (London, 1927–8).

Sir Lewis Namier, *Additions and Corrections to Sir John Fortescue's Edition* . . . (Manchester, 1937).

Arthur Aspinall, ed., *Letters of King George IV, 1812–1830*, 3 vols. (Cambridge, 1938).

A. C. Benson and others, eds., *Letters of Queen Victoria*, 9 vols. (London, 1907–32). (Vols. 1–3 ed. by A. C. Benson and Viscount Esher; vols. 3–9 by G. E. Buckle.)

Also the following secondary sources based on researches at Windsor Castle throw light on some American connexions in the Royal Archives:

Sir Evan E. Charteris, *William Augustus, Duke of Cumberland, His Early Life and Times, 1721–1748* (London, 1913).

——, *William Augustus, Duke of Cumberland, and the Seven Years War* (London, 1925).

M. S. Guttmacher, *America's Last King; an Interpretation of the Madness of George III* (New York, 1941).

Sir Theodore Martin, *The Life of His Royal Highness the Prince Consort*, 5 vols. (London, 1875–80).

Franklin Parker, *George Peabody, 1795–1869, Founder of Modern Philanthropy* (Nashville, Tenn., 1955).

Bradford Perkins, 'George Canning, Great Britain and the United States, 1807–1809', *American Historical Review*, vol. lxiii, pp. 1–22, 1957.

Charles M. Stotz, *The Story of Fort Ligonier* (Ligonier, Pa., 1954).

A volume of letters of John Jay was presented to King Edward VII when he visited the United States as Prince of Wales in 1860, and is in the Royal Library; a microfilm of this was, however, given to the Library of Congress in 1958. A microfilm of two boxes of the papers of William Augustus, Duke of Cumberland, was also presented to the Library of Congress at the same time.

BUCKINGHAMSHIRE

Buckinghamshire Record Office, County Hall, AYLESBURY

TREVOR PAPERS.[1] 5 letters. 1738–40.

Correspondence of Robert Hampden-Trevor, 1st Viscount Hampden and 4th Baron Trevor (1706–83), Minister at The Hague 1739–46.

[1] We are grateful to the Earl of Buckinghamshire for permission to make this report.

(*a*) Horatio [or Horace] Walpole to Robert Trevor. Three letters, 31 Mar., 13 June, and 24 Oct. 1738, on American commerce and navigation, and disputes with Spain concerning them; one letter, 3 Oct. 1740, partly about the French in America.[1]

(*b*) M. de Harlé to Robert Trevor, 25 Mar. 1740 (in French). M. de Harlé, a French Protestant who has left France on account of his religion and is living in Holland, states his desire to go to Virginia to examine the possibility of setting up the manufacture of linen and thread, for the production of the raw materials for which the soil of Holland is not suitable.[2]

HOWARD-VYSE DEPOSIT. 1775–7.

This collection includes some letters and reports, 1775 and 1777, sent from Richard Reeve of Boston to Sir George Howard, M.P., all describing the opening months of the War of Independence.

(*a*) Covering note, 16 May 1775, enclosing copy of a letter written by Reeve to one of the Secretaries of the Treasury. This enclosure, 14 May 1775, with additions, 16 May, gives details of the situation in Boston since the 'skirmish which happened on the 19th [April], between H.M. troops and the rebels in the neighbourhood of this town' (Lexington), and the continued threat of attack by the rebels—interception of letter giving details of plan for such attack to be made on 24 Apr.—Situation in Rhode Island and New York—no communication by land with Philadelphia and the Southern colonies. Rebels' plan is for independence—their forces growing steadily and being supplied with provisions by the country people who receive receipts for what they bring 'which are to be paid for by the Province on some future day'.—'It is certain that Great Britain must now subdue the colonies by force of arms, or relinquish her authority over them, for all appearance of accommodation appears to be now at an end.'—Lord Dunmore's threat to declare the Negroes free at Williamsburg, S.C. (Enclosed is a printed sheet with resolutions of the Provincial Congress at Watertown, Mass., 5 May 1775, to disobey all orders and proclamations, &c., of General Gage.)

(*b*) Letter, 24 June 1775, compares (very favourably) General Howe with General Gage. Intransigence of people in Northern colonies.
     Report, 22 June 1775. Battle of Bunker Hill, 17 June, described in detail. (A list of the officers killed and wounded in this action is enclosed.)—Brief reference to delegates from Southern provinces at General Congress who 'are strenuous and very much in earnest for accepting the proposals of Parliament'.

(*c*) Letter, 25 July 1775, sending report on the subject of 'American matters' and the state of the army. Has not seen General Howe for some time, but he is very well 'commanding a corps upon Bunckers Hill'.

---

[1] Transcripts, H.M.C. xiv (ix), pp. 15, 18, 24, and 56. (Listed as held by the Earl of Buckinghamshire.)   [2] Synopsis, ibid., p. 44.

Report, 25 July 1775. 'The whole system of American politics is now fully disclosed, the Continental Congress has usurped the sovereign power over the colonies. . . .' In order to subdue the colonists 'it is not supposed that there is any necessity for standing upon punctilios with rebels in arms, might it not therefore be a proper measure to emancipate and arm the Negroes in the Southern colonies and to encourage the warlike Indian nations bordering upon them to ravage and lay waste the country?' Boston now 'blockaded completely by the rebels without'. Rebel bombardment of Roxbury, Mass.; their invasion, in long-boats, of Long Island; and their burning of the lighthouse on one of the Brewster Islands. (Enclosed is a manuscript order of battle of the Army at Boston on 16 July 1775.)

(*d*) Letter, 19 Aug. 1775, enclosing 'further intelligence of the transactions in this country'.

Report, 14 Aug. 1775. Troops' brief attack on rebels, on night of 30 July, near Roxbury, Mass. Loss of some forty marines and carpenters, to the rebels, at the lighthouse which they were repairing. Loss of the armed schooner *Diligence*. Other shipping news, &c. An addition of 16 Aug. 1775 reports the return of the transports from the southward with provisions.

(*e*) Letter, 1 Dec. 1775, enclosing further report of state of affairs. Government's disinclination to regard position in its true light. Four months of winter ahead much to be feared owing to 'want of fuel and provisions'. 'The foe most to be dreaded is the North West wind, which rages at this season of the year and forbids all navigation coming upon this coast.'

Report, 15–26 Nov. 1775. Skirmishes with rebels in Canada. Situation in Rhode Island under the rebels. Building of redoubts to protect Boston against attack when Cambridge Bay is frozen. Shipping news. Scarcity of provisions. Rumour that 'Washington has left the rebel Army but upon what account is not mentioned'. News of the position at Marblehead, Mass., 25 November. Controversy between Commanders-in-Chief and the Board of Customs in Boston as to powers under the Boston Port Act. (Ref. 13/7)

(*f*) Manuscript entitled 'Establishment and disposition of His Majesty's land forces at the close of the year 1777 also general state of the army in America to the same period'. (Ref. 13/9*a*)

(*g*) Printed items. (Ref. 13/7)

(i) *A circumstantial account of an attack that happened on the 19th April 1775, on His Majesty's troops, by a number of the people of the province of Massachusetts Bay* (Lexington, Mass.).

(ii) Copy of a letter, Hartford, Conn., 28 Apr. 1775, from Jonathan Trumbull, Governor of Connecticut, on behalf of the General Assembly of that colony to General Gage; with a copy of General Gage's reply from Boston, 3 May 1775.

(iii) *Massachusetts Gazette and the Boston Weekly News-Letter*, Thursday, 30 Nov. 1775.

HOBART PAPERS.[1] *c.* 1776–1803.

Papers of Robert Hobart, 1st Baron Hobart, 4th Earl of Buckinghamshire (1760–1816), soldier and statesman; Secretary of State for War and the Colonies in the Addington administration 1801–4.

(*a*) 'Sketch of the case of Captain Benjamin Roberts', n.d., giving a brief description of his services against the Indians in the Seven Years War and as Superintendent of Indian Affairs among the Six Nations just before the War of Independence.

(*b*) Two certificates, 1798 and 1803, supporting the claims of Captain Daniel Lyman to a consulship in the United States on account of intelligence work by him which led to the interception of French bullion coming from the United States in 1794. (Copies.)

(*c*) Three letters, all 1803, from Captain John Murray, who was trying to recover family property in Virginia. There is a long enclosure, the copy of a letter from Ralph Wormeley of Virginia to Murray concerning Jefferson's change of heart from animosity to cordiality towards Britain, which the writer attributes to American fears that, with France once more in possession of Louisiana, free navigation of the Mississippi will disappear. Should the French treat Monroe 'with hauteur and indignity', says the writer, Monroe has orders to report to London and conclude a treaty.

SHARDELOES PAPERS (AMERSHAM). Letter. 1779.

24 Feb. 1779, from Robert Bourne to William Drake of Shardeloes, about the failure of a 'Rebel descent' upon the Mississippi, the raising of a defence corps by the planters, and the enhancement of land values there.

Hughenden Manor (National Trust), HIGH WYCOMBE

DISRAELI, BENJAMIN, 1st Earl of Beaconsfield (1804–81). Papers.

Disraeli's papers are preserved in thirty large deed-boxes. Most of the boxes contain papers on a related group of subjects, though some are very miscellaneous; there is no detailed list of the whole, only a very general list of the principal subjects in each box. The collection was too large to locate the Americana in it without a full list in the time available. However, the papers were available to Monypenny and Buckle,[2] and the index to volume IV of their work reveals several letters of Disraeli on policy towards America, especially the Civil War and the *Alabama* claims. There are evidently a fairly large group of letters, 1861–5, between Disraeli and other Conservative

---

[1] We are grateful to the Earl of Buckinghamshire for permission to make this report.

[2] W. F. Monypenny, *The Life of Benjamin Disraeli, Earl of Beaconsfield*, 6 vols. (vol. 3 by Monypenny and G. E. Buckle; vols. 4–6 by Buckle) (London, 1910–20).

Party leaders—Beauchamp, Cecil, Derby, Ralph Earle, Edward Bulwer Lytton, Henry Lennox, Malmesbury, Stanley, and others—which discuss the American Civil War, the question of recognition of the Confederacy, armistice proposals, the Lancashire cotton famine, Canadian defences, Laird and the armoured rams, &c.[1]

Sir Harry Verney, Ballams, MIDDLE CLAYDON, Bletchley

VERNEY PAPERS. 3 letters. 1676.

(a) Two letters from Dr. William Denton to Sir R. Verney. On 12 Oct. 1676 he mentions that 1,000 men are being sent to Virginia 'with a pardon to all but Bacon'. On 19 Oct. 'the drums beat for volunteers for Virginia. Here is much talk of a remonstrance from the city.'[2]

(b) 7 Dec. 1676, from John Verney to Sir R. Verney, mentioning Nathaniel Bacon's capture and burning of Jamestown, Va., his taking Sir Thos. Chichely as prisoner, and 'that the Governor Sir Wm. Berkeley was again fled the country'.[3]

Dr. J. Spencer Bernard, NETHER WINCHENDON

BERNARD FAMILY PAPERS.

A large, unsorted collection of family papers, which may include some correspondence of Sir Francis Bernard, Governor of New Jersey 1758–60, and of Massachusetts 1760–71. However, the only eighteenth-century papers found in the brief search possible were those of Scrope Bernard-Morland (1758–1830), M.P. 1789–1802, 1806–8, 1809–30; these included some correspondence, 1790, relating to the Quebec affairs of the Society for the Propagation of the Gospel. A list is being prepared, after which the papers may be available for inspection.

N.R.A. 7343.

---

[1] Many of these are quoted in W. D. Jones, 'The British Conservatives and the American Civil War', *American Historical Review*, vol. lviii, pp. 527–43, 1952–3.

[2] Excerpts, H.M.C. vii, pp. 493–4.

[3] Ibid., p. 467.

CAMBRIDGESHIRE

Cambridgeshire County Record Office, Shire Hall, Castle Hill, CAMBRIDGE

COTTENHAM COMMON RIGHTS. 12 documents.[1] 1596–1842.

Copy of the agreement for the stint, &c., of Cottenham Common, 20 Nov. 1596. Also copy, 1615, by Richard Robinson. Eleven other documents, 1638–1842: copies of the agreement or documents relating to it.

Cunningham states: 'The system [in operation at Cottenham] has interesting analogies with the townships . . . which were soon to be planted . . . in New England. . . . The circumstances of the New England settlers gave the opportunity for the reproduction of similar institutions for the regulation of economic affairs. The system in vogue in Massachusetts, at Chelsea in 1638, at Malden in 1678, or at Lexington was closely allied to that which existed at Cottenham in 1596, and the township, in a new atmosphere and in new surroundings came to play an important part in the constitutional and political history of the United States.'[2]

The Letters of Charles Dickens, Pilgrim Edition, 61 Bateman Street, CAMBRIDGE

DICKENS, CHARLES (1812–70). Letters.

While he was in America, in 1842, Dickens wrote a series of journal-letters to his friend, John Forster, which were the basis of *American Notes*.[3] During his lifetime, Forster had them bound, with various pamphlets and newspaper cuttings Dickens had sent him, in a volume fitted with a lock. After they had been used for his biography of Dickens they were cut out and destroyed. What is left remains in the John Forster Collection in the Victoria and Albert Museum, South Kensington, London, S.W. 7.

Practically all Dickens's extant correspondence with his American friends and acquaintances has remained in American hands. A mere half-dozen of the letters he wrote during his two visits to America, in 1842 and 1867–8, remain in England in private hands, though there are a few more written in England that concern the international copyright controversy. All but

---

[1] See W. Cunningham, 'Common Rights at Cottenham and Stretham in Cambridgeshire', in Royal Historical Society, *Camden Miscellany*, vol. xii, pp. 169–296 (London, 1910), (3rd series, vol. xviii). [2] Ibid., p. 183.

[3] The fuss and bother that resulted from James Spedding's review of *American Notes*, for the *Edinburgh Review*, can be followed in the Macvey Napier papers, in the British Museum (Add. MSS. 34611–31). Most of this has been published, here and there, in one form or another; but a few snippets have not.

one of these have been published. The Editorial Committee of the Pilgrim Edition of the *Letters of Charles Dickens* will publish all his known letters. The first volume is in preparation. It will give the locations of manuscripts.

University Library, CAMBRIDGE

RALEGH, SIR WALTER. The Prerogative of Parliaments, &c. (Dd. 3.85)

In this volume of tracts, written in various hands between the sixteenth and eighteenth centuries, there is 'A Discourse concerning a voyage intended for the planting of Christian religion and people in the northwest regions of America in places most apt for ye constitution of our boddies and ye speedy advancement of a state'. (9 leaves.) 16th century.

HUDSON'S BAY COMPANY. 4 documents. 1678–87. (Dd. 13. 31)

From a volume containing a miscellaneous collection of historical documents. (In French.)

(*a*) No. 5, 1687. Hudson's Bay Company. Memorandum on the claims of the English Crown to the commerce in Hudson Bay, with reply by the French commissioners and a rejoinder by the Company[1] (in parallel columns).

(*b*) No. 5, cont. Abstract of title of the Compagnie de la Baye du Nord du Canada to trade in Hudson Bay with the reply of the Hudson's Bay Company.[2]

(*c*) No. 9. Island of St. Christopher, copy of treaty between English and French representatives, 19 May 1678.

(*d*) No. 11, 1687. Compagnie de la Baye du Nord du Canada: *Mémoire*, a reply to the rejoinder of the Hudson's Bay Company to the French company's reply to the Hudson's Bay Company's memorial.[3]

CHOLMONDELEY (HOUGHTON) MANUSCRIPTS. Sir Robert Walpole's Archive. *c.* 1710–1747. (On deposit)

This collection was deposited in the Library by the Marquess of Cholmondeley in Oct. 1951 for a period of ten years. Some of the papers are duplicates of existing papers in the Public Record Office. A detailed five-volume catalogue of all the letters and papers, together with an index of correspondents, is in the University Library.[4]

---

[1] See *Calendar of State Papers: Colonial Series, America and West Indies, 1685–1688, preserved in the Public Record Office*, no. 1258, p. 369, and no. 1324, pp. 388–9 (London, 1899).   [2] Ibid., no. 1324, p. 389.   [3] Ibid., no. 1369, pp. 405–6.
[4] See also G. A. Chinnery, *A Handlist of the Cholmondeley (Houghton) MSS: Sir Robert Walpole's Archive* (Cambridge, 1953).

American material is found particularly in the following:

(*a*) Trading and colonial papers:

84. Papers relating to the colonies, their settlement, administration and defence, including schemes for expanding; state of the quit-rents in Virginia, &c. 1710–40 (87 items).

87. Papers relating to the colonization of Georgia under General Oglethorpe and relating to some of his other actions in America; forays into South Carolina, &c. 1738–47 (11 items).

(*b*) Army and Navy papers:

7, items 10 and 11. Correspondence relating to Lt. Washington's complaint to the Board of Ordnance, June 1721.

8. Army estimates, particularly relating to the American expedition, 1741–2.

10. Army expenses. American expeditions 1711–15, 1740.

13. Lists of ships taken by the enemy 1688–1713, 1740, including the Quebec expedition.

(*c*) Foreign papers:

26, item 144. Account of negotiations with France about navigation in America. n.d.

(*d*) Treasury, Customs and Excise:

37. Lists of goods imported from Antigua, Barbados, Jamaica, Montserrat, Nevis, St. Christopher, and Virginia. 1715–19 (10 items).

The correspondence, which was not examined, is arranged in chronological order. There are about 3,400 letters in all, many dealing with personal and local affairs. Between 1727 and 1735 subjects covered include diplomatic matters. Throughout the period there are a few letters from the leading politicians of the time.

GEORGIA. 1 volume. 1732–8. (Add. 4269)

Transcripts and notes of official correspondence relating to Georgia, copied by Miss A. E. Seeley for the use of Professor Sir J. R. Seeley, *c.* 1887. They include extracts from Colonial and Foreign Office documents.

WOGAN, LE CHEVALIER DE: PLAN DE LA COMPAGNIE ROYALE AMÉRICAINE. (Bound volume in French.) 1743. (Add. 6572)

'Projet d'accommodement entre l'Espagne et l'Angleterre ... contenant un plan général de commerce entre le vieux et le nouveau monde à l'exclusion de toute contrebande et au profit de tout l'univers.' A plan for an international trading company drawn up under seventy-one articles.

PLUMSTED, ROBERT. Letter-book. 1756–8. (Add. 2798)

Quaker merchant in London. Contains an alphabetical list of addressees and copies of letters to them. Many were merchants in New England.

They include a Quaker cousin in Philadelphia with whom he was doing business, and who introduced him to other American merchants, dealing in logwood, furs, and corn, &c., in exchange for guns, anchors, nails, &c.

H.M. FORCES. Volume of returns. 1782. (Add. 4376)

The returns are arranged geographically under stations. The North American station (pp. 22–26) is divided into the commands of General Sir Guy Carleton, 1 June 1782, and General Haldimand (Canada), 1 July 1782. Returns for cavalry and infantry are given separately. The information is written on the blank sheets of printed forms. An abstract of the total forces is given on p. 41.

KEATING, SIR HENRY SINGER (1804–88). Journal (Add. 3819)

(Typescript made in 1896 by his son, H. S. Keating, M.A., of Trinity College.) Judge. Journal of his travels in Madagascar, Greece, and the United States. Pages 218–340 contain an account of his American journey, July 1830–Jan. 1831. He travelled through New York state into Canada, and back through New England as far south as Philadelphia and Washington. He comments on American habits and customs, modes of travel, religion—including an account of a visit to a Shaker community; the state of American cities, and the military training system at West Point, and such terms as 'Yankees'.[1]

GOOCH, RICHARD. Collectanea. (188 leaves with 15 water-colour sketches at the end, and another copy of Chapter 1.) (Add. 2616)

'America and the Americans', from a collection of six boxes of treatises, published and unpublished extracts, notes, drafts, verses, &c., made 1823–39 by Richard Gooch of St. John's College. Subtitled 'Have at the Americans or: America and the Americans in 1833–4, embellished with 12 engravings, by an emigrant.' It is said to describe the 'manners, customs, habits, climate, fashions, matrimony and courtship, notions of gentility . . .', &c., of the Americans.

ACTON, SIR JOHN EMERICH EDWARD DALBERG, 1st Baron Acton (1834–1902). 5 boxes of notes on America. (Add. 4894–8)

Each item is on a separate numbered slip. They include quotations and extracts from American authors and brief comments on American affairs.

AMERICAN LECTURESHIP. 1865–6. (Cam. b. 865. 1)

A bound collection made by F. W. Maitland of official documents and various papers circulated as part of the controversy concerning the proposal to establish a Lectureship in the History, Literature, and Institutions

---

[1] See also similar manuscript in the Bodleian Library—MS. Eng. misc. c. 29 (S.C. 32396) (p. 382), but in this the relevant pages are 222–353.

of the United States. Henry Yates Thompson was the would-be benefactor; he stipulated that the lecturer should be an American and appointed by Harvard with Cambridge, however, having a right of veto. Charles Kingsley, Professor of Modern History, wrote strongly in support of the proposal. E. H. Perowne bitterly attacked it. Sedley Taylor supported Kingsley but H. R. Baily seconded Perowne and argued that not merely 'Republican' but also 'Socinian' or 'Unitarian' principles would be preached. 'Government, authority, faith, submission, reverence, these are indissolubly bound together, and any shock to one part of the system may be felt throughout the whole.' The Senate defeated the proposal by 110 votes to 82.

HARDINGE PAPERS.

A few letters and papers in this large collection concern the very brief service of the 1st Baron Hardinge of Penshurst as a Second Secretary at Washington, D.C., 1886–7.

Fitzwilliam Museum, Trumpington Street,
CAMBRIDGE

HENDERSON AUTOGRAPH COLLECTION.

Franklin, Benjamin. Copy of a letter, Passy, 24 July 1782, to a M. Durivall: is sending his grandson to execute legal instrument and collect some papers (or money?). Also a single sheet in French, n.d., anon., of biographical notes on Franklin.

ASHCOMBE AUTOGRAPH COLLECTION.

Jefferson, Thomas. Letter, Washington, D.C., 19 June 1807, to Caesar A. Rodney. He asks Rodney to send him General Wilkinson's letter of 21 Oct. Rodney has sent the wrong one: 'It was the one which was sowed up in the shoe-soal of the officer, to which my message referred.' He asks Rodney to call on a Mr. John Gordon and possibly a Mr. Graybell; he urges secrecy, and can assure Gordon that his name will not be known out of the Cabinet. It ends: 'I think it material to break down this bull-dog of Federalism (Martin) and to break down the imprudent supporters of Burr by showing to the world that they are his accomplices.'

Madison, James. Note, 1 Jan. 1817, to Isaac Tichenor, requesting his attendance in the Senate Chamber on 4 Mar.

Monroe, James. Memorandum, n.d., on the case of one George W. Irvine as to whether he was a United States citizen or not, having been born in Massachusetts but having resided abroad. Monroe submits the case to the decision of Col. Humphries and Mr. Hichborn in Paris, who annotate the memorandum in Irvine's favour, dated 3 May 1795.

Polk, James K. Short letter, 24 Nov. 1847, to the Secretary of War,

William L. Marcy, introducing 'the Hon. Mr. Mitchell, formerly a Member of Congress', from Ohio.

Van Buren, Martin. Letter, 13 Apr. 1820, to John V. Henry, enclosing a letter from the Vice-President, Daniel D. Tompkins.

SHARPLES, JAMES (1750?–1811). 2 letters. 1802, 1804. (MS. 13 and 14—1948)
American portrait painter.

Bath, 12 Dec. 1802, to William Strutt of Derby. Discusses his paintings and life in Bath.

London, 2 Mar. 1804, also to Strutt. On painting; also asks for an introduction to General Bentham and talks of his own interest in mechanics.

The Library, Magdalene College, CAMBRIDGE

FERRAR PAPERS.[1] 78 papers. 1617–23.

Papers of the Ferrar family, including those of Nicholas Ferrar and his brother John, active in the affairs of the Virginia Company of London. They include seventy-eight papers—letters from Edwin Sandys and others—relating to the Company, 1617–23.

See also Andrews and Davenport, pp. 429–30.

BIBLIOTHECA PEPYSIANA.

The following catalogues of the collection have been published: J. R. Tanner, ed., *A Descriptive Catalogue of the Naval MSS. in the Pepysian Library at Magdalene College, Cambridge*, 4 vols. (London, 1903–23) (Publications of the Navy Records Society, vols. xxvi, xxvii, xxxvi, lvii); and *Bibliotheca Pepysiana. A Descriptive Catalogue of the Library of Samuel Pepys*, 4 vols. [Volumes edited respectively by J. R. Tanner, E. Gordon Duff, M. R. James, and William J. Carlton.] (London, 1914–40).

See also Andrews and Davenport, pp. 424–30.

H.M.C. Pepys MSS. [70] (London, 1911) includes the following:

(*a*) Two letters, Madrid, 4 Apr. and 21 June 1565, from Robert Huggins to the Earl of Leicester, mention the anger of the King of Spain at the French taking part of Florida and building a fort there, the latter stating that a Spanish expedition has gone to try to recover it. There is also a letter, Padstow, 20 Sept. 1565, from John Hawkins to the Queen, in which he says, 'I have also discovered the coast of Floryda in those parts where there is thought to be any great wealth.'[2]

---

[1] For an account of these papers see *The Records of the Virginia Company of London*, ed. by Susan M. Kingsbury, volumes iii and iv (Washington, D.C., 1933–5).

[2] Transcript, H.M.C. Pepys MSS. [70], pp. 54–55, 61, 65–66.

(b) An undated paper headed 'Expenses in the first plantation of New England', written in a spirit hostile to the Puritan settlers, but advocating a policy of conciliation on the part of (?) Charles II rather than force towards them.[1]

(c) Among papers taken at the battle of Worcester is one (?1649) from Charles II to the colony of Virginia, mentioning its loyalty to the Royalist cause and giving instructions concerning fortifications and collection of duties.[2]

(d) 'A copy of a patent granted by the King of Scots to Sir John Berkely and Sir Willm. Davenett [Davenant] for the office of Treasurer in Virginia',[3] Sept. 1649. (Also in Worcester papers.)

(e) Copy of a commission, dated Sept. 1649, appointing 'Davenant to be Treasurer in Virginia in the absence of Sir Jno. Barclay, whom he made Treasurer in the room of Capt. William Clayburne', a parliamentarian.[4] (Among 'Letters brought from Jersey'.)

Scott Polar Research Institute, Lensfield Road, ## CAMBRIDGE

LEFROY BEQUEST[5] (1941). Letters, journals. 1814–70.

Journals and correspondence of Sir John and Lady Franklin.

(a) Letters, 1814, from James Alexander Gordon to Sir John Franklin (1786–1847), the Arctic explorer, concerning his service in the expedition against New Orleans. (MS. 248/398)

(b) Franklin, Lady Jane (1792–1875). Four travel journals and notes of visits to America; letters, 1846–70. (MS. 248)
Second wife of Sir John Franklin. The travel journals, which contain much social observation and references to American affairs, including the Civil War, are:

(i) Journal of a visit to the United States of America, July and Aug. 1846 (98 pages).

(ii) Journal of travels in America and the Pacific, 1 August 1860–31 May 1862 (6 volumes). Volume 1: United States; volume 4: California.

(iii) Notes made in the United States and Canada, 1860 (121 pages).

(iv) Journal notes, Salt Lake City, 11–18 July 1870 (58 pages).

The letters include many dealing with American search expeditions following the disappearance of Sir John Franklin and an expedition which

---

[1] Transcript, H.M.C. Pepys MSS. [70], pp. 270–1.   [2] Ibid., pp. 262–3.
[3] Ibid., p. 284.   [4] Ibid., p. 302.
[5] This collection of the journals and correspondence of Sir John and Lady Franklin was used extensively in the writing of F. J. Woodward's *Portrait of Jane* (London, 1951).

left England in 1845 to find the Northwest Passage. There are several from the United States Navy Department and United States consulates. The letters of Sophia Cracroft, Lady Jane Franklin's companion, contain descriptive material of their American travels.

HERO and *PENGUIN.* Logs[1] (microfilms). 1820–9. (MS. 321–323)

Logs of the sealers *Hero*, 1820–1 and 1821–2, and *Penguin*, 1829–31, upon which the American claims to the discovery of the Antarctic are based.

HUNTRESS. Log[2] (microfilm). 1820–2. (MS. 440)

Log of American sealer which visited the Antarctic.

The Library, Trinity College, Trinity Street,
CAMBRIDGE

LYNDHURST PAPERS. 3 letters. 1792–1859.

A volume of letters, 1792–1864, inscribed 'Used by Sir Theodore Martin K.C.B. in writing the life of Lord Lyndhurst . . .'[3] (John Singleton Copley, (1772–1863), Lord Chancellor), includes the following letters: Philadelphia, 12 Dec. 1792, from George Washington to John Singleton Copley, Sen. (1737–1815), the portrait painter, thanking him for his print of the death of the Earl of Chatham;[4] 16 Aug. 1845, from Edward Everett to Lord Lyndhurst; Boston, 4 July 1859, from Josiah Quincy to Lord Lyndhurst.

EVERETT, EDWARD (1794–1865). 28 letters.

To William Whewell, Master of Trinity College, Cambridge.

PRINTED MATERIAL.

The Library has a number of seventeenth- and eighteenth-century tracts and printed pamphlets, some of which relate to America.

[1] Originals in the Library of Congress, Washington, D.C.
[2] Original in Mystic Seaport, Connecticut.
[3] Sir Theodore Martin, *Life of Lord Lyndhurst* (London, 1883).
[4] See *Writings of George Washington*, ed. by John C. Fitzpatrick, vol. xxxii, p. 260 (Washington, D.C., 1939).

CHESHIRE

Fawcett Preston & Co. Ltd., Dock Road, BROMBOROUGH, Wirral

BUSINESS RECORDS.

Marine and general engineers, founded in 1758.[1] The only surviving record is an order book (or engine book) which, from 1815, gives details of engines the firm exported for cane roller mills for Southern sugar plantations, and also the engines of some famous American ships, including the *John Randolph*, the *Royal William*, the *Florida*, and the *Alexandra*.

Chester City Record Office, Town Hall, CHESTER

CITY COUNCIL MINUTES. 1584–1788.

1584. Consideration of a letter from Christopher Carlile to the Mayor and citizens informing them of his proposed voyage to America and asking for contributions to the enterprise. Copy of a reply stating that for various reasons they cannot afford to contribute.

1670. Petition from Elihu Yale asking for remission of the fine imposed upon him at the Sessions of the Peace for the City for writing and publishing a scandalous libel against Mrs. Sara Hudson, wife of Gawen Hudson, Alderman. Not granted.

1707. Elihu Yale and Dudley North, his son-in-law, were to be desired to accept the freedom of the City, and were to be entertained at the City's charge.

1788. Decision that an address should be presented to the King asking that a regulation be made in the African slave trade.

MISCELLANEOUS DOCUMENTS.

(*a*) Letter, 1616, from the Council of the Virginia Company to the Mayor, Recorder, and Aldermen of Chester concerning the holding of a lottery in Chester for the benefit of that plantation. (Among the Mayors' Letters.)

(*b*) Draft of bond, 1698, between the part owners of the *Providence of Mostyn* and three merchants of Chester concerning a voyage to Virginia for tobacco. (Among a miscellaneous collection mainly concerning the private practices of various Town Clerks of Chester.)

[1] See Horace White, '*Fossets*': *A Record of Two Centuries of Engineering* (Bromborough, priv. print., 1958).

QUARTER SESSIONS RECORDS.

(*a*) Examination before the Mayor of Hugh Catlyn of Kent, who had been hired by Hugh Cornish of Plymouth for a voyage to Newfoundland to 'the harbour of grace', concerning piracy there. 1609.

(*b*) A number of indictments bear instructions for transportation to the American plantations, and there are a few loose orders for transportation to America, 1766–73.

Trustees of the late 2nd Duke of Westminster, Muniment Room, Eaton Estate Office, ECCLESTON

WESTMINSTER PAPERS. 1634, 1769.

(*a*) 'A commission for the making laws and orders for the government of English colonies planted in foreign parts. Charles I to William, Archbishop of Canterbury [William Laud], Thomas, Lord Coventry and others. 28th April, 10 Car. I'[1] (4½ pages) [1635].

(*b*) Original grant, 1769, by George III of 12,000 acres of land in East Florida to the Rt. Hon. Richard Lord Grosvenor.

Quarry Bank Mill, STYAL, Wilmslow

GREG FAMILY PAPERS.[2] Letter (copy), and memoranda book. 1795–1881.

Samuel Greg began cotton-spinning at the mill about 1784. The collection of Greg family and business records held there includes a copy of a letter, 2 Dec. 1795, from Thomas Greg of Belfast to his son Samuel Greg, relating to disposal of land held by the former and Mr. Cunningham in the 'Province of New York'.

It also includes a memoranda book[3] in which Edward Hyde Greg, the grandson of Samuel, began, about 1881, to give details of the mill from its commencement; on page 10 he notes that 'when other mills were using Brazil cotton . . . S. G. only used American and was the first person who proved that it would make yarn equal to any other', and on pages 11 and 74–75 he discusses the effects of the 1862 cotton famine on prices of, and use of substitutes for, cotton.

---

[1] H.M.C. iii, p. 213.   [2] These are the property of A. C. Greg, Esq.
[3] Used by W. Lazenby, 'The Social and Economic History of Styal, 1750–1850', M.A. thesis, University of Manchester, 1949.

CORNWALL

G. G. Fortescue, Esq., BOCONNOC, Lostwithiel

GRENVILLE PAPERS. Letters. 1783–1814.

Correspondence of William Wyndham Grenville, Baron Grenville (1759–1834), statesman.

(*a*) Dublin Castle, 22 Jan. 1783, from Earl Temple, Lord-Lieutenant of Ireland, to W. W. Grenville, mentions evacuation of Charleston, S.C., and Loyalists leaving America.[1]

(*b*) Various letters, Dublin Castle, Feb. and Mar. 1783, from Lord Temple to W. W. Grenville, which mention trade with and emigration to America.[2]

(*c*) Stowe, 8 Dec. 1786, from the Marquis of Buckingham to W. W. Grenville, includes the following comment: 'I have received a very large packet from Mr. Temple (now Sir John Temple) with a long detail of American misery, discontent and anarchy; and seemingly with a strong inclination of putting his finger into every one of these thirteen pies. . . .'[3]

(*d*) 19 Jan. 1790, from W. W. Grenville to the Lord Chancellor, Thurlow, in which he compares claims of settlers on 'Mosquito Shore' with those of East Florida.[4]

(*e*) Cabinet minute, 30 Apr. 1790, regarding British vessels captured at Nootka Sound, recommending that satisfaction be demanded of Madrid, and that a squadron be fitted out to prevent further outrages.[5]

(*f*) Hollwood, 23 June 1791, from W. Pitt to Grenville, concerning the slave trade and the part of American ships therein.[6]

(*g*) London, 29 July 1791, from P. Colquhoun to Grenville, enclosing an extract from a letter from Colonel William Stephens Smith, 'late Secretary of Legation at the Court of London from the U.S.A.', now in Philadelphia. Smith had apparently been combating 'false impressions', circulated by those hostile to the resumption of normal commercial relations.[7]

(*h*) 5 and 8 Aug. 1791, from P. Colquhoun to Grenville on American trade, and especially the prospect of enlarging British markets.[8]

(*i*) 24 Sept. 1791, from P. Colquhoun to Grenville, stating that he has used his influence with Robert Morris to counteract erroneous and unfriendly

---

[1] Transcript, H.M.C. xiii (iii) (Fortescue (Dropmore) MSS. i [30]), p. 184.
[2] Transcripts, ibid., pp. 190–1, 193, 195, 200.
[3] Transcript, ibid., pp. 275–6.
[4] Transcript, ibid., p. 559.   [5] Transcript, ibid., p. 579.
[6] Transcript, H.M.C. xiv (v) (Fortescue (Dropmore) MSS. ii [30]), p. 104.
[7] Transcript, ibid., pp. 145–6.   [8] Transcripts, ibid., pp. 157–8, 160.

information emanating from Britain, and enclosing extracts from letters received from Morris.[1]

(*j*) 15 Nov. 1791, from P. Colquhoun to Grenville, enclosing letters from Robert Morris: Aug. 27, on the need for a capable British Minister, and John Brown Cutting; 12 Oct., on 'the credit and even opulence of the United States', and its indifference to a commercial treaty with Great Britain.[2]

(*k*) Four dispatches, 1791–3, from Philadelphia, from George Hammond, first British Minister to the United States 1791–5, to Grenville. He considers that Washington's offering the London appointment to anyone will give him [Hammond] sufficient reason to present his credentials. Mentions anti-British tactics of Jeffersonians. That of 2 Feb. 1792 mentions difficulties arising regarding the North West frontier. That of 12 Oct. 1793 on the epidemic in Philadelphia.[3]

(*l*) 5 Jan. 1792, from Henry Dundas to Grenville, recommending Colquhoun (whose Glasgow mercantile house had just failed) for an American consulship, and Grenville's reply, 6 Jan., regretting his inability to do so.[4]

(*m*) The Hague, 9 Nov. 1792, Lord Auckland to Grenville, suggests that American wheat, which is cheap, be imported into Britain to avert scarcity.[5]

(*n*) 15 Aug. 1793, from Grenville to Henry Dundas, on [presumably French] 'prisoners taken aboard an American ship still detained at Liverpool'.[6]

(*o*) Foreign Office Journal of J. B. Burges. Entry for 28 Dec. 1793 makes mention of a call by Pinckney to protest against 'the new instruction to commanders of ships of war and privateers', which would shut American trade out of the French islands, as the Act of Navigation already shut it out from the British.[7]

(*p*) Leghorn, 1794, from Francis Drake to Lord Grenville, enclosing three bulletins, 10 and 27 Feb. and 11 Mar. 1794, from Paris, concerning the American Minister [Gouverneur Morris]; and bulletin, 26–31 May 1794, on England and the United States (bulletins in French).[8]

(*q*) 22 June 1794, from Lord Auckland to Grenville, enclosing an extract from a letter to 'Mr. Elliot, heretofore Lieutenant-Governor of New York' on the character of Jay.[9]

(*r*) July 1794, from Pitt to Grenville, about a meeting held with a group of American merchants to discuss the American debts.[10]

---

[1] Transcript, ibid., p. 197. [2] Transcript, ibid., p. 228.
[3] Transcripts, ibid., pp. 223, 229, 254, 443–4.
[4] Transcript, ibid., p. 249. [5] Transcript, ibid., p. 329.
[6] Transcript, ibid., p. 414. Dundas's reply is on p. 416.
[7] Transcript, ibid., p. 488–9. [8] Transcripts, ibid., pp. 526, 541, 579.
[9] Transcript, ibid., p. 578. [10] Transcript, ibid., p. 607.

(s) 6 Aug. 1794, from Buckingham to Grenville, on impressment of American seamen and the importance of the western posts, particularly Detroit.[1]

(t) Copy, 9 Dec. 1794, from Grenville, recalling George Hammond.[2]

(u) H.M.C. Fortescue (Dropmore) MSS. iii [30]. Contains many letters of importance concerning Anglo-American relations during Grenville's term as Foreign Secretary 1796–1801, including a 'precis [dated Sept.–Oct. 1794] of correspondence relating to alleged breaches of the treaty of peace . . .', pp. 520–8.

16 Aug. and 24 Oct. 1794, touching on Anglo-United States friction regarding Indians and debts respectively, p. 530.

9 Nov. 1794, from Grenville to Portland on the Prize Courts in the West Indies, and their effect on Anglo-American relations, p. 533.

From Jay, 1794–5, pp. 34, 38, 516, 528, 534.

To Jay, 1794–5; from Grenville, pp. 68, 517; from Randolph, p. 529.

28 June 1795, describing Gouverneur Morris's view of the Jay Treaty, pp. 87–89.

7 Oct. 1795, from Grenville to Dundas enclosing article proposed by Jay on American trade to the East Indies, pp. 136–7.

8 Sept. 1796, from P. Bond in Philadelphia to Grenville on good effects of the Jay Treaty, pp. 243–4.

25 Aug. 1797, from Rufus King to Grenville, concerning the expulsion of Senator Blount for a 'project' detrimental to the United States; and reply from Grenville, 30 Aug., pp. 360–1.

(v) H.M.C. Fortescue (Dropmore) MSS. iv [30].

July and Aug. 1798, between Rufus King and Grenville on the United States' quarrel with France, pp. 269, 272–3, 288; and United States intercourse with Santo Domingo, 1799, p. 437.

13 Sept. 1798, and reply, 18 Sept., from Grenville to Cornwallis on American government's wish to buy small arms in England, pp. 314, 317.

(w) H.M.C. Fortescue (Dropmore) MSS. vi [30].

Letters, 1800, from Rufus King and Dundas to Grenville on commissioners appointed to consider claims of British merchants upon United States, pp. 202–3, 370.

Two of Jan. 1800, from Dundas to Grenville, on American trade, pp. 107, 112.

28 Feb. 1800, from Grenville to Liston, British Minister to the United States, deploring situation in United States ('system of the American Government seems . . . to be tottering') and granting him provisional leave of absence, p. 146.

24 and 29 Oct. 1800, from Thomas Macdonald to Grenville; the first dealing with American opinion of Britain, especially as represented by American newspapers; and the second with Secretary of State Marshall, pp. 358–60, 365–6.

---

[1] Transcript, H.M.C. xiv (v) (Fortescue (Dropmore) MSS. ii [30]), pp. 610–11.
[2] Transcript, ibid., p. 651.

12 Feb. 1801, from Rufus King, on probable policy of new United States administration, pp. 444–5.

(x) H.M.C. Fortescue (Dropmore) MSS. viii [30]. This volume contains a large number of letters, 1806, some from Grenville, but most to him from Auckland, and also Holland, concerning chiefly questions of trade with the United States, American trade with the West Indies, and the abortive Anglo-American treaty of Dec. 1806. The impressment of American seamen, and the dispute over 'continuous voyage' are also touched upon. The main references are: pp. 36, 47, 54, 58, 63, 85, 87, 102, 112, 138, 140–1, 263, 265, 285, 290, 293, 296–8, 302, 310, 357, 406, 410–11, 429, 441–2, 446, 458–9, 472, 484–5, 489, 491.

(y) H.M.C. Fortescue (Dropmore) MSS. ix [30]. This volume contains a number of letters, 1807–9, chiefly by Auckland to Grenville, criticizing the Orders in Council and prophesying war with the United States because of them. There is also one letter, p. 141, touching upon the *Chesapeake* incident. The main references are: pp. 143, 146–7, 151, 158, 164, 177–9, 182, 193, 198–9, 200–1, 206, 277, 279, 302, 438–9.

(z) H.M.C. Fortescue (Dropmore) MSS. x [30]. Several letters, mostly from Auckland to Grenville, touching on the War of 1812, written mainly in that year, 1813 and 1814. The major references are: pp. 88, 125, 194, 223, 286, 290, 292–3, 322, 394–5.

Miss E. D. Enys, The Cottage, ENYS, Penryn

ENYS PAPERS.[1] Memorandum, diary. 1783–c. 1800.

(a) 'History of the 29th Regiment of Foot, 1702–1800', a memorandum compiled, c. 1800, by John Enys, who became Colonel of the Regiment in 1797, and served in Canada after the War of Independence: a manuscript of 52 pages in his hand giving an account of the history and movements of the Regiment. There is a table at the end of Regimental officers 1702–1800.

(b) Diary of Colonel John Enys: nine notebooks, 1783–7. The first four diaries relate to a tour of Scotland. In the middle of the fifth diary, May 1784, he receives orders to join his Regiment in America. There follows a detailed account of garrison duty in Lower Canada, Quebec, then Montreal, then several small forts on the Lakes; some comment on French and Indian customs, including an account of the last days of the *voyageur*, St. Luc de la Corne; ends with an account of Prince William's visit to Canada.

H.M. Customs and Excise, FALMOUTH

See H.M. Customs and Excise, London (p. 200).

---

[1] Among an unexamined collection of family papers dating from the sixteenth century the owner kindly allowed us to consult the items listed.

G. C. Fox & Co., 48 Arwenack Street, Falmouth

UNITED STATES CONSULAR APPOINTMENTS AT FALMOUTH.
8 documents. 1794–1900.

Firm of shipping agents, and United States consular agents 1794–1900.
Eight letters of appointment signed by Presidents or Secretaries of State
survive. An earlier inspection by the County Archivist mentions 'American
Consular Letter-books, 1833–54', but these could not be found (Summer,
1957), although it was not possible to inspect all the records of the firm,
scattered around their offices. It seems likely that if a thorough search were
possible records of shipments to America would be revealed, possibly of
mining machinery.

See also Fox Bros. & Co. Ltd., Wellington, Somerset (pp. 406–7).

H.M. Customs and Excise, Penzance

See H.M. Customs and Excise, London (p. 200).

Penzance Library, Morrab Gardens, Penzance

CORNISH PAMPHLETS AND TRACTS (bound into volumes).

Volume 1, pamphlet no. 15 is *Narrative of a Voyage from England to the United
States of North America, with Travels through Part of Eight States; and Remarks on
the Soil, Produce, Prices and Agriculture in General; in the Year 1811*, by James
Hoskin, Farmer (49 pages). (Penzance, printed for the author by T. Vigurs,
1813.)

Earl of St. Germans, Port Eliot, St. Germans

ELIOT PAPERS. Letter. 1775.

31 May 1775, from Edward Gibbon to the 1st Baron Eliot (1727–1804) on
the American rebellion.[1]

Cornwall County Record Office, Gwendroc, Barrack Lane, Truro

EAST CORNWALL WOMEN FRIENDS MONTHLY MEETINGS.
Minutes (1 volume). 1762–88.

The entry under 24 July 1785 records the reading of the epistle from the
Yearly Meeting of Women Friends in America; under 23 July 1786 the

[1] H.M.C. i, p. 41. Printed in *The Letters of Edward Gibbon*, ed. by J. E. Norton,
vol. ii, pp. 72–73 (London, 1956).

entry records the visit of one Rebecca Jones, a Friend from America, bringing a certificate from Friends of the Monthly and Quarterly Meetings of
Philadelphia.

BLEWETT, HARVEY & VIVIAN & CO. Estimates book, 1834–9.

Manufacturers of boilers and pumping engines. The firm, established in the
late eighteenth century, still survives. It had world-wide trading connexions,
and the book shows a shipment of twelve pumping engines to Virginia in
1835.

The Record Office also holds letter-books for 1809–32; letter-books
since 1832 are still in the possession of the firm at Hayle.

(An advertisement in the *West Briton*, 13 Feb. 1835, inserted by the Union
Gold Mines in Virginia asks for engineers and miners for the Virginia gold
mines.)

BOLITHO BUSINESS RECORDS. Lists of business and estate
records, *c.* 1830–1900. Newspaper-cutting book, *c.* 1880–90.

Cornish fishing, tin, and banking firm.

(*a*) There is a full list of the firm's extensive banking, estate, and trading
reports in the Record Office, referring to some 162 volumes. These include
vol. 13, 'Foreign ledger, 1841–1853'; and vol. 25, 'Foreign ledger, 1860–
1880'; these were not examined.

(*b*) Cutting-book, 'Facts and scraps', contains miscellaneous clippings from
English and American newspapers (some unidentified) on, for example, the
state of the American stock market, Dakota tin mining, the McKinley
Tariff; it also contains stockholders' reports on, for example, Louisville and
Nashville Railroad, all evidently referring to the firm's foreign investments.

VIVIAN, SIR ARTHUR PENDARVES (1834–1926). Travel diary
(50 folios), 1877. (Bosahan MSS.)

Third son of J. H. Vivian, a partner in the Hafod copper-smelting works in
Swansea; M.P. for West Cornwall 1868–85. The diary concerns his 1877
trip to Canada and the United States. From Canada he travelled from
Detroit to Chicago, then via Burlington, Omaha, Cheyenne, and Denver,
to Longmont, with hunting in Estes Park and the Black Canyon, &c. This
was a holiday trip and he was mainly interested in hunting, but there are
some passages on the lumber trade in Canada, railways, and Indians. He
wrote a book on the United States, *Wanderings in the Western Land* (London,
1879). His brother, Sir Henry Hussey Vivian, later 1st Baron Swansea, who
went with him on the trip, also published *Notes of a Tour in America from
August 7th to November 17th, 1877* (London, 1878).

Royal Institution of Cornwall, County Museum and Art Gallery, TRURO

CORNISH EMIGRANTS. Memorial book, &c. 1810–   .

The large-scale migration of Cornish miners, following the decline of the copper- and then the tin-mining industries, is well known, as is the export of pumping and mining machinery. Although the County Museum was virtually the county archive until recent years, no primary records of these movements could be found. But the present Curator of the Museum, Mr. H. L. Douch, keeps a book in longhand in which he lists and transcribes all references to emigration to be found in the *West Briton*, 1810–56, and the *Royal Cornwall Gazette*, 1801–56, the sailings of emigrant ships, advertisements for skilled miners and engineers from all over the world, including the United States, and also published letters from emigrants and editorial comments and notices of emigration agents' activities. Mr. Douch is glad to show this book to scholars.

The *Mining Journal*, 1835–1909, of which the Museum holds a complete file, regularly carried advertisements from the United States for Cornish miners, as did the *Cornubian*, 1830–7, a newspaper of which the Museum possesses the only complete file. Various Cornish historical and antiquarian society proceedings in the Museum contain occasional references to migration.

CUMBERLAND

Stead, McAlpin & Co. Ltd., Cummersdale Print Works, P.O. Box 1, CARLISLE

BUSINESS RECORDS. Firm's order books. *c.* 1890–   .

Textile printers, machine and hand-block. The firm has carried on a considerable export trade to the United States since the 1890's. Most of the records, kept in London, were destroyed during the Second World War, but a large number of order books are still available at the Cummersdale Print Works. For each design, listed by number, these show the date of orders, the amount of cloth ordered, and the names of the customers. Although no addresses are given, many of the customers are known to be American.

Mrs. M. Holman, The Dower House, Rheda Estate, FRIZINGTON

WILSON, W. S. American diary. 1830.

The diary, which begins in the West Indies, mainly concerns Wilson's visit to New York city and his subsequent journey up the Hudson and across to Niagara. On his trip upstate Wilson visited the Shaker village near New Lebanon, N.Y., and he gives description and impressions of the religious and social customs of the community. The diary is interspersed with rather startled comments on American equalitarianism, on availability and method of sale of books, and on the strength of political opinions held.

Brig. J. W. Kaye, Millbeck Towers (The Old Carding Mill), Underskiddaw, KESWICK

DOVER, YOUNGHUSBAND & CO. Ledger, day-book.[1] 1824–41.

Woollen goods manufacturers, Millbeck, Keswick. From the ledger, 1823–56, and the day-book, 1830–41, it appears that the firm shipped blankets and other woollen goods to the United States during the period 1824–39. The ledger gives brief details of charges for particular shipments and payments by the American firms for these; 'loss in sale' is a frequent entry. The day-book contains fuller information about shipments made from 1830 onwards, with contents of and charge for each bale noted separately. The goods, apparently shipped mainly through W. P. Bushby of Liverpool (or Bowe & Bushby, or Bushby, Son, & Foster), went to firms in New Orleans— first Curell, Kilshaw & Co., and later S. T. Hobson; New York—Thos. Dixon & Co., George Mackie & Co., Gabriel Mead & Co., W. B. Bend, and Alex. B. McAlpin; Philadelphia—Wm. Scott, John A. Brown, and Harrison & Watson; and Baltimore—A. Brown & Sons, Campbell & McIlvain, and G. B. Hoffman & Brother.

Sir Fergus Graham, NETHERBY, Longtown, Carlisle

GRAHAM PAPERS. 32 letters and papers. 1683–(late 17th century?).

(a) Thirty letters and papers, n.d. but late seventeenth century, relating to Hudson Bay, New England, &c., and disputes with the French.[2]

---

[1] An article by Brig. Kaye, 'The Millbeck woollen industry', based mainly on these two volumes, was published in the 1957 *Transactions of the Cumberland and Westmorland Antiquarian and Archaeological Society*, vol. lvii, N.S., pp. 158-72, 1958.

[2] H.M.C. vii, p. 409.

(*b*) 7 Aug. 1683, from Lord Preston to Secretary Jenkins mentions boundary disputes between Boston and the French, and the French complaints that the English are supplying the Indians with arms.[1]

(*c*) 6 Feb. 1684, mentioning that 'several Scotchmen came . . . to London under the (pretence) or notion of going to Carolina, and were many of them taken here into custody'.[2]

H.M. Customs and Excise, WHITEHAVEN

See H.M. Customs and Excise, London (p. 201).

Rev. P. B. Lyon, St. Mary's, Kells, WHITEHAVEN

MARTIN, GEORGE. 1 volume.[3] 1779–1800.

Solicitor, London. The volume consists of Martin's copies of claims submitted by him and by his father—Samuel Martin, Whitehaven merchant—for recompense for loss of Virginia property; Edmund Randolph's opinion, 1785, on these claims; and Martin's continuing comments on lack of progress in attaining satisfactory results. The property was originally owned by John Martin, at one time representative of Caroline county in the Virginia Assembly, who died in 1761 leaving his estate to his sons Samuel and Lewis and to their sons; the family's 'attachment to the British government' led the Virginia Assembly to confiscate and sell the considerable property, of which inventories are given in the claims, in 1779.

Public Library, Catherine Street, WHITEHAVEN

BRAGG, JOHN. Diary, &c. (1 volume). 1767–88.

Shoemaker, Whitehaven. The items of American interest in this very mixed volume are as follows:

(*a*) Copies of material from a 'Book of Richard Pike's in Manuscript'. Two letters, 1767 and 1771, from Benjamin Ferriss, Quaker schoolmaster of Wilmington, Pa., to his friend Elizabeth Wilkinson concerning personal affairs.

(*b*) Copies of letters[4] from American relatives of Bragg—John Hadwen and his daughters Elizabeth and Dorcas. Five letters, 1774–88, from Newport, R.I., give news of family members.

---

[1] Transcript, H.M.C. vii, p. 287. See also p. 392.
[2] Transcript, ibid., p. 407.
[3] Microfilm held at Colonial Williamsburg. An article on it appeared in the *Whitehaven News*, 20 Aug. 1953.
[4] Microfilms of these in the Library of Congress, Washington, D.C.

(*c*) Diary for 1774–90. Most of the entries for the period 1774–83 relate to the War of Independence. Bragg gives latest news of events leading up to the War and of battles, &c., during the War, with some comment on these; he mentions the arrival of Henry Fleming from Virginia 'with a vessel & crew, passengers &c—all being banished out of that country that durst pretend to be friends to Government' (entry of 6 Sept. 1776); the arrival of a ship from Virginia carrying tobacco intended for France (21 May 1777), and the appearance at Whitehaven during the night of 22 Apr. 1778 of John Paul Jones and his men.

DERBYSHIRE

Duke of Devonshire, CHATSWORTH, Bakewell

DEVONSHIRE PAPERS.

Chatsworth contains the extensive papers of the Dukes of Devonshire, the main bulk of which are as yet unlisted (see, however, H.M.C. iii, pp. 36–45). These include the personal accounts of the Earls of Devonshire, members of the original Virginia and Somer Islands Companies. These were not available for inspection at the time of compilation, but are normally open to inspection by prior arrangement.

Derbyshire County Record Office, County Offices, MATLOCK

QUARTER SESSIONS RECORDS.

Papers dealing with the transportation of felons to America, 1720–72.

Marquess of Lothian, MELBOURNE HALL, Derby

COKE PAPERS. 10 letters. 1625–39.

Papers of Sir John Coke (1563–1644), Secretary of State 1625.

(*a*) 20 Jan. 1626, from Sir Robert Heath, Attorney-General, to Sir John Coke on the decayed state of the Virginia tobacco trade.[1]

(*b*) 29 Nov. 1626, 10 Sept., and 17 Nov. 1627, from Captain Christopher Levett to Sir John Coke, sets forth the advantages to the Crown of New

[1] Transcript, H.M.C. xii (i), p. 250.

England if properly fortified and defended, especially for naval stores and fishing. Seeks a commission to go thither, and 'make that country good against an enemy' at little cost.[1]

(c) 16 Jan. 1628, from Lord Baltimore saying that he has no objection to Levett's request as it will not encroach upon his plantation in Newfoundland.[2]

(d) 4 Feb. 1632, Massachusetts Bay, from Richard Saltonstall to Emanuel Downing, mentioning the commodities—fish, hemp, flax, pitch, tar, potashes, soapashes, masts, pipestaves, clapboards, and iron—in which New England hopes soon to be able to trade, and asking Downing to encourage men to go over.[3]

(e) 12 Dec. 1633, from Emanuel Downing to Sir John Coke, describing the reasons for the settlement of New England and the arguments against the view that 'in time they [New Englanders] will revolt from their allegiance and join in trade with strangers'.[4]

(f) 23 Aug. 1634, from Downing to Sir John Coke, concerning trade with New England and suspicion that the Dutch will try to appropriate it.[5]

(g) 7 May 1635, Jamestown, Va., from Governor Sir John Harvey to Mr. Kemp, charging him to order the Council 'now gathered together' that their assembly is unlawful and that they must disperse.[6]

(h) Extract of a letter, 25 May 1635, from Samuel Mathews 'on the differences between Sir John Harvey (Governor) and the colony of Virginia. The former leaving Jamestown, and the latter appointing Captain John West to act as Governor till His Majesty appoint another.'[7]

(i) 11 July 1639, from Sir Francis Wyatt to Coke, announcing that he is ready to sail to take up his appointment as Governor of Virginia; also draft of Coke's answer.[8]

BUCKINGHAMSHIRE PAPERS. 1770–82.

Contain the correspondence of John Hobart, 2nd Earl of Buckinghamshire (1723–93), who was Viceroy of Ireland 1777–80. Many of the letters to him during that period and earlier contain references to the War of Independence, and to the events that led up to it. (*Letters unless otherwise stated.*)

(a) North American papers include extracts, 1766–8, relating to the Stamp Act crisis; and a representation, 27 Aug. 1765, of the Board of Trade to Council relative to the Virginian Resolutions received in Governor Fauquier's letter of 5 June 1765.[9]

---

[1] Transcripts, H.M.C. xii (i), pp. 287, 321, 331.   [2] Transcript, ibid., p. 337.
[3] Transcript, ibid., p. 449.   [4] Transcript, H.M.C. xii (ii), pp. 38–39.
[5] Transcript, ibid., p. 64.   [6] Transcript, ibid., p. 79.
[7] Ibid., p. 81.   [8] Transcript, ibid., pp. 236–7.
[9] H.M.C. Lothian MSS. [62], pp. 260–1.

(*b*) Copies of Minutes of the Lords of the Committee of Council for Plantation Affairs, upon considering the state of disorder, confusion and misgovernment in the province of Massachusetts Bay, 26 June 1770.[1]

(*c*) Paper, entitled 'Commencement of the American Rebellion', in Buckinghamshire's handwriting but unsigned.[2] [1775?]

(*d*) Letters giving general news about the War, 1776–80.[3]

(*e*) Comments on Irish–American trade. [1777?][4]

(*f*) Letters, 15 and 22 Jan. 1781, and enclosures from Clinton about the threatened mutiny of the Pennsylvanian troops in the American army in 1781.[5]

(*g*) Letter, 21 Jan. 1781, from Peter Holmes, M.P. for the borough of Banagher, King's County, asking Buckinghamshire for a recommendation to a man going to South Carolina to assert his rights to some property there.[6]

(*h*) Letters from Clinton in 1781 and early 1782, the latter group being mainly concerned with Cornwallis's surrender.[7]

(*i*) Three letters from Lord Townshend to the Earl of Buckinghamshire in Feb. 1782, on the Clinton–Cornwallis controversy, and Cornwallis's attempt to have certain letters from him to Clinton brought before the House of Lords. Also 'Notes on the . . . controversy' by Clinton himself; and 'Annotations for Lord Cornwallis's correspondence', containing thirty-three manuscript notes on the controversy.[8]

Godfrey Meynell, Esq., MEYNELL LANGLEY, Derby

ANDRE, JOHN (1751–80). Envelope containing printed poem and letter. 1781.

(*a*) Printed poem, *Monody on Major Andre*, by Anna Seward, 1781.

(*b*) Letter, 1 Oct. 1780, from Andre to General Washington asking to be shot not hung. (Copy?)

N.R.A. 4101.

Mrs. R. Coke-Steel, Trusley Old Hall, SUTTON-ON-THE-HILL, Derby

COKE, EDWARD THOMAS. Travel diaries. 1832.

Diaries and sketches written during a journey to the United States and Canada in 1832. These diaries evidently form the basis of a book published

---

[1] Ibid., p. 289.   [2] Ibid., pp. 291–2.
[3] Ibid., pp. 295–6, 300–6, 309–12, 315–16, 323–4, 326–7, 342–3, 362, 368–9, 378.   [4] Ibid., pp. 306–7.   [5] Ibid., pp. 381–4.   [6] Ibid., p. 384.
[7] Ibid., pp. 387–9, and 396–410 *passim*.   [8] Ibid., p. 411.

in 1833, *A Subaltern's Furlough*, by E. T. Coke, Lieutenant of the 45th Regiment (New York and London, 1833).

N.R.A. 4221.

Sir William Fitzherbert, TISSINGTON HALL, Ashbourne

FITZHERBERT PAPERS. 2 documents. *c.* 1691–2.

Royal warrants for the appointment of Sir William Phipps as Captain-General and Governor-in-Chief of Massachusetts Bay in New England [1691], and of Sir Edmund Andros as Lieutenant and Governor-General of Virginia [1692].[1]

PERRIN, W. S. Correspondence, surveyor's reports and plan. 1774.

Correspondence between W. S. Perrin and Colonel Mercer, and surveyor's reports, upon land on the banks of the Ohio River purchased by Perrin. Includes a surveyor's plan of the land.

N.R.A. 4879.

DEVONSHIRE

J. E. C. Mackrell, Esq., BEECHWOOD, Sparkwell

SEATON PAPERS. 1830–9.

Sir John Colborne, 1st Baron Seaton (1778–1863), was Governor-General and Commander-in-Chief of Canada during the Canadian rebellion of 1838. The collection includes his private letters, official papers, memoranda, speeches, and reports concerning Canada.

N.R.A. 5288.

Mrs. C. Drummond, Oak Lodge, BUDLEIGH SALTERTON

PRATT, JOHN. 14 letters. 1779–1805.

John Pratt served in the 4th (American) Pioneer Regiment during the War of Independence and during subsequent Indian Wars. The letters are military orders or discuss military operations.

N.R.A. 5972.

[1] H.M.C. xiii (vi), pp. 159–60.

H.M. Customs and Excise, DARTMOUTH

See H.M. Customs and Excise, London (p. 199).

City Library, Castle Street, EXETER

EXETER CITY RECORDS.[1] Letters, papers. 1615–1760.

(*a*) 15 July 1615, from Richard Martyn, thanking the Mayor of Exeter 'for your bountifull returne of ther lottery booke' [on behalf of the Virginia Company], and commenting on 'the coldness and backwardness of other places and persons in returning ther books'.[2]

(*b*) Papers, 1623, relating to New England: comprising a letter from Francis, Lord Russell, to the Deputy-Lieutenants of Exeter, and enclosures—a paper entitled 'Reasons shewinge the benefitt of plantinge in Newe England, 1623', and a copy of the King's letter, 8 Dec. 1623, to the Lords-Lieutenants of Somerset, Devon, and Cornwall. The purpose of all these is to secure further settlers for New England.[3]

(*c*) Various items, 1729–64, concerning criminals transported to America.[4]

(*d*) Guinea, 10 Feb. 1737, from Robert Parker to the Chamber of Exeter, mentioning importance of the Royal African Company's forts to the settlements in America.[5]

(*e*) Resolutions to bestow the freedom of the city upon Cornwallis and Simcoe, and Cornwallis's acceptance, both undated. [1782–3?][6]

COCKINGTON PAPERS. Letter-book.

Fragments of the letter-book of Colonel Thomas Gorges (1618–71), Lieutenant-Governor of New England. Include copy of a letter, 28 Aug. 1641, to the elders of the Church at Boston, and letters describing American conditions.

PALK PAPERS. 2 letters. 1769, 1785.

Letters to Sir Robert Palk, Governor of Madras 1763–7, M.P. 1767–8 and 1774–87, including:

(*a*) Madras, 15 June 1769, from Josias Du Pré, containing the sentence: 'Have some mercy, I pray you, upon poor America, or you will repent it by and by.'[7]

---

[1] See also a thesis based primarily on the Exeter City Records and the Devon Collection in the City Library by E. A. G. Clark, 'The estuarine ports of the Exe and Teign with special reference to the period 1660–1860: a study in historical geography', 3 vols. Typescript Ph.D. thesis, University of London, 1957.
[2] Transcript, H.M.C. City of Exeter MSS. [73], p. 99.
[3] Transcript, ibid., pp. 166–71.   [4] Ibid., pp. 237–8.
[5] Transcript, ibid., p. 242.   [6] Ibid., p. 252.
[7] Transcript, H.M.C. Palk MSS. [74], pp. 101–2.

(*b*) Madras, 25 Jan. 1785, from George Baker, mentioning the arrival at Pondicherry of the first United States ship there, coming from Philadelphia.[1]

LETTERS CONCERNING EMIGRANTS FROM DEVON. 3 files containing *c*. 300 letters. 1900–1.

These letters, from persons living in the Empire and the United States, were written in response to a circular published in various newspapers by Sir Roper Lethbridge, the president-elect of the Devonshire Association, asking for information about families of Devonian descent, now settled 'in those lands'.

H.M. Customs and Excise, EXETER

See H.M. Customs and Excise, London (p. 199).

Devon Record Office, The Castle, EXETER

SIDMOUTH PAPERS.[2] 3 volumes, 6 files. 1822–31. (D. 152)

Henry Unwin Addington (1790–1870), a nephew of the 1st Viscount Sidmouth, was British Chargé d'Affaires in Washington 1823–5, and later a British plenipotentiary in negotiations with the United States over the North-East and North-West boundaries with Canada, 1826. American papers included in:

(*a*) Reminiscences, three volumes, 1822–5, include accounts of Congressional debates which Addington attended, the presidential election of 1824; and descriptions of Washington and of trips he made outside Washington; character sketches of leading Americans and of Americans in general.

(*b*) American dispatches and correspondence: 6 files, 1822–31.

(i) Two files, 1823–5, contain copies of his dispatches, chiefly to Canning, and his general correspondence whilst in Washington. Deal with the Monroe Doctrine, the tariff, and the suppression of the slave trade. Include the original of the secret dispatch to Canning of 3 Nov. 1823 about a confidential conversation with John Quincy Adams on the subject of a joint manifesto by Britain and the United States on the revolt in the Spanish colonies as proposed by Canning to Rush in Aug. 1823. Some correspondence with John Quincy Adams and James Buchanan is included.

(ii) Two files entitled 'Negotiations with the U.S.A., 1826–7'. Letters to various members of the government, chiefly to Canning, describing the progress of negotiations with Albert Gallatin on both the North-West and

[1] Transcript, H.M.C. Palk MSS. [74], p. 363.
[2] We are grateful to Viscount Sidmouth for permission to make this report.

North-East boundaries, and the renewal of the commercial agreements of 1815, including projects for conventions on these subjects. Also private correspondence concerning the negotiations, especially the North-East boundary, with notes on surveys and former treaties and agreements. Files contain also printed correspondence on United States–West Indian trade, the boundary negotiations of 1824, the 1824 convention with Russia on possessions on the Pacific coast, copies of Anglo-United States peace treaties from 1783, and a compendium of arguments over the interpretation of the Fifth Article of the Treaty of Ghent, 1814 (i.e. on the North-East boundary), with map.

(iii) Two files entitled 'Letters and other papers relating to the North-East boundary, U.S.A., 1828 and 1829': further private correspondence and memoranda on the North-East boundary negotiations by Addington. Includes: 'Statement respecting the differences between Great Britain and the United States of America under the 5th Article of the Treaty of Ghent destined to be submitted to arbitration as provided by the Convention of the 29th September, 1827'; manuscript volume (250 pages), prepared by him for Lord Aberdeen.—'Skeleton of a project for a second British statement', 1829, manuscript, also by him.—Some papers on the North-East boundary by Sir Howard Douglas, Governor of New Brunswick.—Manuscript copy of the protest by W. P. Preble, American Minister at the Hague, against the award of the Netherlands arbitrator in the North-East boundary dispute, 1831.—Printed *'First statement on the part of Great Britain according to the provisions of the Convention of 29th September 1827 for referring to arbitration the disputed points, under the Fifth Article of the Treaty of Ghent'.*—Printed correspondence on the north-east boundary arbitration of 1831.

FEWINS, GEORGE. 2 letters.[1] 1850, 1851. (D. 132A/PO 822–3)

'Kanses, Jackson county, State of Missouri', 21 July 1850 and Jan. 1851, from Fewins, a carpenter, to the overseers of the parish of Cheriton Bishop, near Exeter, asking that the parish pay for the transportation of his wife and children to New Orleans, where he emigrated because of poverty in England. In the second letter he curses the overseers for refusing, and states with vulgar emphasis that he will not return to England neither to collect his family nor to maintain them.

H.M. Customs and Excise, PLYMOUTH

See H.M. Customs and Excise, London (p. 200).

[1] We are grateful to the Chairman of Cheriton Bishop Parish Council for permission to make this report. Photostats in the collection of Letters of Emigrants to America in the British Library of Political and Economic Science, London School of Economics.

Plymouth Archives Department, Public Library, Tavistock Road, PLYMOUTH

PLYMOUTH CITY RECORDS. Collected papers. 1606–1815.

(*a*) Copy of letters patent by James I for planting two colonies 'on the coast of Virginia and America' to be called the First Colony and the Second Colony, n.d. [1606].[1] (W. 360, f. 57)

(*b*) Copy of orders for the government of the colonies of Virginia, n.d. [1606].[2] (W. 360, f. 95)

(*c*) Letter, 17 Feb. 1609, from the Council of the Virginia Company to the Mayor and Aldermen of Plymouth inviting them to assist the plantation.[3] (W. 359, f. 65)

(*d*) Copy of letter, 5 Feb. 1633, from John Delbridge to the Mayor of Barnstaple about the Turkish pirates. He thinks they will soon attack the fishing boats in Newfoundland and Virginia.[4] (W. 360, f. 30)

(*e*) Letter, 18 Apr. 1815, from J. Beckett to the Mayor of Plymouth, informing him, on behalf of Lord Sidmouth, that Mr. Seymour Larpent and Mr. Charles King have been appointed on behalf of the British and American governments to investigate 'the late unfortunate event' at Dartmoor Prison concerning American prisoners. Draft reply, 20 Apr. 1815, from [Town Clerk] that the Prison is not within the borough's jurisdiction.[5] (W. 362, ff. 64 and 65)

It is almost certain that a complete survey of the Corporation's Account Books would produce other references to Virginia.

Countess of Iddesleigh, PYNES, Exeter

PARKES, JOSEPH (1796–1865). Papers.[6] 1793–*c*. 1863.

Joseph Parkes, politician and Birmingham solicitor. American material in this collection consisting of a large cardboard box of letters and notes, arranged in a number of folders and envelopes, is among the following:

(*a*) Envelope containing about fifty letters, many from Parkes to Sutton Sharpe, about proposed articles by Parkes in the *Jurist*. Letter, 3 May 1829, proposing to write on the jurisprudence of Louisiana, and sending copies to the United States. There are also several letters from Thomas Erskine to his brother, the Earl of Buchan, which include one from Stone (Staffs.?),

[1] Abstract, R.N. Worth, *Calendar of the Plymouth Municipal Records*, p. 223 (Plymouth, 1893). Also H.M.C. ix (i), p. 271 (uu).
[2] Worth, op. cit., p. 228.
[3] Abstract, Worth, op. cit., p. 203. Also H.M.C. ix (i), p. 265 (ww).
[4] Abstract, Worth, op. cit., p. 219.
[5] Abstract, ibid., p. 246. Also H.M.C. x (iv), p. 553 (q).
[6] These are now in the Library, University College, London.

18 Aug. 1793, meditating retirement and retreat to the United States if no change in public affairs occurs, and praising Washington.

(b) Folder of typed copies of letters from Parkes to E. J. Stanley, later 2nd Baron Stanley of Alderney, and replies from Stanley. The letters are mostly about elections and internal Whig politics, but there are occasional American references, e.g. 30 Sept. 1841, from Parkes, 'A Boston steamer will be in Liverpool today or tomorrow. It will probably bring the first day's trial of McLeod and the President's decision on the second edition of the Bank Bill.'

(c) One loose letter, Staples Inn, 9 Feb. 1853, from Parkes to Richard Cobden, describes how in 1830—to aid the Real Property Commission— Parkes had acquainted himself with United States law and legal practice and had published a volume on inheritance, registration, &c., of land in the United States. Proposes to send a copy of this to Cobden.

(d) Envelope containing about twenty letters from Richard Cobden and John Bright. One letter, Rochdale, 9 Dec. 1861, from Bright to Parkes, concerns a speech of his about war with the United States: 'I conclude war is intended here, from the preparations being made and the excitement purposely created. . . . Our ruling class may over-reach themselves.'

(e) Envelope containing several letters from Lord Broughton from Tedworth House, Marlborough. One, 7 Sept. 1862, is on the situation in the United States; he declares that the British Government and public opinion are against the North. Another, 4 Nov. 1863, expresses dismay at the war in the United States.

(f) Envelope containing about fifty letters from Lord Brougham. The letters are nearly all short and some are undated, but there are occasional references to American affairs, particularly c. 1863.

N.R.A. 6313.

Earl Cathcart, SANDRIDGE, Stoke Gabriel

CATHCART PAPERS. Books, journals, miscellaneous papers. 1759–1853.

The American material is mostly from the papers of Sir George Cathcart (1794–1854), general; and Charles Cathcart, 9th Baron Cathcart (1721–76), soldier and diplomat.

(a) Account of an expedition against Quebec under Maj.-General Wolfe, by an engineer, 'P.M.', on that expedition, Apr.–Sept. 1759. (Copied in 1841 from a manuscript lent by Lieut.-General Sir R. D. Jackson, who was Commander of Forces in Canada in 1841.) (45 pages in book form.)

(b) 'Journal de l'expédition contre Quebec, 1759', extending from 1 to 10 May.[1] (35 pages.)

[1] H.M.C. ii, p. 30.

(c) Report on the defence of Canada and Quebec, c. 1763.

(d) Answer of Francis Bernard, Governor of Massachusetts Bay, to the Lords of Trade, 5 Sept. 1763.

(e) Copies of letters, 1766, from Col. Robert Clerk to Lord Shelburne on American affairs.[1]

(f) Copy of Lord Chatham's plan for settling America and asserting the sovereignty of Great Britain over her colonies; reduced into a Bill; presented to the House of Lords; read a first time and rejected 1 Feb. 1775.[2]

(g) Various papers relating to American affairs, 1778–89, including letters from Andrew Elliot, Collector of Customs at New York and Lieutenant-Governor of New York, of both a political and military nature; and letters, 1780 and 1781, from Sir Henry Clinton.[3]

(h) General Wolfe's *Instructions to Young Officers*, &c., 1780 (printed volume).

(i) Eight small books relating to North American history, 1838–53. Contain scraps of material useful for the biography of Charles Murray Cathcart, 2nd Earl Cathcart, general.

N.R.A. 3946.

DORSET

Dorchester Borough Record Office, Town Hall, DORCHESTER

MUNICIPAL RECORDS. 4 papers. 1630–64.

(a) Records of the Justices of Peace. Deposition, 23 Nov. 1630, that Thomas Jarvis, of Lyme, said that 'all the projectors for New England busines are rebells, and that those that are gon over are idolaters, captivated and seperatists'.[4]

(b) Indenture, 11 Mar. 1653, of Henry Hobbs to serve Mr. George Cole, now Mayor, as an apprentice for six years in New England.[5]

(c) Enrolment of apprentice Wm. Parker, bound 9 Mar. 1663, to serve Maximilian Gollop, merchant of Dorchester, for nine years, from 25 Mar. 1664, in New England.[6]

---

[1] H.M.C. ii, p. 30.   [2] Fuller description, ibid., p. 28.
[3] Fuller description, ibid., pp. 29–30.
[4] Charles Herbert Mayo, ed., *The Municipal Records of the Borough of Dorchester, Dorset*, p. 657 (Exeter, priv. print., 1908).
[5] Ibid., p. 547.   [6] Ibid., p. 417.

(*d*) Dorchester Hospital Records. 2 Mar. 1664: 'The steward of the hospitall is desired to disburse unto Mr. Cole the summe of 3*li* for the transportacion of John Barber and his family to New England.'[1]

Dorset Record Office, County Hall, DORCHESTER

CUTLER-RACKETT-CAILLOUEL PAPERS.[2] 46 letters, documents. 1717–61. (NU).

(*a*) Letters from Dr. John Cutler of Boston, mostly 1755–61, to his nephew and niece, Mr. and Mrs. Thomas Rackett, with some, 1744–56, to his sister Abigail Caillouel. Mainly personal, with occasional references to military and naval events during the Seven Years War, and to Indian raids.

(*b*) Two copies of wills of John Cutler of Boston, 1760.

(*c*) Copy of *Boston Gazette and Country Journal*, 24 Sept. 1759.

ABBOTT COLLECTION. Correspondence, account books, &c. *c.* 1795–1832. (Part of the Colfox Collection.)

Andrew Abbott (1743–1819), London potter. His youngest brother, John, went to New Jersey, and a cousin, Joseph Master, settled in Philadelphia; both were Quakers. The correspondence includes four letters, 1812–16, to Andrew Abbott from Joseph Master, Philadelphia; five letters, 1812–17, to Andrew Abbott from his brother John; three letters, 1818–20, to Andrew's daughter Hannah from John Abbott; one letter, 1832, to Hannah Abbott Colfox from a cousin, William Master, in Philadelphia. These letters contain information on conditions of life in Philadelphia, shipments of china, business associates, &c.

An account book, 1795–6, for the late partnership of John Abbott and James Simpson of Philadelphia, contains references to shipments of merchandise, the dispatch of which Andrew appears to have attended to on his brother's behalf. It is followed by an account of cash taken and goods sold out of stock belonging to the late partnership, 1809.

Included with this collection is a typed manuscript by Mrs. E. M. C. Hulls, 'Some notes on Andrew Abbott and his family by his great granddaughter.'

MEATYARD, ROBERT. 2 letters.[3] 1836, 1838.

Written to his mother, Mrs. Mary Meatyard of Twyford, Dorset. The first, Alton, Ill., 22 Mar. 1836, gives an account of his journey to Alton, the price of land, wages of 'mechanics', &c. (NK1). The second, Prasau Creek, Ill., 29 Jan. 1838, is concerned with religious exhortation. (NK2)

WELD PAPERS.[2] 1840–63. (D10)

Mainly letters to Joseph Weld (1777–1863), of Lulworth Castle, about his financial affairs. He had large investments in the Maryland and New York

---

[1] H.M.C. ii, p. 521.   [2] These papers have not yet been catalogued.

[3] Photostats in the collection of Letters of Emigrants to America in the British Library of Political and Economic Science, London School of Economics.

Iron and Coal Co., and a relative, Henry Weld, was an officer at the Company's Mount Savage ironworks. Letters give description of the Company's trade, the operation of the Mount Savage works, and relations with the Baltimore and Ohio Railroad Co. There is an account of assets and liabilities as at 1 July 1863, and a letter, 11 Mar. 1861, on the Morrill Tariff and the prospects of civil war.

Viscount Hinchingbrooke, MAPPERTON, Beaminster

SANDWICH PAPERS.[1] Volume of treaties; letters. 1739–78.

John Montagu, 4th Earl of Sandwich (1718–92), First Lord of the Admiralty 1763–5 and 1771–82. The packet of letters contains copies of letters concerning the attack on St. Lucia and other West Indian islands, 1778. The collection of treaties contains some papers relating to boundaries of Florida, Carolina, &c., 1739.

N.R.A. 5472.

H.M. Customs and Excise, POOLE

See H.M. Customs and Excise, London (p. 199).

S. Wingfield Digby, Esq., SHERBORNE CASTLE, Sherborne

DIGBY PAPERS. 5 letters. 1612, 1755.

(a) Four letters, 1612, from Sir J. Digby at Madrid to W. Trumbull, Sir D. Carleton (two), and Sir T. Edmondes, about Spanish displeasure over the English plantation in Virginia and reputed hostile designs against it.[2]

(b) 26 Aug. 1755, from John Calcraft to Lord Digby on General Braddock's defeat.[3]

H.M. Customs and Excise, WEYMOUTH

See H.M. Customs and Excise, London (p. 199).

---

[1] Some published in *The Private Papers of John, Earl of Sandwich, First Lord of the Admiralty 1771–1782*, ed. by E. R. Barnes and J. H. Owen. 4 vols. (London, 1932–8) (Publications of the Navy Records Society, lxix, lxxi, lxxv, lxxviii).
[2] Transcripts, H.M.C. x (i), pp. 576, 583, 600, and 608.
[3] Transcript, H.M.C. viii (i), p. 226.

DURHAM

The Chapter House, The Cathedral, DURHAM

BACKHOUSE COLLECTION. Letters, minutes, and testimonial.
1785–1838.

(*a*) Letter, 21 Oct. 1785, from Gustus Nassa, a Negro, and seven others,
to the London Meeting for Sufferings of the Society of Friends, being an
address of thanks after reading a book against slavery and of their efforts
to abolish it. Copies of two letters, 19 and 27 Sept. n.y., writer and addressee
not stated, on the state of slaves in Maryland; the writer hopes that the
Friends may work for total abolition.

(*b*) Epistle, 15 June 1816, from Yearly Meeting of Women Friends, Rhode
Island, to same in London.

(*c*) Backhouse–Gurney correspondence: ten letters, 1830–5. Letters to and
from Jonathan Backhouse and his wife, Hannah Chapman Backhouse,
mainly while in New York and Philadelphia, with one letter from Indiana:
four are to their son Edmund in England and one from him; one is from
Jonathan to his wife; and there are single letters from Jonathan's brother
Edmund, H. Gurney, Jane Gurney, and J. Pease. The letters deal mainly
with family and personal news, with occasional comment on English political
matters.

(*d*) Letter, New York, 29 Oct. 1830, from Martha Hawxhurst to William
Hartshorn, criticizing the epistle from the London Yearly Meeting breaking
off communication with the American Friends, who are accused of being
influenced by 'anti-Christian doctrines'; quotes George Fox and William
Penn, and is indignant at the suggestion that Elias Hicks denies Christ.

(*e*) Letter, Westhill-in-Baltimore, 3 Nov. 1835, from I.R.S. (?) to Hannah
Backhouse, describing Yearly Meeting at Baltimore, the decision to send a
certificate of thanks for religious work to Jonathan and Hannah Backhouse
and domestic details about Friends.

(*f*) Testimonial, 27 Jan. 1836, formally addressed to Monthly Meeting at
Darlington and Quarterly Meeting at Durham from Monthly Meeting,
Philadelphia, of work of Jonathan and Hannah Chapman Backhouse as
approved ministers. Signed by Chas. Yarnall and Abigail Nicholson, clerks,
and forty-four members of the meeting. Sent to Jonathan Backhouse at
Darlington.

(*g*) Printed *Copy of a Letter from Joseph John Gurney to Grandchildren of his Aunt,
Jane Gurney*, 25 Dec. 1838. Gives moral advice; mentions 'Hicksism' and
slavery as blots on American escutcheon—otherwise a noble country.

N.R.A. 0628.

National Union of Mineworkers (Durham Area), Miners' Hall, DURHAM

UNION RECORDS (printed).[1] 1877–99.

There are a few references to emigration in the nineteenth-century records of the Durham Miners' Association. A leaflet dated 26 July 1877 announcing the winding-up of a short-lived emigration agency is inserted in the *Minutes and Balance Sheets* volume for July–Dec. 1877. The Union's *Monthly Circular*, Sept. 1899, consists of an address to the members by John Wilson, M.P., on the subject of working conditions and inadequate union organization of miners in the Pittsburgh-Monongahela River areas of Pennsylvania, based on his recent visit there.

Department of Palaeography and Diplomatic, University of Durham, The Prior's Kitchen, The College, DURHAM

GREY OF HOWICK PAPERS.[2] 1777–1911.

This very large collection, in the process of being catalogued, includes the papers of the following:

(*a*) Charles Grey, 1st Earl Grey (1729–1807), general. His papers have not yet been catalogued (Feb. 1960), but are known to include copies of some dispatches and letters of Sir Guy Carleton during the War of Independence.

(*b*) Charles Grey, 2nd Earl Grey (1764–1845), statesman. His correspondence, while Foreign Secretary 1806–7, includes five letters from the American Minister in London, James Monroe.

(*c*) Henry George Grey, Viscount Howick, and afterwards 3rd Earl Grey (1802–94). Two journals kept by his brother, General Charles Grey (1804–70), are included in this group. They cover two visits to the United States, one of these on an official delegacy in connexion with frontier disturbances along the St. Lawrence ('1838. 1st voyage to Canada'), and the other a pleasure trip ('Canada. June 1839. Trip to the States'). The first contains comment on the excellence of travel facilities in the United States, a report on Grey's interview with President Van Buren, impressions of Washington, D.C. The second is a description of roads, scenery, and city sightseeing through Vermont to Boston, New York, Philadelphia, Baltimore, and Washington.

[1] Some of this material was used by Charlotte Erickson, *American Industry and the European Immigrant, 1860–1885* (London and Cambridge, Mass., 1957).
[2] These papers are in the joint custody of the Dean and Chapter of Durham and the University.

(*d*) Albert Henry George Grey, 4th Earl Grey (1851–1917). His correspondence while Governor-General of Canada, 1904–11, includes a great many letters concerning Canadian–American relations. Among the available material (mainly photostats)[1] may be mentioned one box (all photostats), which includes over 200 letters, 1906–8, between Grey and the British Ambassadors in Washington—Sir Mortimer Durand and James Bryce—Theodore Roosevelt, Elihu Root, and others, about the Newfoundland fisheries dispute, Bering Sea fisheries, &c.; and another box (all photostats), containing more than a hundred letters, 1908–10, between Grey and Bryce on the fisheries problems, the boundary waters treaty, possible tariff changes, &c.

The Library, Ushaw College, DURHAM

WISEMAN, NICHOLAS (1802–65). Correspondence: 3 letters.[2] 1827, 1837.

Letters from correspondents in the United States to Wiseman while vice-rector and rector of the English College at Rome:

Kenrick, Peter Richard. Philadelphia, 30 July 1837, on particulars of American editions of Wiseman's works, noting that these have revived Kenrick's desire to have Hebrew, at least, taught in American seminaries.

Larkin, John. Baltimore, 12 Feb. 1827, dealing with the study of Hebrew at St. Mary's Seminary, Baltimore; the state and prospects of the Catholic Church and its priesthood in America; the attitude towards the Catholic Church of Protestant bishops and the press; &c. (11 pages).

Maréchal, Ambrose, Archbishop of Baltimore. Baltimore, n.d. but received by Wiseman on 15 Nov. 1827, on the neglect of Oriental studies among Catholics and the pursuit of such studies at the Baltimore Seminary.

Public Libraries, Ocean Road, SOUTH SHIELDS

FOX COLLECTION. American journals (4 volumes). 1831–68.

George Townsend Fox (1810–86), born at Westoe, South Shields, entered the firm of G. Sands & Hodgson, general merchants, Liverpool, in 1830; he was sent to America by Mr. Sands in 1831.

The journals cover four separate visits: 1831–2, 1834, 1841, and 1868. The first is through the North-East; the second is down the Southern seaboard to New Orleans; the third is to New York and Ohio; and the fourth is through the North-East to Illinois, containing an account of the oil well at Oil City. The volumes contain comment on religion, social customs, cost of travel, &c.; the comparisons he makes in the fourth journal with New York twenty-four years previously are interesting.

---

[1] The originals are held in the Public Archives of Canada, Ottawa.

[2] Printed with introduction and notes by John Tracy Ellis, 'Three American Letters from the Wiseman Papers', *Catholic Historical Review*, vol. xliii, pp. 458–72, 1958.

H.M. Customs and Excise, STOCKTON-ON-TEES

See H.M. Customs and Excise, London (p. 205).

H.M. Customs and Excise, SUNDERLAND

See H.M. Customs and Excise, London (p. 205).

ESSEX

W. Weston Underwood, Esq., The Maltings, ALDHAM, Colchester

WESTON PAPERS. 13 letters, 1 document. 1757–68.

(*a*) Dispatch, 26 Sept. 1757, from Sir Benjamin Keene, Ambassador to Madrid, to William Pitt, including the views of the Spanish Minister on British usurpations in America.[1]

(*b*) Copy of a dispatch, 24 Sept. 1762, Paris, from the Duke of Bedford to Lord Egremont, mentioning navigation of the Mississippi.[2]

(*c*) 'Copy of the preliminary articles of peace friendship & alliance entered into between the English and the deputies of the Seneca Nation by Sir William Johnson . . . Superintendent of Indian Affairs.' 13 Apr. 1764.[3]

(*d*) Copy of an extract from a letter, 21 Sept. 1764, written by Major General Gage to Lord Halifax from New York (enclosed in Mr. Sedgwick's letter of 6 Nov.) in which he describes the conference at Niagara with various Indian tribes, names those which did not attend, and details crimes committed by some of them, against whom punitive expeditions have been sent.[4]

(*e*) Nine letters from Edward Sedgwick to Edward Weston. Three, 1765, concern opposition in America to the Stamp Act; six, 1767–70, concern disaffection in the American colonies, including non-importation measures.[5]

(*f*) 12 Aug. 1768, from Sir James Porter to Edward Weston, including the comment 'I think whatever measures government may adopt with the

---

[1] Transcript, H.M.C. x (i), p. 217.   [2] Transcript, ibid., pp. 222–3.
[3] Ibid., p. 228.   [4] Transcript, ibid., p. 236.
[5] Transcripts, ibid., pp. 382, 384, 399, 402–3, 405–6, 418, 420–1, 422.

Americans; they will succeed without any great difficulty it is at Boston but two or three degenerate wretches who occasion the bustle and when it comes to the push I dare say they will fear the rod.'[1]

Essex Record Office,[2] County Hall, CHELMSFORD

ROUND PAPERS. Letters, business and miscellaneous papers. 1585–1776. (*Letters unless otherwise stated.*)

(*a*) Document entitled 'For Mr. Rauleys viage', *c.* 1585. Apparently written by an experienced soldier giving advice to those undertaking Sir Walter Ralegh's project to colonize Virginia.[3] (D/DRh z1)

(*b*) Thomas Stebbing & Son. Business records. 1743–57. Eighteenth-century linen drapers of Cornhill, London.

(i) Six letters, 1743–4, from Thomas Summersett, master of a packet going to Carolina, to the owners, concerning a voyage to Antigua and South Carolina, with accounts, manifests, and bills of lading. (D/DRc B24)

(ii) Sixteen letters, 1746–65, mostly to Robert Stebbing from John Guerard, of Charleston, S.C., concerning the dry goods trade, with three accounts and three bills of exchange. (D/DRc B26)

(iii) Bills of exchange, 1748–51, drawn in Maryland on London merchants. (D/DRc B27)

(iv) Five letters, 1750–7, from Charles & Alex Stedman, merchants of Philadelphia, concerning the dry goods trade, with six bills of exchange. (D/DRc B29)

(*c*) Perth Amboy, N.J., 14 Nov. 1748, from Governor Belcher of New Jersey to an unknown correspondent, describes the foundation of Princeton, and gives a description of the crops raised in New Jersey.[4] (D/DRg 4/65)

(*d*) 5 Apr. 1757, from Thomas Falconer to Charles Gray, mentions that 'Lord Loudon is gone upon an expedition of some consequence, either against Ticonderago, or some other fort which opens the way to Crown Point'.[5] (D/DRg 4/5)

(*e*) 30 Nov. 1765, from Falconer to Gray, on the unsatisfactory state of the American colonies. Three further letters, 18 Mar. and 19 Apr. 1766, and 25 May 1767, on American affairs.[6] (D/DRg 4/9–11, 4/17)

(*f*) 10 Feb. 1770, from Falconer to Gray, 'discusses arguments of the Bostonians and their friends', &c.[7] (D/DRg 4/24)

---

[1] Ibid., p. 411.

[2] F. G. Emmison, ed., *Guide to the Essex Record Office*, part ii (Chelmsford, 1948).

[3] Printed in A. C. Edwards, ed., *English History from Essex Sources, 1550–1750*, pp. 178–9 (Chelmsford, 1952). (This volume includes colonial documents to 1783.)

[4] Transcript, H.M.C. xiv (ix), pp. 292–3.   [5] Transcript, ibid., p. 295.

[6] Extracts, ibid., pp. 297–9, 300–1.   [7] Extract, ibid., p. 304.

(g) 15 Nov. 1775, from Falconer to Gray, says, 'The examination of Pen was of little consequence, but it proves that the Pensylvanians reject their charter whenever they like and admit it where it is advantagious.' Says 'the sword must decide' the dispute. The Irish may help the Americans. Fears engendered by the Quebec Act. The Glasgow trade will suffer during the suspension of Virginian commerce.[1] (D/DRg 4/31)

(h) 13 Apr. 1776, from Falconer to Gray, considers that the root of the rebellion lies in the expulsion of the French from Quebec.[2] (D/DRg 4/32)

ABDY PAPERS. Will. 1642.

Will of Nicholas Abdy, London merchant, includes a bequest of £120 for twenty boys and girls, taken vagrant in the streets of London, to be conveyed to Virginia, New England, or the West Indies. (D/DAy F4)

AUDLEY END PAPERS. Letters and documents. 1673–1779.

(a) Eight documents, 1673–1749, chiefly relating to New York, including warrants for delivery and reception of gunpowder there, 1673.[3] Letter, 1675, from the Governor, Sir Edmund Andros, concerning revenue. Petition, c. 1680, of the collector of customs for discharge from debt. Copy, c. 1725, of a 1711 Act for affirmation of those who cannot take an oath. Letter, 1736, to a Henry Clay on the purchase of land in New York colony, and factories there (11 pages). Report, 1749, on the state of affairs in New York by Governor Clinton, and copies of his letters on finance and Indians. (D/DBy o26–32)

(b) Three letters, two in 1700[4] and one in 1702, from William Penn to Lord Grey, Governor of Barbados, congratulating him on his administration. (D/DBy o25)

(c) 15 Feb. 1749, from Corbyn Morris to the Earl of Halifax, on the balance of trade with the North American colonies, and on the suppression of their paper currency (7 pages). (D/DBy o53)

(d) 12 Apr. 1779, from Rockingham to Sir John Griffin Griffin, stating that many Americans are in favour of returning to their allegiance.[5] (D/DBy C9/28)

SPERLING PAPERS. Ledger, 1719–58; letter, 1795.

Business records of Henry and John Sperling, furriers of London.

(a) Numerous ledger entries relate to the Sperlings' dealings with American trappers, and trade with the colonies, under such headings as 'Cargoes to Maryland', 'Voyage to New England', &c. (D/DQl)

(b) 13 July 1795, from W. Jackson of Pennsylvania, commenting on American exports for 1791–5. (D/DSe 5)

---

[1] Extract, H.M.C. xiv (ix), pp. 307–8.   [2] Extract, ibid., p. 308.
[3] Printed in Edwards, op. cit., p. 181.
[4] One of these printed in ibid., p. 181.   [5] Printed in ibid., p. 200.

DISNEY PAPERS. 3 documents. 1725–1804.

(a) Declaration of trust, 1725, from Harvard College to Thomas Hollis of sum of £3,670. 13s. 0½d. for the salary and support of a Professor of Divinity, which chair Hollis had founded, and for the support of poor scholars. Further declaration, 1730, for the same sum and for a further sum of £1,170, which Hollis had given to found a professorship of Mathematics and Natural and Experimental Philosophy. (D/DDs F8)

(b) Probate of will and codicils, 1804, of Thomas Brand Hollis, which includes a bequest to 'the college instituted for the promoting of learning in New England'. (D/DDs F9)

TOWER PAPERS. Letters, documents, &c. (photostats).[1] 1732–8

Papers of Thomas Tower (d. 1778), a trustee for Georgia in the colony's early days, include:

(a) Notes (incomplete) on a palaver with the Indians; n.d. (D/DTw o8/5)

(b) Draft charter for Georgia, n.d. (before 1732). (D/DTw o8/1)

(c) Copies of a memorial, of 1 Dec. 1727, on the importance of a fort on the River Alatamaha, Ga. (D/DTw o8/5)

(d) Account, 1732, of a voyage of the Anne with James Oglethorpe and settlers for Georgia aboard.[2] (D/DTw o8/2)

(e) Letters, both 1738, from Oglethorpe to Sir Robert Walpole[3] and Tower about Georgia. (D/DTw o8/3, 6)

(f) Oglethorpe's personal account, 1738, of the mutiny at St. Andrew's Fort, Georgia.[4] (D/DTw o8/7)

(g) Copy of petition, 1742, from the people of Georgia. (D/DTw o8/4)

MILDMAY PAPERS. 2 documents.[5] 1734, c. 1750. (D/DM o1/41)

(a) Memorial on constitutional development in the American colonies laid before the House of Lords, 1734.

(b) Memorandum, c. 1750, by William Shirley, Governor of Massachusetts 1741–56, on the economic and strategic value to Britain of the American colonies.

WITHAM MONTHLY MEETINGS OF THE SOCIETY OF FRIENDS. Certificate.[6] 1751. (D/NF 1/2/13)

Certificate, 19 Aug. 1751, from the East Pennsylvania Monthly Meeting of Friends to the Chelmsford Meeting, certifying the good character of Thomas Wyett, about to journey to England.

[1] Originals sold to Thomas Gilcrease Institute of American History and Art, P.O. Box 2419, Tulsa, Okla.
[2] Extracts printed in Edwards, op. cit., p. 182.
[3] Printed in ibid., p. 183.   [4] Printed in ibid., pp. 183–4.
[5] Printed in ibid., pp. 189–95.
[6] See photograph in F. G. Emmison, ed., Guide to the Essex Record Office, pt. ii, p. 102 (Chelmsford, 1948).

RUSSELL PAPERS. 2 journals of risks. 1759–74.

Business papers[1] of William and Samuel Braund, merchants of London. William Braund (1695–1774) was a director of the East India Company and of the Sun Fire Office, and a Lloyds underwriter. The journals, arranged under names of merchants with an index in the second volume, record premiums paid, in some cases for insurance on voyages to the North American colonies. (D/DRu B7, 8)

SLAVERY RELEASE. 2 documents.[2] 1760–1. (D/DHt A5)

Document, 9 July 1760, signed by Cornelis C. Wynkoop of New York, providing for the liberation of his slave, Fortin Vrelinghuyson, should the latter go on a cruise on board of H.M. ships then fitting out. Also a certificate, 5 June 1761, by the captain of one of these vessels that this has been done.

RIGBY PAPERS. 1772–82.

Papers relating to the clearing of the public accounts of Richard Rigby, Paymaster-General to H.M. Forces 1768–82. One document is 'a certificate of sums issued to Daniel Wier, Commissary General in North America and to his deputies and assistants' there, 1772–82. Total of £2,071,904. 6s. 6d. was issued. Includes entries for forage and other supplies to forces fighting in various parts of the colonies during the War of Independence. (D/DHw 048)

SMYTH PAPERS. 3 letters. 1781, 1785.

Correspondence of Sir Robert Smyth (1744–1802), M.P. for Colchester 1780–90, includes:

(a) Comments on the Franco-American alliance, Jan. 1781, by Dr. Nathaniel Forster, rector of All Saints, Colchester, and Rev. Charles Onley of Stisted Hall, Essex.

(b) Letter, 1785, from John Frederick Sackville, 3rd Duke of Dorset, Ambassador to Paris 1783–9, referring to Adams and Franklin in Paris being 'damned angry' at the British bill to restrain American trade to Newfoundland. (D/DFg 21)

EVANS AND HARVEY-GEORGE FAMILIES' PAPERS. 6 letters and documents. 1793–1808. (D/DU 126/167–72)

Letters and documents from or about John Jee, Jr., who went to the United States in 1793 to escape his creditors in England and apparently died there c. 1808. He settled first in Charleston, S.C., and in a letter, 7 Oct. 1794, to his father, describes the unhealthiness of the Charleston climate, the high mortality there, and his intention of going to New York. Thereafter he vanishes and the letters and documents relate to the administration of his estate.

---

[1] See L. S. Sutherland, *A London Merchant, 1695–1774* (London, 1933) which is based on these papers.   [2] Printed in *Essex Review*, vol. xlv, pp. 120–1, 1936.

SANDFORD AND HUGHES FAMILIES' PAPERS. Letter, journal.
1794, 1796.

(a) 1 Sept. 1794, from R. T. Hughes at Pittsgrove, Salem, N.J., to Sheppard
Sandford, grocer, South Halstead, Essex. Gives interesting details of fruits
grown, price of land, method of farming and quality of soil, timber, shortage
of labour because 'every man thinks himself independent'; comments on
slave trade and European war, news of other emigrants, including Mr.
Choat from Coggeshall. (D/DU 371/12)

(b) Journal, 31 May–9 July 1796 [? kept by R. T. Hughes], of a voyage
from America to England. Includes observations on the choice between a
French guillotine and an English press-gang and on the writer's reading
matter. At end: 'A coppy of a letter to a friend on the present political and
agricultural state of America' with a pencilled note, 'Supposed the Revd.
Jas. Bass'. (D/DU 371/13)

MAITLAND PAPERS.[1] Will. 1802. (D/DMe F1/5)

Copy of will and codicil of John Shoolbred, an eighteenth-century London
merchant, whose son, James, owned a plantation and Negroes in Virginia.
The will shows that these Negroes were mortgaged to John as a security for
James's debts, and a bond for their value was deposited with Mr. Moodie,
British Consul at Charleston, S.C.

PARISH RECORDS.

(a) Earls Colne. Document,[2] 14 May 1711, giving the consent of the
Colchester Workhouse Corporation to a gardener taking his apprentice to
New England. (D/P 209/14/1)

(b) Steeple Bumpstead. Overseers' miscellaneous papers, 1811–57. Memorandum of an agreement, 26 Apr. 1832, between the parishioners and certain
pauper families that the parish will pay for their emigration to America;
and a resolution, 15 May, to borrow £100 for that purpose. (D/P 21/18/5)

(c) Writtle. Overseers' accounts include an item for 1631. 'Layd out for
parrill [apparel] for two boyes that ware sent to Virgeny', £4. 7s. 3d.[3] (D/P
50/12/1)

There is more such emigration material, including emigration circulars
and poor law union accounts, in other parish records in the Record Office.[4]

QUARTER SESSIONS RECORDS.

Agreement, 1741, by two London merchants to transport certain felons to
the colonies and plantations in America, and to procure certificates of

---

[1] See also Papers belonging to Commander Maitland, M.P., Harrington Hall,
Spilsby, Lincs. (p. 117).
[2] See *Essex Parish Records, 1240–1894*, prepared by E. J. Erith, plate ix (Chelmsford, 1950).   [3] Printed in Edwards, op. cit., p. 179.
[4] See M. D. Wainwright, 'Agencies for the promotion or facilitation of emigration from England to the U.S.A., 1815–61', M.A. thesis, University of London,
1951.

landing from the governors or chief customs house officers there.[1] (Q/SBb 156/16)

H.M. Customs and Excise, HARWICH

See H.M. Customs and Excise, London (p. 207).

GLOUCESTERSHIRE

Bristol Record Office,[2] Council House, BRISTOL 1

DEPOSITION BOOKS OF BRISTOL. 6 volumes. 1643–87.

These records contain copies of voluntary sworn statements made before the Mayor and one or more of the Aldermen on a wide variety of subjects, including loss of ships, merchandise quarrels, thefts, &c. The first two volumes,[3] 1643–54, contain a number of references to the Virginia trade, tobacco, and one reference to New England. The unpublished volumes[4] seem likely to contain rather more of this type of information.

SERVANTS TO FOREIGN PLANTATIONS.[5] 2 volumes. 1654–79.

In 1654 the City Council of Bristol ordained that, before embarkation, persons bound as servants for overseas were to be articled and enrolled as were the city apprentices. These two volumes contain the fair copies of this system of enrolment. They include the names, with places of origin, of more than 10,000 servants to foreign plantations who sailed from Bristol to Virginia, Maryland, and other parts of the Atlantic coast. Also an entry on the system in Sessions concern Gloucestershire apprentices bound to serve in Virginia. The City Archives also contain other rough entry books concerned with city apprentices, which note servants bound overseas down to Feb. 1685.

---

[1] Printed in Edwards, op. cit., p. 185.

[2] Once known as the City Archives Department.

[3] Two volumes have been published : *Deposition Books of Bristol*, vol. 1, 1643–7, ed. by H. E. Nott; vol. 2, 1650–4, ed. by H. E. Nott and E. Ralph (Bristol, 1935, 1943) (Bristol Record Society's Publications, vols. vi and xiii).

[4] Extracts from these in P. McGrath, ed., *Merchants and Merchandise in Seventeenth Century Bristol* (Bristol, 1955) (Bristol Record Society's Publications, vol. xix).

[5] Much of this material has been printed in *Bristol and America*, transcribed by R. Hargreaves-Mawdsley (London, 1929). The original documents contain rather more detail.

PENN, WILLIAM (1644–1718). 6 documents. 1681–1713.

These deeds and conveyances were formerly in the archives of the Bristol and Frenchay Monthly Meeting of the Society of Friends. They refer to the lease and sale of land in Pennsylvania, and various agreements between William Penn and others.

VANDERHORST AND DUNCOMBE COLLECTION. *c*. 200 items. 1701–late 19th century.

Consists of deeds, a few letters, and papers (*c*. 200 items) of the Vanderhorst and Duncombe families. Elias Vanderhorst of South Carolina came to Bristol, after the War of Independence, where he became a merchant, and in 1792 he was appointed the first American Consul there. Although most of the documents relate to the affairs of the families in Bristol and South Wales, there is some material concerning slaves and estates in South Carolina and Georgia. There are also official documents relating to Elias Vanderhorst's consulship in Bristol, including a letter of appointment signed by George Washington and Thomas Jefferson.

OPIE PAPERS.[1] 3 letters, few miscellaneous papers. 1704–19.

Three letters, n.d., 5 Nov. 1714, 28 June (?)1719, from John Opie in Virginia to Miss Susannah Opie and Mrs. Eleanor Harte. Also bills and notes of Susannah Opie, 1704–7, concerning the business of her father's estates in Virginia, and the tobacco trade.

JACKSON, ARTHUR. Letters of administration. 12 July 1712.

Administration of the goods of Arthur Jackson of 'Quary Crik, Patomack River, Co. Stafford, Virginia' to Arthur Jackson, his father.

NOBLET RUDDOCK & CO. Bills of lading[2] (1 volume). 1719–21.

General merchants, Bristol. Bills of lading for ships bound to many ports in Europe, Africa, West Indies, and America sent by this firm. The volume has not been examined, but the catalogue references indicate that it might relate to the 'triangular trade'—Bristol, West Africa, North America.

HOBHOUSE PAPERS.[3] Letters. 1723–36.

These are mainly duplicates of those in the Jefferies Collection, volume xiii, in the Bristol Public Libraries (p. 58).

KING, JOHN (d. 1734). Business records. 1716–36(?)

Bristol merchant long engaged in the North American trade. He had interests in the tobacco trade and invested in a Virginia ironworks. The

---

[1] One of these is printed in W. E. Minchinton, ed., *Trade of Bristol in the Eighteenth Century*, p. 140 (Bristol, 1957) (Bristol Record Society's Publications, vol. xx).
[2] Bills of lading for 1720 printed in ibid., pp. 76–81.
[3] See ibid., pp. 74–75, 82–101, 150–1. See also Henry Hobhouse, *Memoirs of the Hobhouse Family* (Taunton, priv. print., 1927).

firm of King continued to flourish in Bristol throughout the eighteenth and nineteenth centuries. It is believed that they were prominent in the slave trade. The City Archives also contain various papers and deeds relating to other members of the family including William Poole King, Samuel King, and Thomas Liston. These contain several references to the Virginia trade and to William Temple of Virginia.

FELTMAKERS AND HABERDASHERS. Minute-book, 1673–1865.

Contains a copy of the famous 'Hat Act', 1732, which limited the number of apprentices bound to the hat-making trade in the colonies, and forbade the export of hats from the American plantations. The incorporation of this Act into the minute-book might suggest that the Bristol hat-makers regarded the Act of considerable importance; but it seems unlikely that this volume contains other references to the American hat industry.

COGHLAN, JOHN. Articles of agreement. 1781.

An authorization for John Coghlan, a Bristol merchant, to privateer against French, Spanish, Dutch, and American colonial vessels during the War of Independence.

City Museum, Queen's Road, BRISTOL 8

GREAT WESTERN. Log-book, 2 Apr.–11 May 1842. (G 2538)

Covers the twenty-third Atlantic crossing of the famous steamship. The outward journey was made from Bristol to New York, and the return voyage was to Liverpool. Except for some references to the disorderly behaviour of the crew and pilot in New York, the log is merely a systematic account of engine speeds, weather conditions, and other nautical information.

H.M. Customs and Excise, BRISTOL

See H.M. Customs and Excise, London (p. 200).

Friends Meeting House, 300 Gloucester Road, BRISTOL 7

BRISTOL AND FRENCHAY MONTHLY MEETING OF THE SOCIETY OF FRIENDS. Records.[1]

Some of the principal classes of records are:

(*a*) Bristol and Frenchay Monthly Meeting:
    (i) Minutes of Men's Monthly Meeting, 1667–

---

[1] Extensive use of the material was made by R. S. Mortimer, 'Bristol Quakerism, 1654–1700'. Typescript M.A. thesis, University of Bristol, 1946.

(ii) Minutes of Women's Monthly Meeting (merged with the Men's Meeting in the nineteenth century).

(*b*) George Fox and other Friends' letters (MSS. vol. v), 1667–73.

(*c*) Certificates of Removal, 1669–

(*d*) Letters of Discipline, 1671–

The present depository is of a temporary nature, and while the records were available for examination only a cursory glance was made at their content. It is to be presumed that they contain scattered Americana similar to that in like classes in the Library of the Society of Friends, London (p. 211). Some of the Minutes relate to a Friends' committee in Bristol for aiding distressed cotton workers during the Civil War. Vol. v of the collection contains two manuscript diaries of George Fox, which are printed in the *Journal of George Fox*, rev. ed. by John L. Nickalls (Cambridge, 1952).

Imperial Tobacco Company (of Great Britain and Ireland) Ltd., East Street, BRISTOL 3

FRANKLYN, GEO. & CO. Letter-book. 1814–20.

Bristol firm of tobacco merchants, which has since been incorporated into Imperial Tobacco. The letter-book contains material relating to the impact of the War of 1812 on the English tobacco industry. It also describes the working of the domestic market and industry.

Moravian Church, Maudlin Street, BRISTOL 1

RECORDS OF PIONEER MISSIONARY WORK IN NORTH AMERICA. 1751–77.

In the archives of the Bristol Moravian Church there are a number of manuscripts relating to the work of the Moravian missionaries in North America. There is an account of their station among the Eskimoes and Indians in Labrador, Sept. 1771–Oct. 1772; and fragmentary material relating to their work in Pennsylvania and Ohio, and to their travels to and from the mission field.

These records are listed in F. M. Blandford, 'Catalogue of the Archives of the Bristol Moravian Church', 2 vols., typescript, submitted for Part III of Diploma in Librarianship, University of London, 1949. (Copies in Bristol University Library and with the Rev. Henry Williams, Moravian College, 87 W. Church Street, Bethlehem, Pa.)

Port of Bristol Authority, Queen Square, BRISTOL 1

STATISTICS OF THE PORT OF BRISTOL (printed volumes).
1885–   .

The Port of Bristol Authority is responsible for the Bristol City Docks,
Portishead Dock, and Avonmouth Dock. The printed annual reports of
the Port's trade give information about Anglo-American trade, in particular
the amount of net register tonnage arriving from and departing for America.
Detailed statistics of trade with America are contained in the Authority's
archives.

Public Libraries, College Green, BRISTOL 1

JEFFERIES COLLECTION.[1] Vol. xiii: letters. *c.* 1722–36.
(B 7957)

Consists mainly of about 150 letters written to Isaac Hobhouse,[2] a leading
Bristol merchant, and his partners, by ships' captains and agents in the
West Indies and the American colonies. Of particular importance are the
letters describing the trade between West Africa and the Southern colonies,
and the relations between New England and the West Indies during 1722–
36. These give details of the commodities carried, and the difficulties involved in this trade. This volume also contains one or two letters relating
to the colonial shipbuilding industry[3] in Boston and Philadelphia, and to
the cost of construction during the 1730's. There is also information on the
efforts of British merchants to restrict a 'cheap money' policy in South
Carolina and Virginia, and their interest in the Indian trade in deer-skins
and hides.

SOUTHWELL PAPERS.[4] (B 11152–61)

Most of this large collection of ten bound volumes of letters and other documents, dating from the late seventeenth century to 1776, relates to the
activities of the Southwell family of Kingsweston, near Bristol, who were
Bristol merchants. The volumes contain scattered references to the colonial
trade, but the relevant material is slight. The volumes covering 1745–76
contain some reference to the tobacco trade with Virginia and Maryland;
and a scheme to revise the duty system on American tobacco which was
first proposed by the merchants of Liverpool. Other references to the tobacco
trade are few and of little value. The volume for 1746–76 also includes a
copy of a pamphlet condemning the smuggling prevalent in the American
colonies.

[1] See W. E. Minchinton, ed., *Trade of Bristol in the Eighteenth Century*, pp. 82–101,
150–1 (Bristol, 1957) (Bristol Record Society's Publications, vol. xx).
[2] See W. E. Minchinton, ed., 'The Virginia Letters of Isaac Hobhouse, Merchant
of Bristol', *Virginia Magazine of History and Biography*, vol. lxvi, pp. 278–301, 1958.
[3] See W. E. Minchinton, ed., *Trade of Bristol in the Eighteenth Century*, pp. 93–94.
[4] See ibid., pp. 152–3.

DICKINSON, CALEB. Copy-book of letters. 1757–8. (B 19718)

Contains some references to Bristol trade with Virginia and Philadelphia. For fuller details *see* the Frankard and Dickinson Papers in the Somerset Record Office, Taunton (p. 405.)

BRISTOL PRESENTMENT BOOKS.[1] (B 10750, &c.) (Published by Samuel Worrall from the Custom House records of the port of Bristol, but they are not official Custom House Papers.) Imports: 1770, 1775–80, 1795–6, 1801–18.—Exports: 1773–80, 1790, 1795–6, 1801–18.—Exports and Imports: 1819–20, 1823–4, 1827–8, 1830–44, 1846–1917.

These volumes are composed of weekly or bi-weekly publications listing imports and exports at Bristol. The nineteenth-century series was published every Monday and Thursday, listing every vessel clearing and entering the port of Bristol. Amongst them are vessels trading between Bristol and America. Details of the goods which were exchanged are given.

MERCHANDISE IMPORTED INTO BRISTOL. 1774–88. (B 21259)

This account book lists vessels which entered Bristol from the American colonies and other ports during 1774; and gives the date of arrival and the commodities carried. This is most probably derived from the Bristol Presentment Books (q.v.); the volume of imports for 1774 is missing in that series.

SHARPLES, ELLEN (WALLACE) (1769–1849). Diary,[2] 1803–36. (B 19728)

Wife of James Sharples, the artist, who painted portraits of Washington and many other prominent Americans. She was herself an artist of considerable talent. She visited the United States twice. This diary, kept 1803–36, covers the time of her second visit, May 1809 to Feb. 1811, when James Sharples died. She met many prominent figures, and her diary gives a useful picture of life in early nineteenth-century New York. After 1811 the diary contains scarcely any material which is directly relevant to the United States.

EARLY BRISTOL NEWSPAPERS.

There is a published catalogue of the Reference Library collection: *Early Bristol Newspapers: a detailed Catalogue of Bristol Newspapers Published up to and including the year 1800 in the Bristol Reference Library* (Bristol, private circulation, 1956).

[1] See ibid., pp. 48–50, 57–71.
[2] For copious extracts from the diary see K. M. Knox, *The Sharples* (London 1931; and New Haven, Conn., 1930).

Red Lodge, City Art Gallery Annexe, Park Row, BRISTOL 1

MARY CARPENTER COLLECTION. Photograph album.

This album was once the property of Mary Carpenter (1807–77), the philanthropist and reformer, who maintained a girls' reformatory school in the Red Lodge. The album is of interest only because it contains individual portraits of all the principal American delegates to the International Penal and Prison Congress held in London in 1872, including such figures as G. S. Griffith and Governor Haines of New Jersey. Mary Carpenter also kept a book in which her friends, visiting the Lodge, were asked to write a few verses. This book is still in the Lodge, but appears to be of little value except to show that a number of prominent abolitionists and reformers held Mary Carpenter in high regard.

W. E. Salt, Esq., Director, Department of Adult Education, University of Bristol, 20A Berkeley Square, BRISTOL 8

CANER, HENRY (?1700–92). Letter-book. 1728–78.

Anglican clergyman. The letter-book contains draft copies of the letters of Caner, who was taken to the colonies as a child. His father built the first buildings of Yale College, from which the son graduated in 1724. The letters date from his acceptance of the Society for the Propagation of the Gospel mission at Fairfield, Conn., in 1728, and continue through his tenure of the rectorship of King's Chapel, Boston, to his return to England as a Loyalist refugee.

The majority of the letters concern ecclesiastical affairs: reports to the S.P.G., letters to the Archbishop of Canterbury and the Bishop of London, and correspondence with other New England clergymen. There are a number of letters to members of his family, to Barlow Trecothick on financial affairs, and to Governor John Wentworth of New Hampshire.

Society of Merchant Venturers, Merchants' Hall, Clifton Downs, BRISTOL 8

(Applications should be made in writing to the Treasurer)

RECORDS OF THE SOCIETY.

Contain material relating to American trade and colonization. A guide to the scope of this material for the seventeenth century is to be found in Patrick McGrath, ed., *Records Relating to the Society of Merchant Venturers of the City of Bristol in the Seventeenth Century* (Bristol, 1952) (Bristol Record Society's Publications, vol. xvii), and in Patrick McGrath, ed., *Merchants and Merchandise in Seventeenth Century Bristol* (Bristol, 1955) (Bristol Record Society's Publications, vol. xix). Among the material there is also a manuscript calendar by J. Latimer, *c.* 1897, useful as a summary of the Society's records. Latimer also wrote *The History of the Society of Merchant Venturers of the City of Bristol* (Bristol, 1903), which may be of value in examining these sources.

The Library, University of Bristol, Queen's Road, BRISTOL 8

MARTIN, HENRY (d. 1721). Inspector-General's Ledger of Imports and Exports from Christmas 1715 to Christmas 1716.

Martin was Inspector-General of Imports and Exports. The ledger is a record of English imports and exports, arranged under the names of the countries with which business was done, and classified in a detailed list of commodities. The American colonies are grouped together as follows: Carolina, New England, New York, Pennsylvania, Virginia, and Maryland. The account of colonial exports is arranged under these headings and relates either to London or the outports. Details are given, including the amount and estimated value of both British and foreign merchandise imported and also the relative values of different products in the economy of each group of colonies. Values are totalled and a series of abstracts give the general balance of trade and the particular balance for each group of colonies.

PINNEY PAPERS

These deal mainly with West Indian trade.[1] But in the letter-books there are a few letters to correspondents in the mainland colonies, including a letter,[2] Bristol, 19 Feb. 1785, from Pinney & Tobin to David Ross & Co., Portsmouth, Va., for whom Pinneys acted as commission agents for the sale of sugar, rice, and tobacco, and who supplied corn to Nevis, West Indies.

W. D. & H. O. Wills,[3] East Street, BRISTOL 3

WASHINGTON, GEORGE. Letter.[4] 1759.

Original letter, 25 Nov. 1759, from George Washington to his English agent, Robert Cary & Co., stating that he will be shipping some tobacco and asking Cary to deal with it in the usual manner.

[1] Richard Pares, *A West India Fortune* (London, 1950).
[2] W. E. Minchinton, ed., *The Trade of Bristol in the Eighteenth Century*, pp. 129–30 (Bristol, 1957) (Bristol Record Society's Publications, vol. xx).
[3] Branch of Imperial Tobacco Company (of Great Britain and Ireland) Ltd.
[4] See *Writings of George Washington*, ed. by John C. Fitzpatrick, vol. ii, p. 338 (Washington, 1931).

Earl Bathurst, CIRENCESTER PARK, Cirencester

BATHURST PAPERS. 1777–1826. (*Letters unless otherwise stated.*)

(*a*) 9 Dec. 1777, from Bathurst to Lord . . ., criticizing the handling of the rebellion, and advocating peace.[1]

(*b*) 13 Aug. 1807, from Vice-Admiral Geo. Berkeley to [?] Bathurst, on warlike preparations and anti-British sentiment in the United States.[2]

(*c*) 24 and 25 Mar., 15 Apr. 1809, from George Canning to Bathurst, on the American embargo and non-intercourse.[3]

(*d*) Bathurst's proposals for modifying the Orders in Council of November 1807, with comments thereon by other Cabinet members. Apr. 12 [1809].[4]

(*e*) 2 Feb., and 10 and 29 Aug. 1810, one from the Earl of Malmesbury and two from George Rose, on Orders in Council.[5]

(*f*) 3 Apr. 1812, from George Rose to Melville, alludes to fur trade between Canada and the United States.[6]

(*g*) 25 May 1812, from Major-General Isaac Brock to the Earl of Liverpool on Canadian preparations to resist United States invasion.[7]

(*h*) 15 Sept. 1812, from Thomas Tackle to Bathurst offering information respecting the policy of the United States to the Indians.[8]

(*i*) Number of additional letters, 1814, from the Earl of Liverpool, concerning the Conference and Treaty of Ghent.[9]

(*j*) Three accounts, 1814, of the Battle of Plattsburg, including opinions of Sir James Yeo and Sir Frederick Philipse Robinson.[10]

(*k*) 4 Oct. 1814, from Castlereagh to Bathurst, in which he deprecates 'spoiling America by acts signally unjust to our own subjects'.[11]

(*l*) Paris, 4 Nov. 1814, from the Duke of Wellington to Bathurst offering to take command in America the following year, if required.[12]

(*m*) 15 Dec. 1814, from Henry Goulburn to Bathurst, about disputes with the American delegates at Ghent over the fishery issue. (A note is added to the effect that this is one of a collection of letters 'from Goulburn to Bathurst written during the negotiations at Ghent; but all except the above are to be found in the *Supplementary Despatches of the Duke of Wellington*, and are therefore not given here'.)[13]

---

[1] Transcript, H.M.C. Bathurst MSS. [76], pp. 16–17.
[2] Transcript, ibid., pp. 63–65.   [3] Transcript, ibid., pp. 86–87, 89–90.
[4] Transcript, ibid., pp. 87–89.
[5] Transcripts, ibid., pp. 139–40, 144, 146.
[6] Transcript, ibid., pp. 170–2.   [7] Transcript, ibid., pp. 174–5.
[8] Ibid., p. 212.   [9] Ibid., pp. 285–8, 294, 302, 319, 320, 324, 370–1.
[10] Transcripts, ibid., pp. 285, 286, 290–4.
[11] Transcript, ibid., pp. 295–6.   [12] Transcript, ibid., p. 303.
[13] Transcript, ibid., p. 316.

(*n*) Quebec, 21 Aug. 1818, from the Duke of Richmond to Bathurst, mentions Canadian border incident, 1818.[1]

(*o*) 6 Aug. 1820, from Bathurst to Viscount Castlereagh, mentions the United States' wish to buy Santo Domingo from Spain.[2]

(*p*) 1 Oct. 1821, from Henry Goulburn to [Earl Bathurst]; and one 22 Dec. 1821, from Liverpool to Bathurst; comment on United States–West Indies trade in 1821.[3]

(*q*) 28 Apr. 1824, from Sir Howard Douglas to Bathurst, giving 'reasons against allowing the Americans free navigation of the St. Lawrence'.[4]

(*r*) Synopsis of letter, 23 July 1824, from Stratford Canning to William Huskisson, on delay in handing over islands in the St. Lawrence to the United States.[5]

(*s*) 7 Nov. 1825, from Wellington to Bathurst, mentions 'the report of the commissioners sent to North America' and also complains of the 'insolence' of the South American states in inviting the North Americans to the congress at Panama and not inviting Britain.[6]

(*t*) 27 Apr. 1826, from Lord Carbery to Bathurst, on emigration from Ireland to the United States.[7]

Corporation of Gloucester, Guildhall, GLOUCESTER

'A BOOKE FOR ENTERING OF LETTERS SENT FROM THE LORDS OF THE COUNCELL AND LORD LIEUTENANT, BEGINNING ANNO DOMINI 1639.' Letter.[8] 1655.

27 Mar. 1655, from Henry Lawrence, President of the Council, to the Mayor and Justices of the Peace of Gloucester, on the prohibition of tobacco planting in England in order to benefit Virginia.

Gloucestershire Records Office,[9] Shire Hall, GLOUCESTER

GLOUCESTERSHIRE AND WILTSHIRE QUARTERLY MEETING OF THE SOCIETY OF FRIENDS. Records. 1670–1866.

As in all Quaker records (*see* Library of the Society of Friends, London, p. 211), these contain numerous references in the minutes to the affairs of

---

[1] Ibid., p. 454.　　　　　　　　[2] Transcript, ibid., p. 485.
[3] Transcripts, ibid., pp. 518, 525.　　[4] Synopsis, ibid., pp. 568–9.
[5] Ibid., p. 572.　　　　　　　　[6] Transcript, ibid., pp. 591–2.
[7] Ibid., pp. 601–2.　　　　　[8] Transcript, H.M.C. xii (ix), p. 510.
[9] *Gloucester Quarter Sessions Archives, 1660–1889, and other Official Records; a Descriptive Catalogue* (Gloucester, 1958).

the Friends in America, particularly in Pennsylvania, to the travels of preachers in America and from America, and records of Gloucestershire Quakers who emigrated. The material thus appears to be of the same general character as that of other Meetings elsewhere; it was not examined in detail. (D 1340)

MISCELLANEOUS PAPERS. *c.* 1784–1830.

(*a*) Printed credentials, *c.* 1784, of Mrs. Ann Stanley, 'daughter to Wm. Stanley, a very learned and emminent physician in Hampshire'. She, being deaf and dumb, returned to England after her father's death in Philadelphia and claimed to be expert in healing all ailments. (Q/SR)

(*b*) Advertisement, prospectus, and poster of lands in Upper Canada with detailed map. Covering letter from Canada Company written on back, 1830. (D 1359)

(*c*) Among the Mullings and Ellett Papers (solicitors) is a printed notice of the New York Emigrant Society, on which is written the name of their English agent in Liverpool, Robinson & Bros., merchants; there is also a letter, 1833, written on the back from J. Pilmere of New York to L. Randall of Chedworth, Glos., demanding the sum of £17 apparently belonging to the Emigrant Society. (D 1388)

PARISH RECORDS.

(*a*) Chedworth. Receipt and Payment Book of the Overseers, 1836–48. Includes payments for emigration to America. (P77/OVI/5)

(*b*) Dursley. Miscellaneous correspondence of the churchwardens with Somerset House regarding ten applicants for poor-rate assistance for emigration, 1840. (P124a/CW4/4)

(*c*) Frampton. Overseers' Accounts Book, 1687–1788. Entry for 1712: 'paid the widow Ffox when she was goeing to New Yorke, £3'. (P149/OV2/1)

QUARTER SESSIONS RECORDS.

Treasurer's Book, 1726–73, gives disbursements for transportation together with individual bonds of transportation to 'His Majesty's colonyes and plantations in America'. Some sixty documents are included, giving names of convicts, offences, and sentences. Also list of convicts transported, 1750–5. (Q/CBL)

Public Libraries, Brunswick Road, GLOUCESTER

SMYTH OF NIBLEY PAPERS. (16524)

John Smyth (1567–1641), antiquarian, steward, and chronicler to the Berkeley family. 'He was chief adventurer in the establishment of a settlement in Virginia and had a good deal to say at meetings of the Virginia

Company.'¹ Although the Library contains a collection of nearly 2,000 of his papers, bound in sixteen volumes and described in the published catalogue to the Gloucestershire collection,² the papers relating to Virginia were sold separately to the New York Public Library (see their *Bulletin*, vol. i, pp. 186–90, 1897). No American material could be found in a fairly thorough search of four likely volumes in the Gloucestershire collection, but some small items may remain.

WHITEFIELD, GEORGE (1714–70). Pamphlets. (13918–14073)

George Whitefield, the Methodist preacher and evangelist, was born in Gloucester. The Library has an extensive collection of contemporary printed material by, for, or against Whitefield, several concerning his evangelizing tours of Georgia, Pennsylvania, and New England.

PARISH RECORDS.

Dursley. Copies of printed notices of meeting to be held in Dursley, 28 Mar. 1839, to consent to raising money for emigration purposes. (RF 115. 50 (4–9))

Earl St. Aldwyn, WILLIAMSTRIP PARK, Fairford

HICKS-BEACH MANUSCRIPTS. Travel journals, letters, 2 printed copies of lecture. 1869–1939.

Papers of Sir Michael Edward Hicks-Beach, later 1st Earl St. Aldwyn (1837–1916), statesman; and his family. The scattered American material amid a very large collection is:

(*a*) Letters, 1869–70, from Sir Michael while in the United States: three to his mother and one to K. Hardy; also a letter of introduction. (2731)

(*b*) Journals, &c., 1869–70, of Sir Michael of a trip to Canada and the United States. (2871)

(*c*) Two printed copies of a lecture on America delivered by Sir Michael on 24 Oct. 1870; also some manuscript notes; and an advertisement of Virginia lands for sale. (3095)

(*d*) Journal, 1905, of a journey by Sir Michael which included America. (2800)

(*e*) Letters, 1934–9, from the 2nd Earl St. Aldwyn to his grandmother, including some from the United States. (2854)
    N.R.A. 3526.

¹ *Commons Debates, 1621*, ed. by Wallace Notestein, Frances Helen Relf, and Hartley Simpson, vol. i, p. 74 ,(New Haven, Conn., and London, 1935) (Yale Historical Publications. MSS. and edited texts, 15).
    ² Roland Austin, comp., *Catalogue of the Gloucestershire Collection: Books, Pamphlets and Documents in the Gloucester Public Library Relating to the County, Cities, Towns and Villages of Gloucestershire* (Gloucester, 1928).

Ruskin Galleries, Bembridge School, BEMBRIDGE, Isle of Wight

WHITEHOUSE, J. HOWARD (1873–1955).[1] Correspondence and papers. 1916–55.

Liberal M.P. 1910–19; Parliamentary Private Secretary to the Chancellor of the Exchequer 1913–15. Whitehouse visited the United States on a number of occasions, including Oct. 1916–Apr. 1917, when he held conversations with Colonel House on the subject of American mediation in the war. Defeated in the general election of 1919, he founded the Bembridge School, putting into practice his own educational theories and devoting much time to trying to establish the teaching of American history as a normal part of English education.

The material, which has not yet been fully sorted, includes the following:

(*a*) American mediation, 1916–17.

(i) Original correspondence with Colonel House.

(ii) Reports of conversations and transcripts of letters between Whitehouse and House, 14 Nov. 1916–14 Apr. 1917. (During this period they were in almost daily communication.)

(iii) Notes on conversations with House, 18 Apr. 1917.

(iv) Reports of interviews, also on the subject of American mediation, with Secretary of State Robert Lansing, Secretary of the Interior F. K. Lane, and Counsellor Polk; views of Oswald Garrison Villard (with information concerning Henry Morgenthau, Jr.) and Sir Cecil Spring-Rice; reports on the interchange of news and views with America, and on the political situation there (this latter prepared for Whitehouse by M. W. Davis).

(*b*) Miscellaneous correspondence, 1916–55.

(i) Letters, 1916–45, from Oswald Garrison Villard.

(ii) Three files of miscellaneous correspondence and papers, 1916–17, consisting of letters to American universities, newspapers and periodicals, newspaper reports on Whitehouse's lectures in the United States, &c.

(iii) Five files of correspondence, 1923–41, concerning the Sulgrave Institution; among the correspondents are J. A. Stewart, H. S. Perris, and Mrs. Duncan-Whyte. (Further correspondence, up to 1955, is likely.) Correspondence with E. E. Browne concerning Whitehouse's gift to New York University in 1926 of an exhibition illustrating English education.

[1] See James S. Dearden, 'J. Howard Whitehouse and Anglo-American Understanding', *Bulletin of the British Association for American Studies*, no. vii, pp. 23–27, 1958.

Reports and correspondence of the sub-committee for teaching American history in English schools.

(iv) Correspondence with American bodies in connexion with the American architecture exhibition held at Bembridge in 1928.

(v) Correspondence, 1938–41, between Whitehouse and the headmasters of English schools concerning the teaching of American history in English schools.

(c) Articles, pamphlets, lectures, &c., by Whitehouse, from 1916 onwards, on American education and other aspects of American life and culture.

The Estate of the late Countess Mountbatten of Burma, BROADLANDS, Romsey

PALMERSTON PAPERS.[1]

The papers of Henry John Temple, 3rd Viscount Palmerston (1784–1865), at Broadlands, are being steadily indexed and listed. Detailed lists were made available to the editors and then the most important sections were examined, including everything relating to the American Civil War and to plans for the defence of Canada in the event of war. The amount of detail now given for each file varies according to the apparent uniqueness and importance of the matter.

Some of the papers are, of course, copies of, or copied in, papers in the Public Record Office and elsewhere, but certainly there are a large number of papers both unique and important.[2]

It is necessary that access to these papers should be very restricted and it must be clearly understood that very special permission is required to see them and that this permission is only likely to be granted in a few cases.

The headings in the following report are the titles of the separate files into which the material has been sorted by the archivist. (*Unless otherwise stated, letters are to Palmerston.*)

(a) United States of America, 1833–4. Letters from Christopher Hughes.

Eleven letters from Hughes, while American Chargé d'Affaires in Stockholm, mostly letters of politesse, but some containing American political news.

(b) United States of America, 1832–41.

Thirty-three letters, mainly between Palmerston and Andrew Stevenson, United States Minister in London 1834–41, but some from Aaron Vail,

---

[1] We are grateful to the late Countess Mountbatten of Burma for permission to make this report.

[2] Some of these papers were used by Sir Charles Kingsley Webster in writing his *Foreign Policy of Palmerston, 1830–1841: Britain, the Liberal Movement and the Eastern Question*, 2 vols. (London, 1951).

United States Chargé in London, to Palmerston. Also three from Martin Van Buren, two slight notes while in England, but a long letter from Washington, D.C., 3 Mar. 1836, on relations between America and France.

(c) North America, 1832–6. Letters to and from Palmerston, Sir Charles Vaughan, Henry Stephen Fox, Charles Bankhead, &c.

Eighteen letters mainly concerned with the French and American quarrel and English steps to mediate between them.

(d) America—letters to and from Palmerston and Henry Stephen Fox, British Minister to Washington, 1835, 1839–41.

Eleven items include:

24 Mar. 1839. John W. Cowell, an agent in the United States of the Bank of England, from Philadelphia, to Timothy Abraham Curtis, Governor of the Bank, transmitting the plan below.

22 Apr. 1839, from Curtis, enclosing 'a Plan' drawn up by Cowell, 24 Mar. 1839, 'for hostile operations against the United States in the event of war with them'.

9 Feb. 1841. Palmerston to Fox, threatening immediate war if McLeod is executed.

4 Mar. 1841. Memorandum as to the laws which exist in the Southern states of the United States with respect to free persons of colour.

16 Mar. 1841. Letter from John Abel Smith enclosing a further memorandum on the same subject as that of 24 Mar. 1839, sent to him by Cowell, who had just returned from the United States. Smith said that the memorandum had been sent to the Horse Guards by Colonel William Napier, who had also submitted a plan of his own, but that the Duke of Wellington had preferred Cowell's. The plan turned upon political and economic means of 'liberating' the South from dependence on the North. Signed and dated, 5 Mar. 1841.

(e) Canada, 1838–9. Letters and reports on Canada from Frederick James Lamb, Ambassador to Austria, to Palmerston.

Ten items, letters and memoranda, relating to the affairs of Lower Canada.

Papers of 1783 on the boundary question are disinterred and discussed.

Letter, 28 Feb. 1838, from Lamb encloses Macgregor's memorandum on the 'Paramount importance of retaining the province of Lower Canada, both as a British possession, and as a counter-poise to American power' (map attached). Also another letter from T. A. Curtis, 27 Mar. 1839, enclosing an extract of a letter from John W. Cowell on the boundary question.

(f) North and South America, 1840–1. Letters from General James Hamilton to Palmerston.

Twenty-two letters, mainly relating to Texas.

(g) America 1842 and 1844. Ashburton Treaty.

'10 Oct. 1842, to Lord Minto on the Webster–Ashburton Treaty.

28 Oct. 1842, to Lord Monteagle on the Treaty.

11 Nov. 1842, from Lord John Russell enclosing letter from his brother William in Vienna on the Treaty.

14 Nov. 1842. Palmerston's reply to the above.

Also drafts or copies of eight dispatches in 1844 to Pakenham on American affairs, particularly on the American annexation of Texas, and a copy of a dispatch of M. Guizot to Count St. Aulaire stating the views of the French government on Texas.

(h) United States of America, 1843–6.

Twenty-four miscellaneous letters including references to Lord Ashburton's mission to the United States, American interest in French aggression on Tahiti, and letters from consuls discussing the character of Polk and public feeling against Britain on the Oregon question. (Most of the letters in this file concern South America.)

(i) North American Boundary Question, 1848–9, 1859–60.

n.d., from Lord Grey, enclosing extract from a letter of Lord Elgin's of 4 May 1848, with Lord John Russell's remarks upon it, concerning admission of American ships to the St. Lawrence.

10 Aug. 1848, from Edward Everett, introducing John Davis, Massachusetts Senator, and assuring Palmerston that 'American sympathy' for Ireland is limited to Irish immigrants.

July 1849. Copy of the note (with supporting papers) on the boundary-line controversy of 1842–3 to lay before Parliament.

24 Dec. 1849, from Sir Henry Bulwer, Washington, D.C., enclosing a copy of a letter he had written to Lord Dundonald from Bermuda about the Mosquito Coast question.

16 July 1859, from the Duke of Newcastle, concerning an American claim and including supporting correspondence.

1 Aug. 1859. Foreign Office memorandum on Monckton Milnes's motion in the House of Commons for protection of American seamen on high seas in mercantile service.

31 Aug. 1860, from J. P. Coppinger, Adjutant of the 9th Regiment, New York City Guard, requesting permission to visit England in uniform.

(j) Central and South America, 1848–62.

Eight letters mainly on South American affairs, though one touches on Mexico and the United States.

(k) United States of America, 1850. Letters to and from Sir Henry Bulwer in Washington.

6 Jan. 1850, from Bulwer on the Nicaragua question.

20 Jan. 1850, from Bulwer on the Canada Bill, the Nicaragua question, and describing conversations with Clayton.

5 Feb. 1850, from Bulwer, sending project for settlement of the Nicaragua question.

18 Feb. 1850, from Bulwer on the Nicaragua and Mosquito Coast questions.

12 Mar. 1850. Bulwer asks whether England intends to keep the Slave Trade Squadron on the coast of Africa.

4 Apr. 1850, from Palmerston in reply to the above letter: Bulwer is to urge the United States government to help in putting a stop to the slave trade.

28 Apr. 1850. Bulwer, in reply to the above, enclosing a copy of Clayton's reply to him about the slave trade.

1 July 1850. Bulwer, discussing the employment of secret service money to ease the passage through Congress of the Reciprocity Bill, thinks better of the idea—safer to employ a lawyer to manage the Bill in the usual manner, rather than to run the risks of bribery.

(*l*) United States of America, 1849–51.

Mainly letters of 1851 from Sir Henry Bulwer, similar to the above, with several on Cuba, one accounting for £182. 19*s*.—spent on the passage of the (Canada) Reciprocity Bill (see 1 July 1850 above), a memorandum on methods of blockading American ports, and a memorandum on conversations between the British Minister at Washington and the United States in 1822–3.

(*m*) Letters from the Earl of Clarendon to Palmerston. America, 1855–6.

Twenty-one letters on routine diplomatic matters; one of 24 Apr. 1855 discusses the right of search in relation to shipment of arms to Russia from the United States; and one of 25 Sept. 1855 discusses American objections to recruitment there for the Crimean War. Also several on Central American boundary disputes.

(*n*) Letters from the Earl of Clarendon to Palmerston. America, 1857–8, 1862.

Seventeen letters, again mostly on routine matters, though several discuss the Clayton–Bulwer Treaty, and there is a recurring complaint that Lord Napier in Washington is 'Yankee bitten'. Anxiety lest the United States get possession of the 'Panama railway'. A single letter of 12 Oct. 1862 concerns Lord Derby's views about America.

(*o*) Letters from the Duke of Newcastle concerning the visit of H.R.H. the Prince of Wales to Canada, 1860.

Nine letters. Newcastle accompanied the Prince; the letters are all from Canada or the United States, which he also visited. There is some discussion about the difficulties in Canada of avoiding violent Orangemen's demonstrations, some discussion of American public opinion, and the enclosure of an extract of a fulsome letter from Charles Sumner about a visit to the Speaker of the House of Commons.

(*p*) Defence of Canada, 1861–4, 1865.

Twenty-three letters, many from Edward Cardwell, all concerning the defence of Canada, prohibition of the export of arms to the United States, the defence of other colonies (i.e. India, Australia, New Zealand) in the event of a general war, or else plans for a Canadian Confederation. They include:

26 Aug. 1861, from Palmerston to Sir George Cornewall Lewis discussing plans for the defence of Canada.

3 and 10 Sept. 1861. Two letters from Lewis on the same theme.

30 Nov. 1861, from Palmerston circulated to members of the Cabinet canvassing the advisability of prohibiting the export of arms, gunpowder, saltpetre, &c., to all foreign countries because of the likelihood of war with the United States.

n.d. (Dec.? 1861.) Copies of the individual opinions of members of the Cabinet on the above question.

n.d. (1863?) Memorandum sent from Cairo, Ill., and extracts from *The Times* of 2 June on 'Iron ships engaged with forts in the present American war'.

3 Jan. 1864, from Lord Westbury, about the probable course of the Mason–Slidell affair.

9 Feb. 1864, from Lord Westbury, about possible intervention in the Civil War: 'let them tear one another to pieces'.

10 Dec. 1864, from Sir George Grey concerning papers circulated by Cardwell on North American confederation.

June 1865, from Cardwell, enclosing a copy of a letter of Lord Monck's about powers to extradite Confederate raiders in Canada.

Memorandum from Cardwell (printed) of a meeting at the Colonial Office on 19 May 1865 to discuss with the Canadian Ministers visiting London the defence of Canada.

(*q*) Defence of Canada and American Civil War, 1861–5.

Sixty-three letters of great interest include the following:

5 May 1861. Palmerston to Lord John Russell (copy) concerning mediation in America, and enclosing a copy of a letter of his of the same date to Edward Ellice, M.P.

4 June 1861. Lord Herbert giving details of arms and troops for Canada.

25 June 1861. Duke of Somerset, concerning naval reinforcements for the North American Station (also letters of 15 July and 19 August on same topic).

27 Aug. 1861. Sir George Cornewall Lewis, concerning arms in the North American provinces.

30 Aug. 1861. Duke of Newcastle, against sending more troops to Canada.

31 Aug. 1861. Duke of Somerset, enclosing 'A list of the ships belonging to the United States stationed in the Gulf of Mexico and upon the Atlantic coasts', 30 Aug. 1861, with comments on the French attack on Vera Cruz.

3 Sept. 1861. Duke of Newcastle, concerning his regret that publicity is given to removal of troops from England to Canada.

10 Sept. 1861. Sir George Cornewall Lewis concerning the Queen's annoyance that she has not had an explanation about additional troops for Canada, and has only seen it in the newspapers.

26 Sept. 1861. Duke of Somerset, about operations against Mexico, enclosing a printed list of the British force in North America.

13 Nov. 1861. Lord Derby, enclosing Sir James Fergusson's account of his visit to the Union and Confederate armies, November 1861 (19 pages).

7 Nov. 1861. Sir George Cornewall Lewis, criticizing plans to recognize the Confederacy.

9 Nov. 1861. Sir George Cornewall Lewis, concerning the supply of new rifles to troops in Canada.

9 Nov. 1861. Edmund Hammond, concerning Americans and the right of search.

30 Nov. 1861. Sir James Fergusson concerning line of march for British reinforcements between Halifax, N.S., and Rivière du Loup, Que.

3 Dec. 1861. Mr. Hammond on the imminent rupture with America, advising a naval show of force.

6 Dec. 1861. Duke of Somerset enclosing three lists of ships required to blockade the United States.

24 Dec. 1861. Sir George Cornewall Lewis, enclosing memorandum of troops at Parkhurst Barracks to protect Queen Victoria from being kidnapped by an American privateer at Osborne, Isle of Wight.

26 Dec. 1861. Mr. Hammond, enclosing a résumé of Lord Lyons's dispatches up to 6 Dec.

31 Dec. 1861. Duke of Somerset, concerning proclamations in the event of war, and enclosing a statement of the number of British troops being sent to North America.

11 June 1862. Palmerston to Charles Francis Adams, the American Minister in London (marked 'confidential'): protests as a 'private gentleman' at outrages at New Orleans, enclosing newspaper cutting of General Butler's famous order.

12 June 1862. Mr. Adams, inquiring in what capacity Palmerston had written.

15 June 1862. Palmerston to Adams, returning to his attack on Butler's New Orleans proclamation.

16 June 1862. Adams, declining to receive Palmerston's letter as a 'private communication', as it contains imputations against the government of the United States.

19 June 1862. Palmerston to Adams, on the same subject (copy).

20 June 1862. Adams, stating that he is sending the correspondence to the government of the United States, and that he cannot in future receive 'private' letters from Palmerston.

10 Sept. 1862. Duke of Cambridge to Sir George Cornewall Lewis, in favour of concentration of troops at Quebec and Montreal.

30 Dec. 1862. Sir George Cornewall Lewis, concerning the defence of Canada, with an enclosure on the cost of permanent works, including purchase of land, recommended by the Defence Commissioners for Canada.

22 Apr. 1863. Mr. Hammond, concerning the capture of the *Dolphin* and the *Peterhoff* by the United States, making use of a neutral island; and enclosing a cutting from *The Times* of his letter, 22 Apr., to Joseph Spence, the owner (?) of one of the ships.

9 July 1863. Palmerston to John Arthur Roebuck, M.P., urging him to adjourn the debate on his motion demanding recognition of the Confederacy.

25 Jan. 1864. Foreign Office paper relating to the *Chesapeake* affair.

7 Mar. 1864. Duke of Argyll, concerning the *Alabama* and Britain's proper conduct, as a neutral, towards her.

12 July 1864. Confidential report (printed) on the defence of Canada, from the commission under the general guidance of Sir John Fox Burgoyne. Initialed 'W. E. G.' (William Ewart Gladstone).

17 May 1865 (received). Memorandum by the defence committee on the report by Lieutenant-Colonel Jervois on the defence of Canada, 1864.

(*r*) America and Canada, 1861–2.
Nine letters covering the same topics as the above.

(*s*) Letters from Lord John Russell to Palmerston. America, 1862–5.

14 Jan. 1862. American affairs are at a standstill.

15 Jan. 1862. Against giving orders to British cruisers to stop American men-of-war which have captured British ships suspected of blockade running.

31 Mar. 1862. Palmerston must stir up the Admiralty: the United States is ahead of Britain in ship construction.

13 June 1862. On Palmerston's letter to Charles Francis Adams about General Butler's New Orleans 'atrocities'.

14 Sept. 1862. American news, enclosing a portrait of 'Stonewall' Jackson, 'the man of the day. It really looks as if he might end the war.'

17 Sept. 1862. 'The time has come for offering mediation to the United States Government, with a view to the recognition of the Confederate states. I agree further that in case of failure, we ought ourselves to recognize the Southern States.'

13 and 15 Oct. 1862. Printed Foreign Office memoranda by Russell urging compulsory mediation. Also printed memorandum, 17 Oct., by Sir George Cornewall Lewis, opposing these, and Russell's answer to Lewis in a further memorandum of 24 Oct.

18 Oct. 1862. The possible recognition of the Confederate states.

20 Oct. 1862. The need to consult Russia and France over forcing mediation on America.

24 Oct. 1862. The chances of joint European action in forcing mediation.

3 Nov. 1862. Little chance of England's mediation being accepted in America.

27 Mar. 1863. The *Alabama*.

15 Dec. 1864. Brief comment on the American situation.

6 Apr. 1865. The *Alabama* claims.

23 Apr. 1865. The budget as affected by American affairs.

(*t*) United States, 1864–5.
Memorandum and five letters. Memorandum, 1864, concerns a question by Roebuck in the House of Commons on alleged Union recruitment in Ireland.

Letter, 29 Mar. 1865, from the Duke of Somerset, encloses an extract from a letter from a shipbuilder in American service describing conversations with Admiral Farragut on the efficacy of various designs of warships. Three letters from Sir George Grey, and one from Lord Wodehouse to Grey, all 1865, concern the Fenians in Ireland and America.

H.M. Customs and Excise, COWES, Isle of Wight

See H.M. Customs and Excise, London (p. 198)

Town Clerk's Office, 17 Quay Street, NEWPORT, Isle of Wight

BAKER, ELIZABETH. 1 document. 1624.

Deed, 1 Oct. 1624, about the emigration to Virginia of Elizabeth Baker.[1]

H.M. Customs and Excise, PORTSMOUTH

See H.M. Customs and Excise, London (p. 198).

H.M. Customs and Excise, SOUTHAMPTON

See H.M. Customs and Excise, London (p. 198)

Southampton Record Office, Civic Centre, SOUTHAMPTON

PETTY CUSTOMS BOOKS.

There are 119 volumes covering 1426–1803. In the volumes for 1723–1803 there are occasional references to exports, mainly salt, to the American colonies, giving name of ship, place of origin, name of master, date of sailing, name of consignor, and type and quantity of goods.

PAGE AND MOODY PAPERS.[2] Documents, 2 printed pamphlets. 1814–23.

(*a*) Contains the financial accounts of the 103rd Regiment of Foot, largely for 1814–23, including regimental pay lists, lists of prisoners taken by the Americans in the War of 1812 (some of whom later settled in the United States), records of deserters to the American side, and court martial proceedings.

(*b*) Two printed pamphlets circulated in Southampton during the War of 1812. Both endeavour to persuade the Corporation to petition the Crown, one in favour of the American cause, one against it.

---

[1] Extracts printed in R. J. Eldridge, *Newport, Isle of Wight, in Bygone Days*, Appendix B, p. 82 (Newport, 1952).

[2] These papers have recently been deposited in the Southampton Public Library.

CORPORATION ASSEMBLY BOOKS AND JOURNALS.

Contain scattered material concerning American trade, notably references in 1754 to relieving American produce entering Southampton from payment of petty customs; and in 1850-60, on the encouragement of American trade.

TRADE COMMITTEE MINUTES.

Included in volume containing minutes of various committees 1847-61, refer to the proposed free unloading at Southampton of American exhibits for the 1851 Great Exhibition, a move designed to encourage the American trade of the port.

See also Town Clerk's Correspondence and Papers below.

TOWN CLERK'S CORRESPONDENCE AND PAPERS. 1850-86.

(*a*) 7 Dec. 1850, from J. Iselin, of the Southampton Dock Co., to J. R. Stebbing, Secretary to the London & South Western Railway Co., in favour of a 'regularity' of sailing vessels from Southampton to California.

(*b*) Four letters, all Dec. 1850, referring to Southampton's request that the American exhibits for the 1851 Great Exhibition be landed there, the Corporation being willing to pay the railway charges to London.

(*c*) Bundle of letters and some printed material, 1884-6, concerning the attempt of Southampton to have its superiority over Plymouth and Liverpool as a packet station for United States mails recognized.

COMMERCE OF THE PORT COMMITTEE[1] MINUTES.

Contain references to the Corporation's anxiety to encourage the trade of the port with the United States, especially in the 1870's; and its campaign to become recognized as the main packet station for American mails.

See also Town Clerk's Correspondence and Papers above.

QUARTER SESSIONS RECORDS AND PAPERS.

(*a*) Examinations and depositions, 1622-44, and some both earlier and later at separated intervals. Those for 1622-44, printed by the Southampton Record Society,[2] contain a number of references to sailings to or from Virginia, as do those of 1648-63.

(*b*) Petition, 19 July 1700, of Gilbert Stokes, an apprentice, to the Mayor and Justices of Southampton, to restrain his master from unlawfully shipping him to Virginia, contrary to his indenture.

(*c*) Papers (unbound) contain a few bonds and orders for transportation of criminals to the American colonies in 1750-60.

[1] Formed in 1874, but until 1884 its minutes were included in Minutes of Various Committees, 1854-84; and subsequently in Minute-Books, 1884-7 and 1892-4. After 1894 its Minutes were printed.
[2] R.C. Anderson, ed., *The Book of Examinations and Depositions, 1622-1644*, 4 vols. (Southampton, 1929-36) (Southampton Record Society Publications, nos. 29, 31, 34, 36).

Hampshire Record Office, The Castle, WINCHESTER

WRIOTHESLEY DEEDS. 2 documents. 1623.

(*a*) Acquittance, 25 June 1623, to Henry Wriothesley, 3rd Earl of Southampton, as Treasurer of the Virginia Company.

(*b*) Grant, 19 Nov. 1623, by the Virginia Company of twenty shares of land in 'old adventure in Virginia' to the Earl of Southampton in recognition of his services as Treasurer of the Company.

MALMESBURY PAPERS. 6 documents. 1674–85.

(*a*) Letter of appointment, 23 Apr. 1674, by Shaftesbury of Andrew Percival as agent for Carolina. New agreement, 2 June 1680, between Shaftesbury and Percival as to the agency. Sale of stock, &c., 2 May 1685, on St. Giles plantation, Carolina, by the trustees of Shaftesbury to Percival.

(*b*) Three copies of articles of agreement, 6 May 1674, between the Lords Proprietors and Treasurer of Carolina for financing the supply and development of Carolina.

WYNDHAM, HENRY (1709–88). 2 account books. 1725–53.

Merchant of Salisbury and Dinton. The account books contain entries on the trade in tobacco with Virginia.

See also his letters in the Wiltshire Archaeological and Natural History Society, Devizes (p. 445).

BOLTON PAPERS. I document.[1] (1782.)

Papers of Thomas Orde, afterwards Orde-Powlett, 1st Baron Bolton (1746–1807), Secretary to the Treasury under Shelburne in 1782. Included is a 'List of Americans applying for allowances whose cases have not yet been considered', 3 June 1782, giving the name, profession, residence, and family of applicants, and names of those persons certifying the application.

HEREFORDSHIRE

Hereford Herd Book Society, 3 Offa Street, HEREFORD

HEREFORD CATTLE.

Complete records relating to the export of Hereford cattle to the United States from 1817 to the present day. (The American Hereford Association has its headquarters at Hereford Drive, Kansas City 5, Mo.)

[1] This has recently been returned to Lord Bolton, Bolton Hall, Leyburn, Yorks.

HERTFORDSHIRE

Earl of Verulam, GORHAMBURY, St. Albans

VERULAM PAPERS.[1] 1768–93.

(a) In a journal of a tour through the Midlands into Wales, probably by the 3rd Viscount Grimston, in 1768, there are remarks in passing about trade with America.[2]

(b) Letter, dated 'XVIII' century [1776?], from J. Mervin Nooth to Viscountess Grimston, mentions a man who has just returned from 'captivity amongst the rebels, and is just returned to New York, with scarce anything more than his skin on his back'.[3]

(c) Letter, New York, 23 Nov. 1779, from J. Mervin Nooth to Viscountess Grimston, complaining of the inactivity of the British forces and the incompetence of their commander, and referring to the alleged dislike of the French by the Americans. Another letter, 18 July 1781, is in a similar vein.[4]

(d) Petition, 20 Oct. 1793, from Thomas Lashley to Verulam for a position as physician with forces going to the West Indies; recounts trading experiences with America.[5]

Marquess of Salisbury, HATFIELD HOUSE, Hatfield

CECIL PAPERS. 4 letters, 2 documents. 1563–1606.

(a) 30 June 1563, from the Queen to the Earl of Sussex, 'in favour of Thomas Stuckly, who is about to make a voyage to discover certain lands in the west towards Terra Florida'.[6]

(b) 22 July 1586, to Lord Burghley mentioning that Drake has 'over-run and spoiled . . . St. John's in Florida' among other places.[7]

(c) Before 25 Mar. 1606, from Sir Walter Cope to Salisbury, mentioning that the Lord Chief Justice [Popham] 'is affectionately bent to the plantation of Virginia' in order to provide a place where idle vagrants might be sent.[8]

(d) Two protests from Plymouth, 10 May 1606: one from Walter Mathewe, the Deputy Mayor, and the other from Sir Ferdinando Gorges, both to

---

[1] Not all the papers are as yet catalogued.
[2] H.M.C. Verulam MSS. [64], pp. 271 and 274.
[3] Ibid., p. 183.   [4] Transcripts, ibid., pp. 127–8, 129–30.
[5] Transcript, ibid., p. 151.
[6] H.M.C. Salisbury (Cecil) MSS. i [9], p. 273.
[7] Transcript, ibid., iii, p. 152.   [8] Transcript, ibid., xviii, p. 84.

Salisbury, complaining about the composition of the Council set up under the Virginia charter.[1]

(*e*) 19 June 1606, from William Udall to Salisbury, stating that the secular priests and lay Catholics (as opposed to the Jesuits) are about to petition the King to allow 300 Catholic households to settle in Virginia.[2]

Hertfordshire County Record Office, County Hall, HERTFORD

As well as the main items listed below, manuscript schedules to the various collections reveal scattered references to early settlers and their families, land sales of later emigrants, and occasional references to American property and funds. The Record Office is establishing an index of such Americana.

COWPER COLLECTION. 2 letters, 2 documents. 1700–23.

(*a*) Copy (?) warrant, New York, 20 Jan. 1700 (?), for additional military establishment for New York. Signed William III and William Blathwayt.

(*b*) Letter of application, Boston, 23 Sept. 1714, from J. Dudley, for the renewal of his grant.

(*c*) 'A modest computation of the pay of H.M. four Companies of Foot posted in New York Province, etc., shewing what commission and other money came to the Governor.' *c.* 1723.

(*d*) Letter, 1723, complaining of the Governor of New York, William Burnet, and particularly of the treatment of the soldiers affected by the difference of exchange.

DACARETTE PAPERS. 3 letters, 4 documents. 1745–87. (In Gorhambury Collection.)

These are a small packet found wrapped in an advertisement (see (*g*) below) for claims to be submitted to the Officer for American Claims, as follows:

(*a*) Letter, 2 Apr. 1745, from Larchevesque, a chaplain of Cendré, near Cléry sur Loire, to his brother, living on the Ile Royale [Cape Breton Island], discussing the governors and other ministers in Canada from whom he might get a job.

(*b*) Letter, 9 Oct. 1749, from Pierre (?) Faribauer, Louisbourg, N.S., to Mme Dacarette at Chibouetouch (Halifax), about winding up her affairs in Louisbourg and selling her boats.

---

[1] Transcript, H.M.C. Salisbury (Cecil) MSS. xviii [9], pp. 133–4.
[2] Transcript, ibid., xviii, p. 173.

(*c*) Letter, 9 Apr. 1750, from Lieutenant John Straton, Greenwich, Kent, to 'ma chère mère' at Halifax, N.S., with news of his voyage home via France and news of her children; also comments on the danger of an Indian and French attack on Halifax.

(*d*) Bill and promissory note, 23 July 1756.

(*e*) Copy of land grant, 8 July 1766, by Benjamin Green, Commander-in-Chief in Canada, to the Sieur Gratian D'Arrigrand: a tract of 20,000 acres near Louisbourg.

(*f*) Grant of 400 acres by D'Arrigrand to Frances Dacarette and Anne Laurence of Halifax for £200, with an excellent plan showing Louisbourg Harbour. 24 July 1766.

(*g*) Copy advertisement of the Office of American Claims, 1787. The packet is endorsed 'Mrs W[alter]', who had American correspondents.[1]

ASHRIDGE II COLLECTION. 1 document. [n.d., ?1752]

'Case of the Rt. Hon. Frederick, Lord Baltimore, Lord Proprietory of the province of Maryland in America, against Messrs. Penn, proprietors of the province of Pennsylvania. 1632–1752.' (10 pages.) Setting out briefly all grants and stages in the affair.

HALSEY COLLECTION. 7 letters, document. 1813–16.

(*a*) Five letters from Lieutenant John Frederick Johnston, R.N., who fought in the War of 1812, written to his mother while he was serving with the British fleet on the Great Lakes, 1813–14.

(*b*) Two letters, 5 and 9 May 1814, to Johnston from Captain Cunliffe-Owen, giving news of the fleet on the Great Lakes (Johnston having been transferred).

(*c*) Manuscript (4 pages) giving a brief account of Johnston's career and death in 1816.

TRANSPORTATION OF PRISONERS.

Contract between the Lords Commissioners of H.M. Treasury and John Stewart, of London, merchant, for transporting malefactors from the county jails of Hertford, Buckingham, Essex, Kent, and Sussex, to America, 3 Feb. 1757.

HERTFORD AND HITCHIN MONTHLY MEETINGS OF FRIENDS. 1798–1852.

Four or five copies of letters and other papers such as were circulated among Quaker Meetings and which contain some minor references to Americans.

QUARTER SESSIONS RECORDS.

Ten volumes of printed calendars cover 1589–1843. Contain numerous references to persons being sentenced to transportation, although in many cases the destination is not given.

[1] See also H.M.C. Verulam MSS. [64], pp. 130, 157, 183.

HUNTINGDONSHIRE

Huntingdonshire County Record Office,[1] County Buildings, HUNTINGDON

MANCHESTER COLLECTION[2] (from Kimbolton Castle). 1 document. 1784.

Includes a memorial of Lord Charles Montagu, sometime Governor of South Carolina, to Commissioners for American Claims, for compensation for loss of lands in Carolina and a request for proportionable quantity in Nova Scotia, 1784; and other papers.

KENT

H.M. Customs and Excise, DOVER

See H.M. Customs and Excise, London (p. 198).

Lord Sackville, KNOLE, Sevenoaks

SACKVILLE PAPERS.

The De La Warr and Cranfield Papers are part of the Sackville collection from Knole. Some of these were reported on in H.M.C. iv (i), pp. 276–317, and H.M.C. vii, pp. 249–60. Since these reports the papers have been moved and rearranged several times. Inquiries about them should be addressed to the Secretary of the Historical Manuscripts Commission.

Kent County Archives Office,[3] County Hall, MAIDSTONE

SANDWICH BOROUGH RECORDS. 1611–1773.

(*a*) Letter, 1611, from Sir Edwin Sandys and twelve others, seeking financial backing for the Virginia Company, with copy of registered list of

---

[1] *Guide to the Huntingdonshire Record Office* (Huntingdon, 1958).
[2] There is a copy of the catalogue of this collection in N.R.A. 0902.
[3] *Guide to the Kent County Archives Office* (Maidstone, 1958).

adventurers and list and numbers of tradesmen to be sent out with Sir Thomas Gates[1] and letter, 1612, containing order to subscribe £25.[2] (Sa/ZB 2/64–68)

(*b*) Returns of persons taking passage from Sandwich to America, 1635–7.[3] (Sa/AC7)

(*c*) Contracts, bonds, &c., for transportation of convicts to the American colonies, including two certificates of landing, 1721–73. (Sa/JQb 145)

TUFTON PAPERS. Volume and 13 estate documents. 1613–67. (U455 E21)

Papers relating to the holding of Sir Nicholas Tufton in Virginia with later questions for opinion of counsel, 1613–*c*. 1667.[4]

LENNARD, SIR SAMUEL (*c*. 1553–1618). Will. 1618. (U312 T17/2)

References to money 'adventures' in Virginia and Newfoundland and money there.

FILMER PAPERS. 21 documents. 1653–83. (U120 C8–9)

Include letters from Henry Filmer, who emigrated to Mulberry Island in Virginia in 1653, to relatives in Kent; and discharge signed by the parish officers of Mulberry Island for legacy left by Filmer to provide communion plate for the Parish Church there.

WYKEHAM-MARTIN PAPERS. Family papers and correspondence: 206 documents. 1672–1820. (U23 C1, 2, 5, 6, 18, 23, 24, 27)

Correspondence of the Culpeper, Fairfax, and Martin families, referring particularly to the family estates in Virginia, the difficulties inherent in owning American property after the War of Independence, and the claims for compensation for loss of the land. Contain also many letters from Bryan Martin (1731–98), who settled permanently in America.

CRIPPS PAPERS. 1 document. 1684. (U17/271)

Conveyance of a part of a share in the province of East Jersey, 1684.

[1] Printed in Alexander Brown, *Genesis of the United States,* vol. i, pp. 461–70 (London, 1890).
[2] Printed in ibid., vol. ii, p. 555.
[3] Transcribed (not fully) in William Boys, *Collections for a History of Sandwich . . .,* 2 vols., pp. 750–2 (Canterbury, priv. print. 1792, repr. 1842). Transcribed and edited, Eben Putnam, 'Two early passenger lists, 1635–7', in *New England Historical and Genealogical Register,* vol. lxxv, pp. 217–26, 1921.
[4] See F. Hull, ed., 'The Tufton Manuscripts and the Virginia Connection ' *Virginia Magazine of History and Biography,* vol. lxv, pp. 313–27, 1957.

KENNETT, MARGARET. 2 letters. 1725. (U352 C1)

Written to her father, Dr. Thomas Brett, giving detailed description of conditions in Charleston, S.C.

TWISDEN FAMILY PAPERS. 2 notebooks. 1776–84.

(a) References in a notebook covering 1776–84, to Sir William Twisden going to America with James Gambier, 1777. (U49 F4/2)

(b) Notebook, by an unidentified writer, includes four pages on the War of Independence, c. 1780. (U49 F3)

MACKESON, JOHN. Correspondence. 1807–14. (U47/34 C1 and U511 C8)

Includes references to his experiences in the West Indies and to the war with the United States, 1812–14.

MARTIN, GEORGE F. (d. 1852). 23 letters. 1834–52. (U442 F/10/2)

Letters from or relating to George F. Martin, who emigrated to Rochester, N.Y., in 1834, and died of cholera in 1852. (There are some later letters from his widow, c. 1869.) Martin refers to the immigration of Irish paupers to the United States, railroad building in New York in 1837, the 'infamous' war with Mexico, &c. There are also letters of advice to his relatives who emigrated to New York in 1850–1.

PARISH RECORDS.

Headcorn (P181/18/27), Marden (P244/12/185), and Staplehurst (P347/18/11). Correspondence regarding emigration of paupers to America and Canada from these parishes. The emigration papers of the parish overseers include notices from shipowners on their terms for transporting the emigrants, applications from the overseers for permission to borrow money against the parish rate to finance emigration, approval of this by the Poor Law Commissioners, lists of emigrants, &c.

QUARTER SESSIONS RECORDS.

(a) Occasional bonds for transportation occur after the Act of 4 Geo. I (1717). (Q/SB)

(b) Certificates concerning apprentices sent to Pennsylvania or Maryland. 1 bundle. 1719. (Q/SB 1719)

Viscount De L'Isle, PENSHURST PLACE, Tonbridge

SIDNEY PAPERS. 2 letters. 1609.

18 and 23 June 1609, from Sir William Browne to Viscount Lisle, mention the possibility of a Lieutenant Saunders joining the second expedition to Virginia under de la Warr.[1]

[1] H.M.C. De L'Isle and Dudley (Penshurst) MSS. iv [77], pp. 130, 132. (Deposited with H.M.C. for editing.)

LANCASHIRE

Public Library, Civic Centre, BOLTON

WHITMAN COLLECTION.[1] Letters; diary (5 volumes); lectures, &c. 1880–1953.

The Bolton group of Walt Whitman admirers, known as the Eagle Street College or the Bolton Whitman Fellowship, had many contacts with Whitman.

Most letters from him were given to the Library of Congress in 1924, but there remain in the library collection one letter, 1885, and two postcards, 1884 and 1885, to Bessie and Isabella Ford; and the draft of a letter, 1889, to Thomas B. Harned. The collection includes several hundred letters, 1880–1921, from Whitman's literary executors, H. L. Traubel, R. M. Bucke, and T. B. Harned to J. W. Wallace, as well as letters to Wallace with a Whitman interest from Robert Blatchford, John Burroughs, Edward Carpenter, Keir Hardie, Ramsay MacDonald, and others; it also includes the correspondence, 1891–1953, of Anne Montgomerie Traubel with Wallace and with Mrs. M. Whiteside.

There are a number of manuscripts of talks given on Whitman by Wallace, and the manuscript diary of his visit to Whitman in 1891. There is also an extensive group of books and periodicals containing the works of Whitman and biography and criticism.

See also the Walt Whitman material in the John Rylands Library, Manchester (p. 103).

H.M. Customs and Excise, HEYSHAM (Lancaster)

See H.M. Customs and Excise, London (p. 201).

The Library, The Athenaeum, Church Alley, LIVERPOOL 1

GLADSTONE COLLECTION. Bill of exchange book, 1784–1805; notebook, 1829.

(*a*) Bill of exchange book, 1784–1805. A large number of these bills were drawn in the United States, particularly in Philadelphia (these mainly by Robert Morris). The business is probably that of Corrie & Co., originally

---

[1] See H. Hamer, *A Catalogue of Works by and Relating to Walt Whitman in the Reference Library, Bolton* (Bolton, 1955).

corn merchants of Liverpool, which John Gladstone (1764–1851) joined in
1786; the firm was subsequently known as Corrie, Gladstone & Bradshaw,
and later as Gladstone & Co.[1]

(b) R. G. (?Robertson Gladstone) (1805–75), 'Journal of a voyage to, and
residence in, the colony of Demerara, with a continuation of the same tour
through the West India Islands & North (U.S. & British) America, & thence
to Liverpool, commencing 12th October 1828, ending August 1829' (notebook of 85 pages). The section dealing with the author's visit to New York,
Philadelphia, Albany, Buffalo, &c., consists largely of an impersonal record
of such facts as layout of streets, number of theatres, major exports of the
ports visited. A list of 'acquaintances formed' is included.

LIVERPOOL REGISTER OF SHIPPING (printed). 2 volumes
(156, 10 pages). 1835, 1838.

These registers were compiled, because of a feeling that Lloyd's paid insufficient attention to local matters, by 'a committee of ship-owners, merchants, and underwriters'. A large number of ships on the American run
are included.

LIVERPOOL ATLANTIC CATTLE TRADE, 1887–90 (printed)
(90 pages). 1890.

This book, marked 'private and confidential: not for publication', is the
'Statement and Evidence of the Liverpool Steamship Owners' Association
and Messrs. F. Leyland & Co.' about conditions on board the ships, sanitary
precautions, &c.

PAMPHLET COLLECTION.

At least sixteen of the pamphlets, published 1769–83, concern political
or military relationships between Britain and America; nineteenth- and
twentieth-century pamphlets of American interest in the collection concern
free trade, the Civil War, and other subjects.

Chamber of Commerce, 1 Old Hall Street,
LIVERPOOL 3

REPORTS (printed). 1851–83, 1886– .

The volumes include annual, committee, and special reports of the Chamber,
and the proceedings of the annual general meeting. Comment on matters
relating to the United States is frequent, since subjects such as the following
were dealt with: revision of international maritime law, Atlantic mail and
cable services, American tariff policy, problems connected with the *Alabama*
case, &c.

[1] See Thomas Ellison, *The Cotton Trade of Great Britain including a History of the
Liverpool Cotton Market and of the Liverpool Cotton Brokers' Association* (London, 1886).

H.M. Customs and Excise, LIVERPOOL

See H.M. Customs and Excise, London (p. 201).

Liverpool Cotton Association, 16 Cotton Exchange Buildings, LIVERPOOL 3

MINUTE-BOOKS, CIRCULARS (printed), MISCELLANEOUS PAPERS. 1841– .

Many of the records of the Association were lost or destroyed during the Second World War, and those remaining are in process of being put in order. The Association has, however, a complete set of its minutes from its founding in 1882, and it is probable that the minute-books of its predecessor, the Liverpool Cotton Brokers' Association,[1] founded 1841, still exist.

In addition, a rough check of other relevant material revealed letter-books for 1872–8 and 1882–95; a minute-book of the Clearing House Committee covering 1910–30; a volume labelled 'European Committee' containing duplicated, typescript, and typescript copies of material concerning conferences held in 1923–6 in Washington, Liverpool, London, and Paris, to discuss the proposals of the United States Department of Agriculture for Universal Standards for Grade and Staple; an 'import book' for 1929–35, showing weekly imports by ship and port of origin; a volume containing papers relating to the 1940 American Cotton Import Committee; file boxes containing outgoing and incoming correspondence, from the late 1920's onwards.

The Association also has the (printed) *American Telegraph Circular* and the *Liverpool Daily Circular* (also a weekly circular), both 1895–1939.

Martins Bank Ltd., Head Office, 4 Water Street, LIVERPOOL 2

BANK RECORDS.[2] 1786–1903.

After an extensive search of the records of Arthur Heywood, Sons & Co. (absorbed 1883), the Liverpool Commercial Banking Company (absorbed 1889), the Bank of Liverpool (original name of Martins Bank), and various Liverpool offices of Martins Bank, officers of the Bank have found the following material:

(*a*) Arthur Heywood, Sons & Co. (established 1773).

(i) Arthur Heywood's private ledger, containing a balancing of the accounts of the copartnership as of 4 Jan. 1786. Three of the entries refer to

[1] See W. O. Henderson, *The Lancashire Cotton Famine 1861–1865* (Manchester, 1934).
[2] Virginia material microfilmed by the Virginia Colonial Records Project.

money due from the United States, the debtors being Andrew Brunner of Philadelphia, Reade & Bogardus of New York, and Donaldson & Stotts of Virginia; the first two are noted as unlikely to pay.

(ii) Two ledgers, covering the years 1791–7 and 1801–12. A quick search showed relevant references only in the account of Richard Heywood and James Currie, which includes entries of sums paid for American stock in 1791 and 1792, and for proceeds of sale of such stock in 1793.

(iii) Four signature-books—1836, 1842, 1847, and one undated. The books contain specimen signatures of customers, with addresses. The only American address noted was that of David Acheson of Washington, Pa., in the 1836 volume.

(*b*) Bank of Liverpool (established 1831).

Minutes of Directors' Meetings, 1831– . The first seven volumes, covering 1831–1903, contain various references to dealings with the United States, among which are the following: copies of letters sent to the Western Bank of Philadelphia and the Union Bank of Louisiana, 21 May 1833; a resolution that the Bank have no dealings in the bonds of Slave States, 26 Mar. 1839; purchase of Indiana Stock and other affairs of the North American Trust & Banking Co., 27 Oct. and 3 Nov. 1840, 9 July 1844, 11 July 1854; discussion concerning the propriety of continuing the account of the Bank of Charleston, 26 July 1844 and 8 July 1845; notes on the Bank's purchase and sale of United States Funded Loans, 1875–82; report of the failure of Martin, Wise & Fitzhugh, cotton merchants of Liverpool and Paris, Tex., 23 Mar. 1897.

Public Libraries, William Brown Street, LIVERPOOL 3

LIVERPOOL TOWN BOOKS.[1]

These records, which are in the process of being published, contain occasional references to America—e.g. in Feb. 1733, concerning a grant to settle prisoners in Georgia; in Sept. 1779, concerning defence measures to be taken against possible attack by John Paul Jones.

NORRIS PAPERS.[2] Letters. 1693–1708.

The letters to Richard Norris (1670–1731), merchant, Mayor of Liverpool, M.P., include some dealing with trade with Virginia, from merchants or agents in London, Dublin, and elsewhere (not America). They note the arrival of the Virginia fleet, and include comment on tobacco crop prospects, tobacco prices, customs costs, the Virginia embargo, salt exports; many of these are from Thomas Johnson, who later was a customs officer in Virginia.

---

[1] See J. A. Twemlow, ed., *Liverpool Town Books, 1550–1862*; vol. i, 1550–71; vol. ii, 1571–1603 (Liverpool, 1918–35).

[2] Some of the letters are printed in T. Heywood, ed., *The Norris Papers* (Manchester, 1846) (Chetham Society Publications, vol. ix).

TARLETON PAPERS.[1] Letters, deeds, and business accounts. 1754–80.

(a) John Tarleton, Sen. (1719–73), merchant, Liverpool. Included are his annual profit and loss accounts for most years from 1749 and those of Messrs. Tarleton & Backhouse, 1786–1810, also incomplete. The Tarleton business, both in John's lifetime and that of his sons, was very varied, including slave trading, privateering, West Indian estate owning, cotton importing, sugar refining, &c. Mention is made in the accounts of 13 June 1754 of money due to him 'by voyage to Philadelphia'; of 26 Apr. 1758 of money due 'brig *John* of Philadelphia' and of money owed 'to Henry Harrison of Philadelphia'; in 1761 there is a reference to 'lead unsold at New York', and in 1776 to 'brig *Fanny* to Pensacola' Fla.; there may well have been later trade with America, since, e.g. accounts with Nicholas Waterhouse, the Liverpool broker, appear in 1810.

(b) Sir Banastre Tarleton (1754–1833), one of the four sons of the above; officer in the British Army during the War of Independence. Two letters written in 1780 to 'my dear brother', one[2] from Winnsboro, S.C., and the other from Camp Camden, S.C. (copy), the latter giving an account of the battle at Camden on 16 Aug. 1780.

CASE & SOUTHWORTH. Sales ledger. 1754–5.

Merchants and shipbrokers, Kingston, Jamaica. The sales ledger includes a few references to cargoes—flour, staves, decanters—from Philadelphia. The collection also includes two account books for the period.

PARKER FAMILY PAPERS.[3] *c.* 600 items: almanac, notebook, 16 bundles (mainly letters). 1760–95.

James Parker (1729–1815), merchant, and his family. Parker went to America as a young man, and became a merchant in Norfolk, Va. He fought as a captain in the British Army during the War of Independence. About two-thirds of the items in the collection relate to his career in Virginia or during the War, or to that of his son Patrick in Norfolk after the War. They include much family correspondence, including letters written by Parker, while a prisoner-of-war, to his wife and 150 letters, from Patrick— mostly from Norfolk—between 1785 and 1795; Parker's diary of the War in the form of letters; and miscellaneous papers concerning prize money accounts. Also in the collection are 'copies of Franklin documents, three Williamsburg imprints (a Purdie & Dixon interleaved almanac of 1771, an annotated copy of the Virginia Association of 1771, and a printed letter of Edmund Randolph dated 1774, indicating that he has assumed Mr.

[1] *See* W. R. Serjeant, 'The Tarleton Papers: a Merchant's Accounts', *Liverpool Libraries, Museums and Arts Committee Bulletin*, vol. vi, pp. 28–31, 1956.

[2] W. R. Serjeant, op. cit., includes a reproduction of this letter on p. 28.

[3] Microfilms are at Colonial Williamsburg, and have also been made for the Virginia Colonial Records Project.

Jefferson's law practice in the General Court), a letter of Robert Morris [re the Boston Tea Party], . . . a letter of James Parker's describing the Arnold-Andre treason case, a letter of William Aitchison's, November 14, 1774, describing the proceedings in Williamsburg after the York River tea party'.[1]

SAMWELL, DAVID (1751–98).[2] 3 letters. 1774–95. (Gregson Collection GRCxvii)

Surgeon, London and on ships. Most of the fifty-six letters in the collection are from Samwell to Matthew Gregson, upholsterer and antiquarian, of Liverpool. A few of these contain comment on Anglo-American relations, 1774, 1775; and on Thomas Paine, 1795.

CURRIE, JAMES (1756–1805). 'Journal of a Voyage from Nixonton No. Carolina to the Island of Saint Martin's.'[3] 1775–6. (Currie Papers Hq 695)

Physician. This journal, kept during the voyage in 1776, includes a balancing of the good and bad experiences of his five years' stay in America. At the end of the notebook Currie has copied from the original manuscript a letter 'which I wrote in Mar: 1775, & which appeared in Pinkney's [sic] Gazette [Virginia Gazette] of 24th of that month'. This letter, sent anonymously, is a defence of the Scots merchants in Virginia against attacks which had been made on them; Currie notes that the letter as he here transcribes it includes some sentences 'which were thought too severe' by Pinckney and so omitted in the publication of the letter.

HOLT AND GREGSON PAPERS. 1778–early 19th century.

This is a collection of nineteen volumes of manuscript and printed material for a history of Liverpool, made by John Holt during the latter part of the eighteenth century and by Matthew Gregson until about 1830. Volume 10 includes statements of monthly imports of cotton from various countries into London and Liverpool in 1792; it also includes a section on docks, shipping, and commerce; and list of the ships, statistics, and documents connected with the slave trade. Volume 19 includes a compilation by Gregson of all vessels that were taken by Liverpool privateers between 28 July 1778 and 13 Apr. 1779; a number of the ships taken are listed as having come from American ports. There may be other relevant material in the papers.

HORNBY LIBRARY AUTOGRAPH LETTERS. 1782–1857.

Of no intrinsic interest, merely letters of politesse from the following:

Barnum, P. T. Bridgeport, 9 Nov. 1848, to J. Nimms.

    [1] J. M. Hemphill II, 'Virginia and the Parker Family Papers', Liverpool Libraries, Museums and Arts Committee Bulletin, vol. vi, pp. 25–27, 1956.
    [2] See H. A. Taylor, 'David Samwell', Liverpool Libraries, Museums and Arts Committee Bulletin, vol. vi, pp. 32–46, 1956, where these letters are quoted.
    [3] Extracts printed in W. W. Currie, ed., Memoir of the Life, Writings, and Correspondence of James Currie, vol. i, pp. 34–38 (London, 1831).

Cooper, James Fenimore. Paris, 15 Aug. 1877, to an unknown correspondent.

Franklin, Benjamin. Passy, 9 Apr. 1782, to F. Nogarei.

Hawthorne, Nathaniel. Liverpool, 10 Aug. 1857, to H. A. Bright.

Irving, Washington. New York, 21 Mar. 1835, to Robert Southey, introducing the Rev. Francis L. Hawks of New York.

SPARLING & BOLDEN. Letter-book. 1788–99. (MD219)

John Sparling and William Bolden, Liverpool merchants. Most of the letter copies are to merchants in Virginia, mainly to John Lawrence & Co. Business affairs dealt with relate to export from Liverpool of nails, twine, salt, linens, and import of tar, turpentine, tobacco; many of the letters refer to attempts to settle debts contracted before the War of Independence. There is also some discussion of other matters, such as French privateering, and yellow fever epidemics and fires in Norfolk, Va.

ROSCOE PAPERS. Correspondence; some manuscript notes, pamphlets, &c. 1794–1831.

William Roscoe (1753–1831), historian, poet, reformer, M.P., of Liverpool. His great interest in prison reform is the major topic of his large American correspondence, but many letters concern current Anglo-American political affairs, and some his commercial interests. (A typescript calendar, arranged alphabetically, is available.)

(a) Correspondence on American prison management and reform, 1816–31.

Letters from Alden Bradford, Gamaliel Bradford, C. A. Busby, John F. Champlin, Thomas P. Cope, Caleb Cresson, Louis Dwight, Thomas Eddy, William Eustis, John Griscom, S. M. Hopkins, Edward Livingston, William Maxwell, James Mease, Josiah Quincy, William Tudor, Gulian C. Verplanck, and Chauncey Whittelsey. There are also drafts or copies of letters from Roscoe, or, in a few cases, letters written on his behalf, to most of these correspondents, as well as to Elizabeth Fry, General Lafayette, and T. I. Wharton.

In addition, the collection includes printed pamphlets and reports, 1795–1826, on American prisons.

(b) Correspondence on other American topics, 1794–1830.

Bradbury, John. Most of the correspondence, 1806–11, concerning his plant collecting trip has been published.[1]

Brougham, Henry Peter (later Baron Brougham and Vaux). 1812–13. At least fourteen of the letters in the extensive correspondence between Brougham and Roscoe include comment on Anglo-American affairs.

Cooper, Thomas. Seven letters from Philadelphia, 1815–19, and one from Columbia, S.C., 1830, include comment on political and scientific affairs.

Daulby, William. Draft letters and copies of letters from 'W. D.', New

[1] See H. W. Rickett, 'John Bradbury's Explorations in Missouri Territory', *Proceedings of the American Philosophical Society*, vol. xciv, pp. 59–89, 1950.

York, 1817–19. Business matters, mainly concerning importing of steel and hardware, exporting of cotton, with some comment on bankruptcies and other indicators of depressed conditions. Also an 1827 letter from Daulby to W. S. Roscoe, and several relating to the settlement of Daulby's affairs after his death.

Eddowes, Ralph. Twenty-four letters, Philadelphia, 1794–1828, concerning family, political, financial, and business (import of white lead) affairs.

Fraser, John, Jr. London, 1 June 1810, on American plants and seeds.

Heywood, Benjamin A. Manchester, 4 Oct. 1794, on his attitude towards the United States and its prosperity.

Jefferson, Thomas. Washington, D.C., 1 Sept. 1806; and Monticello, 27 Dec. 1820, concerning the proposed university in Virginia.

Tartt, William Macdonald. Two letters, Charleston, S.C., 1810 and 1811, during his visit to the United States, concern politics, Benjamin Rush, &c.

Thornely, Thomas. London, 9 June 1812, concerning the Orders in Council; 12 Dec. 1828 mentioning the conversion to Unitarianism of Philadelphia Quakers and quoting a letter from G. M. Justice of Philadelphia on prison discipline.

Tuffen, T. F. (of Tuffen & Pugh, bankers of Bristol). London, 12 Mar. 1812, to Messrs. Roscoe, Clarke & Roscoe concerning James Slater Hall, who has absconded to America.

William Frederick, 2nd Duke of Gloucester. Correspondence, 1806–25, concerning the slave trade and Anglo-American relations.

Wright, Frances, the feminist, reformer and freethinker. Two letters, New York and Allenby, Cumberland, 1820, concern her plays.

(c) Other American correspondence, 1803–31.
Letters from J. J. Audubon, Benjamin S. Barton, William P. C. Barton, E. Bronson, William Ellery Channing, Joseph Charless, W. Creswell, Joseph Delaplaine, Joseph Gilpin, Maximilian Godefroy, William Gracie, Christopher Hughes, John Lowell, William Maclure, Samuel L. Mitchell, John Richardson, Benjamin Rush, Benjamin Silliman, Mrs. Smallcroft, W. C. Somerville, William B. Sprague, George Ticknor, Aaron B. Tucker, Noah Worcester.

(d) A notebook containing manuscript notes about 'the coast of the territory of New Orleans', &c.; and the manuscript journal, 1805–6, of John Williamson, 'who ascended White River in company with his wife, in pursuit of game'. Both these include extensive descriptions of Indian tribes. The notebook also contains newspaper cuttings on this subject.

AMERICAN CHAMBER OF COMMERCE FOR THE PORT OF LIVERPOOL. Minutes (4 volumes, indexed separately). 1801–1908.

The initial purposes of this British organization were the redress of existing and the prevention of future grievances affecting the American trade, and the establishment of regular and settled rules in respect of payments of freights and rates of fees in the customs and at public boards and offices in London. 'The annual survey of the work of the Chamber, the annual financial statement of the Treasurer, meetings of the general committee, of sub-committees and of the financial council, special general meetings and banquets were reported. Important letters received by the Chamber and the replies to them were sometimes recorded in full.'[1]

BROWN, GEORGE ALEXANDER (1803–70). Memoirs and diaries (3 volumes). 1803–63. (E 14734)

Merchant and banker. The first of the three volumes describes Brown's boyhood and schooldays in Baltimore; his work in his uncle's firm—Alexander Brown & Sons, linen merchants, Baltimore—including comment on the decline of the linen trade after 1817; his partnership in a merchant firm in Tampico, Mexico, in 1825, and the vicissitudes of this firm; his establishment in Liverpool in 1829.

The diary entries thereafter, including those in the latter two volumes, concern political, family, and business affairs; some of these include notes of the arrival of American ships, and also reactions to two visits from Hawthorne in November 1855.

McIVER, McVICCAR & McCORQUODALE. Document (2 folios). 1804. (MD 97)

Accounts for the sale, on behalf of this Liverpool firm, of 197 Negroes, signed by Benjamin Maurice Pickering, Savannah, Ga., 28 Feb. 1804.

JOSEPH, JOSEPH. Papers (1 vol.). 1805. (Kf 161)

Silversmith, Liverpool. This volume of privateering papers contains receipts and other papers relating to disposal of prize money; at least one American ship, the *Commerce*, is involved.

HOPE, SAMUEL, & CO.—GEORGE HOLT & CO. 10 ledgers.[2] 1812–66. (MD 230)

Cotton brokers and bankers, Liverpool. The partnership of Samuel Hope and George Holt as cotton brokers and bankers was dissolved in 1821, the cotton side of the business thereafter being known as George Holt & Co. The ledgers contain many entries of sales of sea island and other American cottons; the ledger covering the years 1830–42 includes two pages devoted to 'New Orleans acct.' for the years 1835–40.

BROWN, JAMES. Log-book, letter-book. 1843–8. (Kf 227)

Captain of the Liverpool ship *Gossypium*. The log of the ship covers six voyages from Liverpool to New Orleans and five from New Orleans to

[1] W. O. Henderson, 'The American Chamber of Commerce for the Port of Liverpool, 1801–1908', *Transactions of the Historic Society of Lancashire and Cheshire*, vol. lxxxv, pp. 1–61, 1933.

[2] Mentioned in F. E. Hyde, *Blue Funnel* (Liverpool, 1956).

Liverpool, 1844–6. The letter copies, 1843–8, include those from Brown in New Orleans, to the owners of the ship—John Croft, and Messrs. Clint and Leftwich—concerning prices, progress, &c., in selling the salt and tin-plate which seem to have been the main cargoes, and in buying cotton and 'Indian corn'.

REPORTS ON THE COTTON MARKET (1 vol.). 1848–63. (Kf 259)

Weekly summaries of sales, imports, &c., presumably at Liverpool. A brief comment on trade during each week is included, these frequently referring to the United States—e.g., in 1848 there appear such notes as 'American scarce', 'large receipts at NO', 'demand for sea island', and in 1861 'US a/cs more warlike', 'large export to America', 'anxious of U.S., holders determined to sell'.

MANN, WILLIAM THOMPSON. 'Diary of a Trip to America.' 1848–9. (G6590)

Mann went south from New York to Apalachicola, Fla., via Philadelphia, Washington, D.C., Savannah, Ga., &c.; he took a steamer along the coast to New Orleans, and then went north to Kentucky, Ohio, to Montreal and back to New York. Most of the entries relate to sightseeing or social calls paid.

BUCKLEY-MATHEW, GEORGE B. (1807–79). Correspondence (1 volume). 1850–6. (Ef 216)

M.P., Consul at Charleston, S.C., 1850–3, and at Philadelphia 1853–6. The collection includes letters from the following:

Boucicault, Dion. New York, 14 June 1856.

Bulwer, Sir William Henry. Washington, D.C., 3 May 1851, and New York, 2 Aug. 1851, asking for news of the 'Cuban expedition'.

Butler, A. P. Washington, D.C., 15 Feb. 1852, including discussion of the 'kidnapping traffic', i.e., the capture of free West Indian Negro seamen and their sale in the South.

Crampton, John F. Washington, D.C., 18 Dec. 1851 and 20 Feb. 1852, including discussion of the 'kidnapping traffic'.

Cowper-Temple, W. F. Writing from England, 1855, 'I suppose the American Irish invasion will end in smoke, otherwise we shall have the trouble of sinking them in the Atlantic on their way.'

Gladstone, William. Two letters, 1852, thanking Mathew for information and suggestions; and two, 1856, relating to Mathew's leaving his consular post at the request of the United States government, as a result of his attempted recruitment of Americans for service in the Crimean War.

Grey, Sir Charles E. Jamaica, 20 Jan. 1855, referring to the 'kidnapping traffic', and thanking Mathew for his kindness in the United States, especially his introduction to General Ward.

James, G. P. R. Norfolk, Va., 10 June 1855, including discussion of the 'kidnapping traffic'.

Lytton, Edward Robert Bulwer. 29 Feb. 1854, including discussion of reciprocity.

Sumner, Charles. Boston, 10 Sept. 1854.

Thackeray, W. M. [from America] 7 Jan. [1855].

Letters written to Mathew in America from correspondents in England, containing comment on American affairs, are those from John Bigelow, 1855; the Earl of Ellesmere, 1855; and Miles T. Stapleton (Baron Beaumont), 1854.

The collection also includes a letter from John F. Crampton at the British Legation in Washington, D.C., 9 Sept. 1851, to Daniel Lance, acting Consul at Charleston, S.C., concerning a letter he has had from someone named Randolph which informs him of a plan for releasing Smith O'Brien and other Irish leaders from the penal colony in Tasmania.

BAKER, F. J. and R. L. FREER. 'Account of a Voyage in the *Great Eastern*.' 1862. (G5120)

Included are details of their stay in New York city—Central Park, the magnificence of the shops, &c.—of their journey up the Hudson River and to Niagara and Buffalo.

Reynolds & Gibson, Cotton Exchange Buildings, LIVERPOOL 3

FIRM'S LEDGER. 1809–30.

Cotton brokers, Liverpool. Francis Reynolds's ledger covers the years 1790–2 and 1809–30. There are frequent references to the sale of American cotton during the latter period.

C. E. Turner, Esq., E. W. Turner & Son, Cunard Buildings, Water Street, LIVERPOOL 3

SLAVE TRADE. 2 notebooks.[1] 18th century.

The two manuscripts contain letters of instruction to masters of slaving vessels and replies to these. Although the trade involved was primarily to the West Indies, there is some reference to the mainland—e.g., instructions from the Liverpool owners, 9 July 1768, direct the captain that if he is not able to sell his cargo satisfactorily in the West Indies he is to proceed to Maryland and there contact Messrs. Samuel Gallaway, Thomas Ringold & Co. of Annapolis.

---

[1] Part of the material was published in 'Instructions to Slavers', *Sea Breezes*, vol. xxiii, N.S., pp. 322–7, 1957.

Harold Cohen Library, University of Liverpool, Ashton Street, LIVERPOOL 3

RATHBONE COLLECTION.[1] Papers, letters, &c. 1819–97.

The Rathbone family were Liverpool merchants who dealt with the United States as well as with many other countries. The main documents relating to the United States are as follows:

(a) Thirty-two packets of correspondence, mainly business (cotton, coffee, tea), from New York, Boston, &c., 1819–73.

(b) Two folders of correspondence, mainly personal, between William Rathbone (1819–1902) and his family during his visits to America, 1839–49.

(c) One letter-book: William Rathbone (1787–1868) to 'New England Relief Society',[2] 1847, concerned with the relief of distress in Ireland.

(d) One packet of personal letters, 1895–7, from J. M. Forbes, of Boston, to William Rathbone (1819–1902).

Department of Economics, University of Liverpool, 11 Abercromby Square, LIVERPOOL 7

WATERHOUSE & SONS.[3] Ledger, 1799–1800.

Cotton brokers, Liverpool. (Nicholas Waterhouse was probably the most important cotton broker of the time.) The ledger includes entries relating to the sale of Georgia cotton.

[1] *Catalogue of the Rathbone Papers in the University Library, Liverpool. Part i: Family Papers; part ii: Business papers* (Liverpool, 1959–60). See also E. F. Rathbone, *William Rathbone, a Memoir* (London, 1905); E. A. Rathbone, *Records of the Rathbone Family* (Edinburgh, 1913); S. G. Checkland, 'An English Merchant House in China after 1842', *Bulletin of the Business Historical Society*, vol. xxvii, pp. 158–89, 1953; Sheila Marriner, 'Rathbones' Trading Activities in the Middle of the Nineteenth Century', *Transactions of the Historic Society of Lancashire and Cheshire*, vol. cviii, pp. 105–27, 1957, and her forthcoming *Rathbones of Liverpool* (Liverpool, 1961). S. G. Checkland, 'American versus West Indian traders in Liverpool, 1793–1815', *Journal of Economic History*, vol. xviii, pp. 141–60, 1958.
[2] This is the binder's title for the letter-book which relates to various relief committees in towns in New England—there is no single body with the binder's title.
[3] See S. Dumbell, 'The Cotton Market in 1799', *Economic History*, vol. i, pp. 141–8, 1926. F. E. Hyde and others, 'The Cotton Broker and the Rise of the Liverpool Cotton Market', *Economic History Review*, vol. viii, pp. 75–83, 1955.

Amalgamated Union of Foundry Workers, 164 Chorlton Road, MANCHESTER 16

REPORTS (printed), EXECUTIVE COMMITTEE MINUTES, LETTERS. 1856– .

The Union holds extensive records of the Friendly Society of Iron Founders of England, Ireland, and Wales; and the Associated Iron-Moulders of Scotland. These unions were very active in promoting emigration of members in the nineteenth century, and this is reflected in the printed reports and manuscript minute-books.[1]

The records of the English union, for example, show that the Executive Committee passed resolutions approving members' applications for emigration benefit—to go to New York, Illinois, Pennsylvania, &c.—these being particularly frequent in 1867. The Associated Iron-Moulders of Scotland were very concerned during the 1870's—when their reports often included extracts from the American *Iron Molders' Journal*—to obtain the return of emigration benefit from the many members who had come back from the United States.

The Union also has a file of cards of members emigrating during the 1920's and 1930; in some cases letters or forms of clearance are clipped to these, indicating the emigration of members to the United States and their transfer to the Iron Molders' Union of North America.

Amalgamated Weavers' Association, Chronicle Buildings, 74 Corporation Street, MANCHESTER 4

NORTHERN COUNTIES AMALGAMATED WEAVERS' ASSOCIATION. Minutes of General Council Meetings (printed). 1888.

There are references in the minutes of 1 and 22 Sept. 1888 to the payment of union funds to finance the emigration of a group of weavers, with their children, from Lower Heys Mill, Macclesfield, Cheshire, then on strike, via Castle Garden, N.Y., and the attempt of their employer to prevent their being allowed to land in the United States.

---

[1] See also *The Friendly Society of Iron Founders of England, Ireland and Wales: Centenary Souvenir* (Manchester, 1909). Includes Table 1(c) in the Appendix, showing annual expenditure on emigration, 1855–1908.

The Library, Co-operative Union Ltd., Holyoake House, Hanover Street, MANCHESTER 4

OWEN, ROBERT (1771–1858). Correspondence and papers. 1825–56.

Socialist and philanthropist. Owen visited the United States four times between 1824 and 1828; on the first of these trips he founded New Harmony, Ind. In 1828 he went to help the colonization of land in Texas to be granted by the Mexican Government. He lived in the United States, 1844–7, and most of his children settled there, notably Robert Dale Owen, United States Congressman and diplomat.

The correspondence and papers consist mainly of letters to Owen, 1822–58. Previously organized in bundles, the material is now numbered from 1 to 2,964 and kept in folders by the hundred, in roughly chronological order. There is a good typescript catalogue (164 pages).

Among the numerous individual letters and papers of American interest the following groups stand out:

(a) New Harmony. Conditions, purchase, paraphernalia of Owen's visit (hotel bills, letters of introduction, notes for advice); the first letter is dated 16 Dec. 1825 and the last (a French reference to New Harmony) 10 July 1848.

(b) Mexico and Texas. 1828–50. Concern Owen's projected Texas scheme, 1828–30; Texan annexation and possible British intervention in Mexico, 1844–6; and requests for advice about emigration to Texas.

(c) Emigration. Besides the overlap with (a) and (b) above, there are one or two interesting individual letters, e.g. a scheme of emigration by Robert Gouger, 19 Mar. 1830; and letters, 1847, from W. S. Peters, founder of a colony in Texas, urging Owen to go there and to take many Scots.

(d) Robert Owen in America, 1844–7. Parting wishes to Owen, 1844 (items 1327–37). A section called 'Robert Owen in the U.S.A.' (items 1340–1534) includes requests to speak (e.g. from 'Committee of Socialists at Cincinnati', 31 Oct. 1844); letters of introduction; talk of books; Owen's contacts with Congress; the Oregon question.

(e) Oregon question, 1846. Among the correspondence on this subject is item 1456, 'Confidential correspondence between Robert Owen and Earl of Aberdeen and Sir Robert Peel on new state of affairs between the British nation and the United States'. This comprises three letters from Peel to Owen, three from Owen to Peel, two from Aberdeen to Owen, and one from Robert Dale Owen to his father, all Apr. or May 1846. Peel is very cool to Owen; Aberdeen more friendly. Owen's letter from his son is the most interesting: 'Webster's manifesto . . . on the Oregon question' was enclosed. 'You will see how pointed he is in regard to the utter impossibility of a line South of 49 . . . if the British ministry are not now persuaded how things actually stand, "neither would they be persuaded though one rose from the dead".' In addition there are two foolscap sheets: Last American Proposition, 12 July 1845, and Last British Proposition, 26 Aug. 1844.

(*f*) Spiritualism, 1855–6. Owen was converted to spiritualism by an American medium in 1854, so odd letters touch this gentle aberration, e.g., item 2393 from the American spiritualist Hume, and 2555 and 2541 from Colonel E. Brand.

(*g*) Robert Dale Owen. Letters, 1830–48, touching, *inter alia*, upon national education in the United States, the Panic of 1837, Cuba, and the Wilmot Proviso.

MISSISSIPPI VALLEY TRADING CO. Papers.[1] 1875–7.

Many leaders of the English Co-operative Union were connected with this project. The collection includes articles of association and alterations thereto; contemporary press cuttings on the project; correspondence between Dr. Worrall, manager, American Co-operative Union, and Edward Vansittart Neale, and other letters; pamphlets on direct trade between Mississippi Valley and Great Britain; a tract on the order of the Patrons of Husbandry. There are also extracts of a report of Lieutenant A. Gillmore, Corps of Engineers, on transportation from St. Mary's River on the Atlantic through Okefinokee, Ga., to the Gulf of Mexico. There are also references to the project in the reports of the Co-operative Union Congress and *Co-operative News*.

HOLYOAKE, GEORGE JACOB (1817–1906). Correspondence.[2] *c.* 1879–83.

Co-operator and secularist. A large box contains twelve packets of letters to Holyoake, and some loose letters. Among them are letters from Americans, particularly during and just after the period of Holyoake's two visits[3] to the United States in 1879 and 1882. Included are several from Robert G. Ingersoll; one from Rutherford B. Hayes, addressed to E. E. Barnum, expressing regret at not being able to attend the 'public breakfast' being given in New York in honour of Holyoake; and one from Rosamund Dale Owen, mainly in defence of her father, Robert Dale Owen.

See also the Holyoake Collection in the Bishopsgate Institute, London (p. 125).

---

[1] These papers were used by Clifton K. Yearley, *Britons in American Labor: a History of the Influence of the United Kingdom Immigrants on American Labor, 1820–1914* (Baltimore, 1957) (Johns Hopkins University Studies in History and Political Science, series 75, no. 1).

[2] See Joseph MacCabe, *Life and Letters of George Jacob Holyoake*, 2 vols. (London, 1908).

[3] See his *Travels in Search of a Settler's Guide-Book of America and Canada* (London, 1884).

The Library, Hartley Victoria Methodist College, Alexandra Road South, MANCHESTER 16

BOURNE, HUGH (1772–1852). Journals, minute-book, c. 60 letters. 1800–51 (with large omissions from Journals for 1821–42).

Co-founder, with William Clowes, of the Primitive Methodist Church in Great Britain. The two journals, covering July–Dec. 1844, and Jan. 1845–Mar. 1846, contain accounts of journeys to and from America and of the mission to America and Canada undertaken by Bourne as superintendent preacher of the Primitive Methodist circuits in these countries.[1]

The minute-book of this American mission covers entries 25 Jan. 1844–Dec. 1850. A box of papers contains eighty-two items, about sixty of which are letters from preachers on the American circuits to various correspondents in England, chiefly to William Clowes.

The John Rylands Library,[2] MANCHESTER

AUTOGRAPH COLLECTIONS. Letters and manuscript notes. 1658–1874.

Includes the following (unless otherwise stated, merely letters of politesse):

Audubon, J. J. 12 Dec. 1827, to an unknown correspondent. After giving a brief autobiographical sketch, Audubon asks for the support of 'the learned & wealthy'.

Bryant, George. n.d., to Dr. Raffles. Manuscript of a poem beginning 'While thee I seek protecting powers'.

Bryant, W. C. [Oct. 1848], to Mr. Gourlie.

Cobbett, William. Ross, Herefordshire, 4 June 1830, to Thomas Smith, Liverpool, making arrangements to have a copy of the *Register* published as a pamphlet in New York as quickly as possible. 'It is the *finest blow* that the Borough-villains have got for years.'

Cooper, James Fenimore. Paris, 3 Aug. 1831, to J. D. Hammond.

Franklin, Benjamin. New York, 2 July 1756, to George Whitefield.[3] 'I sometimes wish, that you and I were jointly employ'd by the Crown, to settle a colony on the Ohio'; plans for this utopia.

Irving, Washington. New York, 17 Dec. 1833, to James M. Wayne, Washington, D.C., asking Wayne to present the views of the bearer,

---

[1] See J. T. Wilkinson, *Hugh Bourne 1772–1852* (London, 1952). Chapter x is entitled 'Mission to America', pp. 161–8.

[2] Virginia material microfilmed by the Virginia Colonial Records Project.

[3] Printed in *Evangelical Magazine*, pp. 50–51 (London, 1803), and in *Complete Works of Benjamin Franklin*, ed. by John Bigelow, vol. ii, pp. 466–8 (London and New York, 1887). A copy of the letter is held at Manchester College, Oxford.

Lieutenant Nicholson of the Marine Corps, on better regulation of that service and the Navy generally.

—— London, 10 Feb. 1840, to his niece Rosa.

Lincoln, Abraham. Washington, D.C., 4 Dec. 1861, to Mrs. A. Van B. Nash.

Longfellow, Henry Wadsworth. Cambridge, Mass., 9 Jan. 1850, to an unknown correspondent.

—— Cambridge, Mass., 9 Feb. 1854, to T. Hitchcock.

Mather, Cotton. Manuscript sermon (8 pages), 1701. Manuscript notes (8 pages), 26 May 1702.

Mather, Increase. Manuscript notes (4 pages), 31 July 1658 and 23 June 1668. Manuscript (2 pages), July 1688.

Mather, Richard. Manuscript notes (1 page), n.d.

Motley, J. L. 1 May 1870, to Mr. Neilson.

Penn, John. Philadelphia, 3 Sept. 1768, asking his correspondent to arrange accommodation for him along his route to Fort Stanwix for the 'Congress of the Indians'.

Penn, Thomas. London, 6 June 1769, to Sir William Johnson, informing the latter that his 'grant' has come through.

Penn, William. Philadelphia, 3 Feb. 1684, to Dr. Ralph Tretwell, mainly concerning the navigability of the Schuylkill River and the fertility of the land bordering it.

Rogers, William. Philadelphia, 27 Feb. 1796. He has not yet seen the 'historic defence' written by his correspondent in London; when it arrives he will try to prevent its republication in Philadelphia.

Thacher, Peter. Two letters to Thomas Prince: Middleborough, Mass., 4 Jan. 1722, on family affairs, and 28 Aug. 1722 asking Prince to use his influence with 'his Excellency' so that Thacher may get back his servant Jonathan Wood.

Washington, George. Philadelphia, 9 Sept. 1787, to his nephew George Augustine Washington. State of the crops, question of railing for fences, and other farm and household affairs.

Webster, Daniel. Washington, D.C., 18 July 1823, to Jeremiah Nelson, Newburyport, Mass. Discussion of cases being heard before 'the Commissioners'.

Whistler, James A. M. Oct. 1874, to an unknown correspondent.

Whitefield, George. Savannah, Ga., 18 Jan. 1747, to James Habersham, Charleston, S.C.

Willis, Nathaniel Parker. Morristown, N.J., 5 Apr. 1842, to Theodore Ledyard Cuyler.

MORAVIAN COLLECTIONS. Diaries, minute-books, letters, notes.

Much of the Library's extensive collection of material dealing with the Moravian Church relates to America. Among the manuscripts are, for example, the following:

(a) Headquarters' diary, 1747–64 (eighteenth-century translation from the original German). (Eng. MSS. 945–50)

Relevant entries include those of 19 Jan. 1763, an account of the building up of new settlements in Carolina, 1753–61; and 5 Oct. 1763, text of a letter from Brother Nathanael in New York on missionary activities, the Indian wars, &c.

(*b*) Moravian Church in America (Eng. MS. 1080). Historical and bibliographical notes and papers relating to John Jacob Fries, minister at Bethabara, N.C., including a copy of his diary, 27 Apr.–31 July 1754; Benjamin Mortimer (teacher at Nazareth Hall, Pa., 1791–8; missionary among the Indians, 1798–1812; appointed pastor of First Moravian Church, New York, 1812); and the Mortimer family

SLAVE TRADE DOCUMENT. (1 folio). 1756–73. (Eng. MS. 517)

One of the three sheets in this collection is a list of ships engaged in the slave trade during the years 1749–87, showing 'where slaved', 'where sold', numbers who died, net sales. Four of the cargoes are noted as having been sold in Carolina, and one in Maryland.

WALSH, JOHN (1725?–95). Letter. 1772. (Eng. MS. 724)

Scientist, secretary to Clive. Included in the diary of his visit to France is a copy of a letter, Paris, 21 June 1772, to Benjamin Franklin. It includes his plans for experimenting on torpedo fish, and discussion of French electrical experimentation.

FRANKLIN, BENJAMIN. Letter (copy). 1787. (Eng. MS. 1110)

A volume containing copies of letters to members of the Wedgwood family from various correspondents includes a letter, 15 May 1787, from Franklin to Josiah Wedgwood thanking him for the present of a cameo depicting a slave. (The letter Wedgwood sent with the cameo is printed in vol. ii, p. 566 of E. Meteyard's *Life of Josiah Wedgwood* (London, 1865).)

MICKLETHWAITE, JOHN. Letters and business papers. 1790–1818. (Eng. MS. 1138)

Merchant of Leeds and Ardsley, Yorkshire. The items of American interest are:

(*a*) Printed brokers' circular, 179(?): *An Account of the Nature and Prices of American Stocks*, D. De Berdt & Co., London.

(*b*) Three letters, 7 Aug., 8 Aug., and 8 Aug./10 Sept. 1805, to Micklethwaite from C. Comegys in Baltimore, concerning Micklethwaite's property in Delaware, &c.

(*c*) Philadelphia, 29 Dec. 1818, from John Young to Micklethwaite, asking whether during his visit to the United States he can perform any commissions for Micklethwaite in relation to the latter's property there.

(d) Two letters, 1794, and two legal documents, 1790, 1794, from John Ellis, merchant, of New York, concerning the estate of his sister, Mary Ellis of Barnsley and Liverpool. These came into Micklethwaite's possession because he was, with John Benson of Liverpool, an executor of this estate.

ANTI-SLAVERY COLLECTION. Pamphlets, society reports, periodicals, &c. 19th century. (R 107337)

There are materials relating to the United States in 19 of the 25 boxes in this collection: 10 of these contain anti-slavery pamphlets, 5 contain society reports, 3 contain periodicals (among them a few numbers of anti-slavery journals), and 1 contains leaflets and posters. Some of the pamphlets were published in the United States, but most in England and Scotland; they range from exhortations to the Christian women of the United States, to protests against the building of the *Alabama*, and include speeches by Garrison, first-hand accounts of what it is like to be a slave, political maps of the United States. The annual reports of anti-slavery societies consist of those of American societies as well as of the Birmingham and Midland Freedmen's Aid Association and other British groups.

NICHOLSON PAPERS. Correspondence: including 60 business letters. 1817–26. (Eng. MSS. 1041–5)

The family correspondence of the Nicholsons includes some letters referring to America—e.g., two (nos. 498, 503) in 1817 concern the departure for America of Robert Dent.

There are in addition about sixty business letters[1] from the United States agents of the Liverpool merchant firm (mainly linen) of James & Thomas Nicholson. These were written 1822–6; most of them are from Wood Gibson in New York, with a few each from Sam Mordecai, Petersburg, Va.; J. S. and G. Hobson, Philadelphia; Beckett and Davies, Charleston, S.C.; Francis Thompson, New York; and Peter Remson & Co., New York. The letters report progress, or lack of it, in selling the goods, mainly linens, shipped by the Liverpool firm, and include information about prices, demand, &c.

RAWSON COLLECTION.[2] Minute-book; 2 boxes letters, notes, drafts of speeches, &c. 1825–67. (Eng. MSS. 741–3)

This collection of anti-slavery material consists of the minute-book of the Sheffield Female Anti-Slavery Society, 1825–33; and letters and other papers concerning various aspects of the anti-slavery movement, particularly as connected with the Sheffield group. Included are two letters from Neal Dow; a copy of a letter, 7 Dec. 1859, from Frederick Douglass, giving his views on the Harpers Ferry incident and the use of force in general; a

---

[1] Copies of most of these business letters are in the McLachlan Library, Unitarian College, Manchester (p. 106).

[2] See N. B. Lewis, 'The Abolitionist Movement in Sheffield, 1823–1833', *Bulletin of the John Rylands Library*, vol. xviii, pp. 377–92, 1934.

private circular from the Birmingham and Midland Freedmen's Aid Association giving particulars of four Americans who will be addressing them: George Cabot Ward, Robert J. Parvin, Phillips Brooks, Sella Martin, &c.

GASKELL COLLECTION. 11 letters. 1828–56. (Eng. MS. 730–4)

(a) The two volumes of letters to E. C. and W. Gaskell include the following:

Palfrey, John G. London, 21 June 1856, to Mrs. Gaskell, promising to send her some books on the Salem witchcraft trials when he returns to the United States.

Stowe, Harriet Beecher. Boston, 24 May 1856,[1] to Mrs. Gaskell, introducing her friends, Mr. and Mrs. Webb. Mrs. Webb, the daughter of a fugitive slave, gives dramatic readings.

(b) The three volumes of miscellaneous letters include the following (trivia unless otherwise described):

Bryant, W. C. London, 22 June 1845, to Mr. Fox.

Buchanan, James. United States Legation, London, 29 Dec. 1855, to Nathaniel Hawthorne, requesting Hawthorne to look into the case of H. N. Johnson, who has been kept in prison five months in Liverpool waiting to be sent to New York for trial.

Channing, W. E. Boston, 29 Nov. 1828, to Rev. James Yates.

Emerson, R. W. Manchester, 2 Mar. [1848], to [Mr. Shuttleworth].

Furness, W. H. Philadelphia, 8 Oct. 1854, to H. Bright.

Hawthorne, N. Liverpool, 23 Jan. [1855], to Mr. Bright.

—— Liverpool, 2 Nov. [1855], to H. A. Bright.

Longfellow, H. W. 14 Nov. —, to Mr. Chapman.

Sedgwick, Catharine M. New York, 17 Apr. 1853, to Mr. Bright.

Stowe, Harriet Beecher, to Lady Atherton, n.d.

Webster, Daniel. Boston, 14 May 1833, to Matthew Carey, discusses doctrine of nullification.

STANLEY CORRESPONDENCE. 17 letters. 1871–3. (Eng. MS. 1094)

Fifteen letters were written by Mrs. Sarah Anne Ellis Dorsey (1829–79), author, mainly from Louisiana, to Edward Lyulph Stanley. One letter was written to Mrs. Dorsey by 'J.M.S.' (J. M. Sandidge?) and one by Thomas P. Farrar. The letters 'offer a glimpse at first-hand of life in a Southern State in the years after the American Civil War . . . and they reveal something of the nature of Anglo-American relations during the nineteenth century'.[2]

---

[1] This letter was printed in full in R. D. Waller, ed., 'Letters Addressed to Mrs. Gaskell by Celebrated Contemporaries', Bulletin of the John Rylands Library, vol. xix, pp. 164–5, 1935.

[2] See Marcus F. Cunliffe, 'Notes on the Dorsey–Stanley Correspondence (1871–1873)', Bulletin of the John Rylands Library, vol. xxxvi, pp. 360–85, 1954.

WHITMAN, WALT (1819–92).

(*a*) Miscellaneous letters and papers, 1880–1948, of Charles F. Sixsmith of Anderton, Lancs., respecting his Whitman interests. Included is a group marked 'Summer in Canada 1880', among which are thirty-nine letters to Whitman from various correspondents. (Eng. MS. 1170)

(*b*) Miscellaneous letters and papers respecting Whitman's friend J. W. Wallace, and the Bolton Whitman Fellowship. Included are copies and drafts of fifty three letters, 1887–91, from Wallace to Whitman, six items concerning Mr. and Mrs. Horace L. Traubel, and a typescript 'Diary of Visits to Walt Whitman, &c., in 1891 by J. W. Wallace' (135 pages). (Eng. MS. 1186)

(*c*) Correspondence, 1891–1918, of Horace L. Traubel. (Of the 178 letters, 117 were written in 1892.) (Eng. MS. 1172)

(*d*) The Department of Printed Books holds over 250 books and articles by and about Whitman, a collection of over 150 newspaper and other cuttings relating to Whitmaniana and to members of the Bolton Whitman Fellowship, and an incomplete set of the *Conservator*, edited in Philadelphia by Traubel.

See also the Whitman Collection in the Bolton Public Library (p. 83).

National Union of Vehicle Builders, 44 High Street, Rusholme, MANCHESTER 13

EXECUTIVE COMMITTEE REPORTS (printed).

The Union has an incomplete set of these quarterly reports from 1851. The early reports—of the then United Kingdom Society of Coachmakers— include a few references to emigration; one of these gives the names of ten members making use of the Union's emigration fund, nine of whom went to Australia and only one to America.

Public Libraries, St. Peter's Square, MANCHESTER 2

JEFFERSON, THOMAS. Notes on the State of Virginia (printed). 1782.

Jefferson had 200 copies of this book privately printed in 1782 for his friends. Opposite the title page is the author's presentation inscription to Dr. McMahon, ' . . . unwilling to expose them [the notes] to the public eye he begs the favor of Dr. McMahon to put them into the hands of no person on whose care & fidelity he cannot rely to guard them against publication'.

STUBS, WOOD & CO. Business records.[1] 1796–1827. (On deposit.)

File, pin, &c., manufacturers of Warrington, Lancs. The records of this firm (forty-four boxes containing letters; a number of parcels containing loose, unsorted papers; miscellaneous letter-books, account books, &c.) include letters from Sheffield, Birmingham, &c., from 1796 onwards referring to goods ordered from Peter Stubs for the American trade. Correspondence with agents in New York begins at some time prior to 1821, and continues until 1827, the last year for which letters are available. The letters include some from each of the following: John Sharp, Jr., Philadelphia; Wright, Taylor & Co., New York; T. Sherman, New York.

MANCHESTER CHAMBER OF COMMERCE. Proceedings and minutes.

This body was once known as the Manchester Association of Importers and Exporters. The Library holds 130 volumes, 1821–1945. There are references to trade with the United States scattered throughout the volumes.[2]

AUTOGRAPH COLLECTIONS. Letters and notes. 1841–95.

Include the following, mainly trivia:

Bispham, David S. Leeds, 1 Oct. 1895, to Max Mayer. (Mayer Collection.)

Burritt, Elihu. Draft of an article, 'The loss of capital by war', n.d. (Withers Collection.)

Gaskell, E. C. Manchester, c. 1852, to Mrs. Schwabe, giving her impressions of Harriet Beecher Stowe. (Gaskell Collection.)

Holmes, Oliver Wendell. Boston, 3 May 1888, to Stanley Withers. (Withers Collection.)

James, Henry. London, 17 June 1884, concerning the Municipal Elections (Corrupt and Illegal Practices) Bill. (Withers Collection.)

Lowell, James Russell. Cambridge, Mass., 16 Feb. 1890, to Stanley Withers. (Withers Collection.)

Sargent, John Singer. London, n.d., to Charles Hallé. (Withers Collection.)

Switzer, D. W. K. New York, 14 Dec. 1841, to S. Butler of the Tremont Theater, Boston. (Swain Collection.)

ALEXANDER IRELAND COLLECTION. Newspaper and periodical clippings; letters (5 boxes). 1846–88.

The collection, on Ralph Waldo Emerson, consists mainly of clippings from British and American newspapers and periodicals: reviews of books about

[1] See T. S. Ashton, *An Eighteenth Century Industrialist: Peter Stubs of Warrington, 1756–1806* (Manchester, 1939). Exports of 'P.S. files' to the United States in 1796 and 1797 are mentioned on p. 59.

[2] See, *inter alia*, A. Redford, *Manchester Merchants and Foreign Trade*, vol. ii, 1850–1939 (Manchester, 1956).

Emerson, reports of his lectures, evaluations of his writings, obituaries. It also includes a few letters:

Anon. Eulogy of Emerson, n.d., addressed to 'Christopher North' [John Wilson]. (12 pages.)

Carr, T. 28 Apr. 1888, to Alexander Ireland, including copy of a letter to Carr from George Crawley concerning his acquaintance with Emerson.

Emerson, Annie L. Concord, Mass., 28 May 1882, to Mrs. Conway, giving an account of Emerson's last illness. (Copy.)

Harris, W. T. Concord, Mass., 1 May 1882, to James H. Stirling. A tribute to Emerson. (Copy.)

Lytton, Edward Robert Bulwer, 1st Earl of Lytton. Carlsbad, Austria, 18 July 1882 (to Ireland?), comparing Emerson and Whitman. (Copy.)

SMITH, JOHN BENJAMIN (1794–1879). 3 letters. 1866.

M.P. for Stockport, Cheshire, 1852–74. The sixteen-volume collection of his correspondence includes three letters on the *Alabama* case and Anglo-American relations, two from Smith to Lord Stanley, and one from Stanley to Smith.

CHORLTON UNION (POOR LAW GUARDIANS). 'Register of children emigrated to Canada.' 1906–22.

Contains details—name, under whose auspices emigrated, &c.—of some emigrants to the United States: of children in 1906, 1909, and 1920, and of families in 1921 and 1922.

Typographical Association, Beechwood, Oak Drive, Fallowfield, MANCHESTER 14

EXECUTIVE COUNCIL MINUTES, 1845– . HALF-YEARLY and ANNUAL REPORTS (printed), 1849– . UNION JOURNALS (printed), 1849– .[1]

The Executive Council Minutes of the Association and its predecessors include some references to the United States—e.g., to the use of American composing machines in the 1890's.

A bound volume labelled 'Typographical Circulars, 1849–59' contains many American references. It consists of the following printed documents: the *Address to the Delegates* of the 1849 Sheffield founding conference of the Provincial Typographical Association; half-yearly reports of this Association, 1849–60; Scottish Typographical Association reports, 1853–7; the *Typographical Societies' Monthly Circular*, 1852–61; and the *Typographical Protection Circular*, 1849–53. The *Address* includes discussion of tramping vs. emigration, and a proposed scheme of emigration to 'any of the colonies of Her Majesty, or those of America or elsewhere'. The general functioning

[1] See A. E. Musson, *The Typographical Association* (London, 1954).

of this and later plans is referred to in many of the Provincial Typographical Association half-yearly reports; and letters from branches give the numbers and names of emigrants to the United States (including the Liverpool case in which fares were paid for six 'unfair hands' who were persuaded to emigrate to the United States). Similar material is available in some of the Scottish reports and in the *Typographical Societies' Monthly Circular*. The *Typographical Protection Circular* includes extracts from letters of ex-members giving details of working conditions and wages in America.

A reference of another kind is found in the Bedford branch letter (Provincial Typographical Association eighth report) which notes that at a public dinner the editor of the local newspaper 'with much palaver' proposed the health of Harriet Beecher Stowe; a member of the union, present to report the affair, thereupon 'arose and told the liberal-minded gentleman that . . . he considered him a most exact personification of the Legree of Mrs. Stowe'; a considerable disturbance seems to have ensued.

McLachlan Library,[1] Unitarian College, Daisy Bank Road, MANCHESTER 14

MAYHEW, JONATHAN (1720–66). 3 letters. 1751–61.

Clergyman; early champion of Unitarianism and political liberty in New England. The letters were written from Boston to Dr. George Benson in London. The first, 6 Dec. 1751, deals with the sad state of Harvard College finances, and thanks Benson for his advice concerning tolerance towards 'those of different sentiments in religion'. The second, 7 Jan. 1754, is a discussion of John Taylor's *Scripture Doctrine of Atonement*. The third, 28 Aug. 1761, includes adverse comment on the (flourishing) state of 'bigottry and enthusiasm' in New England.

HULTON, HENRY (*c.* 1731–91). 16 letters (copies). 1769–76.

Government official. Hulton's correspondence with Robert Nicholson, a Liverpool merchant, includes fifteen letters, 1769–76, written by Hulton from in or near Boston, where he had gone as Revenue Commissioner, and one from Halifax, N.S., May 1776, before his embarkation for England.

Copies are also held by Manchester College, Oxford, and fuller details are given in that report (p. 399).

NICHOLSON, JAMES & THOMAS. *c.* 60 business letters from the United States (copies). 1822–6.

The originals are held by the John Rylands Library, Manchester (p. 101).

IRVING, WASHINGTON (1783–1859). Letter. n.d.

London, n.d., apparently to William Godwin. Irving acknowledges receipt of 'your manuscript' which he will forward to America, having already told his New York agent that it will be arriving.

[1] Virginia material microfilmed by the Virginia Colonial Records Project.

GORDON, JOHN (1807–80). 15 American letters. 1831–99.

Unitarian minister.

Bartol, C. A. Glasgow, 30 Sept. 1854, and Edinburgh, 13 Oct. 1854, to John Gordon, Edinburgh.

Channing, William Henry. 5 Apr. 1859, to John Gordon.

Choate, Joseph H. London, 16 Oct. 1899, to Samuel A. Steinthal, London.

Clarke, James Freeman. Boston, 24 Nov. 1860, to J. R. Beard, Manchester.

Rodgers, A. Robertson. New York, 28 Sept. 1831, to George Kenrick, London.

Thomas, Abel C. Nine letters, 1852–77, to John Gordon. Six from London and one from Philadelphia, 1852–3, relate to his preaching engagements, people he has met in England, &c.; the letter of 15 Feb. 1853 asks 'What do you think of a Unitarian preacher [Mr. Solly of Carter Lane Chapel, London] who declined to invite me into his pulpit because I am not as ultra as *he* is on the subject of Negro slavery?' Two letters, Tacony, Pa., 1876 and 1877, give details of his life since the trip to England: 'The war of the rebellion took vital hold of my thots, and I am neither sorry nor ashamed of anything I said or did in that regard.' &c.

AMERICAN LETTERS. Envelope containing 18 letters. 1834–1907.

Allen, Joseph H. London, 27 Aug. 1855, to John Gordon, Edinburgh.

Bellows, Henry W. New York, 5 Nov. 1856 and 19 Mar. 1867, and London, 13 June 1868, to J. R. Beard.

——. 20 June 1868, to James C. Street, Newcastle.

Channing, William Henry. Huntingdon, 19 June 1884, to James C. Street. In answer to a question from Street concerning William Ellery Channing's death-bed attitude towards Unitarianism, Channing states that 'every word and act of his proved conclusively that he remained *serenely happy in his Unitarian faith* to the end'.

Collyer, Robert. Chicago, 23 Mar. 1874, to James C. Street.

——. New York, 20 Sept. 1887, to Thomas Read Elliot.

Conway, Moncure D. Hammersmith, 9 Apr. 1879, to James C. Street.

Dewey, Orville. New York, 22 Apr. 1845, to J. R. Beard.

Douglass, Frederick. Anacostia, D.C., 23 May 1894, to Samuel A. Steinthal, informing Steinthal of the prospective visit to England of Ida B. Wells, and containing a plea for strong English protests against the continuing oppression of Negroes in the United States.

Dow, Neal. Portland, Me., 7 Dec. 1857, to Samuel A. Steinthal.

Gannett, William C. Rochester, N.Y., 27 Mar. 1894, to Christopher J. Street, Manchester.

Hale, Edward Everett. Boston, 22 Nov. 1907, to Christopher J. Street, Bolton.

Hosmer, Frederick L. Chicago, 12 Oct. 1893, to Christopher J. Street, Manchester.

——. Berkeley, Calif., 21 Dec. 1903, to Samuel A. Steinthal.

Howe, Julia Ward. Boston, 19 Feb. 1871, to James C. Street, presenting the purposes and activities of the Woman's International Peace Association, with the hope that a world congress can be held in London if support is forthcoming from such people as Street in England.

Tuckerman, Joseph. Stapleton Grove, near Bristol, 9 Jan. 1834, to J. R. Beard, Manchester.

HERFORD, BROOKE (1830–1903). Sermons (1 volume and 10 separate manuscripts); article. 1876–91.

Unitarian minister. The bound volume contains six manuscript sermons on 'Preaching and pastoral care', originally given at Harvard Divinity School in 1891, and notes for a talk on 'The Ministry', given at Harvard in 1890. Ten sermons in individual envelopes are marked as having been first preached at Arlington Street Church, Boston, 1887–91. The Library also holds a manuscript, 'Account of a visit to the Mammoth Cave of Kentucky, U.S.A. in April 1876' (4 pages).

BURGESS, WALTER H. (1867–1943). Notebooks, loose notes, correspondence (4 boxes).

Unitarian minister; historian. Burgess wrote extensively about the Pilgrim Fathers, and his papers include manuscript notes for a life of William Brewster, correspondence with American descendants of John Robinson, &c.

The Library, University of Manchester, MANCHESTER 13

OWENS, OWEN & JOHN. Business records.[1] 1806–52. (On deposit.)

Manufacturers and merchants, Manchester. The firm exported cotton and woollen goods, umbrellas, hatters' trimmings, and skins; the United States was one of its principal markets. The firm also imported raw cotton and some flour from the United States.

Five letter-books cover 1821–52, and contain copies of letters to Philadelphia, 1821–6, to Thomas Owen, and to New York, successively from 1821 to George Wragg & Co., William Barraclough, Oakeys & Robinson, and John Robinson. Five sales-books, 1819–46, contain invoices of shipments to the two cities. Incoming letters, 1839–45, include letters from New York and New Orleans. Ledgers contain a few references to the firm's early trade with the United States, 1806–18.

---

[1] These records, other than the letter-book for 1845–52, are at present on loan to the Roborough Library, University of Exeter, Prince of Wales Road, Exeter, Devon.

MCCONNEL & KENNEDY. Business records.[1] 1807–35. (On deposit.)

Fine cotton-spinning firm, Manchester. The records of this firm (thirty-one boxes containing letters, receipts, &c.; c. fifty volumes of letter-books, ledgers, &c.) include, from 1807 onwards, correspondence with agents in Savannah, Ga., and/or Charleston, S.C. Letters from the agents are available until 1826: during the first few years of the correspondence these include discussion of the changing political relations between Britain and the United States and the effects of these on raw cotton exports; later letters—of which there are, for example, over 100 in 1825—appear to be confined to discussion of the state of the cotton crop, invoices of shipments, &c. Letters include some from A. L. Molyneux, Savannah; J. Speakman & Co., Savannah; Thomas H. Hindley, New York and Charleston (these are the early ones about political developments); J. & W. Longsdon, Charleston. There are copies of letters from the firm to the agents through 1835.

Department of Economic History, University of Manchester, MANCHESTER 13

W. & J. GALLOWAY. Copies of c. 800 out-letters and estimates. 1840–54.

Engineers of Manchester. The firm supplied machinery to John Lucas of Charleston, S.C., and the correspondence includes two letters, 1840, from the Galloways to Lucas, as well as a considerable number about boilers, &c., ordered by Lucas, written by the Manchester firm to his agent, J. J. Cordes & Co. of Newport, Monmouthshire, 1840–4, and to W. Stuart of Liverpool, who shipped the goods, 1840.[2]

There are also letters from the Galloways to the following: J. S. Worth of New York, 21 Apr. 1848 (including the comment that 'with no other party but yourself do we ever ship abroad any goods on credit'); Messrs. Curtis, Bowie & Co. of Boston, 13 May 1851, concerning an order for boiler rivets, and noting that 'we are weekly sending to New York considerable quantities' of these; and Messrs. Wm. Bailey Sons & Co. of Boston,

---

[1] See G. W. Daniels, 'The Early Records of a Great Manchester Cotton-Spinning Firm', *Economic Journal*, vol. xxv, pp. 175–88, 1915; and his 'American Cotton Trade with Liverpool under the Embargo and Non-Intercourse Acts', *American Historical Review*, vol. xxi, pp. 276–87, 1916. Also Roland Smith, 'Manchester as a Centre for the Manufacture and Merchanting of Cotton Goods, 1820–1830', *Birmingham University Historical Journal*, vol. iv, pp. 47–65, 1953.

[2] See W. H. Chaloner, 'John Galloway (1804–94), Engineer, of Manchester and his "Reminiscences" ', *Transactions of the Lancashire and Cheshire Antiquarian Society*, vol. lxiv, pp. 93–116, 1954. Chaloner quotes the section of Galloway's notes which concern the dealings of his father's firm with John Lucas in 1820; a typed transcript of these notes is in the Manchester Public Libraries.

22 Nov. 1854. There is also a letter, 6 Mar. 1843, to Messrs. Shaw & Crane of Wolverhampton concerning sawmills for 'your friends over the water'; and a group of letters to Messrs. Jas. Cocker & Co. of Liverpool in 1854, one of them asking that 'if the names of your customers in the States is a secret with you (as we understand your letter)—pray be candid enough to forward us by return of post *some* particulars of the claim you profess to have against us'.

Oldham Operative Cotton Spinners, Central Office, Rock Street, OLDHAM

ANNUAL REPORTS (printed). 1871– .

Annual expenditure of the union and its branches, as given in these reports, 1871 onwards, included for some years—e.g., 1872–4, 1876–8, 1900—money 'paid to members for emigrating'.

COTTON FACTORY TIMES. 1885–1937 (complete set).

This Manchester periodical included letters on emigration, reports on American trade conditions, &c.

Lancashire Record Office,[1] The Sessions House, Lancaster Road, PRESTON

BARCROFT PAPERS.[2] (Part of the Parker of Alkincoats and Browsholme Muniments.) 10 letters. 1682–1780. (DDB 61)

Eight letters are from America to relatives in or near Colne, Lancs.: three, 1752–7, from William Barcroft in Virginia refer to payment of an annuity due to him; one, 1 Mar. 1723, from Ambrose Barcroft of Solebury, Pa., give details of management of his estate; and four, 1752–80, from Ambrose Barcroft, Solebury and Philadelphia, concern financial and family affairs. In addition there are: a letter, 1737, to William Barcroft in Virginia; and a letter, 1682, from Ireland to Lancashire, concerning the emigration of Thomas Barcroft to help divide the land in Pennsylvania.

KENYON MUNIMENTS. 2 letters. 1683–4. (DDK e/9)

Both letters are from Roger Kenyon to his father, Roger Kenyon, in Peel, near Manchester. The first, 'Road Island', 30 May 1683, explains how Kenyon has been sold to Mr. Coddington, the Governor's brother, as a three years' servant, and appeals for money to obtain his discharge. The second, 'Marshfeild', Mass., 9 Nov. 1684, written on Kenyon's arrival again in America after a period in England, discusses family affairs.

---

[1] R. Sharpe France, *Guide to the Lancashire Record Office* (Preston, 1948).
[2] Microfilms made by the Virginia Colonial Records Project.

HOUGHTON MUNIMENTS. 21 letters.[1] 1829–46. (DDHt 12)

These letters, written from various places in Pennsylvania, Virginia, Ohio, and New York, are addressed to members of the Morris family in Lancashire. They include details of the voyages, information concerning the weaving trade and the work and wages of blacksmiths, prices of food, &c.

BIRKET(T) FAMILY PAPERS. 14 letters.[2] 1833–59. (DP/265–278)

The letters are written from Peoria and Mount Pleasant, Ill., to relatives in Lancashire. Most are from John Birket. Besides news of relatives in Vermont and Illinois, they include discussion of the religious and financial problems involved in the attempt to provide a Protestant Episcopal Church and school in Mount Pleasant.

CLIFTON MUNIMENTS. 2 letters. 1842. (DD Cl 1192)

Myerscough House, 22 Mar. 1842, from John Cunliffe, includes extensive discussion of the effects of United States and British import duties on cheese, in the light of the difference in quality between the cheeses of the two countries.

Knowsley, 28 Feb. 1842, from Thomas Statter, refers to the shipment of pigs to Kentucky and Tennessee.

PARISH RECORDS.

Include emigrant material, for example, the Minute-Book of the Select Vestry of Barnacre contains the resolution, 21 Mar. 1833, that a meeting be held 'for taking into consideration of a family going into America'.

QUARTER SESSIONS RECORDS.

Among the petitions (QSP) are at least four referring to America; there may be others.

1666. (284/5): Relief for a man who has returned after thirty years in the plantations in America.

1676. (444/25): Relief for the wife of a man 'who is gone into Virginia'.

1686. (625/2): List of servants to go to America.[3]

1708. (968/13): The proposed sending of Robert Gregory as a slave to Virginia.

---

[1] Photostats in the Collection of Letters of Emigrants to America in the British Library of Political and Economic Science, London School of Economics.
[2] Loc. cit.
[3] *Genealogists' Magazine*, vol. xii, p. 234, 1956.

Public Library, Peel Park, SALFORD 5

AMERICAN LETTERS. 10 letters. 1702–1818.

Adams, John. Auteuil, 8 Feb. 1785, to R. H. Lee, concerning which of the great powers are likely to 'treat with us'.

Adams, John Quincy. Washington, D.C., 19 Apr. 1818, to John A. Smith, Secretary of the United States Legation in London, introducing John E. Holbrook, who is coming to Britain to continue his medical studies.

Franklin, Benjamin. London, 22 Aug. 1772, to John Bartram, Philadelphia, on horticultural matters.

Jefferson, Thomas. Monticello, Va., 26 Dec. 1795, to B. F. Bache, Philadelphia, ordering the *Aurora*.

Lafayette, Marquis de. Brunswick Camp, 6 July 1778, to R. H. Lee, Philadelphia, recommending the Marquis de Vienne.

Madison, James. New York, 21 June 1789, to an unknown correspondent in Paris, introducing George James of Virginia.

Monroe, James. New York, 12 Apr. 1785, to an unknown correspondent in London, commenting on the state of arts and sciences in the United States, and requesting information about 'the situation of our affrs. with the powers of Europe'.

Penn, William. London, 27 Apr. 1702, 'to Samuel Carpenter for James Logan, Secretary in Philadelphia', about bills drawn.

Priestley, Joseph. Northumberland, Pa., 16 June 1796, to Benjamin S. Barton, Philadelphia, requesting that the latter see Mr. Dobson about the correct layout of the title-page of *The Doctrine of Phlogiston Established*.

Washington, George. 26 Oct. 1782, thanking Captain John Pray for a gift of oysters.

Public Library, Museum Street, WARRINGTON

PRIESTLEY, JOSEPH (1733–1804). Letters.[1] 1794–1802.

Scientist, educator, writer. Most of the sixty-nine letters, 1789–1802, are from Priestley to his brother-in-law, John Wilkinson; a few are from other persons to Wilkinson; a few are from various persons to Priestley—e.g., copies of two well-known letters from Jefferson. The letters from Priestley to Wilkinson written from America, 1794–1802, contain much interesting material, chiefly on life in the Pennsylvanian backwoods.

[1] Photostat copies are held by the Library of Congress, the Houghton Library of Harvard University, the University of Pennsylvania, and the American Philosophical Society, and there is a typed transcript in the British Museum. A brief description of the material was given in Library of Congress *Information Bulletin* vol. xii, no. 20, 18 May 1953. W. H. Chaloner, 'Dr. Joseph Priestley, John Wilkinson and the French Revolution, 1789–1802', *Transactions of the Royal Historical Society*, 5th series, vol. viii, pp. 21–40, 1958, is based on the letters. These have also been edited with an introduction and notes by F. Beckwith and W. H. Chaloner, but have not yet been published.

MIFFLIN, ANN. Notebook. 1802-3.

Quaker, Philadelphia. The notebook contains an introductory letter, 8 Dec. 1803, to Pim Nevins, and reports of two visits to the Indians: 'Relation of a Visit made to the Indians [in Massachusetts and New York] in 1802 by K. Kirkbude and Ann Mifflin with other Friends, in the course of their Journey to Upper Canada, with some Observations on their Origin &c.' and 'Account of a Visit to some of the Seneca Nation on Allegany Rivers in the 10th mo. 1803, by John Letchworth, Ann Mifflin, Mary Bell, and Company'. The reports consist mainly of accounts of the speeches made by the visiting Quakers, and the Indian replies to these, together with Ann Mifflin's ideas concerning the Indians as descendants of the ten lost tribes of Israel.

Stonyhurst College, WHALLEY, Blackburn

PAPERS OF THE COLLEGE. 3 documents, 7 letters. 1737-1813.

(a) Two conveyances of land in Maryland by the Rev. George Thorold of 'Anairundle' co., Md., 1737, and the Rev. James Charles Thompson, 1795.[1]

(b) Disposition of estates in Maryland by the Rev. Richard Molyneux, 8 Mar. 1758.[2]

(c) Seven letters[3] from the Rev. John Carroll, Archbishop of Baltimore; copies of two letters, 1784 and 1786, to the Rev. J. Berrington; and five letters, 1797-1813, to the Rev. Robert Plowden.

Public Library, Rodney Street, WIGAN

FOLLIOTT, GEORGE. Diary (1 volume), 1765-6. (Part of Edward Hall MS. Diary Collection.)

General merchant, New York. The diary was kept during a visit to England, spent mainly in London. While in London Folliott frequented the Exchange, the New York Coffeehouse, and the Antwerp Club. He discussed American affairs, particularly the question of a molasses tax, with Lord Rockingham. He visited the Victualling Office to arrange contracts for the supply in London of hogs and oxen, and in New York of beer, bread, pork, &c.; he discussed with Mr. Evory a contract for supplying warships at New York. His expenditure on laundry, travel, &c., is noted in some detail, and extensive lists of books bought and sent to New York are included.

[1] H.M.C. x (iv), p. 197.
[2] Ibid., p. 191.
[3] Photostats of these were sent in 1952 to the Catholic University of America, Washington, D.C.

LEICESTERSHIRE

Duke of Rutland, BELVOIR CASTLE, Grantham

RUTLAND PAPERS. Letters. 1611–1780.

(a) 10 Mar. 1611, from Bruz to Rutland says: 'Sir Thomas Dale is departed to Virginia with three hundred men, and the Cumpanye hath spent therein ayght thowsand pownes. They should have sent with them at lest twise as many wemen to have mad a good and spedye plantatione.'[1]

(b) 12 Oct. and 7 Dec. 1676, from Lady Chaworth to her brother Lord Roos, mention Bacon's rebellion.[2]

(c) Various letters, 1763–5, touching upon such matters as operations against the Indians, a description of West Florida, and the Sons of Liberty.[3]

(d) 20 Dec. 1766, from Gage at New York, to the Marquess of Granby, concerning the transport of troops. Also makes a number of complaints [no details of complaints given].[4]

(e) Two letters to the Marquess of Granby: the first, 16 Jan. 1768, from Samuel Martin, recommending his brother for the position of Quartermaster-General in North America; the second, 7 Feb. 1768, from Colonel Charles Hotham, applying for his regiment to be sent to America.[5]

(f) 9 June 1769, from Lieutenant-Colonel Edward Maxwell to the Marquess of Granby, 'as to a prosecution arising out of a conflict of jurisdiction between a court martial and the civil government of the province in the southern district of America'.[6]

(g) Report on West Florida and part of French Louisiana, by John Thomas to General Williamson, 28 Nov. 1769 (11 pages).[7]

(h) A description of the Battle of Bunker Hill. 25 June 1775.[8]

(i) 28 June, 2 Sept., 26 Nov., 26 Dec. 1776, from Edmund Stevens to the Marquess of Granby, describing the fighting on Long Island, divisions on the American side, and the capture of General Lee.[9]

(j) Various letters to the Marquess of Granby, with some mention of American affairs.

[1] Transcript, H.M.C. xii (iv), p. 429.
[2] Transcripts, H.M.C. xii (v), pp. 30, 32.
[3] Transcripts, H.M.C. Rutland (Belvoir) iv [24], pp. 231–5.
[4] Synopsis, H.M.C. xii (v), p. 289.　　　　　[5] Ibid., pp. 300–1.
[6] Ibid., p. 311.　　　　　　　　　　　　　　[7] Ibid., p. 312.
[8] H.M.C. xiv (i), pp. 2–3.
[9] Transcripts, ibid., pp. 5–8. Also letter, 29 Dec. 1776, of Thomas Thoroton to his mother, p. 8.

Aug.—1777, from Lord Robert Manners—French naval movements. 30 Aug. and 9 Oct. 1777, from Edmund Stevens—troop movements and skirmishes in America.

6 and 28 Nov. 1777, from the Marquess of Rockingham—the first mentions the precarious situation of Burgoyne's army and the second 'not a word of news as yet from America through the ministerial channells'.[1]

(k) Philadelphia, 13 Dec. 1777, from E. Stevens to Marquess of Granby, referring to the disaster to Burgoyne, says that only a reinforcement of not less than 25,000 to 30,000 men could reduce the country, but even then he doubts if it could be done.[2]

(l) '1778 [c. April] List of prices of various articles as they were formerly and a few months ago in Pennsylvania, showing in several instances a tenfold increase.'[3]

(m) Long letter, compiled at various dates between 19 July and 14 August 1780, from Lord Robert Manners, with the fleet off Rhode Island, to the Duke of Rutland. Gives a very optimistic picture of the overall British position in the war, which he expects to end in an American capitulation within a year. Gives also a description of the French fleet at anchor off Rhode Island and French fortifications ashore.[4]

(n) 20 Sept. 1780, from Lord Robert Manners, at sea, to the Duke of Rutland, mentions that Cornwallis 'has gained a very complete victory at South Carolina'.[5]

(o) 27 Sept., 4 and 31 Oct. 1780, from Lord Robert Manners, at sea, to the Duke of Rutland, mainly describing the superiority of the French fleet, the poor condition of the English, and the dangerous situation of Cornwallis's army. Also mentions the defection of Benedict Arnold from the American side.[6]

City Museum and Art Gallery, The New Walk, Leicester

VIRGINIA COMPANY. 3 letters. 1618. (BR II/18/12 items 289, 296 and 303)

Letters between the Virginia Company and the Mayor and Aldermen of Leicester concerning local arrangements for the Virginia lottery.

WASHINGTON, GEORGE. 4 letters. 1786–91.

From George Washington to Mrs. Catharine Macaulay Graham: Mount Vernon, 10 Jan. 1786, congratulating her on safe travelling in very bad weather.[7]

---

[1] Transcripts, ibid., pp. 9–10.   [2] Ibid., p. 12.
[3] Ibid., p. 13.   [4] Transcript, ibid., pp. 31–34.
[5] Transcript, ibid., p. 36.   [6] Transcripts, ibid., pp. 37–39.
[7] See *Writings of George Washington*, ed. by John C. Fitzpatrick, vol. xxviii, pp. 370–1 (Washington, D.C., 1938).

Mount Vernon, 16 Nov. 1787, referring to a Mr. Pine's historical paintings, and Washington's own difficulties in framing and forming the Federal
Convention.[1]

New York, 9 Jan. 1790, thanking her for her congratulations on the
Presidency; he reflects for three pages on the responsibilities and difficulties
of his position and the effects of the situation in America of the new government, the increase in commerce and manufactures, &c., and the constitutional effects he thinks it may have in France.[2]

Philadelphia, 10 Feb. 1791, acknowledging receipt of a treatise on education and excusing himself from writing at length because of pressure of
public business.[3]

(One surviving envelope is addressed to Mrs. Macaulay Graham at
'Bracknal' [Bracknell], Berkshire, England.)

Leicestershire Record Office, 57 New Walk, LEICESTER

POOR LAW RECORDS.

Lutterworth Union Minute-book, 1838–40. Minute for 24 Apr. 1838 records
the reading of a letter from the Poor Law Commissioners about the emigration of paupers to the United States.

QUARTER SESSIONS RECORDS.

Forty-nine bonds, 1721–83, and nine orders, 1720–83, for the transportation
of criminals, chiefly to Virginia and Maryland.

LINCOLNSHIRE

H.M. Customs and Excise, BOSTON

See H.M. Customs and Excise, London (p. 206).

Earl of Ancaster, GRIMSTHORPE, Bourne

ANCASTER PAPERS. Letter. 1585.

London, 15 Nov. 1585, from 'Jhohn Stubbe' to Lord Willoughby in
Denmark, mentions the Virginia voyage of Sir Richard Grenville, and
encloses a letter (not printed) concerning it.[4]

---

[1] *Writings of George Washington*, ed. by John C. Fitzpatrick, vol. xxix, pp. 316–17
(1938).   [2] Ibid., vol. xxx, pp. 495–8 (1939).
[3] Ibid., vol. xxxi, pp. 213–14 (1939).
[4] H.M.C. Ancaster MSS. [66], pp. 16–17.

Commander J. W. Maitland, M.P.,
HARRINGTON HALL, Spilsby

FLUDYER MAITLAND & CO. Business papers. 1790–1801.

(*a*) Valuation of lands in Luzerne county, Pa.; Alexandria, Va.; and Skin Bottom, Va.; note of lands about a hundred miles from Philadelphia, n.d.

(*b*) Letter, 2 June 1790, from Miers Fisher of Philadelphia to the firm of Fludyer Maitland & Co. of London, enclosing draft of declaration by John Maitland of London, merchant (trading with George Bridges Brudenell as the above firm), as to the indebtedness to him of William and Luke Morris, merchants, late of Philadelphia.

(*c*) Accounts of John Coles and John Maitland. 22 May 1801. References to Pennsylvania; Alexandria, Va.; and Skin Bottom, Va.

(*d*) Remarks of John Coles on the state of American property and investments. 2 June 1801.

There is also material relating to New Brunswick.

N.R.A. 3640.

Wren Library, Lincoln Cathedral, LINCOLN

The Wren Library, part of the Cathedral Library, is rich in seventeenth-century pamphlets and broadsheets, as well as early printed books. There is, for instance, a rare copy of Captain John Smith's *The Seaman's Grammar* ... (London, 1627); and of more especial relevance:

(*a*) A broadsheet (bound in 'Various Treatises', numbers 5–27): *Proportion of Provisions Needfull for Such as Intend to Plant Themselves In New England, for One Whole Year*. Printed at London for Fulke Clifton, 1630.[1]

(*b*) A photostat of the broadsheet, *The Capitall Lawes of New-England, as They Stand Now in Force in the Common-Wealth, by the Court. In the Years 1641. 1642*. This was the first known codification. The original is now in the library of the Harvard Law School.

Lincolnshire Archives Office, Exchequer Gate, LINCOLN

MASSINGBERD AND MASSINGBERD-MUNDY DEPOSITS. Letters. 1699–1714.

From Elizabeth and Edward Hyrne from Charleston, S.C., to Elizabeth's brother Burrell Massingberd of South Ormsby, Lincs., about trade with

---

[1] See A. M. Cook, *Lincolnshire Links with the U.S.A.*, p. 59 (Lincoln, priv. print., 1956).

South Carolina and the purchase of a plantation between the Bath and Cooper Rivers. (Mass. 21; M.M. 2/1)

MONSON FAMILY PAPERS. Letters, documents, &c. c. 1737–1833.

(a) Papers of John Monson, 1st Baron Monson (1693–1748), Commissioner for Plantations 1737, and of Charles Monson, Deputy Paymaster-General. (Monson 13, *passim*)

(b) Hampton, Va., 1740, from William Blakney [or Blakeney] to Henry Pelham on the condition of troops there, their payment, and embarkation for Jamaica. (Monson 25/2/49)

(c) Correspondence[1] of the 1st and 2nd Barons Monson: including letters from Thomas Pownall, Governor of New Jersey, addressed to John Monson, 2nd Baron Monson (1727–74), which give an account of the colonies but more especially New Jersey, 1754–6. (Monson 25/1/44–48)

(d) Bargaintown, N.J., 29 July 1833, from Louisa Canfield to Mrs. Sarah Stone, Italy Hill, Yates county, N.Y., containing mainly family news. (Monson 25/3/19)

ASWARBY MUNIMENTS (Whichcote Family Papers). c. 80 letters, papers and accounts. 1742–73.

(a) Nathaniel Tregagle, a Cornishman, married a daughter of Sir Paul Whichcote. Papers relating to his affairs in Carolina. Seventy-six estate accounts, bills, and letters concerned with the administration of an estate and the business as importer of Nathaniel Tregagle of Georgetown and Charleston, S.C., 1742–64.—Various letters, papers and accounts marked 'South Carolina', 1759–62, including an alphabetical list of debts due to Tregagle, Georgetown, S.C., 1760.—Copy of Tregagle's will, 4 June 1760, which provides for the manumission of his two Negro slaves, Cubah and Quashebald, with the interest of £100 for their clothing. (Asw 1/23, 10/67)

(b) Letters, Charleston, S.C., 1742–84, from A. Johnston and George Appleby. Some refer to war against Indians. (Asw 1/23, *passim*)

(c) Letter, 1761, from George Appleby to T. Whichcote, describing the war and the difficulties of war-time trade in South Carolina. (Asw 10/67/9)

(d) Bill of exchange drawn by Alexander Rose of South Carolina on Messrs. Berwicke & Co. of London, 1763. (Asw 10/43/20)

(e) Letter, 1773, from William and Mary College, Virginia, on death of Josiah Johnson and copy of his will. (Asw 10/48/6–7)

AMCOTTS DEPOSIT. 1 document. 1779. (Amc 4/6/1)

Deed of partnership, 1779, between Robert Weston Cracroft and his brother Francis, and Robert Bourne, planter, of Katesbourne, W. Fla., to share the profits of planting and the buying and selling of Negroes.

---

[1] Photostats of these items have been sent to the Library of Congress, Washington, D.C., at the request of Lord Monson.

MISCELLANEOUS DEPOSIT. Notebook. 1873–87. (Misc. Dep. 17/18)

Small notebook relating to financing Algernon L. H. Short on his going to Ridgeway, Warren county, N.C.

Lady Muriel Barclay-Harvey, c/o Barclays Bank, STAMFORD

WARREN PAPERS.

Papers of Sir William Warren, the Restoration contractor to the Navy Board for naval supplies, who was accused of making excessive charges. These contain a number of references, 1675, to the cost of masts brought from New England.[1]

LINDSEY PAPERS.

In a list of the yearly expenses of His Majesty 'in times of peace' c. 1679, New York is listed at £1,500 and Virginia at £9,000.[2]

LONDON

Allen & Hanburys Ltd., Bethnal Green, LONDON, E. 2

BUSINESS RECORDS.[3] 1777–1885.

Manufacturing chemists and makers of surgical instruments. The firm, founded in 1715 by Silvanus Bevan and continued by Joseph Gurney Bevan, William Allen, and others, carried on a considerable trade with New York, Philadelphia, and other American cities both before and after the War of Independence. The records held which contain material relating to this trade are as follows:

(a) Letter-books. Eleven volumes, 1774–1849, containing the originals written by the various partners (the letters actually sent to customers were

---

[1] H.M.C. Lindsey MSS. [79], pp. 121, 126, 128, 131, 133, 144, 145, 147–9. (Papers of the late 12th Earl of Lindsey, Uffington House, Stamford, Lincs., now the property of his daughter.)   [2] Ibid., p. 110.

[3] These were used by D. Chapman-Huston and E. C. Cripps for *Through a City Archway: the Story of Allen and Hanburys, 1715–1954* (London, 1954) which includes a chapter on the firm's early trade with America based on research by Whitfield J. Bell, Jr.

copies of these); also a volume of duplicates for 1865–85. Of the volumes examined, the earliest, 1775–8, includes a number of 1777 letters to Donald McLean, William Brownjohn, and William Stewart of New York, about orders and shipping problems; letters to the United States in the 1795–1806 volume mainly concern debts owed the firm; the 1826–49 volume includes much correspondence, 1845–7, with Hull & Bowne of New York, and the volume for 1865–85, letters, 1885, to W. H. Scheiffelin & Co. of New York about the market for their pills in Britain.

(b) Ledgers. Ten ledgers covering, with a few gaps, 1777–1866. Most include the accounts of firms in various American cities; these are particularly frequent in the earlier volumes.

(c) Order and 'waste books'. Twenty order books containing orders for 1777, 1801–4, and 1855–78; eight 'waste books', containing the same information in a different form, are available for 1773, 1776–8, and 1851–71.

MISCELLANEOUS RECORDS.

In addition to the business archives described above the following material is held by the firm:

(a) Pennsylvania Hospital. Photostats of records in the minutes of the Managers' Committee of the Pennsylvania Hospital, and typed transcripts of these. Included are invoices of drugs bought from the Bevans in 1752; letters to Silvanus Bevan and Thomas Hyam, the London agents for the hospital, from Benjamin Franklin and other managers; &c.

(b) William Allen (1770–1843). Correspondence.

(i) Envelope labelled 'William Allen's Letters' includes a copy of a letter, Philadelphia, 4 Mar. 1796, from Joseph Bunghurst to William Cowper, expressing best wishes from Bunghurst and other Philadelphia admirers of the poet. On the copy is written 'N.B. The copy was given to me on the — April 1830 by Eliza Fothergill. Edinburgh. John McCoy.'

(ii) Volume labelled 'Letters of William Allen' includes a letter to Allen from W. Dillwyn, 15 Dec. 1810, containing an extract about Paul Cuffe from a letter from John James and Alexander Wilson of Pennsylvania. It also includes letters to Allen from J. W. Griscom, New York, 1812; Nathan Hunt, Springfield, N.C., 1812; Stephen Pretter, Burlington, N.J., 1843; and Benjamin Silliman, New Haven, Conn., 1815.

(iii) Volume labelled 'African Correspondence' contains copies of correspondence, 1811–19, among Allen, Thomas Clarkson, John Kizell, Henry Warren, Captain Paul Cuffe (American Negro seaman), and others, about the affairs of the African Institution of London and the Friendly Society of Freetown, Sierra Leone. Cuffe's letters concern the attitudes of American Negroes towards emigration to Sierra Leone, news of embarkation for Freetown, &c.

(iv) Folder labelled 'William Allen Letters' includes a letter, New Bedford, Mass., 12 July 1811, from W. Sawyer Wall to Allen, with news of friends and comment on the American political scene.

(v) Volume labelled 'William Allen—letters, notes, diaries, etc.' includes a typed transcript of a letter, 4 June 1812, from Allen to John Griscom, New York, about scientific instruments.

(c) Parcel marked 'Old orders on A & H' includes a document, 22 Nov. 1803, giving John Murray the younger, of New York, power of attorney to act for Joseph Gurney Bevan in collecting debts; and a letter, London, 7 June 1819, from Josiah Forster (to Allen?) on the Quaker Yearly Meeting he has recently attended—his brother's 'concern to visit Friends in America', information about Friends' activities, mainly relations with Negroes, in various states, &c.

Amalgamated Society of Woodworkers, 9–11 Macaulay Road, LONDON, S.W. 4

MONTHLY REPORTS (printed). 1869– .

The 1860 rule providing for emigration benefit for members of the Amalgamated Society of Carpenters and Joiners was never, in fact, utilized, since all the conditions governing it were never realized at the same time. The monthly reports, however, contain material relating to members who went to the United States, and to the branches which the union maintained there until 1924. The American branches, including some in California, sent in monthly reports, printed in the journal, which contained brief comment on the state of the building industry, number of members unemployed, and number receiving sickness benefit. Discussion concerning relations with the American union, the United Brotherhood of Carpenters and Joiners, frequently appeared in the reports in the early part of this century.

Anti-Slavery Society, 49 Denison House, 296 Vauxhall Bridge Road, LONDON, S.W. 1

SLAVERY AND THE ANTI-SLAVERY MOVEMENT. Printed books, journals, and pamphlets (c. 1,200 volumes). 1823– .

The Anti-Slavery Committee was founded in 1823. The Aborigines Protection Society (1837) and the British and Foreign Anti-Slavery Society (1839) amalgamated in 1909 to form the Anti-Slavery and Aborigines Protection Society. (The 'working' title was recently changed to 'Anti-Slavery Society'.)

Journals in the collection include: *Anti-Slavery Magazine* (Derby), 1824; *Anti-Slavery Reporter* (New York), 1825–1950 (1836–40 not published); *Anti-Slavery Record* (New York, for American Anti-Slavery Society), 1835–7; *Anti-Slavery Examiner* (American Anti-Slavery Society), vol. i, nos. 2–8, 1836; Publications of the British and Foreign Anti-Slavery Society, two volumes, *c.* 1840, and *Annual Reports*, two volumes, 1840–52; *Proceedings of Anti-Slavery Conventions*, London, 1840, 1843, and Paris, 1867; *Aborigines Friend and Colonial Intelligencer* (name varies), 1847–1909 (with Annual Reports of the Aborigines Protection Society.

See also Anti-Slavery Papers in Rhodes House Library, Oxford (p. 388).

Bank of England, Threadneedle Street, LONDON, E.C. 2

The Archives of the Bank are not primarily an historical archive, but are a working archive for the daily business of the Bank itself. However, permission to inspect records of an earlier date than a hundred years ago may be granted on occasion for specific scholarly purposes. For records of a later date access is granted only in exceptional circumstances. Applications should be made to the Secretary of the Bank, and the applicant should be sponsored by the academic body concerned in the research.

Sir John Clapham's history, *The Bank of England*, 2 vols. (Cambridge, 1944), made use of all available types of records in the Bank, and so its footnotes and index furnish an easily accessible guide to the Bank's principal records. There are five main series of records, in any or all of which important transactions may figure:

  (i)   The General Court of Proprietors—Minute Books (G.C.B.).
  (ii)   Court of Directors—Minute Books (C.B.).
  (iii) Committee of Treasury Minute Books (C.T.).
  (iv)   Letter Books (L.B.).
  (v)   General Ledgers (G.L.).
  (vi)   Drawing Office Ledgers (D.O.).

In addition, certain other collections in the Bank, such as the Dobree MSS., contain relevant material. The main records are kept chronologically; there is a General Index to the two series of Court Books and to the Committee of Treasury Books. The most important incidents relating to American affairs—leaving aside routine business entirely—appear from Clapham to be:

1836. To help straighten out its affairs on the expiry of its charter, the Bank of the United States was arranging a loan in London. (See the Governor's memorandum for the Chancellor of the Exchequer of 6 Aug. 1836 in the 'Minutes of Correspondence with H.M. Government, 3'.)

1836. The Committee of Treasury Books (C.T.) for this year continually refer to the affairs of the seven English or Anglo-American firms who were most involved in the over-extension of finance for American trade and American loans: Baring, Brown, Lizardi, Morrison, and the notorious 'three W's', Wilson, Wiggin, and Wildes (e.g. C.T. 22, 27 July 1836; and the entry for 26 October shows Baring's American specialist, Joshua Bates, advising the Committee, and also Lizardi's supplying information about bill-drawing at New Orleans). In June 1836 Nicholas Biddle of the Bank of the United States asked for an account and open credit with the Bank of England (C.T. 8 June 1836).

1837. Further entries in the Court Books (C.B.) about the affairs of the 'three W's' in relation to the failure of American credit (see, especially, C.B. Ib., 13 April, 3 and 30 May, 8 and 22 June; the entry for 13 April is a memorial from 200 Liverpool business men and merchants referring to the intense distress that the American panic was causing to the cotton trade).

The Directors sent an agent, John W. Cowell, to America to inquire into debts due from firms in the United States to them, as backers and creditors of English houses. He was to contact the President of the Bank of the United States, then doing business as the United States Bank of Pennsylvania (see C.B. 14 Sept.).

1838. Biddle's request for credit was turned down (C.B. Ib., 15 Feb.) and Biddle complains that the Bank of England would not receive his funds (C.B. Ib., 15 Feb.). Further exchanges in this controversy—C.B. Ib., 22 Feb. and Kb. 19 Apr. But in March of that year the Bank decided to let the American market have gold (C.B. Ib., 15, 22, and 29 Mar.).

1857. The world-wide panic of 1857 started similarly in the American market, and is reflected in the Bank's records for that year. (See especially C.B. Ec., report to the Chancellor of the Exchequer of 1 December 1857. Also the Diary and Letters of Bonamy Dobree, the Deputy Governor, touch on these matters; see the Dobree MSS.)

1881. The American silver question and the international bimetallic controversy led to the American Minister, James Russell Lowell, sounding out the views of the British Treasury, and so in official and more private letters the Governor of the Bank explains to the Chancellor the history and practice of the Bank's silver buying (see especially C.B. Dd., 30 June, and L.B. 19, 30 June).

Barclays Bank Ltd., Head Office, 54 Lombard Street, LONDON, E.C. 3

BANK RECORDS.

Records have been found relating to American investments in the 1870's by the London and Provincial Bank, some in United States stock but mostly in railways, and to similar investments by the London and South Western Bank. The railways concerned are the New York Central; Atlantic and Great Western; Erie, Philadelphia and Reading, and the Grand Trunk.

These two Banks amalgamated in 1917 as the London Provincial and South Western Bank, which in turn amalgamated with Barclays Bank Ltd. in 1918.

Bishopsgate Institute, 230 Bishopsgate, LONDON, E.C. 2

GEORGE HOWELL COLLECTION.

George Howell (1833–1910), bricklayer; secretary of the London Trades Council 1861–2, and of the Reform League 1864–7; Liberal M.P. 1885–95.

(a) Library of 4,138 volumes of books and bound pamphlets on economics, the early history of trade unionism and the labour movement. It includes many early works on emigration generally, slavery, the American labour movement, &c. The pamphlets are mostly bound together by subjects, e.g., 'Emigration 1836–1889'. There are several pamphlets on the *Alabama* dispute, American agriculture and land systems, and Anglo-American trade. Constitutions and rules of trade unions often contain union regulations about emigration of members and assistance from union funds, e.g., *Constitution and Rules of the National Agricultural Labourers Union*, 1874.

(b) Eight volumes of manuscripts, being several drafts for 'Notes on the Life of a Toiler', Howell's unpublished autobiography. Include accounts of the working-class movement's reactions to the Civil War. Incorporate a series of letters, 1870–5, and a review of the years 1876–9, sent to a friend in America.

(c) Diaries, about thirty volumes. c. 1864–1910.

(d) Thirteen letter-books of George Howell and the Reform League, 1865–84; and tin box of letters to Howell. The first four letter-books are concerned with the Reform League; the later ones include Howell's personal letters. There are references to American institutions[1] and to the *Alabama* dispute, 1872. The letters to Howell are indexed under the sender's name, the letters for each year being in a separate envelope; they include a series of letters from Goldwin Smith at Cornell describing American opinion, Republicanism, British emigrants in the United States, &c.

(e) Minute-book of the First International Workingmen's Association, 1866–9.[2] Scrapbook of cuttings and notes made by George Howell on the Association's meetings. List of members, 1865–70.

The minute-book includes many entries of American interest. The minutes of a meeting on 4 Dec. 1866 contain a report of a statement by Orsini on his return from a visit to the United States that Wendell Phillips, Charles Sumner, and Horace Greeley had joined the Association. The Annual Report, 1866–7, of the American secretary of the General Council of the International Workingmen's Association contains references to the Report of the National Labour Congress of working-class delegates of the United States, efforts to open up correspondence between workingmen's

---

[1] See Henry Pelling, *America and the British Left: from Bright to Bevan*, p. 24 (London, 1956).

[2] Certain sections of this Minute-book are restricted from use.

associations in the old and new world, the progress of the eight-hour movement, cheaper postage between the United States and Europe, efforts to finance the emigration of Lyons silk weavers to America, &c. At a council meeting held on 9 July 1867 a letter was read from Mr. Sylvis, president of the United States Iron Molders' Union, offering to organize voluntary contributions from members for London tailors on strike, and describing the establishment of co-operative foundries. On 23 July 1867, 'Citizen Marx has received letters from New York announcing the affiliation of the Communist Club . . . [to the I.W.A.]'. There are reports of the exchange of newspapers, letters from corresponding secretaries of American unions, resolutions to the working men of America, &c.

HOLYOAKE COLLECTION.

George Jacob Holyoake (1817–1906), co-operator and secularist.[1] The collection consists of 359 books and 424 pamphlets dealing with the early co-operative movement and manuscript diaries for 1848–1905. Holyoake visited America in 1879 and 1882,[2] and the diaries give brief entries during the 1882 period. Pamphlets include several on American topics by Holyoake.[3]

See also Holyoake's correspondence in the Library of the Co-operative Union Ltd., Manchester (p. 97).

Board of Trade, Companies Registration Office, S.W. Wing, Bush House, Strand, LONDON, W.C. 2

Since 1856 a file has been begun here for each company at the time of its registration, containing memoranda and articles of association, together with names, addresses, and occupations of shareholders, and details of the financing of the companies. Files for those companies which have been voluntarily dissolved are in the Public Record Office (B.T. 31) (p. 288).

The nature of the materials available is illustrated by the microfilming programme in Bush House of the Bancroft Library (of Western American History) of the University of California at Berkeley. The Bancroft Library has microfilm of the Bush House records of companies operating in Western United States, Central America, and Mexico during the latter half of the nineteenth century and the early twentieth century. The records filmed are not confined to any particular type of activity; they include such diverse enterprises as mining, cattle-raising, colonization, railroads, land speculation, &c.

[1] See Joseph MacCabe, *Life and Letters of George Jacob Holyoake*, 2 vols. (London, 1908).
[2] See his *Travels in Search of a Settler's Guide-Book of America and Canada* (London, 1884).
[3] See C. W. F. Goss, *A Descriptive Bibliography of George Jacob Holyoake* (London, 1908).

The nature of the records is as follows: memoranda of association (names of founders, purposes and reasons for association); articles of incorporation; by-laws; annual financial statements and complete annual lists of stockholders; all changes in corporate structure, officers, addresses, by-laws; reduction or increase in capital, new security issues, balance sheets (after 1909), copies of official meeting calls, and court orders; voluntary wind-up notices, appointments and reports of closing officials or receivers and final reports.

British Museum,[1] LONDON, W.C. 1

The following summary of manuscripts is simply a continuation of Andrews and Davenport, pp. 1–169, and Paullin and Paxson, pp. 494–555. Andrews and Davenport carried their work on the pre-1783 manuscripts down to Additional Manuscript (Add. MS.) 37067 (that is, for all accessions up to 1905); Additional Charter (Add. Ch.) 43062 (to the end of 1895); and Egerton Manuscript (Eg. MS.) 2860 (to the end of 1895). Paullin and Paxson later worked over the same ground for their post-1783 materials and brought their list down to Add. MS. 37951 (to the end of 1909) and Eg. MS. 2860 (to the end of 1905)—with no additions to Add. Chs. And they also brought Andrews and Davenport's work on the pre-1783 materials down to the same dates.

Therefore the following list summarizes the Americana collected by the Museum during 1910–56 for Add. MSS.; 1906–55 for Eg. MSS.; and gives a note on Add. Chs. to the terminal date of the last printed catalogue, 1925.

The entries were compiled with the aid of the following lists: *Catalogue of Additions to the Manuscripts in the British Museum* which in 1958 extended only to the end of 1925[2] (i.e. to Add. MS. 41295, Eg. MS. 3038, and Add. Ch. 66689); page proofs of the volume about to be issued to cover 1926 and 1927 (i.e. to Add. MS. 41477), which was being constantly added to as fresh proofs came from the press and which is, as yet, unindexed; and for accessions since 1927—to the end of 1956 for Add. MSS. and 1955 for Eg. MSS., but without Add. Chs.—there are two scrapbooks, each entitled 'Handlist of Recent Accessions', made up of handwritten or typescript slips giving usually just the title of manuscripts, though in some cases (fortunately most of the important collections) cuttings from the *British Museum Quarterly* give a fuller general description. However, there is one excellent printed catalogue, the *Catalogue of the Gladstone Papers* (1953), which covers Add. MSS. 44086–835. An official booklet describes in detail the complete range of catalogues, both printed and manuscript, *The Catalogues of the Manuscript Collections in the British Museum*, by T. C. Skeat (London, 1951).

It is relatively simple to locate particular subjects for the period covered by the printed and indexed *Catalogue of Additions*. But for the period thereafter, it being thought impracticable (indeed almost impossible) to search all

---

[1] Virginia material microfilmed by the Virginia Colonial Records Project.
[2] By 1960 this has now been extended to 1930.

the papers since 1925, the hunt for Americana was much more empirical—
for the short titles of the scrapbooks often give no clue at all, particularly
in the large collections. We examined scores of volumes, on a remote
likelihood of their containing Americana, which, in fact, contained nothing
relevant. It is likely that we will have missed some items; but it is unlikely
that we have missed any large or important body of Americana. Some of the
collections here listed are, of course, so well known that, as in the Public
Record Office, we have not normally attempted to note the names of published works that have relied on, or which illuminate, particular sections of
these papers; but we have checked that accessions since 1925 which are
mentioned in recent scholarly monographs have been included below.

Three collections were not available for inspection, pending binding, at
the time of the survey (Winter, 1957–8) which probably contain Americana:
the Herbert Gladstone Papers (Add. MSS. 45985–46118), the Stanmore
Papers (Add. MSS. 49199–285), and the Dilke Papers (Add. MSS. 43874–
967).

The principal collections are:

Add. MSS.	38190–489	LIVERPOOL PAPERS
	38931–39164	LAYARD PAPERS
	40181–617	PEEL PAPERS
	42083–8	GRENVILLE PAPERS
	43039–358	ABERDEEN PAPERS
	43383–92	JOHN BRIGHT PAPERS
	43510–644	RIPON PAPERS
	43647–78	COBDEN PAPERS
	43874–967	DILKE PAPERS
	44086–835	GLADSTONE PAPERS
	44992–45022	RUSSELL OF BIRMINGHAM PAPERS
	45728–30	AUCKLAND PAPERS
	45985–46118	HERBERT GLADSTONE PAPERS (An additional section of these, 46474–86, is reserved from public use.)
	46920–47213	EGMONT PAPERS
	47559–601	CHARLES JAMES FOX PAPERS
	48417–589	PALMERSTON PAPERS
	49173–95	SPENCER PERCEVAL PAPERS
	49199–285	STANMORE PAPERS
Eg. MSS.	3324–508	LEEDS PAPERS
LOAN	29	PORTLAND PAPERS

ADDITIONAL MANUSCRIPTS

38144. PAPERS RELATING TO NEGOTIATIONS BETWEEN JAMES II AND THE POPE.

Papers relating to negotiations between James II and the Pope, 1689–90, in
which James (ff. 2b, 3b) says that his Catholicism has caused the Revolution,

also 'Unica turbarum contra nos excitatorum origo est, quod Catholicam fidem complexi simus et eandem in tria regna, et late sparsas per Americam subditorum nostrorum colonias reducere statuissemus'. (The sole source of the disturbances stirred up against us is that we have adopted the Catholic faith, the same faith in three nations, and that we have decided to withdraw the widely scattered colonies of our subjects in America.)

38161. NOTES OF SPEECHES AND DEBATES IN PARLIAMENT, taken by Philip Yorke, 1st Earl of Hardwicke, his son Philip, the 2nd Earl, and others.

f. 141. Questions for the Judges on an Act of Pardon passed by the Massachusetts Assembly, temp. George III.

38190–489. LIVERPOOL PAPERS.[1]

The papers of Charles Jenkinson, 1st Earl of Liverpool (1727–1808), and of Robert Jenkinson, the 2nd Earl (1770–1828).

38193

ff. 65, 184. Two letters from George Canning to Lord Liverpool. In the first, Lisbon, 14 Jan. 1815, Canning gives his opinion of the American peace; he is cool, but concedes that Liverpool has done what is 'wise and necessary'. In the second, Storrs, 30 Aug. 1823, he encloses a letter to him from the American Minister, Richard Rush, from London, 27 Aug. 1823, which states that the United States would look with disfavour upon any attempt by European powers to interfere in South America, suggests that Britain should recognize the independence of the former Spanish colonies, and infers that the United States is willing to consider any suggestions for joint action with Britain about South America.

38197

f. 1. Correspondence of G. Clarke, Deputy Auditor, concerning the revenues of New York, 1718. (Copies.)

38202

f. 342. Refusal by the Assembly of Massachusetts of the offered alternative to the Stamp duty, 1764.

38207

f. 285. Minute of Governors of King's College at New York, 1773. (Copy.)

38221

f. 334. Letter, 1787, of American merchants to (?) the 1st Earl of Liverpool.

[1] N. S. Jucker, *The Jenkinson Papers* (London, 1949), is a useful introduction to this very important collection.

38223

f. 222. Abstract of a letter on Spanish interests in North America, 1788.

38225

f. 162. (*See also* 38394, f. 65*b*.) Reports on memorials from the inhabitants of Vermont, 17 Apr. 1790. (Copy.) Concerns the wish of the inhabitants of Vermont to 'negociate a commercial and friendly intercourse' with 'His Majesty's Dominions'. The report is by S. Cottrell, on behalf of the Lords of Trade, to W. W. Grenville.

f. 315. Copy of a letter, 9 Nov. 1790, from 'an eminent merchant of Philadelphia to his friend in New York', on the industries and commerce of the United States.

38229

f. 340. Project of an Anglo-United States treaty, 1794. This outline of a proposed treaty is unsigned but endorsed 'In Mr. Jay's Aug. 6th 1794'. It is presumably Jay's original draft of what developed into Jay's Treaty.

38252

ff. 3–8, 32, 34, 353, 355. (*See also* 38253, ff. 74, 92, 217; 38256, ff. 176–81, 205; 38257, f. 359; 38267, f. 142; 38271, ff. 16, 18; 38272, f. 343; 38274, f. 246; 38379, ff. 26, 80, 287.) Papers relating to claims of British subjects lately residing in the United States, 1813, 1814, 1818.

38259

ff. 43–58, 91–103, 118, 178. (*See also* 38362, f. 195; 38363, ff. 12, 149; 38365, ff. 153–78.) Papers relating to the War of 1812 and the negotiations for peace, 1812–14. Includes correspondence from Castlereagh and Goulburn.

f. 218. Passengers of the *Jenny* from Rhode Island, 1814.

38284

ff. 232, 238. Correspondence of American Loyalists with the 2nd Earl of Liverpool, 1820.

38303

f. 12. Headed 'Observations on American affairs, 16th September, 1812'—unsigned—urges adoption of a 'lenient' mode of warfare against the Americans; followed by a paper headed 'Extract of a letter dated New York, 27th September, 1818'—unsigned and unaddressed—on the obscurity of American objects in the War.

f. 149. Chronological 'precis of the operations in North America from July 1812 to January 1813'.

K

38329

f. 12. Grant of parts of Maine and New York by Charles II to his brother James, 1674. (Copy.)

f. 17. Headed 'Copy of the 8th article of instructions given by James Duke of York and Albany . . . to Major Andros, Governor of New York, 1st July 1674'. Concerns 'the publick payments and impositions and the course of justice for determining all differences amongst the inhabitants'.

38330

f. 91. Treasury warrant to William Burnet, Governor of New York, 1722, regarding refusal by the Treasurer of the province to render an account to H.M. Auditor-General. Orders the Governor to ensure that the Treasurer do so. (Copy.)

38334

ff. 68, 250. (*See also* 38332, f. 227.) Returns of troops furnished by the several provinces, in eleven colonies, excluding Delaware and Georgia. 1760–2.

f. 134. 'Charges for carrying on the Indian Service . . . in North America', by E. Atkins, Superintendent for Indian Affairs 1756–60. (Incomplete.)

f. 223. State of the present branches of the Customs in North America, with hints for their improvement (after 25 Dec. 1762).

f. 229. Note on the quit-rents of New York, 1762.

f. 273. Lists of Customs officers (twelve officers, including those at St. Augustine, Fla., and Mobile, Ala.), 1762–3.

38335

ff. 1, 14–36, 68–77. (*See also* 38334, f. 297.) Reflections on the settlement and government of British North America, 1763. Regards the colonies as raw material producers. It is in Britain's interest to keep their population down. Their benefits to Britain include the use of British shipping to transport their raw materials and the consumption of British manufactures by the colonies.

ff. 37, 90. Lists of officers in North America absent from duty, 1763.

ff. 40, 82, 148–53, 237, 241. (*See also* 38201, f. 33; 38337, ff. 50, 60; 38373, ff. 80–84*b*, 111*b*–122.) Papers relating to quit-rents in Virginia, 1761–3.

ff. 81, 95*b*–98, 240. Accounts of Virginia tobacco duty, 1763.

f. 87. Drawbacks on foreign goods re-exported from England to North America, 1761.

ff. 103, 144, 154, 327–31. (*See also* 38339, f. 250.) Reports, Treasury minutes, &c., on the customs revenue from British North America, 1763.

f. 209*b*. Number of ships annually cleared from American colonies, 1760–2. Shows number going to or coming from British and foreign ports and total tonnage.

f. 233. Report of the Lords of Trade on the colonization of Florida, 1763. (Copy.)

f. 243. Estimate of tea, sugar, and molasses illegally imported into British North America, (?) 1764.

38336

f. 155. Account of Spanish Florida by Dr. Campbell, c. 1763.

38337

f. 1. Abstract of a Bill for encouraging the trade of British North America, (?) 1763.

f. 60. Quit-rents of the several provinces, Virginia, the Carolinas, Georgia, and New York, 1764.

ff. 162–73b. Extracts from report on whale fishing, fur trade, and bounty on hemp in the American colonies, 1764.

f. 234. Note on the trade of North America, especially imports of Carolinian rice, 1764.

f. 245. Report of seizures of uncustomed and prohibited goods at Philadelphia, Boston, Quebec, and in Virginia, 1763–4.

f. 314. Auditor-General's report on the Quit-Rent Act of New York, 1764.

38338

f. 39. Address, 1764, from the Assembly of New York, to the Lieutenant-Governor, Cadwallader Colden. (Copy.) Expressing loyalty but stating circumspectly that it will be taxed only with its own consent, and asking Colden to point out to the Ministry 'the many mischiefs arising from the Act commonly called the Sugar Act'.

38339

ff. 131, 182–9, 306. Notes on the right to tax the colonies, c. 1765.

f. 180. Change of military establishment in American colonies, 1750, 1765.

f. 235. Agreement of West Indian and North American merchants, 1766.

f. 302. Decrease of British exports to North America since the repeal of the Stamp Act, 1766.

38340

ff. 163–5. Estimates of military expenses in British North America, 1767.

f. 192. Petition, c. 1767, of London merchants trading with North America, representing that their trade has been seriously affected by the Townshend Duties and praying for relief by Parliament.

ff. 201–378b, passim. Papers relating to the collection of Customs in British North America, 1767–71. Includes legal opinion of Jonathan Sewall, Attorney-General of Massachusetts, 1768.

38341

ff. 29, 69, 163, 329. Papers relating to the collection of Customs in British North America, 1767–71.

ff. 104, 135. Proposals for amending the taxation of the North American colonies, c. 1769.

f. 125. Ships entered outwards from London for British North America, 1765–70.

f. 324. Quantities of wheat exported from British North America, 1678–1772.

38342

f. 32. Protest of Massachusetts against the claims of Parliament to authority over the colony, 1773.

f. 34. Paper on the state of unrest in Massachusetts, c. 1773.

f. 39. Paper on the Virginia tobacco trade (after 1773), giving a brief history of the trade during the eighteenth century.

f. 82. Note on the rate of exchange in New England, (?) 1774.

f. 153. Paper on grants of land in North America, c. 1775–6.

f. 157. Paper urging the creation of a special fund for the American colonies. (n.d., but seems likely to be late 1760's.) The document does not make clear the purpose of the proposed fund, but the author's argument is that there should be set up an orderly system of colonial government to prevent the colonies combining and becoming 'untractable' as they are already doing by misapplying Locke's writings.

ff. 161–221, 281. Letters and papers relative to the rebellion of the American colonies, 1774–7, including various declarations and petitions of the colonists, proposals of parliamentary Bills affecting America, &c.

38343

ff. 1–22b. (See also 38342, f. 302.) Account of what the Treasury has done in freighting provision ships for America, with lists of ships, &c., 1775–7.

ff. 117–219b. Papers relating to the War of Independence, 1777, 1778.

38344

ff. 103–24. Plan for a permanent union between Great Britain and her American colonies, 1779, sent by Joseph Galloway, an American Loyalist of Philadelphia, to Charles Jenkinson.

38345

f. 59. Articles 4–6 of the treaty of peace between Great Britain and the United States, 1783.

f. 173. (See also 38346, f. 27.) General orders for intercourse with the United States, 1784–5.

f. 177. Observations on the trade between the West Indies and the United States, c. 1784.

38346

f. 18. Narrative respecting trade between Jamaica and the United States, 1785.

f. 39. Remarks by Committee of Loyalists of New York on proposed Bill for their relief, 1785.

f. 54. King's Advocate's opinion as to granting registration to ships built in the United States, 1785.

f. 67. American ships arrived in the port of London, 1783–5.

f. 87. Paper on the increased price of produce in the United States, 1785.

ff. 279b, 281b. Imports from the United States duty free, or subject to especially low duty, 1786.

38347

f. 104. Proceedings of the Supreme Court of Pennsylvania, 1786.

38348

ff. 65–68b. (See also 38375, ff. 132, 136; 38376, f. 103.) Papers relating to debts due from the United States to British subjects, &c., 1785–9.

f. 116b. Statement of duties imposed on British ships and goods by the United States, c. 1788.

38349

ff. 203, 358–62. Papers relative to British trade with the United States, 1789.

f. 332. Petition of merchants banished from the United States, to the House of Commons, 1789.

38350

f. 97. State of shipping in the United States, 1789.

f. 202. Note on industries in the United States, c. 1790.

f. 215. Statistics of whale oil industry in the United States, 1790.

f. 246. Report of Committee of Council on Trade on commerce with the United States, 1791. (Proof with corrections. Imperfect.)

38352

f. 290. Corn exported by the United States, 1790–3.

f. 381. Objections to admitting American ships to West Indian ports, c. 1793.

38353

f. 301. Order in Council for regulating trade with the United States, 1795. Draft.)

38354

ff. 38–55. 'Project of heads of proposals to be made to Mr. Jay.' 1794.

38356

ff. 1–4. Commercial treaty between United States and Prussia, 1800. (Extract.)

ff. 101–4. Paper concerning West Florida, 1801.

ff. 278–82. Papers concerning American relations with Britain, c. 1807.

38357

f. 31. Paper concerning Napoleon's intentions regarding Florida, 1801.

38363

ff. 155–60b. Memorials to the British government on the American-Canadian frontier, claiming protection for the Indians, 1783, 1794, 1813.

ff. 184–98. (See also 38358, f. 139.) Papers relative to the Commission for American Claims, 1813. Stipulating the duties required of the commissioners in deciding which citizens had a right to claim a share of moneys to be paid by the United States under the treaties of 1783 and 1794.

f. 200. Memorial of American Loyalists pressing for compensation under the decisions of the above Commissions, 1813. (Copy.)

38374

f. 107. Reflections on the rebellious state of New York, 1775.

38375

f. 136. Memorial of Duncan Campbell, Chairman of the Committee of Merchants of London, Bristol, Liverpool, Whitehaven, and Glasgow, trading to Virginia, Maryland, and North Carolina, 'previous to the year 1776', to the Foreign Secretary, complaining of inability to recover debts.

38376

f. 77b. Numbers and tonnage, &c., of ships clearing from Massachusetts Bay, 1787–8.

f. 112. Report on trade with the American colonies (and later with the United States) before and after the War of Independence, 1789.

38387

f. 53. 'Account of all foreign goods exported to the British colonies in America, particularly wines and calicoes', 1762–4, by John Tankyns, Assistant Inspector-General of Customs, 12 June 1765.

38389–93

passim. Minutes of the Committee of Council on Trade relative to intercourse with the United States, 1786–92; e.g. 38389, ff. 63*b*, 68*b*: references to rice exported from South Carolina; and ff. 64, 68*b*.: trade with Georgia, 1786.

38396

'Five representations made by the Board of Trade [to the King] on the fishery and trade of Newfoundland.' Dated 19 Dec. 1718, with heads of a Bill of 24 Dec.; 29 Apr. 1765; 27 Mar. 1766; 17 Mar. 1786; 10 May 1790.

38416

f. 63. Act of the Commonwealth of Massachusetts to prevent the slave trade, 1788. (Printed.)

38465

Letters and papers of William Draper, Treasurer of Greenwich Hospital, 1704–*c.* 1718, with additions. One addition, f. 210, is an 'Account of the number of seamen employed in the merchants' service at the several ports in America, 1763–1772' (dated Receiver's Office for Greenwich Hospital on Tower Hill, 21 Jan. 1778).

See also LIVERPOOL PAPERS SUPPLEMENT, 38564–81.

38510. MISCELLANEOUS PAPERS.

f. 101. Report on descent and property of the Todd family of Caroline county and Dorchester county, Md., with a pedigree from Michael Todd 'about 1693'. (Typewritten.)

f. 126. 'An account of the coast [of America] from Cape Mendosino [on the coast of California] to the Port of Acapulco [on the west coast of Mexico] by Rev. Father Fry [i.e. Fray] Anthony de la Conception, a Carmelite, second cosmographer in the fleet despatched by . . . the County of Monterey . . . Viceking of New Spain in . . . 1602.' (Translation.)

38564–81. LIVERPOOL PAPERS SUPPLEMENT.

38568

f. 46. Lisbon, 9 Dec. 1814, Canning to Liverpool, asking to be kept informed of the progress of the American war, and stating that opinion in Portugal leans 'towards the Yankees'.

38577

f. 1. Grievances of the several provinces of North America, 1769.

f. 39. Papers on the War of 1812 and the negotiations for peace, 31 Aug. 1814.

38650. MISCELLANEOUS PAPERS.

ff. 1–34. Letters relating to North America. 1775, 1780.

f. 1. 7 Aug. 1775 from New York, William Tryon, Governor of New York, to the Earl of Dartmouth, urging a change of policy towards the American colonies. (Copy.)

f. 3. 5 or 6 Dec. 1775, Major-General Richard Montgomery to General Sir Guy Carleton at Quebec, calling upon him to surrender the city.

f. 5. Copies of letters,[1] Richmond, Va., 27 July–13 Sept. 1780, of Thomas Jefferson as Governor of Virginia, mainly referring to military operations. The manuscript (apparently an incomplete letter-book) was found by Benedict Arnold on his capture of the town in 1781.

f. 56. Report, San Ildefonso, Spain, 16 Aug. 1796, of Michel-Ange Bernard Mangowit, late French Consul at Charleston, S.C., to the French Foreign Minister, on the attitude of the United States towards France. (*In French.*)

38712. PAPERS OF EDWARD SOUTHWELL AND OTHERS.

f. 116. Minutes, 1707, of Council at Portsmouth, N.H., concerning a deficiency in the rendering of the accounts of the revenue and expenditure of the province to the Council for Trade and Plantations.

38734–70. HUSKISSON PAPERS.

Papers of William Huskisson (1770–1830), statesman.

38744

ff. 167–9. Extracts and notes concerning trade with the United States, 1823.

f. 251. Instructions, 27 June 1823, from John Quincy Adams to Richard Rush, the United States Minister in London. (Copy.)

38745

ff. 219–23. Letter, 8 Mar. 1824, from Lord Grenville to Charles W. W. Wynn concerning trade with the United States. (Copy.)

ff. 286–93. (*See also* 38746, ff. 1, 7–9.) Letters, &c., relating to the United States-Canadian frontier, 1824.

38746

ff. 67, 71, 73. American Bill for constituting Oregon a territory, 1824. (3 copies.)

ff. 265–8. Paper on commercial intercourse of the United States with England and Russia, 1825.

---

[1] For printed sources of these letters see *Catalogue of Additions to the Manuscripts in the British Museum, 1911–15, sub.* 38650 (London, 1925). Also *The Papers of Thomas Jefferson*, ed. by J. P. Boyd and others, vol. iii, pp. 508–646, *passim* (Princeton, N.J., 1951).

38747

ff. 217–46. Papers relating to proceedings in Congress on commercial regulations, 1826.

38748

f. 3. Letter relating to British trade with the United States, 1826.

f. 10. Act of the General Assembly of Rhode Island to regulate process against banks, &c., 1826. (Copy.)

ff. 214–24. Papers on reciprocity in the carrying trade between British and American vessels, 1826, 1827.

38756

f. 255. Letter on the dependence of the British cotton trade upon the United States, 1828.

38763

f. 93b. Table of regulations of trade between the British colonies and the United States, c. 1824.

ff. 103b–8. Statistics of United States trade and shipping, 1824–5. (Printed.)

38766

f. 208. Comparison of the British and American navies, 1826.

f. 251. Papers relating to America, 1805 and 1822–8. Relate to negotiations on the North-East boundary and of the regulation of the trade of the United States with the British West Indies. Also papers on Spanish America and Canada.

38823. HOBY, SIR EDWARD (1560–1617). Commonplace book. Includes:

f. 1. Instructions for a voyage of discovery to North America, beginning imperfectly at f. 4 with instructions for geographical and scientific observation, followed by 'Instructions for the master' and 'Instructions to be observed by Thomas Bavin', 1582.

f. 5b. 'How the Crowne of England hath most right to all the mayne land and islands alongst the costes of America from the Cape of Florida to 58 degrees northwardes.' n.d.

f. 7. Things known to be in the countries about the river of Norumbega[1] (late sixteenth century).

---

[1] Name applied by sixteenth- and seventeenth-century map makers to undefined region along east coast of North America north of Florida.

38835. TALLACK, WILLIAM (1831–1908). Autograph letters to him.

Secretary of the Howard Association.

ff. 18, 20. Spiegel Grove, Fremont, Ohio, 25 Jan. 1890, and 21 Oct. 1891, from Rutherford B. Hayes.

f. 23. London, 19 Sept. 1884, from James Russell Lowell. Chiefly about meetings or articles on prison reform.

38861. PRIVY COUNCIL MEMORANDA, 1540–1718.

20. Petition of [Peter] Sonmans in a dispute with [Joseph] Ormston concerning lands in East New Jersey. *c.* 1718.

38898–913. HAZLITT PAPERS.

Letters of William Hazlitt, the younger, and his son William Carew Hazlitt (1834–1913).

38906

f. 89. Boston, 11 Apr. 1890, from Francis H. Lincoln to W. C. Hazlitt, on an early Hazlitt working in New England as a portrait painter.

f. 91. Hartford, Conn., 23 Apr. 1890, from Henry Barnard to W. C. Hazlitt, on school textbooks.

38912

f. 13. Boston, 8 June 1908, from Charles Francis Adams, president of the Massachusetts Historical Society, to W. C. Hazlitt, about a manuscript describing New England, 1783–7, said to have been written by Hazlitt's great-aunt, Margaret.

38931–39164. LAYARD PAPERS.

Private and official papers of Sir Austen Henry Layard (1817–94), M.P., Under-Secretary of State for Foreign Affairs 1852 and 1861–6, and first Commissioner of Works 1868–9; and thereafter Minister at Madrid and Constantinople respectively.

Layard was Under-Secretary under Russell, 1861–5, and Clarendon, 1865–6, and as in both cases his superior sat in the House of Lords, he was Government spokesman on foreign policy in the Commons. Thus the papers contain many items relating to the American Civil War, the *Alabama* claims, &c. Major items are as follows. (*Letters unless otherwise stated.*)

38951–62. Correspondence of Layard with Edmund Hammond, who was Permanent Under-Secretary for Foreign Affairs 1854–73.

38951-4. Letters, 1861-75, of Hammond to Layard.

Chiefly of interest as containing the comments of a pro-Southern Englishman on the Civil War. The almost total disappearance of references to
America in the period 1864-5 is significant in view of Hammond's opinions.

38951

f. 2. 29 Nov. 1861, mentions *Trent* incident.

ff. 20, 22. 22 Feb. 1862 (2 letters) discuss the Northern blockade.

f. 52. 21 Apr. 1862, says that Adams has sent one of his periodical
'blustering' communications about 'our countenancing the South', and
'Seward shows his teeth about British designs in Mexico'.

f. 70. 12 June 1862, comments on a complaint from Liverpool merchants
that British ships are being stopped by Northern vessels in British West
Indian waters. Hammond has no sympathy for them as they are carrying
contraband. He mentions General Butler's proceedings in New Orleans
and their adverse effect on British feeling. (*See also* f. 74, letter, 15 June
1862.)

f. 93. 10 July 1862, mentions blockade running.

f. 95. 14 July 1862, mentions serious Northern position before Richmond;
also blockade running.

f. 100. 18 July 1862, states 'Federals have had a most complete licking'.
The South has almost completely established its claim to recognition, but
British should not interfere until 'the Northern cause is more thoroughly
degraded'. If Britain wants to 'pick a quarrel' it can find reason in 'Butler's
proceedings at New Orleans'.

f. 114. 28 July 1862, discusses the finding of funds for a mission to the
Confederacy 'which before many months elapse, we must be prepared to
accredit'. Says also 'the Federal cause is fast going to the dogs'.

f. 130. 17 Aug. 1862, more comments on the very bad position of the
Federals, and the overlarge demands of the United States government for
troops. Hammond thinks that Lincoln is acting deliberately in this in order
to make the North demand peace. (*See also* f. 134, letter, 24 Aug. 1862.)

f. 137. 28 Aug. 1862, mentions the recoaling of Southern ships in British
ports.

f. 143. 9 Sept. 1862, notes the Southern threat to Washington.

f. 150. 18 Sept. 1862, comments on the bad state of the North; and adds
that nearly 4 million bales of cotton are available in the South if means
could be found to export it.

f. 160. 6 Oct. 1862, minimizes the importance of Antietam, and thinks
that emancipation will do little good.

f. 164. 12 Oct. 1862, states that he does not think that recognition of the
South will be necessary, as things are 'working to an early end without it'.
Again criticizes the preliminary Emancipation Proclamation.

f. 170. 17 Oct. 1862, thinks that the mid-term elections may well cause
a 'civil war within civil war'.

f. 174. 18 Oct. 1862, refers to lack of action, except at Corinth, Miss., and threatened retaliation by the South for the Emancipation Proclamation.

f. 182. 24 Oct. 1862, says the next two months will be critical for the North. He has told Lord Lyons, who is returning to the United States, that he will be lucky if he does not arrive in a blood-stained city (i.e. New York at election time). Mentions Gladstone's Newcastle speech.

f. 186. 27 Oct. 1862, states that the idea of recognizing the South has been given up because 'of its inexpediency'.

f. 212. 25 Nov. 1862, states that the *Nashville* must not be allowed to arm herself at Southampton, and mentions her activities in the Channel.

f. 215. 26 Nov. 1862, also on the *Nashville*.

f. 220. 7 Dec. 1862, on the activities of British consuls in the South. Adams has alleged that one of them (Bunch?) has communicated with the Confederates in diplomatic matters.

f. 241. n.d. encloses note, 16 Jan. 1863, from Consul Archibald at New York about the growth of a peace party in the North, especially in New Jersey, which, he thinks, will bring about an armistice by April.

38952

f. 16. 8 Apr. 1863, on the seizure of the *Alexandra*.

f. 39. 27 June 1863, mentions Lee's invasions of Maryland and Pennsylvania.

f. 50. 13 July 1863, thinks only the capture of New York and Philadelphia will bring the war to a speedy close.

f. 63. 26 July 1863. After Gettysburg still thinks there is a good chance of Northern disintegration. (*See also* f. 65, letter, 29 July 1863.)

f. 70. 1 Aug. 1863, expresses first doubts of ultimate Southern success, but says the South has a 'set-off' in the New York riot and the reported removal of Meade. This, if true, he says, proves that Lincoln does not want any competitor for the presidency.

f. 82. 13 Aug. 1863. The Confederates are recovering. The French Mexican scheme will worry the North, but there is no reason why Britain should oppose it.

f. 95. 22 Sept. 1863. The iron-clad issue has been finally disposed of (but contrast f. 99, letter 26 Sept. 1863).

f. 100. 3 Oct. 1863. Smashing defeat of Federals [at Chattanooga, Tenn.]. The Confederates have an abundance of everything and are preparing for a great effort. The iron-clads are obviously Confederate and must be held.

f. 108. 17 Oct. 1863. A great disaster is facing the North in Tennessee. The Southern cause is 'looking up'.

f. 111. 2 Nov. 1863. The difficulties experienced by the government over the *Alexandra*.

f. 153. 1 June 1864, on the *Florida*.

f. 159. 21 June 1864, on a proposed commercial convention with the United States, projected as long ago as 1854 (the Reciprocity Treaty of that year). (*See also* f. 164, letter, 24 June 1864.)

f. 193. 27 Aug. 1864, on McClellan's candidacy for the presidency; the capture of the *Georgia*.

f. 197. 6 Sept. 1864, still says 'a renewal of the Union' is 'out of the question'.

38953

f. 3. 21 Sept. 1864, thinks McClellan's candidacy will cause a 'crash' in the Northern camp.

f. 33. 19 Nov. 1864. American denunciation of the Anglo-American agreement concerning armed vessels on the Lakes, and Northern 'impudence' in pressing for withdrawal of British recognition of Southern belligerency.

38954

f. 1. 19 Nov. 1865, mentions Fenianism in the United States.

f. 127. 21 Oct. 1871, mentions good relations with the United States. Does not have high opinion of the *Alabama* arbitrators.

f. 138. 2 Feb. 1872. The storm raised in Britain by the United States pressing the indirect claims. The Cuban insurrection.

f. 142. 4 Mar. 1872. American surprise at outburst of British feeling over the indirect claims.

f. 148. 20 June 1872, thinks the British view on indirect claims will prevail at Geneva. The proceedings there had better remain secret.

f. 154. 13 Dec. 1872, on the United States, Spain, and Cuba.

f. 163. 22 Feb. 1873, on Daniel Sickles, United States Minister at Madrid.

f. 169. Extract from a letter from Thornton, 11 Mar. 1873, which says that Grant's administration does not 'care a straw' for Cuba.

f. 171. 12 Mar. 1873, on the scramble of American lawyers to recover large sums for British clients from the Mixed Commission on Claims.

f. 184. 22 Apr. 1873, extract from a letter from Thornton, on the unscrupulous financial activities of Sickles.

f. 223. 16 Nov. 1874, mentions the Democratic successes in the 1874 elections.

38987–96. General correspondence, 1861–9.

38987

f. 184. Memorandum, 8 Sept. 1861, headed 'Convention with the United States'. States that there is little chance of the United States accepting the convention (? on maritime rights).

f. 198. 10 Sept. 1861, Montreal, from W. F. Williams to Layard, on impending anarchy in the United States and anti-British sentiment there.

f. 218. Memorandum, 20 Sept. 1861, on Southern plan to withhold cotton from Britain, and Northern suspicions of British intentions in Mexico.

f. 271. Memorandum, 27 Sept. 1861, on 'right of search'.

f. 301. Memorandum, 20 Oct. 1861, on recognition of Confederacy. Likely that South will win independence, in which case it will be a valuable market for British manufactured goods, but the war thus far has been too indecisive to make recognition feasible.

f. 343. Memorandum, 16 Nov. 1861, from Hammond to Layard on the Northern blockade.

f. 355. Memorandum, 24 Nov. 1861, discussing question as to whether Britain could detain the *Nashville*.

f. 373. Memorandum, 27 Nov. 1861, on the *Trent* incident.

f. 392. 5 Dec. 1861, from the Rev. Dr. John Waddington to Layard deprecating any British sympathy for the South, and possible war with the North.

f. 410. Memorandum, 17 Dec. 1861, on possible understanding with the South.

f. 424. Memorandum (n.d. but Dec. 1861), on the request from Delane, the editor of *The Times*, for information regarding Russell's avoidance of the term 'United States' to Mason and Slidell, the Southern Commissioners. Apparently from Layard to Russell, with reply written at the end by Russell.

38988

f. 9. 7 Jan. 1862, United States Legation Vienna, from J. L. Motley to Layard, on the folly of war between Britain and the United States, which no one in the United States desires.

f. 190. 11 July 1862, Montreal, from W. Williams to Layard, on McClellan's defeat in the Peninsula, Va.

f. 216. Memorandum, 29 July 1862, on the *Alabama*. States that she slipped out to sea just before the arrival of the law officers' opinion that she should be detained.

f. 220. Note, 30 July 1862, from Russell to Layard. A 'pity' the *Alabama* escaped.

f. 386. 27 Nov. 1862, Vienna, from J. L. Motley to Layard, on Confederate raiders and blockade runners.

f. 390. 28 Nov. 1862, from the Rev. Dr. John Waddington to Layard. Hopes that the British government will give no aid to the slavery cause.

38989

f. 18. 12 Jan. 1863, Montreal, from W. Williams to Layard, on Burnside's defeat. Says the South hates Britain as much as does the North.

f. 48. 7 Feb. 1863, Norwich, from W. Elwin to Layard, on French proposal of mediation between North and South. (*See also* f. 178, n.d. (? June 1863).)

ff. 264–341 *passim*. Memoranda and notes, 19 Aug.–9 Sept. 1863, addressed to Layard on the question of the iron-clad rams fitting out at Liverpool, and the arguments for and against their detention. Chiefly from Russell and Sir Roundell Palmer. Also one from Layard to William Stuart, Secretary of the Legation in Washington.

f. 333. Note, 7 Sept. 1863, from Palmerston to Layard on British subjects allegedly employed on the *Alabama*.

38990

f. 6. A peace plan to end the Civil War (n.d. but 1863).

ff. 62–69. A series of undated cryptic notes on the Civil War (? on recognition of the Confederacy).

38991

f. 128. Request, n.d. (presumably to Layard), by Russell, for the exact dates of the law officer's opinion on detention of the *Alabama*, and of Layard's telegram to Liverpool ordering detention.

f. 129. Unsigned memorandum, 14 Mar. 1865, presumably by Layard, in reply, giving dates and circumstances. Blame for delay is put upon Charles Francis Adams.

f. 159. Memorandum, n.d. (? 25 Apr. 1865), unsigned (? by Russell), on the assassination of Lincoln.

f. 336. Note, 7 Aug. 1865, from Russell, on Seward's hostility to Britain.

f. 388. 19 Aug. 1865, London, from Russell to Layard. United States will not press demand for *Alabama* compensation to the point of war, and Russell thinks that the question may well 'drop out of sight'.

f. 392. 22 Aug. 1865, from Layard to Russell, on delay in completing the draft on the *Alabama* to be given to Adams. (The printed version of this draft, dated Aug. 1865, is in 39157 f. 79.)

38997–39011. Correspondence of Layard while British Minister at Madrid Oct. 1869–Mar. 1877. Contains the following relevant to the United States-Spanish tensions over Cuba, the *Virginius*, &c.

39001

f. 403. Two notes, (? 4 Apr. 1872) from Daniel Sickles to Layard, the first on 'rascals [? Spanish] bleeding us', the second on the Geneva Arbitration.

39003

ff. 329–33. Two notes, 15 Oct. 1873, from Sickles to Layard, on the Cuban customs regulations. Further note, 25 Oct. 1873, on United States-Spanish friction over Cuba—especially on the slaves there.

39005

f. 222. 19 Mar. 1874, Washington, D.C., from Sir Edward Thornton to A. G. Dunlop, British Consul-General in Havana, says United States government and 'the sensible part of the population have no wish whatever to acquire Cuba', but if affairs like that of the *Virginius* continue to occur, it will be difficult to suppress public clamour.

39007

f. 246. 14 Jan. 1875, Washington, D.C., from Thornton to Dunlop, similar in tone to 39005, f. 222 (above)—Spain should not provoke the United States.

39101–20. Semi-official correspondence with British Ministers and Consuls, 1861–6.

39101

f. 66. Draft letter, Liverpool, 15 Sept. 1861, from T. M. Mackay to Layard, on the seriousness of the American conflict for Europe, especially the threat of the cessation of cotton supplies.

f. 104. 19 Sept. 1861, Liverpool, from Mackay to Layard, on effects of stoppage of cotton.

f. 237. 7 Nov. 1861, from Mackay to Layard, hopes Napoleon III will take initiative in recognizing the Confederacy.

f. 248. 8 Nov. 1861, London, from Mackay to Layard. Thinks a war with the United States would be popular with the commercial classes.

39102

ff. 15, 26. 4 and 6 Dec. 1861, Liverpool, from Mackay to Layard. Preparations for transfer of 'Yankee' ships to nominal ownership of Englishmen in view of impending Anglo-United States war.

f. 30. 9 Dec. 1861, Liverpool, from Mackay to Layard. War threat receding. Britain's right to demand end of Northern blockade.

f. 33. 10 Dec. 1861, from Sir J. Harding to Layard, on precedents in *Trent* incident.

f. 161. 14 Jan. 1862, New York (misdated, should be 1863) from Sir James Caird to Layard: Northern determination, American relief for Lancashire; advises against foreign interference in Civil War.

39103

f. 284. Copies of two anonymous letters. One, London, 30 July 1862, from an American living in voluntary exile in England, thanks (?) Layard for his efforts on behalf of 'humanity' and 'justice' in America. The other, St. Louis, Mo., 31 July 1862, tells of conditions in the border states (Union ill treatment of anyone suspected of Confederate sympathies, &c.) and prays for British intervention to end the War.

39104

f. 225. 27 Dec. 1862, Washington, D.C., from a British officer stationed at Montreal (signature illegible) to Layard. His opinions of the Federal Army formed on a visit to the Army of the Potomac before Fredericksburg. Potentially excellent soldiers, but dirty, undisciplined, ill equipped, &c.

39105

f. 183. 25 Mar. 1863, Western Circuit, Taunton, from Sir Robert Collier to Layard, giving his opinions of the legal aspects of the detention or non-detention of the *Alabama*.

39106

f. 117. Letter and memorial, Paris, 25 and 21 May 1863 respectively, from Alex. Barclay to Layard, on advisability of British recognition of eight of the Southern States as a separate nation (i.e. Virginia, North and South Carolina, Georgia, Florida, Alabama, Mississippi, and Tennessee). This arrangement, the writer thinks, would be accepted by both American belligerents and by France.

f. 172. 5 June 1863, Paris, from Barclay to Layard, on same subject as f. 117 above, with views of Southern representatives in Paris (they expect no help from Britain or France).

f. 334. Memorandum, *c.* 10 July 1863, about the visit of the pro-Confederate M.P.'s, Roebuck and Lindsay, to Napoleon III, and his attitude on recognition of the independence of the South.

39107

f. 225. 18 Sept. 1863, Washington, D.C., from William Stuart, Secretary of the Legation at Washington, to Layard, on communications with the State Department on the rams. Fears that Seward may have sent 'blustering instructions' to Adams had he not communicated news of the rams' detention immediately upon receipt.

39108

f. 183. Note on the jurisdiction of American consuls in Great Britain, 1864.

39109

f. 9. 2 Mar. 1864, Liverpool, from William Rathbone, Liverpool shipowner, to Layard, on the implications of the rams incident for international law.

f. 277. 'Mem: as to case of *Tuscaloosa*' (? by Layard). On question of prize at sea re Confederate raiders (with printed letters). (? 23 Apr. 1864.)

39110

f. 99. 20 May 1864, Liverpool, from William Rathbone to Layard, that it would be in Britain's interest to forbid the use of her ports to all Confederate vessels which may previously have caused a breach of her neutrality—e.g. by fitting out in British ports.

f. 308. June 1864, New York, from John Gilmary Shea to (?) Layard, on the military situation, and prospects for the 1864 presidential election. Maintains that Lincoln's chances are very strong.

39111

f. 36. 9 July 1864, New York, from John G. Shea to (?) Layard, on the confused and divided state of the Democratic Party; unrest in New York city; Irish immigration into the United States; the military situation.

f. 66. 13 July 1864, New York, from Shea to (?) Layard, that Democrats seem to be working for a revolution to force the North to sue for peace.

f. 264. 9 Sept. 1864, Montreal, from W. Williams to Layard, mentions Sherman's capture of Atlanta, Ga.

39112

f. 218. 28 Nov. 1864, Washington, D.C., from J. Hume Burnley, British Chargé at Washington, to Layard, on a conversation with Seward on the capture of the *Florida*, with a postscript on the sinking of that vessel.

f. 245. 1 Dec. 1864, Washington, D.C., from Burnley to Layard, on Seward, and 'the matter of the exequaturs'; also the *Florida* incident.

39113

f. 66. 20 Jan. 1865, Montreal, from W. Williams to Layard, thinks the Civil War may last another year; wants Southern independence *and* emancipation of slaves.

39114

f. 189. 25 Mar. 1865, London, from James Whitbread to Layard, on a report that certain emigrants sent out by the Discharged Prisoners Aid Society have been arrested in New York.

f. 290. 4 Apr. 1865, Washington, D.C., from J. Hume Burnley to Layard, on an article in the *North American Review*, vol. lxxxii, pp. 478–512, 1856, on the Monroe Doctrine, unsigned, and a discussion on it.

ff. 392 and 432. 17 and 25 Apr. 1865, London, from William Tasker Smith, British Consul at Savannah, Ga., to Layard, asking for transfer to Richmond, Va.

See also 42711.

39168. MISCELLANEOUS PAPERS.

f. 95. 'O Star of France', poem by Walt Whitman. The printed text, first published in 1872, differs considerably from the present draft. (Holograph.)

f. 128. Letter, 1 Feb. [1774] from William Fraser, Under Secretary of State, to the Earl of Holderness, on the Massachusetts petition praying the King to remove Governor Hutchinson and Lieutenant Governor Oliver. Presented by Franklin to 'the Council' and rejected.

39190. MACKENZIE PAPERS, vol. iv.

ff. 204–11. Include letters, Boston, 10 and 28 Dec. 1774, 16 Feb. 1775, of Major John Pitcairn of the Marines (killed at Bunker Hill, 1775) to Lieutenant-Colonel John Mackenzie of the Marines, recounting his difficulties in America.

39245. WODEHOUSE PAPERS.

f. 20. Letter, 22 Feb. 1615, from the Privy Council to the Deputy Lieutenants of Suffolk, promoting a lottery for benefit of Virginia.[1]

39255. MISCELLANEOUS PAPERS.

f. 26. Appointment of Jacob Mark, of Maryland, as United States Consul at Cork, 16 Dec. 1817; signed by James Monroe, President, and John Quincy Adams, Secretary of State; with paper seal. Engraved.

39304–16. BERKELEY PAPERS.

Papers of George Berkeley (1685–1753), Bishop of Cloyne, and his family. Berkeley lived in America from Jan. 1729 until the autumn of 1731. The papers include:

39306

ff. 140b–63. Notes for sermons preached at Newport, R.I., 1729–31.[2]

39311

ff. 12–13. Letter, London, 23 June 1729, from Martin Benson to Berkeley about ideas in England as to what Berkeley and his wife are doing in Rhode Island.[3]

ff. 17–20. Letter, 1730, from Rev. Samuel Johnson of Stratford, Conn., on Berkeley's philosophical theories.

ff. 158–9. Copy of a letter, London, 4 May 1764, from Sir Alexander Cuming, chief of the Cherokees, to the Earl of Bute, asking for alleviation of his poverty. (Enclosed in a letter from Cuming to George Berkeley, son of Bishop Berkeley, 8 May 1764.)

39316

ff. 31–33. Indentures of sale of two slaves to Berkeley, 7 Oct. 1730, with confirmation, 17 Oct. 1731, by Governor Joseph Jenckes of Rhode Island.

39561. C. G. LELAND COLLECTION, vol. x.

ff. 71–79. 'The cattle-range idiom' for a projected dictionary of Americanisms. List of words with meanings, apparently compiled in the late 1880's.

[1] H.M.C. xiii (iv), p. 437.
[2] Printed in *The Works of George Berkeley, D.D.*, ed. by A. C. Fraser, vol. iv, pp. 634–9 (Oxford, 1871).   [3] Printed ibid., pp. 170–2.

39577. AUTOGRAPH LETTERS.

f. 57. 20 July 1869, London, from J. L. Motley to J. A. Froude, declining an invitation and referring to his historical studies.

f. 64. 4 June 1898, from Bret Harte to Miss Froude, declining an invitation.

39855. CUMING, SIR ALEXANDER (1690?–1775). Autobiographical notes. 1 volume (42 folios).

Cuming went to South Carolina in Dec. 1729 and drew up a scheme for the reform of its currency system. In Mar. 1730 he crossed the Cherokee Mountains, and was received by the Cherokees as their law giver. He returned to England taking with him seven chiefs of the Cherokees. On 18 June 1730 he presented them to George II, who received their submission.

39869. MISCELLANEOUS PAPERS ON NAVAL MATTERS.

'Abstract of the general printed Sailing and Fighting Instructions and Vice-Admiral Arbuthnot's Additional Signals, 1779 . . . for the North American Station.' Arbuthnot was commander of the Station 1779–81.

f. 45. 'General observations on the coast of South Carolina': an account of bays, shoals, islands, &c., from Winyah Bay, S.C., to Tybee Island, Ga.

f. 49b. 'General observations on the weather on the coast of South Carolina.'

f. 50. Short accounts of 'Fishing ground'; Nantucket Island; George's Bank; . . . a shoal in Delaware Bay on which the *Santa Magritta* struck, 11 Dec. 1781.

39908. AUTOGRAPH LETTERS OF ALL THE PRESIDENTS OF THE UNITED STATES FROM WASHINGTON TO WILSON.

Up to and including Hayes, the letters are inlaid in a printed book, *The Presidents of America*, by H. W. Smith and John Fiske (Boston and New York, 1879).

The only letters of more than calligraphic interest are:

(a) 30 Nov. 1812, Headquarters (?), Franklinton, La., from William Henry Harrison to his father-in-law John C. Symmes of Cincinnati, Ohio, about provisioning the army in the North-West.

(b) 17 June 1817, Quincy, Mass., from John Adams to James Madison, on universal suffrage and on tyranny in Europe.

(c) 3 Mar. 1840, Washington, D.C., from John Quincy Adams to Nathaniel F. Williams of Baltimore, sending him two copies of the *National Intelligencer* containing Adams's two letters of 1839 to the petitioners 'who had entrusted me their petitions, memorials or remonstrances to the House of Representatives . . . during the preceding session of Congress', which session, he says, proved unsatisfactory 'to both the great parties to the slavery, abolition, and petition controversies'.

(*d*) 26 Mar. 1840, Nashville, Tenn., from James K. Polk to Samuel H. Loughlin, on the coming Democratic Convention in Baltimore.

(*e*) 2 Mar. 1843, Springfield, Ill., from Abraham Lincoln to Richard Symmes Thomas, Jr., about a rumour that Lincoln did not wish to be a candidate for Congress; a Bill forming electoral districts in Illinois. Suggests that Thomas become a delegate for his county to the district Congressional convention. Reports a Whig meeting, and has hopes that the Whigs will soon control the State of Illinois.[1]

(*f*) 27 Jan. 1845, Washington, D.C., John Tyler to his daughter, mentions his pleasure at the passage through the House of the joint resolution for annexing Texas, and hopes that it will pass the Senate.

(*g*) 13 Dec. 1851, Washington, D.C., from Andrew Johnson to A. O. P. Nicholson, on prospects for the 1852 Democratic Convention.

(*h*) 30 Apr. 1883, New York, from U. S. Grant to General Adam Badeau, on defensive potentialities of Havana. He thinks it would be easy for a first-class power, and especially the United States, to capture it in a war.

39954. OWEN, SIR RICHARD (1804–92).

Superintendent of the Natural History Department of the British Museum 1856–83.

Non-scientific correspondence: letters to Owen with some draft replies by him, *c.* 1838–89. Of American interest is his correspondence with James Russell Lowell, f. 636, and J. L. Motley, f. 493.

40108–22. HONE PAPERS.

40122

ff. 47, 50. Correspondence of French and Spanish diplomatists on the independence of the American colonies, consisting of English translations. Two brief notes, 10 Mar. 1778 and 27 May 1779. Although the above is the catalogue description, an endorsement on one of the manuscripts says that they are 'draft letters to King George III'. The first is slight; the second more important, relating to Spain's attitude to the conflict in America.

40177–80. GRENVILLE, GEORGE NUGENT-TEMPLE-, 1st Marquis of Buckingham (1753–1813).

Letter-books while he was Lord-Lieutenant of Ireland 1782–3 and 1787–9.

40177

Volume 1, 1782–3. Two letters to Lord North. The first, 19 May 1783, states that Grenville is enclosing a copy of a memorial of Messrs. Mitchell

---

[1] See *Collected Works of Abraham Lincoln*, ed. by R. P. Basler, vol. i, p. 309 (New Brunswick, N.J., 1953).

and Anderson, Dublin merchants, concerning the export of wines to 'Charlestown in America', to be submitted to H.M. Commissioners of Revenue. The subject of the memorial, he says, affects the whole commercial intercourse 'between this kingdom and America'. With the second letter, 30 May 1783, he sends the Commissioners' report to North, and in both letters he says that, as the law now stands in Ireland, all trade with America is precluded on any other footing than that of a foreign nation.

40181–617. PEEL PAPERS.

Papers of Sir Robert Peel (1788–1850), statesman. (*Letters unless otherwise stated.*)

40192

ff. 176–8. Numbers of Irish emigrants to America, 1813–16.

40312

f. 81. 14 Dec. 1829, London, from Peel to Aberdeen, in which he doubts the wisdom of allowing American students unrestricted access to the State Papers, as their study may exacerbate anti-British feeling in America. (Copy.)

f. 83. 31 Dec. 1829, London, from Peel to Aberdeen, asking for statistics of British trade with the United States. (Copy.)

f. 114. 27 July 1830, Foreign Office, from Aberdeen to Peel, and Peel's reply, Whitehall, 28 July 1830. (Copies.) On a note from Mr. McLane, the American Minister, concerning Anglo-United States trade.

f. 294. 14 Feb. 1838, Argyll House, from Aberdeen to Peel, on the North-East boundary question as it stood in 1830, and the arbitral award of the King of the Netherlands in 1831.

40333

f. 32. Remarks by J. D. Hume on duties upon United States goods, 1828. (Copy.)

40365

f. 12. *Education for the Ministry in the American Episcopal Church*, 1824. (Printed.)

40455

Correspondence, 1845–6 *passim*, between Aberdeen and Peel on Oregon, Mexico, California, and tariffs.

40464

f. 335. Memorandum on trade with the United States, by Lord Ashburton, 1843.

40467

f. 302. Statement of wheat exported from the United States to Britain through Canada, 1842.

40468

ff. 209–13. Stanley to Peel, 5 Sept. 1845, and Peel to Stanley, 7 Sept. 1845, on Canadian-American relations and defence of the Great Lakes.

40469

f. 278. Memoranda concerning the trade and resources of the United States, 1841, 1842. Contain some statistics, e.g. the number of persons employed in manufacturing and agriculture; investments in woollen and cotton manufactures, &c. Describes high and low tariff groups; production of wheat, &c.; prospects of British trade with Illinois, &c., via the Mississippi (endorsed 'from General Duff Green').

f. 282. London, 6 Oct. 1842, from General Green to J. Macgregor, on American high-tariff agitation.

40492

f. 306. 22 Oct. 1841, from Ashburton to Peel, on Daniel Webster and the British Minister, Henry Fox.

40497

f. 382. Headed 'England and America No. 1'. Treatise, with statistics of Anglo-United States trade, 1835–40, on the United States tariff, especially as it affects Britain, with several comments on the American production of corn.

40500

ff. 239–44. 20 Jan. 1842, from Lord Ashburton to Peel, written just before Ashburton's departure for the United States, where he was to negotiate the Webster–Ashburton Treaty, enclosing a paper headed 'The case of the *Creole*', concerning American ships carrying slaves from Virginia to Louisiana putting into British West Indian ports because of bad weather, &c., or slave revolt on board.

There are no letters from Ashburton while in the United States.

40511

ff. 114–33. Letters and papers from James Buchanan, Consul at New York, consisting of a printed pamphlet by Buchanan (published anonymously), *War with England* (New York, 1838), on averting war over Canadian border incidents; two letters, June 1842, from Buchanan to Peel and Edward Drummond on his retirement and on emigration to Canada; a printed pamphlet by Buchanan on this latter subject, *Letter to . . . Sir Charles Bagot* (New York, 1842); and an 1842 clipping from the Quebec *Gazette* of a letter of Buchanan's on emigration.

40516

ff. 115–17. 28 Sept. 1842, from Peel congratulating Ashburton on the success of the mission, and one of Ashburton's thanks in reply.

40517

ff. 1–10: 13, 16, and 22 Oct. 1842; and 40492, f. 250: 18 Oct. 1842 [a misplaced letter]. There is some correspondence on the subject of a suitable honour to be awarded to Ashburton in recognition of his services in the United States.

40523

f. 99. New York, 3 Nov. 1842, from J. Horsley Palmer, Governor of the Bank of England, to Walter Forward, United States Secretary of the Treasury, relating to United States currency, &c., and the possible measures to improve American banking and currency systems in the absence of a Bank of the United States.

40526

f. 432. Washington, D.C., 29 Mar. 1843, from Daniel Webster, then Secretary of State, to Edward Everett, Minister to Britain, on a possible commercial treaty between Britain and the United States, and Webster's views on the tariff.

40562

ff. 292, 293. Memoranda on prices of Louisiana sugar, 1845.

40563

f. 394. Memorandum relative to the Oregon boundary question, 1845.

40574

ff. 380–5b. Two letters from Edward Everett to Peel. The first, Boston, 29 Sept. 1845, on his voyage home at the termination of his service as Minister to Britain, the good grain harvest and poor potato crop of the United States in 1845. The second letter, Boston, 28 Nov. 1845, again mentions crops, recession of the threat of a Mexican war, and his assumption of the presidency of Harvard. Peel's reply, Drayton Manor, 16 Oct. 1845, mentions the bad state of the potato crop, especially in Ireland.

There is a great deal of correspondence between Everett and Peel, 1837–48, and especially during Everett's term as Minister 1841–5, but most of them are no more than slight notes. (See 40423, 40504, 40518, 40520, 40524, 40528, 40531, 40532, 40534, 40540, 40547, 40554, 40556, 40557, 40559, 40562, 40565, 40566, 40569, 40571, 40597, 40600.)

f. 448. Report on the United States harvest, 1845, with remarks on potato disease.

f. 448b. *Prices current of grain, flour, and meal in the United States, 1845.* (Printed.)

40576

f. 87. Copy of a dispatch, Washington, D.C., 13 Sept. 1845, from Sir Richard Pakenham, British Minister to the United States 1843–7, to

Aberdeen, in which he gives the opinions of the American Secretary of the Treasury as to the probable influence of the elections of 1844 on the tariff. Secretary Walker believes that the new House will have a low tariff majority, but local issues will, as always, complicate the voting. Walker also believes the present tariff to be detrimental to revenue.

40581

ff. 425–31. Official correspondence of the United States with Britain relative to the slave trade, 1843. (Printed.)

ff. 432, 434. Everett's dispatches, both undated, to Webster and H. S. Legaré, on slave trade.

40588

ff. 70–71. Copy of a letter, 19 Jan. 1846, from F. C. Matthiesson, Charleston, S.C., to Thomas Bazley, Manchester, concerning tariffs and Anglo-American relations; forwarded to Peel by Edward Tootal.

ff. 161–8. Three letters, 1846, from Robert Owen to Peel, concerning the Oregon question.

40590

f. 338. 28 Apr. 1846, from Everett to Peel, mentions Oregon question.

40602

f. 28. Letter relative to gold diggings in California, 1849. (Printed.)

40611

ff. 117–50. Papers relative to the North-West boundary negotiations, 1824–6. (Printed.)

40612

f. 117b. 'A statistical account of the population, product, &c. of the United States of America for the year 1840 distinguishing each state.' Gives for each state: number of senators; number of representatives in this and 'the next' Congress; population in 1820 and 1840; area; capital invested in manufactures of wool and cotton; production in 1840 of wheat, oats, Indian corn, meat cattle, swine, cotton and tobacco; number of persons employed in trades and agriculture. (Apparently sent to Peel by Gladstone in 1842.)

40690. MISCELLANEOUS PAPERS. (*Letters.*)

f. 21. Middlebrook, 5 Apr. 1779, from George Washington to George Clinton, Governor of New York, concerning the movement of troops from Minisinck, N.Y.[1]

[1] See *Writings of George Washington*, ed. by John C. Fitzpatrick, vol. xiv, pp. 337–8 (Washington, D.C., 1936).

f. 23. West Point, N.Y., 10 Oct. 1779, from Washington to Clinton, concerning preparations for an expedition against New York.[1]

f. 27. Philadelphia, 18 Jan. 1781, from Major-General Baron von Steuben, offering an appointment as aide-de-camp to Major Benjamin Walker.

ff. 87–110. To, and relating to, Dr. J. G. Cogswell, Superintendent of the Astor Library, New York, largely written during his visits to Europe to purchase books for the Library, 1825–58. Among the writers are W. H. Prescott, Washington Irving, and Edward Everett. Mostly slight personal notes, also some enclosing books or about forthcoming publications or reviews.

40760. FRANCIS PAPERS, vol. v.

Letters and papers of, and relating to, the Rev. Philip Francis (1708?–73) and his son, Sir Philip Francis (1740–1818).

ff. 220–70. Correspondence,[2] 9 Nov. 1755–5 Sept. 1756, of Major-General William Shirley, Governor of Massachusetts Bay, with Henry Fox, William Wildman Barrington, Major-General Sir William Johnson, Horatio Sharpe, Governor of Maryland; Major-General James Abercromby, Commander-in-Chief North America 1758, and John Campbell, 4th Earl of Loudon. (All copies.)

41064. QUIETUS TO 'JAMES (EDWARD) OGLETHORPE, ESQ., General and Commander-in-Chief of His Majesty's Forces in South Carolina and Georgia in America upon his account thereof between the 22nd of September 1738 and Michaelmas 1743'.

Official certified copy from the record in the Roll of Foreign Accounts of 32 Geo. III at the Pipe Office. Oglethorpe's bills were disputed by the Treasury and the account was not settled until 25 Feb. 1792, more than four years after his death. Vellum roll, 1792.

41178. MISCELLANEOUS LETTERS AND PAPERS.

D.f. 19. Brief letter, London, 26 Sept. 1870, from Jefferson Davis to George Bryan Jennings, of personal interest only.

E.f. 26. Letter, 16 May 1854, from Nathaniel Hawthorne, as United States Consul at Liverpool, to James Buchanan, United States Minister in London, protesting against the levying of British income tax on his consular fees. There is also a letter, 19 May 1854, from Lord Clarendon, as Foreign Secretary, to James Wilson, Financial Secretary to the Treasury, requesting that immediate attention be paid to Hawthorne's claim.

---

[1] *Writings of George Washington*, ed. by John C. Fitzpatrick, vol. xvi, pp. 452–3.
[2] Most of these letters are printed in *Correspondence of William Shirley*, ed. C. H. Lincoln, 2 vols. (New York, 1912).

41206–52. CAMPBELL-BANNERMAN PAPERS.

Letters of Sir Henry Campbell-Bannerman (1836–1908), Prime Minister 1905–8.

41211

f. 284. New York, 7 Oct. 1904, from James Bryce to Campbell-Bannerman, says that Roosevelt is expected to win the 1904 election.

ff. 359, 369. 26 Dec. 1906, 17 Jan. 1907, 8 Apr. 1908, from Bryce to Campbell-Bannerman, on the appointment of Bryce as British Ambassador to the United States, and a letter (copy) 28 Dec. 1906, from Campbell-Bannerman to Bryce. In the letter of 8 Apr. 1908 Bryce regrets that Campbell-Bannerman has had to resign.

41295. MISCELLANEOUS PAPERS.

f. 20. Certificate by John Wesley to Richard Whatcoat and Thomas Vasey of their appointment as Elders for the work of the ministry in America, 2 Sept. 1784.

41340. MISCELLANEOUS PAPERS.

f. 125. Letter, 10 Feb. 1913, from Henry James to Miss E. Lea, giving his opinion (which is unfavourable) of 'Ouida' (Marie Louise de la Ramée).

41346–41475. MARTIN PAPERS.

Papers of the Martin family, planters of Antigua, 1714–1878, including many late eighteenth- and nineteenth-century naval papers (but not the War of 1812). There is possibly more scattered Americana in this large collection.

41352

'Letter-book of Josiah Martin, the elder, originally of Antigua, but after 9 July 1739 of "Rockhall" Far Rockaway, Long Island, North America', 19 Mar. 1729–8 Dec. 1740. Also some accounts.

41361

Correspondence, 21 Dec. 1752–19 Nov. 1785, of Josiah Martin (nephew of Josiah, the elder; see 41352), Governor of North Carolina 1771–6, mainly with his brother, Samuel Martin, junior. The letters are chiefly concerned with Josiah's financial difficulties, from which Samuel had often to rescue his brother. Samuel's influence obtains for Josiah the governorship of North Carolina, but Josiah continues to plead for money and further offices. The letters, mostly written in the 1770's, also touch on the defection of New York from the other colonies and their reproaches of it—especially recriminations between Boston and New York; sale of patents by the governor of New York; boundary disputes between New York and Connecticut; riots in North Carolina under his predecessor Tryon; the revenues of the various colonies;

his flight to a warship in Cape Fear River, N.C., in 1775; his return to Long Island; and the expedition of General Clinton to invade South Carolina, which army Josiah accompanied.

41567. MISCELLANEOUS PAPERS.

ff. 212–47b. Sixteen letters, 3 Apr. 1861–31 Mar. 1863, from George Henry Herbert, of Newcastle-upon-Tyne, while serving with the Northern Army in the Civil War, to his relatives in England. Herbert served first in Virginia under General Butler and took part in the attack upon Fort Hatteras. While later stationed at Roanoke Island he gives a very favourable picture of Union prospects in the early part of 1862. Subsequently there are descriptions of the evacuation of Fredericksburg, the preliminaries to the battle of Antietam, and the battle of South Mountain. He describes in much detail the 'thrashing' taken by the Federals at the battle of Fredericksburg. Early in 1863 his attitude is one of disillusionment—'instead of fighting for a principle, we are fighting for a set of scheming politicians, army contractors and would-be Generals'.

41760. GREVILLE LETTERS.

Twenty letters, London (and one from Paris), 15 June 1855–10 June 1856, from Charles Cavendish Fulke Greville (1794–1865), the diarist, to Sir Charles Ash Windham serving in the Crimea. Deal, *inter alia*, with differences with America, chiefly the activities of British recruiting agents in the United States, which in the spring of 1856 seemed likely to threaten war.

42083–8. GRENVILLE PAPERS.

Some 500 original letters of the Grenville family, 1767–77, chiefly of Richard Temple Grenville, afterwards Grenville-Temple, Earl Temple (1711–99), but also of his brother George (1712–70), including the latter's political diary.

This correspondence of the author of the Stamp Act and his brother contains many glancing references to the American question amid letters predominately on other topics. Only the specifically American items are noted below since the diary and most of the correspondence have been published in *The Grenville Papers*, ed. W. J. Smith, 4 vols. (London, 1852–3). (*Letters unless otherwise stated.*)

42083

The political diary of George Grenville, 1761–8. It contains only a few brief references to parliamentary debates on American affairs, 1765–7.

42084–7

28 Feb. 1767, from the Earl of Suffolk to George Grenville on the Duke of Bedford's motion in the House of Lords for all correspondence of the several governors in America.

17 July 1768, from George Grenville to Mr. Pownall, on the possibility of seating American members in the House of Commons; also the general situation in America.

15 Oct. 1768, from Commodore Hood to George Grenville on the extension of his American command, and his probable dispositions in view of the threatening state of affairs in America; also the landing of Gage's troops at Boston.

27 Oct. 1768, from Mr. Whately to George Grenville, on prospects of revolution at Boston (*see also* same to same, 28 Oct. 1768).

1 Nov. 1768, from Mr. Knox to George Grenville, says 'the revolt of New England is now unquestionable'.

7 Nov. 1768, from John Temple, a Commissioner of Customs at Boston, to George Grenville, on his disagreeable position.

15 Dec. 1768, from Knox to George Grenville, on negotiations with the colonies over the Townshend Duties.

3 Jan. 1769, from Whately to George Grenville, on the spread of disaffection to Virginia and South Carolina.

15 Apr. 1769, from Hood to George Grenville, on the former's forbearance in order not to exacerbate American feeling.

5 Aug. 1769, from Whately to George Grenville, on a report that the troops are retiring from Boston.

2 Sept. 1769, from Hood to Earl Temple, on the worsening situation at Boston over the duties.

19 Sept. 1769, from Knox to George Grenville, mentions the duties.

22 Sept. 1769, from Whately to George Grenville, on a report by ex-Governor Bernard on the situation in Massachusetts.

3 Dec. 1769, from Whately to George Grenville, on a plan for an American parliament; also on American non-importation.

24 Sept. 1777, from Lord Chatham to Temple, in which he says, whatever the result of the conflict with the colonists, 'poor England will have fallen upon her own sword'.

42257–496. STEVENS TRANSCRIPTS.

Benjamin Franklin Stevens (1833–1902), an American bookman and antiquarian, devoted many years to collecting transcripts of papers and letters relating to American history between 1744 and 1784. The transcripts, which amount to somewhere between 45,000 and 50,000 leaves, are taken from various sources, including the British Museum, the Public Record Office, French and Dutch archives; but the greater portion are from private collections, particularly the Lansdowne[1] and Carleton[2] Papers. However, these papers in the British Museum are only some of the raw materials for the various series of transcripts now housed in the Library of Congress. There is a very incomplete index which accompanied the deposit.

42711. MISCELLANEOUS PAPERS.

P. Eighteen letters, unbound, 1845–57, from Sir Austen Henry Layard to Miner K. Kellogg, the American artist and art critic. Mainly about archaeology and art in general, but there is a little about American art.

---

[1] Now in the William L. Clements Library, Ann Arbor, Mich.
[2] Now in the Public Record Office, London.

There are seven letters, 1845–57, in the LAYARD PAPERS—Add. MSS. 38976, ff. 222, 373; 38977, f. 355; 38983, f. 75.

43039–358. ABERDEEN PAPERS.

George Hamilton Gordon, 4th Earl of Aberdeen (1784–1860), statesman. While Foreign Secretary 1841–6, he negotiated the Oregon Treaty of 1846.

There may be other smaller items of Americana amid this large collection, but the principal American papers appear to be:

43121

Letter-book containing abstracts or copies of the official dispatches to the British Minister in the United States, Charles Vaughan, June 1828–Nov. 1829 (32 pages). Mentions Mexican affairs; the Canadian boundary islands —their division between the United States and Britain under the Treaty of Ghent; the North-Eastern boundary arbitration under the convention of 1827; detention at Key West, Fla., of slaves taken from a Spanish vessel by a British ship.

43122

As 43121 above, from Vaughan, May–June 1828 (13 pages). Appointment of American arbitrators on North-Eastern boundary; the Tariff of 1828; opposition in Congress to wishes of John Quincy Adams; slowness of Britain in handing over boundary islands allotted to the United States by the Treaty of Ghent.

43123

Diplomatic correspondence and papers relating to the United States, 1841–6, arranged as follows:

f. 1. Correspondence, described as mainly 'private', of Aberdeen as Foreign Secretary, with Ashburton, chiefly concerning the latter's special mission to the United States as negotiator of the Webster–Ashburton Treaty.

f. 212. Similar correspondence with Henry Stephen Fox, Nov. 1841– Nov. 1843, and Richard Pakenham, Oct. 1843–July 1846, successive British Ministers to the United States. The correspondence with Pakenham relates to the settlement of the Oregon question.

f. 312. Correspondence, Apr. 1842–Aug. 1845, with William Peter, Thomas Colley Grattan, and William Ogilby, British Consuls at Philadelphia, Boston, and Charleston, S.C., respectively.

f. 370. Correspondence, Oct. 1841–Oct. 1846, with Andrew Stevenson, Edward Everett, and Louis McLane, successively American Ministers to Britain.

43126

Correspondence of Aberdeen, with:

f. 31. Captain Charles Elliot, British Chargé d'Affaires in Texas, Sept. 1842–May 1846.

f. 88. William Kennedy, British Consul at Galveston, Tex., Sept. 1841–July 1844.

f. 113. General James Hamilton and General G. W. Terrell, successively Plenipotentiaries in London for the Republic of Texas, Oct. 1841–Sept. 1842, and June 1845.

43154

Letter-book containing abstracts or copies of the official dispatches which were sent by Aberdeen to the successive British Ministers to the United States, Fox and Pakenham, Sept. 1841–May 1846. The subject most frequently touched upon is that of the division of Oregon, over which relations can be seen worsening after the accession of Polk to the presidency; and the Disputed Territory Fund. Other subjects represented are the McLeod trial; the investigation by British warships of suspected slavers flying the American flag; the Ashburton mission and Webster–Ashburton Treaty; the *Creole* case (in which slaves bound for New Orleans took control of the ship transporting them and sailed it to Nassau); attacks by American citizens on British vessels on the Great Lakes; Texas, and especially slavery there.

43155

Letter-book containing abstracts or copies of the official dispatches which were sent to Aberdeen by the successive British Ministers to the United States, Aug. 1841–June 1846. In addition to the topics dealt with in 43154, including considerably more about the McLeod trial and Texas, there are remarks about Tyler's break with his Cabinet and party in Congress; various messages, Bills, &c., for which several letters are covers; joint Anglo-American naval action for the suppression of the slave trade—the whole-heartedness of the United States in this is suspect; the occupation of Monterey, Calif., by American naval forces under the impression that war with Mexico had broken out; Hawaii.

43356

Confidential memoranda and papers printed during Aberdeen's tenure of the office of Foreign Secretary for Cabinet use, dealing with the United States—i.e. North-West boundary and Canadian fisheries.

43357

Similar to 43356, concerning the slave trade.

43377. MISCELLANEOUS PAPERS.

H. Slight note, 26 Oct. 1904, from Theodore Roosevelt to Edmund Lauterbach.

43383–92. JOHN BRIGHT PAPERS.

John Bright (1811–89), radical leader, M.P. for Durham, Manchester, and Birmingham 1843–85. Two volumes of his correspondence consist of letters from the United States and from American representatives in Europe, nearly all from supporters of the Federal cause during the Civil War, expressing their gratitude for Bright's advocacy of the Northern cause in opposition to the general trend of British opinion, and discussing the progress of the war. Other volumes contain occasional references to American affairs.

43390

ff. 1–49. Thirteen letters, 1861–8, from John Bigelow, first from France and then from America. He discusses, *inter alia*, French attitudes and policies to the Civil War; Gladstone's unfriendly attitude to the North (sending Bright a list of subscribers to the Confederate Cotton Loan in England for him to verify if Gladstone's name properly belonged there); the building of Confederate ships in England; and sends copies of letters concerning the Southern Independence Association in Britain.

ff. 50–122. Seventeen letters, 1853–87, from Edward L. Pierce, ranging through topical political events, particularly Massachusetts' politics and the problem of the ex-slaves. Also much on Charles Sumner, of whom Pierce wrote a biography.

ff. 123–286. Sixty-four letters, 1861–8, from Sumner; also enclosures of letters to Sumner by various people, including William H. Seward. They discuss, *inter alia*, Sumner's irritation with Britain's attitude during the Civil War; the *Trent* incident; emancipation (Lincoln holds back because of the border states); removal of McClellan; criticism of Seward; disputes in Lincoln's Cabinet over naval policy; British building of ships for the Confederacy (Sumner appears prepared to have the North go to war with Britain); case of Alfred Ruberg, a Birmingham youth imprisoned for 'piracy' against the North and later pardoned by Lincoln at Bright's request; Sumner's and Lincoln's plans for reconstruction of conquered Confederate states; the presidential campaign of 1864; *Alabama* claims; confiscation and break-up of large plantations; Lord Lyons and strained Anglo-American relations; armed vessels on the Lakes; possible effect of death of Lincoln on national affairs; his (Sumner's) belief that Andrew Johnson is in agreement with Sumner's policy on reconstruction, and his later 'immense disappointment' in Johnson; American finances after the war; rumours of an American expedition against the French in Mexico; the 'folly' of Johnson's plans for reconstruction; the struggle between President and Congress over reconstruction in 1866; the Philadelphia 'Union' Convention of 1866; Sumner's opinion, 1868, that Johnson 'is as bad as J. D. [Jefferson Davis]'; the currency question in 1868.

43391

The whole volume consists of miscellaneous letters, 12 Jan. 1853–14 Oct. 1887, to Bright from Americans. The correspondents include Charles

Francis Adams, Henry Adams, George Bancroft, Salmon P. Chase, Schuyler Colfax, Neal Dow, Dorman B. Eaton, William M. Evarts, Cyrus W. Field, Horace Greeley, Reverdy Johnson, Hugh McCulloch, John Lothrop Motley, Charles Eliot Norton, George Peabody, G. P. Putnam, William H. Seward, Governor James Smith of Rhode Island, Lewis Tappan, Amasa Walker, John Greenleaf Whittier.

Most of the letters are for the Civil War years and express gratitude to Bright for his advocacy of the Northern cause, and communicate views on the progress of the struggle.

43392

Contains miscellaneous memoranda, notes for speeches, &c., by Bright, including:

f. 131. An extract 'from a letter of Jefferson's—March 1810', on the characters of the sovereigns reigning while he was in Europe.

f. 159. Notes, n.d., on the size of the United States and of various states, and a comparison in size with European nations.

f. 170. *Considerations on the Military Position of Great Britain with respect to the United States*, 28 May 1869. (Printed.) A review of the defence potentialities of Canada, against any possible American attack.

43510–644. RIPON PAPERS.

The papers of George Frederick Samuel Robinson, 2nd Earl and 1st Marquess of Ripon (1827–1909), who, as Earl de Grey, was chairman of the Joint High Commission on the *Alabama* and other claims, which drew up the Treaty of Washington, 1871.

Letters mentioning the claims are found scattered throughout the non-Indian portion of the Papers; the more important of these groups are noted below. In addition, the Papers include letters from Thomas Hughes (*see* 43548–9).

43510

Contains two draft memos, 29 May 1872, by Ripon to the Queen on matters arising from the Treaty of Washington.

43514

ff. 78, 81, 102, 104. Correspondence with Gladstone, 1870–8. Contains four letters, 3 Apr.–28 Nov. 1871, on the dismissal of Sumner from the chairmanship of the Senate Foreign Relations Committee; Macdonald and the Canadian fisheries; and claims of British holders of Confederate Bonds.

43519

ff. 110–212, *passim*. Correspondence, 27 Feb. 1871–12 Mar. 1873, with Sir Stafford Northcote (with an enclosure from Lord Lisgar to Northcote,

6 May 1871, on Sir John Macdonald), on the Treaty of Washington, the claims, the Geneva Arbitration, Fenians, &c.

43528

ff. 1–88. Correspondence, 7 Feb. 1871–4 Dec. 1872, with Lord Tenterden. Mostly from Tenterden to Ripon, a few written while they were both serving on the Joint High Commission at Washington in 1871, but most subsequent to their return. On rules laid down in the Treaty of Washington, the indirect claims, and the Geneva Arbitration.

43542

f. 17. Letter, 22 Sept. 1902, from James Bryce to Ripon, on Andrew Carnegie's method of making benefactions.

43548–9

Correspondence, 1857–88, of Lord and Lady Ripon with Thomas Hughes, including a letter from Hughes, 14 Nov. 1870, concerning his meeting in Boston with Julian Harney, the Chartist poet, and a number in 1880–1 concerning his Rugby, Tenn., venture.

43621–40. General correspondence of Ripon, 1849–1909.

43622

A few letters, Apr. 1863–Feb. 1871, concerning de Grey's arrival in America, chiefly of the welcome he received, but also including one from Thornton, the British Minister, on meeting the President, and a long one from Edward Armstrong of New York on the *Alabama* claims, in which he says that the replacement of wood by iron is the chief cause of the American shipping decline.

43623

Letters, Mar.–May 1871, almost all from Americans; mainly slight notes including some from Bayard, Edmunds, Fish, Schurz, and Sumner. Numerous begging letters and invitations to attend masonic functions; also letters from Mrs. Jane P. Thurston, who claims to own the state of Maine. Chiefly important for several letters from Sir John Macdonald on the Canadian viewpoint in the Washington negotiations, and a few from people setting forth their reactions to the Treaty.

43624

Letters, June 1871–Apr. 1872, including letters from Macdonald on Canadian indignation over the Treaty of Washington; correspondence with Fish and Bernard; and references to the indirect claims.

43625

Letters, May 1872–Dec. 1875, including correspondence with Bernard, Rush, Cyrus W. Field, Thornton, &c.; copies of letters to Bayard; letters on the Johnson–Clarendon Convention, the British case at Geneva, the indirect claims controversy, the Clayton–Bulwer Treaty, the proceedings at Geneva; several letters of congratulation at the dropping by the United States of the indirect claims; also a letter of 'Washington gossip', Dec. 1872, from Henry Stafford Northcote, including an explanation of how Horace Greeley received the Liberal Republican nomination in 1872.

43647–78. COBDEN PAPERS.

Richard Cobden (1804–65), statesman.

There may be more odd items of Americana in this large, unindexed collection, but the principal items appear to be those listed below.

43659

Letters from Cobden to the Rev. Henry Richard:

f. 83. London, 12 July 1861, on the blockade of the South and its effect on cotton supplies.

f. 86. Midhurst, 17 Aug. 1861, commenting that the Federal Government is more accommodating since Bull Run, and mentioning Northern taxes.

ff. 102, 131. Midhurst, 17 Oct. and 7 Dec. 1861, on the blockade.

ff. 126, 138, 140, 142. Midhurst, 3 and 18 Dec. 1861 and 10 Jan. 1862, on the *Trent* incident.

43676

ff. 79–104. Typed copies of letters, 28 May 1861–5 Jan. 1862, from Richard Cobden to John Slagg, mainly on the Northern blockade, the cotton famine, and the *Trent* incident.

ff. 115–58, *passim*. Typed copies of letters, 9 May 1862–12 Feb. 1865, from Cobden to Slagg, chiefly on cotton, and on European sympathy for the Confederacy. Also, f. 139, a letter from H. Sanford to Cobden which says that the North lacks 'grim earnestness' and has not really felt the war yet, but will not terminate the conflict until the whole South submits.

ff. 159–260. Typed copies of letters, Mar. 1848–Mar. 1865, from Cobden to Charles Sumner, on 'peace campaigns'; Brooks's attack on Sumner; recession (Cobden regrets that the North did not let the South go in peace, but admits obstacles to this course); the capture of Mason and Slidell; cotton; maritime disputes and precedents (especially of right of search, and blockade); confusion of British opinion over the Civil War; American tariffs; the necessity of lifting the Northern blockade, which is bringing misery to Europe and turning people against the North; desirability of Northern recognition of the South as a belligerent; strained Anglo-American relations after the *Trent* incident; British sympathy with emancipation; building of Confederate ships in Britain; Sumner's denunciation of Britain and France in 1863; the arming of Negroes; the character of Lincoln; the Thirteenth Amendment. There are a few slight American references in the letters of Cobden to Ed. Alexander, Jr., which comprise the rest of the volume.

43677

ff. 78–84. Typed copies of letters, from Cobden to Henry Catt. In the first, 16 Dec. 1861, Cobden regrets that he cannot attend a meeting of Brighton working men called to deplore the possibility of war with the United States, and argues in favour of arbitration. In the second, 18 Dec. 1861, he advises the working men to send a memorial in favour of arbitration to Palmerston.

43678

A few letters from Americans about Cobden, written after his death.
    See also 43807–8.

43688. MISCELLANEOUS LETTERS.

U. 29 Dec. 1890, Oliver Wendell Holmes, Sen., to F. D. Flory of London.
    Y. Papers described as 'a collection of American literary autographs'. There are eight in all, but only five of the letters appear to be from American literary figures—all poets. They are: Fitz-Greene Halleck, New York, 29 Dec. 1826, to J. W. Olcott, a slight note on financial matters. Paul H. Hayne, Augusta, Ga., n.d., to an unknown correspondent, about a cheque. Charles Fenno Hoffman to R. W. Griswold, no place, n.d., about Sir Walter Scott. Sidney Lanier, Macon, Ga., 21 Aug. 1867, to his publishers. Henry Timrod, Orangeburg, S.C., 10 Apr. 1856, to Oscar Keeler, enclosing a stanza.

43722. STURGE PAPERS.

Joseph Sturge (1793–1859), Quaker philanthropist and abolitionist.
    Two letters from Richard Cobden to Sturge:

f. 122. 7 June 1856, on Anglo-American differences, war fears, and the evil influence of *The Times* on Anglo-American relations.

f. 320. 3 July 1859, comparing American banking and railroad management with British.

43742. MONCK, SIR CHARLES STANLEY, 4th Viscount and 1st Baron Monck (1819–94).

Governor General of Canada 1861–8.
    Letters, 1867–8, from Lord Monck and others to the 3rd Duke of Buckingham and Chandos, mainly on a reported threat of an invasion of Canada by Fenians from the United States. (*See also* 41860.)

43807–8. COBDEN, RICHARD (1804–65). Diaries in America,[1] 1835 and 1859.

---

[1] *The American Diaries of Richard Cobden,* ed. by Elizabeth H. Cawley, with an introductio (Princeton, N.J., 1952.)

43841. ACCOUNT BOOK OF THE CAPTAIN OF THE *MONGOVO GEORGE*, a Liverpool schooner, while engaged in the slave trade, 1785-7.

Entries, June 1785-Jan. 1786, detail various purchases of slaves on the west coast of Africa; and, reversing the volume, the subsequent sales in America, Oct. 1786-Apr. 1787. Also included is a copy of instructions left with a mercantile house in New Orleans, authorizing the firm to collect moneys due the slaver in America and to remit them to William Denison, a Liverpool merchant.

43846. TRISTAN DA CUNHA RECORDS.

A collection of documents, 1817-21, relating to the annexation and colonization of this island due to its having been used as a raiding base by United States cruisers during the War of 1812. The documents are printed and described by D. M. Gane in 'The Early Records of Tristan da Cunha; the discovery in New London', *United Empire*, vol. xxiv, pp. 589-98, 651-8, 709-13, 1933.

43874-967. DILKE PAPERS.

The papers of Sir Charles Wentworth Dilke (1843-1911) were not available for inspection in 1958.[1] From his book, *Greater Britain: a Record of Travel in English-Speaking Countries during 1866-1867* (London, 1868), American correspondence would be expected. Roy Jenkins, M.P., has, however, made use of these papers in *Sir Charles Dilke, a Victorian tragedy* (London, 1958).

44085. MISCELLANEOUS PAPERS.

C. Letter, 1794, written from America by Samuel Hart, an English settler in New Jersey. Deals with land and crops, and describes outbreak of yellow fever.

44086-835. GLADSTONE PAPERS.

The papers of William Ewart Gladstone (1809-98) comprise some 750 volumes, the largest collection of any Prime Minister found in the British Museum. The following list relies almost entirely on the special and separately printed *Catalogue of the Gladstone Papers* (London, 1953); and the following is by no means complete, for Gladstone had numerous minor American correspondents—but most of these can be readily located in the admirable index to the *Catalogue*. (*Letters unless otherwise stated.*)

44133-4. Correspondence with Clarendon.

44133

ff. 194-229 *passim*. 28 Feb., 22 and 26 Mar., 15 and 20 May 1869, from Clarendon to Gladstone on Reverdy Johnson and the *Alabama* claims convention.

[1] These papers have now been catalogued.

44134

ff. 64–166 *passim*, ff. 201–5. 15 and 23 Oct., 24 and 27 Nov., 4 and 24 Dec. 1869; 18 and 23 Jan., 17 Mar., 15 and 18 May 1870, Clarendon to Gladstone on the claims, negotiations over which were at a standstill after the Senate's rejection of the Johnson–Clarendon Convention.

44136

ff. 146–75 *passim*, ff. 248–74 *passim*. Correspondence with Cobden. Ten letters, six from Cobden to Gladstone, 11 Dec. 1861–20 Feb. 1865, and four from Gladstone to Cobden, 13 Dec. 1861–22 Feb. 1865. Include a long letter from Cobden pleading with Gladstone to use his influence against war with the United States over the *Trent* incident. Also letters on emancipation in the border states; the Northern blockade; the proposed Atlantic cable; a comparison of the British and American navies; the defence of Canada and armaments on the Great Lakes.

44168

Correspondence with Granville.[1]

ff. 36, 62, 114–17, 229, 246–80 *passim*. Twelve letters, 27 Jan. 1871–30 June 1872, mostly from Gladstone to Granville, but including letters from Granville to Gladstone; Granville to Northcote; Sir Alexander Cockburn, British arbitrator at the Geneva Convention, 1872, to Granville; and Robert Schenck, United States Minister in London, to Granville. Chiefly on appointments to the Washington Commission; the Treaty of Washington; the indirect claims; and the Geneva Arbitration.

44183

Correspondence with Edmund Hammond, permanent Under-Secretary for Foreign Affairs 1854–73.

ff. 438, 472. Two letters from Hammond to Gladstone. The first, 26 Mar. 1869, on a draft to be sent to Thornton, presumably on the Claims Convention, altered at Bright's suggestion, and on American activities off Cuba. The second, 3 Sept. 1872, on the Geneva award.

44217

Correspondence with Sir Stafford Henry Northcote, Conservative leader in the House of Commons, and member of the Washington Commission.

ff. 115–37. Four letters (and one enclosure from Lord Lisgar to Northcote), Washington, D.C., 17 Mar.–21 Apr. 1871, from Northcote to Gladstone. Deal with the San Juan question; Canadian fisheries and reciprocity; the committee system of Congress; the *Alabama* claims; the danger to a settlement arising from the adjournment of the Senate between April and May.

---

[1] Printed in *The Political Correspondence of Mr. Gladstone and Lord Granville, 1868–1876*, ed. by Agatha Ramm, 2 vols. (London, 1952).

44249

f. 49. Newark, N.J., 16 Apr. 1868, from James Roosevelt Bayley, Roman Catholic Bishop of Newark, to Cardinal Manning, on American attitudes on the Irish question and its effect on Anglo-American relations.

44272

Correspondence with Palmerston. Two letters, 9 Jan. and 24 Sept. 1862, from Palmerston to Gladstone; two letters, 25 Sept. 1862 and 8 Oct. 1863, from Gladstone to Palmerston. Deal with the *Trent* incident. Palmerston suggests and Gladstone agrees that the time has come to offer mediation in conjunction with France and Russia, and that, should the North refuse and the South accept, Britain should recognize Southern independence; in his 1863 letter Gladstone says that the Queen 'did not appear to lean towards over-reconciliation of the Federal government' in the rams issue.

44285

Correspondence, 1887–97, with William Henry Rideing, editor of the *North American Review*.

44286

Correspondence with Earl de Grey, later 2nd Earl and 1st Marquess of Ripon, Chairman of the Joint High Commission.

ff. 110–14. Letter, 21 Mar. 1871, from de Grey to Gladstone, on the work of the Commission, especially on the *Alabama* claims and San Juan boundary; also on the Grant–Sumner quarrels. (Copy in RIPON PAPERS, 43514, f. 73, q.v.)

44292

Correspondence with Lord John Russell, 1st Earl Russell (1792–1878).

ff. 43–56 *passim*, 84–87, 162–81 *passim*. Eight letters, 30 Oct. 1861– 17 Sept. 1865, from Russell to Gladstone; and two letters, 2 and 6 Sept. 1865, from Gladstone to Russell. On cotton; the *Trent* incident; Sumner's accusations that Britain had encouraged the South to take up arms; Gladstone's Newcastle speech—'Jefferson Davis and other leaders of the South . . . have made a nation'—for which Russell mildly rebukes him; recognition of the South; American claims for depredations of Confederate cruisers and Britain's refusal to go to arbitration in 1865.

44303

f. 190. Ithaca, N.Y., 14 May 1871, from Goldwin Smith to Gladstone, on the good effect of the Treaty of Washington on American public opinion.

44352–526. Gladstone's general correspondence, 1826–98.

Scattered American references include the following :

44400

f. 192. [New York], 8 Apr. 1863, from William Adams, American clergyman, to Cyrus W. Field, on the war aims of the North and British misunderstanding of them.

44412

f. 274. (*See also* 44442 f. 117.) London, 7 May 1867, from Charles Francis Adams, American Minister to Britain, to Gladstone, introducing John Sherman.

44420

f. 180. Copy of a letter, 1869, to the Duke of Argyll from J. L. Motley, referring to and refuting some accusation that he had called Gladstone a liar in a dispute which had accidentally reached the American press.

44427

f. 232. Also 44428 ff. 90, 96, 182, 211, 213, 276, 290; 44439 f. 23. (*See also* 44766, f. 201.) Letters, 1870–3, from J. L. Motley to Gladstone. Mostly slight notes, with some mention of possible mediation in the Civil War reparation disputes of American interests, and of Fenian prisoners in England.

44428

ff. 282, 284. Official memoranda, 1870, on the *Trent* case from Lord Tenterden to Gladstone, showing how the draft of the Cabinet's proposed dispatch to Lord Lyons, then British Minister at Washington, was in 1861 altered by the Prince Consort.

44433–50

44433, ff. 235, 264; 44434, ff. 1, 82; 44435, f. 49; 44437, ff. 43, 148; 44438, f. 305; 44442, ff. 33, 324; 44445, ff. 194, 213; 44447, f. 319; 44448, ff. 88, 231; 44449, ff. 3, 11; and 44450, f. 194. Correspondence, 1872–6, between General Robert Schenck, United States Minister to Britain, and Gladstone. One or two letters are personal notes or letters of introduction; some of the earlier letters contain references to the indirect claims. The main interest of the correspondence lies, however, in 44437, f. 148, 44442, f. 324, and the letters in 44445–9; these deal with Gladstone's attempts to obtain from Hamilton Fish, through Schenck, a statement that the use made of his allegedly anti-Northern sentiments during the Civil War in the American case at the Geneva Arbitration did not imply that the United States considered him unfriendly towards it. Schenck finally obtained from Fish a letter in which the Secretary of State says that he believes that Gladstone had no 'consciousness of hostility' towards the North but was simply reflecting the general feeling of middle and upper class Britain at the time.

44452

f. 35. New Britain, Conn., 6 Oct. 1876, from Elihu Burritt, American philanthropist, to Gladstone, on the teaching of Sanskrit.

44490–525

Scattered through these volumes is correspondence with Andrew Carnegie, 27 Apr. 1885–8 June 1897. Fourteen letters and a telegram from Carnegie to Gladstone; five letters from Gladstone to Carnegie. Mostly personal notes—e.g., on Gladstone's health, Carnegie's hopes that Gladstone will write an autobiography, &c. Other subjects dealt with are the possibility of a general arbitration treaty between the United States and Britain, which Carnegie expects to see signed when Gladstone and James G. Blaine are in office at the same time; a contribution by Carnegie to Liberal Party funds; the presentation to Lord Acton of his library during his lifetime, which Carnegie financed; the inevitability, according to Carnegie, of Canada's joining the United States; the Venezuela dispute of 1895; an appeal by Gladstone to Carnegie to help the Bodleian Library, and Carnegie's refusal.

44524

f. 23. Memorandum by A. and E. Howland on religious persecution in New England, 1684.

44527–51. Letter-books. Copies of Gladstone's letters written while he was holding various offices under the Crown, 1835–94.

There are few letters of American significance; even the letter-books for the Civil War period (chiefly 44531–4) appear to contain very little of importance. Major items include:

44536

30 Mar. 1869, to Clarendon, on an 'outrageous' proposal of Reverdy Johnson—presumably on the claims—and the way in which the 'indefensible' frontier of Canada forces Britain into a submissiveness to the United States. 11 May 1869, to the Duke of Argyll, on Motley and Sumner. 12 May 1869, to Clarendon on Motley.

44537

23 and 25 Oct., 22 Nov. 1869, to Clarendon, on Fish's dispatch to Motley on the *Alabama* claims.

44538

24 and 25 Dec. 1869, 20 and 24 Jan., 18 Mar. 1870, to Clarendon on the *Alabama* claims and the San Juan boundary; highly critical of Sumner, but has hopes of Fish. 28 June 1870 on the same subjects, to Sir John Young.

44539

9 Jan. 1871, to Granville, on possibility of arbitration of claims; composition of Washington Commission, and progress of negotiations. 3 and 4 Apr. 1871, to Earl de Grey at Washington, on the Commission. 30 Mar. and 3 Apr. 1871, to Sir Stafford Northcote, also on the Commission.

44540

12, 13, 14, 17, and 21 Apr.; 1, 2, 3, 11 May 1871; to Granville on the wording of the preamble of the Treaty of Washington—especially on the word 'rebellion'; San Juan boundary; fisheries; importance of British Commission's leaving Washington before the Senate meets; Fenian raids into Canada.

44563–635. Gladstone's official papers, including memoranda prepared for the use of the Cabinet, 1834–95. (Mostly printed.) The following contain material concerning the Civil War:

44593, ff. 47, 55, 83, 84, 86, 99, 104.
44594, ff. 26, 36, 44, 115.
44595, ff. 66, 72, 77, 82, 84, 86, 94.
44597, f. 32.
44599, f. 97.
(*See also* 44511, f. 23; 44752, ff. 51, 305, 342; 44754, f. 120.)

Examples of the type of material contained in this group are:

44593

Instructions to Lord Lyons respecting hostilities in the U.S., 1861. (Printed.)
Judicial Decision on the blockade of U.S. Ports by Judge Dunlop, 1861. (Printed.)
Various printed memoranda on the *Trent* incident, 1861, especially as regards precedents.

44595

Present Conditions of Affairs in the U.S. by Russell, 13 Oct. 1862. (Printed.)
Report of a Chicago meeting held on 20 Sept. 1862 to discuss the first Emancipation Proclamation. (Printed.)
Various memoranda, Oct.–Nov. 1862, by Sir George Cornewall Lewis, Gladstone, and Russell, arising from Russell's memorandum of 13 Oct. 1862, cited above, chiefly on recognition of the Confederacy. (Printed.)
Report on travels in the West, by H. Percy Anderson, 1862. (Printed.)

44601–20

The following contain material on the *Alabama* claims and the Treaty of Washington: 44601, f. 17; 44603, ff. 71, 83; 44610, f. 45; 44617, f. 8; 44618, ff. 51, 86, 113; 44619, ff. 29, 62, 88, 98, 126; and 44620, ff. 48, 94. (*See also* 44107, f. 322, 44760, f. 194, and 44761, f. 181.)

Examples of the type of material contained in this group are: 44617, *Memorandum Explanatory of some of the Articles of the Treaty of Washington*, by Lord Tenterden, 1871. (Printed.) 44618, Various memoranda on the meaning of certain parts of the Treaty of Washington, especially on the claims. (Partly printed.) 44619, Various memoranda on the indirect claims, and the Geneva Award, 1872. (Mostly printed.)

Miscellaneous subjects are dealt with in the following: 44616, f. 149. Manuscript memorandum on the Southern states, 1871. Discusses whether or not they 'rebelled'. 44617, f. 169. *The Case of the Confederate Cotton Bondholders.* An 18-page printed pamphlet, 1871, giving the opinions of the Lord Chancellor, Attorney-General, and others.

44625

f. 110. Manuscript memorandum entitled 'Extracts from Cushing's *Manual*', on cloture in the United States, 1880.

44633

ff. 36, 45, 59. (*See also* 44497, f. 367, and 44768, f. 14.) Papers on the American attitude to the Irish question, 1884–6. Include a clipping from the *Daily News*, 1886, entitled 'American sympathy with Home Rule'; an extract from a letter, 11 June 1886, from E. L. Godkin to James Bryce; and a list of public bodies in the United States which had sent communications on Home Rule, 1886.

44636–48. Cabinet minutes.

Minutes by Gladstone of Cabinet meetings which he attended as Chancellor of the Exchequer and as Prime Minister, 1853–94. Included are also notes and minutes made by other members of the Cabinet.

These were available only with the written permission of the Cabinet Office, and were not examined.[1] It was, however, known that 44638–640, covering 1870–2, contain minutes on the *Alabama* claims and the Treaty of Washington; and 44636 probably contains material on the Civil War.

44649–80. Notes and memoranda for speeches, &c.

44654

f. 201. (*See also* 44746, f. 26.) Memoranda, 1856, concerning opposition to recruitment in the United States for the British army. 44746 appears to contain three drafts of a motion on this subject.

44681–714. Gladstone's literary works (original manuscripts).

44690

f. 55. Address on the cotton famine and distress in Lancashire and Cheshire, delivered at Chester, 27 Dec. 1862.

44701

f. 251. 'The Future of the English-Speaking Races', published in the American *Youth's Companion*, Nov. 1888.

---

[1] This restriction has now been lifted.

44702

f. 296. A review of Mrs. S. D. Smedes' *Memorials of a Southern Planter* (Baltimore, 1887),[1] published in the *Nineteenth Century*, Dec. 1889.

44703

f. 296. Corrected proof sheets, followed, f. 305, by manuscript additions of an article in the *Nineteenth Century*, Nov. 1890, entitled 'Mr. Carnegie's Gospel of Wealth' (published in London, 1890).

44734

ff. 1, 260; and 44735, f. 2. (*See also* 44575, f. 71, printed.) Memoranda on commercial relations with the United States. For example, claim of United States for repayment of duties on rough rice, 13 Jan. 1844; and the commercial aspects of the Treaty of Ghent.

44752

Memoranda (manuscript), 1862–3, on public opinion in the United States, effect of foreign opinion on the United States; possible British intervention to end the Civil War; possible joint action with France and Russia to the same end; recognition of the Confederacy; the United States public debt; the Foreign Enlistment Act, the iron-clad rams, and British neutrality.

44773

f. 96. Memorandum entitled 'For fair play all round', on tariffs, 1889. Argues against American protectionism.

44790

f. 131. Autobiographical memorandum, 'Some of my errors', 1894. One of the subjects treated is his attitude towards the Civil War.

44791

f. 29. In 'Recorded errors', 1896, again mentions his attitude towards the Civil War.

f. 131. 'First period of leadership, 1865–75 and to 1880', 1897. The section headed 'First Cabinet, 1868–74' contains remarks on the claims question.

44793

f. 158. Notes by Gladstone on *Letters* of 'Massachusettensis', n.d. 'Massachusettensis' was Daniel Leonard, who published his *Letters to the Inhabitants of the Province of the Massachusetts Bay* in 1775.

44889–90. MISCELLANEOUS PAPERS.

Manuscript of Nathaniel Hawthorne's *The Marble Faun*, which was published in 1860, first under that title and then as *Transformation*.

[1] Published in London in 1889 as *A Southern Planter*.

44914. MISCELLANEOUS PAPERS.

Chart and record of a voyage to America in the S.S. *Oceanic*, by Charles
Kingsley, 1874.

44992–45022. RUSSELL OF BIRMINGHAM PAPERS.[1]

William Russell (1740–1818) and his son, Thomas Pougher
Russell (1775–1851), of Birmingham, were friends of Joseph
Priestley, and exporters to the United States. They migrated
to the United States in 1795 and lived there until 1800.

A full list of contents of the papers is given in 44992. They include seven
letters from Priestley—one written from Philadelphia; and a letter, 28 Sept.
1798, from George Washington on agricultural matters.[2] Also:
  Bundle xviii, item 11. George Russell's accounts with Thomas Russell,
1803–12. Gives the latter's expenses as George Russell's American agent.
  Bundle xx, item 9. Duplicate copy of an Act of the Maryland Assembly
in favour of William Russell, Annapolis, Md., 3 Nov. 1793.
  Accounts xiv. Labelled '1812–18. Waste Book June 1812.' William
Russell's French farming accounts and other miscellaneous accounts in
France, England, and America, 20 June 1812–Jan. 1818. Entered by
William Russell until Dec. 1817; continued by Thomas Russell.
  Accounts xxii. Labelled 'Waste Book 1813–21'. Thomas Russell's yearly
accounts of his own business ventures in France, England and America,
6 Nov. 1813–5 Nov. 1821.
  Accounts xxiii. Labelled 'Journal 1813–23'. Thomas Russell's yearly
journals of accounts in France, England, and America, 6 Nov. 1813–1 Nov.
1823. Duplicates material in Accounts xxii up to 1821.
  See also Russell Diaries, Birmingham Public Libraries (p. 438).[3]

45498. MISCELLANEOUS PAPERS.

f. 12. Letter, 29 Nov. 1857, from Herman Melville to an unknown correspondent regretting that he cannot keep an appointment.

45728–30. AUCKLAND PAPERS.

Papers of William Eden, 1st Baron Auckland (1744–1814),
who was one of the Peace Commissioners sent to America in
1778.

45728

Two letters from Lord North to Eden. The first, 18 Sept. 1775, praises
General Gage, Governor Tryon of North Carolina, and Governor Campbell

---

  [1] See S. H. Jeyes, *The Russells of Birmingham in the French Revolution and in America,
1791–1814* (London, 1911).
  [2] See *Writings of George Washington*, ed. by John C. Fitzpatrick, vol. xxxvi, pp.
469–70 (Washington, D.C., 1941).
  [3] Other Russell Papers, mostly those relating to their America sojourn, are
owned by the Pennsylvania Historical Association.

of New York for their actions in America, and details the troops to be sent there. The second, 1777, refers to Eden's appointment to the Peace Commission under Lord Carlisle. Also a letter, 30 Mar. 1778, from Eden to North, giving the conditions on which he is prepared to go to America with the Commission.

Fifteen letters, 1777–8 and undated, from Alexander Wedderburn to Eden (one incomplete, but apparently from Wedderburn); and seven, 1778, from Eden, unaddressed but presumably to Wedderburn. The earlier letters contain general comments on American affairs—e.g. the procrastination of the Howes, the apparent policy of wearing down the rebels rather than defeating them, the Franco-American treaty, the possibilities of peace. Then two letters on the composition of the Peace Commission, and another in which Wedderburn reports a rumour that North is of the opinion that American independence must be granted. Most of the others are written by Eden while in America, in which he describes the evacuation of Philadelphia, which he thinks needless and which convinces him that the government did not intend to give the Peace Commission a fair chance— he complains bitterly of this 'shameful treatment' and (?) Wedderburn writes answering his complaints; the blockade of New York—to where the Commission moved—by d'Estaing; the American evacuation of Rhode Island; the 'race' between the fleets of Howe and d'Estaing for Boston, which the French won; General Howe's pessimism on American affairs, and his poor strategy; Eden's belief that some exertion on Britain's part would speedily end the rebellion as the Americans are already, Sept. 1778, feeling that they have neither 'a grievance [nor] a just object'; the failure of the Peace Commission. In another letter, n.d., Wedderburn introduces to Eden someone who has a plan for 'an accommodation with the Americans'.

Nine letters and papers, 1777, sent by Hugh Elliot in Berlin to the Earl of Suffolk. These, which are marked 'most secret', &c., and are partly in code(?), concern the connexions of France and Spain with the Americans. Some are transcripts of intercepted communications from A. Lee. (Three are in French.)

Three letters, 18 Dec. 1777–9, two from Berlin and one from London, from Elliot to Eden. On the 'close correspondence' between Prussia and the Americans, and various naval actions in 1779—one against John Paul Jones. Elliot suggests that Britain should grant independence to her American colonies, and then force the independence of all French and Spanish American colonies.

45729

Letter, Madrid, 26 Feb. 1789, from Eden to Lord Sheffield, on a reported Russian settlement on the California coast.

There are also AUCKLAND PAPERS in 46490.

45985–46118. HERBERT GLADSTONE PAPERS.

These were not available for inspection in 1958 pending binding.

46196. ROLLO PAPERS.

Letter 'C. Townshend', from the War Office to Lord Rollo in America, 25 Feb. 1762, informing him that he has been breveted colonel by the King.[1]

46474–86. HERBERT GLADSTONE PAPERS.

Not available for inspection.

46840. MISCELLANEOUS PAPERS.

Diary of the siege of Quebec by an American force, written by J. Danford, a member of the garrison, 10 Nov. 1775–6 May 1776.

46920–47213. EGMONT PAPERS.

Papers of the Perceval family, principally collected by Sir John Perceval, Viscount Perceval and 1st Earl of Egmont (1683–1748).

47032

Letter-book, 1727–30, including copies of correspondence, 1729–30, mainly between George Berkeley and Perceval, concerning the former's Rhode Island visit to purchase land in order to supply a proposed college in Bermuda.[2] Berkeley's letters include description of Newport, R.I., and his activities there.

47053

Papers, 1764, concerning Nova Scotia estates.

47054

Papers, late eighteenth century, concerning estates in Nova Scotia, Florida, and elsewhere.

47060–71

Diaries, 1730–47, of Viscount Perceval (from 1733, 1st Earl of Egmont).[3] These contain much information about the early days of the colony of Georgia. (Perceval was the first president of the trustees of the colony.)

47287. LIEVEN PAPERS, vol. lii.

Papers of Prince Christopher Lieven (1774–1839), while Russian Minister to Britain, include American letters, 1818–27.

Bundles 3 and 4. Two letters to Lieven from Pierre de Poletica, the Russian Minister to the United States, and two draft replies, Nov. 1819–Mar. 1822

[1] H.M.C. iii, p. 407.
[2] Extracts, H.M.C. vii, pp. 242–4. The correspondence has been printed in Benjamin Rand, *Berkeley and Percival*, pp. 237–68 (Cambridge and New York, 1914).
[3] Published in three volumes in H.M.C. Egmont MSS. [63].

(in French). The first letter from Poletica at Washington, D.C., mentions
a packet to be sent to Count Nesselrode, and says that he (Poletica) has been
comparing information from Madrid with John Quincy Adams. The second
letter is personal, and the draft replies illegible.

Bundles 7 and 8. Three slight notes, London, Dec. 1818–24, from Richard
Rush, the American Minister, to Lieven.

Bundle 10. Four slight notes, 1826–7, from Albert Gallatin to Lieven.
Also a letter, 1 Apr. 1833, from Aaron Vail, United States Chargé d'Affaires
in London, about a commercial treaty (presumably between the United
States and Russia) about to be signed by the President. (All in French.)

47559–601. CHARLES JAMES FOX PAPERS.

Charles James Fox (1749–1806), statesman. His papers include:

47561–3

Scattered references to the peace negotiations with the Americans in Paris,
1782–3. The letters are chiefly to Fox from the Duke of Manchester and are
concerned mainly with the French and Spanish aspects of the negotiations.
The most important letters from the American standpoint are nine, 10 May–
9 July 1782, to Fox from Thomas Grenville in Paris; also copy letter,
London, 10 June 1782, Fox to Grenville (47562, ff. 1–34). These letters
illustrate the British wish to detach America from France in the negotiations,
which Grenville thinks will be difficult in view of Franklin's attitude. 47563
contains an undated and unsigned memorandum on the American–Spanish
commercial convention of 1802.

48212. MISCELLANEOUS PAPERS.

B. Long letter, 29 Oct. 1866, from William V. Walton of 'Hooyelles parish',
La., to his brother in England, describing his experiences as a Confederate
soldier. The letter is, as he says, 'an account of the War as seen and experienced by myself' while serving with the 2nd Louisiana Infantry. He describes
the Peninsula campaign, and especially 'Stonewall' Jackson's part therein,
and the battles of Malvern Hill, Cedar Mountain, Fredericksburg, Chan-
cellorsville, Winchester, and Gettysburg. The South, he says, lost because
it had insufficient manpower and no navy. He also includes remarks on
the injustice of reconstruction, high prices, poor crops, and the incompetence
of the Negroes.

48417–589. PALMERSTON PAPERS.

The papers of Henry John Temple, 3rd Viscount Palmerston
(1784–1865), run to some 173 volumes and are not yet fully
indexed. This list should, therefore, be regarded as illustrative
rather than exhaustive. There are no papers later than 1850 in
the collection, but see report (pp. 67–73) on the papers held at
Broadlands, Hampshire.

The Foreign Office letter-books (133 volumes) include:

48495

'To North America', 1835–41. Copies of dispatches to Ministers Vaughan and Fox, and to Chargé Bankhead. Chief topics dealt with are Britain's offer of mediation in American–French dispute over French blockade of Mexican ports; Canadian fisheries; the selling into slavery of a coloured British subject in Florida; Canadian boundary; armed incursions into Canada by American citizens, and the *Caroline* incident.

48575

'To and from U.S.A.', 1846–9. Copies of dispatches, chiefly from but also to, Ministers Pakenham and Crampton. Major matters dealt with are the Oregon question; the Mexican War—especially as regards blockade and possible British mediation; arrests of Negroes on board British ships calling at Charleston, S.C., and New Orleans, La.; United States tariff; Buchanan, whom Pakenham thinks neither 'honest [nor] sincere'; Canadian boundary, especially as regards the Strait of Juan de Fuca; the Wilmot Proviso; the United States militia; Central America, especially the Mosquito Coast; postal rates between Britain and the United States; disputes between the administration and General Taylor and Scott; the peace treaty with Mexico; rumours of Britain's desire for California; establishment of American relations with the Papacy; the slavery issue in Congress; the isthmian canal; rescues and attempted rescues of Irish insurgents by Irish–American mobs; the presidential election of 1848; Canadian reciprocity and fisheries; measures to prevent filibustering against Cuba.

48576

'To and from U.S.A.', 1849–50. To and from the Minister, Sir Henry Bulwer. Major topics dealt with are commerce between the United States and Canada; killing of cattle in the Falkland Islands by American seamen; the Clayton–Bulwer Treaty; United States disputes with Portugal over the destruction of an American privateer, the *General Armstrong*; the threatening situation over Cuba; hostilities between Haiti and the Dominican Republic; clashes along the Juan de Fuca Strait and Puget Sound; slavery debates in Congress; the Compromise of 1850; Anglo-United States friction in Central America; filibustering; Cuba and Nicaragua; the characters of Taylor and Fillmore.

49063. MISCELLANEOUS PAPERS.

Collection of autographs (no letters) of Presidents of the United States and their wives, from General Washington to General Eisenhower.

49173–95. SPENCER PERCEVAL PAPERS.

Spencer Perceval (1762–1812) became Chancellor of the Exchequer in 1807 and was Prime Minister from 1809 until his death. The twenty-three bundles of unbound correspondence and papers include:

N

49177

Correspondence with James Stephen. Various letters from Stephen, 1807–10, contain comment on the Orders in Council, which Perceval originated and drafted. A memorandum, 'Coup d'Oeuil on an American War', Dec. 1807, is a discussion by Stephen of American politics and an attack on the United States for its pro-French policies.

49178

Papers relating to the Orders in Council: notes, statistics, &c.

49179

Papers relating to the message of the President of the United States: printed *Documents accompanying the Message of the President . . . to the two Houses of Congress* . . . (Washington, D.C., 1810), about the Berlin Decrees, Orders in Council, right of search, &c. Chiefly composed of letters from William Pinkney and Secretary of State R. Smith.

49199–285. STANMORE PAPERS.

These were not available for inspection in 1958 pending binding.[1]

EGERTON MANUSCRIPTS

2952. MISCELLANEOUS PAPERS.

A. Letters of Samuel Langhorne Clemens ('Mark Twain') to the publishing firm of Chatto & Windus.

f. 1. Hartford, Conn., 7 Oct. 1881, referring to the publication of *The Prince and the Pauper*.

f. 3. Hartford, Conn., 1 Sept. 1883, writing of his new book, *Adventures of Huckleberry Finn*, as a 'rattling good one'.

f. 6. Elmira, N.Y., 17 Sept. 1888, referring to *A Connecticut Yankee in King Arthur's Court*.

f. 7. 27 Jan. 1892, giving instructions as to the publication of 'six newspaper letters', which he had been writing from Europe.

2972. LE MARCHANT, SIR JOHN GASPARD (1803–74). Correspondence.

Soldier and administrator. Lieutenant-Governor of Nova Scotia 1852–7, connected with the raising in the United States and elsewhere in North America of a foreign legion for service in the Crimean War, 1855–6, &c. Some of the letters are addressed to his secretary, Lewis M. Wilkins. The writers include John F. T. Crampton, British Minister to the United States, whose first two letters, 1853–4, refer to the fishery and reciprocity questions;

---

[1] These papers have now been catalogued.

Joseph Howe, Nova Scotia statesman; Lieutenant John W. Preston; C. H. Stanley, British Consul in New York; and others.

At the beginning of the volume, f. 1, is an opinion (?given in 1842) on the American Neutrality Act of 20 Apr. 1818; and at the end, f. 414, is the *New York Herald*, European edition, 25 Sept. 1855.

2978. HEATH AND VERNEY PAPERS, vol. I.

5. f. 10. 'A comparison . . . between the contract made by the companies for Virginia and Summer Islands, in the year 1622, and the contract lately made by some undertakers who were the chief breakers [sic] of the former.' An analysis of a new contract for the exploitation of the tobacco plantations in Virginia and Somers Islands, drawn up apparently soon after the revocation of the charter of the Virginia Company in 1624.

3324-3508. LEEDS PAPERS.

Correspondence and papers of the family of Osborne, Dukes of Leeds, including the papers of Robert D'Arcy, 4th Earl of Holderness.

These 185 volumes, acquired in 1947, supplement Add. MSS. 28040-95.[1] They were formerly at Hornby Castle, where they were the subject of a report by the Historical Manuscripts Commission, which clearly, however, did not cover all the deposited collection.

The papers are not yet listed, so it was not practicable to examine them; the entries below refer to the H.M.C. report. (*Letters unless otherwise stated.*)

(*a*) 1675, from Sir William Berkeley, Governor of Virginia, against a patent granted to Lord Culpeper [Colpeper].[2]

(*b*) Eight articles by Edward Randolph against the government of Boston: 'that the Bostoners have no right either to land or government in any part of New England, but are usurpers', &c.[3] n.d. *c.* 1676.

(*c*) 1676, from Edward Randolph, Boston, giving an account of trade, army, &c.[4]

(*d*) Copy of a writ, 1676, issued by Governor Berkeley for the electing of a new Assembly; with notes of memorials on the condition of Virginia.[5]

(*e*) 27 Mar. 1677, from the Commissioners of Virginia forwarding petitions &c.[6]

(*f*) Extract from a memorial by the dissenters in New England presented to the King by Increase Mather, Samuel Newel, and Elizabeth Hutchinson, and read before him in July 1688.[7]

---

[1] See Paullin and Paxson, pp. 546-7.
[2] H.M.C. xi (vii), p. 10.
[3] Ibid., p. 38.
[4] Ibid., p. 11.
[5] Ibid., p. 14.
[6] Ibid., p. 19.
[7] Ibid., p. 31.

(g) 28 Feb. 1690, from the Earl of Effingham about his commission and departure for Virginia.[1]

(h) Narrative of hostilities committed by the French on the Ohio in 1754, with papers relative to the negotiations in 1755 relating to these.[2]

(i) 27 July 1759, from Captain Peter D'Arcy, giving an account of the capture of the French fort at Ticonderoga.[2]

(j) Short notes, 26, 27, and 28 May 1785, from John Adams to Pitt on his arrival in England as first American Minister.[3]

(k) 16 Dec. 1785, Pitt to the Marquis of Carmarthen (Francis Osborne, later 5th Duke of Leeds), concerning a memorial from Adams of which Pitt says 'the demand seems itself fairly founded upon the treaty', but that the English also have claims which must go hand in hand, particularly 'satisfaction respecting the debts due from America to our merchants'.[4]

ADDITIONAL CHARTERS

59151

Sale by the trustees for the Free Society of Traders in Pennsylvania to Jeremiah Langham of Bucks. county, of 2,000 acres of unlocated land in Pennsylvania, 15 Feb. 1725. Signatures and seals of vendors.

66210

Extracts from the records of the court of New Haven, Conn., relating to James Davids al. John Dixwell (d. 1690), of Folkestone, Kent. Copy attested by Gurdon Saltonstall, Governor of the colony, 1710. Signed.

LOANS

29. PORTLAND PAPERS.

The collection mainly contains late sixteenth- to early eighteenth-century papers of various members of the Harley family, including those of Sir Robert Harley (1579–1656), his sons Sir Edward Harley (1624–1700) and Sir Robert Harley (1626–73), and his grandson, Robert Harley, 1st Earl of Oxford (1661–1724). There are over 300 volumes, thirty-nine of which contain papers arranged chronologically in two series, 1582–1724 and 1625–1708.

Much of the collection was, before its transfer to the British Museum, the subject of reports by the Historical Manuscripts Commission in H.M.C. xiv (ii) and xv (iv), and in the ten volumes of the Portland MSS. [29]. As the collection has not been listed, it was not practicable to check the relevant

---

[1] H.M.C. xi (vii), p. 32. [2] Ibid., p. 45.
[3] Ibid., p. 55. [4] Ibid., p. 54.

material listed by the H.M.C. However, the following, drawn from the H.M.C. reports, are almost certainly still in the collection. (*Letters unless otherwise stated.*)

(*a*) 28 May 1608, from Lord Eure to Sir Robert Harley, says that the Virginia ship is returned, and Captain Newport has brought over Captain Wingfield.[1]

(*b*) 3 Nov. 1662, from Sir Robert Harley to Sir Edward Harley, describing plans for a settlement 'in the West Indies, on that part which adjoynes to Virginia next to Florida . . . Sir George Cartwright is engaged in the thing'.[2]

(*c*) 7 Aug. 1691, from Sir Thomas Clarges to Robert Harley, says, 'I cannot but be troubled for our plantations in America, for if the ships which were going there with provisions are taken, with their convoy, I know not how they or the ships we have there can subsist.'[3]

(*d*) 18 Aug. 1694, to Robert Harley from an unknown correspondent, 'the Queen has signed a revocation of that part of Colonel Fletcher's commission relating to Pennsylvania, as also a warrant to restore William Penn to that colony, who intends to go there about a month hence'.[4]

(*e*) 12 Oct. 1697, from W. Snowe to Robert Harley, 'The news from Virginia is that Admiral Nevill and Mees, Captain Lilcot, Holmes, Belwood, Dyer, Studley and Fisher are dead, and all the Dutch captains but one, with 1,500 seamen [of Nevill's squadron]'.[5]

(*f*) 30 Jan. 1699, from William Penn to Robert Harley, pleading for fair treatment for the colonists.[6]

(*g*) Boston, 5 and 7 Mar. 1700, from the Earl of Bellamont to various people, mainly about piracy and Captain Kidd.[7]

(*h*) Two letters from William Penn to Robert Harley, the first dated 27 Aug. 1701, the second undated but apparently in the same year. The first sets forth the advantages of proprietory governments; the second is an account of the trade of the colonies.[8]

(*i*) The case of Sir Matthew Dudley and others concerning their petition for the incorporation of a company to import naval stores from North America. 1704.[9]

(*j*) ?1704, from Sir Henry Ashurst to (?)Robert Harley, recommending that Major General Waite Winthrop be appointed Lieutenant-Governor until a Governor is sent over.[10]

[1] H.M.C. xiv (ii), (Portland MSS. iii [29]), p. 5.
[2] Transcript, ibid., p. 268.   [3] Transcript, ibid., p. 471.
[4] Ibid., p. 553.   [5] Ibid., p. 590.   [6] Transcript, ibid., pp. 601–2.
[7] Transcripts, H.M.C. Portland MSS. viii [29], pp. 69–77.
[8] Transcripts, H.M.C. xv (iv), (Portland MSS. iv [29]), pp. 19–21 30–32.
[9] Transcript, H.M.C. Portland MSS. viii [29], pp. 164–5.
[10] H.M.C. Portland MSS. x [29], p. 62.

(*k*) 9 Feb. and 3 Mar. 1704, from William Penn to Robert Harley on affairs in the colonies.[1]

(*l*) Report, 31 May 1705, from the Board of Trade on a petition from merchants of Virginia and Maryland, against the projected establishment by certain merchants of a monopoly of the tobacco trade with Muscovy.[2]

(*m*) 30 Dec. 1710, from P. Schuyler to an unknown correspondent concerning missions to the Indians.[3]

(*n*) 10 May 1711, from Thomas Coutts to Dr. Arbuthnot, 'concerning a proposal he had made for advancing the revenue upon tobacco which he thinks will bear testing by the Commissioners of the Customs and the merchants trading to Virginia'.[4]

(*o*) July 1711, from Daniel Defoe to the Earl of Oxford, says that the advantages of planting settlements in America have been made obvious by the success of New England, New York, &c., which are both strong and healthy.[5]

(*p*) New Haven, Conn., 10 Sept. 1711, from Gurdon Saltonstall to the Earl of Oxford, describing the raising of troops in the northern colonies for an expedition against Canada.[6]

(*q*) Two letters, New York, 1712, from Caleb Heathcote to the Earl of Oxford. The first, 21 June, is on the abuses and mismanagements in relation to the men-of-war stationed for securing the American coasts and trade, and the supply of naval stores; the second, 8 July, complains that the great danger in America, both to Church and State, lies in the Charter governments, and goes on to give a description of the sad state of the Church of England in America, particularly in Connecticut.[7]

(*r*) 20 June 1713, from Thomas Coram to the Earl of Oxford, supporting the plea of some disbanded officers to be allowed to settle in Acadia.[8]

Business Archives Council, 9 King's Bench Walk, LONDON, E.C.4

HUTH, FREDERICK, & CO. LTD. Business records. 1836–94.

Merchant bankers, London; dissolved in 1936. The Council holds a large box containing letters, receipts, wills, &c., relating to the firm's investment connexions in the United States, Latin America, Spain, Portugal, Australia, and elsewhere. The following relevant items were found:

[1] Transcripts, H.M.C. xv (iv), (Portland MSS. iv [29]), pp. 79–81.
[2] See further ibid., pp. 191–2.   [3] Transcript, ibid., p. 649.
[4] Ibid., p. 686.   [5] H.M.C. Portland MSS. v [29], p. 67.
[6] Transcript, ibid., p. 89.
[7] Transcript, ibid., pp. 186–91 and 199–200.
[8] Transcript, ibid., p. 297.

(*a*) Packet labelled 'J. W. Perit, Girard Bank', containing sixteen letters, 1836–7, from John W. Perit in Philadelphia, mainly about negotiating loans in Europe for the Bank. Also in the packet is an 1836 letter from Perit's son, P. W. Perit, announcing his establishment in Philadelphia.

(*b*) Packet labelled 'D. 131. North American Trust & Banking Co.', containing a copy of the 1839–48 accounts of this New York Company with Huth's; a brief summary of the correspondence between the two firms, 1839–41; an agreement, 1841, between Huth's and James Murray, attorney for the New York firm, about the disposal of Arkansas and Indiana state bonds; a letter, Philadelphia, 23 Jan. 1841, from C. Macalister to Murray, about the possibility of a joint arrangement between his own firm and a London house for the sale of American securities in London.

(*c*) Packet labelled 'D. 168. Documents relating to agreement with the Bank of Florida'. Papers, 1843–4, concerning the arrangements made by the Union Bank of Florida, Richard K. Call of Tallahassee, Fla., and David Meinertzhagen, a partner in Huth's, for the turning over of plantations and slaves in Florida to Meinertzhagen.

(*d*) Packet labelled 'D. 270. W. Gruning's Correspondence with George Peabody concerning $40,000 Pennsyla. 5% Stock', 1851.

(*e*) Envelope labelled '1178. Papers relating to the Washington Iron Co. a/c Duke of Riansares'. Papers concerning the 1862 transfer by John Fallon of the Washington Iron Co., Clinton county, Pa., to the Duke. Included are detailed lists of the Fallons' personal property; and of fixtures at the company; of debts due; and of land held.

(*f*) Envelope labelled '3337. Letter of John Arbuckle relating to Credit to Arbuckle Bros. New York', 12 Oct. 1882. The credit was to be made available against shipments of coffee from 'the Brazils' to New York.

(*g*) Packet labelled 'Deposit receipt from the Bank of Montreal, New York Agency, for $50,000 Chicago & Indiana Coal Ry. Co., $50,000 Duluth & Iron Range Ry. a/c F.H. & Co.', containing letters and documents giving details of various American stocks (not confined to those noted) held for Huth's through John H. Davis & Co., New York, by the New York agency of the Bank of Montreal, 1889.

(*h*) Envelopes labelled '4111. Letter of Guarantee of the National Cordage Co. of New York' and '4151. Letter of the National Cordage Co. of New York'; 1889. The latter contains two letters from the New York firm to Messrs. G. Amsinck & Co., Huth's representatives in New York.

(*i*) Envelope labelled '4766. Letters of American Trading Compy., New York, and Galbraith & Co., Manchester, relating to credit', 1894. The credit was for the shipment of 'Manchester staple goods' to Japan and/or Shanghai.

There are also a few other items such as shares in the Texas & German Emigration Co.

See also the firm's records held at University College, London (p. 341).

Christy & Co. Ltd., 8–10 Lower James Street, Golden Square, LONDON, W.1

BUSINESS RECORDS. 4 documents (printed). 1790, 1816.
Hat manufacturers.

(a) Bond, 12 May 1790, between David Ross and Thomas Pleasants of Virginia, and Phineas Bond, regarding the debts of Thomas Edwards, deceased partner of Ross & Pleasants. Mentions various transactions with Storrs & Christy, the first being in 1785. (Printed.)

(b) Schedules of duties under the United States tariff of 1816, with two identical forms of declaration for import of goods into the United States. (Printed.)

Congregational Library, Memorial Hall, 15 Farringdon Street, LONDON, E.C.4

SPRAGUE PAPERS. Sermons and letters. 1683–1863.

Dr. William Buell Sprague (1795–1876), clergyman, biographer, and collector of manuscripts and pamphlets, of Massachusetts and New York; author of 150 books, including *Annals of the American Pulpit*, 9 vols. (New York, 1857–69).

His papers include sermons, 1683–1797, by American divines; and about 190 autographs and autograph letters of American divines, missionaries, and statesman, 1704–1863 (MS. 11 C1). For these, see Andrews & Davenport, pp. 347–9. In addition Sprague's papers include:

Letters from Sprague to Joshua Wilson, London. About a hundred letters, 1828–55, with four letters from Wilson to Sprague, 1834, 1836, and 1861. Most of Sprague's letters concern books and periodicals which he is sending to Wilson, or which the latter has sent to him. There is also some discussion of Sprague's autograph collections and of American political and religious affairs. (MS. 11 C14)

GREY, ZACHARY (1688–1766). Correspondence: 4 letters. 1725–75. (MS. 11 C 3)

Rector of Houghton-Conquest, Bedfordshire.

Boston, 10 Dec. 1725, from John Checkley, describing his attempts to convert certain Indian tribes from Roman Catholicism to Anglicanism.

Boston, 7 May 1726, 18 May 1727, and 5 June 1735, from Timothy Cutler, the first two on the progress of the Church of England in New England and the third on heresies rampant there.

WHITEFIELD, GEORGE (1714–70). Correspondence: 5 letters. 1745–54. (MS. 11 C 9)

Methodist preacher. Whitefield made preaching tours of the American colonies in 1738–9, 1740–1, 1744–8, 1751–2, 1754–5, 1763–5, and 1769–70. He was appointed minister of Savannah, Ga., in 1739, and founded an orphanage there in 1740.

15 Jan., 3 June 1745, and 30 Oct. 1754, from James Davenport in New Jersey, the first two describing the state of religion in his area as 'dead', and the third, to Mrs. Whitefield, telling of her husband's evangelistic activities in New Jersey.

Charleston, S.C., 25 Jan. and 4 May 1752, are from John Edwards; the first is personal, the second deals with the religious situation in Charleston.

PALMER, CHARLES RAY. Letter. 1898.

New Haven, Conn., 31 Mar. 1898, from Charles Ray Palmer, son of Dr. Ray Palmer, the author and hymn writer, to Rev. J. Griffiths of Gainsborough, Lincs. Comments on the apparent imminence of war over Cuba and the silver party's support of it.

MISCELLANEOUS LETTERS AND PAPERS.

The letters are mainly personal in nature, written by Americans or from America; also an appeal to the American churches on behalf of evangelistic work in Paris by Horatius Bonar, the hymn writer (MS. 11 C 53); and a remonstrance from the English Congregational Churches to the churches in South Carolina, on John L. Brown's death sentence for assisting a slave to escape, 1844 (Z2g30H). Included are:

(a) Letter, Philadelphia, 8 May 1847, from Albert Barnes, the American Bible commentator. (MS. 11 C 53)

(b) Several letters from the Rev. J. Waddington concerning appeals for funds, some to the United States, for the building of the Pilgrim Fathers' Church, Southwark, in the 1850's. Waddington visited the United States in 1859, but makes no comments on his visit. (MS. 11 C 53)

(c) Letter, 12 Sept. 1896, from Thomas F. Bayard, United States Ambassador in London, to the Rev. J. Griffiths of Gainsborough, Lincs., introducing Senator George F. Hoar; and an undated note by Senator Hoar. (MS. 11 C 53)

Corporation of London Records Office,[1] Guildhall, LONDON, E.C.2

The Corporation's records, listed in Andrews and Davenport, pp. 280–3, as part of the Guildhall collection, are vast; but the following classes appear to contain the most significant American items:

[1] Philip E. Jones and Raymond Smith, *A Guide to the Records in the Corporation of London Records Office and the Guildhall Library Muniment Room* (London, 1951).

JOURNAL OF THE COMMON COUNCIL.[1]

(a) Fourteen miscellaneous petitions, motions, addresses, 1618–1762, dealing with such matters as transportation to Virginia, the tobacco trade, and military successes—e.g., Cape Breton, 1758, and Belle Isle, 1761. See Andrews and Davenport, pp. 280–1.

(b) A number of letters, petitions, addresses, remonstrances, &c., 1775–83, to and from the Mayor and Corporation during the War of Independence. See Andrews and Davenport, pp. 281–2.

COMMON HALL BOOKS.

Include addresses to the King, 1775, concerning the War of Independence. See Andrews and Davenport, pp. 282–3.

MAYOR'S COURT.

(a) Files of original Bills *temp.* Edward III (but mainly *temp.* Elizabeth) —1733. (317 files.) May contain items concerning American trade and transportation to America. Unindexed, but a manuscript list giving the chronological limits of each box is available in the Office.

(b) Depositions in the Mayor's Court. There are fifty-five boxes, 1640– c. 1835, containing material variously known as 'depositions', 'affidavits', 'certificates', 'affirmations' (when by Quakers), &c. Many of these deal with overseas trade and some may have reference to America. Unindexed, but a manuscript list giving the chronological limits of each box is available in the Office.

QUARTER SESSIONS RECORDS.

(a) Servants' indentures (3 boxes), 1718–40, with a few items for 1749–59. Memoranda or certificates of agreement to serve a stipulated number of years—three to seven, but usually four—in America or the West Indies. These certificates, of which there are nearly 3,000, give the age and native town of the contracting person, and are signed or marked by him; they state also to which colony he is bound, and sometimes a particular wage is laid down.

(b) Register of servants' indentures (1 volume), 1718–32. Names of those persons voluntarily binding themselves to go to the colonies and plantations in America. (A comparison of the register with the memoranda discloses more names in the former than appear on memoranda; in a very few cases there are memoranda with no corresponding entries in the register.)

[1] Journals 31, 32, 33 (1618–26) have been microfilmed for the Memorial Library of the University of Wisconsin, and journals 38, 39, 40, 41 *x*, 45 (1638–63 complete) for the Henry E. Huntingdon Library; the negatives are with the Corporation.

(c) Bonds for transportation of felons. Single items, 1667–70, 1680, 1698, 1715–35. Bonds, with two sureties, given to the justices of the peace by mariners and others that they would transport to America felons thus sentenced, or pardoned on condition of transportation.

(d) Certificates of landing at American ports (44 items), 1718–36. Certificates of the naval officers of the American ports, chiefly in Maryland and Virginia, where felons were landed, giving their names and numbers landed, the names of the ships carrying them and of the ships' commanders, and, usually, the names of those who had died during the voyage.

MISCELLANEOUS PAPERS.

(a) A few miscellaneous items relating to the sending of children and vagrants to Virginia, 1618–19. See Andrews and Davenport, p. 283.

(b) A petition, after 1643, from Plymouth to Parliament regarding the injurious effects of Dutch competition on western trade. See Andrews and Davenport, p. 283.

(c) Five collections of manuscripts relating to French Protestant refugees, some settling in America, c. 1680–1710. See Andrews and Davenport, p. 283, for some which were formerly in the Guildhall Library.

(d) Notes on freedoms and entertainments connected with America, 1853–1945. (Misc. MSS. 23. 33)

Coutts & Co., 440 Strand, LONDON, W.C.2

RUSSELL PAPERS.[1] c. 200 letters. 1767–1806 (mainly 1773–5).

The collection consists mainly of letters addressed to James Russell, a merchant, of 2 Hylords Court, Crutched Friars. Mrs. Ann Russell, for whose executors the papers are now held, is assumed to be his widow. (Although there are two accounts with Coutts & Co. in the name of James Russell, neither can be definitely identified with James Russell of 2 Hylords Court.)

Most of the correspondence and papers is from agents and firms in Maryland and Virginia, and the letters concern cargoes of tobacco, with occasional mention of other freight such as wheat; and various other matters, such as the collection of debts and requests for manufactured goods to be sent from England. Some also contain comments on the political situation, full of loyalty to the King and criticism of his ministers. A few are dated from the West Indies and from Europe, mostly from ports in England, Scotland, France, and the Netherlands.

Of particular interest are the names of two later Governors of Maryland: Thomas Sim Lee and George Plater; also of Richard Henry Lee and of Thomas Pownall, the Governor of Massachusetts and writer on colonial

---

[1] Microfilmed by the Virginia Colonial Records Project.

affairs. The correspondents also include members of the Fendell, Galloway, Jenifer, Johns, and Warfield families of Maryland, and the Washington family of Virginia.

There are also some bonds and legal papers relating to New York; their connexion with Russell's correspondence is not obvious. Among them are four bonds, 1775–6, to the Loyalist, the Rev. Charles Inglis, then assistant to the rector of Trinity Church, New York, and from 1787 first Bishop of Nova Scotia.

Further details as to names of correspondents are in N.R.A. 5612.

The Library, H.M. Customs and Excise, King's Beam House, Mark Lane, LONDON, E.C.3

Since this report incorporates, not merely extends, the work of Andrews, vol. ii, pp. 111–30, and since the records are singularly complex, an extended introduction has been thought useful.[1]

INTRODUCTION

At Michaelmas 1671 the English customs in general were finally taken out of farm, although certain of the minor farms were not finally wound up until some years later. A board of commissioners was vested by royal letter patent[2] with full power and authority to manage, levy, and collect the duties in England and Wales.

The customs of Scotland were not taken out of farm until the Union, but in 1707 a board of commissioners was set up in Scotland, likewise by royal letter patent. An Act of 1723[3] provided that the English and Scottish customs might be placed under the management of a single commission for 'the whole United Kingdom' (of Great Britain); the current patents were therefore cancelled, and a single commission was set up accordingly.[4] In 1742, however, the existing joint patent was cancelled by royal warrant,[5] and separate boards were again appointed in respect of England and Scotland.[6] This arrangement continued until 1823 when an Act[7] was passed to consolidate the customs boards and the excise boards of England and Scotland and the revenue board for Ireland, into two boards only, one of customs and one of excise, both for the whole of the United Kingdom.

Although an Act of 1672[8] authorized the English commissioners to control the collection of duty upon enumerated goods shipped in the plantations

[1] See Introduction (p. xxx).
[2] Pat. roll: 23 Car. II, p. 2, no. 1, mem. 35, *dorsa* (27 Sept. 1671).
[3] 9 Geo. I, cap. 21.
[4] Pat. roll: 9 Geo. I, p. 2, no. 12 (27 June 1723).
[5] Royal sign manual, 25 Aug. 1742.
[6] Pat. roll: 15 Geo II, p. 5, nos. 3 and 4 (9 Sept. 1742).
[7] 4 Geo. IV, cap. 23.   [8] 25 Car. II, cap. 7.

but not brought to England, the authority was never apparently explicitly stated (either in the statutes or in any of the early patents) for the English Board of Customs to control the plantation customs generally. Nevertheless, special collectors of customs were appointed in America and the West Indies, and such officials were directly under the control of the commissioners in England until 1767, when a board of American commissioners was created with headquarters at Boston.[1] The collectors of Bridgetown (Barbados), Roseau (Dominica), Grenville Bay (Grenada), Kingston and Montego Bay (Jamaica), Sandy Point (St. Christopher), and the ports of Montserrat and other Leeward Islands remained subject to the old board, but those of Accomac, Bermuda, Boston, Beaufort, Brunswick, Chester and Patapsco, Charleston, Halifax, James River, upper and lower, Mobile, Nantucket, New York, New Haven, Newfoundland, New London, Potomac, Philadelphia, Patuxent, Pensacola, Piscataqua, Plymouth, Pocomoke, Rhode Island, Rappahannock, Sunbury, Salem and Marblehead, Savannah, Salem and Cohenzie (Cohansey), and York River were transferred to the establishment books of the board in America.

In England the outports were divided, for purposes of administrative convenience,[2] into 'the Northern ports', which were those from the Thames 'north-about' to Barmouth on the river Mawddach in West Wales; and 'the Western ports', which were those from the Thames 'south-about' to the river Mawddach.

In the head office, the principal officials in the two 'departments' were 'the Northern clerk', and 'the Western clerk'. When the English commission first assumed responsibility for plantation affairs, the plantation ports were laid to 'the Western department' which became 'Western and plantations', and the clerk the 'Western and plantation clerk'.[3] Later a separate 'plantation clerk' was appointed, and he in time was conceded an 'assistant plantation clerk'. In certain other departments or branches separate officials were appointed in respect of the plantation business, for example, the 'solicitor of debts standing out in the plantation receipts'. The 'surveyor of the Acts of Navigation' was not specifically a plantation official, as the navigation laws (or Acts of trade) had to be enforced in relation to Europe, Africa, and Asia also.

After 1767 (when the separate board of American commissioners was set up at Boston)[4] the particular staff in the London Custom House dealing with plantation affairs could be reduced, for example, by the discon-

[1] Pat. roll: 7 Geo. III, p. 5, no. 11 (8 Sept. 1767). See also Edward Channing, 'The American Board of Commissioners for the Customs', *Proceedings of the Massachusetts Historical Society*, vol. xliii, pp. 477–90, 1909–10; and D. M. Clark, 'The American Board of Customs, 1767–1783', *American Historical Review*, vol. xlv, pp. 777–806, 1939–40.

[2] E. E. Hoon, *The Organization of the English Customs System, 1696–1786*, p. 69 (New York, 1938) (American Historical Association Publications).

[3] When Dr. Hoon said (ibid., p. 194) that 'the western ports were concerned primarily with the plantation . . . trade', she could not have meant the 'Western' ports in this technical sense, for such important plantation ports as Liverpool, Lancaster, and Whitehaven were 'Northern ports' in this classification.

[4] Pat. roll: Geo. III, p. 5, no. 11 (8 Sept. 1767).

tinuance of such offices as the 'assistant plantation clerk', and the 'assistant to the husband of the four-and-a-half-per-cent'.[1]

The board of commissioners in England was legally concerned with the enforcement of the Acts of Trade and with the collection of the plantation duty imposed by the Act of 1672.[2] This duty was established not so much as a source of revenue as to prevent direct trade with the continent of Europe; the collections therefore in the earlier years, particularly from Virginia and Maryland, where the large rivers and the great distances rendered the work of the collectors difficult, were very meagre, the whole produce of the imposition being little more than sufficient to defray the officers' salaries and the incidental charges for boat hire.[3] After 1696, with the increased number of collectors and the improved condition of the service, the amount became larger and the net returns sufficient to constitute an item in the commissioners' states of the revenue.[4]

The English Commissioners of Customs had no real power of appointment to ports in the plantations, but they were able to control the personnel of the establishment through their right to nominate and approve. They named the leading customs officials in America, and approved or disapproved of the minor officials selected by the surveyors general there, but in all cases the actual appointment lay in the hands of the Treasury.

Appointments were either 'on the establishment' or 'by incident'. Of the 'established officers', some of the principal officials of the ancient ports of England and some of the plantations held by patent: others held by commission out of the Treasury, and others (by the end of the colonial period, by much the major part) by warrant to the Commissioners of Customs to issue their deputation to the persons named. The 'incident officers' were normally appointed by the Commissioners of Customs. Executive deputies to titular patentees were variously appointed, usually by nomination of the patentee or the Treasury, or upon recommendation to the commissioners, and (latterly at least) always subject to the satisfaction of the commissioners as to competence and so forth.

Officials on the plantation establishment received their authority, pay, leave of absence, instructions, and power to hire boats and boatmen, by means of Treasury warrants. From 1767 to 16 Oct. 1783 this method of procedure was changed by the creation of the American board. During those years, some of the incidental officers, but not those on the establishment, were appointed by the board in England, others by the surveyors general in the colonies, with the approval of the American board, and still others by the American board itself.[5] The commissioners in England not only drew up special instructions for the colonial officials, but also wrote the general instructions to the governors, so far as these instructions concerned the part which the governors were to play in upholding the collectors and surveyors in the performance of their duties. The same was true of all

[1] British Museum Add. MSS. 8133 C.
[2] 25 Car. II, cap. 7.
[3] Blathwayt's Journal, Library of Congress transcript, i. 354.
[4] For references see T38/346–7 in Andrews, vol. ii, p. 217.
[5] See papers no. 767 (p. 197).

colonial laws that affected trade. Such laws were sent by the Board of Trade to the customs commissioners for approval and ratification.

Before Pitt's consolidation of the customs duties and his constitution of the consolidated fund in 1787,[1] the system of assessing, collecting, and accounting the customs duties was necessarily a very complex matter. The legislature's practice of appropriating the *net* yield of particular enactments to specific purposes led inevitably to great complexity in accounting, for the same goods were usually chargeable under a number of heads, each one of which being required by law to be assessed and accounted separately. That the gross yield of certain of the plantation ports or English outports was occasionally hardly enough to bear the costs of administration is, however, of no particular significance, for certain of the enactments were not intended to be revenue producing, and certain of the regulations were frankly cautionary and preventive.

In London there have been a number of Custom Houses, all of them on more or less the same site. The fact that three of them were almost completely destroyed by fire—in 1660, 1715, and again in 1814—is not without effect on the surviving records.

Various bundles and volumes containing Custom House accounts may now be found in the Public Record Office, among the Colonial Office Papers, the Treasury Papers,[2] and the series described below (composed of original Custom House documents) the greater part of which appear to have been earlier deposited in the Treasury. Some 565 volumes were transferred thence to the Custom House in 1835, and of these 438 were removed to the Rolls House in 1848 and the remainder in 1851. Many volumes were brought directly from the Treasury Chambers in 1846, 1847, and 1853. A number of volumes were returned to the Custom House in 1853 and 1854.

The bundles in the Treasury series that contain customs accounts will be found in Treasury, classes 38 and 64,[3] to which the searcher may be referred; those of the Board of Trade series may be found among the Colonial Office Papers, class 390: 6–11, already described, but of which a supplementary account is given here, together with a brief entry of a few volumes now in the modern Board of Trade series.

Also, there are in the Customs Library today about 40 volumes of correspondence to or from the outports, 1673–1783; 19 volumes of minutes of the Scottish Board of Customs, 1723–83 (see p. 196); a collection of customs papers, seizures after 1814 (which contain many documents relating to smuggling in the Canadian provinces and the seizure of American vessels trading contrary to the Navigation Acts); digests of Board's minutes from 1696; 55 volumes of annual ledgers of the Inspector-General of Imports and Exports, 1682–1776; 32 volumes of counsels' opinions, dating from 1701; complete board's minutes, out-letter books, and other records, dating mostly from 1814 (the date of the last of the fires noted above); and a number of

---

[1] 27 Geo. III, cap. 13.

[2] Though no Customs In-books have survived, many of the letters received by the Board can be traced through the Treasury Out-Letter Books: (Customs) (T11) from 1667. See Andrews, vol. ii, p. 209.

[3] T38/339–66; T64/137–54 and 238–57.

volumes relating to the plantations establishment. There are also complete and detailed lists of all records held in the outports (part only of which are referred to below), and collections of bound typewritten representative transcripts of the outport letter-books the originals of which are located in the ports themselves.

I. PUBLIC RECORD OFFICE

(a) BOARD OF TRADE SERIES.

Custom House Accounts: C.O. 390/6–11

6. 1677–1731. Custom House Accounts: an entry book of the Board of Trade, containing tables of exports and imports, arranged under the name of colony or subject: Newfoundland (fishery and inhabitants), Jamaica (goods), Barbados (goods), Leeward Islands (goods), Virginia (goods exported and shipping), Maryland (goods exported), Italy, Spain, Portugal ('State of the trade'), East India (goods and ships), Coinage, Naval stores (from all countries, including the plantations, 1701–23). Also a 'Scheme of the fishery of Newfoundland', 1720, 1722–7, 1729–31, by Capt. Percy. Also tables of goods imported and exported, Jamaica, 1718–22.

7. 1670–1729.

8. 1712–17.

9. 1725–71.

A Board of Trade volume, containing the original reports sent from the Custom House at the request of the board in the years 1760–72. There would seem to be some duplicating of information in the lists. Early returns are of hemp and rice imported, 1752–62; hats exported, 1735–8, 1750–3, 1759–62; beaver skins, imported and exported, 1735–8, 1750–3, 1759–62; beaver wool, exported, 1735–8, 1750–3, 1759–63; beaver skins, imported, 1749–63.

Miscellanea. First Committee. Papers. BT6/80–81 and 83–88.

80. 1783–4. America: commercial intercourse (correspondence).

81. 1783–6. America: commercial intercourse (minutes, &c.).

83. 1784. America and West Indies: commercial intercourse (minutes, &c.).

84. 1784–5. America and West Indies: commercial intercourse (correspondence).

85. 1784–6. American intercourse with Great Britain.

86. 1783–4. American intercourse with Great Britain (Custom House accounts).

87. 1783–5. American intercourse with Newfoundland and Nova Scotia.

88. 1804–7. America and West Indies: commercial intercourse.

(b) CUSTOMS SERIES: INSPECTOR-GENERAL'S ACCOUNTS.

In England the collection of primary material for the express purpose of the compilation of statistics of foreign trade was commenced by the Inspector-

General of Imports and Exports[1] in 1696. The new office was charged to produce 'a true account of the importacions and exportacions of all commodities into and out of this Kingdom, and to and from what places the same are exported and imported'.

Customs 2 (10 volumes). 1696–1702. Accounts of imports and exports, specifying the trade from London and the outports, to and from the English plantations.

Customs 3 (80 volumes). 1697–1780. Ledgers of imports and exports showing: I, Importations, and II, Exportations, through (a) London and (b) the outports, of (i) foreign goods and (ii) English goods, all separately (and additionally) distinguished.

Customs 4 (94 volumes). 1792–1899. Ledgers of imports—under countries.

Customs 5 (162 volumes). 1811–99. Ledgers of imports—under commodities.

Customs 6 (22 volumes). 1832–53. Ledgers of imports into colonies—under countries.

Customs 8 (140 volumes). 1812–99. Ledgers of exports of British merchandise—under countries.

Customs 10 (97 volumes). 1809–99. Ledgers of exports of foreign and colonial merchandise—under countries.

Customs 16 (1 volume). 1768–73. Ledger of imports and exports: America. Valuable and informative annual analytical accounts of the vessels (with their description, tonnages, and voyages) entered and cleared the several ports of North America, the shipment of goods in the British and foreign West Indies, general overseas, and coastwise trades; all based upon returns rendered by the American Board of Customs at Boston.

Customs 17 (30 volumes). 1772–1808. States of navigation. Statistical tables showing *inter alia* the number, tonnage, and voyages of British and foreign ships entering and clearing at British ports, from or to oversea places; with detailed accounts, in quantities and values, of merchandise shipped, including that to and from British and foreign America, distinguishing England from Scotland.

(c) ESTABLISHMENT REGISTERS.

Quarterly salary-books, in respect of Lady Day, Midsummer, Michaelmas, and Christmas quarters (1 volume per quarter), of the English customs establishment.

Customs 18 (607 volumes). 1675–1813. Two volumes in particular, no. 310 for Midsummer 1767, and no. 312 for Christmas 1767, include an 'Establishment of the Officers of His Majesty's Customs in the Plantations', the latter to the date of the establishment of the American Board (8 Sept. 1767). In the Customs Library (see 767, p. 197) is another volume showing the American establishment just prior to that date.

---

[1] See G. N. Clark, 'The Inspectors-General of Imports and Exports', in *Guide to English Commercial Statistics, 1696–1782* (London, 1938) (Royal Historical Society Guides and Handbooks, no. 1).

(d) EXCHEQUER PORT-BOOKS.[1]

These are the most important source for the study of English maritime trade, both overseas and coastwise, in the sixteenth and seventeenth centuries. After 1696 interest transfers to the records of the Inspector-General of Imports and Exports (see p. 196). The port-books, however, were not intended to be either commercial records or statistical returns; they were part of the financial records of the customs administration.[2] They are vellum books of varying size and thickness, usually about 11 inches by 15 inches, returned into the Exchequer by the principal officers at the various head-ports and 'creeks' in response to an order of 1564. The series (of 1464 bundles) contains altogether between 14,000 and 15,000 books. They vary greatly in physical condition, some being well preserved, others little injured, but a few hardly legible. Although some of the books from certain of the creeks are in English from the commencement, the entries until the end of the sixteenth century are generally in Latin—but in a Latin Dr. N. J. Williams calls 'a patois known rarely outside the custom house'. About half the surviving books relate to the overseas trade, and half to the coastwise trade. The great value of the books for colonial history lies in the record they contain of the nature and distribution of colonial staple products and of goods exported from the English outports to America. This record is not confined to the direct trade between Great Britain and America, but includes also a very large body of material showing the reshipment and re-exportation of colonial staples to other parts of Great Britain and Ireland and to the Continent, and the transportation of such commodities inland as well as by water. For the British coastwise trade the books are indispensable, and of this traffic American staples formed an important part. Furthermore, in these books are hundreds of names of vessels, either plantation- or English-built or taken as prize, that were concerned in the trade and passenger traffic between England and America, and these books date back to the beginning of that history.[3]

A good idea of the character of the information contained in this class of record can be obtained from the introduction and text of R. W. K. Hinton's *The Port Books of Boston: 1601–1640* (Lincoln, 1956) (Lincoln Record Society, vol. 50) and E. A. Lewis's *Welsh Port Books: 1550–1603* (London, 1927). For a good critical study and demonstration of their value as historical sources see N. J. Williams's papers,[4] Francis Shaxton and the Elizabethan Port-Books', in the *English Historical Review*, vol. lxvi, pp. 387–95, 1951; and 'The London Port Books' in *Transactions of the London and Middlesex Archaeological Society*, vol. xviii, pp. 13–26, 1955.

[1] For an informative introduction see G. N. Clark, 'Note on the Port Books', in op. cit.

[2] N. J. Williams, 'The London Port-Books', in *Transactions of the London and Middlesex Archaeological Society*, vol. xviii, pp. 13–26, 1955.

[3] For a note on the port-book entries of the *Mayflower* see R. G. Marsden's memorandum, *First Report of the Royal Commission on Public Records*, vol. i, part ii, p. 49 (Cd. 6395/1912). There is also a port book exclusively concerned with tobacco, which has been printed in N. J. Williams, 'England's Tobacco Trade in the Reign of Charles I', *Virginia Magazine of History and Biography*, vol. lxv, pp. 403–49, 1957.

1–160. London. 1665–97.

161–84. Berwick. 1606–1784.

185–302. Newcastle upon Tyne. 1579–1798.

303–86. Hull, including Scarborough and Grimsby. 1565–1644, 1654–1787.

387–424. Boston (Lincs.) 1565–1773.

425–70. Lynn. 1565–1794.

471–586. Great Yarmouth, with Blakeney, Dunwich, Walberswick, Southwold, Aldborough, and Woodbridge. 1565–1780.

587–637. Ipswich, including Colchester and Malden. 1565–1736.

638–736. Sandwich and Deal, with Rochester, Milton, Faversham, and Dover. 1565–1756.

737–813. Chichester, with Folkestone, Hythe, Romney, Rye, Winchelsea, Hastings, Pevensey, Matching (Meeching, now Newhaven), Lewes, New Shoreham, Arundel, and Littlehampton. 1565–1731.

814–63. Southampton and Portsmouth. 1565–1758.

864–924. Poole, including Lyme and Weymouth. 1565–1759.

925–1009. Exeter, with Dartmouth, Barnstaple, Bideford, and Ilfracombe. 1565–1788.

1010–80. Plymouth, with Looe, Fowey, Penryn, Truro, Helston, Mount's Bay, St. Ives, and Padstow. 1565–1758.

1081–1127. Bridgwater and Minehead. 1566–1776.

1128–1240. Bristol. 1565–1788.

1241–69. Gloucester. 1581–1776.

1270–97. Cardiff, including Chepstow, Neath, and Swansea.

1298–1322. Milford, including Bury, Carmarthen, and Cardigan. 1565–1784.

1323–1447. Chester, including Beaumaris, Conway, Caernarvon, Liverpool, and Lancaster. 1565–1789.

1448–61. Carlisle, with Whitehaven. 1611–1743.

1462–4. Uncertain ports.

II. CUSTOMS LIBRARY[1]

(a) Board's Minutes and Letter-books (English, later Great Britain, later United Kingdom).

1319–32 (14 volumes). Digest of Board's Minutes, 1696–1869.

Originally compiled for Sir William Musgrave, Commissioner 1763–86, and continued thereafter; the only complete chronological record of the Board's administration throughout the period.[2]

---

[1] It is particularly to be noted, with reference to sections 3 and 4 of the Public Records Act of 1958, that the place of final deposit of the records noted below has not, at the time of writing, yet been decided.

[2] E. E. Hoon, *The Organization of the English Customs System, 1696–1786*, p. 293 (New York, 1938) (American Historical Association Publications).

Board's Minutes.

1268–75 (9 volumes). Receiver-General's Minutes. 1716–84.

887–96 (10 volumes). General Business Minutes. 1734–1813.

9743–10068 (316 volumes). Board's Minutes. 1814–85.

The above minute-books record the board's general business, including, for example, the incidents during the Civil War, 1861–5.

1480–1542, and 1621 (64 volumes). Scottish Board Minutes 1723–1828.

References to plantation trade generally, especially tobacco from Virginia and Maryland, rum from New England, and coffee from the West Indies; registry of plantation-built ships, prizes and privateers (including John Paul Jones in the Forth—1779).

Board's Letter-Books.

8714–940 (227 volumes). Western letter-books, 1787–1872.

Copies of out-letters to the various ports, from London 'south-about' to Cardigan.

8988–9170 (183 volumes). Northern letter-books, 1812–72.

Copies of out-letters to the various English ports, from London 'north-about' to Aberystwyth.

8647–705 (59 volumes). Scottish letter-books, 1823–72.

Copies of out-letters to the various Scottish ports.

7704–26 (23 volumes). Treasury letter-books, 1814–64.

Copies of out-letters from Board of Customs to Treasury.

There are also other letter-books, &c., in other series.

(b) 1683–1735 (53 volumes): Inspector-General's Ledgers of Imports and Exports, 1682–1776.

Tables showing both quantities and values[1] of the separately specified commodities imported and exported, through London and the outports, from and to the several overseas places (distinguishing, e.g. Carolina, Florida, Georgia, New England, New York, Pennsylvania, &c.).

(c) Opinions of Counsel. England: 200–6, 17796 and 21618–38 (29 volumes), 1701–1841. Scotland: 1547–9 (3 volumes), 1760–83.

Occasional informative discussions regarding application and interpretation of laws of trade, the nationality of vessels built in America between 1776 and 1783 ('in some of the provinces in America at the time when they were in actual Rebellion'); and the precise legal status of particular vessels and seamen in immediate post-1783 period.

(d) Plantation Records.

760. Plantations Ledger. 1767–75. Showing yields, incidences, and balances under various headings in the different collections (including the collectors'

[1] It is now generally understood, of course, that these 'values' were notional values.

names). (James River, lower part, James River, upper part, York River, Rappahanock, South Potomac, North Potomac, &c.)

767 (1 volume). General Establishment of all the Officers employed in the Service of His Majesty's Customs in America [1767], including notes as to source of emolument, whether 'established' or 'incidental', and if the latter, whether appointed by the board in England, the board in America, or the surveyor general confirmed by the board in America.

768 (1 volume). Customs Establishment: American Colonies. 1767–71.

766 (1 volume). Customs Establishment: American Colonies. 1771–6.

Quarterly salary accounts of the Boston headquarter establishment and of the ports from Newfoundland to Bermuda.

III. OTHER CUSTOMS RECORDS

THE OUTPORTS

The following notes on the material in the main English and Scottish outports are intended only to indicate in general terms the nature of their contents, the earlier records of Greenock alone, for example, number no less than 300 volumes, some of which are very bulky. The statutory registers of British merchant ships date mostly from 1786 (the date of the first Act of general registry),[1] but occasionally commence earlier (e.g. Liverpool and Campbeltown) and occasionally later (e.g. Bristol, Dartmouth, and Plymouth). Because in the year 1786 the law required the re-registry of every foreign-going British merchant vessel then afloat, the records contain many registries of plantation-built vessels, and in the later period references to American vessels captured by British privateers, and British vessels lost to American privateers. There are also occasional references to trade during the currency of 'the Prohibitory Acts',[2] to the departure of 'artificers' contrary to the provision of the Acts of 1718, 1749, and 1785,[3] and, particularly in certain of the Scottish ports (e.g. Campbeltown and Stornoway) to emigration generally.

The value of much of the outport material generally, therefore, is not confined to pre-1783 records. The later volumes of letter-books and registers are important also, for example, for the War of 1812 and for the trade of the United States as late as the period of the Civil War. As noted above, there are in the Customs Library in London sets of typewritten representative transcripts of the various letter-books, both inwards and outwards, selected from each of the main outports, to illustrate their general character. There are also in the Library full hand-lists of all material available in each of the outports. A list of these outport records is to be found[4] in the *Appendix to the Second Report of the Royal Commission on Public Records*, vol. ii, part ii, pp. 242–8 (Cd. 7545/1914). It should, however, be noted that neither that list nor the one that follows is complete. Access to these papers is obtainable

---

[1] 26 Geo. III, cap. 60.

[2] 16 Geo. III, cap. 5, and 17 Geo. III, cap. 7.

[3] 5 Geo. I, cap. 27; 23 Geo. II, cap. 13; and 25 Geo. III, cap. 67.

[4] But see Rupert C. Jarvis, 'Local archives of H.M. Customs', *Bulletin of the Society of Local Archivists*, no. 9, pp. 1–14, 1952.

only through application to the Librarian of H.M. Customs and Excise, *never* by direct application to the outports.[1]

No. of volumes

Dover

Board to Collector, from 1746	20
Collector to Board, from 1784	88
Other letter-books, order books, &c., from 1792	7
Registers of British ships, from 1824	9
Other records, from 1693	9

Of little American significance, except for the clandestine trade in tobacco, mostly in contravention of the Acts of Trade.

Portsmouth

Board to Collector, from 1726	140
Collector to Board, from 1748	151
Other letter-books, order books, &c., from 1810	15
Registers of British ships, from 1824	9
Other records, from 1689	8

Few direct references to American affairs: return of stamps from Nova Scotia on repeal of Stamp Act; passage of continental emigrants from Rotterdam (via Portsmouth for quarantine) for Philadelphia, 1774; arrival of Parker's fleet from South Carolina after Americans' attack on Charleston harbour—with casualty list—1776; taking of the American privateer, *Rising States*, 1777; discharge of cargo of American prize *Thomas Koulikan*, loaded with guns, shot, drugs, 'and many other things for the use of the Americans', 1778; shipment of 'considerable sums of money for the service of His Majesty's Forces in America', 1778, &c.

Southampton

Board to Collector, from 1756	128
Collector to Board, from 1714	126
Other letter-books, order books, &c., from 1814	16
Registers of British ships, from 1855	15
Other records, from 1728	18

Little of direct American interest, but much information about clandestine trade in American tobacco from the Channel Islands, in contravention of the Acts of trade.

Cowes

Board to Collector, from 1703	79
Collector to Board, from 1749	60
Other letter-books, order books, &c., from 1703	27
Registers of British ships, from 1786	10
Other records, from 1810	7

[1] It is particularly to be noted, with reference to sections 3 and 4 of the Public Records Act of 1958, that the place of final deposit of these records has not, at the time of writing, yet been decided.

Little of American interest, but much referring to contraband, and some reference to privateers, quarantine, &c., and to the clandestine trade in American tobacco from the Channel Islands in contravention of the Acts of trade.

No. of volumes

Poole

Board to Collector, from 1760	6
Collector to Board, from 1820	16
Other letter-books, order books, &c., from 1758	28
Registers of British ships, from 1845	3
Other records, from 1793	4

The earlier records were lost in a fire at the Custom House in 1813, but those surviving are very informative about the affairs of Newfoundland and the whale fisheries.

Weymouth

Board to Collector, from 1694	117
Collector to Board, from 1716	103
Other letter-books, order books, &c., from 1812	37
Registers of British ships, from 1786	8
Other records, from 1801	6

A remarkably complete body of port record.

Exeter

Board to Collector, from 1676	121
Collector to Board, from 1743	50
Other letter-books, order books, &c., from 1822	20
Registers of British ships, from 1786	10
Other records, from 1738	12

Much information about the affairs of Newfoundland, the whale and other fisheries of Greenland and Newfoundland, and some references to mid-eighteenth century trade (e.g. in rice, deer-skins, &c., with Carolina), and the later activities of the American privateers.

Dartmouth

Board to Collector, from 1675	112
Collector to Board, from 1775	38
Other letter-books, order books, &c., from 1800	4
Registers of British ships, from 1824	16
Other records, from 1687	14

References (in 1775) to the guard to be placed upon all ports to prevent the shipment of 'any goods, especially gunpowder or other military stores' being 'clandestinely put on board' any vessel bound for North America, to the proclamation of 22 Apr. 1779, relating to the trade of New York, and Newport in Rhode Island, &c.

No. of volumes

Plymouth

Board to Collector, from 1775	229
Collector to Board, from 1799	4
Other letter-books, order books, &c., from 1818	16
Registers of British ships, from 1824	13
Other records, from 1835	5

Of special interest for the War of 1812, particularly with regard to contraband and prize of war, the seizure or retention of American vessels on suspicion, the infringement of the Acts of trade (in the unshipment of tobacco in the Channel Islands), &c.

Falmouth

Board to Collector, from 1780	134
Collector to Board, from 1867	5
Other letter-books, order books, &c., from 1853	15
Other records, from 1817	25

Mostly about the packet service, with little of American interest.

Penzance

Board to Collector, from 1722	119
Collector to Board, from 1738	35
Other letter-books, order books, &c., from 1849	6
Registers of British ships, from 1786	8
Other records, from 1777	4

Much information about the French wars, and illicit trade generally.

Bristol (including Barnstaple and other creeks)

Board to Collector, from 1717	90
Collector to Board, from 1727	56
Other letter-books, order books, &c., from 1816	71
Registers of British ships, from 1786	25
Other records, from 1760	23

The greater part of the earlier records of the port of Bristol itself (as distinct from its creeks) were lost in the burning down of the Custom House during the Reform Bill riots of 1831.

The earlier Barnstaple records, from 1727, refer to the American tobacco and Newfoundland trades, including returns of the names of vessels, and quantities of tobacco in hogsheads, from Virginia and Maryland (separately) in each of the years 1722–32; other references to later trade with America; and privateers generally, and the shipment, in 1776, of grain as stores to the army.

Cardiff

Board to Collector, from 1689	93
Collector to Board, from 1746	23
Other letter-books, order books, &c., from 1813	7
Registers of British ships, from 1824	22
Other records, from 1704	32

Of little or no direct American relevance except as regards the activities of 'wreckers' plundering cargoes of tobacco, cotton, sugar, coffee, ginger, and other plantation produce.

No. of volumes

Swansea

Board to Collector, from 1709	155
Collector to Board, from 1730	43
Other letter-books, order books, &c., from 1806	17
Registers of British ships, from 1824	18
Other records, from 1711	23

Only occasional references to American affairs, as when the *Gloucester Lass* left Swansea 'for Boston in New England with eighty chalder coals' duty-paid, but foundered in the bay, 1755; or when the brigantine *Sally* (a prize 'taken from the Americans') from Boston with cargo and ten passengers, bound for London, was forced into Swansea 1776; or the ship *James and Peggy*, a transport of Leith, from New York in ballast for London, arrived in Swansea, 1777.

Caernarvon (including its creeks)

Board to Collector, from 1714	103
Collector to Board, from 1757	53
Other letter-books, order books, &c., from 1806	23
Registers of British ships, from 1840	22
Other records, from 1817	13

Many references to illicit trade with Isle of Man (before 1765) in American and East Indian produce, contrary to Acts of trade.

Liverpool

Registers of British ships, from 1739	152

For the text of the port letter-books, to and from the Board, &c., see *Customs Letter Books of the Port of Liverpool, 1711–1813*, ed. by R. C. Jarvis (Manchester, 1954) (Chetham Society Publications, third series, vol. vi). There is much information about colonial and plantation trade and shipping generally, the whale fisheries, tobacco, trade practices, the slave trade, the privateers, the Prohibitory Acts, and so forth, transatlantic ship-ownership and shipbuilding.

Heysham (Lancaster)

Letter-books, order books, &c., from 1715	6
Registers of British ships, from 1786	12
Other records, from 1689	1

Many references to the eighteenth-century colonial and plantation trade and shipping.

Whitehaven

Board to Collector, from 1703	19
Collector to Board, from 1730	32

No. of volumes

Other letter-books, order books, &c., from 1779   42
Registers of British ships, from 1786   10
Other records, from 1771   13

Many references to plantation and colonial trade and shipping, particularly the tobacco and lumber trades and shipbuilding. Occasional brief references to American affairs, e.g. to 'prisoners from North America' ('tall lusty young men' but 'very ragged and shabby') taken in the Ohio Expedition in 1755, to affairs generally during the War of Independence, e.g. to the detailed operation of the Prohibitory Act, the seizure of American vessels in 1778, the return of General Burgoyne's ships, 13 May 1778, to Paul Jones's attack on the port, and so forth.

Dumfries

Board to Collector, from 1727   76
Collector to Board, from 1708   16
Other letter-books, order books, &c., from 1788   8
Registers of British ships, from 1824   10
Other records, from 1782   5

Eighteenth-century legal trade with Virginia consisted of only about four arrivals a year, but there was extensive illegal traffic, via the Isle of Man and Ireland.

Ayr

Board to Collector, from 1740   5
Collector to Board, from 1729   30
Other letter-books or order books, from 1812   27
Registers of British ships, from 1855   5
Other records, from 1798   5

Extensive trade with America and the West Indies in tobacco, sugar, and rum, with considerable transhipments to Norway and France; up to 1765 much illicit trade in these goods with the Isle of Man, and thereafter with goods 'coloured' for exportation (e.g. to Norway) and relanded (e.g. in Scotland or Ireland); references to Prohibitory Act, 1776, to the prevention of the 'embarkations of Rebellious subjects, gunpowder, and all ammunition to America', 1775; to the licensed trade, 1778–9; and to American privateers in the Clyde, including Paul Jones, elsewhere referred to as 'the Pirate' or 'the Villain', but here as the 'Captain'. Trade appears to have dwindled away after 1783.

Greenock

Board to Collector, from 1723   342
Collector to Board, from 1749   81
Other letter-books, order books, &c., from 1749   26
Registers of British ships, from 1786   68
Other records, from 1707   39

From opening period, a large trade in tobacco, and later in sugar and rum; extensive export trade, ostensibly to Europe, but actually to be clandestinely relanded; references to evasions of the Prohibitory Act; the watch placed upon emigrants and other passengers; to the shipment of military stores and reinforcements; to the privateers generally and to Paul Jones in particular in 1778; to the D'Estaing's operations in the West Indies in 1779; and to the news brought by incoming vessels about American affairs generally. The ship registry of the *Comet* and other transatlantic vessels.

No. of volumes

Glasgow

Board to Collector, from 1773	86
Collector to Board, from 1811	26
Other letter-books, order books, &c., from 1812	38
Registers of British ships, from 1808	48
Other records, from 1799	21

Much information about shipbuilding, ship-ownership.

Campbeltown

Board to Collector, from 1738	60
Collector to Board, from 1749	47
Registers of British ships, from 1763	13
Other records, from 1764	7

Contain interesting information about local emigration to America, both before and after independence.

Stornoway

Board to Collector, from 1780	30
Collector to Board, from 1765	26
Other letter-books, order books, &c., from 1800	5
Registers of British ships, from 1788	9
Other records, from 1828	13

Contain interesting information about local emigration to America, both before and after independence.

Lerwick

Board to Collector, from 1790	91
Collector to Board, from 1791	11
Other letter-books, order books, &c., from 1845	13
Registers of British ships, from 1837	4
Other records, from 1818	8

Of little or no American interest.

Inverness

Board to Collector, from 1781	58
Other letter-books, order books, &c., from 1866	12
Registers of British ships, from 1789	25
Other records, from 1707	16

Of little or no American interest.

No. of volumes

Aberdeen

Board to Collector, from 1733	98
Collector to Board, from 1721	32
Other letter-books, order books, &c., from 1801	23
Registers of British ships, from 1824	23
Other records, from 1708	23
(Plus unbound 'Ages and capacities' from 1771)	

There is little of direct American interest, but there are a number of references to the Greenland fishery, and to the interruption of shipping by the privateers off the coast in the 1780's—but no direct reference to Paul Jones.

Montrose

Board to Collector, from 1708	52
Collector to Board, from 1724	29
Other letter-books, order books, &c., from 1710	59
Registers of British ships, from 1824	7
Other records, from 1841	3

These records date from the Union of Scotland and England in 1707, and contain many references to the considerable eighteenth-century trade in tobacco, and to the whale fisheries.

Dundee

Board to Collector, from 1708	206
Collector to Board, from 1735	39
Other letter-books, order books, &c., from 1792	33
Registers of British ships, from 1824	31
Other records, from 1716	19
(Plus unbound 'Ages and capacities' from 1833)	

These records date from the Union of Scotland and England in 1707, but there is disappointingly little about the early whaling trade and the distant fisheries, which contributed so largely to the growth of Dundee as a port.

Alloa

Board to Collector, from 1744	19
Collector to Board, from 1736	14
Other letter-books or order books, from 1718	106
Registers of British ships, from 1838	3

Much trade with West Indies; list of customs officers in Virginia and Maryland empowered to sign tobacco manifests, 1752, alteration in port routine accounts and returns, on establishment of Board of Customs in America, 1769; certificate under the Act of 1780, that the ports and towns of New York and Charleston are 'now under the protection of His Majesty's arms', 1780.

No. of volumes

Leith (including Dunbar)

Board to Collector, from 1707	309
Collector to Board, from 1834	108
Other letter-books, and order books, from 1885	22
Registers of British ships, from 1824	7
Other records, from 1707	6

References to the tobacco and rum trade with New York, Georgia, and other colonies; to the 'many embarcations' for America, 'some of them with money arms and ammunition', 1775; to the interception and seizure of letters and papers from the 'persons now in rebellion in America', 1775; to John Paul Jones's squadron in the Forth, 1779; and to the Loyalists from New York, 1783.

Newcastle upon Tyne

Board to Collector, from 1706	27
Collector to Board, from 1724	120
Other letter-books, order books, &c., from 1725	164
Registers of British ships, from 1786	41
Other records, from 1764	19

Principally the coal trade, including vessels bound for New York in 1777 with coal; some references to the whale fisheries and the privateers (mostly French); and to the tobacco trade from Virginia and Maryland as early as 1727.

Sunderland

Board to Collector, from 1740	103
Collector to Board, from 1732	65
Other letter-books, and order books, from 1810	4
Registers of British ships, from 1786	43
Other records, from 1832	3

Relating principally to the coal trade, but some references to the whale fishery and the privateers, principally French; and, for example, a report of the harbour, light, buoyage and clearances dues payable by American vessels in 1789.

Stockton-on-Tees

Board to Collector, from 1675	71
Collector to Board, from 1736	35
Other letter-books, order books, &c., from 1838	6
Registers of British ships, from 1838	6
Other records, from 1748	7

References to the plantations and whale fisheries from the very beginning of this series.

Whitby

Board to Collector, from 1816	42
Collector to Board, from 1721	10

No. of volumes

Other letter-books, order books, &c., from 1715   16
Registers of British ships, from 1786   41
Other records, from 1808   4

Many and detailed references to the Greenland whale fishery.

Hull

Board to Collector, from 1799   118
Collector to Board, from 1843   24
Other letter-books, order books, &c., from 1733 213
Other records, from 1756   18

References to plantation and colonial trade (e.g. Virginia tobacco trade), to the late eighteenth-century privateers, and details of the doings of Paul Jones on the eve of the *Serapis* action.

Boston

Board to Collector, from 1732   99
Collector to Board, from 1766   14
Other letter-books, order books, &c., from 1862   1
Registers of British ships, from 1824   9
Other records, from 1815   8

Have been said to be possibly of genealogical interest to American families originating in this part of Britain.

King's Lynn

Board to Collector, from 1700   124
Other letter-books, order books, &c., from 1728   25
Registers of British ships, from 1832   10
Other records, from 1817   4

Many references to smuggling, and to lights, lighthouses, and light dues, but little of plantation, colonial, or American interest—notwithstanding that George Vancouver's father, and his brother and biographer, were once in charge here.

Great Yarmouth

Board to Collector, from 1662   114
Collector to Board, from 1702   110
Other letter-books, order books, &c., from 1731   99
Registers of British ships, from 1834   15
Other records, from 1777   8

Of importance in the continental and fishing trades in the eighteenth and nineteenth centuries, particularly with regard to wreck salvage, &c.— but little of plantation, colonial, or American interest. A reference, however, to American privateers in the North Sea in 1777.

No. of volumes

Harwich

Board to Collector, from 1699	129
Collector to Board, from 1713	89
Other letter-books, order books, &c., from 1794	28
Registers of British ships, from 1824	10
Other records, from 1699	10

Of importance in the continental trade of the late eighteenth and early nineteenth centuries, particularly the packet service and refugee immigrants, but only very occasionally anything of plantation, colonial, or American interest. There is, however, a reference, for example, 30 Nov. 1775—the brig *Despatch* of New York, from Malaga to Hamburg with wine, to the shipment from Hamburg to New York of 'arms and ammunition for the use of the American rebels'.

Dr. Williams's Library, 14 Gordon Square, London, W.C.1

The Library is primarily theological, but contains many historical and other works. The following is additional to the material listed in Andrews & Davenport, pp. 343–6 (which are mainly the papers of the Rev. Richard Baxter (1615–91)):

JOLLIE PAPERS. 3 letters. 1681–8. (12.78)

Dedham, Mass., 29 Apr. 1681 and 2 Nov. 1682, from W. Adams, of religious interest.

Watertown, New England, 26 Sept. 1688, from John Bailey to Henry Bailey, giving some details of Indian attacks on the settlers; and of attempts to convert the Indians to Christianity which, he feels, is effort wasted.

LINDSEY, THEOPHILUS (1723–1808). 8 letters. 1788–94. (24.86)

Letters to Lindsey from the United States, chiefly concerning Unitarianism, with three of merely personal interest.

(*a*) Four letters, all from Boston, from James Freeman, first Unitarian minister of King's Chapel, Boston, and a founder of the Massachusetts Historical Society:

29 Mar. 1788, referring to the adoption of the Constitution and matters connected with this.

15 Oct. 1788, commenting adversely on the American bishops.

16 June 1793, touching on religious liberty in the United States.

13 June 1794, dealing with Unitarianism in America.

(*b*) Letter, 1789, from J. Smith of Cambridge, Mass., remarks that the new government enjoys the confidence of all the people, and will clear the national debt.

PRIESTLEY LETTERS. Volume of correspondence, letters. 1794–1832. (12.13)

(a) Volume of correspondence from Joseph Priestley, while resident at Northumberland, Pa., from 1794 until his death in 1804. Letters, 1794–1803, to Theophilus Lindsey and Thomas Belsham, dealing chiefly with Priestley's religious activities and writings, but containing incidental references to American politics, including the respective strengths of the Federalists and anti-Federalists, and the violence of American party feeling. There are some references to Washington and John Adams. The passage of Jay's Treaty occasions a remark on the conduct of business in Congress. There are some sidelights on the Alien and Sedition Laws, under which Priestley considered himself in danger as a friend of France, a view which appears to be supported by a letter from Jefferson, 18 Jan. 1800,[1] part of which is transcribed in the correspondence, regretting the 'persecution' to which Priestley has been subjected; and also asking Priestley's advice on the foundation of a university in Virginia. There is praise for Jefferson's administration; and a brief comparison of the American and English forms of government, to the advantage of the American. In 1803 Priestley expresses the opinion that events are moving in the direction of Negro emancipation, and mentions the Southerners' fears of slave insurrections. The Louisiana Purchase is mentioned, and the view expressed that even if Britain had occupied Louisiana, the increasing population of the United States 'would in time have burst thro' that feeble barrier'.

(b) Letter, Philadelphia, 17 Aug. 1832, from James Taylor to the Rev. Hugh Hutton, extra-illustrator of the *Life and Correspondence of Joseph Priestley* (London, 1832), includes comments on the consequences of the re-election of Jackson. (12.79–80)

KENRICK PAPERS. 4 letters. 1810–23. (24.107)

Letters to Thomas Belsham (1750–1829), Unitarian minister, from correspondents in the United States.

Boston, 14 July 1810, from W. Buckminster, mentions the rejection of the Erskine agreement, says that neither Britain nor the United States really wishes to compose the differences between them.

Boston, 11 Dec. 1813, from Samuel Cary, on the increase of Roman Catholicism in the United States, and the growth of intolerance.

Boston, 25 June 1816, from Francis Parkman, on Unitarianism.

Baltimore, 20 June 1823, from Jared Sparks, the editor and historian, comments on Jefferson's opinion of Christianity. Contains quotations from a letter from Jefferson to Sparks ('over two years ago') in which Jefferson adheres to the principle of first-century Christianity without the erroneous accretions of later centuries.

---

[1] Printed in *The Writings of Thomas Jefferson*, ed. by P. L. Ford, vol. vii, pp. 406–10 (London and New York, 1897).

HEYWOOD, ROBERT (1786–1868). Travel diary.[1] 1834. (28.158)

Heywood left England for America on 1 May and returned on 11 Oct. 1834. He travelled from New York via Philadelphia, Baltimore, Washington, D.C., through Kentucky, by steamer to Cincinnati, thence to Columbus, Ohio, Wheeling, W. Va., Pittsburgh, Pa., Buffalo, N.Y., and Niagara, into Canada, and back via Ticonderoga, N.Y., Albany, N.Y., Boston and Newport, R.I., to New York. The diary is of some interest to the social historian but does not deal with political or economic matters.

ESTLIN PAPERS. 1840–84. (24.120–7)

Mary Estlin was the daughter of Dr. J. B. Estlin (1785–1855), a prominent ophthalmic surgeon of Bristol, a Unitarian reformer, and anti-slavery supporter. She was a member of the Bristol and Clifton Auxiliary Ladies Anti-Slavery Society and maintained an extensive correspondence with abolitionists in the United States, which she visited in 1868; after the Civil War she transferred her energies to the women's rights campaign.

The most important items are:

(a) Minute-book, 1840–61, of the Bristol and Clifton Auxiliary Ladies Anti-Slavery Society. References to slavery in the United States, the raising of funds to assist fugitive slaves, and the American Anti-Slavery Society.

(b) Part of a letter, n.d., from Parker Pillsbury, American reformer travelling in Ireland, on the evils of slavery and the reluctance of the clergy and politicians to fight it.

(c) Letters, 1844–51, of anti-slavery interest, to Dr. Estlin from James Martineau; Mr. Donaldson of Cincinnati, mentioning also Oberlin College and Negro education; Dr. S. G. Howe of Boston; Joshua Coffin of Newbury, Mass.; W. E. Whiting (letter to unnamed person—Estlin?—1847); Dr. Joseph Sargent in 1850, deploring the visit of George Thompson, British abolitionist; and Frederick Frothingham of Cambridge, Mass.

(d) Letters, 1851–84, to Mary Estlin.

1851–83, from Mrs. M. W. Chapman of Massachusetts, dealing with certain political events of the day as they affect the abolitionist cause. (Also copies of some letters from Mrs. Chapman to others.)

1852–84, chiefly to Mary Estlin from Sarah Pugh. References to anti-slavery; the transfer of abolitionists' energies after 1865 to the women's rights movement; moral education and anti-vice campaigns; and, in a letter of 1879, the exodus of Negroes from the deep South to the West.

1853–4, from Mary Grew and Abby Kimber, referring to the anti-slavery movement.

c. 1854–81, about William Lloyd Garrison from Oliver Johnson, Abby Kimber, Sarah Pugh, and Maria Weston Chapman. (There is also the

[1] Privately printed (limited edition of 100 copies), *A Journey to America in 1834* (Cambridge, 1919).

ENGLAND · LONDON

copy of a letter on Garrison by the Rev. Samuel Alfred Steinthal to an
unknown person.)

Oberlin, Ohio, 1862, from the Rev. John Keep, describing Oberlin
College.

Roxbury, Mass., 1863–9, from William Lloyd Garrison, mainly personal,
with comments on political events of the period.

New York, 1863, from Mattie Griffith, giving an eyewitness account of
the New York Draft Riots.

New York, 1869 and 1872, from Oliver Johnson, editor and reformer, on
the Grant administration.

Boston, 1869, from Anne Waterston, rejoicing over Grant's election, and
including references to J. L. Motley.

1877–81, from Frank J. Garrison, include references to his father, the
woman's suffrage movement, and Chinese immigration.

(e) Letters, 1852–69, from Mrs. Harriet Beecher Stowe (also to Mrs. E. L.
Follen, Joseph Sturge (copy), and Miss Wigham (copy)) include acknowledgements of donations from England for her scheme to establish a school
for Negro children in Mandarin, Fla.

(f) Letters, 1858, from Samuel May, Jr., the anti-slavery advocate, to
various people, including copy of one to R. D. Webb on the American
Anti-Slavery Society and the *Advocate*.

(g) Letters from Mary Estlin, while in America in 1868, to Rebecca Moore.
References to William Lloyd Garrison, Gerrit Smith, and other anti-slavery
leaders whom she visited; the division of the anti-slavery movement, now
concentrating on the betterment of the Negroes' conditions, between those
advocating better education and those wishing to ensure intelligent use of
the suffrage; an account of an address by Anna Dickinson criticizing the
Republican Party; an account of schools in New York; and reports brought
back by teachers returning from the South.

(h) Letters, 1868–9, and poems by Dr. Ann Preston (1813–72), one of the
first graduates of the Female Medical College of Pennsylvania and later
its Dean and Trustee.

Women's Service Library, Fawcett Society, Fawcett House, 27 Wilfred Street, London, S.W.1

AMERICAN WOMEN SUFFRAGISTS. Letters: volume 10:
'Emancipation of women: United States of America, 1876–
1948': and other letters, 1865–97, from a general autograph
collection.

These letters show that there has been a continual, detailed, and lively
exchange of help and information between American and British women's
suffrage movements. Of particular interest are letters from:

Catt, Carrie Chapman, president of the International Woman Suffrage Alliance and of the National American Woman's Suffrage Association;

Gilman, Charlotte Perkins, publisher of the *Forerunner*, author and lecturer, who made a lecture tour of England in 1913;

Marion, Kitty, suffragist and birth-control pioneer, mainly to Alice Park concerning, *inter alia*, the politics of the American birth-control movement and reminiscences about the early days of the women's suffrage movement;

Park, Alice, whose letters contain much comment on women's suffrage campaigns in various states, notably New York and California, and also allude to financial help of American women in keeping the British movement alive during the First World War.

PAMPHLETS AND NEWSPAPER CUTTINGS.

This collection includes obituary notices, and contains many relating to the American suffrage and other women's movements. The pamphlets include two bound volumes of American Suffrage Tracts 1845–64, containing the *Proceedings of the Woman's Rights Convention* held at Syracuse, N.Y., 8–10 Sept. 1852; an *Address adopted by the Woman's Rights Convention* held at West Chester, Pa., 2–3 June 1852—Woman's Rights Tracts 1–10 including Samuel J. May, *Rights and Condition of Women*, 1845; *Speeches of Wendell Phillips Esq. and of Abby Kelley Foster*, 1851; Paulina Wright Davis, *Education of Females*, 1851; Anon., *Enfranchisement of Women*, 1850; Mrs. Oakes Smith, *Sanctity of Marriage*, 1851; Mrs. Nichols, *Responsibilities of Women*, 1851; speech of Mrs. M. J. Gage at the Woman's Rights Convention, Syracuse, N.Y., Sept. 1852; *Letter from Angelina Grimké Weld*, 1852; *Letters from Mrs. Elizabeth C. Stanton*. There are many later pamphlets and tracts published by various American women's suffrage organizations.

Robert Fleming & Co. Ltd., 8 Crosby Square, LONDON, E.C.3

BUSINESS RECORDS. 1 volume. 1901–9.

Bankers. The firm holds a volume which includes simply a list of American railroads in whose financing Robert Fleming assisted, 1901–9. Among the major investments, ranging from 1 to 3 million dollars, were those in the Atchison Railroad, Bangor & Aroostook, Carolina Clinchfield, Chicago Great Western Railway Syndicate, Kansas City, Fort Scott; Kansas City Street Railway, Pennsylvania Railroad and Union Pacific (these two through Kuhn, Loeb & Co.), Western Pacific, and the Wisconsin Central.

Library of the Society of Friends,[1] Friends House, Euston Road, LONDON, N.W.1

The Religious Society of Friends (Quakers) have had at all times, of course, a uniquely close transatlantic connexion; see, for example, Frederick

[1] Virginia material microfilmed by the Virginia Colonial Records Project.

B. Tolles. *The Atlantic Community of the Early Friends* (London, 1952) (*J.F.H.S.* Supplement no. 24). The Library shows how faithfully they have followed the injunction of George Fox to be 'a record keeping people'. It contains the largest of all collections of manuscripts relating to the Quaker movement from the mid-seventeenth century to the present. There is an extensive card catalogue, indexed under personal names, places, subjects, &c. Copies of many Quaker manuscripts in places other than the Library (especially many in the United States) are available.

Much of the American material was used in the preparation of an Oxford University D.Phil. thesis by A. T. Gary, 'The political and economic relations of English and American Quakers, 1750–85', 1935, which contains an extensive bibliography and a critical account of sources (a copy is available in the Library). From time to time relevant material has been printed or described in the *Journal of the Friends Historical Society* (*J.F.H.S.*).

To list all references to America would be impracticable; the following describes the main categories of records and the main directly American material. But for the Manuscripts of William Penn, an important item, see Andrews & Davenport, pp. 351–4, which was the only collection they described. The arrangement is as follows:

1. Official manuscript records and correspondence of the Society of Friends.
2. Major collections of manuscripts containing items relating to America.
3. Quaker journals.
4. Miscellaneous correspondence and documents relating to America.

OFFICIAL MANUSCRIPT RECORDS AND CORRESPONDENCE OF THE SOCIETY OF FRIENDS. 1668– .

(*a*) London Yearly Meeting: Minutes 1668– (in progress).

More than sixty volumes containing a full account of the history, activities and opinions of the central English organization of Friends, which 'are of fundamental importance for any study of the attitude of the Society, particularly in its international and political aspects'.[1] They contain also transcriptions of a number of travel journals relating to America, the writers of which travelled through most or all of the colonies, but were concerned mainly to record Meetings visited and spiritual experiences gained. Included are transcriptions of the following:

Atkinson, Aaron. Visit in 1698–9. L.Y.M.M., vol. ii, pp. 312–14.[2]

Baldwin, William. Visit in 1709. L.Y.M.M., vol. iv, pp. 211–18.[3]

Chalkley, Thomas. Travels, 1707–11. L.Y.M.M., vol. iv, pp. 65–73, pp. 294–6.[4]

Frankland, Henry. Visit in 1730–2. L.Y.M.M., vol. vii, pp. 340–4.[5]

[1] A. T. Gary, 'The political and economic relations of English and American Quakers, 1750–85', p. 424, D.Phil. thesis, University of Oxford, 1935.

[2] Printed in *J.F.H.S.*, vol. xiv, pp. 31–32, 1917.

[3] Printed in *J.F.H.S.*, vol. xv, pp. 27–30, 1918.

[4] Printed in *J.F.H.S.*, vol. xi, pp. 84–85, 1914.

[5] Printed in *J.F.H.S.*, vol. vii, pp. 27–29, 1910.

Hopwood, Samuel. Visit in 1741–4. L.Y.M.M., vol. ix, pp. 314–22.[1]

Peckover, Edmund. Visit in 1742–4. L.Y.M.M., vol. ix, pp. 322–39.[2]

(*b*) London Meeting for Sufferings: Minutes 1673–   (in progress).

These are the records of the executive committee of the Yearly Meetings and contain the official Anglo-American correspondence of the Society of Friends. In the eighteenth century, especially, it maintained a constant system of detailed correspondence with the colonial meetings.

(*c*) London Yearly Meeting: Epistles Sent. 10 volumes of transcripts. 1683–1934.

Contain the letters sent from the London Yearly Meeting to American Yearly Meetings. Although mainly exhortatory, they touch on other subjects, such as slavery.

(*d*) London Yearly Meeting: Epistles Received. 11 volumes of transcripts. 1683–1916.

Include answers from Yearly Meetings in America to the London Yearly Meeting. Subjects touched on briefly include Indian education, slavery, the Civil War, &c.

(*e*) London Yearly Meeting: 'Christian and Brotherly Advices'. 1 volume. 1738.

Contains advice on special problems which was sent intermittently to the colonies. Arranged under headings such as 'discipline', 'Negroes', 'smuggling', 'trading', &c.

(*f*) Testimonies concerning ministers. 7 volumes. 1728–1872.

Contains memorials of Quaker missionaries presented to the Yearly Meeting after their deaths.

(*g*) London Yearly Meeting of Ministers and Elders: Minutes. 9 volumes. 1757–1906.

Contains reports on the missionary journeys and activities of Quaker ministers.

(*h*) Letters to and from Philadelphia. 2 volumes of transcripts. 1757–1857.

Contains correspondence between the London and Philadelphia Meetings for Sufferings.

---

[1] Printed in *Bulletin of the Friends' Historical Association*, vol. xxxix, pp. 91–99, 1950.

[2] Printed in *J.F.H.S.*, vol. i, pp. 95–109, 1903/4.

(*i*) Casual correspondence. 1 volume. 1785–1881.

Contains copies of various Yearly Meetings and other letters, some of which were sent to or from Meetings in America. Several of these refer to the slavery question, e.g. two of 1834, one touching on the respective powers of the federal and state governments in the matter, and one on colonization in Liberia (pp. 204–11).

(*j*) Minutes of various Quarterly and Monthly Meetings. 1668/9—(in progress).

For specimens of the contents of Monthly Meeting minutes see the printed *Minute Book of the Monthly Meeting of the Society of Friends for the Upperside of Buckinghamshire, 1669–1690* (Aylesbury, Bucks. Archaeological Society, 1937), which contains a number of references to Quakers about to go to America and desiring certificates (original minutes are in Friends House); and *The First Minute Book of the Gainsborough Monthly Meeting of the Society of Friends 1669–1719*, ed. by Harold W. Brace. 3 vols. (Hereford, for the Lincolnshire Record Society, 1948–51). Most such records are kept by the Meetings concerned or deposited with local record offices; a check list of these local records of locations is kept at Friends House.

(*k*) Registers of English Quaker births, marriages, and burials. *c.* 17th century—(in progress).

Up to 1836 the Registers are entered under the names of the various county Quarterly Meetings; after this all the Registers are amalgamated into a single sequence for all the Quarterly Meetings. The Registers, which give also some details of place of residence and occupation, are of assistance in identifying little-known Friends.[1]

MAJOR COLLECTIONS OF MANUSCRIPTS CONTAINING ITEMS RELATING TO AMERICA. (*Arranged chronologically.*)

(*a*) A.R.B. (Abram Rawlinson Barclay) Manuscripts. 2 volumes (also 2 volumes of transcripts). 1654–88.

Collection of 250 letters, 1654–88, of early Friends, containing a number of items concerning America—e.g. an account of a journey 'by land and water' from Virginia to New England in 1658 (ARB/13); and a letter, 1686, from John Archdale in North Carolina to George Fox, describing the country (ARB/68).[2]

(*b*) Spence Manuscripts.[3] 3 volumes. 17th century.

Volumes 1 and 2 comprise the manuscripts of the 'Journal' of George Fox (1624–91) and volume 3 consists of numerous letters to and from the Fell

---

[1] Gary, op. cit., p. 427.
[2] These manuscripts are being printed in *J.F.H.S.*; see vol. xxvii, 1930, in progress.
[3] See W. C. Braithwaite, *Beginnings of Quakerism*, Appendix B (London, 1912).

family. Volume 1 of Fox's 'Journal' contains letters from his friends describing travels in America.

(c) Gibson Manuscripts. 10 volumes and portfolios. 1660–1861.

Contain original letters, drawings, news cuttings, &c., collected by Thomas Thompson of Liverpool. Include many letters from Friends in America, and also a grangerized copy of the printed journal of Thomas Story of Philadelphia, to William Penn; and correspondence between Story and James Logan of Philadelphia.[1] Also a letter, 1 Dec. 1674, from Penn to George Fox.

(d) W. C. Braithwaite Manuscripts. 1661–end of 18th century.

Contain the transcripts of the documents examined by William Charles Braithwaite, historian of the Quaker movement. Include items relating to early Quakerism in America, and also his draft of a chapter on 'Work in America', which was not printed in his *Beginnings of Quakerism* (London, 1912) in order to avoid overlapping with Rufus M. Jones and others, *The Quakers in the American Colonies* (London, 1911).

(e) Reynolds Manuscripts. 1 volume. 1663–early 18th century.

Contains the correspondence of the Reynolds family, Anglo-American merchants in London and Philadelphia. Mainly of religious interest. Late eighteenth or early nineteenth century copies of documents, 1663–1779, compiled by Richard Reynolds (1735–1816), of Coalbrookdale and Bristol.

(f) Southwark Manuscripts. 6 volumes. 1667–1777.

Contains letters and other data relating to the history of London Friends; some of the material bears upon American matters.

(g) Penn Manuscripts. 2 albums. 1682–1779.

Miscellaneous assortment of originals, transcripts, facsimiles, engravings, and newspaper clippings. There are also many other manuscripts relating to Penn in the Library and catalogued under his name. See Andrews & Davenport, pp. 351–4.

(h) Swarthmore Manuscripts.[2] c. 1400 original documents. 17th century.

Illustrate seventeenth-century Quakerism. Include many letters to Margaret Fell from Friends both at home and overseas. There are also transcripts of later date.

---

[1] Printed in the *Bulletin of the Friends' Historical Association*, vol. xv, 1926, supplement.
[2] See Braithwaite, op. cit., Appendix B.

(i) John Thompson (1797–1877). Manuscripts (5 volumes). 18th century.

Contain the correspondence of the Thompson family, Anglo-American merchants of Philadelphia in the eighteenth century.

(j) Gurney Manuscripts.[1] 1772–1850.

Mainly letters written to Joseph John Gurney (1788–1847) while on his famous ministry in America for the English Society of Friends to refute the teachings of the Hicksites, 1836–40. The principal correspondents are Anna Gurney, Amelia Opie, Elizabeth Fry, and the Buxton family—also a few letters from William Wilberforce, Joseph Sturge, and J. G. Whittier. There are also many from J. J. Gurney describing the course of his ministry, American life and topography, slavery, &c. A few other family papers relating to America, mainly of an earlier period, are included.

QUAKER JOURNALS. (*Arranged chronologically.*)

(a) Mary Weston (1712–66). Travel journal[2] (a transcript made from the original by her son-in-law, John Eliot), 1735-52. (138 folio pages.)

Toured the colonies preaching to Quaker Meetings, 1750–2. The journals mainly describe her preachings and spiritual experiences; they contain a list of Meetings visited in New Jersey, Maryland, Pennsylvania, Virginia, and the Carolinas; also maps of her tours; a few family letters; and some verses in her honour by Thomas Merryworthy.

(b) Rachel Wilson[3] (1720–75). Journal of a visit to America (copies, both manuscript and typescript; original in private possession). 1768–9.

Visited American Meetings, chiefly in Pennsylvania, Virginia, and the Jerseys. The journal is of almost exclusively religious interest.

(c) Elizabeth Robson[4] (1771–1843). Travel diaries, letters and family papers: 26 volumes. 1813-43.

Preacher. Wife of Liverpool linen merchant, himself a Quaker Elder. Travelled extensively and was twice in America, 1824–8 and 1838–42, visiting probably every Meeting of the Friends. Diaries mostly describe these Meetings, contain much of the 'Hicksite' controversy, and also on mission meetings with soldiers, sailors, miners, Indians, and Negroes; a list

---

[1] These manuscripts, which are on loan to the Library, form part of the extensive Gurney and Barclay Family Papers still at Bawdeswell Hall, Norfolk (pp. 351–2).

[2] See also 'Mary Weston's Journal', *J.F.H.S.*, vol. iv, p. 130, 1907.

[3] See John Somervell, *Isaac and Rachel Wilson, Quakers of Kendal, 1714–1785* (London, 1924).

[4] See also 'Elizabeth Robson', *J.F.H.S.*, vol. xiv, pp. 75–78, 1917.

of Meetings visited in Philadelphia in 1828; and some general description of American life. The diaries for the first trip, 1824–8, are originals, but for the second, 1838–42, are transcripts made by her son, Henry Robson, shortly after her death as part of a nine-volume manuscript 'Memoir'.

(*d*) Richard Smith (1784–1824).[1] Journals: 7 volumes (transcribed from the originals shortly after his death). 1817–24.

Small trader and Quaker missionary. Went to the United States in 1817, settled for a short while at Smithfield, Ohio, and then journeyed back to the coast on foot. The journals are very detailed, both personal and social, reflecting an odd and observant mind. Fascinating account of Indian settlements in Ohio and Isaac Hervey's mission at Wapakoneta, Ohio. While at Smithfield he joined the Friends; he returned to England in 1820, and in 1823 he offered himself for service with the Friends' 'Committee on African Instruction', obviously from seeing the plight of the American coloured peoples. He died of fever in Birkow in Gambia in 1824.

Also a memorial to Smith by the Staffordshire Monthly Meeting; and eighteen manuscripts connected with him, including a few of his letters from America to his father and brother.

(*e*) Joseph Crosfield (1821–79). Letters written during American journeys, 1845 and 1865–6: 2 volumes of typewritten copies (originals held by the Crosfield family).

During his first journey in 1845 Crosfield travelled chiefly in Ohio, Indiana, Illinois, Kentucky, Virginia, and North Carolina, visiting prisons, asylums, schools, and institutions for coloured people. The letters contain a certain amount of material of topographical and sociological interest.

The second journey, in 1865–6, was mainly in the South, especially in Tennessee and North Carolina, and the letters contain some observations on the Civil War and its aftermath.

(*f*) Robert Lindsey (1801–63) and Sarah Lindsey (1805–76). American travel journals:[2] 5 volumes, 1846–51; 7 volumes, 1857–61.

On the first visit, 1846–51, Robert Lindsey was accompanied by Benjamin Seebohm. Their journey was confined largely to the Eastern and Middle-Western states. Sarah, his wife, accompanied him on the second visit, and wrote six volumes of the journals. In 1857–61 they visited also California and Oregon. The interest is chiefly religious, but descriptions of the country, and observations on slavery, are included.

[1] See also J. D. Crosfield, 'Richard Smith and his Journal', *J.F.H.S.*, vol. xiii, pp. 49–58, 89–98, 129–41, 1916; and vol. xiv, pp. 15–25, 59–69, 108–21, 161–7, 1917.

[2] Extracts from the journals have been printed in the *Travels of Robert and Sarah Lindsey* (London, 1886).

(g) John Candler (1787–1869). Journal of a visit to the West Indies and the United States: 1 volume. 1850.

Quaker minister. Visited the United States with his wife in 1850 after a tour of the West Indies, and his account of America occupies about a quarter of his journal. He visited New York, Long Island, Philadelphia, Baltimore, and Washington, D.C., and then travelled through Ohio and Indiana. The journal contains some description of the cities and country visited and of agriculture in the Middle West; some observations on the Compromise of 1850, the Senate debate on which Candler attended while in Washington. Here he also interviewed Zachary Taylor on the slavery question.

(h) Priscilla Green (1802–77). Letters from America: 1 volume. 1856–8.

Quaker minister. Worked in the United States, 1856–8. The letters are mainly of religious interest, but touch on the slavery issue.

MISCELLANEOUS CORRESPONDENCE AND DOCUMENTS.

(a) Miscellaneous correspondence. 1666–c. 19th century.

Forty portfolios of originals and/or copies of unofficial Quaker correspondence during the last three centuries. Important from the standpoint of American studies are:

(i) Copies of letters, 1766–76, from Dr. John Fothergill to William Logan and James Pemberton before and during the War of Independence.[1]

(ii) Copy of a letter, 31 Mar. 1776, from David Barclay to Benjamin Franklin.[2]

A few examples of other relevant items:

(iii) Accounts of Quaker travellers, e.g. Elizabeth Hooten in 1666, (Port 3/80) Susanna Wright in 1714 (Port 14/88) and Joseph Gill in 1734 (Port 2/43).

(iv) Quaker address to the Governor of Pennsylvania in 1756 against war with the Indians.

(v) Letter, 18 Jan. 1773, from Patrick Henry to Anthony Benezet, admits the evils of slavery but says that he personally cannot do without slaves (Port 17/28).

(vi) Letter, 1834, from North Carolina Friends, on the raising of funds to buy slaves and sending them to free states.

(vii) Biographical notes on the Thompsons of Liverpool, owners from 1817 to 1830 of the Black Ball Line, the first regular passenger and mail service between Liverpool and New York.

---

[1] Originals in the Library of the Historical Society of Pennsylvania.
[2] Original in the possession of the American Philosophical Society.

(*b*) Thomas Broadbank (1752–1808). Miscellaneous documents. 1720, 1801.

Some correspondence, 1801, relative to the shares of Thomas Broadbank in the Pennsylvania Land Company; and some share transfers, signed Thomas Story and dated 1720.

(*c*) Lewis Tappan (1788–1873). Letter. 1840.

Abolitionist. Letter, 25 Mar. 1840, deals with Prussian immigrants to the United States bound for Milwaukee, and refers also to the evils of slavery.

(*d*) John Greenleaf Whittier (1807–92). 6 letters and manuscript poems. 1842–91.

American poet and abolitionist. Letters deal with slavery and slave trade, capital punishment, pacifism, and his ancestry. The poems are 'Unity' and 'Abolition rhymes'.

(*e*) Elihu Burritt (1810–79). 2 letters (photostat copies; originals in private possession). 1861–2.

Both letters are to Henry Richard. The first, 26 May 1861, is concerned chiefly with dissensions among American pacifists caused by the Civil War. The second, 27 Oct. 1862, gives a more general account of the war itself, Northern opinion, and the Emancipation Proclamation.

(*f*) William Jones (1826–99) and Katherine Jones (1850–1929). Letters (unbound). 1889.

Written during a world tour, 1889–90, in the cause of promoting arbitration of international disputes. The letters from the United States, 1889, include references to the Pan-American Congress, and an account of their interview with President Harrison.

General Post Office, St. Martin's le Grand, LONDON, E.C.1

TREASURY LETTER-BOOKS. 623 volumes to date. 1686– (in progress). (Volumes to 1859 are indexed individually, after that cumulatively; volumes from 1891 are mainly in typescript.)

Copies of letters passing between the Postmasters-General and the Lords Commissioners of the Treasury. After 1783 the letter-books cease to be of interest for the internal history of American mails, but contain much scattered material relating to such matters as contracts, e.g. with Cunard, for, and costs of, packets to carry mails across the Atlantic, frequency of

such services, postal rates, illegal conveyance of letters, and the forwarding
of letters for America from the Continent.

See further, Andrews & Davenport, pp. 273–5, which deal with the first
ten volumes to 1783; Paullin & Paxson, pp. 476–8, for volumes to 1859.

PACKET REPORT BOOKS. 6 volumes. 1807–37. (Index for
each volume.)

Supplement the Packet Minute Books below.

PACKET MINUTE BOOKS. 218 volumes. 1811–1920.[1] (Index for
each volume, 1811–63; cumulative index for 1864–1920.)

Indexed under 'United States' will be found all the important material
relating to transatlantic mail services for the period covered, such as
dates of sailings, irregularities of dispatch, surcharges due, establishment
of a direct mail route to California via Panama, &c. See Paullin & Paxson,
p. 479, which describes the volumes for 1811–59.

AMERICAN LETTER-BOOKS.[2] 38 volumes, May 1849–June
1871; Jan.–June 1876; Jan.–June 1879; Jan.–Dec. 1884; Jan.–
Dec. 1889; Jan.–Dec. 1894; Jan.–Dec. 1899; Jan.–June 1904;
July–Dec. 1905; July–Dec. 1910. (The last four are in typescript.) (Each volume contains an index.)

Copies of letters sent from the General Post Office to both British American
and United States post offices on all aspects of postal communication
between the hemispheres. See Andrews & Davenport, p. 276, for separate
American letter-book, for 1773–83, not in the main series.

For other series, containing slight references to American business, see
Andrews & Davenport, pp. 275–6, and Paullin & Paxson, pp. 478–80.

Glyn, Mills & Co., 67 Lombard Street, LONDON, E.C.3

TRANSFER OF SHARES. Printed document. 1692.

Relates to the transfer of shares in West Jersey, 4 Apr. 1692.

ROBSON, ROBERT (b. 1754). Letters and documents. 1800–5.

Robson, a notary public, occupied 67 Lombard Street before Glyn's acquired
it in 1821. The papers he left there contain a number of letters from LeRoy,
Bayard & M'Evers of New York; Thomas M'Euen & Co. of Philadelphia;

---

[1] A catalogue (duplicated) of the Packet Minute Books, 1811–1900, has been
produced; the second volume, 1901–1920, is in preparation.

[2] In this and several other series, volumes survive only at five-yearly intervals.
The intervening volumes were pulped for salvage during the Second World War.

the United States Register's Office; and the Bank of the United States. They deal with investment, the transfer of shares, lawsuits concerning debts between British and American nationals, administration of estates, current exchange rates and quotations, the bankruptcy of an American company which had British creditors, and the collection of dividends in the United States for British investors. There are also statements of Robson's account with the Bank of the United States; and correspondence about the renewal of share certificates lost at sea in 1803 with the packet *Lady Hobart*. In a letter, 22 Sept. 1800, LeRoy, Bayard & M'Evers assure Robson that British fears that funds will fall, should Jefferson be elected, are groundless as Jefferson will attempt no major changes in the government, will not involve the United States in war with Britain, and will be economical.

GOLD STANDARD DEFENCE ASSOCIATION. Papers. 1895–1901.

It seems highly likely that these papers (account books, letter-books, letters, lists of subscribers, pamphlets, &c., in a large tin box; as yet unsorted and uncatalogued) contain correspondence relevant to the silver controversy in the United States in the 1890's. A very cursory examination revealed two letters from Professor F. W. Taussig in 1897, a copy letter to the Director of the United States Mint, and a pamphlet on bimetallism in America.

CURRIE, BERTRAM WODEHOUSE (1827–96). Memoirs, 2 volumes (privately printed). 1901.

Currie, a partner in the bank of Currie & Co., which amalgamated with Glyn's in 1864, travelled extensively in America in 1850. He was one of the British delegates to the International Monetary Conference in Brussels, 1892, called at the request of the United States government to discuss the possibility of international bimetallism. Currie opposed bimetallism, and in 1895 he founded the Gold Standard Defence Association. Volume 1 includes the letters written by him while in the United States, 27 Apr.–26 Nov. 1850; also papers connected with the Brussels Conference. Volume 2 is his journal for 26 Apr.–12 Aug. 1850.

Guildhall Library,[1] Basinghall Street, LONDON, E.C. 2

NEW ENGLAND COMPANY.[2] Papers: miscellaneous collection of charters, books of account, minute-books, journals, ledgers,

---

[1] Philip E. Jones and Raymond Smith, *A Guide to the Records in the Corporation of London Records Office and the Guildhall Library Muniment Room* (London, 1951).
[2] See William Kellaway, 'The Archives of the New England Company', *Archives*, vol. ii, pp. 175–82, 1954, and his *New England Company, 1649–1776* (London, 1961).

general correspondence, &c. (Most of the records are incomplete, or contain large gaps.) 1649– .

Originally created by Ordinance in 1649 as the Society for the Propagation of the Gospel in New England, and chartered by Charles II, 7 Feb. 1662, as the 'Company for Propagation of the Gospell in New England and the parts adjacent in America'. The New England Company, as it is usually known, is the oldest Protestant missionary society still in existence. Its funds were spent largely on salaries of missionaries to the Indians, among whom were John Eliot, Thomas and Experience Mayhew, and John Cotton.

The Company functioned continuously until the War of Independence, but at the beginning of the War it discontinued its payments to New England, and after the War its funds were diverted to Canada.[1] Thus, although the Company's records are still in progress, only those relating to the colonial period are of value in the study of American history. These are as follows:

(a) Treasurers' individual and sundry accounts, 1649–1728 (1 file). An account of moneys received and disbursed, 1649–55 (double sheet). Treasurers' general accounts, 1659–84 (incomplete, 4 ternions). Treasurers' general and estate account books, 1660–1764 (3 volumes). Treasurers' ledgers: volume 1, 1726–65; volume 2, 1764–1801. Treasurers' journals: volume 1, 1764–1801.

(b) Loose court minutes with some committee minutes, 1655–1816, with lacunae 1729–43, 1808–15 in one box. General court and committee minute-books: volume 1, 1770–1816, and index volume, 1770–1830. Also a photostat of the court minute-book, 1655–85, now in the Library of the Massachusetts Historical Society.

(c) Original correspondence[2] relating to affairs in New England, 1657–1714, one large folio; this is an artificial collection made c. 1896. Each letter has a printed transcript mounted opposite the original. Includes several letters from John Eliot, the Hon. Robert Boyle, a principal benefactor of the Company, and the Commissioners of the United Colonies; one letter from the President and Fellows of Harvard College; and one from a group of sixteen Indians of Natick, Mass., to Eliot. Also the journals of Experience Mayhew relating to missions to the Indians, 1713 and 1714.

(d) General correspondence, 1668–1818. Principally in-letters, with some draft out-letters (1 box). Letter-book, 1762–72, chiefly copies of out-letters.

(e) Correspondence[3] from Boston, mainly by the Commissioners to the

[1] William Kellaway, 'The Archives of the New England Company', *Archives*, vol. ii, p. 176.

[2] This correspondence has been printed in John W. Ford, ed., *Some Correspondence between the Governor and Treasurers of the New England Company in London and the Commissioners of the United Colonies in America* (London, 1897).

[3] 'The correspondents include such distinguished colonial figures as Adam Winthrop and Samuel Sewall, and their letters often shed an interesting light, not only on the work of the missionaries and the Company's affairs, but also upon colonial society', Kellaway, op. cit., p. 179.

Company in London, relating principally to Indian affairs, 1677–1761 (2 files).

(*f*) Official copy minutes of the Commissioners for Indian Affairs at Boston, 1699–1784 (1 file). (Increase and Cotton Mather were commissioners.) Accounts of Indian stock, i.e. receipts and disbursements of the Company's Commissioners at Boston, 1657–1731 (2 files).

In addition to the above the collection contains:

(*g*) Charter of incorporation by Charles II, and a contemporary office copy of the same, 7 Feb. 1662.

(*h*) Several series of muniments of title for the Company's properties, dating from 1543 onwards; the only American deeds are those for Martha's Vineyard, Mass., 1671–1730. A transcript, made in 1910, of a volume (among the Rawlinson MSS. C934 in the Bodleian Library[1]) of papers relating to the proceedings of the Company, 1649–56.

ROBERT HOOKE PAPERS. Essay (87 pages). 1666.

Entitled 'American pirates'. Chiefly concerned with the West Indies, and only incidentally with the mainland. This is part of a translation of Exquemelin's *De Americaensche Zee-Rovers*.

GUILD RECORDS.

Of the twelve 'great' companies, records of the Fishmongers (complete) and Grocers (rough minute-books from 1638) are in the Library. Also the records of most of the minor guilds: Carpenters, Joiners, Masons, Plaisterers, Painter-Stainers, &c. Items relating to Virginia appear in the seventeenth century.

DISSENTING CONGREGATIONS IN THE CITY.

Records of Baptists, Congregationalists, Protestant Dissenters, French Protestants, Independents, Scottish Presbyterians, some late seventeenth century but mostly eighteenth century. Minute-books, lists of members, &c., might yield details about members emigrating to America.

DAVISON, NEWMAN & CO. Business records. 1753–1897.

Grocers and importers of West Indian produce, founded in 1650; carried on business at the Sign of the Three Sugar Loaves and Crown, Gracechurch Lane. The firm was taken over by the West Indian Produce Association in 1911. Its dealings with the mainland colonies, and later the United States, were incidental, but the collection contains papers relating to its agents in Boston, and in Charleston, S.C. The firm's current account with its Boston agent, Henry Lloyd, for 1772–3, is framed, because one item mentions Francis Rotch, the master of the *Dartmouth*, one of the ships involved in the Boston Tea Party. A file of seventy to eighty letters and copies, 1791–1816, from John Ward, the Charleston agent, consists mainly of enclosures

[1] See Andrews & Davenport, pp. 405–6.

with bills, but there is some discussion of current news—e.g., on 4 Jan. 1794 Ward refers to the recovery of British debts, and the adverse effect of the French Revolution on American commerce.

PEABODY MEMORIAL COMMITTEE. Minute-book. 1866–70.
Minutes of meetings of the Committee held to consider the erection of the statue of George Peabody, the American philanthropist, in London.

The Museum, Gunnersbury Park, LONDON, W.3

COLLINSON, ADMIRAL SIR RICHARD (1811–83). Letter. 1837.
Collinson served from 1828 on ships employed on survey work mainly on the South American coast. A letter, 20 Nov. 1837, written to his father from H.M.S. *Sulphur*, San Francisco, says, 'This is the country for emigration... Bullocks are killed for their hide and tallow... deer in thousands... Geese and ducks in myriads, corn in abundance. It only wants one million of inhabitants instead of 20,000 to make it the nation of the Pacific Ocean. At present the inhabitants consist of uneducated Spaniards without the slightest energy—Kentucky backwoodsmen and Englishmen of very doubtful character who would just as soon make 500 per cent as any Jew in the United Kingdom.'

Henry George School of Social Science, *and the* United Committee for the Taxation of Land Values Ltd., 177 Vauxhall Bridge Road, LONDON, S.W.1

JOURNALS AND PRINTED PAPERS.[1]
These propagate the doctrines of Henry George (1839–97), American economic and political reformer. No manuscript materials appear to be available, however the printed records include:

(a) The volumes of the *Single Tax*, monthly organ of the Scottish Land Restoration Union, vols. i–vii, 1894–1901, continued as *Land Values*, monthly organ of the Movement for the Taxation of Land Values, vols. viii–xix, 1902–19, continued as *Land and Liberty*, monthly organ of the United Committee for the Taxation of Land Values, vol. xx, 1919– (in progress), form a continuous series. They contain much information about the progress of Henry George's ideas and include contributions from American sympathizers.

[1] This material was used by Elwood P. Lawrence, *Henry George in the British Isles* (East Lansing, Mich., 1957).

C. Hoare & Co., 37 Fleet Street, LONDON, E.C.4

BRAY, DR. THOMAS (1656–1730). Accounts: 1 notebook.
1700–4.

Clergyman. The notebook contains various accounts, mainly 'benefactions, missions, and libraries' for Maryland. Part I contains Bray's accounts for 1700 and 1701, with the report of the committee of the Society for the Propagation of the Gospel which examined these; Part II brings the accounts up to Lady Day, 1704; Part III relates to libraries 'rais'd or augmented' both abroad and at home.

MISCELLANEOUS HOLDINGS. 1775–93.

(a) Two papers, written in Boston, 14 June 1775. One certifies, on behalf of the Governor, Thomas Gage, that Peter Oliver is Chief Justice of Massachusetts Bay; and the other is a power of attorney given to Hoare's by William Burch, one of the Massachusetts Bay Commissioners of the Customs.

(b) 'Suffering Clergy': three letters, 1776 and 1777. The Bank acted as the agent for a fund collected in England to aid the 'suffering clergy' in America, and three letters reporting to the Bank the drawing of £50 from this fund are held. These are from W. Serjeant, Boston; William Clark, Boston ('Missionary for the Venble. Society etc. in Stoughton & Dedham, New England'); and John Tyler, Norwich in New England.

(c) Three papers relating to the purchase of $5,000 in United States loan stock by William Rawson & Co. of London, 5 Feb. 1793, through George Morewood of New York.

BANK'S LEDGER. 1789–1895.

The ledger entries give details of investment by Hoare's Bank in the following American concerns:

American Debentures, opened 18 Nov. 1789;
St. Paul–Minneapolis Railway, opened 1891, closed 11 Aug. 1896;
United States Brewery Co., opened 1892;
Pennsylvania Railway Co., opened 4 Jan. 1892, closed 13 July 1895;
New York Central Railway, opened 4 Jan. 1892, closed 11 July 1895;
Chicago, Milwaukee, and St. Paul Railway, opened 14 Jan. 1892, closed 13 July 1893;
Illinois Central Railway, opened 17 Feb. 1892, closed 14 Mar. 1892;
United States Government 4 per cent., opened 3 Apr., closed 10 Apr. 1895.

The Library, House of Commons, Westminster, LONDON, S.W.1

As will appear under the entry for the House of Lords Record Office, that other place is the main repository of Parliamentary Records.[1] But there are

[1] The Library of the House of Commons was, of course, destroyed in the fire of 1834.

two series peculiar to the House of Commons. It must be borne in mind that the Library of the House of Commons is a private one intended solely for the use of Members of Parliament, yet despite its private nature and its primary duty to assist Members, the Library has been willing on occasion to help *bona fide* students to use material which does not exist in any other accessible source. The two series are:

UNPRINTED PAPERS. 1851–to date.

The vast majority of these consist of Statutory Instruments which are later published; the unpublished material is simply that which government departments have thought to be of so little public interest as not to be worth publishing. All these papers are indexed, of course, in the printed *Journals* of the House (see introduction to House of Lords Record Office, below) and thus their titles can be traced. But it appears that students only very rarely find any need to consult the unpublished items. Students wishing to do so, however, should apply to the Speaker through the Librarian.

DEPOSITED PAPERS.

These are papers deposited by Ministers in the Library for the information of Members, usually in connexion with a parliamentary question. Since they are occasionally deposited subject to the condition that they are not to be published, the Library invariably refers outside inquirers to the issuing department. The existence of such papers can be established through the *Official Report of Parliamentary Debates, House of Commons* (Hansard).

The Record Office, House of Lords, Westminster, LONDON, S.W.1

The House of Lords Record Office in the Victoria Tower at Westminster is (as is plainly not widely realized) the general archive of Parliament. The Commons (see above) possess no Record Office of their own. Apart from two series of records which have been deposited in the Commons library, practically all original parliamentary papers of post-1497 date that have been kept by or restored to the parliamentary record officers have come to rest in the vertiginous confines of the Victoria Tower.

All intending searchers are asked to write to the Clerk of the Records at least two days before their first visit, explaining the nature of their research and, if possible, the specific documents they wish to consult. No special passes or introductions are required.

The materials are immense in both mass and variety; but they can be approached through four main guides within the House of Lords Record Office.[1]

[1] Documents to 1693 were calendared by the H.M.C. (see full list of their reports in Andrews & Davenport, p. 189). Material to 1714 calendared in *Manuscripts of the House of Lords* (New Series), vols. i–x, 1693/5–1712/4 (in progress) (London, 1900–53). This calendar is to be continued shortly for records later than 1714.

1. *General Index to the Journals of the House of Lords*, 1509–to date, taken together with the *General Index to the Commons' Journals*, 1547–to date. These make a complete guide to the formal history of parliamentary transactions. A parliamentary journal, however, is a highly artificial composition, made up from the records and minutes of the clerks some time after the frequently crowded, informal, and even nocturnal events; it does not lie, but it may not always tell the whole truth. There are two sets of papers that stand between the transactions of the Lords and the final record, and which may sometimes be instructively compared with the latter. These are the Manuscript Minutes, and the Clerks' Assistants sheets. The Minutes have been printed since 1828.

2. *Indexes to the Lords' and Commons' Journals*. That is, the index at the back of each sessional volume,[1] which have been found to be somewhat easier to use, and perhaps more reliable, than the *General Index* series.

3. *Index to Accounts and Papers, Reports of Commissioners, Estimates, &c.* A great deal of historical source material coming before Parliament is contained in the printed series of accounts of numerous transactions delivered to either House. Reports known to have been submitted in this form, or to have subsequently been ordered to be printed, may sometimes be more easily found through the *Index to Accounts and Papers* than in the other indexes mentioned, though strictly speaking everything mentioned in the *Accounts* indexes for the Lords and Commons must be duplicated in one of the others.

4. 'House of Lords Papers.' Manuscript List in the H.L.R.O. Search Room. This list (which continues in brief form the printed Calendars, 1497–1714, mentioned in the footnote, p. 226) is planned to include everything preserved in the Victoria Tower—that is, every document in the parliamentary archives. It has by diligent perseverance been brought down to 1840 and inches its way forward every day.

It will be useful to note the differences between the parliamentary transactions as recorded by the *Journals* and the extant documents as recorded in the Manuscript List. There have been many transactions of which no account has got into the archives. Some of the papers seem to have missed their way at the beginning; others have strayed; but some, fortunately, have been brought back, as in the case of the important Braye Manuscripts, acquired 1952–6, from Lord Braye. Students should go to the *Journals* to find out what happened in Parliament and then to the Manuscript List to find out whether the relevant documents have been preserved. It may be added that while the index entries are self-explanatory, those in the Manuscript List are very brief, and will be of most use to those who already know fairly well what kind of detail they are looking for and in what categories it will fall.

Records pertaining to American history before 1714 are calendared in the volumes noted;[2] those before 1783 are listed in Andrews & Davenport, pp. 189–272; the succeeding period to 1903 is covered by Paullin & Paxson,

---

[1] Only from 1820 for the *Lords' Journals*. [2] See footnote, (p. 226).

pp. 326–60. In the present survey, the work of Andrews & Davenport *has been taken as read*, but that of Paullin & Paxson has been *supplemented* by two further lists:

(*a*) A fuller guide just for 1787 to 1840 has been provided through a search of the Manuscript List referred to above, which did not exist in Paullin & Paxson's day. This, of course, is a *supplement* to their list and *not* a replacement.

(*b*) The list of references has been brought down from 1904 to 1923 by use of the indexes to the sessional *Lords' Journals*.

The example of Paullin & Paxson has been followed in omitting references to slavery and the slave trade. Many of these references, which are numerous throughout the period, refer to the United States, many do not. Students of those subjects will want to treat them in their entirety, which would not have been practicable here. Trade returns are also omitted for similar reasons (these are normally found in the first quarter of each year). The texts of treaties have also been excluded, as these have been published in the Treaty Series since 1892. Further equipment for the study of the parliamentary records is provided by four pamphlets issued gratis by the House of Lords Record Office:

Report for 1953. One of the annual accounts of the state of the archives, recent accessions, plans, and work in progress; this includes an analysis of the papers of 1819.

The Journals, Minutes and Committee Books of the House of Lords (London, 1955). (Record Office Memorandum No. 13.)

List of Main Classes of Records (revised Oct. 1959). (Record Office Memorandum No. 1 (D).)[1]

A Guide to House of Lords Papers and Petitions (London, 1959). (Record Office Memorandum No. 20.)

P. and G. Ford, *A Guide to Parliamentary Papers* (Oxford, 1955), may also be referred to, though it does not concern itself with manuscript records.

The sessional *Lords' Journals* are hereinafter referred to as L.J.

Additions to Paullin & Paxson, pp. 329–60, from 'House of Lords Papers' Manuscript List, 1787–1840.

1787, Apr. 2. American Debts Bill. (L.J. 37, p. 644)

1789, July 20. Tobacco Duty Bill: petition against, of several manufacturers of tobacco. (L.J. 38, p. 505)

1789, July 23. Tobacco Duty Bill: petition against, Corporation of London (rejected) Evidence (printed and manuscript). (L.J. 38, p. 509)

1789, July 31. Tobacco: accounts of imports and exports, &c. (L.J. 38, p. 514)

1790, May 5. Tobacco Duty Bill: petition against, of manufacturers of tobacco in the Port of London. (L.J. 38, p. 618)

---

[1] A complete guide to the House of Lords Record Office is in course of preparation (1960).

1790, May 5. Trade with North West coast of America and Southern Whale Fishery: motion for state of. (L.J. 38, p. 622)

1790, May 7. Tobacco and snuff: accounts re. (L.J. 38, pp. 625–7)

1790, May 10. Southern Whale Fishery: state of. (L.J. 38, p. 626)

1790, May 14–28. Tobacco Duty Bill: evidence taken at Bar, with printed copy. (L.J. 38, p. 633)

1790, May 21. Tobacco, account of, delivered for home trade. (L.J. 38, p. 647)

1790, May 31. Tobacco: accounts re; three accounts. (L.J. 38, p. 657)

1790, Dec. 23. Whale fisheries and Northern lighthouses: two accounts. (L.J. 39, p. 33)

1792, Feb. 29. Whale fisheries: accounts. (L.J. 39, p. 291)

1793, Jan. 7. Whale fisheries and Northern lighthouses: two accounts. (L.J. 39, p. 512)

1794, Mar 24. Whale fisheries and Northern lighthouses: two accounts. (L.J. 40, p. 86)

1794, May 26. Differences between the United States and Indian tribes, motion for address for instructions to Lord Dorchester re (negatived). (L.J. 40, p. 215)

1795, Feb. 19. Whale fisheries and Northern lighthouses: two accounts. (L.J. 40, p. 308)

1796, May 14. Cotton wool imported: account delivered. (L.J. 40, p. 745)

1796, Oct. 19. Explanatory article to American Treaty. (L.J. 41, p. 24)

1797, Mar. 16. Whale fisheries and Northern lighthouses: accounts re. (L.J. 41, p. 130)

1799, May 27. West India Islands: motion for accounts of imports and exports, &c. Secret committee, report from. Annexed, printed. (L.J. 42, pp. 222–4)

1799, June 21. Vessels which entered and cleared West India Islands: account. (L.J. 42, p. 279)

1799, July 1–4. London Port Bill. Petitions, in support, of planters, merchants, and ship owners in West Indian trade; against, of London sugar refiners; and of ship owners trading from London. (L.J. 42, pp. 302–13)

1800, Feb. 25. Whale fisheries and Northern lighthouses: accounts. (L.J. 42, p. 380)

1800, July 10. Foreign wheat imported into Port of London: account. (L.J. 42, p. 620)

1801, Dec. 4. Whale fisheries: accounts. (L.J. 43, p. 423)

1803, Feb. 10. Convention with America. (L.J. 44, p. 53)

1807, June 29. American commerce: Order in Council re. (L.J. 46, p. 218)

1807, June 30. American commerce: motions for accounts respecting, &c., four motions. (L.J. 46, p. 224)

1807, July 18. American trade with Ireland, papers: five returns with a covering letter. (L.J. 46, p. 269)

1808, Feb. 4. Message from President of United States to Congress: motion for address for. Declaration of H.M. plenipotentiaries to America: motion for address for (negatived). (L.J. 46, p. 427)

1808, Feb. 15. Neutral vessels brought in under Orders of Council, motion for account of; Orders of Council: motion for a committee to consider. (L.J. 46, p. 436)

1808, Feb. 18. Message of President of the United States to Congress, &c.; and communications with America re French decree, three motions re. (L.J. 46, pp. 442–3)

1808, Feb. 26. Neutral vessels brought in under Orders of Council, &c.: two motions for. (L.J. 46, p. 454)

1808, Mar. 7. Answer to Mr. Madison's note: motion for address for (negatived). (L.J. 46, p. 471)

1808, Mar. 8. Orders of Council re neutral commerce: motion on (negatived). (L.J. 46, p. 473)

1808, Mar. 10. Vessels entered and cleared Port of London: account of. (L.J. 46, p. 477)

1808, Mar. 17. Orders in Council: motion for committee on (negatived); Orders in Council: petition against, from merchants of Kingston-upon-Hull. (L.J. 46, p. 494)

1808, Mar. 18. Orders in Council: petition against, of merchants and manufacturers of Manchester; annexed, motion for petitioners to be heard by Counsel (negatived). (L.J. 46, 504)

1808, Mar. 22. Orders in Council: motion to refer to a Committee of Whole (withdrawn). L.J. 46, p. 506)

1808, Mar. 23. Orders in Council: motion for them to be referred to Committee of Whole, with petitions. Motion for amendment to this. (L.J. 46, p. 508)

1808, Mar. 24. Orders in Council: motion for address for. (L.J. 46, p. 510)

1808, Mar. 28. Orders in Council: message to Commons for evidence. (L.J. 46, pp. 516–17)

1808, Mar. 29. Orders in Council: motions re, five motions (negatived). (L.J. 46, pp. 523–4)

1808, Mar. 31. Orders in Council: copies of six orders. (L.J. 46, p. 527)

1808, May 5. Orders in Council: evidence of Commons on. (L.J. 46, p. 595)

1809, Jan. 23. Orders in Council: motion for address for correspondence with the United States respecting. (L.J. 47, p. 15)

1809, Feb. 10. America: two motions for addresses for papers re. (L.J. 47, p. 37)

1809, Feb. 17. America: motion for address re (negatived). (L.J. 47, p. 50)

1809, Feb. 23. Letter from Canning to Pinkney and answer: motion for address for. (L.J. 47, p. 58)

1809, Apr. 17. America: motions re (negatived). (L.J. 47, p. 148)

1809, Apr. 26. America: motions for address for papers re (negatived). (L.J. 47, p. 180)

1809, May 3. America: motion for address re (negatived). (L.J. 47, p. 221)

1810, Feb. 1. America: list of papers re, ten papers. (L.J. 47, p. 434)

1810, Feb. 5. America: two motions for papers re. (L.J. 47, p. 435)

1810, After Feb. 16. Ireland: account of vessels and men and boys employed in them that entered and cleared ports of Ireland in three years ended 5 Jan. 1810, &c. (No L.J. ref.)

1810, May 25. Trade and navigation commercial licences: motions for accounts respecting. (L.J. 47, pp. 699–700)

1810, June 5. British and foreign ships in Commission and in ordinary, returns of: schedule and four returns. (L.J. 47, pp. 730–1)

1811, Mar. 28. Dollars: papers re. (L.J. 48, p. 158)

1811, Mar. 29. Dollars: paper re circulation of bank dollar tokens. (L.J. 48, p. 162)

1812, Jan. 9. Naval timber, &c.: accounts re, four accounts. (L.J. 48, p. 516)

1812, Feb. 24. Orders of Council: re specie and grain, eight orders. (L.J. 48, p. 596)

1812, Feb. 25. Vessels and tonnage, &c.: motion for account re. (L.J. 48, p. 598)

1812, Feb. 28. Message from Commons for attendance of Lord Grenville at committee re American claims. (L.J. 48, p. 609)

1812, Mar. 5. Message from Commons for Earl of Liverpool to attend committee re American claims. (L.J. 48, p. 620)

1812, Mar. 5. Revenue, trade and navigation, &c. (Ireland) accounts re: list and three accounts, one missing. (L.J. 48, p. 621)

1812, Mar. 23. British and foreign manufactures: motion for statement re. (L.J. 48, p. 662)

1812, Apr. 10. Imports and exports, grain and spirits (Ireland), motion for accounts re. (L.J. 48, p. 697)

1812, Apr. 13. Cottons, &c.: statement re. (L.J. 48, p. 700)

1812, Apr. 24. Orders in Council: declaration of Prince Regent re. (L.J. 48, p. 761)

1812, May 5. Same entry. (L.J. 48, p. 810)

1812, May 14. Imports and exports between Great Britain and the United States: account of, motion for. (L.J. 48, p. 838)

1812, June 12. Committee on petitions against Orders in Council: papers laid before. (L.J. 48, p. 894)

1813, Feb. 18. America: motion for an address re. (L.J. 49, p. 95)

1813, Mar. 31. British naval force on American stations: motion for statement of the. (L.J. 49, p. 245)

1813, Apr. 7. American coast, motion for, account of ships on the. (L.J. 49, p. 281)

1813, Apr. 12. Troops in America—ships taken by the Americans, &c.: motion for six papers re. (L.J. 49, p. 294)

1813, May 1. Court martial of officers and crew of the *Java*: motion for address for proceedings of the. (L.J. 49, p. 337)

1813, May 14. War with America: motion for a committee re (negatived). (L.J. 49, p. 391)

1813, June 23. Cotton Trade (Ireland) Bill (printed with manuscript amendment). (L.J. 49, p. 528)

1814, Apr. 4. Ships of war built in private yards, and oak timber. (L.J. 49, pp. 774–5)

1814, Nov. 15. War in America: motion for five papers re. (L.J. 50, p. 13)

1814, Dec. 1. American War: papers, list and five papers. (L.J. 50, pp. 34–35)

1815, Feb. 9. American War: motions for papers re. (L.J. 50, pp. 49–50)

1815, Feb. 15. Frigates *Prompte* and *Psyche*: motion for letter re. (L.J. 50, p. 50)

1815, Feb. 20. American War: papers re. (L.J. 50, p. 54)

1815, Apr. 5. Duties on foreign articles imported: account of. (L.J. 50, p. 124)

1815, Apr. 13. Negotiations for peace with America: motion for address re (negatived). (L.J. 50, 146)

1815, Apr. 17. America: motion for address respecting peace with. (L.J. 50, p. 151)

1815, May 2. North American Station: order for returns of ships for the. (L.J. 50, p. 193)

1816, June 10. Stamped dollars: minute of Court of Directors of Bank of England. (L.J. 50, p. 682)

1819, Apr. 26. Cotton goods and yarn exported 1785–1818: account of. (L.J. 52, p. 305)

1819, June 10. Canadian trade accounts. (L.J. 52, p. 678)

1820, June 6. Select committee on foreign trade: evidence. (L.J. 53, p. 110)

1820, July 7. Report on foreign trade. (L.J. 53, p. 266)

1820, July 13. Timber, &c.: Baltic and American trade accounts. (L.J. 53, p. 294)

1821, Feb. 16. Foreign trade accounts. (L.J. 54, p. 46)

1821, Feb. 21. Select committee on foreign trade appointed. (L.J. 54, p. 57)

1821, Feb. 26. Report from House of Commons on foreign trade. (L.J. 54, p. 67)

1821, Apr. 11. Exports to Denmark and North America: accounts delivered. (L.J. 54, p. 188)

1821, Apr. 11. Report from Commission on foreign trade. (L.J. 54, p. 188)

1821, May 9. Timber duties: petition from New Brunswick. (L.J. 54, p. 394)

1821, July 11. Foreign trade: minutes of evidence, one box. (L.J. 54, p. 582)

1822, May 6. Grain and flour imported, &c.: accounts. (L.J. 55, p. 151)

1822, May 14. Grain and flour imported, &c.: accounts bundle. (L.J. 55, p. 179)

1822, May 17. Foreign grain and flour imported: account of. (L.J. 55, p. 182)

1822, May 24. Grain and flour imported and warehoused in Ireland. (L.J. 55, p. 200)

1822, June 19. West Indian and American Trade Bill. (L.J. 55, p. 253)

1824, Feb. 23. Exports to North American colonies: accounts ordered. (L.J. 56, p. 42)

1824, May 14. Exports to South and North America: accounts. (L.J. 56, p. 227)

1824, June 21. Emigration from Ireland: reports ordered re. (L.J. 56, p. 450)

1825, Apr. 13. Vessels moored in Port of London: account of. (L.J. 57, p. 535)

1825, May 4. Accounts of ships entered into Port of London and account re transit trade, delivered. (L.J. 57, p. 746)

1825, May 11. Vessels laden with grain: account delivered. (L.J. 57, p. 784)

1825, May 13. Vessels entered London Docks and Commercial Dock: account of. (L.J. 57, p. 803)

1825, June 3. Memorials from Canadian legislature on corn laws, delivered. (L.J. 57, p. 977)

1825, June 28. Corn, grain and flour, ships and vessels: accounts delivered, six papers. (L.J. 57, p. 1181)

1825, June 30. North American corn and grain imported. (L.J. 57, p. 1201)

1826, Apr. 12. Imports and exports, Scotland and Ireland: accounts ordered re. (L.J. 58, p. 179)

1826, Apr. 25. Exports from Ireland. (L.J. 58, p. 241)

1826, May 9. American Steam Navigation Bill. (L.J. 58, p. 309)

1826, May 11. Foreign grain in warehouse. (L.J. 58, p. 323)

1826, Nov. 29. Export and import of grain in foreign countries: address re. (L.J. 59, p. 27)

1826, Dec. 1. Price of wheat, foreign oats, &c., admitted for home consumption, &c.: accounts delivered. (L.J. 59, p. 29)

1826, Dec. 7. Emigration petitions re Glasgow Emigration Society, Govan, Camachie Emigration Society, Paisley Emigrant Society. (L.J. 59, p. 36)

1826, Dec. 8. Report of House of Commons on emigration, communicated. (L.J. 59, p. 38)

1826, Dec. 12. Foreign grain admitted for home consumption: account of. (L.J. 59, p. 40)

1827, Feb. 9. Foreign and British vessels importing corn and flour; foreign exchanges and gold and silver coinage: accounts re ordered. (L.J. 59, p. 56)

1827, Feb. 15. Foreign corn: account re ordered, six papers. (L.J. 59, p. 76)

1827, Feb. 20. Foreign grain: accounts ordered, three papers. (L.J. 59, p. 88)

1827, Feb. 26. Foreign and colonial corn and flour imported: six papers. (L.J. 59, p. 102)

1827, Feb. 27. Foreign corn: further accounts re delivered. (L.J. 59, p. 115)

1827, Mar. 2. Ships entered ports of London and Liverpool. (L.J. 59, p. 124)

1827, Mar. 2. Foreign grain. (L.J. 59, pp. 124–5)

1827, Mar. 5. Timber and corn imported from America, vessels entered and cleared: accounts delivered. (L.J. 59, p. 133)

1827, Mar. 8. Import of foreign grain: select committee appointed, two papers. (L.J. 59, p. 145)

1827, Mar. 9. Wool imported and re-exported and woollen manufactures exported: accounts ordered. (L.J. 59, p. 151)

1827, Mar. 12. Grain: regulations of foreign countries re export and import. (L.J. 59, p. 154)

1827, Mar. 12. Foreign and British corn: nine papers. (L.J. 59, p. 155)

1827, Mar. 19. Foreign oats, &c., imported; woollen manufactures exported; sheep exported: papers delivered. (L.J. 59, p. 174)

1827, Mar. 22. Foreign and British wool and woollen manufactures: four papers. (L.J. 59, p. 183)

1827, Apr. 10. Foreign wool and grain: accounts re. (L.J. 59, p. 248)

1827, May 7. Foreign grain: further papers re. (L.J. 59, p. 278)

1827, June 1. Message to House of Commons for second report on emigration. (L.J. 59, p. 375)

1828, Feb. 1. Wool imported; cotton, linen and woollen goods, leather goods and unwrought leather exported: accounts ordered. (L.J. 60, p. 16)

1828, Feb. 21. Wool, &c., exported: account of ordered. (L.J. 60, p. 58)

1828, Mar. 5. Second report of House of Commons on emigration communicated. (L.J. 60, p. 97)

1828, Apr. 1. Duties on foreign corn account; foreign grain re-exported; importation of foreign oats. (L.J. 60, p. 153)

1828, Apr. 1. Wool, &c., exported: account re. (L.J. 60, p. 155)

1828, May 13. Foreign wool imported into London. (L.J. 60, p. 442)

1829, May 8. Grain and wool imported; British manufactures exported: accounts delivered. (L.J. 61, p. 442)

1829, June 1. Coals, &c., exported: account of delivered. (L.J. 61, p. 529)

1830, Apr. 26. Flour imported into Liverpool, navigation: accounts rendered. (L.J. 62, p. 218)

1830, May 6. Foreign wheat, barley, and oats admitted for home consumption: accounts. (L.J. 62, p. 333)

1830, May 11. Foreign trade with China: account delivered. (L.J. 62, p. 366)

1830, June 14. British articles exported in American vessels to China and the East Indies: statement ordered. (L.J. 62, p. 720)

1830, June 16. Return by British consuls of grain prices: address for. (L.J. 62, p. 726)

1830, June 29. Return by British consuls on foreign grain. (L.J. 62, p. 787)

1830, July 12. Commercial intercourse at Canton, correspondence. (L.J. 62, p. 866)

1831, Feb. 8. Commercial intercourse at Canton, correspondence re, delivered. (L.J. 63, p. 211)

1831, Mar. 9. Tobacco imported and exported: papers delivered. (L.J. 63, p. 305)

1832, Jan. 19. Emigration: returns of people emigrating from the United Kingdom to North America, &c. (L.J. 64, p. 23)

1832, Aug. 9. Emigration reports, address. (L.J. 64, p. 439)

1832, Aug. 15. Exports and imports from Haiti; annexed, price of sugar after revolution in Santo Domingo. (L.J. 64, p. 464)

1833, Apr. 30. Foreign wheat: account delivered. (L.J. 65, p. 224)

1833, May 1. Grain imported from America: account of. (L.J. 65, p. 227)

1833, May 8. Foreign wheat: accounts respecting. (L.J. 65, p. 262)

1833, Aug. 7. Foreign affairs, secret service and embassies: accounts re delivered, five papers. (L.J. 65, p. 554)

1835, Aug. 21. North American Association Bill amendments. (L.J. 67, p. 602)

1836, Mar. 15. Accounts delivered, referred to Agriculture Committee: prices of wheat at Mark Lane 1815–35, foreign grain; grain imported from Ireland and America, &c. (L.J. 68, p. 68)

1836, Mar. 30. Foreign grain imported into American colonies, &c.: account of, delivered and referred to Committee on agriculture. (L.J. 68, p. 101)

1837, Mar. 22. Foreign grain, &c.: account of. (L.J. 69, p. 151)

1837, June 2. Emigration: address for papers. (L.J. 69, p. 364)

1838, Mar. 9. Exports and imports, North American provinces. (L.J. 70, p. 150)

1838, May 22. Emigration: address for papers. (L.J. 70, p. 354)

1838, July 9. Lower Canada: papers re delivered. (L.J. 70, p. 524)

1838, Aug. 2. Affairs of Canada. (L.J. 70, p. 661)

1839, Feb. 25. Return of grain imported. (L.J. 71, p. 66)

1839, Mar. 11. Indians in America: address for papers re. (L.J. 71, p. 104)

1839, Mar. 19. Ships off coast of Mexico: return re delivered. (L.J. 71, p. 147)

1839, July 26. Returns of wheat, flour, &c., delivered. (L.J. 71, p. 537)

1839, Aug. 15. (a) Return of sugar from foreign states; (b) report of Board of Customs to Board of Trade re sugar. (L.J. 71, p. 608)

1840, Feb. 24. Land and emigration commissioners. (L.J. 72, p. 64)

1840, May 14. Emigration to Canada: papers delivered. (L.J. 72, p. 297)

1840, May 19. Wheat and flour, importation of: account. (L.J. 72, p. 316)

Additions to Paullins & Paxson, 1904–23.

Treaties and conventions have been omitted since they have been published since 1892 in the Treaty Series.

1904, Feb. 2. Correspondence on Alaska Boundary; map to accompany same. (L.J. 136, p. 12)

1906, Dec. 6. Correspondence on Newfoundland fisheries. (L.J. 138, p. 448)

1907, Mar. 18. Probation system: memorandum on probation system as at present in force in the United States. (L.J. 139, p. 63)

1908, Jan. 29. Notes exchanged with American Ambassador on Newfoundland fisheries. (L.J. 140, p. 10)

1911, Apr. 4. Cost of living in American towns. Report on inquiry by Board of Trade into working-class rents, housing and retail prices, together with rates of wages in certain occupations in principal industrial towns of the United States; with introductory memorandum and comparison of conditions in the United States and the United Kingdom. (L.J. 143, p. 120)

1913, Apr. 24. Proposed new customs tariff. New United States Tariff Bill with comparison of proposed and existing rates of duty. (L.J. 145, p. 73)

1914, July 16. Notes exchanged between H.M. Ambassador at Washington and the United States Government on the subject of oil properties and mining rights in Mexico. (L.J. 146, p. 311)

1917, Apr. 18. United States: Entry into Albania. Resolution of appreciation on entry of the United States into war, 'in joining Allied powers'. (L.J. 149, p. 85)

1919, Oct. 29. American Aviation Mission Report. (L.J. 151, p. 415)

1921, Apr. 7. Correspondence on alleged delay by British authorities of telegrams to and from the United States. (L.J. 153, p. 99)

1923, July 12. Dispatch from H.M. Ambassador at Washington enclosing memorandum on effects of prohibition in United States. (L.J. 155, p. 216)

1923, Nov. 13. Dispatch from H.M. Ambassador at Washington reporting conditions on Ellis Island immigration station. (L.J. 155, p. 291)

Hudson's Bay Company, Beaver House, Great Trinity Lane, LONDON, E.C.4

ARCHIVES.[1] 1668–1870.

The Company was chartered in 1670; its fur-trading posts were at first set up in the Hudson Bay area, but gradually attempts were made at exploration, trading, and settlement farther afield, so that by 1870, the date of the Deed of Surrender to the Crown of the Company's territory, there had been posts established in what are now Minnesota, Montana, Idaho, Oregon, Washington, Alaska, Honolulu, and most of the present Canadian provinces, as well as exploration in California and elsewhere. The expansion west of the Rocky Mountains was due in part to the new methods resulting from the merger in 1821 with the North West Company of Montreal, the Hudson's Bay Company's chief rival.

The Company's archives are very extensive, but vary in completeness

---

[1] The following works have made extensive use of material in these archives:

J. B. Tyrrell, ed., *Journals of Samuel Hearne and Philip Turnor* (Toronto, 1934) (Champlain Society, vol. xxi).

Maurice S. Sullivan, *The Travels of Jedediah Smith* (Santa Ana, 1934).

Arthur S. Morton, *A History of the Canadian West to 1870–71* . . . (London and New York, [1939]).

Grace Lee Nute, *Caesars of the Wilderness. Médard Chouart, Sieur des Groseilliers and Pierre Esprit Radisson, 1618–1710* (New York and London, [1943]).

Marcel Giraud, *Le Métis Canadien. Son rôle dans l'histoire des provinces de l'Ouest* (Paris, Institut d'Ethnologie, 1945).

Charles E. Hanson, Jr., *The Northwest Gun* (Lincoln, Neb., Nebraska State Historical Society, 1955).

John A. Hussey, *The History of Fort Vancouver and its Physical Structure* (Tacoma, Washington State Historical Society, 1957).

Rev. Gaston Carrière, *Les Missions catholiques dans l'Est du Canada et l'Honorable Compagnie de la Baie d'Hudson (1844–1900)* (Ottawa, 1957).

John S. Galbraith, *The Hudson's Bay Company as an Imperial Factor, 1821–1869* (Berkeley, Calif., 1957; Cambridge, 1958).

from year to year and post to post. Among them may be found records relating, for example, to the 'interlopers' from New England, including the case of Benjamin Gillam in 1682; the relationships with the United States resulting from the foundation of the Earl of Selkirk's Red River colony, which included land now part of North Dakota and Minnesota; exploration, fur-trading, relations with the Indians and with American settlers in much of what are now the states of Washington, Oregon, Idaho, and Montana; the question of the North-West boundary settlement. The archives—for which catalogues are available—are divided into six classes, as follows:

A. London records. Minute-books, correspondence books outward, correspondence with H.M. Government, inward correspondence, ledgers, order-books, lists of employees, &c.

B. Post records. Journals, correspondence books, correspondence inwards, accounts, dispatches, &c.

C. Ships' records. Mainly logs.

D. Governors-in-Chief of Rupert's Land. Correspondence and journals of William Williams, Sir George Simpson, Eden Colvile, Alexander G. Dallas, and William Mactavish.

E. Miscellaneous records. Journals, diaries, &c., of Pierre Radisson, James Isham and Andrew Graham, Peter Fidler, Colin Robertson, Nicholas Garry, Duncan Finlayson, John McLoughlin, Jr., Henry Berens, James and Joseph James Hargrave; and papers relating to the Red River Settlement and the Vancouver Island Colony.

F. Records of companies associated with or subsidiary to the Hudson's Bay Company. Miscellaneous papers relating to the North West Company, Puget's Sound Agricultural Company, International Financial Society Ltd., Russian American Company, Assiniboine Wool Company, Red River Tallow Company, Vancouver Island Steam Saw Mill Company, Vancouver Coal Mining Company, Buffalo Wool Company.

Microfilms of most of these are held in the Public Archives of Canada. Since 1938 the Hudson's Bay Record Society (until 1949 in conjunction with the Champlain Society of Toronto) has published an annual volume of material from the archives. These volumes also contain very full introductions and biographical material. Among the volumes which have been published are *Minutes of Council, Northern Department of Rupert Land, 1821–1831* (vol. iii); *Peter Skene Ogden's Snake Country Journals, 1824–1825 and 1825–1826* (vol. xiii); George Simpson's report of an 1828–9 visit to the Company's Columbia district, in *Part of Dispatch from George Simpson Esqr. Governor of Rupert's Land to the Governor and Committee of the Hudson's Bay Company, London* (vol. x); *The Letters of John McLoughlin from Fort Vancouver to the Governor and Committee, 1825–1846* (vols. iv, vi, and vii); *London Correspondence Inward from Committee, 1825–1846* (vols. iv, vi, and vii); *London Correspondence Inward and Eden Colvile, 1849–1852*, from Red River (vol. xix); and E. E. Rich, *The History of the Hudson's Bay Company, 1670–1870*, 2 vols. (London, 1958–60) (vols. xxi–xxii).

See also Andrews & Davenport, pp. 369–71.

Huguenot Library, University College, Gower Street, LONDON, W.C.1

Applications for permission to use the library should be made to the Hon. Librarian, Huguenot Society of London, University College.

This library was formed from the library of the Huguenot Society of London and from the library and archives of the French Hospital, formerly at Hackney, now at Rochester, Kent. It contains books on the early Huguenot settlements in the United States, biographies, dictionaries, and privately printed histories of the Huguenot families in America. Pamphlet material of general Huguenot interest is particularly strong for the seventeenth century.

There are the following papers:

AUFRÈRE PAPERS.[1] 1683–1758.

A collection of personal papers of the Rev. Israel Antoine Aufrère (1667–1758), minister of the French Reformed Church, exiled in London, together with some letters of the Rev. Claude Groteste de la Mothe, minister of the Savoy Church, London. The letters give some information about refugee French congregations in America, and the activities of the Society for the Propagation of the Gospel in Foreign Parts.

LAFAYETTE, MARQUIS DE (1757–1834). Letter. 1828.

Letter, dated La Grange, 17 Sept. 1828, to 'M. Duponceau à Philadelphie', introducing M. Capoulade of Bordeaux.

See also the publications of the Huguenot Society of London: *Proceedings*, vol. i, 1885/6–in progress; and *Quarto Publications*, vol. i, 1887–in progress.

The Library, Inner Temple, LONDON, E.C.4

MASERES MANUSCRIPTS. Document[2] (77 pages). 1758.

'Instructions for Georgia. 1758.' Includes copies of various documents as follows: Extract of Sir William Gooch's answer to the queries of the Board of Trade, in 1749; instructions to Henry Ellis, Captain General and Governor of Georgia in 1758; orders and instructions to Ellis 'in pursuance of several laws relating to the trade and navigation of . . . Great Britain, and our colonies and plantations in America', July 1758; and a list of ships which have entered ports in Georgia 'with the particular quantity and quality of the loading of each vessel'.

---

[1] See Winifred Turner, ed., *The Aufrère Papers, Calendar and Selections* (London, Huguenot Society, priv. print., 1940) (Huguenot Society, Quarto Series, vol. xl).
[2] H.M.C. xi (vii), p. 304.

Institution of Mechanical Engineers, 1 Birdcage Walk, LONDON, S.W.1

TAWS, LEWIS. Letter.[1] 1851.

19 May 1851, from Lewis Taws, of J. P. Morris & Co., Philadelphia, to James Nasmyth, engineer, at Patricroft, Lancs., concerning the prospective visit to Manchester of George Scott, who 'is well acquainted with our operations, having built for him a number of machines for the manufacture of bricks, the best machines I have yet seen for that purpose'.

Islington Public Libraries, Holloway Road, LONDON, N.7

PRICE, HENRY EDWARD (1824–1908?). Diary (1 volume).

Price, an inmate of the workhouse at Warminster, Wilts., was sent to America, under the Poor Law emigration scheme, in May 1842, and returned to England in 1848. From 1850 he was a cabinet-maker in Islington.

The diary, which was apparently written a considerable time after the events, describes the cargo and passengers on the ship, his employment as a varnisher and polisher, and as a cabinet-maker in New York, Staten Island, and Oswego. Touches on the coming of the telegraph to New York, Phineas Barnum, mesmerism, and racial segregation (e.g., in trams). Two letters from a friend in Buffalo, N.Y., 1847–8, are included.

ISLINGTON LITERARY AND SCIENTIFIC SOCIETY. 3 papers (1 printed).

Include papers read to the Society on 'The life of Washington', by Thomas Gale, and 'Was America known to the ancient world?', by Thomas Calvert Girtin (d. 1874). Also a printed notice sent to the Society's members advertising a dramatic reading from Uncle Tom's Cabin on 6 Oct. 1856 by Mrs. Mary E. Webb, 'a coloured native of Philadelphie'.

Lambeth Palace Library, LONDON, S.E.1

The extensive papers of the Bishops of London, who were virtually the diocesan heads of the Episcopal Church in America during the colonial period, were until recently divided between Lambeth Palace and Fulham Palace—and thus were separately described by Andrews & Davenport, pp. 286–301 and 302–329.[2] The slightest glance at their list shows the

---

[1] Photocopy in the James Nasmyth Collection, Public Library, Eccles, Lancs.

[2] Virginia material has been microfilmed by the Virginia Colonial Records Project.

great importance of this archive for almost every aspect of colonial history—few things were not, or could not be made, relevant to the affairs of the Church. However, it is clear that not all the papers can have been available to Miss Davenport. Large sections of the papers, mainly unlisted, were in 1957 found to be in considerable disorder, having undergone much accidental and random rearrangement.

The archive authorities, however, have now begun to restore order to these papers and the Rev. Dr. William W. Manross, associate-editor of the *Historical Magazine of the Protestant Episcopal Church*, has begun work on a comprehensive catalogue.[1]

Lloyds Bank Ltd., Head Office, 71 Lombard Street, LONDON, E.C.3

BANK RECORDS.

The fullest use of the Bank's records has recently been made by R. S. Sayers, *Lloyds Bank in the History of English Banking* (Oxford, 1957).[2] From this, it appears that there was not any major involvement of Lloyds in American financial affairs, but there are occasional references to the United States in the records, as follows (the page numbers refer to Professor Sayers's book):

p. 131. Lloyds asked Hanbury, Taylor, Lloyd & Bowman for advice on which of the American stocks was considered to be the safest and what price should be paid for it, 1839. (Taylor & Lloyds: letter, 14 Sept. 1839.)

p. 183. Lloyds found that stock exchange securities deposited by stockbrokers were mostly American stocks which had taken a bad fall, and so asked for additional cover, 1841. (Taylor & Lloyds: letter, 1 Nov. 1841.)

p. 184. Securities deposited, 1884, by Mills, Cave, Baillie & Co., Bristol, with Barnetts, Hoares, Hanbury & Lloyd, proved to be worthless certificates substituted by one of the stockbrokers, who had abstracted the true documents in order to cover his unsuccessful speculations in North American railway stocks. (Barnetts, Hoares: letters, Mar. 1884.)

p. 186. Hanbury, Taylor, Lloyd & Bowman went into American bonds as early as 1817. (Taylor & Lloyds: ledger, 1817.)

p. 187. After Francis Lloyd's visit to America, 'the bank was in 1827 persuaded by Rathbones of Liverpool to sell, in America, some of their United States Government bonds and to invest the proceeds in raw cotton'.

---

[1] In these circumstances it has not been thought worth while, contrary to our usual practice, to list the few addenda to Andrews & Davenport which we were able to find.

[2] Footnote references to material in the Bank's records have been omitted from Professor Sayers's book, but are available as a supplement, *Reference Notes*, at the Bank itself, the British Museum, the British Library of Political and Economic Science, London School of Economics, the Marshall Library of Economics, Cambridge, the Bodleian Library, Oxford, the Library of the Institute of Bankers, London, and Birmingham Public Libraries. For permission to use the records, application should be made to the Secretary of the Bank.

(Taylor & Lloyds: letters, 11 Aug., 26 and 28 Sept., and 30 Oct. 1827, and 19 July 1828.)

p. 187. Gloucestershire Banking Co. thought of buying United States Government bonds, 1838. (Gloucestershire Banking Co.: minutes, 1 June and 6 July 1838.)

p. 188. Bucks. & Oxon Bank held American bonds, 1869. (Bucks. & Oxon Union Bank Ltd.: balance sheet, 31 Dec. 1869.)

There may also be relevant material in the Liverpool Union Bank board minute-books, which contain information about cotton brokers (p. 93); and in Twining & Co. security registers (kept at Lloyds' Law Courts Branch), concerning investment in North America (p. 107).

London County Record Office, County Hall, Westminster Bridge, LONDON, S.E.1

There is no large body of American material deposited in the L.C.C. Record Office, though records are constantly being added. There are the usual types of parish records arranged alphabetically under metropolitan boroughs. A brief examination of estate records showed scattered references to colonial Americans involved in land transactions. Included among the records of the Boards of Guardians (taken over by the Council in 1930) are registers of children sent to Canada, &c., in the late nineteenth and early twentieth centuries. Among the L.C.C.'s own papers are:

MINUTES OF PROCEEDINGS. *c.* 100 volumes. 1889-to date.

Bound indexes to Council Minutes cover 1889-1937. A brief survey showed that the kind of material contained in the Minutes includes accounts of visits by Council officials to America, e.g. 1904, Chairman of Highways Committee appointed Council's representative at opening ceremony of New York Tramway Subway; 1905, report on American tramways by above to be published. Exchange visits by teachers, e.g. 1907, visit of inquiry to educational institutions, reports submitted by teachers; 1908, visits of teachers from United States, free admission to Council's classes for teachers. 1917, gift of copies of President Wilson's New Declaration of Freedom received from British-American Peace Centenary Committee. 1925, report of visit of Council's architect to America.

London Library, 14 St. James's Square, LONDON, S.W.1

PREVOST, AUGUSTINE (1723-86). Journal (50 leaves). 1774.

Major-General Prevost was apparently Governor pro tem. of Pennsylvania awaiting the arrival of someone whom he repeatedly calls 'His Lordship'. The journal, Apr.-Sept. 1774, contains details of travel through Pennsylvania, Maryland, and Virginia, and of negotiations in conjunction

R

with George Croghan, the Indian agent and trader, with the Shawnee Indians.

READE, CHARLES (1814–84). Papers, clippings.[1] c. 1860–84.

Author. Reade suffered from 'pirating' in America, and his papers include his manuscript, 'The Rights and Wrongs of Authors', on the absence of international copyright. They also include numerous clippings of reviews, &c., of his work from American sources, and material on a libel action, 1868–9, against an American magazine, in which an American jury awarded him 6 cents damages.

ASHBEE, CHARLES ROBERT (1863–1942). Memoirs, 1884–1938, with letters (6 volumes). (Carbon typescript)[2].

Architect, designer, and town planner; founder of the Guild of Handicraft; civic adviser to the Palestine Administration 1918–22; author of numerous books on the arts, and also of *The American League to Enforce Peace* (London, 1917).

Ashbee visited the United States seven times, travelling through all the Northern and Western states, and the Memoirs contain full descriptions of these visits and provide a picture of America as seen through an artist's eyes. The first visit, in 1896, was to lecture on the arts. The second lecture tour, in 1900, was made on behalf of the National Trust, and Ashbee met many American leaders. The third visit, in 1908, was for his Guild of Handicraft, an artistic colony in Gloucestershire, lately saved from dissolution by the American millionaire Joseph Fels. The fourth, fifth, and sixth visits—two in 1915 and one in 1916—were made as a representative of the 'Bryce Group', first to encourage Americans to join the Group in an organization to guarantee peace after the war, and later to assist in the formation of the American League to Enforce Peace. The account of these visits is relevant to an understanding of the attitude of neutral America. Ashbee interviewed Bryan and Roosevelt; also Brandeis, Frankfurter, and other eminent jurists; and many German-Americans. On the seventh and final visit, in 1923, he lectured on the Arab-Zionist question and also the arts.

London Missionary Society, Livingstone House, 42 Broadway, LONDON, S.W.1

UNITED STATES CORRESPONDENCE. 104 letters (1 box). 1799–1840.

Ninety-three letters from the United States, five copies of letters from London, and six from other parts of the world, to America or concerning

---

[1] The collection is described by E. G. Sutcliffe, 'Charles Reade's Notebooks', in *Studies in Philology*, vol. xxvii, pp. 64–109, 1930.

[2] Copies also in King's College Library, Cambridge (original typescript), and the Library of Congress, Washington, D.C.

Americans. The period mainly represented is 1807–11. Concerned with matters of mutual interest, which include the question of the dispatch of American missionaries under the auspices of the Society. There are requests for literature, applications for appointments, and letters of reference. A few early letters refer to work with the Indians and frontiersmen (e.g. in Kentucky); a few contain comments on the state of religion in America, and there is an occasional reference to the political situation, e.g. non-intercourse and the War of 1812.

MORRISON, ROBERT (1782–1834). Journal. 1807.

Missionary in China. Entry for 1807 contains brief comments on his visits to New York and Philadelphia *en route* from Britain to China, and the gift to him by Oliver Wolcott of a passage to China.

London Museum, Kensington Palace, LONDON, W.8

SUFFRAGETTE FELLOWSHIP COLLECTION.

A collection of papers donated by the Suffragette Fellowship. Included is a file on the international women's suffrage movement which contains correspondence, *c.* 1921, with Alice Paul, Chairman of the National Woman's Party in the United States, and the typewritten autobiography of Kitty Marion describing the part she played in the birth-control movement in the United States.

Macmillan & Co. Ltd., St. Martin's Street, LONDON, W.C.2

HUGHES, THOMAS (1822–96). Letters.[1] 1877–95.

Author of *Tom Brown's Schooldays*. The collection contains 115 letters, 1863–97, mainly from Hughes (a few are from his wife or daughter) to George Macmillan and to various other members of the Macmillan family and firm. A few of the 1881 letters refer to the colony founded by Hughes in Rugby, Tenn., and there is one letter, 14 Sept. 1887, written from there.

In a letter of 14 Sept. 1877, Hughes asks George Macmillan for books on 'the labour question' for Abram S. Hewitt, the ironmaster, a member of Congress; about ten letters, 1885–6, were written while Hughes was working on a biography of Hewitt's father-in-law, Peter Cooper, manufacturer, philanthropist, founder of the Cooper Union in New York; and relate to the difficulties raised by Hewitt and his wife.

[1] See E. C. Mack and W. H. G. Armytage, *Thomas Hughes* (London, 1952), and W. H. G. Armytage, 'New Light on the English Background of Thomas Hughes' Rugby Colony in Tennessee', *East Tennessee Historical Society's Publications*, No. 21, pp. 69–84, 1949.

The letters of 18 and 29 Mar. 1887 concern the error made by Hughes in his biography of James Fraser, Bishop of Manchester, in saying that William Ewart Gladstone—rather than his cousin, William Gladstone—was a subscriber to the Confederate Loan. A group of letters in 1894 relate to the unauthorized publication[1] in the United States of a letter from Hughes to James Russell Lowell.

JAMES, HENRY (1843–1916). *c.* 100 letters. 1877–1914.

The letters, written to Frederick Macmillan or to the firm, mainly concern the publication of James's books. There are also a few notes, 1910, from William James.

Methodist Missionary Society, 25 Marylebone Road, LONDON, N.W.1

'LETTERS OF SPECIAL INTEREST.' 1736, 1788.

(*a*) Letter from Georgia, 5 Feb. 1736, from Charles Wesley to Mrs. Sally Kirkham Chapone, chiefly about his spiritual condition.[2]

(*b*) Letter, Bath, Va., 15 Aug. 1788, from Francis Asbury, first Bishop of the Methodist Episcopal Church, to 'my dear Winscom', describing his circuit ('a thousand miles'), mentioning that he has just opened a school, and expatiating on the need for cordial Anglo-American relations.

COKE PAPERS. Certificate; letter. 1784, 1806.

(*a*) Certificate, 2 Sept. 1784, signed by John Wesley, appointing Thomas Coke superintendent of Methodist work in America.

(*b*) Letter from New York, 7 May 1806, from Francis Asbury to Thomas Coke, describing his extensive travels through Eastern America, and mentioning the work beyond the Mississippi. Asbury says, 'in Delaware the millenium is certainly begun. They can live without slavery or liquid fire', and 'American sinners are the greatest sinners upon earth'.

LETTERS. 1802–31.

Chiefly concerned with the progress of Methodism in America.

(*a*) Twenty-four letters from New York, Virginia, Georgia, South Carolina, Maryland, Washington, D.C., Pennsylvania, and Rhode Island (none from a well-known figure), 1802–6, 1815–17 (included in a box marked 'Canada, 1802–1818'). Deal chiefly with spiritual experiences, the number of conversions, mentioning also mission work among Negroes, and camp meetings.

---

[1] In *True Manliness: from the Writings of T. Hughes*, selected by Emma E. Brown' with an introduction by James Russell Lowell (Boston, 1880).

[2] Printed in Frank Baker, *Charles Wesley as Revealed by his Letters*, pp. 21–23 (London, 1948) (Wesley Historical Society Lectures No. 14).

(*b*) Seven letters from New York, 1827–8, 1830–1 (included in box marked 'Home, 1825–1831'), from the headquarters of the Missionary Society of the Methodist Episcopal Church, New York, to the Wesleyan Methodist Missionary Society in London. Chiefly business matters and copy resolutions. Mention missions in South America and Liberia.

ORDINATION CERTIFICATES.

Joshua Marsden to the office of Elder in the Methodist Episcopal Church of America, signed by Francis Asbury, 1 June 1802; and to the office of Deacon in the same, signed by Richard Whatcoat, Associate Bishop, 2 June 1802.

Midland Bank Ltd., Poultry, LONDON, E.C.2

BANK RECORDS.[1]

The Bank holds an extensive collection of records mainly relating to nineteenth-century joint-stock banking in England and Wales; a duplicated 'Catalogue of Historical Material' lists these. The amount of material for each of the banks which later became part of the present Midland Bank varies, the principal classes of records being minute-books of directors' and of shareholders' meetings, with some ledgers, registers, letter-books, &c.; only very rarely have the accounts of individual customers survived.

Typed and manuscript extracts from some of the minute-books are available, these having been copied—and some used—for the history of the Bank. From these, it appears that there is brief scattered comment on American affairs in some of the minute-books—e.g., on the finding of gold in California, and the disruption of trade caused by the Civil War and the Spanish-American War. Several banks in Lancashire had close links with the cotton trade.

The only specifically American reference in the duplicated list is to a 1910 letter in the records of the Birmingham and Midland Bank to the Philadelphia National Bank concerning the opening of the first foreign account with the London and Midland Bank. A number of possibly likely volumes were, however, chosen from the list, and examination of these showed there to be relevant material as follows:

(*a*) North and South Wales Bank. A volume of diary notes, 1851–89, on matters relating to the Bank and banking developments includes a copy of a letter, 5 Nov. 1880, from Mr. Billinghurst of the London and Westminster Bank, whose advice had been asked about investment in, *inter alia*, United States 4 per cent. Funded Stocks.

(*b*) Bradford Banking Co., Bradford. References occur in records to the opening of credits with overseas banks; the chairman's speech to

[1] See W. F. Crick and J. E. Wadsworth, *A Hundred Years of Joint Stock Banking* (London, 1936)—a history of the Bank.

shareholders in 1857 comments on 'the high price of wool, cotton and silk' and contests the view that this is due 'to the influx of Californian and Australian gold . . . in enhancing the monied value' of real and personal property.

(c) Leyland, Bullins & Co., Liverpool.[1] 'Ledger No. 14', 1887–94, includes the accounts of a large number of firms in Galveston and Houston, Tex., New Orleans, New York, Philadelphia, and Savannah, Ga., as well as the accounts of an 'adventure in cotton' from Augusta, Ga., and one from Galveston, and an 'adventure in seedcake' from New Orleans; the entries give only amounts for 'sundries', 'cash', and 'balance'. Many of the accounts appear to have been transferred from Lemonius & Co., Liverpool, liquidated in 1887.

Moravian Church in Great Britain and Ireland, 5 Muswell Hill, LONDON, N.10

ARCHIVES.

The British headquarters of the Church in Fetter Lane, London, was destroyed by enemy action in 1941.[2] The surviving papers are in process of being listed and reassembled.

The records now available in London consist of bound volumes, and of packets of unbound papers, as follows:

(a) Bound volumes of minutes (some in German), extracts from or translations of minutes, miscellaneous collections of material concerning bishops, &c.; eighteenth and nineteenth centuries. There is likely to be relevant material scattered throughout these, since, from the time of the 1735 settlement of Moravians in Georgia, the Church was very active in missionary work in America, especially among the Indians and the Eskimoes. The eighteenth-century translation of the 'Headquarters Diary' for 1747, for example, includes, for 12 June, references to correspondence with Lord Baltimore about land in Maryland and to plans for settlements in Pennsylvania and Georgia.

(b) Two packets contain contemporary extracts from 1745 and 1747 'prayer day' proceedings in London. Included is material concerning missionary work among the Indians and other activities of the Brethren in America, mainly in Pennsylvania, in the form of letters (including one from George Whitefield, 4 Mar. 1745), reports, and journals.

---

[1] There is likely to be further relevant material in the records of this Bank. See L. S. Pressnell, *Country Banking in the Industrial Revolution* (Oxford, 1956), p. 534, for the financing in 1812 and 1818 of a merchant in the Virginia trade.

[2] The existence of relevant records at the Fetter Lane headquarters was noted in the preface to Andrews & Davenport, p. vi.

Morgan Grenfell & Co. Ltd., 23 Great Winchester Street, LONDON, E.C.2

The firm of Morgan Grenfell, merchant bankers, is willing to make its older records available to senior research students, subject to approval of any proposed published use. However, a list of queries concerning the role of George Peabody and Junius Morgan in the floatation of various American issues in the London market, or of investments in American railroad stock, revealed that almost all their papers had been repatriated to New York, as has Junius Morgan's business correspondence with J. P. Morgan.

Inquiries should be addressed to the Manager.

John Murray (Publishers) Ltd., 50 Albemarle Street, LONDON, W.1

INTERNATIONAL COPYRIGHT. 1842, 1852.

The firm's files of the following authors contain letters on the subject of international copyright.

(a) Charles Dickens. A letter (printed), 7 July 1842, concerns attitudes in the United States towards international copyright legislation; letters of 2 Aug. 1842 and 18 May 1852 are also on international copyright.

(b) Edward Bulwer Lytton. A letter (copy), 14 June 1852, from Sir John Crampton, the British Minister in Washington, to Lytton, says that things in America are at the most favourable stage for the passage of international copyright legislation. Another letter, 19 June 1852, from Crampton to Lytton, states that 'the public feeling is very much changed on the subject since Mr. Dickens was here', and discusses the relationship of federal and state jurisdiction and action in the matter. There is also a letter, 9 July 1852, from Lytton, concerning subscriptions to a fund for the copyright cause, and an undated memorandum headed 'Mem. Am. Copyright', listing contributions to the fund.

(c) Philip Henry Stanhope, Viscount Mahon (later 5th Earl Stanhope). Seven letters, Mar.–May 1842, on the wording of the Copyright Bill and its passage through Parliament.

National Maritime Museum, Romney Road, Greenwich, LONDON, S.E.10

The manuscript material in the National Maritime Museum has been brought together from a variety of sources, including public and semi-public records, private papers and collections of documents made by persons interested in particular aspects of naval history. The following is a summary of American material found in official Admiralty records, including the collection of ships' plans and drawings; personal papers and library collections; Lloyd's Register; and ships' logs. It is by no means exhaustive as the collection is very large and is still growing.

ADMIRALTY RECORDS

(a) Orders from Admiralty to Navy Board, 1688–1815; Navy Board Replies 1738–1831. 1,492 volumes.

A great deal of American material would be found in these records. Some information on such topics as the supply of timber and naval stores, shipbuilding practice, and charting of the North American coast has been extracted by the Custodian of Manuscripts for specific purposes, such as exhibitions held at the Museum. The following are examples:

(i) Naval Stores, 1696–1784.

Admiralty to Navy Board. 31 Dec. 1696, instructions for agents to investigate the supply of naval stores in New England. (ADM/A/1837)

Admiralty to Navy Board. 17 Dec. 1701, trial to be made of turpentine imported from New England, with a report on it from the officers at Deptford Yard. (ADM/A/1887)

Admiralty to Navy Board. 3 Jan. 1728, opinion asked for on Thomas Coram's petition concerning his work in promoting supply of naval stores in America, and settlement of shipwrights, &c., in New England. Draft reply. (ADM/A/2159)

Navy Board to Admiralty. 26 Apr. 1748, contract with Messrs. Hennikers for masts from New England, forwarded for the grant of a royal licence. (ADM/B/138)

Navy Board to Admiralty. 30 Oct. 1772, report on Mr. Duer of New York's plan for obtaining masts from New York and the proposal from shipbuilders of New York for building a frigate for His Majesty's service, the latter again not recommended. (ADM/B/187)

Navy Board to Admiralty. 17 Apr. 1777, details of bounties paid on import of naval stores from America. Copy of reply sent to Treasury. (ADM/B/194)

Navy Board to Commissioner Duncan at Halifax. 1 May 1784, asking for report on naval stores available in his neighbourhood. Commissioner Duncan's reply (letter-book copy). (HAL/F/2)

(ii) Timber, 1700–73.

Admiralty to Navy Board, 13 Dec. 1700, letter and papers from Lord Bellamont, Governor of New England, on timber supplies. Has sent specimens to England, sets out advantages of using American timber. Asks for a report on his proposals. (ADM/A/1878)

Admiralty to Navy Board, 1 Apr. 1740, letters and report from David Dunbar, Surveyor of Woods in America, forwarded for opinion. Concerned with supply of masts for His Majesty's Navy. (ADM/A/2282)

Navy Board to Admiralty, 19 Apr. and 17 Oct. 1771, report on information about American timber received from Roger Fisher of Liverpool, author of pamphlet *Heart of Oak, the British Bulwark* (London, 1763; 2nd edition 1771). Praises American live oak and pitch pine. (ADM/B/185)

Navy Board to Admiralty, 30 Apr. 1773, report on undesirability of building ships in North America. Messrs. Begbie & Manson, shipbuilders, of Hobeau, S.C. have offered to build a 32-gun ship with live oak and pine timber and desire employment in refitting navy ships. Navy Board gives unfavourable opinion of American materials and workmanship. (ADM/B/187)

(iii) Charting the North American Coast, 1720–37.

Capt. J. Gascoigne was employed by the Admiralty on a survey of the North American coast. The log of his ship *Aldborough* kept during this period records details about coastline, harbours, surveying practice, &c. (ADM/L/A/79) (ADM/A/2161)

(iv) Shipbuilding practice, 1747.

Navy Board to Admiralty, 4 Mar. 1747, report on building 44-gun ship in New England. Builder—Col. Meserve. Also report on repairing of the *Bien Aime* by Benjamin Hollowell of Boston. (ADM/B/138)

(*b*) Correspondence between the Commissioners for taking care of sick and hurt seamen and the Admiralty relating to the American prisoners of war. 2 volumes; some loose papers. 1777–83. (ADM/M/404, 405)

The arrangements for the care of prisoners of war were at this time the responsibility of the Commissioners appointed for taking care of sick and wounded seamen. There are letters in these volumes on the arrangements for setting up and staffing a prison at Plymouth; petitions from prisoners requesting permission to serve on British ships, and pardons for prisoners 'on condition of their entering and continuing to serve us in our Royal Navy'. From autumn 1778 negotiations were under way for the exchange of prisoners. Authorizations from the Lords Commissioners of the Admiralty to Commissioners for taking care of sick and hurt seamen for exchanging prisoners include names and ranks and ships on which the prisoners had served; a letter, 25 July 1778, from David Hartley, concerns a report from Benjamin Franklin on English prisoners held at Brest; a letter from Passy, 1 Jan. 1779, from Franklin signifies agreement for arrangements for exchanging prisoners. (Hartley and Franklin were principal agents appointed to arrange exchanges of prisoners.)

(*c*) Emigration of American Loyalists, 1783–5. From the volume of Treasury Transport letters, Jan. 1783–Dec. 1789. (ADM/O.T./1)

These transport orders sent from the Lords Commissioners of the Treasury to the Admiralty include detailed orders for moving American Loyalist families to other British colonies, for example Bahamas and Nova Scotia.

(*d*) The Museum holds the Admiralty collections of ships' plans of ships built for or purchased by the Royal Navy, 1700–1900. A list has been compiled of the plans of American-built ships which the Royal Navy captured or purchased, and also of ships of the Royal Navy captured by the Americans. There are thirty-eight names in these two lists.

PERSONAL PAPERS

KEPPEL, ADMIRAL THE HON. AUGUSTUS (1725–86). Coast of North America: order books. 1754–5. (46. MS. 9580)

Appointed Commander-in-Chief, North American Station 1754 The order books contain copies of instructions sent out by Keppel; included are instructions for sending a small party of seamen up the Potomac to join General Braddock's troops and assist them in crossing rivers and building vessels on the Great Lakes, Mar. 1755; and for the examination of all ships passing through Hampton Roads, Va., May 1755.

HOOD, ADMIRAL VISCOUNT (1724–1816). Log books, 1760–95; letter- and order books, 1767–95; letters received, 504 letters, 1771–1815. (50. MS. 0096)

Samuel, 1st Viscount Hood, Commander-in-Chief North America 1767–70. Sent to join Graves in New York 1781–2. Letters include a memorandum in Hood's writing on the events of 5 Sept. 1781, dated Coast of Virginia, 6 Sept. 1781.[1]

GRAVES, ADMIRAL THOMAS (1725–1802). Log book; loose papers; drafts of letters to the Admiralty, 1764–82; private papers, 1782–95. (MS. 9365)

Later 1st Baron Graves. Served with Vice Admiral Byron's squadron in North America 1778, and on the North American Station 1781–2. Orders of sailing, instructions, rendezvous, &c., are to be found in the papers 1781–2.

CORNWALLIS, ADMIRAL SIR WILLIAM (1744–1819). Letters received; journals; order and letter-books. 1770–9.

(a) Letters received[2] (35. MS. 0105). These are mainly letters addressed to Sir William Cornwallis, a naval captain during the War of Independence, and a brother of Lord Cornwallis. The letters thus touch upon both military and naval aspects of the War, although not to any important extent.

(b) Orders received while commanding the *Isis* on the North American Station 1777, with some draft replies. This book is one of the sixty-one volumes of Cornwallis Papers known as the Cornwallis West Collection. (MS. 9575)

STARKE, LIEUTENANT JOHN: 'The case of Lieutenant John Starke of H.M. Navy', together with a short sketch of the

---

[1] Printed in *Letters Written by Sir Samuel Hood . . . in 1781–2–3* (London, 1895) (Navy Records Society Publications, vol. iii). See also *Letters to the Ministry from Governor Bernard, General Gage and Commodore Hood* (London and Boston, 1769).

[2] This collection was formerly the property of Major R. F. Wykeham-Martin and is reported in H.M.C. Various Collections vi [55], pp. 297–434.

operations of the war in Canada in which he was employed during the years 1775–1776–1777 (34 pages). (49. MS. 129)

Starke's service was in the defence of Quebec, on the St. Lawrence River and on Lake Champlain. His memorial was written to show to Lord Sandwich, to gain employment.

COLLIER, ADMIRAL SIR GEORGE (1738–95). Journal, papers. 1776–9.

(a) Personal journal of the war in America, 1776. (35. MS. 0085.) Sir George sailed for America in the *Rainbow* in 1776, carrying reinforcements of Hessian troops. Soon after arrival he was sent by Lord Howe to Halifax, N.S., where he took command as senior officer. The notebook contains jottings of incidents and remarks which he used for letters he sent back to England. It shows a clear change of confidence in the American situation between August and September 1776.

(b) 'A Detail of Some Particular Services Performed in America during the Years 1776–1779 by Commodore Sir George Collier, Commander-in-Chief on the American Station.' Compiled from journals and original papers by G. S. Rainier (Collier's secretary) (174 pages). (MS. 9612.) A note at the end suggests that this narrative was intended for publication. The text was carefully written and corrected in several places.

WARREN, ADMIRAL SIR JOHN BORLASE (1753–1822). Correspondence with Lord Melville during the War of 1812: 34 letters. 1812–14. (MS. 9622)

Admiral Warren commanded the North American Station 1812–14. These private letters to Lord Melville include accounts of the progress of the sea war, of the effects of the blockade on American trade, of the treatment of British merchants and prisoners of war, &c. Warren encloses newspaper cuttings from American newspapers with his own marginal comments, and many intercepted American letters containing comments on the war.

HULBERT, GEORGE REDMOND (1774–1825). Letter-books, account books, and letters received. 1813–23. (MS. 56/040)

Naval agent and Admiral's secretary. Served with Admiral Warren 1808, 1810–14. Hulbert acted as agent for several prizes. There is information about the procedure followed in the collection and distribution of prize money, &c.

CODRINGTON, ADMIRAL SIR EDWARD (1770–1851). Personal papers referring to Codrington's service while commanding H.M.S. *Tonnant* in American waters, 1814–15, including official letters and order books. (MS. 9278)

Served on the American Station 1814–15. Included are a bundle of private letters[1] describing the destruction of Washington, the taking of Alexandria, the failure at Baltimore, the New Orleans expedition of 1815. There are plans and orders for the New Orleans expedition and for landing troops.

MILNE, ADMIRAL SIR ALEXANDER (1806–96). Papers. 1860–4. (49. MS. 117)

The Milne Papers, while including some papers of other members of the family, cover in detail the career of Sir Alexander Milne, Commander-in-Chief, North American and West Indian Station 1860–4; First Naval Lord 1866–8, 1872–6; member of the Committee appointed to deal with claims arising from the *Alabama* dispute. Records for the time when he was commanding the North American and West Indian Station are very full. There are also papers collected together by Milne whilst at the Admiralty, which include memoranda on naval policy. American material includes:

(a) Nine volumes of letter-books containing copies of Milne's letters to the Admiralty, 14 Jan. 1860–5 Apr. 1864. Fully indexed.

(b) Three volumes of letter-books containing copies of Milne's letters to ambassadors, governors, consuls, &c., 13 Mar. 1860–10 Apr. 1864. There are letters to British ambassadors, consuls and commanders of United States forces on the seizure of British ships by American cruisers, and on questions of contraband, &c., memoranda on policy to be followed by British ships in blockaded ports and when involved in incidents arising from the Civil War; and letters asking British Consuls for confidential information on shore defences of ports and harbours within their consular jurisdiction.

(c) Several parcels of letters received by Milne, 1860–4, include a selection of Admiralty letters marked by Milne 'Very important letters on the American Command'. These include c. 100 letters, confidential reports, &c., on the seizure of ships, the right of search, *Trent* case, Newfoundland fisheries, &c., and also several of Milne's own memoranda: Memorandum relative to the North American and West Indian Station for the information of his successor, deals with the defence of Canada, the Canadian canal system, the reception of British ships in American ports, &c. (115 pages). Memorandum relative to the Civil War in America, containing detailed notes on the effects of the war on the Station and discussion of various cases including the *Alabama* and matters arising from blockade-running, &c. (72 pages). Précis of papers relating to the Civil War in America (67 pages).

(d) Dispatch box containing about fifty letters, 1861–2, 1864, from Lord Lyons, British Minister in Washington, dealing with the interests of British citizens, prize-court captures, American opinion on war events and war news, &c.; seven letters from William Stewart about the *Alabama* and the *Blanche*; many letters from the Duke of Somerset, First Lord of the Admiralty,

---

[1] See *A Memoir of the Life of Admiral Sir Edward Codrington with Selections from his public and private correspondence*, edited by his daughter Lady Bourchier, 2 volumes (London, 1873).

with some draft replies by Milne, including a bundle inscribed by Milne 'most important letters from Duke of Somerset in case of war with the United States, 1861–1862'. About fifty letters, Jan. 1860–Apr. 1863 (these were returned to Milne after Grey's death) from Milne to Sir Frederick Grey; several pressed copybooks of private out-letters, 1860–2.

(e) Papers collected together by Milne during his period at the Admiralty include many memoranda on naval policy, among which are:

(i) Folder on the 'Newfoundland Fisheries, 1840'. Including Milne's own printed report and various letters and notes on the Newfoundland and Nova Scotia fisheries.

(ii) Folder on 'Naval Policy in North America, 1861–1866'. Mostly printed reports dealing with the defence of Canada in the event of war with the United States; but including a manuscript list of vessels suitable for the protection of the North American Lakes, 1865.

(iii) Folder on the 'Alabama Case, 1863–1872'. Including a bundle of about fifty letters from Lord Lyons in Washington, 1863, and many letters addressed to Milne as a member of the Alabama claims committee, 1872. There are manuscript notes of the proceedings of the committee and several printed reports.

LLOYD'S REGISTER OF BRITISH AND FOREIGN SHIPPING. Surveyors' reports and plans of ships, from American ports: Baltimore, 1 report, 1890; New York, 1 report, 1898; Philadelphia, 2 boxes, 1880–1901; Portland, Ore., part of one box, 1898–9; San Francisco, part of one box, 1877–1900. (Printed forms filled in in manuscript.)

The reports occasionally have ships' plans and correspondence as enclosures.

SHIPS' LOGS.

A large collection of the logs of both merchant and warships. While the logs kept by officers of ships of the Royal Navy were preserved by the Admiralty, there was no central repository for the records of merchant ships until the middle of the nineteenth century. In consequence the latter are a haphazard collection, but the former provide a continuous record from the late seventeenth to the early nineteenth century. The following are examples of logs with American interest:

(a) Personal journals. 'Journal from Bristol towards South Carolina in the ship Lloyd. Jan.–Oct. 1768'. One volume covering two voyages. An illustrated journal kept by the master, Nicholas Pocock, marine artist. There is some description of trade with South Carolina in rice, turpentine, skins, &. The ship was owned by Richard Champion. (MS. 56/051)

(b) An official Admiralty log. 'A Journal of the proceedings of His Majesty's Ship Eagle by Captain Henry Duncan commander. 1776–1780.' One volume. (ADM/L/E/11.) The ship was ordered to New York and anchored off Chester in the River Delaware. In Nov. 1777 the log records fighting between the rebels on Mud Island and royal troops, and describes the supplying of the army with provisions, &c.

(c) 'Journal of a voyage in the *Isaac Hicks*, merchant ship (Captain Dickenson) from Liverpool to New York, kept by a passenger.' Feb.–Apr. 1829 (8 pages). An account of an eighty-six day crossing. (50. MS. 0165)

National Society of Brushmakers, 77 Kingsland Road, LONDON, E.2

UNITED SOCIETY OF BRUSHMAKERS. Minute-books.

The minute-books, available from 1815 onwards, contain references to emigration to America from the 1820's.[1] From 1834 the Society's general articles make provision for any member wishing to emigrate to make application for assistance to the Society, and, if approved, to be granted £15. There are references in the minutes to votes on applications for assistance, temporary suspension of assistance in 1830–1, and the methods of financing the scheme.

The Plunkett Foundation for Co-operative Studies, 10 Doughty Street, LONDON, W.C.1

PLUNKETT, SIR HORACE CURZON (1854–1932). Papers: correspondence, 1883–1932; diary, 1881–1932.

Advocate of agricultural co-operation, Anglo-Irish statesman. Plunkett actively ranched in the American West in the 1880's (retaining some financial interests long afterwards) before devoting his life to the cause of agricultural co-operatives, first in Ireland and then in Britain and America as well. In this cause he formed intimate friendships in the 1900's with leading American politicians and social reformers, notably Colonel House, Theodore Roosevelt, Gifford Pinchot, and Charles McCarthy of Wisconsin. These friendships led to important unofficial correspondence and conversations by Plunkett in the First World War, concerned both with press information work and with relaying the views of leading British politicians to House and Wilson, particularly on the Irish question as it affected Anglo-American relations—he was the chairman of the abortive Irish Convention of 1917.

Some of Plunkett's papers were destroyed during the troubles of 1923, but most of his public correspondence seems to have survived. There is no list, but the papers were arranged in alphabetical files under the names of

[1] See William Kiddier, *The Old Trade Unions: from Unpublished Records of the Brushmakers*, 2nd edition, pp. 93–97, 108, 197 (London, 1931).

correspondents (together with copies of Plunkett's replies) by Miss Margaret Digby, for her *Horace Plunkett: An Anglo-American Irishman* (Oxford, 1949). (Miss Digby also quotes from the fifty-two volumes of his diary, which cover the whole period.) Comment on American affairs can be found throughout Plunkett's war-time letters on the Irish question to British statesmen. The principal correspondents, however, are:

Frewen, Moreton. Chiefly about a dozen letters, 1883–5, concerning the affairs of the Powder River Cattle Company of Wyoming, of which Frewen was the founder and promoter, and Plunkett later a partner. Frewen was an active promoter in the London market of many American ventures, M.P. for North-East Cork 1910–11, author of pamphlets on the silver question, Anglo-American trade, &c.[1] Some of the letters are from Frewen in London to an agent in Cheyenne, and some from Frewen in Wyoming to C. F. Kemp, the London manager (some of these latter include confidential unsigned enclosures about extra-legal tactics to be used against farmers and Texan interlopers). All of the above letters are in a single 'Miscellaneous File'. Also, in the main alphabetical series, are the originals of some letters from Plunkett to Frewen, 1881–6, some from Cheyenne and some from England, on the paper of the Frontier Land and Cattle Company, Cheyenne, Wyo., the letter-head of which gives Plunkett as President, A. Gilchrist as Vice-President, E. S. R. Boughton as Treasurer, and John Chaplin as Secretary. Also some twenty letters, 1917–18, between Frewen and Plunkett on the Irish question and English politics.

Roosevelt, Theodore. Six letters to and seven from Roosevelt, 1906–17. Mostly about conservation and rural affairs, with supporting papers including copies of other letters, several from or to Gifford Pinchot. (1 file. In this file there is also a slight note from Franklin Delano Roosevelt, 10 May 1918, thanking Plunkett for sending him the Proceedings of the Irish Convention.)

Byrne, James. 1908–28. The early letters are mostly about the affairs of the Western Live-Stock and Land Company, in which Plunkett had an interest; the later correspondence turns to international affairs and Byrne's financial support for Plunkett's co-operative organizations in Ireland.

Pinchot, Gifford. Many letters, 1908–18, covering the whole range of his and Pinchot's common interests in agricultural reform. (Large file.)

Grey, Albert Henry George, 4th Earl Grey. 1908–17, on Anglo-American relations, mostly while Grey was Governor-General of Canada. (1 file.)

Lowell, A. L. 1909–28. Interesting on American opinion, 1914–17. (Large file.)

Bryce, James. Over fifty letters, 1909–21, covering many aspects of Anglo-American relations, particularly Ireland and America in 1917; some discuss the work of Charles McCarthy.

[1] Frewen's founding of the company is described in long footnotes to Howard B. Lett, 'Diary of Major Wise: Hunting Trip in the Powder River Country in 1880', *Annals of Wyoming*, vol. xii, pp. 85–119, 1940.

Godkin, Lawrence. 1909–18. As well as the whole range of topics covering American opinion and the War, specific letters concern the Ambassadorial appointments of Page and Spring-Rice in 1913. (1 file.)

Wallace, Henry. 1909–16, on agricultural reform and politics; Wallace's letters are on the notepaper of *Wallace's Farmer*. (1 file.)

Page, Walter Hines. 1909–14, on Anglo-American relations.

McCarthy, Charles. 1911–19. This would seem to be an extremely interesting source on agriculture and political reform in the Progressive Era. (Large file.)

Hill, James J. Chairman of the Great Northern Railway Company. Three letters, 1911–14.

Chaplin, John. Letter, 13 Apr. 1911, from Plunkett to Chaplin about the affairs of the former Frontier Land and Cattle Company, the successors of which, Plunkett claims, owe him some $60,000.

House, Edward. 1913–32. The most important are the war-time letters in which Plunkett undertook to keep Wilson and House informed on English official and semi-official opinion. Extracts from many, but by no means all, of these have been printed in *The Intimate Papers of Colonel House*, arranged by Charles Seymour, 4 vols. (Boston, 1926; London, 1926–8). House, indeed, writes several letters to Plunkett about the composition and reception of these volumes, reminiscing about himself and Wilson. (2 large files.)

Wilson, Woodrow. 1913–23. Mostly reports by Plunkett to Wilson on English opinion in war-time, similar to those to House, though the earlier letters are on agricultural reform. Wilson's replies are brief and formal. (1 file.)

Walter, Karl. 1916–18. Long reports to and from Plunkett about the work of the Reciprocal News Service in London, which Walter headed, in interpreting British opinion to the Mid-Western press and vice versa—the purpose for which the agency was established. (1 file.)

Spring-Rice, Cecil and Thomas. 1916–17, on Anglo-American relations.

Ladenburger & Thalmann. Some correspondence, 1917, between Plunkett and this New York firm about his Western investments.

Young, Conrad. 1925–7, about the affairs of the Nebraska and Wyoming Investment Company, Omaha, Neb., of which Plunkett was President and Young Manager. (1 file.)

Presbyterian Historical Society, Church House, 86 Tavistock Place, LONDON, W.C.1

THE ARCHIVES, *and* W. B. SHAW LIBRARY.

The Library contains many early printed works on American Presbyterianism, including biographies and histories of the American churches. It contains the *Journal of the Presbyterian Historical Society*, Philadelphia, and some other volumes of reports, minutes, and proceedings of the American Presbyterian churches.

There is a certain amount of manuscript material, including Baptismal Registers of all English Presbyterian Congregations back to 1698, in the Archives. It is available for reference but not yet indexed since the destruction of the original library and archives in 1945. Anyone wishing to see the documents should write to the Hon. Secretary of the Society.

Public Record Office, Chancery Lane, LONDON, W.C.2

The Public Record Office is the consolidated official depository of the separate archives of the various departments of the British government and of the central courts of law. Its holdings of relevance for American history have been described in the guides by Andrews & Davenport, Andrews, and Paullin & Paxson, which include elaborate notes on the administrative history of the departments concerned and also general descriptions of lists, indexes, and other aids to finding material; *this information is not repeated here.* Some recent changes concerning Crown copyright and rules respecting the public use of the records are set out in a leaflet of 'Regulations', Jan. 1959.

Since these earlier guides were published, however, there has appeared M. S. Giuseppi's official *Guide to the Manuscripts Preserved in the Public Record Office*; vol. i: *Legal Records*; and vol. ii, *State Paper Office and Public Departments* (London, 1923, 1924). A new edition of this work is expected shortly; meanwhile there is an annotated copy in the Round Room of the Record Office. Also, Hilary Jenkinson's *Guide to the Public Records: Introductory* (London, 1949) is useful, as is V. H. Galbraith, *An Introduction to the Use of the Public Records* (London, corrected edition, 1952).[1]

The report which follows, then, attempts to indicate merely the main categories of material added since the earlier guides were compiled. The method used was, in general, to compare the printed, typescript, and other lists and indexes to the departmental records with the earlier guides to Americana, and to note additions, whether of complete classes or of material within a class.[2] This dependence on available lists of varying degrees of

[1] See also *The British Public Record Office: History, Description, Record Groups, Finding Aids, and Materials for American History with Special Reference to Virginia* (Richmond Va., Virginia State Library, 1960). This reprints Special Reports 25–28 of the Virginia Colonial Records Project; it is now an essential introduction to the P.R.O.

[2] No attempt was made to cover legal records, except in the cases of the High Court of Admiralty, the Court of Bankruptcy, and the Court of Chancery. For a description of the various classes of legal records probably or certainly containing Americana, see Virginia Colonial Records Project, op. cit., and Giuseppi, op. cit., vol. i, pp. 89–91, 241, 270.

detail makes it probable that some relevant classes or items have been excluded; this is certainly the case as regards the Foreign Office records, since in general only items specifically described as relating to the United States were included, whereas the Foreign Office correspondence with, e.g., Venezuela (F.O. 80) undoubtedly contains material relevant to the Anglo-American Venezuela dispute of 1887–96. The editors are well aware that ideally all papers, or at least doubtful list entries, should have been searched, that lists are often an inadequate guide—but to have done so would have been a labour quite as large as the whole of the present volume.

It should be noted when using the earlier guides that, since these were prepared, changes have been made in the classification, numbering, &c., of some records, and also that certain material described as being in other depositories has been transferred to the Public Record Office; no attempt has been made here to survey these changes in detail.

Since this report was prepared, the Public Records Act of 1958 has come into force. Under its terms records are being transferred by Departments to the Public Record Office within thirty years of their creation and, in general, becoming open to inspection when fifty years old. There has in consequence been a notable accession of material since this *Guide* was compiled and it is not possible here to include many entries beyond 1902, the previous 'open-date' for most Departmental records. For an account of recent transfers see *120th Report of the Deputy Keeper of the Public Records*, 1958 (1959), and the *First Annual Report of the Keeper of Public Records on the Work of the Public Record Office and the First Report of the Advisory Council on Public Records*, 1959 (1960).

Aliens who wish to use the records are required to return a completed application form to the Public Record Office, and then to ask their Embassy or Legation to apply to the Foreign Office for a letter of introduction on their behalf; a student's ticket is issued when this letter is received by the Public Record Office.

Reports have been prepared on the following:[1]

> Admiralty
> Admiralty, High Court of
> Agriculture and Fisheries, Ministry of
> Bankruptcy, Court of
> Chancery, Court of
> Colonial Office
> Copyright Office
> Exchequer
> Exchequer and Audit
> Foreign Office
> German Foreign Ministry Records (Copies)
> Gifts and Deposits
> Health, Ministry of

[1] See separate report on H.M. Customs and Excise (pp. 188–207), and Introduction (p. xxx). Custom House Records, wherever located, have for scholarly convenience been treated in a single report.

Home Office
Privy Council
Trade, Board of
Transport, Ministry of
Treasury
Treasury Solicitor
War Office

ADMIRALTY

Lists, &c.: P.R.O. *Lists and Indexes No. XVIII: List of Admiralty Records* (1904), with additions and corrections.

'Admiralty: Supplementary List' (typescript).
'List of Admiral's Journals' (typescript and duplicated).
'Admiralty: Ships' Logs', 3 volumes (manuscript).
'Admiralty: Ships' Logs to 1902' (duplicated).

Ad. 1/5691–7643. SECRETARY'S DEPARTMENT: IN-LETTERS. 1858–1902.

Included are reports of courts martial, letters from admirals, captains, government departments, &c.; indexes and digests are available in Ad. 12. Examination of Ad. 1/5871 (1864) showed it to include correspondence about American ships in the Rio Grande, eighty-seven pages on the Civil War in a memorandum by Sir A. Milne on transferring the command of the North American and West Indian Station to Sir J. Hope, &c.

Ad. 7. SECRETARY'S DEPARTMENT: MISCELLANEA.

7/624 Lakes and rivers of Canada: defences. 1861–2.
7/625 Captain Warden's report on Canada. 1845–6.
7/626 United States defences: seaboard, lakes, and Canadian frontier. 1845.

Ad. 13. SUPPLEMENTARY.

13/1–63 Out-letters.[1] 1814–69.
  Registers to these are available, for 1860–8, in Ad. 13/66–67. Examination of Ad. 13/66, the register for 1860–3, showed it to contain, under 'United States', thirteen pages of lists of letters, on the subjects of the blockade, the slave trade, &c.

13/184/9. *Standing Orders for the Squadron Employed on the North American and West Indian Station* (Halifax, N.S., 1862), with inserted manuscript notes.

Ad. 50. ADMIRALS' JOURNALS.

Journals for the North American and West Indian Station for 1854–85 are in Ad. 50/300–7; those for 1885–1909 are in Ad. 50/349–53.

  [1] The Library of Congress holds photostats of part of volume 13/4: Instructions to Rear-Admiral Sir Houston Stewart, Commander-in-Chief North American and West Indian Station, 3 Feb. 1857 and 7 Feb. 1860.

Ad. 53. SHIPS' LOGS.

There may be scattered material in these volumes, which are open without restriction as to date.

Ad. 110–13. VICTUALLING DEPARTMENT.

Out-letters, minutes, accounts, and registers all provide details for provisioning the eighteenth century fleet on the American station, giving prices and contractors' names, &c.

Ad. 116. SECRETARY'S DEPARTMENT: CASES.

116/86, 113, 122. Newfoundland fisheries. 1897–1901.

HIGH COURT OF ADMIRALTY

Lists, &c.: 'High Court of Admiralty: Class List' (manuscript).

H.C.A. 35/1–89. SLAVE TRADE: GOVERNMENT REPORTS. 1821–91.

Examination of H.C.A. 35/78 (1860–3) showed it to include copies of letters and reports to the Treasury from H. C. Rothery, Admiralty Registrar, about the New York slave ship *Tavernier*, and the proposed British and American regulations for the suppression of the slave trade.

H.C.A. 36. SLAVE TRADE: ADDITIONAL PAPERS.

Parliamentary papers and printed copies of treaties; some correspondence, drafts, &c. Much of the material relates to the 1876 Royal Commission on fugitive slaves.

MINISTRY OF AGRICULTURE AND FISHERIES

Lists, &c.: 'Ministry of Agriculture and Fisheries—List II' (typescript).

M.A.F. 7/3. MISCELLANEOUS AGRICULTURAL STATISTICS. 1730–1883.

Included are, e.g., statistics of number and estimated weight of cattle, sheep, and swine imported from the United States in 1883.

COURT OF BANKRUPTCY

Lists, &c.: 'Court of Bankruptcy: Class List' (typescript and duplicated).

B.3. COMMISSIONS: FILES. 1759–1911. (Mainly 1790–1842.)
B.4. COMMISSIONS: DOCKET BOOKS (REGISTERS). 1710–1849.

The registers contain summary particulars relating to the issue of commissions and renewed commissions of bankruptcy—see, e.g., W. E. Minchinton, ed., *The Trade of Bristol in the Eighteenth Century* (Bristol, 1957) (Bristol Record Society's Publications, vol. xx), which gives on pp. 184–9 a list of the bankruptcies of Bristol merchants, 1711–70, taken from B. 4/1–20; a few of the merchants and their creditors are noted as being resident in Virginia or elsewhere in America. The files relating to some of the cases listed in the registers have survived, and the names of the bankrupt firms involved are given in the class list for B. 3.

COURT OF CHANCERY

C. 66. CHANCERY ENROLMENTS: PATENT ROLLS.

Andrews, vol. i, Appendix A, pp. 268–73, traced the passage of a Patent through the seals to its final issue and enrolment. Of the various series of enrolments, the Patent Rolls, which include grants to discover colonies, charters of trading companies, appointments of colonial officials, and instructions to governors, are the most important.

C. 103–16. MASTERS' EXHIBITS.

Lists, &c.: 'Lists of Chancery Masters' Exhibits' (photostat).

In suits before the various Masters of the Court of Chancery, papers put forward as exhibits sometimes remained with the Court. They are listed under the names of the plaintiff, the defendant, and the places concerned. The following are only the obviously relevant papers where America is mentioned in the list; numerous mentions of merchants' papers in London, Bristol, and the West Indies would probably repay a detailed search.

104/13–14. Isaac v. Defriez. Invoices, receipts, journals, and freight books relating to the shipping business of Nathan Simson in New York and London. Some in Hebrew. 1700–26.

105/19. Love v. Cohen. Commercial correspondence and price lists. Jamaica and Philadelphia. 1784–8.

105/39. Grants of land under the colonial great seal, plans, and valuations. East Florida. 1767–83.

110/163. Fleming v. Lynde. Mercantile correspondence and accounts. North America and West Indies. 1753–68.

110/168. Holway (? Holman) v. Hynman. Letters relating to the Holman family. United States. 1785–1800.

110/186. Williams v. Wallaby. Letters of marque, accounts, and correspondence concerning the ship *Oliver*. London and North America. 1758–67.

COLONIAL OFFICE

Lists, &c.: 'List of Colonial Office Records to 1902', 10 vols. (typescript).
　　　　　'List of Colonial Office Records: Supplementary List', 2 vols.
　　　　　　　(typescript).
　　　　　'List of Colonial Office Registers: 1886–1902' (duplicated).

'Colonial Office: Indexes to Correspondence: 1815–1870' (duplicated).

Most of the Colonial Office papers are arranged by colony, with classes within each of these sections for in-letters, out-letters, Acts, sessional papers, &c. Material can, for example, be found for Canada in C.O. 42, for British Columbia in C.O. 60, and for Vancouver Island in C.O. 305. There are also classes for 'Colonies (General)' which include Canadian and other material. In addition, relevant items are to be found in the following classes:

C.O. 386. EMIGRATION: LAND AND EMIGRATION COMMISSION—ENTRY BOOKS OF CORRESPONDENCE, ETC.

386/81–86. Letters to the Colonial Office: North America. 1840–76.

C.O. 537. SUPPLEMENTARY.

537/137–44. British North America. 1834–60.

537/139. Upper Canada: dispatch, &c., about destruction of the United States steamship *Caroline*. 1838.

537/140–3. Canada: confidential dispatches, private letters, &c., from and to Sir Charles Bagot, Governor-General 1841–3, and Sir C. T. Metcalfe, Governor-General 1843–5 (some are copies or drafts).

C.O. 807/1–84. CONFIDENTIAL PRINTS: NORTH AMERICA. 1871–91.

Included is relevant material concerning fisheries, reciprocity, extradition, &c.

C.O. 808. CONFIDENTIAL PRINTS: AUSTRALIA.

808/82. Fiji: land claims of American citizens: correspondence. 1885–92.

C.O. 811. CONFIDENTIAL PRINTS: WEST INDIES.

811/29. Reciprocity negotiations with the United States: memoranda. 1885.
811/43. United States demand for reciprocity: correspondence. 1890–1.

COPYRIGHT OFFICE

IND. 6012–38. FOREIGN REGISTERS.

A series of registers lists the names of foreign products, inventions, compositions, &c., made copyright in Great Britain. 1847–1912.

EXCHEQUER: KING'S (OR QUEEN'S) REMEMBRANCER

Lists, &c.: 'Exchequer K.R. Class List', 2 volumes (manuscript and typescript).

154/4/17. Invoice of goods shipped in the *Sivilla Merchant*, bound for Virginia, *c.* 1640.

E. 157. LICENCES TO PASS BEYOND THE SEAS.

Included are a number of registers, 1624–77, containing the names and, in some cases, other information, about passengers for Holland, New England, Virginia, and Maryland; the only ports of embarkation noted in the class list are the port of London and Gravesend. Most of the material has been printed; see, *inter alia*, J. C. Hotten, ed., *The original lists of* . . . [*persons emigrating*] *to the American Plantations, 1600–1700* (London, 1874), and C. B. Jewson, *Transcript of Three Registers of Passengers from Great Yarmouth to Holland and New England, 1637–1639* (Norfolk, 1954) (Norfolk Record Society vol. xxv).

E. 190. PORT BOOKS. See report on H.M. Customs and Excise (pp. 194–5).

EXCHEQUER: LORD TREASURER'S REMEMBRANCER

E. 371. ORIGINALIA ROLLS.

These rolls, from the medieval period, contain enrolments of charters, grants and patents, &c., and pleadings and proceedings relative to tenures and estates until 1851; among them are to be found some colonial charters, &c.[1]

EXCHEQUER OF RECEIPT

E. 407. MISCELLANEA.

407/15. Contract for victualling the garrisons of Placentia and Annapolis Royal. 1720.

407/82. Petitions under the hand of the Bishop of London for the payment to clerks in holy orders taking up appointments in America of the bounty of £25. 1743–70.

EXCHEQUER AND AUDIT

Lists, &c.: P.R.O. *Lists and Indexes No. XLVI: List of the Records of* . . . *the Exchequer and Audit Department* (1921), with additions and corrections.

'Exchequer and Audit, 1838–1850' (typescript), covering all classes except A.O. 2, for which a list is available on request.

---

[1] See Edward Jones, *Index to Records called the Originalia and Memoranda on the Lord Treasurer's Remembrancer's Side of the Exchequer* . . ., 2 vols. (London, 1793–5), for the period from Henry VIII to the reign of Anne, a copy of which is in the Round Room of the Record Office.

A.O. 2. ACCOUNTS DECLARED AND PASSED, IN BOOKS.

A.O. 2/1, 7, 12, 18, 20, 24, 30, 32 include accounts, 1828–36, of T. Crafer, paymaster of pensions to Loyalists. The class also includes the accounts of governors, agents, commissariats, &c., in New Brunswick, Upper Canada, &c.

A.O. 3. ACCOUNTS VARIOUS.

3/276. Compensation to Loyalists and other refugees. 1788–1837.

A.O. 16. MISCELLANEA.

16/44. Exemplification of 1775–7 accounts of Lord Dunmore, Governor of Virginia. 1801.

FOREIGN OFFICE

Lists, &c.: P.R.O. *Lists and Indexes No. LII: List of Foreign Office Records to 1878* (1929), with additions and corrections.

'List of F.O. Records, 1879–1885', 2 volumes (typescript).
'F.O.: List of Records after 1885', 4 volumes (typescript).
'F.O. Addenda: Embassy and Consular' (typescript).
'F.O. Addenda: Various' (typescript).
'F.O.: Registers of Correspondence' (typescript).
'Catalogue of F.O. Lists' (typescript).

F.O. 2. GENERAL CORRESPONDENCE: AFRICA.

2/318–24, 484, 485, 621, 622. Consular and other reports, drafts, &c., from America. 1900–2.

2/686. Boer agents in the United States. Outrage on British ship *Mechanician* at New Orleans. Libel action against Consul A. C. Vansittart. 1901–2.

F.O. 5/755–2625. GENERAL CORRESPONDENCE: AMERICA, UNITED STATES OF. 1861–1905.

This very extensive class, the most important of the F.O. series, consists of the original dispatches, reports, &c., to the Foreign Office from British Ministers (from 1893, Ambassadors), Consuls, Chargés d'Affaires, and other agents of the government in the United States; of correspondence with American Ministers (from 1893, Ambassadors) and other agents in Britain; of miscellaneous correspondence from individuals; and of drafts or copies of letters sent by the Foreign Office.[1] See F.O. 84 for such correspondence concerning the slave trade. See also F.O. 115 for the archives of the British Legation and Consulates in the United States.

[1] The Library of Congress holds photostats or microfilms of many of these volumes.

Dispatches and other communications from Ministers, &c., may be found for particular years by use of the lists noted above, and so are not itemized here.[1] In 1890, for example, the list shows, for the Washington and London Legations:

5/2079. Sir J. Pauncefote [British Minister]. Diplomatic drafts.

5/2080. Sir J. Pauncefote. Diplomatic dispatches, 1–100.

5/2081. Sir J. Pauncefote and Mr. [Henry G.] Edwardes [Secretary of the Legation]. Diplomatic dispatches, 101–71.

5/2082. Sir J. Pauncefote. Diplomatic telegrams and paraphrases.

5/2083. Sir J. Pauncefote. Consular and treaty.

5/2084. Sir J. Pauncefote. Commercial. Drafts.

5/2085–9. Sir J. Pauncefote. Commercial. Dispatches, vols. 1–5.

5/2093–4. Domestic. Mr. [Robert T.] Lincoln [American Minister] and Mr. Henry White [Chargé d'Affaires]. Diplomatic, vols. 1–2.

5/2095. Domestic. Mr. Lincoln, Mr. White, and Mr. Robert S. McCormick [Second Secretary of Legation]. Consular, commercial, and treaty.

5/2096–2102. Various. Diplomatic, consular, commercial, treaty.

Similar headings are to be found for the other years of the period, through 1903, during which the British Ministers were Lord Lyons, 1861–4; Sir Frederick Bruce, 1865–7; Mr. (later Sir) Edward Thornton, 1868–81; Lionel Sackville-West, 1881–8; Sir J. Pauncefote, 1889–1902; Sir M. Herbert, 1902–3; and Sir M. Durand, 1903; and the American Ministers to London were George Mifflin Dallas, 1861; Charles F. Adams, 1861–8; Reverdy Johnson, 1868–9; J. L. Motley, 1869–70; Robert C. Schenck, 1871–6; Edwards Pierrepont, 1876–7; John Welsh, 1877–9; James Russell Lowell, 1880–5; Edward John Phelps, 1885–9; Robert T. Lincoln, 1889–93; Thomas F. Bayard, 1893–7; John Hay, 1897–8; Joseph H. Choate, 1899–1902.

Consular and/or vice-consular reports[1] are available annually from 1861 to 1902 for the following cities: Baltimore, Boston, Charleston, S.C., Galveston, Tex., New Orleans, New York, Philadelphia, San Francisco. In addition, there are such reports for other cities as follows: Buffalo, N.Y., 1861–71; Chicago, 1861–2, 1867–9, 1884, 1886–1902; Mobile, Ala., 1861–87, 1895, 1898, 1900; Pensacola, Fla., 1876–9, 1881, 1884, 1886–7, 1889, 1892, 1894, 1897–8, 1900–2; Portland, Me., 1861–85, 1898, 1899; Portland, Ore., 1873, 1882, 1894–1902; St. Louis, Mo., 1863–6; Savannah, Ga., 1861–3, 1865–6, 1868–86, 1888, 1900. For 1899–1902 there are annual reports from Havana, Honolulu, Manila, Puerto Rico, and Santiago de Cuba. There are also occasional reports throughout the period from other cities.

The volumes of such reports show a great diversity of subject matter and form. In a volume for 1862 (F.O. 5/846), for example, the section for the Portland, Me., consulate includes: drafts of letters from the Foreign Office to the Consul; letters from the Consul about transit of British troops through Portland to Canada, property in Maine of a British subject, &c.; printed

---

[1] Microfilming of some of the volumes was being carried out for the Bancroft Library, University of California, Berkeley 4, at the time the records were surveyed.

material sent to the Foreign Office by the Consul, such as pamphlets containing speeches of the Governor of Maine, printed annual reports of the State Superintendent of Schools and of the Maine Bank Commissioners, &c. The section of the volume containing consular reports from Richmond, Va., includes the statement of Mr. Zacharie, a New Orleans merchant, on being forcibly taken from a British schooner while *en route* from Havana to Matamoros, Mexico; and letters from the Consul about the Confederate sequestration Act, the encounter between the Confederate *Virginia* and the Federal *Cumberland*, military movements, reactions in the South to the Emancipation Proclamation, &c. Clearly some of these files would furnish interesting and important material for the history of American politics and opinion generally, as well as commercial intelligence.

In addition, F.O. 5 contains a large body of material relating to specific subjects, as follows:

Alaska:

5/1638.[1] Cession of Alaska by Russia to the United States. 1835–68.

5/1639,[1] 1640,[1] 1971, 1972, 2133, 2287, 2383, 2384, 2415–17, 2479, 2510. Alaska boundary: correspondence, vols. 1–13. 1872–7, 1886–1902.

Civil War Claims:

5/1236–95. Claims arising out of the Civil War, vols. 1–60. 1861–71.

5/1296–1312. Conferences at Washington, D.C.: correspondence, archives, &c.[2] 1870–1.

5/1390–1409, 1554, 1555. Geneva Arbitration, vols. 1–22. 1871–3.

5/1410–16. Geneva Arbitration: log books, vols. 1–7. 1872.

5/1417–26. Geneva Arbitration: archives, vols. 1–10. 1871–2.

5/1570.[1] Treaty of Washington: three rules. 1871–6.

5/1602–29. Claims Commission: drafts, dispatches, reports, &c. 1871–7.

Extradition:

5/1673–8,[1] 2042, 2104. Extradition treaty: negotiations, vols. 1–8. 1870–90.

5/1708–16, 1749, 1781, 1864, 1865, 1896, 1973. Extradition: correspondence, vols. 1–15. 1875–86.

5/2478. Supplementary extradition treaty. 1893–1901.

5/2516. Extradition: trial for offence other than that for which extradition was granted. 1893–1902.

Fenians:

5/1125. Claim of Mr. Burns for damage done by Fenians. 1866–7.

5/1334–51,[1] 1427,[1] 1535,[1] 1556,[1] 1599,[1] 1706,[1] 1707, 1745, 1746, 1776–80, 1816–20, 1860–3,[1] 1928–32, 1975, 2044, 2359. Fenian Brotherhood, vols. 1–48. 1864–97.

Many of these reports contain shrewd and detailed evaluations of the role of 'Ireland-in-exile' in American politics.

5/2348. Dynamiters. 1896–7.

---

[1] The Library of Congress holds microfilms of these.
[2] The Library of Congress holds photostats of F.O. 5/1297–1304.

Fisheries:

5/1093. Fishery Commission, vol. 2. 1860–6.

5/1458–65. Canadian fisheries, vols. 1–8.[1] 1867–73.

5/1557–69,[1] 1630,[1] 1631,[1] 1671,[1] 1672,[1] 1782, 1897–9, 1933, 1934, 1965–70, 2009–13, 2045–9, 2072, 2103, 2132, 2169–71, 2207, 2278. North American fisheries, vols. 1–47. 1873–95.

5/1632–7. Halifax Commission: miscellaneous papers.[1] 1875–7.

5/1748. Halifax fisheries. 1878–80.

5/1821–7. Fortune Bay, Newfoundland, and fisheries dispute, vols. 1–7. 1875–82.

5/1974, 2014, 2015, 2050, 2051, 2073–7, 2105–12, 2134–45, 2173–83, 2211–18, 2251–60, 2279–86, 2308–15, 2349–56, 2385–7, 2418, 2453, 2512. Seizure of fishing vessels in Bering Sea, vols. 1–89. 1886–1902.

5/2184, 2208–10. Seizure of fishing vessels in Bering Sea: drafts and dispatches. 1892–3.

5/2219–30. Bering Sea arbitration: archives, vols. 1–11, 13. 1891–3. (For volumes 12 and 14–16 see F.O. 97/542–5.)

5/2231, 2358. Bering Sea: miscellaneous. 1893, 1897.

5/2250. American claim concerning fishing schooner seized by Newfoundland authorities. 1891–4.

5/2277. North Pacific seal fishery: Order in Council, 1893; Bering Sea award: Order in Council, 1895. 1893, 1895.

5/2318. Professor Thompson's report on Bering Sea seals. 1896.

5/2622, 2623. Newfoundland fisheries, vols. 1–2. 1902–5.

North-West Boundary and Hudson's Bay Company:

5/809–16, 1466–77, 1505, 1506, 1532, 1666–70. North-West boundary and island of San Juan: correspondence, &c., vols. 1–29.[2] 1846–78.

5/1352–5. Hudson's Bay Company, vols. 4–7.[3] 1859–71.

Ships:

There are a large number of entries in F.O. 5 relating to cases of particular ships, including F.O. 5/1000–3, Case of the ironclads built at Birkenhead, 1863–4; F.O. 5/1235, Case of the *Peterhoff*—trade between neutral ports, 1863–71; F.O. 5/1317, Case of the *Georgia* at Liverpool, 1864–71; F.O. 5/1318–32, *Alabama*, vols. 1–15, 1862–71; F.O. 5/2514, Seizure of the American fishing vessel *Frederick Jerring Jr*—jurisdiction in territorial waters, 1896–1902.

In addition, F.O. 5 contains the following miscellaneous material:

5/934. Case of free Negro emigration. 1862–3.

5/937. Proceedings of American cruisers at St. Thomas. 1863.

5/996, 1045. Case of Mr. J. O'Neill. 1864–5.

5/997. Island of Sombrero. 1863–4.

5/1004. Case of Captain Sherwin. 1862–4.

5/1006, 1007. Trade with Bahamas. 1862–4.

[1] The Library of Congress holds microfilms of these.
[2] Microfilms or photostats in the Library of Congress.
[3] Photostats in the Library of Congress.

5/1008. Confederate ships sold to British subjects.[1] 1863–4.

5/1046. Case of Mr. J. Hardcastle. 1863–5.

5/1047. Seizure of cotton at Savannah, Ga. 1865.

5/1053. Confederate enlistments. 1863–5.

5/1056–8. St. Albans, Vt., raids. 1864–5.

5/1089–92. Commercial negotiations and reciprocity treaty. 1858–66.

5/1099. Gunboats on Canadian Lakes. 1864–6.

5/1101. Case of Burley's extradition. 1865–6.

5/1124. Case of imprisonment of Mr. Shaver. 1862–7.

5/1149–53. Blockade runners: imprisonment of British subjects. 1863–8.

5/1155. Case of William Ross and Colonel Grenfell. 1861–8.

5/1181. Matamoros, Mexico, seizures. 1863–9.

5/1231. Case of Mr. Purvis. 1864–71.

5/1233. Case of Mrs. Molyneux. 1865–71.

5/1356[2]–7. Naturalization treaty. 1868–71.

5/1453–5. Emigration convention. 1868–73.

5/1456–7. Mr. Stewart's cotton claim. 1866–73.

5/1534, 2005, 2006, 2146. Copyright. 1852–75, 1880–7, 1889–91.

5/1571. British legation house at Washington, D.C.[2] 1857–76.

5/1572. Abduction of John Blair. 1876.

5/1600, 1601. Consular convention between Britain and the United States. 1869–77.

5/1641. Claims against Major David, late Vice-Consul at Pensacola, Fla. 1876–7.

5/1643. Correspondence concerning the Philadelphia exhibition. 1873–7.

5/1717. Louisiana quarantine. National Board of Health, 1879.

5/1747. Transit trade, Canada and the United States. 1874–80.

5/1866. Bankruptcy of A. Collie. Claim of Mr. Young, trustee, on the American government.[2] 1882–3.

5/1900. Alleged kidnapping of Alfred Sheldon. 1884.

5/1963, 1964. Murder of J. H. Tunstall in New Mexico. 1878–86.

5/2007. Sovereignty over Pedro Cays, Jamaica; and the case of the *Nathalie.* 1884–7.

5/2008. Pre-emption, homestead, and exemption laws. 1886–7.

5/2016. Regulations for liquor traffic. 1887.

5/2041. Merchant shipping conventions. 1882–8.

5/2043. Report on status of aliens and foreign companies in the United States. 1886–8.

5/2078. International Marine Conference at Washington. 1889.

5/2172. Merchant seamen: Deserters Convention. 1889–92.

5/2232. Registration of trade marks in Great Britain: complaints of American citizens. 1892–3.

5/2316. Arbitration: American addresses to the Queen. 1896.

5/2317. Navigation of the Great Lakes (collisions). 1895–6.

5/2357. Claims of American citizens to lands in Fiji. 1879–97.

---

[1] Photostats in the Library of Congress.
[2] Microfilms in the Library of Congress.

5/2419. Robert Francis: property in Cuba. 1880–99.

5/2420, 2452, 2480, 2511. Crimping in American ports. 1898–1902.

5/2421–4, 2482. Joint commission for the settlement of questions pending between Canada and the United States. 1898–1901.

5/2454. Immigration and exclusion of Chinese. 1881–1900.

5/2483. Bankruptcy declaration. 1899–1901.

5/2513. St. Louis, Mo., Exhibition, 1904. 1901–2.

5/2515, 2517. War between the United States and Spain: ships' claims and mediation proposals. 1898–1902.

5/2518. Claim of Cayuga Indians against New York state. 1897–1902.

5/2519. Transit of Canadian prisoners through American territory. 1901–2.

5/2520. Pan-American conferences. 1900–2.

5/2613–15. Philippine claims. 1899–1905.

5/2616–19. Cuban claims. 1898–1905.

5/2620. Illegal detention of Mr. Kenneth Harper at Honolulu. 1903–5.

5/2621. Cay Sal: question of sovereignty. 1898–1905.

5/2624. Case of the Rio Grande Irrigation and Land Company. 1904–5.

5/2625. American claims (including Standard Oil Company) against Great Britain. 1884–1905.

F.O. 50. GENERAL CORRESPONDENCE: MEXICO.[1]

50/189, 203, 214. Consular reports from California. 1845–7.

F.O. 55. GENERAL CORRESPONDENCE: COLOMBIA.

55/248, 249, 250, 271, 281, 282, 290, 291, 299, 320, 336, 346, 356, 360, 365, 385, 386, 392, 398, 399, 405, 406, 420, 432. Panama and Nicaragua Ship Canals (Clayton–Bulwer Treaty, &c.), vols. 1–24.[2] 1868–1905.

F.O. 58. GENERAL CORRESPONDENCE: PACIFIC ISLANDS.

58/241, 279, 288, 304, 309, 319. Designs of the United States on Hawaii, vols. 1–6. 1886–98.

F.O. 64. GENERAL CORRESPONDENCE: PRUSSIA.

64/1516, 1517. German telegraph cables to America. 1898–1900.

F.O. 72. GENERAL CORRESPONDENCE: SPAIN.

72/1266, 1267. Aid to Cuban insurgents: case of American vessel *Mary Lowell* seized in British waters. 1869–70.

72/1307. Cuban insurrection: mediation of Britain and the United States. 1870–1.

[1] Microfilms of F.O. 50/1–531 are in the Bancroft Library, University of California, Berkeley 4.
[2] Parts of F.O. 55/392, 405, and 406 are printed in C. S. Campbell, Jr., *Anglo-American Understanding, 1898–1903* (Baltimore, 1957).

72/2091–7, 2159. War between the United States and Spain: observance of neutrality.[1] 1898–1901.

72/2143. Fees levied by H.M.'s consular officers in Spain while in charge of American interests. 1898–1900.

F.O. 83. GENERAL CORRESPONDENCE: GREAT BRITAIN AND GENERAL.

Information, &c., from the United States is noted as being included in the following:

83/179, 187, 390. Consular service. 1856–9, 1871–2.

83/295. Technical and industrial education. 1867–8.

83/333, 336, 379. Industrial classes. 1869–72.

83/340. Land tenure. 1869.

83/376. Inventions and patents. 1872.

83/396. British trade. 1872.

83/480. Conventual and monastic institutions. 1874–5.

83/720. Homicidal crime. 1880.

83/762. Interchange of documents. 1880–1.

83/1046. Port tonnage and light dues. 1885–8.

83/1571. Sixtieth anniversary of the accession of Queen Victoria. 1896–7.

83/2077. Bishops' licences, &c. 1868–1902.

83/2168. Arbitration treaties. 1904–5.

83/2204–26. Law Officers' reports. 1781–1876.[2]

Also included in the class are:

83/1888, 1889, 2166. Washington and Rome Postal Congresses. 1897, 1906.

F.O. 84. GENERAL CORRESPONDENCE: SLAVE TRADE.

There is ministerial and consular correspondence from the United States for the period 1861–92. In addition is the following material:

84/1436. Fugitive Slaves Commission (1814–26): compensation paid by British government for slaves removed from America in 1814.

84/1700. United States: Machada claims correspondence. 1879–84.

F.O. 93. PROTOCOLS OF TREATIES.

93/8/17–119. Papers concerning various American treaties. 1842–1908.

[1] Letters from F.O. 72/2097 are printed in G. P. Gooch and H. Temperley, eds., *British Documents on the Origins of the War*, vol. i, pp. 105–7 (London, 1927).

[2] The Library of Congress holds photostats of these. Abstracts are printed in A. D. McNair, ed., *International Law Opinions*, 3 vols. (Cambridge, 1956). Extracts from or transcripts of F.O. 83/2204–10 are printed in A. D. McNair, *Law of Treaties: British Practice and Opinions* (Oxford and New York, 1938).

F.O. 94. RATIFICATIONS OF TREATIES.

Various items between F.O. 94/341 and 876 are for American treaties, 1842–1906.

F.O. 95. MISCELLANEA: SERIES I.

95/684. Correspondence between British sovereigns and American presidents, about appointments, deaths, &c. 1817–34.

F.O. 96. MISCELLANEA: SERIES II.

96/143–6. Accounts of expenses of North American Boundary Commission. 1843–6.

96/200. Anglo-American arbitration memorial. 1896.

F.O. 97. GENERAL CORRESPONDENCE: SUPPLEMENT.

97/37–47. Depredations of American ships in the Guano islands; law officers' reports on Civil War claims, &c. 1859–68.

97/431. Slave trade (including draft of American slave trade treaty). 1862.

97/439–40. Geneva arbitration: archives. 1872.

97/465–70. Fisheries: Halifax Commission: affidavits, &c. 1850–77.

97/471. Consular convention between the United States and Great Britain. 1878–82.

97/472–5. Fenian Brotherhood: press incitements. 1881–5.

97/476. North American fisheries. 1870–87.

97/541. Falkland Island fisheries. 1883–92.

97/542–5. Bering Sea arbitration. 1820–93.

97/546. New Zealand land claims of William Webster, an American citizen. 1887–94.

97/606. America: imprisonment of Joseph Weir. 1897–1904.

F.O. 99. GENERAL CORRESPONDENCE: MOROCCO: SERIES II.

99/159. Case of Mr. Scott, a British subject in American employ, refusing to acknowledge jurisdiction of H.M.'s Consul. 1871–3.

F.O. 115. EMBASSY AND CONSULAR ARCHIVES: AMERICA, UNITED STATES OF: CORRESPONDENCE

115/238–1284. Correspondence with the Foreign Office, United States government, Consuls, &c.[1] 1861–1903.

Registers are available in F.O. 117 for these.

---

[1] Photostats of many of the volumes to 1877 (F.O. 115/617) are in the Library of Congress. The Bancroft Library has microfilmed the volumes relating to the American West.

F.O. 128. EMBASSY AND CONSULAR ARCHIVES: BRAZIL: CORRESPONDENCE.

128/199. Foreign naval commanders (United States, France, Italy, and Portugal) and rebel Brazilian naval commanders. 1893–4.

F.O. 162. EMBASSY AND CONSULAR ARCHIVES: CHILE: PUNTA ARENAS: CORRESPONDENCE.

162/2. Papers concerning the claim of the Falkland Islands Co. against Richard T. Green, owner of the American schooner *Enola C.* (copies). 1899.

F.O. 185. EMBASSY AND CONSULAR ARCHIVES: SPAIN: CORRESPONDENCE.

185/687. Commercial negotiations between Spain and the United States. 1887.

F.O. 198. EMBASSY AND CONSULAR ARCHIVES: TURKEY: MISCELLANEA.

198/21. American Civil War. 1862–8.

F.O. 275. EMBASSY AND CONSULAR ARCHIVES: AMERICA, UNITED STATES OF: MANILA.

275/1. Philippine Islands: cessation of Spanish rule upon seizure by the United States. 1898.

F.O. 281. EMBASSY AND CONSULAR ARCHIVES: AMERICA, UNITED STATES OF: NEW YORK: CORRESPONDENCE.

281/1–45. Correspondence with Washington Legation, Foreign Office, &c. 1816–1911.

Registers to these for 1847–1911 are at F.O. 283.

F.O. 282. EMBASSY AND CONSULAR ARCHIVES: AMERICA, UNITED STATES OF: NEW YORK: LETTER-BOOKS.

282/1–36. Copies of letters to the Foreign Office, Board of Trade, Washington Legation, &c. 1842–94.

F.O. 284. EMBASSY AND CONSULAR ARCHIVES: AMERICA, UNITED STATES OF: NEW YORK: SHIPPING.

284/1A. Register of British vessels entering Philadelphia. 1787–9.

284/1B–11. Movements of British ships: registers. 1858–81.

F.O. 285. EMBASSY AND CONSULAR ARCHIVES: AMERICA, UNITED STATES OF: NEW YORK: MISCELLANEA.

285/1. Correspondence (mainly slave trade, &c., from the Foreign Office) and papers. 1834–42.

285/2. Subject index to Foreign Office dispatches, &c. 1871-8.

285/3-4. Extradition cases. 1893-1901.

F.O. 301. ARCHIVES OF COMMISSIONS: AMERICA: FISHERIES.

301/1-9. Correspondence, minutes, &c. 1873-6, 1887-8.

F.O. 302. ARCHIVES OF COMMISSIONS: AMERICA: NORTH-WEST BOUNDARY.

302/1-29. Correspondence, accounts, &c. 1872-6.

F.O. 305. ARCHIVES OF COMMISSIONS: BRITISH AND AMERICAN CLAIMS, 1871.

305/1-98. Papers relating to particular claims; correspondence, awards, printed papers, &c. [Names of claimants are in *Lists and Indexes No. LII.*] 1871-5.

F.O. 312. ARCHIVES OF COMMISSIONS: SLAVE TRADE: CAPE TOWN.

312/23, 26, 29, 40. British and American letter-books, minute-books, accounts, &c. 1862-70.

F.O. 315. ARCHIVES OF COMMISSIONS: SLAVE TRADE: SIERRA LEONE.

315/16. Minute-books: American. 1862-8.

F.O. 317. ARCHIVES OF COMMISSIONS: MISCELLANEOUS.

317/2. Register of correspondence of the commission at Washington. 1871.

317/4, 5. Bering Sea Commission: register of correspondence and notes of evidence. 1891-2.

F.O. 331. EMBASSY AND CONSULAR ARCHIVES: AMERICA, UNITED STATES OF: HONOLULU.

331/1-55, 59. Correspondence with the Foreign Office, Hawaiian authorities, &c. 1824-94.

F.O. 333. EMBASSY AND CONSULAR ARCHIVES: AMERICA, UNITED STATES OF: MISCELLANEA.

333/1. List of archives. 1791-1856.

333/2, 5, 6. Registers of correspondence: E. Seymour Bell, British commercial agent in Chicago and New York. 1900-8.

333/3, 4, 7-9. Foreign Office annual reports—confidential prints. 1906-13.

F.O. 360. HOWARD DE WALDEN PAPERS.

Included in F.O. 360/4 is a copy of a private letter, 6 July 1826, from George Canning, Secretary of State, to C. R. Vaughan, Minister to the United States, about the Northwest coast of America.

F.O. 362. GRANVILLE PAPERS.

The papers of Granville George Leveson-Gower, 2nd Earl Granville (1815–91) include:

362/1. America, drafts. 1870–4.

F.O. 363. TENTERDEN PAPERS.

The collection consists of five volumes of private papers of Charles Stuart Aubrey Abbott, 3rd Baron Tenterden (1834–82) while Under-Secretary of State for Foreign Affairs. Included are:

363/1. Francis Ford. About twenty letters from Halifax, N.S., and Newfoundland about United States and Canadian fisheries. 1876–7.

363/3. F. R. Plunkett: three letters from the British Legation in Washington about the American political scene and American attitudes towards Russia, Germany, Mexico, &c., 1877. H. C. Rothery: about thirty letters, mainly from New York, about fisheries, the case of the *Virginius*, &c. 1873–4.

363/4. Sir Edward Thornton. About seventy letters from Washington, D.C., on Canadian–American relations, American politics, American relations with Spain, &c. 1874–9.

363/5. R. Bourke. Letter to Lord Derby on the Halifax Fisheries Commission and the Treaty of Washington, and Tenterden's notes on this. 1876.

F.O. 366. CHIEF CLERK'S DEPARTMENT: CORRESPONDENCE.

366/210–14. Accounts: extraordinaries, United States. 1825–66.

366/300. Accounts: Washington Mixed Claims Commission. 1871–4.

366/570. Correspondence (papers): Washington High Commission, Geneva Arbitration, San Juan boundary. 1871–5.

366/725. Messengers: Washington, &c. 1867–88.

F.O. 374/1–17A. PEACE CONFERENCE OF 1919–20. ACTS OF THE CONFERENCE. PUBLISHED 1922–35.

Reports and other official proceedings of the Peace Conference and of its several commissions and committees.

F.O. 519. COWLEY PAPERS.

519/203. Semi-official and private correspondence of Henry Richard Charles Wellesley, 1st Earl Cowley (1804–84), British Ambassador at Paris, including letters from Sir John Crampton from Washington, D.C.

(11 Dec. 1855 concerning *New York Herald* articles thought to be written
from the Paris Embassy) and from Spain (15 Sept. and 13 Nov. 1861,
commenting on probable United States role in Cuba and Mexico).

F.O. 550. EMBASSY AND CONSULAR ARCHIVES: AMERICA, UNITED STATES OF: SAVANNAH, GA.

550/1. Register of inward and outward correspondence. 1880–9. (The
archives themselves are missing.)

F.O. 610–14. PASSPORT OFFICE RECORDS.

Volumes simply listing applications for passports and giving names of
recommenders and destinations; these might be relevant to tracing the
movements of specific individuals to the United States. 1795–1905.

F.O. 621. EMBASSY AND CONSULAR ARCHIVES: AMERICA, UNITED STATES OF: BOSTON.

621/1–5. Registers of correspondence. 1903–14. (The archives themselves
are believed to have been destroyed.)

GERMAN FOREIGN MINISTRY RECORDS (COPIES)

Lists, &c.: 'German Foreign Ministry: Class List', 3 volumes (photostat).

G.F.M. 1–23. COPIES OF GERMAN FOREIGN MINISTRY RECORDS. 1863–1944. (Also some other German official holdings.)

Large sections of these German records were captured by the Allies in 1945
and later removed to Britain for safe keeping during the Berlin blockade.
The originals have now been returned to the custody of the Federal Republic
of Germany.

All the main political files were examined and films were made of the
documents considered to be of historical interest, while the archives were in
Allied custody. Those of 1920–44, together with certain major topics in
the preceding period, were filmed chiefly by the American, British, and
French governments, while the filming of the remainder was sponsored by
other governments, universities, and research institutes. Copies (paper prints
or microfilms) of all the films made are held by or are in course of transfer
to the Public Record Office. G.F.M. 10, for example, contains the bulk of
the German-American diplomatic papers centring on the Bismarck era, and
was filmed by the University of California, so that copies are to be found
there too.

*A Catalogue of Files and Microfilms of the German Foreign Ministry Archives,
1867–1920* (New York, 1959), sponsored by the Committee for the Study of
War Documents of the American Historical Association, contains full details
of film references and a topical index.

For the period after 1920 catalogues of the filmed files of the various German departments will also be available in the Record Office. During the period 1920–36 the Ministry was organized on the basis of regional departments of which Department III handled political and economic relations with America. After the reorganization in 1936 political and economic relations were handled by Division IX of the Political Department (Pol IX) and Division VIII of the Economic Policy Department respectively. Other important collections containing material on America are those of the Foreign Minister; the State Secretary; the German Embassy in Washington; the Reich Chancellery; Department IIIᴅ, 1920–36, and Political Division M.C., 1936–41, dealing with mixed claims; and the papers of Ritter, Wiehl, and Clodius, of the Economic Section of the Foreign Ministry.

For the period 1933–41, *Documents on German Foreign Policy*, Series C (1933–7) and Series D (1937–45) (London, H.M.S.O., and Washington, D.C., G.P.O., 1950–in progress) include the principal documents on German relations with America. Each volume contains an appendix listing the files used, together with their film reference numbers.

GIFTS AND DEPOSITS

Lists, &c: Most of the following are described in 'Gifts: P.R.O. 30 Class List' 2 vols. (typescript); where separate lists are available, this is noted.

P.R.O. 30/6. CARNARVON PAPERS.[1]

Henry Howard Molyneux Herbert, 4th Earl of Carnarvon (1831–90), was Under-Secretary for the Colonies 1858–9, and Colonial Secretary 1866–7 and 1874–8. His papers include:

30/6/26–31. Correspondence: Canadian government, &c. 1874–8.

30/6/71. Confidential Prints (Cabinet and various departments): fugitive slaves, &c. 1833–77.

P.R.O. 30/9. COLCHESTER PAPERS.

The collection includes the papers of Charles Abbot, 2nd Baron Colchester (1798–1867). Among these are:

30/9/1/4. Correspondence with William Sandom about Canadian affairs. 1839–42.

30/9/6/1/13. Correspondence, memoranda, &c., about American military activities on the Canadian border. 1841–6.

P.R.O. 30/11. CORNWALLIS PAPERS.[2]

Bundles 60–283 have been deposited since Andrews's report on the collection; of these, bundles 60–110 contain Americana, as follows:

[1] A separate list is available.
[2] Microfilms of these are in the Library of Congress.

30/11/60–71. Letters to Cornwallis from Lord George Germain, Sir Henry Clinton, Lt.-Col. Alured Clarke, Lt.-Col. Balfour, Francis Rawdon (later successively Baron Rawdon and Marquis of Hastings), and others. 1778–81.

30/11/72–94. Letters from Cornwallis to Clinton, Germain, Balfour, and others; correspondence with American commanders about prisoners, &c. 1780–4.

30/11/95–100. Correspondence of Clinton with Maj.-Gen. Phillips, Maj.-Gen. Leslie, George Washington, &c.; miscellaneous letters. 1777–81.

30/11/101–5. Miscellaneous papers: Cornwallis's proclamations and warrants concerning the Carolinas, intelligence reports, intercepted letters, &c. 1778–81.

30/11/106–10. Miscellaneous items: papers of Gen. William Davidson; and material concerning South Carolina (currency depreciation, dispatches from Balfour at Charleston, copy of the accounts of John Cruden, Commissioner of Sequestered Estates, &c.). 1780–2.

P.R.O. 30/22. RUSSELL PAPERS.[1]

The papers of Lord John Russell, 1st Earl Russell (1792–1878), who was Foreign Secretary during the Civil War, include, in addition to the following, correspondence and papers (chronologically arranged, 1804–78) and correspondence with the Cabinet (1859–65); there is likely to be additional American material among such classes.

30/22/34–38. United States: Correspondence—Legation in Washington. 1859–65.

30/22/39. United States: Correspondence—Legation in London and miscellaneous. 1859–65.

30/22/96. United States: Correspondence (drafts)—Legation in Washington (including two 1859 letters from Lord Lyons). 1859–62.

30/22/97. United States: Correspondence (drafts)—Legation in Washington, 1863–5, and Legation in London and miscellaneous, 1859–65.

P.R.O. 30/26. MISCELLANEOUS.

30/26/58/3. Exchequer. (?) [American Loyalist Claims Commission]. Warrant for payment, No. 3247. Archibald Hamilton. 18 Mar. 1789.

P.R.O. 30/29. GRANVILLE PAPERS.[2]

This collection of the papers of various members of the Granville family includes the following of Granville George Leveson-Gower, 2nd Earl Granville (1815–91), Colonial Secretary 1868–70, and Foreign Secretary 1870–4 and 1880–5:

30/29/67. Correspondence with Sir Roundell Palmer and Lord Westbury about the *Alabama* claims arbitration. 1871–2.

[1] Some of the relevant correspondence has been published in *The Later Correspondence of Lord John Russell, 1840–1878*, ed. by G. P. Gooch (London, 1925).
[2] A separate list is available.

30/29/80. Correspondence: United States: British Legation in Washington. 1870-4.

30/29/81. Correspondence: United States: Legation in London, &c. 1871-4.

30/29/106. Correspondence with Lord Tenterden, mainly about the United States. 1871-4.

30/29/142. Correspondence: Cabinet. Including letter from Earl Spencer, Lord-Lieutenant of Ireland, enclosing copy of the *United Irishman* of New York, 10 June 1882.

30/29/154. Correspondence: United States. 1880-5.[1]

30/29/196. Correspondence (drafts): United States, &c. 1880-5.

30/29/215. Letter-book: in- and out-letters, précis, drafts, &c. United States, &c. 1851-2.

30/29/221-38. Confidential Prints (Foreign Office). United States.

30/29/221-34. Papers connected with the Geneva Arbitration Tribunal of 1871.

30/29/235-6. German arbitration: North-West boundary. 1842-72.

30/29/237. North American fisheries. 1803-73.

30/29/238. Miscellaneous. 1783-1872.

30/29/271. Confidential Prints (Foreign Office). United States: Newfoundland fisheries. 1879-82.

30/29/272. Confidential Prints (Foreign Office). United States: Miscellaneous. 1880-4.

There may also be relevant material in the classes containing the 2nd Earl's Cabinet and other correspondence from 1839 onwards.

P.R.O. 30/32. LEEDS PAPERS.

The fifty-six volumes of this collection mainly contain the papers of Sir Thomas Osborne, successively 1st Earl of Danby, Marquis of Carmarthen, and 1st Duke of Leeds (1631-1712), while Lord High Treasurer 1673-9. Included are Treasury minutes, warrants and orders, customs quarter bills, &c. There is likely to be some Americana among these; for the basic series of Treasury records which they supplement see Andrews, vol. ii, pp. 136-265.

P.R.O. 30/36. STUART PAPERS.

The papers of William Stuart, Chargé d'Affaires and Secretary of the Legation in Washington 1861-3, include the following:

30/36/1-2. United States: dispatches to the Secretary of State, and entry book to these. 1862.

30/36/10. United States out-letters: entry book; &c. 1858-71.

---

[1] See P. Knaplund and C. M. Clewes, eds., 'Private Letters from the British Embassy in Washington to the Foreign Secretary, Lord Granville, 1880-1885', *Annual Report of the American Historical Association*, 1941, vol. i, pp. 73-189.

P.R.O. 30/39. DOCUMENTS OF UNKNOWN OWNERSHIP.

30/39/1. Surgeon Richard Hope. Fifteen letters to relatives in England from Quebec, Boston, New York, and the *British King* off Staten Island. 1770–82. Hope was Surgeon of the 52nd Regiment of Foot 1756–76, when he was transferred to the staff of the hospitals for the forces in North America. With the letter of 20 Aug. 1775 is a copy of the *Massachusetts Gazette and Boston Weekly News-Letter* for 17 Aug. 1775.

P.R.O. 30/42. NICHOLL PAPERS.

Sir John Nicholl (1759–1838) was King's Advocate General 1798–1809, and these papers consist mainly of his rough drafts and notes for reports and opinions on the matters referred to him by the Privy Council and the Home and Foreign Secretaries. Included are:

30/42/3/10, and 4/8, 4/11, 5/1, 7/8, 10/1, 12/3. Drafts of reports to the Privy Council concerning trade with America, including licences for importing from Florida and exporting to New Orleans and elsewhere. 1799–1806.

30/42/17/2, and 18/7, 20/5, 21/5. Drafts of reports to the Home Secretary, as follows:

30/42/17/2. American ships clearing for India. 1799.

30/42/18/7. Blockade of Cadiz and American trade to Spain. 1800.

30/42/20/5. Maritime matters affecting British ships in United States ports: twenty-five papers (copies of documents showing relations between Anthony Merry and James Madison). 1804.

30/42/21/5. Licence to import flour-milling machinery from the United States into Cadiz; and violation of neutral waters of the United States. 1806.

30/42/22/3, and 22/7, 22/10, 23/3, 24/4, 24/7, 25/11, 26/5, 26/8, 28/1, 28/10, 29/4, 29/5, 29/11–14, 29/17, 33/4–7, 34/3. Drafts of reports to the Foreign Secretary about America. 1799–1808 (The originals of some of these may be found among the Law Officers' Reports in F.O. 83/2204–5.)

P.R.O. 30/46. EYRE PAPERS.

The collection includes the papers (P.R.O. 30/46/9–20) of Maj.-Gen. Sir William Eyre (1805–59) while in command of the forces in Canada 1856–9; some of these concern the Red River Settlement, Fort Garry, &c.

P.R.O. 30/47. EGREMONT PAPERS.[1]

The diplomatic and political papers of Sir Charles Wyndham, 2nd Earl of Egremont (1710–63), who was Secretary of State for the Southern Department 1761–3, include:

---

[1] The Library of Congress holds microfilms of P.R.O. 30/47/14 and 30/47/22. The Illinois Historical Survey, University of Illinois, holds photostats of P.R.O. 30/47/11, twenty letters, 1761–3, from the Comte de Viry, Sardinian Ambassador to London, about negotiations for peace with France.

30/47/14/1. Virginia: memorial of Armistead Churchill, and other papers. 1761–3.

30/47/14/2. South Carolina and Georgia: journals of expeditions; surveys; appointments of officers. 1703–63.

30/47/14/3. Florida: report on the expedition against St. Augustine, 1739–40; and notes on the settlement of the colony by the British, 1763.

30/47/14/4. Louisiana: survey of the coast and the Mississippi River. 1757–8.

30/47/14/5. New Spain: projects of attacks on various Spanish settlements.

30/47/14/6. America, general: papers concerning appointments; proposals of Henry Ellis for attacks on various enemy possessions; &c. 1760–3.

30/47/15–16. Canada: various. 1759–63.

30/47/22/1. Board of Trade: report on trade with colonies and plantations in America. 1733–4.

30/47/22/2. Board of Trade: letters and reports about the government of Canada and of Florida. 1763.

30/47/24. Board of Trade: military: details of disposition of forces, North America, 1763.

30/47/25. Board of Trade: postal. Letters concerning packet boats to North America and West Indies. 1763.

30/47/27–29. Semi-official and private correspondence. 1749–63. (These include a number of letters of congratulation on the war, 1760–2, and letters asking for appointments in America.)

P.R.O. 30/48. CARDWELL PAPERS.

Papers of Edward Cardwell, Viscount Cardwell (1813–86), who was Secretary for the Colonies 1864–6, and Secretary of War 1868–74. Included is correspondence, 1864–6, on Canadian Confederation (30/48/6/39 and 40); there may be some relevant material in other of the Colonial Office and War Office correspondence and memoranda in the collection.

P.R.O. 30/50. NEVILLE AND ALDWORTH PAPERS.

Among these are the papers of Richard Neville Aldworth (assumed name of Neville in 1762) (1717–93) as Under-Secretary of State 1748–51, including:

30/50/39. Miscellaneous colonial correspondence, 1748–51. Letters from Hugh Davidson in Halifax, N.S., about relations with the Indians and with New England merchants; notes about correspondence with Governor Belcher of New Jersey; a letter from Corbyn Morris suggesting regulations for currency in the American colonies; &c.

30/50/43. Relation of negotiations for a convention with Spain. Included are notes, copies of letters, &c., relating to Spanish plans for attacking South Carolina, and other matters relating to 'Spanish depredations' in America, 1737–46.

There may also be some relevant material in his papers as Secretary to the Embassy in Paris 1762–3, during the period of negotiating a peace treaty for the Seven Years War.

P.R.O. 30/55. CARLETON PAPERS.[1]

Records of British Army Headquarters in America, 1775–83. The 107 volumes contain the official notes at British Headquarters in America of General Thomas Gage, Sir William Howe, Sir Henry Clinton, and Sir Guy Carleton, as successive commanders-in-chief in America.

MINISTRY OF HEALTH

Lists, &c.: 'Ministry of Health: Class List' (typescript).
'Ministry of Health: Poor Law Union Papers (M.H. 12)', 2 vols. (typescript).

M.H. 1–4. POOR LAW COMMISSIONERS FOR ENGLAND AND WALES: MINUTE-BOOKS. 1834–47.

M.H. 12. POOR LAW UNION PAPERS. 1834–1900.

Material about parish-assisted emigration under the new Poor Law of 1834 is to be found in these classes.[2] For example, M.H. 12/8156, containing the papers of the Aylsham Poor Law Union, Norfolk, for 1834–7, includes lists of persons emigrating, with occupations and destinations (mainly Upper Canada, but in at least one case New York), letters from the Poor Law Commissioners in London, letters from individual parishes within the Union about the financing of emigration, &c.

M.H. 13. GENERAL BOARD OF HEALTH AND LOCAL GOVERNMENT OFFICE: CORRESPONDENCE.

Included in M.H. 13/252 is correspondence, 1853–4, between the General Board of Health and the Colonial Land and Emigration Commissioners, with letters (originals, drafts, and copies) about the outbreak of cholera on the American emigrant ship *Silas Greenman*, and concerning the general problem of mortality on emigrant ships leaving Liverpool.

M.H. 19. POOR LAW COMMISSION, POOR LAW BOARD, AND LOCAL GOVERNMENT BOARD: GOVERNMENT OFFICE CORRESPONDENCE.

19/22. Emigration Commissioners. 1836–76.
Among the correspondence about emigration to Canada and the extracts

---

[1] These were formerly in the Royal Institution, see H.M.C. *Report on American Manuscripts in the Royal Institution of Great Britain* [59], 4 vols. (London, 1904–9). They were acquired by an American owner in 1929, were rearranged and rebound by the New York Public Library for Colonial Williamsburg, who presented them to H.M. Queen Elizabeth II in 1957. There are copies of these documents in the British Museum—Stevens Transcripts, Add. MSS. 42257–496.

[2] See Introduction (p. xxxi).

from reports from Mr. Buchanan (the emigration agent in Quebec) are a few scattered references to the United States.

HOME OFFICE

Lists, &c.: 'Home Office and Signet Office, 1838–1900' (typescript).

'Home Office Registered Papers (H.O. 45) Subject Index, 1841–1855', 2 volumes (photostat).

'Home Office Domestic: Registered Papers (Old Series) Subject Index, 1856–1871' (typescript).

'Home Office Registered Papers (H.O. 45), 1871–1878' (typescript).

'Home Office Registered Papers (H.O. 45), 1879–1900' (typescript).

H.O. 5. ALIENS' ENTRY BOOKS.

These, noted by Paullin and Paxson, p. 226, as containing occasional references to American aliens, are now available to 1900.

H.O. 45. REGISTERED PAPERS.

The subject indexes listed above show relevant material under such headings as 'disturbances', 'emigration', 'extradition', 'foreign', 'Ireland (Fenians)', 'ships', and 'war'. Included are, for example, the following:

45/6877. Disaffected Irish in the United States and Canada. 1859.

45/7232. Extradition: case of American fugitive slave Anderson in Canada. 1861–2.

45/7261. Civil War. General papers, mainly concerning recruiting in England, and the fitting out of ships in England. 1861–6.

45/7523 and 7523A. Distress and riots in cotton districts of Lancashire and Cheshire. 1863.

45/7799. Fenian movement. Chiefly concerning designs of Fenians in the United States and shipment of arms to Ireland. 1865–70.

45/9294/8148. Arming of Confederate ships in the Channel Islands, 1863. Correspondence with the Foreign Office about the *Alabama* claims, 1871–2.

45/9422/59279. Address from the Irish people to the American President. 1876–7.

45/9584/87022. Mormon emigration to the United States: steps to warn emigrants of American law on polygamy. 1879–85.

45/9635/A29278. State-aided emigration of Irish pauper families, and their return to the United Kingdom by the United States government. 1883–5.

45/9660/A42380F. Dispatch from H.M. Consul at Chicago reporting trial of anarchists. 1886.

45/9832/B9588. Emigration of Mormons to the United States. 1890–1.

45/9986/X69316 and X69316A. Spanish-American War: British declaration of neutrality; detention of American destroyer. 1898–9.

H.O. 134/1–27. ENTRY BOOKS: EXTRADITION. 1873–98.

Examination of H.O. 134/1 showed it to include copies of letters to the Foreign Office about the Extradition Treaty between Britain and the United States, warrants to police and magistrates for the apprehension of American citizens, &c.

PRIVY COUNCIL

Lists, &c.: 'P.C. 1: Unbound Papers', 4 vols. (typescript).
'Parliament and Council: List of Records' (typescript).

P.C. 1. UNBOUND PAPERS.

The following (petitions, drafts, reports, &c.) is the relevant material apparently additional to that seen by Andrews and Davenport, pp. 170–87, and by Paullin and Paxson, pp. 292–325, except that the papers in P.C. 1/46–57 have been excluded since they were covered by James Munro in his *Acts of the Privy Council—Colonial Series: Vol. VI. The Unbound Papers* (London, 1912). The available list for this class contains much more detail for the colonial than for the later period, and this fact is necessarily reflected in the following:

1/14. Petitions concerning Pennsylvania, Newfoundland, &c. 1712.

1/15. Draft proclamation about possible invasion of Britain. 1779.

1/18. Order removing prohibition on importation of corn from the United States. 1789.

1/19. Reports on American legislation on duties. 1791.

1/20. Act for regulating trade with the United States. 1793.

1/21. Quarantine papers, including some for Pennsylvania; letter with copy of order re warehoused American rice; petitions about payment of bills drawn in North America. 1794.

1/34. Emigration to America. 1796.

1/35. Emigration. 1796.

1/37. Export of gunpowder and saltpetre to New York, 1796; emigration, 1797.

1/38. Trade with the United States. 1797.

1/39. Emigration. 1797.

1/40. Appeals in cases of seizure of American vessels. 1797.

1/41. Emigration; provisions for Newfoundland; alleged capture of American ship *Mentor* after peace preliminaries (twelve papers); removal of property from East and West Florida to Great Britain. 1798.

1/42. Removal of British property from East and West Florida to the Bahamas. 1798.

1/43. Licence to import cotton in American ships, 1798; American-cargoed prize ship, 1799; Jesuit estates in Canada, 1799.

1/44. Entry of American ships. 1799.

1/45. East Florida Vice-Admiralty Court: concerning the *Fame*. 1799.

1/58–60. A large group of Board of Trade and other reports, petitions, representations, &c., concerning the various colonies, on such subjects as boundaries, relations with Indians, appointments of governors and other officials, repeal of laws, land grants, &c. P.C. 1/58 covers the period, 1701–61, with a few earlier items about Massachusetts Bay; P.C. 1/59, 1762–9; P.C. 1/60 (where relevant items are considerably fewer), 1769–78.

1/61. Papers concerning Jesuit estates, 1769–91; papers concerning Prince Edward Island, chiefly complaints against Governor Patterson, 1783–5; papers concerning New Brunswick, Cape Breton, Nova Scotia, Quebec, Newfoundland—land grants, &c., 1784–5; papers concerning East Florida, 1785; West Indian trade with the United States, 1785–6.

1/62. Papers concerning Prince Edward Island, 1786–91; West Indian trade with the United States, 1787–90; slave trade, 1788.

1/63–66. Miscellaneous papers about trade with the United States, appointments of officials for Canada, &c., 1791–9. P.C. 1/63 includes an account of Capt. Meares's voyage on the Northwest coast of America, and P.C. 1/65 includes a memorial from T. Hasyard, an American Loyalist.

1/1924. Patent rights in Canada of the American inventor [Morse] of the electro-magnetic telegraph. 1846–7.

1/3130–53. Material similar to that in P.C. 1/58–60. 1706–82.

1/3161–3. Papers concerning Nova Scotia. 1767–84.

1/3164–7. Papers concerning Prince Edward Island. 1763–86.

1/3182–4. Papers concerning Newfoundland. 1708–76.

1/3474–4467. Roughly chronological series, 1800–44. Relevant headings among the brief summaries of bundle contents given in the available list include:

> 1/3477. American grain crop. 1800.
> 1/3583. Fever at New York. 1803.
> 1/3646. Fever at Charleston, S.C. 1805.
> 1/3730, 4060, 4146. Emigration. 1806–18.
> 1/4025. Importation of flax seed from America. 1813.
> 1/4109–11. Booty taken at Chesapeake, Ocracock [Ocracoke] Bay, and Georgia. 1816–21.
> 1/4182, 4203. Hudson's Bay Co.: settlers. 1820–1.
> 1/4210. Public health in America. 1821.

There are also many headings referring to trade with the United States or American shipping.

P.C. 4/1–17. MINUTES. 1670–1928.

For discussion of these, and comparison of them with the Registers (covered by Paullin and Paxson), see R. B. Pugh, 'Privy Council Minutes Newly Transferred to the Public Record Office', *Bulletin of the Institute of Historical Research*, vol. xxii, pp. 11–21, 1949.

P.C. 5/14–16. PLANTATION BOOKS. 1784–1806.

There are likely to be references to the United States scattered throughout these; the volume inspected (P.C. 5/16) consisted of copies of instructions to the governors of West Indian islands, Newfoundland, &c., occasionally relating to trade or fishing arrangements with the United States.

P.C. 6/9. MISCELLANEOUS BOOKS: WAR MATTERS.

The volume, which consists of a list of communications received and brief minutes relating to these, contains a section labelled 'North American (United States) Civil War'. The letters noted as having been received mainly concern the shipment of gunpowder and lead to various parts of the world, those from firms generally being requests for permission for particular shipments, and those from government departments being queries on such matters as the sending of munitions to the United States from the Continent.

P.C. 7/1–54. LETTER-BOOKS: ENTRY BOOKS OF OUT-LETTERS. 1825–99.

7/10 War matters, &c. 1859–77.

This volume includes copies of answers to the types of communications noted as being received in P.C. 6/9.

Most other volumes in P.C. 7 are noted in the available list as being on 'General Matters'; indexes are, however, to be found in the individual volumes.

BOARD OF TRADE

Lists, &c.: 'Board of Trade: Class List' (typescript) gives holdings in all classes.

'Board of Trade Records: 1846–1885' (duplicated) contains much more detailed descriptions of some of the records available for that period in B.T. 1 and a few other classes.

'Board of Trade: B.T. 31', 10 volumes (typescript).

B.T. 1/358–560. IN-LETTERS AND FILES, GENERAL. 1840–63.

The following, based on the duplicated list, shows the type of subjects covered in this class; further items may be found by use of B.T. 4/13–40, containing registers and indexes for 1840–64.

1/467/2205. American tariff for Mexican ports. 1847.

1/468/322. Postage on letters to the United States. 1848.

1/470/2506. Vancouver Island: grant to Hudson's Bay Co. 1848.

1/472/1298. Application from W. A. Adair, an American citizen, to send his brig *Eureka* through the St. Lawrence to the Atlantic. 1849.

1/473/2261. Prince Edward Island: relaxation of the treaty between the United States and Britain regulating the fisheries. 1849.

1/477/1395. United States: engaging of seamen. 1850.

1/478/1952. Statement of Vancouver Island Steam Sawing Mill & Agricultural Co. 1850.

1/479/2448. Adoption of one of the harbours of Ireland as a port of embarkation for America. 1850.

1/479/2767. Atlantic–Pacific ship canal convention: copy of convention between Britain and the United States relative to the establishment of a ship canal between the Atlantic and Pacific in Nicaragua; and copy of the dispatch from Sir Henry Bulwer.

1/479/2870. Letter from Norfolk, Va., consulate concerning an outrage by a British ship's captain on a New Brunswick Negro seaman. 1850.

1/480/3299. Jamaica: duty on American vessels with coals. 1850.

1/485/1572. Granting of subsidy to promote steamship service between Nassau and America. 1851.

1/498/2161. London, Liverpool & North American Screw Steam Ship Co.: statistics of ships cleared to New York from London and Liverpool, and protest against charter of Mr. Cunard. 1852.

1/500/26. Consideration of charter of London, Liverpool & North American Screw Steam Ship Co. 1852.

1/502/338. Bavaria: emigrants to America. 1853.

1/515/1468. Vancouver Island and the United States. 1854.

1/532/2166. Sandwich Islands: effect of treaty with the United States on trade with the United Kingdom and Vancouver. 1855.

1/545/1726. Electric telegraph: claim of Mr. Morse for use of his invention. 1857.

1/545/2049. United States–Peruvian treaty concerning whalers in Peruvian ports. 1857.

1/547/709. London & Virginia Gold and Copper Mining Co.: registration as a foreign company. 1858.

1/557/771. Opening of port of New Orleans and effect on cotton trade. 1862.

1/560/1076. Illegal imprisonment: appointment of assessors to assist law officers to decide case against United States. 1863.

1/560/1423. Telegraph line through Asiatic Russia to connect European and American systems. 1863.

B.T. 2/4–5, 11–14. IN-LETTERS, FOREIGN OFFICE. 1838–45.

No detail is given about these in the available list. Examination of one volume (B.T. 2/13: 1841–4) showed it to be unindexed and to contain mainly covering letters from the Foreign Office together with copies of dispatches from Consuls in the United States and elsewhere.

B.T. 3/29–64. OUT-LETTERS, GENERAL. 1840–63.

The available list gives only the destination of the letters in each volume— e.g. Colonial Office, Customs, Miscellaneous Offices and Individuals. One volume (B.T. 3/33: 1844–7) of this last type examined showed only a few routine letters concerning American tariffs, and concerning trade in the Columbia River area.

B.T. 6. MISCELLANEA.

6/34. Canada: extracts from reports by J. W. Duscomb, 'the Commissioner appointed to inquire into the state of the Customs establishments on the Lower Canada Inland Frontier'. 1844.

6/80–81, 83–88. See report on H.M. Customs and Excise (p. 192).

6/151–2. Lists of machinery, permission for the exportation of which was considered by the Board, including date, name of applicant, description of machinery, place to which exportation is desired (including the United States and specific American ports), and decision taken. 1825–43.

6/274–8. Miscellaneous papers. 1838–46.

There are likely to be scattered references to the United States among these. Examination of B.T. 6/278 showed, for example, that it included a letter from English ironmasters, dated 2 July 1844, complaining of the high American duty on English iron.

6/290. Coasting trade: notes of action taken by other countries to remove restrictions.

The volume includes copies of reports from Crampton of conversations with the American Secretary of State, Marcy, on this matter, 1854.

B.T. 12/1–42. COMMERCIAL DEPARTMENT: OUT-LETTERS. 1864–1900.

There are probably scattered references to the United States among these volumes, all of which are indexed. The volume for 1871 (B.T. 12/8), for example, contains copies of letters to the Colonial Office about Canadian tariff policies and consequent trade relations with the United States, as well as answers to various routine inquiries about American tariffs. Indexes to the out-letters from 1897 are available in B.T. 36.

B.T. 15/1–25. FINANCE DEPARTMENT: CORRESPONDENCE AND PAPERS. 1865–85.

There are a few minor items here—e.g.:

15/9/5449. Charleston, S.C., Consul: payment of legal expenses incurred in resisting extortionate claims by crew of British vessel. 1873.

B.T. 26/1–1305. STATISTICAL DEPARTMENT: PASSENGER LISTS INWARDS. 1878–88, 1890–1953.

B.T. 27/1–1740. STATISTICAL DEPARTMENT: PASSENGER LISTS OUTWARDS. 1890–1953.

B.T. 31. COMPANIES REGISTRATION OFFICE: FILES OF DISSOLVED COMPANIES.[1] 1856–1948.

Each file contains the memorandum and articles of association of the company, with names, addresses, and occupations of its shareholders, and a few papers relating to its voluntary winding-up. A good many firms with American interests are included—e.g. the list of companies registered in 1873 includes such firms as Direct United States Cable Co. Ltd., Chicago Silver Mining Co. Ltd., Anglo-Californian Bank Ltd., and Central City (Colorado) Mining Co. Ltd.

B.T. 32/1–15. REGISTER OF PASSENGER LISTS RECEIVED. 1906–51.

B.T. 35/1–18. COMMERCIAL DEPARTMENT: INDEXES AND REGISTERS OF CORRESPONDENCE. 1897–1902.

The correspondence to which these relate has not been transferred to the Public Record Office, but a considerable number of references to the United States appear in the registers.

MINISTRY OF TRANSPORT

Lists, &c.: 'List of the Records of the Ministry of Transport' (typescript).

M.T. 9. BOARD OF TRADE MARINE DEPARTMENT, 1856–1902.

After 1850, Acts for the inspection and survey of passenger steamers gave the Board of Trade certain executive duties specially connected with merchant shipping. The Marine Department was created as a separate department of the Board of Trade in 1850, and now forms part of the Ministry of Transport. The class list for the years 1886–90 illustrates the kind of material available.

9/283. Emigrants. Carriage of passengers in vessels previously used in carrying cattle. 1886.

9/285. American legislation relating to the advance of seamen's wages, allotments, owners' liability, &c. 1886.

[1] The Bancroft Library holds microfilms for selected documents relating to Western history.

9/294. Engagement and discharge of crews. Engagement at New York and other United States ports of seamen in British ships bound for China. 1886.

9/303. Dietary scale of emigrant ships. 1887.

9/324. Transit of Buffalo Bill's Wild West Show to the United States, and status of attendants, &c. 1888.

9/328. Extensive crimping at San Francisco. 1888.

9/381. Riotous conduct, larceny, and receiving by American cattlemen on board S.S. *Chicago*. 1890.

TREASURY

Lists, &c.: 'Treasury: Class List 1838–1902' (typescript).
'T. 1: Treasury Board Papers, 1557–1902', 2 volumes (typescript).
'Treasury Board Papers: Registers, 1777–1902' (photostat).
'Treasury Out-Letters (T. 5–28, 97, 101): 1838–1902' (photostat).

T. 1/3237–9921. IN-LETTERS: TREASURY BOARD PAPERS.[1] 1838–1902.

These can be used by means of the indexes to be found in T. 2, T. 3, and T. 108. Examination of T. 108/4, the subject register for 1866–70, showed only a very few minor items of relevance.

T. 5–28. OUT-LETTERS.

These classes contain copies of letters to various government departments. Examination of T. 11/113 Out-letters: Customs, 1860–3, showed that relevant matter—e.g. concerning British ships leaving Charleston, S.C.—was mainly in the form of letters transmitting Foreign Office material. Examination of T. 12/2 Out-letters: Foreign Office, 1860–3 showed letters about the Liverpool fitting-out of gunboats for the Confederacy, the duty-free entry of breadstuffs sent from the United States for Lancashire, &c.; again these are mainly covering letters for documents forwarded.

T. 29/397–619. MINUTES. 1838–70.

There may be scattered relevant material among these.

T. 39. ACCOUNTS: TREASURY CHEST.

There may be relevant material in T. 39/9–14, which contain accounts for Canada, 1846–71. Included in T. 39/24 are accounts for Fort Garry, 1846–9, and for New York, 1855–6.

[1] The Library of Congress has a transcript of T. 1/5083/18349: Expenses of Lord Ashburton's mission, 12 Sept. 1845.

TREASURY SOLICITOR

Lists, &c.: 'Treasury Solicitor: Class List' (typescript).

T.S. 12. WEST NEW JERSEY SOCIETY.

Correspondence, minutes, accounts, deeds, maps, and plans, 1675–1921. Also manuscript and printed volumes of Joseph Paine's history of the Society, 1895. The Society was formed about 1691 as a company for the purchase of land in West and East New Jersey, Pennsylvania, New England, and elsewhere.

WAR OFFICE

Lists, &c.: P.R.O. *Lists and Indexes No. LIII: Alphabetical Guide to War Office and Other Military Records* (1931).

P.R.O. *Lists and Indexes No. XXVIII: War Office* (1908), with typescript insertions.

'War Office: Supplementary List', 2 volumes (typescript).

'War Office: Miscellaneous Papers. W.O. 32, Bundles 1–2838' (photostat).

'Index to W.O. 32' (typescript) (a partial and select list).

'Amherst Papers (W.O. 34) Calendar', 6 volumes (typescript).

'W.O. Ordnance: Index to In-Letters' (typescript).

W.O. 6. OUT-LETTERS: SECRETARY OF STATE.

6/133. Arming of militia and inspection of field officers for militia in British possessions in North America. 1808.

6/154. Disclaimer by the United States as to giving orders for hostilities in British possessions in North America. 1814.

W.O. 28. HEADQUARTERS RECORDS.

28/303–17. Canada. 1811–17.

W.O. 32. REGISTERED PAPERS, GENERAL SERIES.

32/136. Cuba: military attaché's report on Spanish-American War. 1898.

32/209. Geneva Convention: Red Cross Convention—maritime warfare, Spain and the United States. 1898.

32/257. Canada: mobilization report, Esquimalt. 1900.

32/273. Canada: garrison of Halifax, N.S. 1904.

32/275. Canada: various reports and proposals concerning defences. 1897–1904.

32/317. Canada: enrolment of pensioners for service at Fort Garry. 1848.

32/420. North America: general considerations by the Honours and Distinctions Committee of the Indian Wars, 1763–4. 1910.

32/500. Canada: provision of armament and garrisons for defence of Esquimalt. 1891.

32/910. America: terms of emigration of British German Legion. 1856.

32/1027. President Roosevelt's objections to formation of depots for horse purchasing. 1904.

32/1034. Bermuda: proposed route via New York for military details. 1911.

32/1082. Sanction for payment of pension in the United States. 1901.

32/1117. United States: inquiry as to position of cables in Australia and New Zealand. 1913.

W.O. 33. REPORTS AND MISCELLANEOUS PAPERS.[1]

This class, which covers the period 1853–96, includes the following:

33/10. Unsatisfactory contract for supply of rifles by American firm. 1861.

33/11. Defence of British possessions in North America: report of Commissioner and memorandum by Sir John Burgoyne. 1862.

33/12. Peace, &c., suggestions concerning the Civil War. 1862.

33/14. Report on American military affairs. 1864.

33/15. Report on defences and British naval stations in North Atlantic. 1865.

33/20. Military position of Britain with respect to the United States. 1869.

33/21–22. Correspondence, instructions, and reports on the Red River expedition and settlement. 1870–1.

33/26. Report on American submarine mining establishment. 1874.

33/45. Army estimates: notes on procedures in parliaments of various countries, including the United States. 1886.

33/47. Fortifications and armaments of Halifax, N.S. 1887.

33/49. Tour through the United States and notes on principal government establishments, &c., there by Major G. S. Clarke, R.E. 1888.

33/55. Report on military aspects, &c., of frontier with the United States, 1893; and defence works at Esquimalt, 1895.

33/56. United States: land forces. 1896.

W.O. 34/1–260. AMHERST PAPERS.[2] 1712–84.

The collection consists mainly of the official correspondence of Jeffrey Amherst, Baron Amherst (1717–97). Most of the material relates to his period in charge of the British forces in America, 1758–63 (correspondence with governors of the various colonies, with French officials in North America, &c.), and to his later role as Commander-in-Chief and adviser on

---

[1] These, and additional relevant printed material, are also in the War Office Library.

[2] The Library of Congress holds microfilms of nearly all of these.

the American war, 1778–82 (letters from Germain, Lord North, Cornwallis, &c.). See the six-volume calendar for details.

W.O. 36/1–4. AMERICAN REBELLION: ENTRY BOOKS. 1773–99.

These are the documents described in the report on the War Office Library given on p. 188 of Andrews and Davenport.

W.O. 40. SELECT UNNUMBERED PAPERS.

40/1. Capt. Preston and eight others prosecuted on charge of causing a riot, Boston, 1770. Destruction of tea in Boston Harbour by the Sons of Liberty: report by O.C. troops, 1773. Report of Gen. Carleton on the condition of affairs at Quebec, 1776. Garrisons of Chambly and St. Johns not blamed for surrendering, 1777.

40/2. German recruits for service in America: reports by Maj.-Gen. Fawcett, 1780. Exchange of prisoners of war: lists of officers, 1781.

40/5. Charleston, S.C.: application for the return of the bells of St. Michael's, taken by the English. 1783.

40/5. Extracts from report of the Committee of Council of Quebec on the population, its health, need of medical aid, &c. 1787.

40/6. Newfoundland: a corps of volunteers raised for the defence of Fort Townsend. 1793.

40/10. British half-pay officers in America allowed to enter into the service of the United States. 1798.

40/12. America: troops under Lord Amherst not given prize money. 1799.

40/27. Ferdinand Smyth Stuart: statement of his services, losses in America, &c. 1807.

40/32. Instructions from Lt.-Col. Bruyeres, R.E., to Lieut. Gangreben for the defence of Fort Niagara and the frontier. 1814.

W.O. 44. ORDNANCE: IN-LETTERS.

In addition to the items listed below, this class also includes in-letters from various parts of Canada up to 1855.

44/239. American frigate *Chesapeake* purchased and registered in the Royal Navy list. 1815.

44/502. Mr. Howe, United States: plan for drowning magazines in case of fire. 1852.

44/504. Improvement in the navigation of the St. Lawrence. 1834.

44/506. Lieut.-Col. Kearney, United States Army, permitted to ascertain positions of points on the British shores of Lake Erie and the Northern Lakes for a hydrographical survey, 1845. Settlement in 1846 of the boundary between the United States, Canada, and New Brunswick, as established by the treaty of 1842.

44/532. Warrant for distribution of prize money for capture on Lake Huron in 1814 of the American vessels *Tigress* and *Scorpion*. 1818.

44/539. Dr. Alexander Jones, United States: invention of breech-loading carbine. 1842.

44/540. Surrender of Detroit and Michilimackinac reported to the Board of Ordnance by Maj.-Gen. Glasgow, R.A. 1813.

44/541. Employment of engineers on the boundary survey between the United States and Canada. 1844.

44/622. J. Christopher, United States: process for improving the quality of iron for ordnance. 1855.

44/623. W. Baynton, United States: method of making castings for ordnance. 1855.

W.O. 71. JUDGE ADVOCATE GENERAL'S RECORDS: COURTS MARTIAL: PROCEEDINGS.[1]

This class contains proceedings and papers for 1668–1850. Included are, e.g.:

71/19, 126. Trial and acquittal of Lieut.-Gen. James E. Oglethorpe. 1746.

71/61. Trial of Col. the Hon. Cosmo Gordon for neglect of duty at Springfield, North America. 1782.

W.O. 72. JUDGE ADVOCATE GENERAL'S RECORDS: CORRESPONDENCE RELATIVE TO COURTS MARTIAL.

Included is, e.g.:

72/103. Inquiry into failure of Albany expedition of Lieut.-Gen. John Burgoyne. 1778.

W.O. 80. MISCELLANEA: MURRAY PAPERS.

Sir George Murray (1772–1846) was Governor of the Canadas in 1814, Colonial Secretary 1828–30, and later Master-General of the Ordnance. His papers include:

80/4. Original correspondence, including correspondence with Sir James Kempt, Governor-General of Canada 1828–30; and a letter of 18 Dec. 1844 to Edward Everett acknowledging receipt of maps and surveys.

80/11. Miscellaneous papers on the defence of Canada. 1815–19, 1839–46.

W.O. 81. JUDGE ADVOCATE GENERAL'S RECORDS: CORRESPONDENCE: LETTER-BOOKS.

There are 112 volumes, covering the period 1715–1865; most contain an index. Included are the following:

---

[1] The Library of Congress holds photostats from W.O. 71/131: Proceedings of court martial held at Loyal Hannon, 26 Oct. 1758.

81/8, 9. Court martial of Maj.-Gen. Lord Charles Hay, North America. 1759.

81/13. Lieut.-Gen. John Burgoyne: failure of Albany expedition. 1778.

81/64. Transportation to Bermuda from America of soldiers under sentence. 1824.

81/111. Possession of passenger's ticket for New York not proof of desertion. 1864.

W.O. 106. DIRECTORATES OF MILITARY OPERATIONS AND INTELLIGENCE.

106/17. Correspondence and papers concerning the withdrawal of international troops from North China, including papers about the March 1906 meeting of representatives of the United States, Britain, and other countries to arrange withdrawal.

106/25. China: revolution and civil war: analysis of disturbances—alleged headquarters of reformers' group in England and America, 1903; attack on American mission at Peking, 1905; protection of American interests—troop reinforcements for Manila, 1906.

106/40. Defence and operational plans.

Included is a section on North America, 1896–1910: e.g., defence of the Canadian frontier, Feb. 1897; conditions of a war between the British Empire and the United States, Jan. 1908; &c.

W.O. 107. QUARTERMASTER GENERAL: PAPERS.

107/6. Canada expedition: troop movements, &c. 1861–2.

107/9. Red River expedition: journal, &c. 1870.

W.O. 108. SOUTH AFRICAN WAR: PAPERS.

108/81. Miscellanea: purchase of ordnance from Germany, Austria, France, North and South America. 1899–1900.

Royal Academy of Arts, Piccadilly, LONDON, W.1

BENJAMIN WEST (1738–1820). 4 sketch books.

Historical painter. Born in the United States, West spent the years from 1763 onwards in England; he was a foundation member of the Royal Academy, which was founded in 1768. Of the four sketch books held, three are undated and the fourth is inscribed 'Sketches when travelling in France in 1802'.

Royal Agricultural Society of England, 35 Belgrave Square, LONDON, S.W.1

BOARD OF AGRICULTURE. 16 volumes, including 9 minute-books, 2 letter-books, and a register of letters received. *c.* 1789–1810.

Predecessor of the Royal Agricultural Society. Much of the work of the Board of Agriculture (1793–1822) was concerned with county agricultural surveys, but the interest of its members in improved agricultural practices led to a certain amount of correspondence with the United States or about American methods.

The register of letters received, 1793–1819, includes reference to a number of letters of this sort, on such subjects as machinery, gypsum, hemp, peas, and Virginia white thorn. The actual letters, however, are no longer in the possession of the Royal Agricultural Society.

The two letter-books cover the years 1793–1800 and 1810–22, and include copies of some letters from the Board to American correspondents—e.g., to Mr. Jay of New York, in 1796; to Thomas Jefferson in 1789 and 1798; and to Mr. Pinckney and Dr. Logan in 1810.

The minute-books of the Board—covering most of its existence—consist mainly of notes that letters have been received or sent; occasionally there is slightly more information here about the letters listed in the register.

The Library, Royal Artillery Institution, Woolwich, LONDON, S.E.18

'A JOURNAL CONTAINING THE MANNER, METHOD AND EXECUTION OF THE DEMOLITION OF THE FORTIFICATIONS OF LOUISBOURG.' 1 volume. 1760. (MS. 6)

Daily journal, June–Nov. 1760, of the demolition. Mainly reports of the numbers and ranks of carpenters, miners, and others employed, and the work accomplished.

HOWE, SIR WILLIAM, 5th Viscount Howe (1729–1814). 1 volume. 1777–8. (MS. 58)

General orders, 27 Sept. 1777–21 Feb. 1778, of the Army in North America under General Howe. The volume contains orders concerning deserters from the American Army, marching orders, &c.

PATTISON, JAMES (1724–1805?). 5 volumes. 1777–81.

Pattison served with the British Army in North America during the War of Independence, and was commander in New York 1779–80.

(*a*) 'Brigade orders, Royal Artillery, from September 28 1777 till February 21 1778 by Brigadier General James Pattison.' Similar to the Howe volume above. (MS. 57)

(*b*) 'Warrants. Bills of Lading. Record of Commissions. Day Book.' This volume contains warrants by Pattison, 1777–80; bills of lading concerning supplies for the artillery, 1779; record of commissions, 1779–80; and a day book for Pattison's New York command, 1779–80. It also contains 'Orders and regulations of the Superintendent General of the police of the city of New York and its dependencies authorized by Major General Jones', 1778–9. (MS. 11)

(*c*) Letter-books containing copies of letters sent by Pattison, 1777–81.

(i) Letters, Philadelphia and New York, 1777–8, to the Board of Ordnance, Viscount Townshend, Samuel Cleaveland, and others, mainly about deserters from the American Army, rumours of strife in Congress, &c. (MS. 7)

(ii) Letters, mainly from New York, 10 Jan. 1779–11 Jan. 1781, to Amherst, Clinton, Germain, Lt.-Col. Innes, Townshend, and others, concerning the progress of the war.[1] (MS. 9)

(iii) Letters, New York, 10 July 1779–18 Aug. 1780, to a large number of correspondents, mainly about Pattison's administration of New York.[1] (MS. 9)

'BOOK OF RETURNS ETC. FOR THE CORPS OF ARTILLERY IN CANADA COMMENCING THE 1ST JULY 1778.' 2 volumes. 1778–83. (MS. 19)

One volume contains orders, monthly returns of forces, &c.; and copies of letters, Quebec and elsewhere, 1778–83, from Forbes Macbean to Pattison, Townshend, and others, concerning defences, supplies, &c. The other volume lists ordnance and ordnance stores at the various posts in Canada in 1778 and 1783.

Royal Commonwealth Society, Northumberland Avenue, LONDON, W.C.2

NORTH WEST COMPANY. Miscellaneous papers.[2] 1794–1821.

The North West Company, a group of fur-traders operating from Montreal, was the major rival of the Hudson's Bay Company until the two merged in 1821. The following manuscripts deal with such subjects as navigability of rivers, customs and attitudes of various Indian tribes, adequacy of beaver supply, &c.

[1] Microfilm held by the Library of Congress, Washington, D.C.
[2] Listed in *Subject Catalogue of the Library of the Royal Empire Society*, vol. iii (London, 1932). Hudson's Bay Company, London, has a microfilm of the collection.

(*a*) Duncan M'Gillivray:

(i) 'Journal'[1,2] kept during 1794–5 at Fort George on the North Saskatchewan River (88 pages).

(ii) 'Some account of the trade carried on by the North West Company',[2,3] unsigned [1808] (23 pages).

(*b*) David Thompson:

(i) 'Narrative of the expedition to the Kootenai and Flat Bow Indian countries, on the sources of the Columbia River, Pacific Ocean', 1807[2,4] (27 pages).

(ii) 'Remarks on the countries westward of the Rocky Mountains', 1813 (4 pages).

(*c*) Willard Ferdinand Wentzel, 'An account of Mackenzie's River', 1821 (7 pages).

Royal Geographical Society, Kensington Gore, London, S.W.7

CORRESPONDENCE AND OTHER PAPERS. 1830–80.

Large numbers of letters from corresponding American societies or individuals, but for the most part simply requests for, or acknowledgements of, the periodical publications of the Society or covering dispatch of American publications. In addition, the following letters (the Society's archives are not yet fully indexed so that other items may exist):

(*a*) 22 June 1850, from John Charles Frémont, acknowledging receipt of the Society's medal.

(*b*) Twenty-four letters, 1852–63, from American Ministers in London— mostly from George Mifflin Dallas. Mainly letters of thanks for books, invitations, &c.

(*c*) Washington D.C., 17 Apr. 1852, from Henry R. Schoolcraft to Sir Roderick I. Murchison, about the career of General William Clarke, the American explorer, who had just died.

(*d*) Eight letters, 1855–8, from the American Geographical and Statistical Society asking for advice or concerning papers read before the respective societies.

[1] Published as *The Journal of Duncan M'Gillivray*, ed. by A. S. Morton (Toronto, 1929).   [2] Photostats held by the Public Archives of Canada.

[3] The 'Account' was printed in the *Report* of the Public Archives of Canada for 1928. According to A. S. Morton, *A History of the Canadian West to 1870–71*, p. 936 (London, 1939), the manuscript 'was revised by William M'Gillivray to suit the occasion and published as *On the Origin and Progress of the North West Company* (London, 1811)'.

[4] Published under the title 'The Discovery of the Source of the Columbia River' in the *Quarterly of the Oregon Historical Society*, vol. xxvi, pp. 23–49, 1925.

(e) Long letter, 12 Dec. 1874, from Henry Nichols of New York, asking for an appointment to the Society's next expedition to the North Pole, and suggesting that the only way to reach the Pole is by balloon.

(f) Seven letters, 1878, from T. W. Goad, about papers on his explorations in New Mexico.

(g) Two letters, Oct. 1880, from the *New York Herald* asking the Society's opinion on the probable safety or otherwise of Lieutenant Schwalke's American Arctic expedition in the *Jeannette*, of which there has been no news for some time.

Royal Horticultural Society, Vincent Square, LONDON, S.W.1

DOUGLAS, DAVID (1798–1834). 2 journals and a summary of one of these.¹ 1823–7.

Botanist and traveller. The journals kept by Douglas during two trips to North America as collector for the Royal Horticultural Society are held in the Society's library. The first of these relates to a trip to the United States in 1823, and the second (together with Douglas's own summary of it) to a period spent in Washington, Oregon, &c., 1824–7. The journals consist of daily accounts of plants, birds, &c., seen; and of transport and other difficulties.

Royal Institution of Great Britain, 21 Albemarle Street, LONDON, W.1

RUMFORD LETTERS. 31 letters. 1798–1807.

Sir Benjamin Thompson, later Count von Rumford (1753–1814), the American-born scientist and adventurer, founded the Royal Institution in 1799. The letters are mostly written during absences from London. All except five are addressed to William Savage, clerk of the Royal Institution, who looked after Rumford's affairs in his absence. They all deal with either personal or routine matters.

Royal Mint, Tower Hill, LONDON, E.C.3

NEWTON PAPERS. 1 document. [c. 1701.]

'Proposals for coyning half-pence and farthings of copper for the English plantations in America. n.d. [c. July 1701] [Note by Sir Isaac Newton].'²

---

¹ These were published with some additional material as *Journal kept by David Douglas during his Travels in North America, 1823–1827* (London, 1914).

² H.M.C. viii (i), p. 78 [kkk]. (Listed as held by the Earl of Portsmouth.)

Royal Society,[1] Burlington House, Piccadilly, LONDON, W.1

This list is supplementary to Andrews & Davenport, pp. 355–68, their introductory paragraphs being particularly useful.

LETTERS AND PAPERS COLLECTION.

The manuscript catalogues of the Letters and Papers include entries up to 1806; subsequent entries will be found in the general card catalogue. Papers which have been printed in the *Philosophical Transactions* can be easily traced through its indexes.

Letters and papers of American interest, 1781–1897:

(*a*) There are a number of letters from and papers by Sir Benjamin Thompson, Count von Rumford, who was born in America, but these do not appear to have any specific bearing on America. 1781–1812.

(*b*) Letter, Passy, 30 Aug. 1783, from Benjamin Franklin to Sir Joseph Banks, president of the Royal Society, on the first hydrogen balloon[2] (5 pages with 2 postscripts).

(*c*) Letter, Passy, 8 Oct. 1783, from Franklin to Sir Joseph Banks, on a hot air balloon[3] (2 pages).

(*d*) Paper entitled 'Of the earthy substance found near Niagara Falls and vulgarly called "spray" ', by Robert McCausland. Nov. or Dec. 1784 (10 pages).

(*e*) Paper entitled 'Of the nature and customs of the Indians of North America', by Robert McCausland. Read 16 Feb. 1786[4] (9 pages).

(*f*) Paper entitled 'Halos and Parhelia of the sun seen in 1771 in North America' by Alexander Baxter. Read 7 Dec. 1786[5] (5 pages including 1 page of figures).

(*g*) Paper entitled 'Observations and conjectures on the state, motion and phenomena of heat in the earth' by Samuel Williams, Professor of Mathematics at Harvard University. 1790 (4 pages).

(*h*) Paper entitled 'Analysis of a mineral from North America containing metal hitherto unknown', by Charles Hatchett. Read 26 Nov. 1801[6] (20 pages).

---

[1] Virginia material microfilmed by the Virginia Colonial Records Project.
[2] Printed, with the first postscript, in *Proceedings of the American Antiquarian Society*, vol. xviii, pp. 260–3, 1906–7.
[3] Printed, ibid., pp. 263–5.
[4] Printed in *Philosophical Transactions*, vol. lxxvi, pp. 229–35, 1786.
[5] Printed in ibid., vol. lxxvii, pp. 44–46, 1787.
[6] Printed in ibid., vol. cxii, pp. 49–66, 1802.

(*i*) Letters, 1868–97, from the following American scientists were traced through the general card catalogue; in most cases they were simply letters of thanks for election to the Royal Society, or for award of one of its medals; or concern the distribution of publications: Alexander Agassiz, James Dwight Dana, Josiah Willard Gibbs, Benjamin Apthorp Gould, Asa Gray, Samuel Pierpont Langley, Simon Newcomb, Hubert Anson Newton, Benjamin Peirce, and Henry Augustus Rowland.

BOYLE, HON. ROBERT (1627–91). 8 letters. 1670–88.

Natural philosopher and chemist. A founder of the Royal Society and a governor of the New England Company.

(*a*) Volume ii contains seven letters, Roxbury, Mass., 30 Sept. 1670–7 July 1688, from John Eliot, the missionary to the Indians, to Boyle, dealing with 'the religious walking and wayes of the praying Indians' and the translation of the Scriptures into their language.

(*b*) Volume v contains a letter, 13 Aug. 1676, from Katherine, Viscountess Ranelagh, Boyle's sister, to Eliot, giving him sympathy and moral counsel.

CATESBY, MARK (1679?–1749). 22 letters. 1722–5. ('Dr. Sherard's Phil. Letters', nos. 163–84.)

Naturalist. The twenty-two letters, 1722–5, from Catesby to William Sherard, are from America—mainly Charleston, S.C.—where Catesby was on a plant-collecting trip.

BLAGDEN, SIR CHARLES (1748–1820). 21 letters. 1779–1817.

Physician. Served in that capacity with the British Army in the War of Independence. In this large collection of twenty-three box files of letters and papers, there are nineteen letters from American correspondents, and two copies of letters from Blagden to Americans, 1779–1817. Most are brief notes, letters of introduction or of admission to learned societies, but some letters are from brother officers in America, written to Blagden after his return to England in 1780, describing the military and naval situation in that year, and later the peace negotiations of 1783 and the exodus of Loyalists to Nova Scotia.

There are two letters from Robert Walsh: the first, Philadelphia, 26 June 1810, sets out Walsh's views on American politics, which, he thinks, are conducted by 'contemptible men'—although he excepts Madison from this description, he thinks that even he labours under unreasoning anti-British prejudice. The second, Baltimore, 4 Apr. 1817, gives a glowing account of American progress and prosperity, with some description of Monroe and John Quincy Adams. Other correspondents include John Adams, John Andre, George Clark, Rufus King, Archibald Lee, D. Paine, R. Patterson, E. Pearson, and F. Smyth.

HERSCHEL, SIR JOHN FREDERICK WILLIAM (1792–1871).
American correspondence: 62 letters (59 to him and 3 copies or drafts from him). 1829–71.

Astronomer. A few items deal only with the exchange of publications; the other topics almost all concern astronomical matters, except a comment on a proposed biography of James Grahame, author of a *History of the United States* (London, 1836). The correspondents are: Cleveland Abbe, George Bancroft, George Phillips Bond, Nathaniel Bowditch and his executors, Alvan Clark, John William Draper, Edward Everett, Asa Gray, Edward C. Herrick, Elias Loomis, Peter Lesley, Matthew Fontaine Maury, Benjamin Peirce, Eliza Susan Quincy, Josiah Quincy, William C. Redfield, J. D. Runkle, Charles W. Tuttle, Samuel Tyler, Daniel Vaughan, and Robert Winthrop.

SABINE, GENERAL SIR EDWARD (1788–1883). 45 letters from American correspondents; and 5 papers on American subjects by Sabine. 1832–64.

Army officer. Served in the War of 1812 in the Niagara campaign. Astronomer, geophysicist, and President of the Royal Society 1861–71.

The letters deal with the following subjects: the work of the United States Coast Survey and the establishment of observation stations in Maine, Florida, and Washington state; solar spots and magnetic disturbances; eclipses; a newly found species of American pine tree; the climate, topography and flora of Upper California; magnetic and meteorological observations; Matthew F. Maury, with some criticisms of his scientific work, and his 'desertion to the rebels' in 1861; Chicago and its growth; the foundation and work of the Smithsonian Institution; the feasibility of a Pacific railroad in 1853; American weather; the Civil War. The correspondents are: Alexander Dallas Bache, George Phillips Bond, David Douglas, an Englishman sent to California by the Royal Horticultural Society, William H. Emory, James Melville Gilliss, J. D. Graham, Joseph Henry, Peter Lesley, M. A. Renwick.

The five papers are:

(i) 'Observations taken on the Western Coast of N. America, by the late Mr. David Douglas, with a Report on his Papers by Major Edward Sabine, R.A.' 1837 (8 folios). Chiefly an account of Douglas's botanical and geographical activities in California, &c.

(ii) 'Report on Mr. David Douglas's Papers . . . by Major Edward Sabine, R.A.' 1837 (10 folios). Geographical observations on the Columbia River and its tributaries, and in California, with several tables giving latitudes and longitudes.

(iii) 'A memorandum on various "points"—a relic from Sabine's active service on the United States–Canada frontier.' n.d. A list of frontier posts, or possible frontier posts, with locational data, &c.

(iv) 'American birds.' Includes species from Canada and Greenland (list of 31 folios). n.d.

(v) 'Lists of American and British birds', with explanatory notes (9 folios). n.d.

METEOROLOGICAL ARCHIVES.

Include observations made at Gardiner, Me., in 1839; Boston in 1725–6; Cincinnati in 1840; Hudson, Ohio, 1839; Burlington, Vt., 1839.

MANUSCRIPTS (GENERAL) SERIES.

Include astronomical observations made at the United States Naval Observatory, Washington, D.C., by Lieut. J. M. Gilliss. 1840–1.

Royal Society of Arts,[1] John Adam Street, LONDON, W.C.2

The Royal Society of Arts was founded in 1754 as the Society for the Encouragement of Arts, Manufactures, and Commerce.[2] Among its major early objectives was the development in the American colonies of potash and pearl-ash manufacture, mulberry tree growing and silk manufacture, &c.; premiums were awarded for such activities or for importing such goods into England.

GUARD BOOKS. 1754–70.

The communications considered by the Society to be most important at the time of their receipt were preserved in fourteen guard books. Subject and author card indexes to these have recently been completed, those for volumes 1–11 being based on a contemporary chronological index. The correspondence, &c., from or about America is as follows:

An Englishman. 7 Nov. 1758. Growth of tea in America.

Anon. n.d. Reasons for producing opium in Georgia.

Anon. n.d. Culture of spices, tea, and silk in the colonies.

Anon. n.d. An account of the expenses of the filature in Georgia in 1757.

Anthill, Edward. New Brunswick, N.J., 9 May and 28 Aug. 1766, concerning vineyards; and 28 Feb. 1769 and n.d., concerning his agricultural improvements.

Appleton, N. Boston, 31 Mar. and 28 July 1766. Silk-worms and silk.

Baker, H. 17 Feb. 1762. Matapany tea sent by Dr. Brooke of Maryland.

Barnes, H. Boston, 4 Jan. 1766. Sarsaparilla from Massachusetts.

Bernard, Francis. Boston, 13 Aug. 1763, recommending Mr. Willard, a maker of potash; and 28 Aug. 1767, two letters concerning potash produced by William Frobisher.

---

[1] Virginia material microfilmed by the Virginia Colonial Records Project.

[2] See D. Hudson and K. W. Luckhurst, *The Royal Society of Arts, 1754–1954* (London, 1954), and D. G. C. Allan, 'The Origin and Growth of the Society's Archives, 1754–1847', *Journal of the Royal Society of Arts*, vol. cvi, pp. 623–9, 1958.

Blodget, Samuel. Boston, 20 Jan. 1766. Pearl-ash.

Bridgen, Edward. London, 23 Oct. 1765, urging premium for importing hemp from America.

Broadfield, E. Philadelphia, 10 Dec. 1763, sending sturgeon.

Bull, William. Charleston, S.C., 6 Aug. 1765, certifying that Jean Louis Gibert has produced thirty-five pounds of silk; and 20 Jan. 1770, concerning vines planted in South Carolina by Christopher Sherb. *See also* Garth.

C., F. C. n.d. Bees and wool in Virginia.

Caiger, E. Charleston, S.C., 15 Sept. 1766. Silk in Georgia.

Campbell, Archibald, 3rd Duke of Argyll. n.d. Two letters concerning the New England five-leaved pine.

Carter, Charles. Virginia. Seven letters, two of 1762 and five undated, on a variety of subjects.[1]

Clap, Thomas (and Jared Eliot). New Haven, Conn., 2 June 1760. Silk in Connecticut.

Colden, Cadwallader. New York, 6 Feb. 1761. Winter food for cattle.

Collinson, Peter. 10 Nov. 1763. Provincial garden in West Florida.

Committee for Promoting Arts, Williamsburg, Va. 14 Feb. and 16 Nov. 1759. Minutes.

Crevet, John. Philadelphia, n.d. Papers concerning rewards for encouraging industry in Pennsylvania.

Cushing, Thomas. Boston, 6 Sept. 1766, requesting advice about potash manufacture; and copy of a letter, July 1767, acknowledging receipt of pamphlets on this.

Daux, J. A. London, 1760, concerning a sawmill for clearing lands in America.

Delemare, J., and others. London, 29 Mar. 1755. Certificate concerning the quality of some Georgia silk.

Dick, Charles. Virginia, 22 June 1762 and n.d., on pearl-ash, and an undated letter on the 'polite arts'.

Duane, James, and others. New York, 30 Mar. 1765. Foundation in New York of a society for encouraging arts.[2]

Eliot, Jared. Seven letters, Killingworth, Conn., 1761 and 1762, mainly on black iron sand. Also an undated extract from his essays on field husbandry in America, and an extract from a letter, 26 Mar. 1760, on grapes and wine-making. *See also* Clap and Ruggles.

Ellis, Henry. Georgia, 27 June 1758. Silk, olives, madder.

Ellis, John. Georgia. 16 Dec. 1761. Rhubarb.

Ellis, John and Henry. Georgia, n.d. List of plants for manufacturers that would grow in Georgia, Carolina, and the Bahamas.

English, J. South Carolina, 15 Nov. 1760, on premiums offered for the colonies.

---

[1] See R. H. Hilldrup, 'A Campaign to Promote the Prosperity of Colonial Virginia', *Virginia Magazine of History and Biography*, vol. lxvii, pp. 410–28, 1959.

[2] Extracts printed in K. W. Luckhurst, 'The Society's Early Days: New Light from its Correspondence', *Journal of the Royal Society of Arts*, vol. cii, pp. 292–313, 1954.

Evans, Lewis. Philadelphia. 1 Nov. 1754, on settling plantations in America.

Fauquier, Francis. Williamsburg, Va. An undated letter concerning Zant grapes and, with others, a certificate, 6 Aug. 1763, concerning William Carter's vineyards.

Fearon, Benson. 9 Oct. 1764, certifying that he has received two planks, which have been laid at Mill Creek on the James River, Virginia (as part of the Society's tests concerning destruction of ships' bottoms by worms).

Ferguson, James. Belfast, 7 May 1767. American potash.

Franklin, Benjamin. Five letters, 1755–66: 14 May 1755, on the establishment of a society in America;[1] 15 June 1756 (copy of letter of 27 Nov. 1755), concerning membership in the Society of Arts;[2] 12 Aug. 1763 concerning Mr. Willard's methods of potash production; 2 Sept. 1764 noting the sending of sturgeon; 29 Oct. 1766 enclosing a letter from William Alexander ('Earl of Stirling'), New Jersey, 31 July 1765, about Aaron Miller's compass.

Frobisher, William. Boston, 21 and 25 Aug. 1767 and 13 May 1768, on potash.

Gale, Benjamin. Five letters, Killingworth, Conn., 1763–8, on black grass, his drill plough, and other subjects.

Garden, Alexander. Letters, extracts, and copies, South Carolina, 1757–60 and undated, on various subjects.

Garth, Charles. Three letters, 1770, concerning Christopher Sherb's vine-planting (one includes an extract from a letter of William Bull on this subject).

Gibert, Jean Louis. Silk Hope, S.C., n.d. His production of cocoons.

Gilpin, F. Philadelphia, 16 May 1769. A letter to Franklin about windmills for pumping in mines or ships.

Goddard, James Stanley. n.d. American isinglass.

Habersham, James, and J. Otolonghe. Georgia, 20 May 1756. Premiums for silk in Georgia.

Harrison, G. 18 June 1766. Black grass and sand from Dr. Benjamin Gale.

Harvey, Joel. Connecticut, 20 Aug. 1764. A description of a corn-threshing machine.

Homes, William. London, 16 Jan. 1764, proposing various premiums for America.

Hyam, Thomas. London, 12 Sept. 1760. Import of hemp from Philadelphia.

Ingersoll, Jared. London, 24 Dec. 1760, on the cultivation of maize in North America (8 pages); and 13 Mar. 1765, concerning Joel Harvey's threshing machine.

Johnston, James. Berkeley county, S.C., 22 Oct. 1770. Christopher Sherb's vine-planting.

Leadly, John. London, 1765, certificate of sale of New York potash, and a 1766 affidavit of the quality of pearl-ash imported by Sir W. Baker.

Lewis, William. 27 Jan. 1767, concerning American potash, and an undated paper containing experiments on Virginia saltpetre.

[1] Copy. Original presented to American Philosophical Society.

[2] Printed in Luckhurst, op. cit., pp. 297–9.

Livingston, Philip, and Peter Remsen. New York, 3 May 1765. Establishment of a potash works.

Ludwell, Philip. Virginia, 21 Apr. 1760. Articles to be produced in America.

Maine, David. London, 26 Mar. 1760. Seeds for Carolina and Georgia.

Mascarene, J. Cambridge, Mass., 10 Feb. 1766. Potash.

Mason, A. n.d. Proposing to write a description of North America.

Mayhew, Jonathan. Boston, 20 Jan. 1766, concerning pearl-ash, and an extract from another 1766 letter.

Moffat, Thomas. Newport, R.I., 26 Jan. and 26 June 1761. New England climate.

More, Samuel. 16 July 1763. Rough draft of experiments on Virginia saltpetre.

Neave, Messrs. E. London, 7 Nov. 1760. New England potash.

Neilson, James, and William Oake. New Jersey, 28 Aug. 1765. Certificate concerning Edward Anthill's vineyards.

Otolonghe, Joseph. Georgia, 3 May 1756, on silk. *See also* Habersham and Otolonghe.

Pattison, Nat. and others. London, 18 Dec. 1765. Certificate of the quality of J. L. Gibert's South Carolina silk.

Perrie, J. London, 21 Mar. 1766. New England sarsaparilla.

Peters, M. Dublin, 24 Aug. 1766. Ohio grass seed.

'Phylopatria'. 10 Apr. 1760. Import of hemp, iron, &c., from America.

Pinckney, Thomas. 1 Apr. 1755. Mulberry trees in Carolina and Georgia.

Pringle, Robert. South Carolina, 24 Aug. 1759. South Carolina logwood.

Quincy, Edward. Boston, 17 Oct. 1766, certificate concerning pearl-ash made by Samuel Blodget; 30 June 1765 on various matters; and an undated certificate concerning pearl-ash.

Remsen, Peter. *See* Livingston and Remsen.

Ruggles, Thomas. n.d. A method for marking sheep, originally sent from Jared Eliot to Mr. Collinson..

Rutherford, William. New York, 29 Mar. 1766, on trade with the colonies.

Rutherford, William, and William Smith. n.d. Articles to be encouraged in the colonies.

Schuyler, Philip. New York, 24 Jan. 1765. Letter to P. Skeene concerning the erection of a hemp mill.

Selden, Cary. Virginia, 27 Aug. 1765. A certificate of John Bennet, pilot, that two planks delivered to him have been sunk in Mill Creek, Virginia, and then taken to London (part of the Society's tests concerning destruction of ships' bottoms by worms).

Shakespear, John. 30 Nov. 1765. Letter sent with some American hemp.

Shipley, William. 15 July 1755. The importance of vines, hemp, &c., to South Carolina and to England.

Shubrick, Thomas. London, 4 Feb. 1765. The possibilities for use in making red dye of a root from the Indian country in America.

Skeene, P. New York, 14 Feb. 1765. Indian dye and potash.

Smith, William. *See* Rutherford and Smith.

Stoker, V., and others. n.d. Certificate that silk imported by J. L. Gibert is of his own growth.

Tryon, William. North Carolina. Extract from letter, July 1767, to Edward Bridgen, concerning Mr. Stansfield's sawmill.

Wentworth, John. New Hampshire, 20 July 1767. Extract from a letter acknowledging receipt of pamphlets on potash.

Whitworth, Sir Charles. 31 July and 24 Aug. 1755, concerning letters from Alexander Garden.

Willis, Thomas. n.d. Experiments on American isinglass.

Woodin, Thomas. South Carolina, 28 Oct. 1766, on various matters, and a copy of a letter of the same date on lucerne.

Woodmanson, Charles. Carolina, 23 May 1763, on various matters.

Wright, Jermyn and Charles. Georgia, 27 Oct. 1766, concerning vineyards, and 30 May 1768, concerning balsam found in Georgia.

Young, Henry. Georgia, 23 Dec. 1766, on leek taw or Chinese vetch introduced into Georgia by S. Bowen.

There are also in the guard books some Customs' and other documents relating to the importation of silk, hemp, &c., from America; a 1765 list (printed) of premiums offered in New York province; and undated descriptions of the timber sent to North America by the Society.

LOOSE ARCHIVES. 1755–1840.

The cataloguing of this collection of c. 5,000 unbound papers was not quite complete in Jan. 1958, when the Society was visited; there may, therefore, be some Americana additional to that given below. Card indexes by author and by subject have been and are being prepared; the cards in the subject index are classified first by the Society's standing committees (including 'Colonies and Trade'), and then by subject.

Baker, Benjamin ('an American refugee'). Letter, received 12 Apr. 1779, describing his geometrical instruments.

Box, George. London, ?1759. Draft of a letter to Alexander Garden thanking him for observations on the soil and climate of Carolina.

Bromwich & Co. London, 15 Mar. 1775. Letter concerning a 'Carolina stain'.

Cheffins, Richard. London, 5 Mar. 1806, about his 'American borers'.

Clarke, Isaac W. 11 Sept. 1808, on hemp in Canada.

Colpitts, Thomas. Liverpool. 24 May 1797. Brown cotton in North Carolina.

Davies, Lieut.-Col. London, 6 Feb. 1792. Northwest Passage.

Dossie, Robert. 1767. Manuscript of his 'Observations on the Pot-Ash brought from America . . . to which is subjoined Processes for Making Pot-Ash and Barilla, in North America'. Published in London, 1767, and related papers and minutes.

Fawkener, W. (of the Privy Council). London, 22 Feb. 1791, concerning new methods of manufacturing potash and pearl-ash in Quebec, enclosing copies of letters, from Motz, Macdonald, and Nooth (q.v.).

Flindall, Murray. Bay of Quinte, Upper Canada, 23 May 1823. Letter and drawings concerning his axe and drill, with remarks on life in Canada.

Fraser, John. London, 17 Nov. 1788, on an 'extraordinary grass' which

Thomas Walter of South Carolina has discovered; and 30 Nov. 1789 presenting a book on the new American grasses.

Glenny, James. Quebec, 1791. Copies of memorials to the King and to the Privy Council on his new method of producing potash, and a copy of an account of this method.

Habersham, James. Savannah, Ga., 20 May 1756. Mulberry trees in Georgia.

Habersham, James, and Joseph Otolonghe. Savannah, Ga., 23 Oct. 1758, reporting payment for cocoons.

Hampton, Samuel. Philadelphia, 23 Jan. 1790. His standards of invariable weights and measures.

Lane & Booth. London, 15 and 30 Jan. 1765, on potash.

Lawrence, Robert. Washington, D.C., 28 Nov. 1840, concerning the laws and constitution of the National Institute for the Promotion of Science.

Long, Borden. Longueuil, Upper Canada, 10 Apr. 1808, concerning his perpetual motion machine (with an introductory letter from I. W. Clarke).

Macdonald, Arthur. Quebec, 8 Jan. 1791, copy of a report to the King on James Glenny's new method of producing potash, and a copy of a letter of 24 Nov. 1790 to H. Motz concerning potash.

Mease, James. Philadelphia, 2 Apr. 1801, concerning the possibility of introducing British machinery into the United States, with observations on scientific education there.

Motz, Henry. Copy of a letter of 24 Nov. 1790 to Scrope Bernard [-Morland] about potash.

Nooth, J. Mervin. Copy of a letter of 24 Nov. 1790 to Sir Joseph Banks about potash.

Otolonghe, Joseph. Savannah, Ga., 20 and 24 May 1756, about mulberry trees in Georgia, and 1759 listing persons receiving premiums for cocoons. See also Habersham and Otolonghe.

Paine, Thomas. Rotherham, Yorks., 25 May 1789, to Sir George Leonard Staunton about single-arch bridges (enclosed in a letter from Paine, 30 Apr. 1790).

Percy, Sir Hugh, 2nd Duke of Northumberland. 9 Mar. 1802, about Canadian hemp.

Pettibone, Daniel. Philadelphia, 24 May 1810. His improvements in domestic heating.

Rose, Lewis. Savannah, Ga., 1 Sept. 1792. New species of cinchona.

Solly, R. M. London, 20 May 1823, presenting a pot of American grasses.

Stewart, James. London, 23 Aug. 1774, on 'American productions'.

Tatham, Col. William. Letters, London, 1801–2, mainly on Canadian hemp.[1]

Walter, John. London. Letter, received 1 Dec. 1784, concerning his new method of printing, mentioning encouragement from Franklin.

Walter, Thomas. Santee, S.C., 24 Dec. 1787. Two copies of his pamphlet on American grass.

[1] See D. G. C. Allan, 'Colonel William Tatham, an Anglo-American Member of the Society, 1801–4', Journal of the Royal Society of Arts, vol. cviii, pp. 229–33, 1960.

Watson, John. 3 June 1755. Receipt for £18 to be used for rewarding the planting of white mulberry trees in Georgia.

West, Benjamin. London, 1 and 16 Nov. 1796, concerning his portrait of Samuel More.

In addition to the above, there are a large number of certificates relating to the export from America and import into England of potash and sturgeon; letters on behalf of various American bodies acknowledging receipt of the Society's *Transactions*; letters from the Society to Alexander Garden about cork trees sent to Carolina, 6 Feb. 1760, and to Thomas Hyam about his hemp imports, 6 Oct. 1760; and a petition sent during the 1750's to the parish of St. Peters, Purisburgh, S.C., about the encouragement of the cultivation of silk.

TRANSACTIONS.

(a) Dr. Templeman's Transactions.

Peter Templeman (1711–69), who became the secretary of the Society in 1760, compiled an 'Historical Register of the Transactions of the Society. . . .' in two volumes, covering 1754–8. This contains extracts from letters received, reports of matters discussed, lists of members, &c. An author and subject card index, combined with that for the Society's later manuscript transactions, is available. There is some material of American relevance similar to that listed above.

(b) Manuscript Transactions.

The early transactions of the Society, 1770/1–1783/4, are in manuscript form. The card index to these shows a small amount of American material, again similar to the above.

MINUTES.

There are manuscript minutes of the Society from 1754, and minutes for standing committees (including 'Colonies and Trade') from 1758. The minutes throw light on the Society's attitude towards the correspondence received by it, and include discussion of premiums to be offered.

LETTERS RECEIVED.

The four volumes contain contemporary copies of, or copies of extracts from, some of the letters received by the Society, 1767–78. These letters have not yet been compared with those in the guard books and the loose archives, but there may be some among them whose originals are not in either of these two groups.

LETTERS SENT.

Four volumes contain contemporary copies of letters sent by the Society, 1770–1850.

Royal United Service Institution, Whitehall, LONDON, S.W.1

MILITARY MANUSCRIPTS.

Vol. 99: Proceedings of the general court martial held at Brunswick, N.J., 1778, by George Washington, for the trial of Maj.-Gen. Charles Lee (212 pages).

Vol. 125:

No. 91. Lists showing British Army strength 'in their retreat from Philadelphia', 1777; at the 'Repulse of Stono Ferry, S. Carolina', 1779; and 'during the seige of Savannah', 1779 (2 pages).

No. 110. 'America: State of the Provincial Army on the 31st of May 1776', giving the number of men and the stations of the various regiments (6 pages).

No. 149. Letter, Kingston, Surrey, from Edward Baynes, Adjutant-General, 23 June 1813, giving a report of Lieut. Fitzgibbon's capture of a 'considerable detachment of the American Regular Army under Lieut. Coln. Boerstler' (1 page).

WOLSELEY, GARNET JOSEPH, 1st Viscount Wolseley (1833–1913). Correspondence.

Soldier. The two boxes of correspondence between Wolseley and his wife contain letters covering 1870–1911, and thus do not include material relating to Wolseley's visit to the United States during the Civil War. There are twenty-one letters from Canada in 1870, however, and these contain some references to the progress of the Red River expedition—which he led—against Louis Riel.

St. Mary of the Angels, Moorhouse Road, LONDON, W.2

MANNING, HENRY EDWARD (1808–92). Papers.

The papers of Cardinal Manning are somewhat depleted due to accidental destruction during the War, and a few were dispersed into private hands at an earlier period; but the substantial remainder are now in process of being sorted, though they are not likely to be generally available for inspection for a few years yet. The main American connexions revolve around Manning's correspondence with American bishops about the social question, particularly his defence of some of Henry George's doctrines (whom Manning had met and sympathized with)[1] against attacks of some

---

[1] Shane Leslie quotes some of Manning's correspondence about Henry George in his *Cardinal Manning: His Life and Labours*, revised edition, pp. 151–7 (New York and Dublin, 1954).

of the American bishops, and also his defence of the Knights of Labor. (So far no correspondence has been found with the American bishops that relate closely to Irish politics.)

(a) Six letters, 1885–8, from Bishop Keane of Richmond, Va., four of which are from Rome, Easter 1887. Keane went to Rome as part of a delegation to counter the efforts of Cardinal Taschereau of Quebec and Archbishop Corrigan of New York to get the Knights of Labor put under ecclesiastical censure. From Keane's letters it appears that Manning played a large part in preventing Papal intervention.

(b) Nine letters, 1885–8, from Archbishop Corrigan, mostly concerned with Henry George and the affair of McGlynn, a priest who gave active political support to George. A letter, 30 Nov. 1886, describes the role that Father McGlynn played in George's campaign for Mayor of New York; another, 23 Dec. 1886, is an anthology of objectionable quotations on property from *Progress and Poverty*. Three letters also relate to the difficulties of work among Italian immigrants.

(c) Ten or more letters, 1886–7, from Archbishop Walsh of Dublin refer to the conduct of Archbishop Corrigan and the McGlynn case. They develop into a discussion of those points in George's theories on which both Manning and Walsh agreed. One letter also touches on German attempts in Rome, through the Archbishop of Milwaukee [Michael Heiss], to gain special treatment for German Catholics in America.

(d) Five letters, c. 1887, from Cardinal Gibbons, Archbishop of Baltimore, mainly concerned with the Knights of Labor.[1]

There are also some other letters, c. 1870–80, on the same themes from various American correspondents.[2]

Copies of Manning's replies to most of the above, and some of the original replies, are also in the collection.

Literary Secretary, the Salvation Army, International Headquarters, Denmark Hill, LONDON, S.E.5

Most of the Salvation Army records were destroyed during the Second World War by enemy action.

BOOTH, EVANGELINE (1865–1950). 5 typewritten letters. 1904–5.

New York, Dec. 1904–Apr. 1905: four to General William Booth and one to Bramwell Booth, dealing with the Salvation Army's farm colonies in

---

[1] See John Tracy Ellis, *The Life of James, Cardinal Gibbons, Archbishop of Baltimore, 1834–1921*, 2 vols. (Milwaukee, Wis., 1952).

[2] See John Tracy Ellis's note on Manning's and Gibbons's papers in English and Irish ecclesiastical archives, *Catholic Historical Review*, vol. xxxvi, pp. 332–3, 1950.

Colorado, California, and Ohio, which were established in 1898. They refer
to the mission of Rider Haggard, who was sent out by the British government to inspect the colonies in 1905, and whose report was issued as a
blue book by the Colonial Office in the same year.

Printed material on these colonies is available in the volumes of *All the
World* for 1902, 1904, and 1905, which may be consulted in the Library.

Sion College,[1] Victoria Embankment, London, E.C.4

RECORDS OF THE PROVINCIAL ASSEMBLY OF LONDON.
1 volume. 1647–60. (ARC/L40. 2/E17)

(*a*) Entry for 27 Dec. 1649 (page 102 verso), 'Ordered that papers concerning New England be committed to ye care of ye grand Committee'.

(*b*) Entry for 21 Jan. 1650 (page 103 recto), '*R*[esolved] that it shall be
referred to the Grand Comittee to consider whether there shall be a letter
drawn up for the promoting the businesse of New England, and that the
report be given in in writing to the Province.' (Doubtless arising from the
Ordinance of 1649 for the establishment of the Society for Propagation of
the Gospel in New England.)

(*c*) The entry in the minutes for 19 Mar. 1659 accepts a proposal, that came
from the New England Company, to print the Bible 'in the Indian language'
—what became the 'Massachusetts Bible'. 'Dr. Reignolds bee desired to
call the Ministers of the citty together for the carrying on of this grand
affaire.'

BRAY, DR. THOMAS (1656–1730). Papers (1 volume).[2] 1699–1705. (ARC/L40. 2/E16)
Commissary of the Bishop of London in Maryland 1700. Active in the
work of evangelizing the plantations and educating the Negroes. Papers
mostly concerned with the Church in Maryland. Contents listed in Andrews
& Davenport, pp. 336–8.

CUTLER, TIMOTHY (1684–1765). Letter (5 pages).[3] 1739. (72 ff. 22)
Cutler was rector of Yale 1719–22, and later an episcopal clergyman in
Boston. The letter, 28 May 1739, is to someone unnamed, but addressed
as 'My Lord' (probably Edmund Gibson, Bishop of London), and contains
a highly critical account of the effects of the doctrines of Jonathan Edwards.
He gives examples of reported fanaticism, but thinks that the revival will
have no lasting effects.

[1] Virginia material microfilmed by the Virginia Colonial Records Project.
[2] Used by the Rev. H. P. Thompson for his book, *Thomas Bray* (London, 1954).
[3] This is bound with a volume of pamphlets, but is marked as a manuscript
in the pamphlet catalogue under 'Americana'.

PAMPHLET COLLECTION.

The Library contains a large collection of pamphlets—catalogued under 'Americana', 1641–1878 (but mostly eighteenth century). This includes pamphlets by Increase Mather, R. Baylie (a friend of Roger Williams), Jonathan Edwards, John Adams, and Thomas Clarkson. There are also printed letters of George Whitefield, accounts of actions in the French wars of the seventeenth and eighteenth centuries, reports of missions to Indians, and pamphlets on emigration, the tobacco trade, the establishment of Georgia, expeditions north of California in 1790, and the War of Independence.

Society for Promoting Christian Knowledge,[1]
Holy Trinity Church, Marylebone Road,
LONDON, N.W.1

Almost all the relevant documents relate to the colonial period and have been briefly described in Andrews & Davenport, p. 331. The actual missionary work in the colonies took place only from 1698 to 1701, when this work was taken over by the Society for the Propagation of the Gospel in Foreign Parts (see p. 313); after 1701 the Society's main work in America was the dispatch of books and pamphlets. The relevant material is not extensive. It can readily be traced through the card index. Additional material includes the following:

NEWMAN LETTERS.[2] New England letters (5 volumes), 1721–43; miscellaneous letters (9 volumes), 1735–43.

These are copies of letters sent by Henry Newman (1670–1743), Secretary of the S.P.C.K. 1708–43. (The archives also contain typed transcripts.)

SALZBURG EMIGRATION PAPERS. 8 volumes and some loose letters. 1731–71.

Accounts and correspondence relating to the settlement of German Protestant exiles in Georgia from 1731 onwards.

EMIGRATION COMMITTEE MINUTES, 1882– (in progress). (7 volumes to 1936.) LADIES EMIGRATION COMMITTEE MINUTES, 1879–1921 (2 volumes).

There are scattered references in the Society's minutes and annual reports of the first half of the nineteenth century to occasional help given to

---

[1] Virginia material microfilmed by the Virginia Colonial Records Project.

[2] Leonard W. Cowie, *Henry Newman: an American in London, 1708–43* (London and New York, 1956), has made full use of all these papers and contains an excellent bibliography showing other archives possessing Newman papers.

emigrants, mostly concerned with counselling emigrants at Plymouth and Liverpool, but in 1868 the Society's Liverpool chaplain began to make the round trips across the Atlantic to care for the spiritual needs of emigrants; in 1882 the Emigration Committee was created to supervise this work.[1]

Society for the Propagation of the Gospel in Foreign Parts,[2] 15 Tufton Street, LONDON, S.W.1

The Society was founded in 1701 and the American colonies were its chief field of missionary activity until the War of Independence. A guide to the Society's records is in preparation.

(Arrangement of 'A' to 'X' MSS. is alphabetical, *not* chronological.)

'A' MSS. Letters received (contemporary copies): 27 volumes.[3] 1702–36 (with a few earlier documents).

Letters from missionaries, would-be missionaries, potential supporters of the Society, those requiring its assistance (e.g., in books or cash), civil officials in the colonies, &c. Describe missionary activities; shortage of equipment; personal and civil affairs (the latter mainly from Governors and Lieutenant-Governors); work among Indians and Negroes, especially the education of Indian children; the cruelties of slavery; the building of churches; crops (e.g., tobacco in Virginia); &c. There are also offers of legacies, letters of complaint, requests for ministers, letters of introduction, &c. Include some letters of, or about, Francis Nicholson, who was Governor or Lieutenant-Governor of five colonies.

See also Andrews & Davenport, p. 332.

'B' MSS. Letters received (include the originals of many of the 'A' MSS. and a few miscellaneous documents): 25 volumes, bound under colonies,[4] 1702–99; also 16 or more boxes of unbound papers, 1701–1800.

Covered by the description of the 'A' MSS. above. The later letters include references to difficulties encountered by the Society's missionaries during and after the War of Independence. Vol. 5 contains papers relating to Thomas Tomlinson's attempts at running a school at New Bern, N.C., 1763–71.

See further details in Andrews & Davenport, pp. 332–3.

[1] See also W. O. B. Allen and E. McClure, *Two Hundred Years: the History of the Society for Promoting Christian Knowledge, 1698–1898*, pp. 402–21 (London, 1898). Contains extracts from reports by the Plymouth and Liverpool chaplains.

[2] Virginia material microfilmed by the Virginia Colonial Records Project.

[3] The Library of Congress, Washington, D.C., has both transcripts and microfilms of vols. 1–26.

[4] The Library of Congress has both transcripts and microfilms of vols. 1–25.

'c' MSS. Miscellaneous unbound manuscripts relating to the American colonies: 16 boxes. 1630–1811.

Include much correspondence, mostly pre-Revolution, from and to missionaries: early deeds to lands in America, 1691–1727; treatises on the state of the church in various colonies; certificates, testimonials, petitions from Indians and others; lists of subscribers to local churches; papers relating to charity schools; accounts, bills of exchange, receipts, and grants of salaries. The contents of the boxes are as follows: Box 1: New York, 1708–85. Box 2: North and South Carolina, 1712–84. *Also* 'Short remarks on Indian trade, Virginia'. Box 3: Connecticut, 1635–1796. Box 4: New England, 1630–1780; and New Hampshire, 1760–1811. Box 5: New Jersey, 1709–91; Maine, 1762–89; Maryland, 1760–2. Box 6: Massachusetts, 1711–98. Box 7: Pennsylvania, 1712–84. Box 8: (i) Rhode Island, 1712–85; (ii) Rhode Island, 1760–1800. Box 9: America generally, 1723–33; Georgia, 1758–82; Vermont, 1763; Virginia, 1711–13. Two boxes contain legal deeds. Three boxes of 'Unbound American papers'. One box bills of exchange and receipts. One box 'American papers—New York'. A box labelled 'S.P.G. and Government—North America, 1715–1830', contains only two papers relating to what is now the United States.

'D' MSS. Letters received: United States, 1852–9 and 1871–4, and America, 1875–7 and 1880–1930: 56 volumes.

These volumes contain miscellaneous letters concerned with such topics as co-operation in missionary work between the Church of England and the Protestant Episcopal Church in America; common days of prayer; the West Indian bishoprics; letters of introduction; and requests for historical information.

'G' MSS. Letters sent (copies): United States: 2 volumes. 1851–1928. (Also include a few letters from the United States.)

Deal with such matters as donations to the Society from the United States; visits of American prelates to Britain; requests for information by historians of individual churches and organizers of centenary and other celebrations; sale of the Society's property in the United States; &c.

'X' MSS.

Nos. 141–53: Letters sent (copies): 13 volumes. 1773–1833. Mostly to the Society's missionaries. The first two volumes, 1773–8 and 1778–84 (nos. 141 and 142), are devoted almost exclusively to America and deal particularly with the affairs of the English church in the rebel colonies. The succeeding volumes deal to a lesser extent with United States affairs—mainly with adjustments made by individual missionaries after the War of Independence.

No. 167: Letters (typescripts) relating to S.P.G. property in Vermont, New Hampshire, Connecticut, New Jersey, and Pennsylvania: 1 file. 1855–1907. Contains also a calendar of the manuscripts relating to the properties scattered throughout 'D' MSS. and 'G' MSS.

No. 171: Photostat of will, 1727, of Governor Francis Nicholson, bequeath-
ing most of his property, especially in New England, Pennsylvania, and
Virginia, to the Society, of which he was a member.

No. 234: Edmund Hobhouse (1817–1904). Five letters, 3 Oct.–12 Nov.
1853, to his parents, written while visiting the United States with an S.P.G.
delegation. Hobhouse attended a Protestant Episcopal convention in New
York, and then travelled to Philadelphia, Baltimore, through up-state
Maryland, Washington, D.C., Norfolk, Va., Wilmington, N.C., Charleston,
S.C., and Savannah, Ga., visiting Protestant Episcopal bishops, clergymen,
churches, and other institutions. Letters contain numerous observations on
slavery.

REPORTS OF THE SOCIETY (printed), 1704– . ANNIVER-
SARY SERMONS, 1702– .

The Reports of the Society contain lists of the names of the missionaries in
America up to the War of Independence, extracts from their letters, and
other material relating to the state of the church in the colonies.

JOURNALS AND MINUTES OF THE SOCIETY AND ITS COM-
MITTEES.[1] 1701– . (Some include abstracts of letters received.)

(a) Journal. Since 1701 the S.P.G. has kept a Journal, that is, a record of
the minutes of the meetings of the Society as a whole. The early volumes often
record the discussions and resolutions concerning such matters as the
appointment of missionaries to work in the plantations, their work there
and payment to them. The later volumes contain occasional references to
American bishops, S.P.G. property in America, &c. For much of the period
there are two copies of the Journal, as follows:

  (i) Rough copy, 1714–1833: 107 volumes.
  (ii) Fair copy, 1701–1833; changes to rough copy, 1833–1932: 62
volumes from 1701 to 1932. (Another fair copy of 1701–17 is bound in two
large folio volumes.)
  Appendixes to the fair copy contain copies of important documents.

(b) Minutes of the meetings of the Standing (i.e. executive) Committee of
the S.P.G., 1702– . Sometimes two copies exist, as with the Journal of the
Society:

  (i) Rough copy, 1714–1819: 64 volumes.
  (ii) Fair copy, 1702–58: volumes 1–8. Changes to rough copy, 1833–
1938: 3 unnumbered volumes, 1833–8, and volumes 21–76, 1839–1938.

----

[1] The Library of Congress has prints or photostats of volumes 1–24 of the fair
copy of the Journal, and microfilm of volumes 23–54 and App. B. of this; microfilms of volumes 1–8 of the fair copy of the Minutes of the Standing Committee
and of volumes 28–49 of the rough copy of these.

ACCOUNTS AND ACCOUNT BOOKS. 1701–   .

Include entries of payments to missionaries, many of whom worked in the American colonies before the War of Independence.

See Andrews & Davenport, p. 333.

FULHAM PAPERS: Letters from abroad to the Bishop of London. Letter. 1820.

Volume 1 of the four volumes contains a letter, Charleston, S.C., 22 June 1820, from Frederick Dalcho, giving an account of the progress of the Protestant Episcopal Church in the United States since its foundation in 1789.

MANUSCRIPTS OF DR. BRAY'S ASSOCIATES.

Those of American interest cover the period before the War of Independence.

See Andrews & Davenport, pp. 334–5, for a full description.

PRINTED MATERIAL IN THE LIBRARY.

Large collection of (mainly) sermons dating chiefly from the latter half of the nineteenth century, delivered in America or by American ministers, especially of the Protestant Episcopal Church, visiting Britain. Also annual reports of American churches and mission boards, reports of conferences, &c.

Diocese of Southwark, Bishop's House, St. George's Road, LONDON, S.E. 1

ARCHIVES.

Stonor, Monsignor Christopher (d. 1795). From 1748 to 1790 Stonor was agent in Rome for the affairs of the English Catholics. For information about the American material in the volume (MS. 37) of his copies of documents, 1759–90, held in the Diocesan Archives, *see* Andrews & Davenport, pp. 340–1, in the report on the Westminster Archdiocesan Archives.

Lady Spring-Rice, 36 Argyll Road, LONDON, W.8

SPRING-RICE, SIR CECIL ARTHUR (1859–1918). Correspondence: 39 manuscript or typescript and 75 photostat letters. 1887–1918.

Diplomat, Ambassador to Washington 1913–18. Mostly personal correspondence between Sir Cecil Spring-Rice and Mr. and Mrs. Theodore Roosevelt.

N.R.A. 5574.

Stationers' Hall Registry, Stationers' Hall Court, LONDON, E.C.4

The Records of the Stationers' Company contain a few references to the Virginia lottery and other minor connexions with Virginia. The records are printed in *The Records of the Court of the Stationers' Company, 1602–40*, edited by William Jackson (London, 1957).

Trinity House, Tower Hill, LONDON, E.C.3

EARLY TRANSACTIONS AND MINUTE-BOOKS.

These records were saved although the rest of the library was completely destroyed by enemy action in 1940. They are described in Andrews & Davenport, pp. 277–9, and in H.M.C. viii (i), pp. 235–62.

University of London Library, Senate House, Malet Street, LONDON, W.C.1

Printed *Catalogue of the Manuscripts and Autograph Letters in the University [of London] Library* (London, 1921), together with the *Supplement, 1921–1930* (London, 1930); also a typescript catalogue 'Additions to the manuscripts and autograph letters received in the University of London Library since 1930', is available in the Library.

PRIVY COUNCIL PAPERS. 2 papers. 1609. (MS. 20)

The papers in this volume, covering *c.* 1600–25 (where dated), are apparently transcripts in contemporary handwriting. They include the following:

No. 15. 'The coppie of a comission made by Duke Montmorancye Lo: of Dampvill and Admirall of France unto the Lo: Raverdiere for createinge of him Vice Admirall, and freeinge of his shippes and provisions made for his voyage unto Guyana and other parts of Affrica and America in the yeare of o^r Lord 1609.' (ff. 159v.–161v.)

No. 16. 'The coppie of a comission made by the Lord of Raverdiere by vertue of the K[ing] of Frances letters unto Robert le Brette Lo: Dubose, constituteinge the said Lord Dubose his Lieftennant in the countries of Guyana and other parts of America in A° 1609.' (ff. 162–3v.)

H.M. CUSTOMS REVENUES. 1 volume. 1679–1760. (MS. 46)

The gross and net produce of all the branches of the revenue under the management of the Commissioners of H.M. Customs. It includes tables of sums yielded, e.g. from enumerated duties from the American plantations,

1704–11, and there are other American references. A pencil note on one of the end-papers says that this volume was specially drawn up by the officers of the Crown for the private use of successive Chancellors of the Exchequer.

HUDSON'S BAY COMPANY. 1 volume. *c.* 1801. (MS. 147)

Bound volume of extracts from documents originally written 1684–1719. This is stamped with the Company's coat of arms. The documents are petitions, proclamations, reports of court decisions, &c., relating to the Company; for example, a petition to the King against interlopers, 1688; abstract of the rights of the Crown of England to Hudson Bay in 1699.

VALUE OF TRADE OF GREAT BRITAIN AND IRELAND. 1 volume of statistical tables. 1698–1765. (MS. 126)

The table giving the value of exports and imports to Great Britain compared with the excess of each country. From 1747 to 1762 gives separate figures for each colony under the general heading of 'Plantations'. There are various other entries for the plantations. The manuscript has bookplates of John Baker Holroyd, 1st Earl of Sheffield.

COMMITTEE OF PRIVY COUNCIL FOR TRADE AND PLANTA-TIONS. Report, 1703 (1 volume). Minutes, 1823–7 (5 volumes).

(*a*) MS. 78. Volume entitled 'Report from the Commissioners of Trade and Plantations, 16 December 1703', presented to the House of Lords. As well as details about the trade of each colony the report contains information on defence measures taken to protect the subjects and the trade of the American colonies during the war against France and Spain. There is also a copy of 'Proposals to the Lords Commissioners for Trade and Plantations about the surrender of my province of Pennsylvania', drawn up by William Penn.

(*b*) Minutes (5 volumes). (M.S. 159.) These volumes consist mainly of brief statements that reports from, *inter alia*, British consuls in the United States or letters relating to trade with that country have been received; in a few cases there is included also the Committee's minute or letter dealing with the issue raised—e.g. a discussion, 5 Mar. 1824, of American duties on rolled and hammered iron, containing the suggestion that the British should threaten as a reprisal to treat American cotton as a manufactured product for tariff purposes.

GEE, JOSHUA (d. 1730). Memorials relating to the trade of the plantations. *c.* 1720. (MS. 99)

From a bound volume of papers covering various features of mercantilist policy. In a note on a fly-leaf in the handwriting of George Chalmers, Scottish antiquarian, Joshua Gee is described as a London Quaker merchant, frequently consulted by the government on matters of trade, manufacture, and the colonies, who wrote tracts and *The Trade and Navigation of*

Great Britain considered (London, 1729). The papers were, he says, preserved in the archives of the Board of Trade, but never printed.

(*a*) 'Memorial from Mr. Joshua Gee relating to the trade of the plantations, particularly with respect to iron, copper, hemp, flax, boards, timber, and to the enumerated commodities which are now restrained to be first imported into Great Britain', 1721.

(*b*) 'Memorial to the Honourable the Lords Commissioners for Trade and Plantations.' The answer of Joshua Gee to the Board of Trade on the subjects proposed to him by the Board respecting the trade, raw produce and manufactures of the Colonies and about producing naval stores in the Colonies. (In a letter of the Board, 20 Feb. 1728.)

ROYAL AFRICAN COMPANY. Petition. 1742. (MS. 109)

A petition to the King in Council for a Charter to enable the Company 'to fit out one or more ship or ships of force for the attacking surprising taking or destroying the ships goods settlements factories or lands of the Spaniards or any other of your Majesty's enemies in America'. Dated 'African House March yᵉ 26th 1742'.

GLEN, JAMES (1701–77). 'Answers . . . to the queries from the . . . Lords Commissioners for Trade and Plantations'. *c.* 1749 (1 volume). (MS. 114)

Governor of South Carolina 1743–56. A detailed description of the climate, soil, administration, trade, Indian tribes, &c., of South Carolina, with some statistical tables of exports and imports, &c.

PORTEUS LIBRARY.

The library collected by Beilby Porteus (1731–1809), Bishop of London 1787–1809, contains over 150 uncatalogued volumes of pamphlets. They contain an extensive section on the War of Independence, and another on the West Indian slave trade. Thirty-eight volumes of pamphlets are specifically entitled 'Slave Trade', and range in date 1772–1807. It is probable that a considerable number of works in both these categories are also in the Goldsmiths' Library.

HOLROYD, JOHN BAKER, 1st Earl of Sheffield (1735–1821). (MS. 139)

A French translation of Lord Sheffield's *Observations on the Commerce of the American States*, 1784.

ABSTRACT OF SHIPS REGISTERED IN THE BRITISH DOMINIONS, 1788–93 (6 volumes). (MS. 230)

Section 5 of each volume contains an examination taken at the Committee of the Council for Trade and Plantations with the opinions of insurers and underwriters on the shipping and manner of navigation of Britain compared with that of the nations of Europe and the United States. A comparison is made of premium rates, &c.

IRVING, THOMAS. 'State of the navigation revenues and commerce of Great Britain.' 1790 (1 volume). (MS. 140)

A report made to Pitt by Thomas Irving, 12 Dec. 1791. It includes the number of United States ships from each state entering and clearing British ports; a report on the condition of British trade with the American states; a comparison of British and foreign shipping entering and clearing the ports of the American states.

AUTOGRAPH LETTER COLLECTION.

No. 47. P. E. Du Ponceau. Philadelphia. 19 Nov. 1831, to J. Vaughan, Esq., asking him to send the enclosed [a copy of *An historical review of the . . . Silk Culture, Manufacture and Trade in Europe and America*, &c. (Philadelphia, 1831), in which the letter is inserted] 'to your excellent nephew'.

No. 51. Henry George. New York, 16 Sept. 1891, to Swann Sonnenschein & Co., relating to the publication of his *The Condition of Labor: an open Letter to Pope Leo XIII* (New York, 1891).

No. 75. Thomas Babington Macaulay, 1st Baron Macaulay. London, 14 Oct. 1853, to Augustus de Morgan, thanking him for some papers, 'I am afraid that I shall not live to write the history of the American war. Indeed heaven knows when I shall have done with King William.'

No. 147. Henry James. London, 1886–98, to 'Lady Blanche'.

MANTON MARBLE COLLECTION.[1] 190 file boxes of newspaper clippings and pamphlets and 26 boxes of scrapbooks. Mainly 1860–90.

Manton Marble (1835–1917), editor and owner of the Democratic New York *World*, 1862–76; part author of Tilden's platform of 1876 and also of the Democratic platform in 1884; he was sent abroad by President Cleveland in 1885 to sound European governments on bimetallism. The collection consists of his own library of press clippings. Boxes 1–26 are 'biographies' of persons, notably Tilden; 27–51 are 'political series'; 52–187 are 'special collections'. The 'special collections' contain what must be a unique coverage of the silver controversy and also of the Election Commission over the disputed presidential election of 1876. The collection would be invaluable for any life of Tilden, work on bimetallism, or the Democratic Party after the Civil War, especially in New York. He appears to have clipped every important comment or story on these topics.

[1] This collection was part of a bequest made to the Institute of Historical Research in 1921 by Marble's step-daughter, Lady (Martin) Conway. A typescript catalogue in two volumes is in the library, giving the general content of each box and a detailed inventory listing each clipping up to Box 101. There is also a chronological card index to the boxes 27–51, 'political series'.

GOLDSMITHS' LIBRARY OF ECONOMIC LITERATURE.
Printed material, pamphlets and broadsides.

The Goldsmiths' Library, presented to the University of London by the Goldsmiths' Company in 1903, is a valuable collection of more than 60,000 books and pamphlets of the sixteenth to nineteenth centuries, in English and other languages, covering a wide field of economic, historical, and social interest. It is naturally particularly strong in English material on trade and finance. Besides works of particular interest for American studies, such as a large number of pamphlets on the causes of the War of Independence and the War of 1812, the library's collection of early works on trade and on emigration is relevant, and it possesses also a collection of works on slavery. For the period after 1800, this collection is of approximately 400 volumes, among which there are 49 volumes of bound pamphlets. There are approximately 30 bound volumes of pamphlets on bimetallism, 1876–1904.

The Ludlow Collection of nineteenth-century trade union pamphlets contains material relevant to trade union assistance to emigrants. Broadsides in the Library are listed in a *Catalogue of the Collections of Proclamations and Broadsides in the University Library* (London, 1930), and include several on trade and economic affairs in the plantations.

Muniment Room, Imperial College of Science and Technology, LONDON, S.W.7

HUXLEY PAPERS. 62 letters, notebook. 1864–95.

The papers of Thomas Henry Huxley (1825–95) are listed in W. R. Dawson, *The Huxley Papers, a Descriptive Catalogue of the Correspondence, Manuscripts and Miscellaneous Papers . . .* (London, 1946). Huxley kept in touch with many of the American publicists of the new scientific movements associated with himself and Darwin, as well as receiving numerous random letters from American admirers (or vilifiers), an astonishingly large number of which are preserved. Most of the letters are to Huxley; there are comparatively few from him. The main American correspondents are:

Agassiz, A. Twenty-nine letters, 1874–95, exchange of scientific news and schemes for the promotion of science.

Fiske, John. Eleven letters, 1873–93.

Gilamn, Daniel Coit. Four letters, all of 1876, and concerned with Huxley's address at Johns Hopkins University in that year.

Lowell, James Russell. Fourteen letters, 1880–7, one is about the Copyright Treaty, together with a draft of Huxley's reply.

Yeomans, Edward Livingston. Four letters, 1864–71, about the sale of scientific books, particularly Huxley's, in America.

There is also a small notebook that is a diary kept by Huxley on his American tour of 1876.

Y

British Library of Political and Economic Science, London School of Economics, Houghton Street, LONDON, W.C.2

JEVONS COLLECTION.

One hundred and thirty-four volumes, mainly of eighteenth and nineteenth century pamphlet and other printed matter, including a large number on a variety of American economic and social subjects. A list is available, and all the items are included individually in the catalogue of the Library and in the *London Bibliography of the Social Sciences*.

LETTER COLLECTION, Volume II. 3 letters. 1794, 1872.

(*a*) Two letters, 1794, from William Wilberforce to George Hammond, the British Minister in Washington. One, 15 Mar., seeks a job in America for someone, and the other, 23 June, introduces the son of Sir George Strickland who is touring America.

(*b*) 4 Dec. 1872, from Pierre Girard, London agent of the New York *World*, to C. C. Cattell, asks for information concerning republicanism in England to pass on to readers in the United States. Following a republican conference at Sheffield he wants to know whether a class of politically minded persons who really desire republicanism exists, and if so how they propose to act. Relays Froude's comments on the powerful effect of American opinion on English politics.

BRAY, JOHN FRANCIS (1809–97).

Social reformer. Bray, born in the United States, went to England with his father in 1822; he returned to America in 1842. The Library holds the following material by or about Bray:[1]

(*a*) Bray Collection. 4 volumes. 1823–1943.

One of these volumes contains the typescript (carbon copy) account by Miss Agnes Inglis, Ann Arbor, Mich., 13 June 1943, of her visits in 1937 and later to Bray's daughter-in-law, Mrs. Anna Bray, in Pontiac, Mich., and of the manuscripts and other material relating to Bray found there. It is these letters and papers of which the Library now has photostats or originals.

The remaining three volumes contain notes by Miss Inglis; photostats or original clippings by or about Bray from the *Leeds Times* and from various American labour and socialist periodicals; a manuscript notebook used by Bray for French lessons (he visited Paris in 1842) and as a scrapbook for

[1] Much of this material has been used by M. F. Lloyd-Prichard for the introduction to Bray's *A Voyage from Utopia* (London, 1957). See also H. J. Carr, 'John Francis Bray', *Economica*, n.s. vol. vii, pp. 397–415, 1940; and M. F. Joliffe, 'John Francis Bray', *International Review of Social History*, vol. iv, pp. 1–36, 1939.

news-cuttings on astronomy and other scientific subjects; and photostats of letters from and to Bray. Included is the photostat of a letter from Bray to his mother, 1823; and photostats of letters to Bray from his brother, Charles Frederick Bray, Boston, 1835–42, from Elihu Finnie, Leeds, 1883 and 1894, and from Karl Reuben, Pittsburgh, Pa., 1893, 1895, and 1896.

(*b*) Original manuscripts of articles and books by Bray:

'A voyage from Utopia to several unknown regions of the world by Yarbfj translated from the American', 1842.[1]

'Common sense for farmers' (incomplete), *c.* 1870.

'Machine-made Christians', *c.* 1870.

'The wage workers' declaration of rights', *c.* 1870.

'A new declaration of independence', *c.* 1875.

'The God of the Jews and the God of the universe; (and, Matter for thought)', *c.* 1880.

'Brief sketch of the life of John F. Bray', 1890–1.

The Library also has Bray's own copy of his *Labour's Wrongs and Labour's Remedy* (Leeds, 1839), with manuscript notes.

WEBB TRADE UNION COLLECTION.

The collection consists of manuscript and printed material collected for use in the Webbs' *History of Trade Unionism* (London, 1894), *Industrial Democracy* (London, 1897), &c. It contains manuscript notes and letters and printed trade union reports, rules, &c.; a list is available. The collection is in five parts: Section A. Chiefly manuscript material; Section B. Non-serial printed matter; Section C. Rules; Section D. Printed reports and other periodical material; Section E. Miscellaneous additional material.

The main American relevance of the collection is the material about trade union sponsored emigration to the United States.[2] In Section A the volumes of notes on various unions and industries include some reference to emigration, mainly copied from printed matter—see, e.g., volume XI for the Amalgamated Society of Carpenters Emigration Fund, and volume XVI for the Amalgamated Society of Engineers Emigration Fund; Section A also includes, in volume XLVII, seven pages of notes, 1913–14, on women in trade unions in the United States. The large collection of rules and journals in Sections C and D contain, for some unions, information on the subject of emigration, including, in C. 86, the manuscript rules, n.d., of the Potters' Emigration Society, London District Committee.

FARRER COLLECTION ON BANKING AND CURRENCY. 1864–98.

Sir Thomas Henry Farrer, 1st Baron Farrer (1819–99), was an active opponent of bimetallism and one of the founders in 1895 of the Gold Standard Defence Association. The collection consists of eleven volumes of

---

[1] Published in London, 1957.

[2] This material has been used by W. S. Shepperson, *British Emigration to North America* (Oxford, 1957), and by C. Erickson, *American Industry and the European Immigrant, 1860–1885* (London and Cambridge, Mass., 1957).

manuscript and printed letters and papers, and of news-cuttings. These mainly concern Indian currency, but an examination of the typescript calendar showed the following relevant material (*Letters unless otherwise stated*):

Volume I, items 1–2. 28 Sept. and 9 Oct. 1897, Charles Francis Adams to Farrer, giving an opinion on the importance of a statement of British policy on the Indian currency question.

Volume I, item 55. 8 Jan. 1897, E. L. Godkin to Farrer, concerning the visit to England of Senator Edward Oliver Wolcott, a bimetallist.

Volume III, item 55. 4 May 1894, Cecil [Spring-Rice?] to Stephen [Spring-Rice?], on American monetary policy and the free coinage of silver. (Typescript.)

Volume III, item 108. 13 Nov. 1898, Horace White to Lord Farrer, on financial conditions in the United States and India.

Volume VI, item 3. Horace White, *Answers to Questions of the Gold and Silver Commission*, 29 Sept. 1887. (Printed.)

Volume VI, items 6–7. [Sir David Miller Barbour], *Course of Trade between England and the United States*, Aug. 1887; and *Alteration of the Relative Scale of Prices in England and the United States*, Sept. 1887. (Printed.)

Volume VI, item 29. 21 Sept. 1887, David Ames Wells to Farrer, concerning the monetary conditions of California. (Printed.)

Volume VIII, item 56. Statistics of English and American national banks, the data for the latter covering 1864–93. *c.* 1894.

HUGHES, THOMAS (1822–96). Microfilm. 1880–93.

A microfilm presented by the Tennessee State Archives in 1959 of letters, newspapers, and pamphlets relating to Thomas Hughes and the foundation and management of the attempted colony of Rugby, Tenn.

PASSFIELD PAPERS. 1873–1938.

The papers of Sidney Webb, 1st Baron Passfield (1859–1947), and his wife, Beatrice (Potter) Webb (1858–1943).

I. Diaries.

Fifty-eight manuscript notebooks (each with two typescript copies) contain Beatrice Webb's diaries for 1873–1943.[1]

Volume 1 includes a precocious account of her first visit to the United States, Sept.–Dec. 1873. Her account is mainly topographical although while in Chicago she visited public schools; and in Salt Lake City she showed interest in Mormonism.

[1] See *My Apprenticeship* [to 1892] (London, 1926); *Our Partnership* [1892–1911], ed. by Barbara Drake and Margaret Cole (London, 1948); *Beatrice Webb's Diaries, 1912–1924*, ed. by Margaret Cole (London, 1952); and *Beatrice Webb's Diaries, 1924–1932*, ed. by Margaret Cole (London, 1956).

Volumes 17 and 18 are wholly concerned with the visit of Mr. and Mrs. Webb to the United States, 29 Mar.–10 July 1898; and volume 19, pp. 1–10 (of the typescript copy) with their stay in the recently annexed Hawaii, 13–20 July 1898. The Webbs ranged from New York to San Francisco. They made a special point of visiting universities and colleges. Among those they met, and in most cases interviewed, were Charles Francis Adams, Jane Addams, Governor Altgeld of Illinois, Senator Bailey, D. R. Dewey, President Eliot of Harvard, Worthington C. Ford, E. L. Godkin, Professor Jenks, Robert Lincoln, Henry Cabot Lodge, Seth Low, Josiah Quincy, Thomas B. Reed, Theodore Roosevelt, Albert Shaw, Morse Stephens, Von Holst, Mayor Van Wyck of New York, Lester Ward, Woodrow Wilson, Governor Wolcott of Massachusetts, and Carroll D. Wright. While in Washington, D.C., they attended sessions of both the House and the Senate, and observed the war fever over Cuba. They interviewed Reed and Wilson on the workings of American national government; stayed at Hull House in Chicago; and probed deeply into Mormon beliefs and practices in Salt Lake City, Utah. But their chief concern was the study of American municipal government, and for their reports and views of this topic the diary is invaluable. They devoted much time to observing the operations of Tammany Hall in New York.

Volume 18, pp. 58–70, is an essay entitled 'Superficial notes on American characteristics'.

II. Letters.

(a) Postcard from New York, 17 Sept. 1888, and a letter from Boston, 13 Oct. 1888, to Graham Wallas, written by Sidney Webb during his brief visit to the United States. The letter describes the Massachusetts Institute of Technology and Harvard University, and gives a detailed account of the wages of workers in the *Atlantic Monthly* printing works. Webb is of the opinion that Cleveland will carry all the doubtful states in the presidential election.

(b) Seven letters written during the Webbs' visit to the United States in 1898. Four from Beatrice Webb to Lady Kate Courtney and one to Mary Playne cover much the same ground as the diary entries. A letter, 26 Apr., from Sidney Webb to George Bernard Shaw, discusses the visits to Washington, D.C., and to various universities, and describes the American machinery of central government as 'infantile'; another, of 5 June, describes Chicago as 'viler than tongue can tell and hopeless as the Inferno'.

(c) Two letters to Beatrice Webb and one to Sidney Webb written by Sir Charles Philips Trevelyan while both they and he were in the United States in 1898. He touches on the corruption of Pittsburgh, Pa., city government and the attitudes to organization, &c., of the steelworkers; the filthiness of Chicago; war fever; the progress of the campaign for municipal ownership of utilities in the West. He met and describes Altgeld and William Jennings Bryan.

(d) Typescript copy of a six-page letter, c. Mar. 1924, from Beatrice Webb to a Miss Thomas on the differences in Britain and the United States on the questions of the regulation of women's labour and equal pay.

(e) Typewritten letter, Knoxville, Tenn., 14 Feb. 1938, from Herman Finer to Beatrice Webb, describing his work as director of an 'Administrative Study of the Tennessee Valley Authority'.

(f) Letter, Cardiff, 17 Sept. 1938, from Selig Perlman to Beatrice Webb, on American 'industrial government', especially in the coal industry.

VII. Articles and books.

Beatrice Webb, 'Round the English-speaking world', 1930's. A draft chapter in typescript intended for inclusion in *Our Partnership* but omitted by the editors (see their Preface, p. v). Written in the mid-1930's, it is simply a more polished version of the diary. The first 102 pages (with footnotes, which are not, of course, in the diary) relate to the American part of the journey.

AMERICAN ANARCHISM.

Material collected and notes made *c.* 1945–7 by A. W. Smith in the course of work on American anarchism, mainly in the era 1890–1920. There are letters from American informants, principally Agnes Inglis of the University of Michigan, supplying biographical information, and also originals and photostats of obscure anarchist leaflets and other publications. Notes and pamphlets on and by John Francis Bray are to be found, and also, for example, on George Henry Evans and family, in relation to Spenceanism and Shaker doctrines.

MOREL, EDMUND DENE (1873–1924). Papers.[1]

Political reformer; founder of the Union of Democratic Control. (This organization is said to have had some initial success in the United States, and it is likely that a thorough search of the very large collection of Morel's papers would yield some letters from Americans on its general work.)

Morel visited America in the last quarter of 1904 to arouse support for an investigation into Belgian misrule in the Congo Free State. Specifically, he addressed the Universal Peace Conference in Boston, October 1904, and interviewed Theodore Roosevelt and his Secretary of State, John Hay, on the topic. A file in the collection, 'Congo Reform Association: America', contains correspondence and papers (64 manuscript and 104 typed letters, and 8 printed papers), 1904–11. Most of the correspondence arises either directly from the visit, or from the associations established as a result of it. The letters, many to and from prominent journalists and publicists, show vividly how Morel built up in a very short time an effective lobby. A student of American attitudes towards imperialism would find this collection useful, particularly:

(a) A series of wide-ranging and thoughtful letters from Robert E. Park, the sociologist, as secretary of the Massachusetts Commission for International Justice.

[1] See Robert Wuliger, 'The idea of economic imperialism, with special reference to the life and works of E. D. Morel', Ph.D. thesis, University of London, 1953.

(b) A series from Thomas S. Barbour of the American Baptist Missionary Union.

(c) Two long letters from Senator J. T. Morgan of Alabama, 29 June and 6 Oct. 1904, both dealing candidly with the American Negro problem and speculating on the possibility of encouraging the emigration of educated American Negroes to help administer a reformed Congo Free State.

(d) 'Report of the Honorary Secretary of the Congo Reform Association on his visit to the United States', written by Morel for his British committee some time early in 1905, and containing an account of his short interview with Theodore Roosevelt, and of a longer and more informative one with John Hay.

LETTERS OF EMIGRANTS TO AMERICA. 1745–1911.

Approximately 400 original letters and photostat and typewritten copies of letters are deposited in the Library by the British Association for American Studies. The letters were collected by the editors during the compilation of the present work.[1] Unless otherwise stated, the entries below are photostats and the originals are still in private hands.

The letters commonly contain information about the Atlantic crossing, comparative prices, land values, the state of crops and industry, wages, advice to prospective immigrants and family news; where the writer describes some particular event, this is mentioned below.

29 June 1745
Lieut.-Col. Arthur Noble, Louisbourg, N.S., to Edward Noble (in Ireland?). Officer in regiment of New England troops. Describes the military engagements leading up to the capture of Louisbourg.

3 Feb. 1752
J. W. Noble, Boston, to an unknown correspondent (in Ireland?). Suggests opening up trade with the recipient in Irish linen and woollen goods in return for butter from Boston.

5 June 1775
James Aitken, Wilmington, N.C., to his father, John Aitken, Glasgow. Presbyterian minister and schoolteacher. His plans for buying a plantation and slaves; local people drilling regularly.

1785–1869
c. 150 letters from the Fridge and Murdock families of Philadelphia, later Baltimore, to relatives living in Elgin and Forres, Scotland. Alexander Fridge emigrated to Philadelphia in 1785 and later set up a dry goods business in Baltimore. The letters contain much information about life, politics, and trade in Philadelphia and Baltimore; and American investments made on behalf of Scottish relatives. (Originals.)

11 July 1786
John Wilson, Philadelphia, to Jonathan Dixon, Cockermouth, Cumberland. Trade and politics. (Original.)

[1] Some of these letters are being prepared for publication for the Association by Dr. Charlotte Erickson.

1815–21, 1855–6
Nine letters from Samuel Mearbeck to relatives in Sheffield. A cutler and would-be farmer. The first four letters concern his attempts to cross the Atlantic, and include an account of a shipwreck. Mearbeck sold plated goods which he had brought with him, and with the profits bought land in Randolph county, Va. The last two letters include accounts of conditions of life in the Allegheny Mountains. Also six letters, 1855–6, between executors and lawyers concerned after Mearbeck's death with his estates in Buchanan county, Va. (Typescripts. Typescripts also in Sheffield City Libraries.)

10 Feb. 1815
Robert Gamble, off Mobile, Ala., to Thomas Woodward, Diss, Norfolk. Describes the expedition against New Orleans.

1816–30
Fifteen letters from T. L. Ogden, New York, to Mr. or Miss Lawrence, c/o Forde & Co., Liverpool. Stockbroker and land agent. The letters are about American investments made on behalf of the Misses Lawrence. Ogden was also interested in settling land on an estate in the St. Lawrence area and during the 1820's his letters tell of improvements to the land, the type of settlers required and answer queries raised by prospective immigrants.

Three letters, 15 Jan.–14 Nov. 1817, from Samuel Williams, broker, of London, to Forde, Liverpool, about the purchase of Louisiana stock. (Originals.)

1820–5
Eight letters from Nathaniel Haley to his father Jeremiah Haley, Great Horton, Liverpool. Lead miner and trader. He seems, after much wandering, to have established himself as a lead miner in Missouri, trading lead for whisky, flour, beef, &c., in Cincinnati, and trading these on the return journey. Comments on social conditions.

23 June 1820
James Stott, New York, to his wife in Bolton, Lancs. Recent immigrant. (Typescript.)

1829–46
Twenty-one letters to Jonathan Morris, a joiner of Tyldesley Banks, near Bolton, Lancs., from brothers and sisters in America. Andrew and Jane Morris emigrated in 1829 and worked as weavers in cotton factories, first in Germantown and Philadelphia, later on power looms in Rochdale. They were joined by other members of the family, all weavers, except one steam boiler maker. In 1837 a slump in cotton led other members of the family to leave Massachusetts and buy land in Ohio, where they grew tobacco, except for one brother who started his own woollen factory. Much information about weaving processes and farming. (Originals in Lancashire Record Office, Preston.)

20 Mar. 1829
Jonas Booth, New Hartford, Oneida county, N.Y., to a brother and sister (in Yorkshire?). Emigrated 1828; working in cotton mills in winter and mowing during summer; simple social observation. (Typescript.)

23 June 1829
E. Nudham, Albany, N.Y., to John Blackman, Maidstone. Recent immigrant.

29 Aug. 1829
Joseph Hirst, Equality, Gallatin county, Ill, to his son, Samuel Hirst, near Leeds. Saltmaker. Urging son and family to join him.

1831–1876
Fourteen letters from William and Rev. Thomas Corlett to Thomas Corlett, Orrisdale, Kirk Michael, Isle of Man. William Corlett emigrated with his family in 1827 to a Manx settlement at Newburgh, Ohio, as a farmer. His son became a schoolteacher, and later a clergyman of the Protestant Episcopal Church. (Originals in the Manx Museum, Douglas, Isle of Man.)

1831–8
Nine letters from John Fisher, Michigan, to his mother and brother, Brooke, Norfolk. Farmer. Impressed by freedom from taxation and church-tithes; opinions on the rebellion in Canada, currency problems, and slavery. (Originals in Ipswich and East Suffolk Record Office, Ipswich.)

8 Jan. 1832
Hannah, William, and Jane Young, nr. York, Canada, to relatives at Ellerby-nigh-Whitby, Yorks. Recent immigrants; tavern-keeping; intending to buy land and trade in cattle.

1833–59
Fourteen letters from Walter and John Birket(t), Peoria and Mount Pleasant, Ill., to relatives near Preston, Lancs. Farmers (John was also working a small coal mine on his land). The letters complain of the currency crisis and land tax; they try to raise English support for building a Protestant Episcopal Church and school in Mount Pleasant; urge Lancashire clothworkers to settle with them rather than with the Mormons in Nauvoo, Ill. (Originals in the Lancashire Record Office, Preston.)

10 Jan. 1833
Charles Johnston, Perth Amboy, N.J., to Thomas Tryon, Northants. Recent immigrant. Working on a claybank, and harvesting. (Original in Northamptonshire Record Office, Northampton.)

30 Sept. 1833
Edward Trayes, Cleveland, Ohio, to his wife in Lancashire. Recent immigrant. Tavern-keeping. (Typescript.)

19 Feb. 1834
H. J. M. Nudham, Monroe township, Ohio, to W. Barns, Staplehurst, Kent. Dairyman and farmer.

1834
Two letters to Mr. Poulton, Sen., Hounslow, Middlesex. One, 10 Mar. 1834, from his son George Poulton, Troy, N.Y., a schoolteacher. The other, 26 May 1834, from his daughter-in-law Mary Poulton, Lockport, N.Y., Recent immigrants. Misfortunes.

1836, 1838
Two letters from Robert and Betsy Meatyard to Mrs. Mary Meatyard, Twyford, Dorset; one, 22 Mar. 1836, from Alton, Ill., and the other, 29 Jan. 1838 from Prasau Creek. Recent immigrants. (Originals in the Dorset Record Office, Dorchester.)

1837–56
Ten letters from or about John Hesketh, Pittsburgh, Pa., area, to his brother Robert Hesketh, Manchester. Selling confectionery. Attacks banking principle; worried by currency problems; Canada question; economic situation during 1840's; criticism of Mormons.

c. 1840–50
Mary Collings to her sister. Diary of a voyage from Appledore, nr. Bideford, Devon, to New York.

1840
Three letters from James Booth, New York, to his wife near Huddersfield, Yorks. Cloth trader on business visit to New York and Toronto.

1842, 1845
Two letters to Daniel Carpenter, Wotton-under-Edge, Glos. One, 16 Feb. 1842, is from his son Reubin, Winterville, Jefferson county, Ohio. The other, undated but postmarked Boston, 1845, is from his son Thomas, a soldier.

1843–9
Seven letters from Thomas Wozencraft, Watkinson and Cedar Hill, Ga. Six are to his son John, Kington, Herefordshire, and one to David Lewis, Carmarthen. Farmer and cotton planter. Failure of crops; scarcity of money; low land values; threats of war; facing ruin.

1844–54
Eight letters from Stephen and Ann Longstroth to Thomas Longstroth, Settle, Yorks. Carpenter. Settled first in Rockport, Mo.; then became Mormons and joined the settlement in Nauvoo, Ill. Information about the building of the city, Mormon life and customs; accounts of the murder of the prophets Joseph and Hiram Smith, 1845, and of the expulsion of the Mormons from Nauvoo and the trek to Salt Lake City, Utah, 1849.

1 Mar. 1844
William Walters, Governors Island, N.Y., to Charles Walters, Stockport, Cheshire.

9 Mar. 1844
W. C. Beardsall, South Walpole, Haldimand county, Upper Canada, to
Mr. and Mrs. Foster, Sheffield. Farmer and gunsmith. Describes flora,
fauna, food, &c., of Upper Canada; describes the town and its inhabi-
tants and social occasions; his opinion of emigrant societies and schemes.
(Original in Sheffield City Libraries.)

24 Sept. 1845
James Beck, Dinsmore, Shelley county, to his nephew James A. Beck,
Gilford, County Down. Farmer. State of politics and agriculture.

28 Sept. 1845
E. Gilby, Union Rock county, Wisconsin Territory, to Mrs. Gilley,
Whitton Power, Rothbury, Northumberland. Farmer.

5 July 1846
Rebecca Butterworth, 'Backwoods of America', to W. W. Barton,
Rochdale, Lancs. Misfortunes; returning to England.

1848–65
Three letters from John Griffiths, Illinois, to relatives in Shropshire.
Farmer. One letter, Nauvoo, describes how most of their English neighbours (presumably Mormons) have moved to the West, but they themselves have not been molested by mobs (1850). Greatly upset by the
death of Lincoln; high profits from farm due to war.

1848, 1854
John Norman, Harlem, N.Y., 30 Jan. 1848, to John Philpot, Walpole,
Suffolk. Also a letter, 10 May 1854, from Mary Smith, Harlem, to Mr.
Self, Woodbridge, Suffolk, about the death of John Norman. (Originals.)

1849–56
Four letters from Ann Whittaker, Monroe county, Ill., to her brother
James Smith, near Leeds, Yorks. Farmer's wife. Baptist affairs; state of
crops; cholera epidemics; floods.

1849–52
Four letters from James Roberts, Waterville, Conn., to his children in
Sheffield. Cutler. Gives news of other Sheffield men working in the knife
trade, and describes a knife factory. Sends messages to Chartist friends
in Sheffield. Describes how sixteen workmen, all from Sheffield, are
forming their own company, all the shareholders to be working men.
(Photostats also in the Sheffield City Libraries.)

1850, 1851
Two letters from George Fewins, Jackson county, Mo., to the overseers
of Cheriton Bishop, Devon. Carpenter. Asks for his family to be sent out
to him at the cost of the parish, or not at all. (Originals in Devon Record
Office, Exeter.)

24 Jan. 1850
John and Mary Thomson, Wingville, Wis., to a brother in Fifeshire. Farmers. Disapproving a prospectus inducing people to come to Wisconsin; their own opinion of prospects. (Typescript. Original in Library of the State Historical Society of Wisconsin, Madison 6.)

3 Mar. 1850
W. O. Williams (?), Covington, Ky., to W. Edwards, Pontypool, Mon. Bookkeeper in a wholesale drug store in Cincinnati. Information about local industries, steam ferries, &c., with a map.

1850
Two letters, 15 May and 19 Sept. 1850, from John Yates, Hall Town, Va., to Messrs. W. E. Bleaymire, Penrith. Property owner. Claims to English estates. (Originals.)

7 Sept. 1850
Henry Craig, Ohio City, to relatives. Farmer

21 Sept. 1851
Isaac Goodchild, South Kingstown, R.I., to his brother Richard Goodchild, near Newbury, Berks. Farmer.

14 Oct. 1851
'E', Jail Hospital, Chester, Pa., to Rev. Bleaymire, Penrith, Cumberland. Needing money. (Original.)

1852–4
Nine letters from John Ronaldson, East Braintree, Mass., and Schagticoke, N.Y., to his wife Elizabeth in Fife, Scotland. Flax journeyman (hackler). Dissatisfied with wages and conditions in linen industry; fear of import duties on linen goods being removed, 1853. Returned to Scotland in 1854.

1853, 1854
Two letters from — Salkield, Salt Lake City, Utah, to John Salkield, mason and bricklayer, of Tickhill, Yorks. Mormon. Describes Salt Lake City; discusses principles and history of Mormonism.

1857–73
Four letters from Ch. Aglionby, Charles Town, Va., to Messrs. Bleaymire, Penrith. Farmer. Property in England and losses during the Civil War. (Originals.)

1857–61
Four letters from John and David Hughes to their parents in Wales. Two are from David Hughes, Boston, 28 Sept. 1857 and n.d.; he describes the Atlantic crossing; he is working in a shop in Boston, and sends news of relatives and other Welshmen, sending a message in Welsh for a friend. Letter, 20 Oct. 1861, from John Hughes, Mianus, Conn., comments on the effects of the Civil War on business and describes how railways are transforming transport. An undated and unsigned extract from a letter

describes the quarrel between the actors Macready and Edwin Forrest, and the riots accompanying Macready's appearance in New York. Also describes prospects in Wisconsin.

28 July 1857
Alfred Green, New Rochelle, N.Y., to his mother in London. Impressions of New York en route for Canada.

1861–85
Twelve letters from Radcliffe Quine to relatives in the Isle of Man. Quine emigrated to the Atlantic coast of the United States in 1841; 1854–8 he worked in California as a ship's joiner; 1858–68 in British Columbia, goldmining; 1868 onwards travelled in the United States and South America, finally settling in Seattle, Wash., in the shipbuilding industry. The first letter is from Victoria, British Columbia, and the rest from Seattle. (Originals in the Manx Museum, Douglas, Isle of Man.)

1862–5
Corporal G. L. McCullock, 37th Regiment, New York Volunteers, United States Army General Hospital, Baltimore, 27 Mar. 1862, to his mother, Mrs. Martha McCullock, Ashton-under-Lyne, Lancs.: account of the Battle of Bull Run, where he was wounded and taken prisoner. Also a letter from his Captain, 18 June 1864, telling of his death on active service; and a letter, 14 June 1865, from the United States Treasury about Mrs. McCullock's eligibility for her son's war bounty.

1864–80
Four letters from Ann and Alfred Jones, Missouri, to C. R. Wace, solicitor, Shropshire. Farmers. Mostly about property in England. (Original.)

20 Jan. 1864
John Wiles, Camp of the 152nd Regiment, New York State Volunteers, Army of the Potomac, near Stevensburg, Va. Army life and conditions in the Southern states. (Original.)

1867–79
Seven letters from Thomas J. Bradley, Walden, N.Y., President of the New York Knife Co., to his business partner, James Roberts (*see* p. 331), and to relatives in Sheffield. Orders corkscrews and tweezers and asks for blade forgers and cutters to be sent out. (Photostats and other related letters in Sheffield City Libraries.)

4 Apr. 1870
James Glover, Buchanan, Allegheny, Pa., to Samuel Cleand, near Belfast. Emigrated 1870. Two sons have share in a factory; description of local industry.

23 Nov. 1870
Robert Savery, Phoenix, Ariz., to Richard Scarlett (in London?). Farming and irrigating government land. (Original.)

1871, 1891
Two letters from B. and A. E. Sheldon, Sheldon's Grove, Ill., to relatives in Lancashire. Farmers.

1872–4
Four letters from John and C. W. Bishop, Penn Yan, N.Y., to relatives in Framlingham, Suffolk. Farmer and butcher.

1876–80
Seven letters from W. Butcher and his daughter Marianne to relatives in Bristol. On two visits to relatives living in Brockton, Mass.; travel details; one letter from Washington, D.C.

28 Feb. 1877
Lizzie —, Plymouth, Mass., to Lewis Brown.

1879–87
Five letters from H. Reid (and her family), New York, to her sister in England. Owner of grocery business in Brooklyn.

1882–5
A large number of letters from W. B. Cowan and J. I. Cowan, Iowa and Wyoming, to relatives in Ireland, describing their experiences in learning American techniques of farming and then establishing a farm in Iowa. Also include accounts of ranch work, excursions to Wyoming, considerable discussion of farm prices and comments on habits of neighbours and on fellow Britishers in America. (Typescripts and microfilm.)

1885
Mr. Stewart of Edinburgh. Two-volume travel diary, with photographs. Visited Quebec, Montreal, Toronto, Niagara, Pennsylvania, and New York. Notes many social and business customs; describes people met, buildings, oil wells, &c. (Microfilm.)

1888
Three letters from J. W. Jendwine, Bowman's Bluff, N.C., to Mr. Wace, solicitor, Shropshire. Gentleman farmer. Farming conditions, information about borrowing money in United States; tries to borrow money to start a general store. (Original.)

28 Feb. 1911
W. R. Mellor, Secretary, Nebraska State Board of Agriculture, Lincoln, to the Mellor family, Oldham, Lancs. (Typescript.)

The Library, University College, Gower Street, LONDON, W.C.1

BENTHAM, JEREMY (1748–1832). Manuscripts.

Bentham's papers came to University College through John Bowring, his executor—see a *Catalogue of the Manuscripts of Jeremy Bentham in the Library of University College, London*, compiled by A. Taylor Milne (London, 1937).

The Americana is here listed under boxes and folders and is, indeed, listed rather than surveyed, since the labyrinthian character of the papers almost defeats summary. (*Letters unless otherwise stated.*)

Box 9, folder 3. Epping, 5 Oct. 1818, from Governor William Plumer of New Hampshire to Bentham, stating that he has communicated Bentham's papers to the legislature which has referred them to a committee.

Box 10, folder 26. 25 Jan. 1830, from Bentham to Southwood Smith, concerning a revised and augmented version of Edward Livingston's penal code for Louisiana[1] (copy sent by Livingston to Bentham, 10 Aug. 1829). Livingston has asked Bentham to prepare an article on his code for the *Jurist*, and Bentham passes the request on to Smith.

Box 12, folder 2. Correspondence, 1817. Five letters from W. Vaughan and two from J. Adams Smith to Bentham; letters from Bentham to John Quincy Adams (two), Francis Place, and Vaughan. Vaughan and Bentham were interchanging books and papers, Vaughan furnishing Bentham with information about the United States. John Adams Smith, nephew of John Quincy Adams, was on terms of friendship with Bentham and sent him information, pamphlets, and papers from the United States. Bentham requests John Quincy Adams to forward copies of his codification circulars to various people in America, including the President, Vice-President, Secretary of the Treasury, Professor Cooper of Philadelphia and governors of twenty states; a draft letter from Bentham to Adams asks for information about legal and religious matters.

Box 12, folder 3. Correspondence, 1817–18. Letters to Bentham from Henry M. Francis, Francis Place, Richard Rush, and J. Adams Smith (two); letters from Bentham to Francis (one copy, one draft) and to Smith. Mostly concerned with the circulation in the United States of Bentham's codification proposals. Letter, J. H. Hoe to Smith, asking as to receipt of packet of letters in the United States. Portion of *Niles' Register* (already in Bentham's possession), 9 May 1818. Letter concerning actions of General Jackson, unaddressed, unsigned, undated.

Box 12, folder 4. Correspondence, 1821. Four (one copy) letters from Richard Rush to Bentham, and three from Bentham to Rush; mostly making appointments to meet, but a few have information about the United States. Two letters from J. Adams Smith to Bentham concerning the exchange of pamphlets and tracts. Draft of a letter, 5 Aug. 1821, from Bentham to the editor of the *National Calendar* of the United States, requesting an index to the calendar (not sent).

Box. 12, folder 6. Correspondence, 1822. Letter from Bentham to Rush; two letters from Rush and three from J. Adams Smith to Bentham. Concern exchange of pamphlets, introductions, invitations, &c.

Box 12, folder 9. Correspondence, 1823. Three letters to Bentham from Rush and two from Bentham to Rush: deal with the arrangement of a meeting for Bentham to give Rush some news (about Spain?). Letter,

[1] *A System of Penal Law for the State of Louisiana* (Philadelphia, [1833]).

Philadelphia, 27 Aug. 1823, from Charles Jared Ingersoll to Bentham; account of recent happenings in the United States said to be (but not) enclosed.

Box 12, folder 10. 29 May 1823, from Bentham to Smith, inviting the American Consul, Hunter, to dine with him; and Smith's reply, 30 May.

Box 12, folder 12. 4 Dec. 1823, from Bentham to Rush, requesting a second copy of the New York constitution and assistance in transmitting a paper to 'your secretary of secretaries' (Copy). Rush, in replies of 5 and 8 December, promises to help.

Box 12, folder 13. Five letters to Bentham from Rush and three from Bentham to Rush, Jan. and Feb. 1824. Rush is about to open negotiations with the British government 'of great scope and more than common interest'. Bentham has lent Rush a copy of a letter from 'Col. L.S.' (Stanhope), and wants to borrow American books.

Box 12, folder 16. 18 June 1824, from Henry M. Francis to Bentham, introducing a Mr. Phillips, an officer of the American Army, and asking that Bentham explain the chrestomathic plan of education to him 'for the benefit of my countrymen'.

Box 17, folder 4. Extracts from Lord Sheffield's *Observation of the Commerce of the American States* (London, 1783). In Bentham's hand, with page references; five sheets. These extracts form part of the outlines of the different projects begun by Bentham on the *Manual of Political Economy, c.* 1790–1800.

Box 21, folder 4. 1811–1819.

(*a*) Draft of a letter, first sheet of postscript dated 9 Aug. 1811 and second sheet 1 Oct. 1811, from Bentham to President Madison discussing constitutional amendment and asking for various books and law reports.

(*b*) Information in Bentham's hand from Aaron Burr about legal codification; entered under places from which Burr wrote and containing notes on when to write to him, through whom, and under what alias, Oct. 1811.

(*c*) June 1817, from Bentham to John Quincy Adams on the law of libel, religious freedom, and the Unitarian and Trinitarian controversy in the United States. Adams answers in the margins of the same letter.

(*d*) Form of a letter of credence compared: from the United States President, and from George III. 1819.

Box 21, folder 5. 'Tabular Digest of the Constitution of the Anglo-American United States', June and Nov. 1818 (*c.* 60 pages). The manuscript, most of it in a copyist's hand, is largely from a work by Dr. William L. Smith of South Carolina, *Comparative View of the Constitutions of the Several States* (Philadelphia, 1796).

Box 21, folder 6. Parliamentary Reform Bill, United States election table notes (*c.* 15 pages). Bentham's comments, Oct. and Nov. 1818, on American constitutions, modes of voting, &c.

Box 21, folder 7. Collectanea. United States passport. *National Gazette*, 9 Nov. 1820. Governor's message, Pennsylvania, 1816. *National Intelligencer*, 15 May 1817. Letter of Secretary of Treasury transmitting estimate of appropriations, 1817. Printed testimony in the case of an ejectment pending for the recovery of Dr. William Oxley's estate in the city of Philadelphia, 1821, 1823, 1827 (17 items, none in Bentham's hand); these give information about politics and morals in the United States.

Box 23, folder 1. United States Constitutional Code: Bicameral system, anti-senatica. This is a marginal outline only. (7 sheets) Nov. 1829.

Box 24, folder 15. Tripoli. Bentham to John Quincy Adams, 10–23 Jan. 1823. Fourteen sheets in Bentham's hand, beginning 'The Barbary powers are a constant plague to you. I am not without hopes of seeing you rid of it'. Support of United States wanted in attempt to reform the government of Tripoli. (There is codification material on the backs of several sheets.)

Box 24, folder 16. Tripoli. Hassuna D'Ghies, Ambassador from the Sovereign of Tripoli at the Court of St. James, to John Quincy Adams, Secretary of State. Jan. and Feb. 1823. Ostensibly written by D'Ghies, but written for him by Bentham, this is a request to the United States to back the reform party in Tripoli. Bentham's manuscript is written on the back of cancelled codification offer manuscript. (58 pages copy and outline, 65 pages Bentham's manuscript.)

Box 44, folder 2. Rudiments of the United States Constitutional Code: marginal notes in Bentham's hand. 15–17 Mar. 1823 (3 sheets).

Box 44, folder 3.[1] United States Constitutional Code: An attack on the second chamber. Also codification material on back of sheets. 17 Mar. 1823–12 Feb. 1825.

Box 44, folder 4. United States Constitutional Code. Attack on second chamber, &c. In hands of various copyists; copied 1822–30.

Box 44, folder 5. United States Constitutional Code. Appendix in folder inscribed '1830 June 7, U.S. Antisenatica'. With further copy of manuscripts concerning second chamber. *c.* 1823–4. About twenty-five sheets, in copyist's hand.

Box 64, folder 2. Penal code: Neal's extracts. Apr.–Aug. 1826 (*c.* 120 sheets). These are brief digests in copyist's hand apparently intended by John Neal, American lawyer, to serve as a guide to penal law in the United States.

Box 158, folder 4. United States codification offer, 1811: Bentham to the people of the United States and to the President. Letter, 1817, Bentham to Madison (35 sheets). Marginal outlines in copyist's hand, with a few insertions in Bentham's hand.

Box 169, folder 19. *c.* 1781 from Bentham possibly to Benjamin Franklin Draft of a letter, probably not sent, about future codification.

[1] Part of the material in this folder was published in C. W. Everett, ed., *Anti-Senatica. An Attack on the American Senate, sent by Jeremy Bentham to Andrew Jackson* (Northampton, Mass., 1926) (Smith College Studies in History, vol. xi, no. 4).

OGDEN MANUSCRIPTS COLLECTION. Letters. 1808-78.

(a) Two letters from Aaron Burr to Jeremy Bentham: 22 Aug. 1808, 'It has been my misfortune to attract the attention of Lord Hawkesbury' (2nd Earl of Liverpool); is sending articles to Bentham which may assist in the cross-examination. 21-28 Dec. 1808, describing his travels in Oxford and Birmingham, and the people he has met *en route*.

(b) John Bright. 826 letters, 1847-78, to his second wife, Margaret Elizabeth Leathman. Bright often refers to American affairs, particularly immediately before and during the Civil War, but only in a commonplace manner.

(c) Harriet Martineau. Eleven letters addressed to William Tait, publisher of *Tait's Edinburgh Magazine*, are inserted in a copy of the first edition of Harriet Martineau's *Autobiography, with Memorials by Maria Weston Chapman* 3 vols. (London, 1877). Letter, 16 July 1837, deals with the reception of her book, *Society in America* (London, 1837), and comments on the work still to be done in the cause of abolition in America.

BROUGHAM, HENRY PETER, 1st Baron Brougham and Vaux (1778-1868). Correspondence. 1809-65.

Statesman. A collection of *c.* 50,000 letters to, and a great many from, Lord Brougham, *c.* 17,000 of which have been catalogued to date (Aug. 1957).[1] The letters reflect Brougham's extremely wide range of interests and activities, particularly in the causes of law reform, abolition of the slave trade and slavery, and education, as well as international affairs. Although he had some American correspondents and there are a number of letters dealing with American legal matters, the greatest number of letters with American interest to emerge so far are between Brougham and British correspondents. These include people with whom he corresponded over a period of years and who discussed all political affairs, including American, and British abolitionists and opponents of the slave trade. An index to the letters under the name of the sender is being compiled; an inspection of this index to date reveals as of especial interest:

(a) American correspondents. Edward Everett. Six letters, 1838-53. James A. Hamilton, lawyer and politician. 13 Mar. 1842. Thomas Jefferson. Copy of a letter, 25 Apr. 1824, to Rush. A. Stevenson. Two letters, 1829. Charles Sumner. Three letters, 1838-9. Lewis Tappan. Two letters, 1839, 1843. B. B. Thatcher, author and lawyer. Two letters, 1838.

(b) Letters on American legal matters. John Bell, Manchester, 3 Aug. 1830. John Christophers, 2 May 1851. Robert Dodge, 15 June 1847. Thomas Falconer, county court judge and legal author. Four letters, 1843-54. David Graham, American lawyer and author. 19 Jan. 1850. Henry Hiort, 27 Feb. 1839. Henry Knill, 14 Nov. 1837. John Charles Laycock. n.d., but endorsed 1847. John Livingston, 1 Feb. 1851. R. Shelton

[1] At the time of publication more than twice as many had been catalogued, which it was not possible to re-examine.

Mackenzie, author and journalist. Three letters, 1842–50. William Pentland, 6 Aug. 1850. Silas Moore Stilwell, American lawyer and financial writer. 10 June 1842.

(c) Some British correspondents discussing American affairs:

Baring, Alexander, 1st Baron Ashburton. A number of letters, 1842–7, including: 24 Sept. 1842, on the treaty he has negotiated with the United States; 6 Sept. 1843, on relations with the United States; 26 Sept. 1843, on Lord Palmerston's 'flippant opinions of America', his estimate of Thomas Jefferson; 27 Jan. 1844, American policy in Oregon and Texas.

Cassell, John, publisher and popular educator. Three letters: 25 Nov. 1859, leaving for America, the social science movement; January, endorsed 1860, on conditions in the United States; 2 Nov. 1860, on the success of his visit to the United States.

Copley, John Singleton, Baron Lyndhurst, Lord Chancellor. Many letters, 1828–62, including 20 Aug. endorsed '1852, the Yankee question settled'; n.d. [1852], the 'American affair'; n.d. endorsed 1858, ships of war sent to the American coast; n.d. [1858], right of search; 30 Sept. endorsed 1859, American policy; 12 Nov. endorsed 1859, relations with the United States, a contemporary account of Lord Chatham's speech on the American situation; n.d., endorsed 1861, the American situation; 18 Aug. 1862, Americans offended with Lord Brougham; 2 Sept. endorsed 1862, Northerners confident that the South will accept the abolition of slavery; 8 Oct. 1862, Lincoln and the Southern slaves; 24 Oct. endorsed 1862, Civil War; 18 Aug. endorsed 1863, bitterness of American feeling towards Britain; n.d. [1863], settlement of Northerners in South prolonging the Civil War; n.d. endorsed 1863, victory of Vicksburg great blow to South.

Gladstone, William Ewart. Three letters: 31 July 1843, Slave Trade Suppression Bill; 15 Jan. 1862, Seward's dispatch and the attitude of British law officers to his doctrine; 12 Sept. 1864, hopes success at Atlanta, Ga., will not encourage the federal cause too much.

Hall, Basil (1788–1844), naval captain and author. Letter, 31 Oct. 1828, on his visit to New York, American mechanics' institutes, Carvells of New York, best agent for the publications of the Society for the Diffusion of Useful Knowledge.

Law, Edward, 1st Earl of Ellenborough. Many letters, 1831–65, including: 9 Dec. 1845 and Dec. 1861 on France and America; 21 Jan. 1863 on Lincoln's Proclamation, 'one of the most wicked acts in history'.

Martineau, Harriet. Four letters. Three, 1836, on American copyright, and one, 21 Nov. 1858, on the American Anti-Slavery Society.[1]

Parkes, Joseph. Many letters, 1834–60, particularly on the Civil War.

There are also letters from Lord Brougham, 1 Aug. 1812 to T. Thornely on the War of 1812, and 30 Sept. 1842 to Lord Grey on the American offer on the Boundary Question in 1833.

(d) Letters about slavery and the slave trade with particular reference to America. (Many of these are taken from series of letters covering a period

[1] See R. K. Webb, *Harriet Martineau, a Radical Victorian* (London, 1960).

of years.) Sir Thomas Fowell Buxton. Five letters, 1827–44. Louis Alexis Chamerovzow, secretary of the British and Foreign Anti-Slavery Society. Several letters, 1855–65. Thomas Clarkson. Several letters, 1814–43. Thomas Denman, 1st Baron Denman. Many letters, 1842–51, including several on the African Squadron. George Hamilton Gordon, 4th Earl of Aberdeen. Letters, 1830–58. Hunter Gordon, 1842–4. Joseph Sturge, 1837–59. William Wilberforce, 1809–32. Zachary Macaulay, 1811–37.

There are letters from various anti-slavery societies to Brougham, mainly 1830–40, which, though largely concerned with the West Indies, also contain American references; there are also four letters, 1859–62, from the Young Men's Anti-Slavery Society.

(e) Letters containing miscellaneous information about America. Antonio de Anina to Professor Manvers, 20 Apr. 1857, about life in Memphis, Tenn. Thomas Dodds, 18 July endorsed 1835. United States newspapers; comparative prices. Henry Jones, 6 Feb. endorsed 1838. The poems of Phillis Wheatley. G. Joy, 19 Apr. 1848. Orders in Council and the United States. J. Larish, 19 Oct. 1812. News from Philadelphia of impending attack on Canada. James Lock, 23 May 1822. Russia, America, and England. George McHenry, 27 Aug. 1861. Sending a copy of a speech by Jas. A Bayard. Thomas Martin, 1 Aug. 1812. England and America. John G. Parker, 25 Aug. 1842. Sad case of Americans transported to New South Wales.

(f) Emigration.

Although Brougham was interested in emigration and corresponded with various emigration societies, there are few direct references to emigration to America. Letters from James Mill, 5 Feb. 1831, from John Bright, 5 July 1842, and from Alexander Mundell, 26 Feb. 1831, make general observations on emigration.

SOCIETY FOR THE DIFFUSION OF USEFUL KNOWLEDGE.
Papers.

Adult education society, founded by Lord Brougham and patronized by leading Whigs and Radicals. There are detailed references to this unlisted collection of letters, papers, receipts, minutes, letter and account books, 1826–46, in Monica C. Grobel, 'The Society for the Diffusion of Useful Knowledge', 4 volumes, Ph.D. Thesis, University of London, 1933.

The Society's papers throughout throw considerable light on Anglo-American publishing problems, the relative cost of production and the copyright controversy. There is correspondence relating to the republication in the United States of various of the Society's series (Carvell's of New York published the 'Library of Entertaining Knowledge'). A letter, 30 Mar. 1833, from Condy Raquet, a leading citizen of Philadelphia, perhaps demonstrates the success of the Society's publications in Philadelphia; a letter, New York, 25 July 1841 from Professor George Tucker of the University of Virginia to George Long concerns the law of copyright and Tucker's plan for two novels, one designed 'to lessen the prejudice between North and South'. Minutes of 17 Jan. 1833 show James Mill expressing concern at English ignorance of American affairs and moving a resolution in favour of a 'free interchange' of 'literary productions' between the two countries; apparently a deputation then visited the American Minister in London. Committee minutes of 1831 give information about assistance to various American societies, and letters from Alonzo Potter to T. Coates, 20 July [1837] and 25 May 1841 concern the American Society for the Diffusion of Useful Knowledge.

HUTH, FREDERICK, & CO. LTD. Business records.[1]

Merchant bankers, London; dissolved in 1936. The Library's collection of the firm's records consists of 266 volumes,[2] 1812–1904. Huth's world-wide dealings included some with the United States, particularly, it appears, in cotton and in state bonds.

(a) Letter-books. Letters from the London office were written in English, Spanish, or German, and of the 179 volumes of copies of letters sent from there, sixty-six are 'English letters', 1827–51. Most of the letters to the United States are, of course, in this group, but there are apparently also some in the volumes of 'German letters' and 'Spanish letters'. Each volume contains an index, and from these it appears that there was correspondence with firms in New York, New Bedford, Mass., Philadelphia, Baltimore, Richmond, Va., Mobile, Ala., New Orleans, Tallahassee, Fla., and other American cities. Subjects dealt with include the financing of cotton shipments, credit arrangements in Europe for the firms, purchase and sale of American securities. Unfortunately, a large proportion of the copies are so faded as to be illegible.

(b) Letters. A volume of letters, Jan.–June 1839, to the London firm from Frederick Huth & Co., Liverpool, contains references to flour, cotton, corn, and rice from the United States, and discussion of American agencies and the ways in which other firms—Barings, Browns, &c.—handle American business.

There is also relevant material in the ledgers, the volumes listing bills payable and receivable, &c.

See also the firm's records held by the Business Archives Council, London (pp. 182–3).

CHADWICK, SIR EDWIN (1800–90). Papers.

Sanitary and administrative reformer. The large collection of letters, memoranda, drafts of speeches, &c., has been roughly sorted into about 200 boxes, under subjects such as education, fire prevention, poor law, sanitation, &c., but there are some boxes of unsorted correspondence.

---

[1] The letters from Huth's agents and partners in or about the United States used by R. C. McGrane, *Foreign Bondholders and American State Debts* (New York, 1935) do not appear to be in this collection.

[2] Including thirteen Glyn, Mills and Co.'s cash books.

Examination of a few boxes, notably those labelled 'Correspondence: letters from abroad', 'Correspondence from writers abroad', 'Sanitation: Germany, America, Paris, . . .', 'Statistics, including notes on American statistics', showed that Chadwick was in touch with American individuals and organizations interested in the problems of public health and education and was exchanging pamphlets and statistical information with them. The dates of the letters range from 1854 to 1887, though most are during the 1870's and 1880's. Chadwick received letters from such notable educators, and civil and sanitary engineers, as John Billings, J. Eaton, Charles Emery, Rudolph Hering, Mayor Hewitt of New York, Edward Jarvis, and George Waring; and from Boards of Health, Bureaux of Education, the American Social Science Association, the *Sanitarian* (a monthly magazine devoted to the preservation of health, mental and physical culture), &c. Chadwick was also engaged in compiling comparative vital statistics between America and Britain, based on information supplied to him by local correspondents in the United States.

MISCELLANEOUS CORRESPONDENCE.

Early correspondence of the College, 1825–40. Contains a few letters from T. H. Key and George Long, members of the academic staff who had previously held posts in the University of Virginia. Letter, 10 Oct. 1827, from Long briefly describes his teaching course there; and from James Joseph Sylvester who subsequently became Professor of Mathematics at the University of Virginia.

Wellcome Historical Medical Library, Wellcome Building, 183 Euston Road, LONDON, N.W.1

WELLCOME, HENRY SOLOMON (1853–1936). Personal and business archives.

Manufacturing chemist. Wellcome, who was born in Wisconsin, attended the Philadelphia College of Pharmacy, and then worked with firms in various parts of the United States and in South America. In 1880 he joined another American, Silas M. Burroughs in an agency in London for the sale of American pharmaceutical products. The firm soon began manufacturing its own compressed drugs, and branches were later established in various cities of the world, including New York; Wellcome also founded various research institutions. He became a British subject in 1910, and was knighted in 1932.

His extensive records include letters from his mother, material relating to his Philadelphia period, business records, &c. Applications by scholars to use the archives should be made by letter to the Director.

AUTOGRAPH COLLECTION.

The collection contains about 100,000 items, arranged in folders alphabetically by name of author; no list is yet available. It is probable that the collection includes more relevant material than that noted below.

Barton, Benjamin Smith. Philadelphia, 1 Nov. 1791, to Count de la Cépède about oviparous quadrupeds and serpents. Philadelphia, 2 Sept. 1799, to Messrs. Robinson, London booksellers. 19 Mar. 1810, to Dr. John C. Lettsom about the possibility of joining the Royal Society. London, 1 Mar. 1811, to Dr. Lettsom about the copper-plate of the Pennsylvania Hospital diploma.

Holmes, Oliver Wendell, Sen. Five letters, 1872–92, including two to Dr. John Milner Fothergill in London.

Morse, Samuel F. B. United States Telegraph Office, Washington, D.C., 14 May 1846, to M. Arago, Secretaire Perpetuel de l'Académie des Sciences.

Peabody, George. Salem, Mass., 25 Feb. 1867, to Edward Haslewood about Mississippi Bonds.

Priestley, Joseph. Eight letters, 1777–94, including one of 6 Apr. 1794 to Thomas Cooper about their proposed settlement in the United States and Cooper's religious beliefs.

Rush, Benjamin. Philadelphia, 30 Nov. 1794, to Dr. James Currie of Liverpool, about yellow fever in Philadelphia, the insurrection in western Pennsylvania, &c.

Smith, Nathan. Hanover, N.H., 27 May 1808, to Dr. John C. Lettsom, introducing Lyman Spalding.

Spalding, see Waterhouse.

Washington, George. A list of medicines and household commodities to be sent from England, dated 20 Sept. 1759.[1]

Waterhouse, Benjamin. Cambridge, Mass., 6 Sept. 1800 to Lyman Spalding, Portsmouth, N.H., and Spalding's answer of 10 Sept.[2] Also a letter from Waterhouse, 14 Apr. 1801,[3] to an unknown correspondent, comparing Jefferson and John Adams and containing discussion of other political and scientific affairs.

West India Committee, 40 Norfolk Street, LONDON, W.C.2

MINUTES. 1769–1816.

There is scattered material in these minutes relating to the supply of lumber and provisions from America, the effects of the War of Independence on

---

[1] *Writings of George Washington*, ed. by John C. Fitzpatrick, vol. ii, pp. 330–6 (Washington, D.C., 1931). Letter from Mount Vernon of that date to Robert Cary & Co. includes the list as 'Invoice of sundries to be sent ... for use of George Washington'.

[2] Facsimiles of these letters appear in E. A. Underwood, 'Edward Jenner, Benjamin Waterhouse, and the introduction of vaccination into the United States', *Nature*, vol. clxiii, p. 826, 1949.

[3] Part of this letter printed in Underwood, op. cit., p. 827.

West Indian trade, &c. See the description of 'West India Committee, Minutes, West India Merchants' in H. C. Bell, D. W. Parker, and others *Guide to British West Indian Archive Materials, in London and in the Islands, for the History of the United States,* pp. 318–19 (Washington, D.C., 1926).

Archdiocese of Westminster, Archbishop's House, Ambrosden Avenue, LONDON, S.W.1

ARCHIVES IN THE KEEPING OF THE ARCHBISHOP OF WESTMINSTER.

(*a*) Section A: Main Series. This section of the archives consists of seventy-six volumes and boxes containing a very miscellaneous group of manuscripts (and some printed matter), mainly in chronological order, covering 1509–1850. A general index is available through 1700 (vol. 37), and later volumes through 1808 (vol. 53) have individual indexes. Andrews & Davenport, pp. 339–40, list some of the available material to 1791; one of these items—a letter from General Retz to Charles Shireburn, 23 May 1744 could not be found at the time of the present search. Other relevant material—mostly letters (unless otherwise stated) to the London bishops—is as follows:

Vol. 20, no. 59. Advices on the present state of English Catholics . . . and in the Dominions. *c.* 1626.

Vol. 31, no. 208. Suppression of the Jesuits: names of the Jesuits in Maryland and Pennsylvania, enclosed in a letter of submission by Thomas Sanders. 1773.

Vol. 40, nos. 173–4. Printed papers: *The Defence of John Ury* and *New Lightmen,* Philadelphia, *c.* 1781.

Vol. 42, nos. 39, 45, 53, 54, 70. Bishop James Talbot: correspondence concerning North America. 1783–5.

Vol. 42, no. 108. *Act of Incorporation of Roman Catholics in Philadelphia.* 13 Sept. 1788. (Printed.)

Vol. 46, nos. 169, 200. 20 Mar. and 19 May 1796, granting faculties in the 'American Islands' to the Capuchins.

Vol. 49. Correspondence, 8 July and 8 Oct. 1798, of Rev. Leonard Neale of Philadelphia concerning the marriage of Bird-Quin.

Vol. 54. 27 Nov. 1811, from the Vicars Apostolic to John Carroll and the American Bishops concerning the troubles with Bishop Milner.

Vol. 55. 25 Feb., 2 Mar., 4 May, and 15 June 1812, from Carroll, Bishop Thomas Smith, &c., on the above.

Vol. 57. 9 Sept. 1815, from John Connolly, Bishop of New York.

Vol. 60. 2 May 1819, from Ambrose Maréchal, Archbishop of Baltimore.

Vol. 63. 10 Nov. 1822, giving Rev. Francis P. Kenrick's report of the distress of the Bishop of Bardstown, Ky. (B. J. Flaget) about the collection being made in England for his church.

Vol. 64. 1 Oct. 1823, from Henry Conwell, Bishop of New York.

Vol. 65. 14 Jan. 1824, concerning the presence in Liverpool of the 'unhappy Hogan' (William Hogan, the leader of the Philadelphia schism); and a letter, 11 Oct. 1824, giving information about another leader of the schism, Thadeus O'Malley.

Vol. 66. 1 Jan. 1825, from Henry Conwell from Philadelphia. Letter, 12 Apr. 1825, from Edward Fenwick, Bishop of Cincinnati, Ohio, giving information about the new cathedral there and about Ohio in general.

Vol. 66. A document in Latin concerning Thadeus O'Malley, 25 July 1825. A letter, 23 Dec. 1825, from Ambrose Maréchal concerning Catholic affairs in Washington, D.C., and in Philadelphia (in French).

Vol. 67. 19 Mar. 1826, from Henry Conwell.

Vol. 68. 29 Jan. 1827, from Henry Conwell. Letter, 11 July 1827, from Joseph Rosati, Bishop of Tenagra, from Missouri. Letter, 29 May 1827(?), from John Dubois, Bishop of New York.

Vol. 69. 8 Mar. 1829, from T. J. Donague, Pastor of St. Joseph's Church, Philadelphia, urging that Rev. W. V. Harold not be sent to Cincinnati, Ohio; the letter is written on the back of a printed leaflet consisting of a letter 2 July 1828, about the matter from Harold to Henry Clay, Secretary of State. A Rome notary public's statement about Henry Conwell (in Italian), 18 Mar. 1829.

Vol. 70. 28 Oct. 1831, from James Whitfield, Archbishop of Baltimore, commenting on the number of Protestants attending Catholic schools.

Vol. 71. 10 Apr. 1832, from James Whitfield concerning provision of schools and churches. Copy of a letter, 3 Sept. 1831, from Rome to Henry Conwell (in Latin), but enclosed in a letter of 8 Nov. 1832.

Vol. 73. A document, 20 June 1846, showing Nicholas Wiseman's election as an honorary member of the American Ethnological Society, and a letter, 26 June 1846, concerning this from J. R. Bartlett, the Society's corresponding secretary.

There are also in the collection a number of early nineteenth-century letters from Quebec, Montreal, and elsewhere in Canada, relating mainly to administrative matters in those areas.

(b) Section B: Miscellaneous Archives.

B. 3. Robert Gradwell (1777-1833), Rector of the English College at Rome and the agent in Rome of the Archbishops of Baltimore and Quebec: letters, 1819-27. The bound volume consists almost entirely of letters written from Rome to Bishop Poynter in London. Although most of the very full correspondence deals with the affairs of the English College and with various problems of the Catholic Church in England and in Rome, there is some discussion of religious affairs in the United States, especially after Gradwell's appointment in 1821 as agent of Ambrose Maréchal, the Archbishop of Baltimore. The main American matters referred to are the appointments of Bishops for Philadelphia and Carolina; the Philadelphia schism and its leaders William Hogan, Thadeus O'Malley, and Abbé Inglési; and the property conflicts between the Jesuits and the Archbishop of Baltimore.

B. 33–46. Fourteen volumes containing about a thousand letters, chrono-logically arranged 1701–84, mainly correspondence of the agents in Rome of the English Vicars Apostolic. These volumes are not yet indexed, but American material is likely to be slight. Examination of the first and last volumes showed that in B. 33 had been inserted a notebook containing copies of letters sent by Bishop James Talbot, including a letter of 29 Mar. 1763 to the Acadians at Southampton, and one of 9 June 1770 to the Bishop of Quebec about the Acadians (both these in French); B. 46, no. 73, is a letter, 15 Mar. 1764, from Bishop Richard Challoner, to Christopher Stonor, the Rome agent, about the state of the Catholic religion in the American colonies.

(c) Section H: Pamphlets. There are twenty-six bound volumes of pam-phlets, including eight pamphlets, 1635–1824, relating to Catholicism in America.

Archives Department, Westminster Public Libraries, Buckingham Palace Road, LONDON, S.W.1

WESTMINSTER CITY COUNCIL ARCHIVES.

Among these extensive archives only one reference to America could be traced: 'Warrant of the Trustees incorporated to encourage the development of the colony of Georgia, America, appointing the minister, churchwardens and gentlemen of the parish of St. Margaret to gather money for the said purpose.' 1733.

MIDDLESEX

Middlesex County Record Office, 1 Queen Anne's Gate Buildings, Dartmouth Street, LONDON, S.W.1

Only a short general note on these records appears in Andrews & Daven-port, p. 284, under Westminster Guildhall or Session House, where they then were.

More detail will be set down here, to show the kind of minor information that can be found in most County Archives which possess the records of the Courts of Quarter Sessions and large estate collections. Such minor informa-tion has not been generally noted elsewhere.

QUARTER SESSIONS RECORDS.

In the first half of the seventeenth-century offenders sentenced to death were sometimes reprieved on condition which they left England for the colonies. Such sentences were recorded in the Sessions Rolls or Registers. An early example of such a case is that of Stephen Rogers in 1617, sentenced to be hanged for manslaughter but 'reprieved for Virginia' because the plantation needed carpenters. Again, in July 1663, twenty-three persons gained the King's pardon on condition that they left England in two months for the colonies. A number of such cases are recorded in the published calendars to the Middlesex Sessions records.[1]

Other classes of official records which contain reference to America are:

TRANSPORTATION BONDS. 1682–1837.

These give the names of ships and ships' owners, the names of the felons transported therein, and the colony to which they were destined.

INDENTURES. *c.* 1,000. 1683–4.

These are indentures of persons willing to serve in the plantations of America in accordance with the Order of the Privy Council of 1682. They give name and place of origin of the apprentice, the name of the master to whom he is bound and his trade, the colony in which he is to serve, and the period of the apprenticeship. This class has been much used in the past by American historians and genealogists.

MIDDLESEX SESSIONS PAPERS. 1689– (Listed up to 1751 but there is no index yet.)

For example, petition of Robert Nevell *v.* Captain Dodson of the *Robert Samuel* for abuse *en route* for Maryland. R. Nevell obtained a warrant against Captain Dodson on arrival in Cecil county and brought him before a Justice of the Peace there. Several men had to stay in Maryland because of abuses from Captain Dodson. (MSP Aug. 1697, petition 24)

DEPOSITED FAMILY AND ESTATE PAPERS.

(*a*) Papers, 1724–9, concerning the lease of 10,000 acres of land in Pennsylvania by William Aubrey, merchant, of London, and his wife Letitia (one of the daughters of William Penn) to John Knight of Westminster. (Acc. 262/St. 57/47–57)

(*b*) Various certificates and affidavits, 1800–37, proving marriages or deaths of members of families in America. (Acc. 69, 1815–28)

(*c*) Five bills of exchange, 1827–9, payable to William B. Wood, signed Juliana Simpson. (Acc. 69/1829–33)

[1] J. C. Jeaffrison, ed., *Middlesex County Records, Old Series (Extracts), 1549–1687*, 4 vols. (London, 1886–92), and W. Le Hardy, ed., *Middlesex County Records, New Series, 1612–1618*, 4 vols. (London, 1935–41).

(*d*) Memorandum of release, Duke of Buckingham and Chandos to Thomas Grenville, for money paid as compensation for loss of Florida estates to Spain, 22 Feb. 1834. (Acc. 262/St. 57/63–67)

(*e*) Letters of administration of the goods of Mrs. Juliana Wood, wife oɪ William Burke Wood of Philadelphia (intestate), 7 July 1837. Administration to Charlotte Howis, widow, and attorney of William Burke Wood, in the Prerogatory Court of Canterbury. (Acc. 69, no. 1742)

(*f*) Five letters, 24 July 1849–4 Mar. 1850, from Henry Howick of Bridgeport, Conn., about the Howick family of Sussex, England. (Acc. 333/8/12)

(*g*) Downton Family Papers. Letter, affidavit. 1850, 1851. (Acc. 333/21/1)

(i) Letter, 8 Nov. 1850, from William Downton to F. I. Kent, solicitor, about his father, mother, and brother (John Downton). Written on the back of a printed announcement (1 Jan. 1850) from Robert Low & Son, of the Strand, London, that Mr. Jules Hauel, manufacturing perfumer, Chestnut Street, Philadelphia, had been restrained by a United States Circuit Court decree from making and selling an imitation of Low's Brown Windsor Soap.

(ii) Affidavit by Jackson Sparrow of Covington, Ky., residing in 'St. Geo. Hanover Square, Middlesex, England', concerning James Downton of Hampton, Middlesex, deceased (Jackson Sparrow's father-in-law), and John Downton who emigrated to the United States in 1831 and died unmarried in 1841 in the town of Jackson near New Orleans. 6 Aug. 1851.

(*h*) Letter, 2 May 1855, from Henry Butts, Goshen, Cincinnati, Ohio, to his mother in Devonshire. Mentions legacy, weather, health, family matters, &c. 'We have some notion of getting our Daguereotypes taken . . .'. (Acc. 319)

(*i*) Bicknell Family Papers, of Maplewood, South Orange, N.J. Death certificate, 11 Oct. 1874. Letters of administration, 19 Oct. 1880. Inland revenue account with next of kin, 3 Dec. 1880. (Acc. 361/2–4)

(*j*) Letters, Apr.–Dec. 1886, as to raising £1,000 from trust funds to buy a farm in America. (Acc. 351/102–14)

(*k*) Rickards Family Papers. 1887–98. (Acc. 448)
    Mortgage bonds, share certificates, and minor papers, 1887–98, relating to lands in Kansas, Missouri, and Colorado, including some relating to the South West Kansas Land and Irrigation Company and the Syndicate Lands and Irrigating Corporation, Colorado.

(*l*) Letters, 1893–4, from Henry Rankin written on paper headed 'Waterbury Watch (Sales) Co. Ltd., 7 Snow Hill, London E.C. Factory, Waterbury, Conn. U.S.A.'. (Acc. 333/39/7)

SESSIONS PAPERS OF THE SESSIONS GAOL OF DELIVERY AT NEWGATE (MIDDLESEX PRISONERS) HELD AT THE OLD BAILEY. 1755–96. (Fully listed but not yet indexed.)

For example, information per William Platt re ship *Philippa* bound for Georgia and East Florida, 1775, with arms, &c., consigned to individuals there. On 7 July 1775 met by an armed schooner off Tybee Bar, Ga.; forced to stop and give arms to champions of American liberty in Savannah, Ga., by order of 'The Provincial Congress of the province of Georgia', which then ruled the province, leaving the Governor powerless. Lively account of conditions in Georgia in summer, 1775. (Old Bailey S.P./1777/ 4*a* & 4*b*)

MISCELLANEOUS LETTERS. 3 letters. 1822–5.

Letters (in French) from Madame de Coigny to Lady Jersey, wife of the 5th Earl.

11 Sept. 1822. Mentions return of Lafayette to France covered with glory earned in America fighting for liberty (with transcript). (Acc. 510/615)

18 Apr. [1824?]. Asking for the new novel by 'the American Walter Scott of the day', James Fenimore Cooper. (Acc. 510/630)

3 Nov. 1825. Comments on Lord Wellesley's second marriage to an American. (Acc. 510/664)

NORFOLK

Parish Church, ALBY, Norwich

EMIGRANT RECORDS.[1]

Some documents in the Church safe relate to an emigration loan of £100 at 5 per cent. raised in 1836.

Parish Church, BACTON, Norwich

EMIGRANT RECORDS.[1]

Receipts and payments in connexion with the emigration of a resident, *c.* 1849.

[1] For a general note covering the treatment of parish records see the Introduction (p. xxxi). Even these Norfolk parish reports are incomplete, illustrative more than exhaustive. A register of parish records in the diocese is in progress. Permission to view records must be obtained from the incumbent of the particular parish, but it is best to write in the first instance to the Secretary, Norwich Diocesan Advisory Board, The Palace, Norwich.

Col. Q. E. Gurney, BAWDESWELL HALL, Bawdeswell

GURNEY AND BARCLAY FAMILY PAPERS.

A daughter of David Barclay (1728–1809), banker and merchant, specialist in the American trade, married the father of Hudson Gurney (1775–1864), M.P. and antiquarian, the first of several subsequent alliances between Gurneys and Barclays. So it appears that there are three generations of each family's papers now at Bawdeswell and at Barclays (Gurney's) Bank, Norwich, mostly sorted in the 1850's by Hudson Gurney. A few of the papers of Joseph John Gurney, Quaker philanthropist and missionary, are on deposit in the Library of the Society of Friends, London (p. 216). A limited inspection revealed the following American items at Bawdeswell Hall:

(a) Commercial letters, 1769–72, to David and John Barclay (in box marked 'Richard Gurney's Executorship', bundle marked '14'). Letters from their agent John Gibson of Philadelphia. General commercial correspondence, mainly on banking, with some references to trade in tea, paper, glass, cottons, and linen. Two letters dated 1770 indicate steps taken in face of American non-importation resolution. Much concern over the debts of one Daniel Wister.

(b) Banking letters, 1790–1800, to and from David and John Barclay (in box marked 'Old Deeds', bundle marked '3'). Letters on various banking subjects from their agent John Ashley of Philadelphia. Letter-book of replies from the Barclays also. Ashley's detailed accounts with the Barclays, and lists of debts outstanding to the bankers.

(c) Banking letters, 1769–70, to David and John Barclay (in large black box, bundle marked '11'). More letters on banking affairs, mainly from the Philadelphia (?) firm of Gibson & Asheton, but also from some others. There are some references to the tea trade.

(d) David Barclay papers, the other folder of miscellaneous papers in metal box marked 'Mary Gurney's Executorship'.

(i) Copy of letter, 14 Mar. 1764, from Franklin to Dr. J. Fothergill, from Philadelphia, teasing Fothergill for his 'impiety' in saving men by medicine, 'contrary to the plans of Providence', from the just consequences of their own excesses; also reporting on the intolerance of the Philadelphia mob to the Quakers—their belief that the Quakers were selling arms to the Indians, and on the ineptness of the new Royal Governor and the general political situation. (No. 3.)

(ii) Letter, 29 Apr. 1767, from Anthony Benezet of Philadelphia to Barclay, enclosing a treatise on the slave trade and hoping that it may be put in the hands of 'persons of interest and power' to expose the 'corrupt motives and most wicked methods' of the trade. He also alludes to the fear of a slave rebellion, 'a subject of too tender a nature to be exposed to view'. (No. 5.)

(iii) Certificate of David Barclay's membership of the Pennsylvania

Society for Promoting the Abolition of Slavery, 1790, signed by James Pemberton.

(iv) A printed pamphlet by David Barclay, *An Account of the Emancipation of the Slaves of Unity Valley Pen, in Jamaica* (London, 1801) (20 pages).

(*e*) Peace negotiations, 1774-7: Dr. Fothergill, David Barclay, and Lord Hyde with Benjamin Franklin. Memoranda and letters (20 items). These papers relate to the fruitless peace negotiations of 1774-7. The items have been numbered 1-22.[1]

(i) Memorandum. 'Hints for Conversation Upon the Subject of Terms, that may probably produce a *durable* Union between Great Britain and her Colonies', 4 Dec. 1774. This paper is missing, but something of the same title is in Lettsom's *Works of Fothergill*, vol. iii, p. lxxvii (London, 1784), and a slightly differing version in A. H. Smyth's *The Writings of Benjamin Franklin* (New York, 1905-7), included in a letter, 22 Mar. 1775, to his son, vol. vi, pp. 318-99.

(ii) Letter, 13 Dec. 1774, from Lord Hyde to David Barclay, on receipt of a copy of the 'Hints'. (No. 2.)

(iii) Memorandum in Barclay's hand, 'Remarks on Hints'. (No. 3.)

(iv) Memorandum 'Plan for Conciliation', a revision of the 'Hints' showing substantial concessions to the Americans if the 'Dignity of Parliament . . . be preserved.' (No. 4.)

(v) Letter, 5 Feb. 1775, from Lord Hyde to Barclay, regretting the receipt of less favourable terms. (No. 5.)

(vi) Draft of a letter, 6 Feb. 1775, from Fothergill to Lord Dartmouth, explaining the reasons for the breakdown of the negotiations with Franklin. Partly written in Barclay's hand, partly by another, with numerous emendations. (No. 6.)

(vii) Memorandum in Barclay's hand, '*A Plan* which it's believed would produce a permanent Union between Great Britain and her Colonies', 16 Feb. 1775. (No. 7.)

(viii) Letters and yet one more 'Plan', 1775-6, between Fothergill, Barclay, and Hyde concerning further efforts made by Barclay and Fothergill, after Franklin had departed, to reach an agreement. (Nos. 8-16.)

(ix) Copy of a letter, 12 Feb. 1781, from Benjamin Franklin to Barclay, praising the work of Dr. Fothergill on hearing of his death. (No. 17.)

(x) Three letters, 1783-6, from Lord Clarendon to Barclay, expressing his doubts about Lettsom's publication of an account of the negotiations in his life of Fothergill.[2] (Nos. 18-20.)

(xi) Letter from the new Lord Clarendon to Barclay, 30 Oct. 1790, acknowledging Barclay's condolences on the death of his father. (No. 21.)

(*f*) Joseph John Gurney, letters from America,[3] 1837-40 (in large box,

---

[1] Most of these have been printed in R. Hingston Fox, *Dr. John Fothergill and His Friends*, Appendix A, pp. 393-408 (London, 1919).

[2] J. C. Lettsom, *The Works of John Fothergill: volume 1, Some Account of the late J. Fothergill, M.D.* (London, 1783).

[3] Gurney, Joseph John, *A Journey in North America, described in familiar letters to Amelia Opie* (Norwich, priv. print., 1841).

portfolio C, items numbered 531–61). Joseph John Gurney wrote long journal letters to his family while on his ministry for the English Society of Friends to refute the teachings of the 'Hicksites'. Travelled through the Carolinas and New England, visiting Washington and New York. Many references to Friends Meetings. Letters 533, 535, 539–40, 547, and 561 are particularly interesting on slavery and the American Anti-Slavery Society. Visited many institutions, e.g. Sing Sing and a lunatic asylum at Worcester, Mass. Much impressed by the factory system at Lowell (541). Discusses the burning of the Pennsylvania Hall, Philadelphia, following abolitionist meeting in July 1838 (539). Visits Washington and meets Webster, Polk, Clay, and J. Q. Adams (536), and addresses President and Congress (537). A copy of a letter of thanks, 13 June 1839, from President Van Buren (551). Many scattered comments on agriculture, landscape, and manners.

R. W. Ketton-Cremer, Esq., FELBRIGG HALL, Cromer

WINDHAM, WILLIAM (1750–1810). Paper.[1] 1778.

Draft of a protest, 28 Jan. 1778, drawn up by Windham and Thomas Coke, M.P., opposing the raising of a fund to help carry on the War of Independence.

Parish Church, GREAT DUNHAM

EMIGRANT RECORDS.[2]

Twenty-five papers concerning the emigration of fifty persons, 1836.[3]

Parish Church, GREAT RYBURGH, Fakenham

EMIGRANT RECORDS.[2]

Churchwardens' and overseers' accounts of charges on the rates for £400 in 1836 for emigration. Also correspondence with the Poor Law Commissioners. (There are earlier papers for 1809 and 1810 concerning enclosures in the parish.)

---

[1] Quoted in R. W. Ketton-Cremer, *Early Life and Diaries of William Windham*, p. 188 (London, 1930).
[2] See note (p. 349).
[3] See *Eastern Daily Press*, 4 Jan. 1958, for an article summarizing these.

H.M. Customs and Excise, GREAT YARMOUTH

See H.M. Customs and Excise, London (p. 206).

Parish Church, GUESTWICK, Dereham

EMIGRANT RECORDS.[1]

Papers relating to an emigration loan of £200 in 1836 to send poor persons to Quebec.

Brigadier H. Long, O.B.E., M.C., The Estate Office, HEYDON, Norwich

BULWER, SIR HENRY (1801–72). Papers: 3 dispatch boxes.[2]

William Henry Lytton Earle Bulwer, Baron Dalling and Bulwer (1801–72) (better known as Sir Henry Bulwer); diplomat. The papers mainly relate to his service as Minister at Madrid 1844–9, and then to his time at Constantinople 1857–65. Some papers relate to his earlier travels and residence in Paris, but none directly to his time as Minister in Washington 1849–52. Each of the boxes contains upwards of a thousand letters, including many from, as well as to, Palmerston, Addington, Peel, Aberdeen, &c. There is a rough pencilled list of contents on top of each box.

Box 1: Madrid, 1844–9. Letter, 25 Jan. 1849, from Palmerston offers Bulwer the post of Minister in Washington, which 'would have the advantage of getting you honourably out of the embarrassment as to the question of returning or not returning to Madrid'. A copy of a letter, 10 Nov. 1849, from Bulwer to Palmerston, acknowledges receipt of H.M. Government's instructions relating to his American mission and of Palmerston's own instructions (these instructions could not be found, but they might easily be misplaced among other bundles which it was not possible to examine thoroughly in the time available). A letter from Mr. David Lutyens, who examined the papers in 1955, to the owner, speaks of a most interesting letter relating to Bulwer's American mission in this box, but this also could not be found.

Box 2: Constantinople, 1857–65.

Box 3: Constantinople, 1858–65. A printed copy, headed 'For use of the Foreign Office, 27 July 1854' of James Buchanan's note from the United States Legation in London, 22 July 1854, entitled *Remarks in Reply to Lord Clarendon's Statement of May 2nd, 1854*; there are marginal notations in Sir

---

[1] See note (p. 349).
[2] These papers have now been listed in N.R.A. 6790 and are on temporary deposit at the Institute of Historical Research, London.

Henry Bulwer's hand. Also a copy, n.d., of a letter of Bulwer to Lord Clarendon, urging caution on the above matter—American complaints about British expansion in Central America, particularly on the Mosquito Coast and the island of Roatán, allegedly contrary to the terms of the Clayton–Bulwer Treaty.

Parish Church, HINDOLVESTON, Dereham

EMIGRANT RECORDS.[1]

A notice of a vestry meeting concerning emigration, *c.* 1836. There may be entries in four volumes of overseers' books.

Earl of Leicester, HOLKHAM

This is a private library[2] built by successive owners upon the basis of Sir Edward Coke's library (see W. O. Hassall, ed., *A Catalogue of the Library of Sir Edward Coke* (London, and New Haven, Conn., 1950) (Yale Law Library Publications Series, no. 12); many papers of Thomas Coke, 'Coke of Norfolk', are also there. As the Librarian is only at Holkham at varying times of the year, it is essential to write well in advance for permission to work in the library.

CHRISTOPHER COLUMBUS. Letter. 1493.

One of seven known contemporary copies of Columbus's own account of his discovery of America, written as Admiral of the Fleet of the Ocean. The original is in Seville. This copy is connected with Planck's first edition— also at Holkham—having the same errors as the title.

BARGRAVE, JOHN. *c.* 1625.

A copy of a petition of John Bargrave, planter in Virginia, to the House of Commons concerning the Virginia Company; it is inserted loose in Sir Edward Coke's own copy of *For the Colony in Virginea Britannia, Lawes Divine, Morall, and Martiall* (London, 1612).

COKE, THOMAS WILLIAM, 1st Earl of Leicester (1752–1842). Letters from Americans. Three guard-books. 1810–34. Vol. iii contains 47 letters to Coke. Vol. i contains accidentally 2 letters, 1837.

Coke of Norfolk, the agricultural reformer, was a patron of the American cause in Norfolk politics and in the House of Commons during the Revolutionary era. A print of George Washington at Holkham is inscribed: 'Every night during the American War did I drink the health of George Washington

---

[1] See note (p. 349).
[2] Virginia material microfilmed by the Virginia Colonial Records Project.

as the greatest man on earth.' No letters, however, relating to this earlier period appear to survive: most of the 'Letters from Americans' refer to agricultural reform, though many air strong Whig politics too.

The annual sheep-shearing at Holkham was almost a place of pilgrimage for Americans visiting Europe who were interested in agricultural reform; Coke's methods, and his agricultural shows, were clearly of great influence in America. The letters (arranged chronologically) are from the following:

King, Rufus. 29 July 1810, asking for advice about purchase of cows and discussing the Napoleonic War and American commercial policy.

Logan, George. 'Stenton', Pa., 2 June 1812, concerning his private mission to attempt a reconciliation between the two countries. He discusses the hopes for peace and the common importance of maintaining the agricultural interest over the 'moral and physical evils of the manufacturing system'. Also a letter, 24 Mar. 1817, referring to his stay at Holkham and to a new drilling machine. And a third similar letter, 19 Oct. 1819.

Caton, Richard. Three letters, 20 Mar. 1817, 16 June 1821, 20 May 1833, mostly about exchange of agricultural machinery, animals, products, and information. Caton was a Baltimore merchant, born in England, whose daughters all married into high English society.

Rush, Richard, American statesman and Minister to London. Four letters. 1819–23, concerning agricultural reforms.

Lyman, Theodore, philanthropist. 6 Aug. 1819, concerning agriculture.

Williams, Charles, Vermont statesman. 6 Aug. 1819, concerning agriculture.

Mease, James, physician and author of Pennsylvania. 14 Sept. 1819, concerning agriculture.

Parish (or Farish), David. Annapolis, N.S., 28 Apr. 1820, announcing that Coke had been made an honorary member of the Montreal Agricultural Society and enclosing a note to that effect from a Mr. Gillespie.

King, Charles. n.d., introducing William Beach Lawrence.

Lowell, John, Boston merchant. 15 Nov. 1821, announcing that Coke had been made an honorary member of the Massachusetts Society for Promoting Agriculture.

Pomeroy, S. W. Brighton, nr. Boston, Mass., n.d., concerning agriculture.

Hughes, Christopher, diplomat. Twenty-two letters, 1823–32, mostly personal and about mutual friends, or rather great acquaintances, though occasional political gossip. He encloses copies of three letters of Lafayette to himself.

Hunter, John Dunn. London, 15 Feb. 1824, flattering Coke. Hunter was the adventurer who falsely claimed to have been raised by the Kickapoo Indians and who was fêted by the Royal Society in London.

Harper, Robert Goodloe, United States Senator. 10 Apr. 1824, concerning agriculture.

Weeks, Ezra. 20 Dec. 1824, asking Coke to allow William E. West, American artist, to paint his portrait.

Bainbridge, William. 30 Aug. 1825, introducing James Potter of Savannah, Ga., James Hamilton of Philadelphia, and James Hamilton Couper of Charleston, S.C., to see the improvements and stock at Holkham.

Barbour, James, statesman, Minister to London. 20 Sept. 1829 letter of thanks for a visit to Holkham.

Fisher, John, a New York farmer. Two letters, 10 and 31 Mar. 1831, re-calling a visit to Holkham thirty years previously and telling of his delight at now finding Coke's breeds of sheep and cattle all over New York.

D'Evereux, General. Paris, 17 May 1831, introducing a Colonel Thorn of New York.

Jackson, Andrew. 1 Oct. 1834, praising Coke and introducing a Mr. Bradford of Massachusetts.

The first volume of the three guard-books also contains, accidentally, two American letters, both written from London. One from Richard Rush, 22 July 1837, congratulating Coke on his elevation to the peerage, and the other, 21 July 1837, from A. Stevenson on the same subject.

PRINTED MATERIAL: pamphlets, &c.

Several bound volumes of miscellaneous English seventeenth-century pamphlets containing many items of American interest, some rare: e.g. three copies of the English edition of *The Simple Cobler of Aggawam* (London, 1647); a number of religious tracts, e.g., *Severall questions of Serious and necessary Consequence . . . unto M. John Cotton of Boston in New-England* (London, 1647); several accounts of the New England and Virginia settlements, including John Underhill's *Newes from America* (London, 1638). One volume is particularly noteworthy for its accounts of Virginia including *Virginia Richly Valued . . .* translated out of Portuguese by Richard Hakluyt (London, 1609). *A True Relation of such Occurrences and Accidents of Noate as hath Happened in Virginia . . .* by Captain Smith (London, 1608), and several proclamations dated 1610 by the 'Counsell of Virginia', advertising for 'sufficient, honest and good artificers'.

H.M. Customs and Excise, KING'S LYNN

See H.M. Customs and Excise, London (p. 206).

Parish Church, LITTLE BARNINGHAM, Norwich

EMIGRANT RECORDS.[1]

Correspondence and detailed accounts concerning the emigration of fifty-two people in 1836 at the cost of £203. 3s. 7½d. The security of the rates was given for a loan of £200, with the consent of the Poor Law Commissioners. The accounts show the cost of each stage of the migration. One family paid own passage. Other parishes were concerned in these accounts.

[1] See note (p. 349).

Parish Church, LYNG, Norwich

EMIGRANT RECORDS.[1]

Correspondence, bills, and detailed accounts concerning the emigration of members of the parish in 1836 under the terms of the Poor Law Act of 1834. Similar details to Little Barningham (q.v.).

Public Library, St. Andrew Street, NORWICH

NORFOLK AND NORWICH COLLECTION.

This local collection virtually serves also as a county record office. A thorough examination of several catalogues and indexes revealed no important items of American relevance, somewhat surprising considering the deep Puritan-Whig-Radical (and thus pro-American) tradition of Norfolk and, specifically, the large number of locally printed nineteenth-century American travel books and emigrant guides to be found in the Library. There are also local pamphlets on the emigration controversy in relation to pauperism of the 1830's; and, of course, several first editions of works by Thomas Paine (1737–1809), who was born in Thetford, Norfolk. In addition, there are:

(a) Norwich Mechanics Union. Minutes, 1824–41. Scattered entries on purchase of books and subjects of lectures, &c., especially 1833–7, show an interest in the allied topics of the Poor Law, emigration, and America.

(b) Solomon Lincoln, junior. Manuscript of the *History of Hingham, Mass.* Printed at Hingham, Caleb Gill, junior; and Farmer and Brown 1827. (Rye 136 34 A 6)

(c) Fred Henderson (1867–1957). Press cuttings, 1933–5.
Socialist publicist and Norwich alderman. Henderson toured the United States and Canada in 1933 and again in 1934–5. There are numerous cuttings about these tours, including his address to the Wisconsin State Legislature of 12 Feb. 1935; to the Taylor Society in New York of 8 Dec. 1933; and to the Eighteenth National Convention of the Socialist Party of America, 1934, in Chicago. There are also separate American editions of 1934 of his *Case for Socialism* by the Socialist Party of the United States, Chicago, and the New York State Socialist Party.

(d) Letter, 1917, from Mayor of Norwich, Conn., to the Mayor of Norwich, England, concerning the entrance of America into the War. (MS. 20213 38 C 3)

[1] See note (p. 349).

Parish Church, SAXTHORPE, Norwich

EMIGRANT RECORDS.[1]

Overseers' book contains account of sale of cottages belonging to the parish in 1836 to defray part of the cost of the loan for sending poor persons to America. £350 was borrowed in all, from a private individual, who was repaid in yearly instalments. The churchwardens' accounts also touch on this transaction, which can be followed through, in both sets of books, for the years 1838–40.

NORTHAMPTONSHIRE

Earl Spencer, ALTHORP, Northampton

SPENCER, GEORGE JOHN, 2nd Earl Spencer (1758–1834). Correspondence: 8 letters. 1774–83.

Eight letters concerning the War of Independence.

(a) Six letters from Sir William Jones, tutor at Althorp, concerning the debates in Parliament on the American question; they repeatedly urge the need of granting the Americans their independence and of Britain entering into 'a family compact with the United States'. One also contains a description of Franklin at Paris.

(b) Letter from Patrick Campbell, writing from America on the military situation there in 1777.

(c) Letter from Earl Spencer to his son (?), asking him to attend Parliament.

(d) Other letters in the three boxes for 1774–83 touch on American affairs, but to a slighter degree.

SPENCER, GEORGIANA, Countess (Poyntz) (1737–1814). Correspondence: 31 letters. 1774–8.

(a) Six letters, 18 May 1774–6 Oct. 1777, from George Bussy Villiers, 4th Earl of Jersey. Contain various items of news concerning debates on, and battles in, America; e.g. two in Oct. 1778 describe the Battle of Long Island.

(b) Twenty-five letters, 20 July 1775–26 Oct. 1778, from the Hon. Mrs. Howe, who was a sister-in-law to General Sir William Howe and Admiral Lord Richard Howe, and thus in a position to pass on various scraps of news about the American war.

[1] See note (p. 349).

ASGILL CORRESPONDENCE. 9 letters (8 copies).[1] 1782–3. (Filed with the correspondence of Georgiana, Countess Spencer.)

The original letter, Lancaster, Penn., 29 May 1782, is from Captain Greville, a prisoner in American hands, to his mother. He describes in detail the circumstances leading up to the taking by lot of Captain Asgill, a fellow prisoner, to be a scapegoat for the murder of the American Huddy by Loyalists. There is also a copy letter (n.d. but 1783) from Lady Asgill to Lieut.-Col. James Gordon, Asgill's superior officer, expressing her gratitude for her son's release.

The seven other copies of letters—one from Gordon to General Sir Guy Carleton; four from Herman Witsius Ryland, Acting Paymaster for Prisoners of War, to Asgill; and two from Asgill to Ryland—are concerned with the financial implications of the episode.

SPENCER, FREDERICK, 4th Earl Spencer (1798–1857). Correspondence. 17 letters. 1857.

Seventeen letters from his son, John Poyntz Spencer, later 5th Earl Spencer, during a visit to the United States and Canada, 26 July–23 Nov. 1857. Two letters are apparently incomplete.

John visited Boston; New York; Trenton Falls, N.Y.; Saratoga, N.Y.; Quebec; Niagara Falls; Detroit, Mich.; Chicago; St. Paul, Minn.; the Mammoth Cave, Kentucky; St. Louis, Mo.; New Orleans, La.; and Washington, D.C. He gives detailed descriptions of the towns in which he stayed, and in some cases of the country through which he travelled; visited West Point and met Winfield Scott; lectured at a Negro colony called Backstone in the North, and visited an Indian camp in Minnesota. He also describes American sympathy with Britain over the Indian Mutiny, the dominance of the slavery issue in American politics, the economics of cotton cultivation in the South, the aftermath of the Panic of 1857, the so-called 'Mormon War', Congressional feeling about the Clayton–Bulwer Treaty, and the working of the Federal government. He expresses the opinions that the United States will soon obtain Cuba to the ruin of the Louisiana sugar industry, and that Britain's links with the North are far stronger than those with the South.

SPENCER, JOHN POYNTZ, 5th Earl Spencer (1835–1910). Correspondence. 1857.

Small bundle of letters relating to his American trip, July–Oct. 1857; some from Americans, e.g. Edward Everett, R. H. Dana, G. M. Dallas, but only of personal interest, letters of introduction, &c. Also some American naturalization forms; and state election tickets brought back as souvenirs from Ohio.

[1] See also H.M.C. ii, p. 20.

Duke of Buccleuch, BOUGHTON HOUSE, Kettering

BUCCLEUCH AND QUEENSBERRY MUNIMENTS. 1696–1708 (?).

(a) Two letters, both from New York, 20 Sept. 1696, and almost identical, from Colonel Robert Livingston to the Duke of Shrewsbury, and the Earl of Romney respectively, on the activities of Captain Kidd.[1]

(b) A long, undated letter, c. 1700, from J. Nelson to Shrewsbury, especially on the dangers to the colonies from the French. Also a paper by Nelson on 'the methods or ways I propose for the reduction of Canada unto the obedience of the Crown'.[2]

(c) A number of papers written by Richard Daniel and others, apparently for the benefit of the Duke of Shrewsbury, on the American colonies, especially recommending the establishment of a Commission responsible for them. There are papers on New England, 'the American Colonies', and New Albion.[3]

Northamptonshire Record Office, Delapre Abbey, London Road, NORTHAMPTON

BRUDENELL PAPERS.[4] 3 agreements. 1582–3.

Agreement, 9 June 1582, between Sir Humphrey Gilbert and two others, in which Gilbert gives them authority to search out and govern lands between the 'Cape of Florida and Cape Britton'. Two further agreements, 1582 and 1583, between the same parties on colonization in America.

GRAFTON PAPERS. Document. 1649.

Letters patent of Charles II, 1649, granting land between the 'Rappahanocke and Potawomeck Rivers and Chesapayocke Bay' to Ralph, Lord Hopton and others.

ISHAM PAPERS. Letter. 1673.

2 Oct. 1673, from Dorothy, Lady Long, to Sir Justinian Isham, mentions that New York, 'a town lying near Verginia' has been 'taken by the Duch'.

BROOKE PAPERS. 2 documents, &c. 1735.

Grant of a tract of land in South Carolina to Alexander Talley. Seal of province and plan, attached. 1735.

---

[1] Transcripts, H.M.C. Buccleuch and Queensberry MSS. ii [45], pp. 405–8.
[2] Transcripts, ibid., pp. 723–33.   [3] Transcripts, ibid., pp. 733–9.
[4] Printed in D. B. Quinn, ed., *The Voyages and Colonial Enterprises of Sir Humphrey Gilbert* (London, 1940) (Hakluyt Society, 2nd ser., vol. lxxxiv).

FINCH-HATTON PAPERS. Documents. n.d.; 1745.

(*a*) Motion, n.d. [first half of seventeenth century?] against restoring the 'Old Virginia Company'. (3731)

(*b*) Copy of orders by Sir Peter Warren, Vice-Admiral, Commander-in-Chief of British naval forces 'employed in North America to the northward of Carolina', during the operations against Louisbourg, N.S., 1745, with a list of ships engaged in the action. (281. ff. 160*b*–165*b*)

FITZWILLIAM PAPERS. Papers of Edmund Burke: letters, notes and draft speeches on American affairs. 1753–81.[1]

These papers came from Milton, nr. Peterborough, the seat since 1857 of the younger branch of the Fitzwilliam family; and are obviously complementary to the group from the Fitzwilliam (Wentworth Woodhouse) Muniments now in the Sheffield City Libraries (pp. 463–5). The papers on American affairs, dealing mainly with the Stamp Act and War of Independence, include:

(*a*) Accounts of quitrents paid from various colonies, 1753–63.

(*b*) Petitions from the American colonies against the Stamp Act, and copy of correspondence about the Act.

(*c*) Statement of distribution of Army in North America, 1765.

(*d*) Account of bullion received from Philadelphia and New York, 1765.

(*e*) Resolution of Pennsylvania Assembly, 1766, about grant of aids to the King.

(*f*) Reports on validity of Acts of New York Assembly, 1773.

(*g*) Accounts of exports and imports of New York, 1774.

(*h*) Resolutions of freeholders of Cork against proceeding to extremities against the colonists, 1776; and many similar petitions, letters of advice, &c., including one from Bristol, 1778.

(*i*) Copies of letters of General Clinton, 1777, about Burgoyne's defeat.

(*j*) 'Letters on the temper of the British Nabobs towards America', 1777.

(*k*) Extracts from letters of Lord George Germain, 1781.

(*l*) Petitions of John Trumbull for release from prison, 1781.

FITZWILLIAM CORRESPONDENCE. Letter. 1793.

Halifax, N.S., 23 Mar. 1793, from John Wentworth, Governor of Nova Scotia 1792–1808, to Lord Fitzwilliam, mentions a defeat of the American Army by the Indians, with a loss of six hundred men slain. (And other letters concerning Nova Scotia.)

[1] See *The Correspondence of Edmund Burke*, to be published in 10 vols. (Cambridge and Chicago); vol. 1, Apr. 1744–June 1768, ed. by Thomas W. Copeland (1958); vol. 2, July 1768–June 1774, ed. by Lucy S. Sutherland (1960); vol. 3, July 1774–June 1778, ed. by George H. Guttridge (1961).

AMERICAN SOCIETY FOR MELIORATING THE CONDITION OF THE JEWS. Document. 1830.

Instructions issued, 1830, in New York by the Society to the Rev. Judah I. Abraham, 'missionary to the Jews, on the borders of the Mediterranean'.

TRYON PAPERS. Letter.[1] 1833.

Perth Amboy, N.J., 10 Jan. 1833, from Charles Johnston to Thomas Tryon of Bulwick, Northants. Mentions wages paid for harvesting, the climate; and compares prices with those in England. Asks Tryon to advise his (Johnston's) brother to go over.

ELLESMERE PAPERS. Maps.

Manuscript map of the 'Potowmack and James Rivers showing their several communications with the navigable waters of the New Province on the River Ohio', n.d. Other printed maps of American ports and coast line, 1775-7.

PETERBOROUGH QUARTER SESSIONS RECORDS.

Include royal pardons to certain men sentenced to death, commuting their sentences to transportation to America, 1773.

PARISH RECORDS.

(a) Newnham. Notebook of the Rev. Thomas Green, vicar of Badby with Newnham, with particulars of his parishioners at Newnham. Several members of the Shaw family are noted as having gone to America in the 1830's.

(b) Sywell. Agreement, 6 Jan. 1830, by five ratepayers to pay a sixpenny rate 'to be applied in conveying paupers or poor persons belonging to the parish to the United States of America'.

NORTHUMBERLAND

Duke of Northumberland, ALNWICK CASTLE, Alnwick

NORTHUMBERLAND PAPERS. 1607-1816.

(a) Council in Virginia to the Council of Virginia in London, giving an account of what has been accomplished in the first seven weeks of settlement—fortification, building, planting, further exploration, &c.—and a favourable account of the country. 22 June 1607, Jamestown.[2]

---

[1] Photostat in the Collection of Letters of Emigrants to America in the British Library of Political and Economic Science, London School of Economics.
[2] Transcript, H.M.C. iii, pp. 53-54.

(*b*) Letter, 29 July 1607, from Captain Christopher Newport to Robert Cecil, Earl of Salisbury, on former's return from Virginia.[1]

(*c*) Letter, Jamestown, Va., 17 Aug. 1611, from George Percy, to the Earl of Northumberland, his brother, thanking him for past financial assistance, and asking for more, as his position 'cannot be defrayed with small expense'.[2]

(*d*) Account of the raising of money for the building of a free school at Charles City, Va., 1621–2.[3]

(*e*) Letter-book of Earl Percy. Various letters and papers, 1774–80, relating to the War of Independence.[4]

(*f*) Rebel orderly book (1–13 Sept. 1776), taken at the island of New York, 1776. (This title is in the handwriting of Earl Percy.)[5]

(*g*) Diary of operations of the Lord Howe's fleet and army in America (Connecticut, Dutch Island, North Goat Island, &c.) 29 July–31 Aug. 1778.[5]

(*h*) 'Memoir on the commercial intercourse between the United States of America and the British Islands and Colonies in the West Indies, Signed James Leith, Captain General.' n.d. (1814–1816?)[6]

(*i*) 'Journal of a voyage of a thousand miles down the Ohio (1809–), and an account of the Five Nations, etc., from an early period to the conclusion of the late war between Great Britain and America, by Major John Norton (Teyoninhokarawen), 1816; dedicated to the Duke of Northumberland. 2 volumes, pp. 967, followed by a vocabulary.'[6]

R. H. Carr-Ellison, Esq., HEDGELEY HALL, Alnwick

CARR, RALPH. Business papers.[7] 1737–83.

Merchant, Newcastle upon Tyne. There are sixty or seventy volumes of copy letter-books, 1737–83; these include some letters to America, but most of the relevant business correspondence appears in two separate volumes containing Carr's American letter-copies, 1748–75. Included are letters to Edmund, Henry, and Josiah Quincy, Philip Livingston, Samuel Wentworth, and others.[8] 'The chief exports to America were coal, crown glass, bottles, lead, iron and woollen goods; and the chief import appears to have been tar.' There are also some original miscellaneous letters, including one from Thomas Hutchinson in 1774.[9]

---

[1] Transcript, ibid., p. 54.   [2] Ibid., p. 58.   [3] Ibid., p. 66.
[4] Ibid., p. 108.   [5] Ibid., p. 124.
[6] Ibid., p. 125.
[7] See H.M.C. xv (x), pp. 92, 94–96, 98–99.
[8] Other New York and Boston correspondents are listed ibid., p. 92. Notes from the American letter-books are given on pp. 94–96.
[9] Transcript, ibid., p. 98.

H.M. Customs and Excise, NEWCASTLE UPON TYNE

See H.M. Customs and Excise, London (p. 205).

NOTTINGHAMSHIRE

The Department of Manuscripts, The Library, University of Nottingham, University Park, NOTTINGHAM

MIDDLETON MANUSCRIPTS. 1611–31.[1]

On 2 May [1611] the King had granted letters patent to the Earl of Northampton, Sir Percivall Willoughby, and others to make a plantation and establish a colony in Newfoundland.

(*a*) Bundle of papers, 1611–31, connected with the Newfoundland venture: correspondence, estimates, inventories.

(*b*) 'A journall from the first September [1612] until the last of Aprill 1613 in C[a]pe ... wher the colonie is kept.' This journal gives a day to day report of the weather, the voyages made, and the activities undertaken in Newfoundland.[2]

NEWCASTLE MANUSCRIPTS.[3]

Manuscripts of the 2nd, 3rd, 4th, and 5th Dukes of Newcastle, 1720–1864.

(*a*) Among the forty-four bundles of letters, documents, and copies of documents of the 2nd Duke, Henry Fiennes Clinton (1720–94),[4] are the following:

(i) Clinton, Sir Henry (1738?–95). Over 100 letters and copies of letters and documents. 1775–82.

General, M.P. for Boroughbridge 1772–74 and for Newark 1774–84 (both seats controlled by his cousin, the 2nd Duke of Newcastle). On

---

[1] We thank Lord Middleton for permission to make this report.

[2] H.M.C. Middleton MSS. [69], p. 284.

[3] We thank the Trustees of the Duke of Newcastle for permission to make this report.

[4] Catalogue of the 2nd Duke's Manuscripts compiled as an appendix to his thesis by Clive Priestley, 'The Life and Career of Henry Fiennes Pelham-Clinton, 1720–1794, Ninth Earl of Lincoln and Second Duke of Newcastle-under-Lyme.' Typescript, M.A. thesis, University of Nottingham, 1958.

Howe's return to England after the capture of Burgoyne at Saratoga, Clinton became Commander-in-Chief in North America. The majority of the letters are addressed to the Duke of Newcastle, but the correspondence contains copies of others to Sir William Howe, Lord George Germain, Lieut.-Col. Webster, Vice-Admiral Arbuthnot, and Lord Cornwallis; here are also a number to Clinton's sisters, Richard Reeve, Major-General Edward Harvey, Mr. Carter, and Lord John Pelham Clinton, transmitted by them to the Duke. One paper, presumably the work of Benedict Arnold, is superscribed 'Rules and articles to be observed on this bold and noble attempt to join Sir Henry Clinton'. The correspondence as a whole takes the form of a commentary on the course of the war and on Clinton's feelings, particularly his dissatisfaction with fellow officers and with his own position both before and after his appointment to the senior command in May 1778. Newcastle being his political patron, Clinton poured out to him all his complaints and clearly regarded his letters as confidential. In addition to accounts of military engagements between June 1775 and the attempted relief of Yorktown in Oct. 1781, the correspondence contains vigorous criticism of the government, Howe, Arbuthnot, and Cornwallis. Newcastle is kept informed of Clinton's intentions of resigning, and throughout the war the Duke's replies seem to have urged Clinton to stay at his post. Clinton used the Duke, however, as a channel to the King, requesting release in October 1779 and again in November 1780. The manuscripts include a short and sharp exchange between Lord North and the Duke on 3 and 4 Mar. 1778 (2/25–2/32), showing the latter's concern when he considered that Clinton had a legitimate grievance. The correspondence is chiefly interesting for the light it throws on Clinton's thoughts throughout the war, especially on the virtual military impossibility of subduing the rebellion.

(ii) Phillips, William (1731?–81). 12 letters. 1775–80. Major-General, M.P. 1775–80 for Boroughbridge, a seat controlled by the Duke of Newcastle, of whom he was an active supporter and political client. The letters cover the period when Phillips served with Carleton and Burgoyne in America, being taken prisoner at Saratoga, N.Y. The letters describe and make vigorous comment on the conduct of the war, particularly on Burgoyne's ill-fated advance from Canada. Some are from prison. The last letter, New York, 14 Oct. 1780, refers to Clinton's secret correspondence with Benedict Arnold and his feelings on the capture and execution of Major Andre. (These letters are found as: Bundle 1, nos. 37, 41, 42; Bundle 9, nos. 4, 16, 18, 20, 24; Bundle 11, nos. 14, 75, 123, 129.) There are twenty-three other letters from Phillips, 1768–75, in some of which he comments on the American situation.

(iii) Letter, Pay Office, 7 Nov. 1776, from Richard Rigby to the Duke of Newcastle. Has dined with Lord Lincoln; news from America; another campaign needed; meeting between Howe, Adams, and Franklin; fears of warlike preparations in France. (11/33)

(iv) Letter, Cleveland Court, 6 Aug. 1777, from Edward Harvey to the Duke of Newcastle. 'I can't say that I have heard any thing about Howe & Cornwallis that is alarming. Instead of attacking Washington, Howe has embarked his whole Jersey army leaving sufficient posts att N. York etc., and is proceeding on some expedition. It is to be hoped & credited, (till we hear the contrary) that what he has fix'd on, is the most eligible plan'; expects Ticonderoga to fall without resistance. (35/2)

(*b*) Henry Pelham Fiennes Pelham Clinton, 5th Duke of Newcastle (1811–64), was Colonial Secretary 1852–4 and 1859–64. For both periods there are letter-books and papers relating to North America, including correspondence with Governors-General of the British territories. These papers do, of course, cover relations between Canada and the United States. As Colonial Secretary he accompanied the Prince of Wales on his tour of British North America and the United States in 1860, and the papers include a letter-book containing copies of letters written to the Queen during the visit, and a quantity of newspaper cuttings.

N.R.A. (Catalogue in preparation.)

MELLISH MANUSCRIPTS.[1] 2 bundles of letters; 3 printed sheets; list of pamphlets. 1772–84. (Bundles 171–2.)

Papers belonging to Charles Mellish (*c.* 1737–96), M.P. for Pontefract 1774–80 and for Aldborough 1780–4.

(*a*) Bundle of fifty-four letters, 1772–82, to Charles Mellish from various persons in England and America on North American affairs, including the War of Independence.

(*b*) Nine letters, 1773, 1776–81, from Sir Henry Clinton in America to Charles Mellish, on the War.

(*c*) List of pamphlets (not the actual pamphlets) concerning America, 1776.

(*d*) Proposals made to non-commissioned officers and soldiers of the Pennsylvania line at Princeton, N.J., 7 Jan. 1781. (Printed sheet.)

(*e*) Trenton, N.J.: order of the Board of Committee concerning the discharge and enlistment of soldiers, 10 Jan. 1781. (Printed sheet.)

(*f*) Printed newsheet published by James Rivington, printer to the King, 17 May 1781, New York (endorsed 'New York Gazette, 1781').

N.R.A. 0893.

PORTLAND MANUSCRIPTS.[2]

There is no well-defined group of manuscripts relating to American affairs. On the other hand, reports and comments are embedded within the general political correspondence, especially among the papers of William Henry Cavendish Bentinck, 3rd Duke of Portland (1738–1809), during the period of the War of Independence (e.g., in letters of William Burke and Rockingham).

N.R.A. (Catalogue in preparation.)

[1] We thank the Mellish Trustees for permission to make this report.
[2] We thank the Duke of Portland for permission to make this report.

OXFORDSHIRE

Duke of Marlborough, BLENHEIM PALACE, Woodstock

SUNDERLAND PAPERS.

Papers of Charles Spencer, 3rd Earl of Sunderland (1674–1722), statesman. (*Letters unless otherwise stated.*)

(*a*) 11 Oct. 1684, from Lord Preston to the Earl of Sunderland on hostilities between French and Bostonians.[1]

(*b*) Letters and papers, 1706–9, relating to New York and New Jersey. (C2–45 and 46)[2]

(*c*) Miscellaneous letters and papers, 1706–9, relating to the plantations. (C2–49)[3]

(*d*) Letters and papers, 1706–9, relating to Maryland. (C2–50)[3]

(*e*) Letters and papers, 8 Nov. 1706–12 Sept. 1709, relating to Virginia. (C2–47)[2]

(*f*) Letters and papers, 24 Sept. 1707–10 Feb. 1710, relating to New England. (C2–44)[2]

(*g*) 1 June 1709, from the Council of Trade to Sunderland about large numbers of German Protestant refugees from the Palatinate arriving in England, some of whom were sent to New York and North Carolina. (C1–38)[2]

(*h*) 'Papers respecting the relief and settlement of the distressed Protestant Palatines in the colonies of America.' (*c.* 1709?)[4]

(*i*) 'Orders and instructions to Edward Nott, Esq., Lieutenant and Governor General of Virginia, in America.' (32 pages.) (1710.)[2]

Bodleian Library, OXFORD

The following summary of manuscripts is additional to the entries in Andrews & Davenport, pp. 372–421. Since their report, the *Summary Catalogue of Western Manuscripts* has been continued to 1915 (vol. vi, part 2). Vol. i (historical introduction and conspectus of shelfmarks) and vol. vii (index) were published in 1953. For accessions see *Bodleian Quarterly Record*, vols.

[1] H.M.C. viii (i), p. 30. [2] Ibid., p. 47.
[3] Ibid., p. 48. [4] Ibid., p. 59.

i–viii, 1914–38; continued as *Bodleian Library Record* from 1939. Typescript catalogues of accessions are available in the Library.

The material is arranged as follows:

Collections belonging to the Bodleian Library:

    (1) Bankes Papers
    (2) Locke Papers
    (3) North Papers
    (4) Bryce Papers
    (5) Miscellaneous Collections

Collections deposited in the Bodleian Library:

    (6) Nalson Papers
    (7) Dashwood Papers
    (8) Clarendon Papers (United States)

BANKES PAPERS.

The official papers of Sir John Bankes as Attorney-General 1634–40 purchased by the Library from Lord Bledisloe in 1960; see *Quarterly Review*, Jan. 1951, and *Bodleian Library Record*, iii. 179; iv. 313–23. There is a typescript list of the whole collection compiled by I. Gray, and a detailed calendar and index are in process of being compiled.[1]

5/29. Copies of minutes of the Council of New England, 1635, 1638. Agreements on division, allotment of lands in New England (bundle 23 [uncalendared] also contains extracts of this).

5/30. n.d. ? Apr. 1635. Agreement setting out lands in New England allotted to Sir Ferdinando Gorges, with careful delimitation of said lands.

7/7. Brief note on the Charter of Massachusetts Bay. n.d., in or after Trinity Term 1635.

7/8. Copy of the *quo warranto* exhibited against the Massachusetts Bay Company in King's Bench, 1635.[2]

7/9. Copy of sentence given in King's Bench, 1624, in *quo warranto* proceedings against the Virginia Company.[3]

7/11. Copy of the sentence concerning Matthew Cradock given in suit in King's Bench of Rex *v.* Massachusetts Bay Company (see 7/8 above), 1635.[4]

7/12. A similar copy concerning John Venn.

7/13. Copy of charter of Massachusetts Bay, 4 Mar. 1629.[5]

---

[1] The entries in the calendar relating to Virginia have been duplicated and circulated in a Memorandum from the Alderman Library, Manuscripts Division, University of Virginia, 1953.

[2] Printed in translation in T. Hutchinson, *A Collection of Original Papers Relative to the History of Massachusetts Bay*, vol. i, pp. 114–16 (Albany, N.Y., 1865).

[3] See Alexander Brown, *The First Republic in America*, pp. 585–9, 601–3 (Boston, 1898).

[4] Printed in Hutchinson, op. cit., vol. i, p. 117.

[5] Printed from original in *Records of the Governor and Company of the Massachusetts Bay*, ed. by N. B. Shurtleff, vol. i, pp. 3–19 (Boston, 1853).

8/1. Abstracts of the patent of incorporation of the Council of New England of 3 Nov. 1620; of the royal grants of Avalon to Sir George Calvert, 7 Apr. 1623; and of Maryland to Lord Baltimore, 20 June 1632; and of grants from the Council of New England of Cape Trebizond, Laconia, Piscataqua, and River Bishopscotte, 1622–32; also a note on laws relating to 'plantations in Virginia', and list of legal officers to whom patents for the colonies had apparently been submitted for consideration.[1]

8/2. Copy of representation and petition of the Commissioners for Virginia appointed on 27 June [1631].[2]

8/3. 1635. Lists of charges made by the Virginia Company against Sir John Harvey, the Governor, and against Lord Baltimore's deputies, annotated with page and line references to other papers relating to these disputes.[3]

8/4. ? 1635. Petition, apparently of planters of Virginia, then in England, to Privy Council on the alleged infringement of their rights and territories by Sir Robert Heath and Lord Baltimore.

8/6. n.d. 'The names of the chiefest planters that have both ventured their lives and estates for the plantation of Virginia.'

8/7. 1635. Order of the Commissioners for the Plantations that patent for Massachusetts Bay should be questioned by *quo warranto* or *scire facias*. (8/17 is a certified copy of this.)

8/8. 1634. Orders of Commissioners of Plantations for delivery of all patents to Attorney-General [Bankes] for examination.

8/9. Abstracts by Bankes of the letters patent of 20 June 1632, granting Maryland to Lord Baltimore,[4] and of the charter of Massachusetts Bay of 4 Mar. 1629.

8/10. ? 1635. An abstract of the terms of the letters patent by which Charles I granted to Sir William Alexander a proportion of the mainland of New England [with marginal notes and additions by Bankes].[5]

8/12. n.d. Notes by Bankes endorsed 'Desires of the planters of New England'.

8/15. n.d. after 12 June 1634. 'Motives and reasons for the petition of the Governor and Company of New Albion' [midway between New England and Virginia]. (See 8/16 below.)

8/16. n.d., after 21 June 1634. Abstract of the [Irish] patent of 21 June 1634 made by advice of Sir Thomas Wentworth, 1st Earl of Strafford, granting to [then follows list] 'all that isle called Isle Plowden or Long Isle, and 40 leagues square of the mainland next adjoining commonly called North Virginia' this is to be called New Albion.

8/18 n.d. ? 1637. List of persons against whom a *quo warranto* was exhibited in King's Bench in Trinity Term 1635, for claiming to have certain liberties and franchises as freemen of the Society of Massachusetts Bay; 'with notes of what has been done by any of them and what against them'.[6]

---

[1] See *Calendar of State Papers, Colonial Series, 1574–1660*, pp. 24, 42, 28, 102, 135, 152 (London, 1860).

[2] See ibid., p. 136.   [3] Ibid., p. 211, and 8/19 below.

[4] Printed in W. MacDonald, ed., *Select Charters and other Documents Illustrative of American History, 1606–1775*, pp. 53–60 (New York, 1899).

[5] See *Calendar of State Papers, Colonial Series, 1574–1660*, pp. 195, 204 (8/13 is another copy of this).   [6] Ibid., p. 251, and also 7/8 and 7/11–12 above.

8/19. Copy of 'A breviat of the declaration of the planters in Virginia, dated the 1st of July 1635' a fuller version of 8/3 above in a different order.

8/20. n.d. ?1636. Fragments of an abstract of, or notes for, the drafting of an official document relating to Virginia, perhaps renewal of Sir John Harvey's commission as governor, with marginal notes and endorsement by Bankes.

13/27. 1638. Proceedings upon a petition of the defendants in a suit in the Star Chamber of the Attorney-General vs. John West, Samuel Mathews, William Tucker and others, protesting against the commissioners nominated by Robert Evelin to examine witnesses in Virginia.

Bundle no. 36 [uncalendared]. 'Memorandum concerning alleged irregular legal proceedings by the Massachusetts Company', undated. [Fragile and defective.]

42/33. Order of the King in Council to prepare a proclamation 'for the restraint of disorderly transporting His Majesties subjects unto any of the plantations within the parts of America'. 23 Apr. 1637. Extract.

50/44. 1638. Warrant for a commission to Sir Francis Wyatt creating him Governor of Virginia in succession to Sir John Harvey.

51/36, 37. Warrants for grants of lands in New England to the Duke of Lennox, and others; the first, 31 May 1635, does not specify the lands; the second, 18 June 1638, adds a grant to the Earl of Stirling, which is defined as 'lands adjoining New Scotland . . . with Mattoacks or Long Island . . ., Cole Island, Sandy Point, Hell Gate, Martin's [Martha's] Vineyard, Elizabeth Islands, and Block Island'.

54/23. 1637–8. Warrant for a grant to Robert Evelin of the office of Surveyor-General for the colony of Virginia, void by the death of Gabriel Hawley.

54/33. Petition of Capt. Richard Morrison to be appointed governor of Point Comfort Castle, Virginia, and warrant accordingly, 13 Feb. 1638.

LOCKE PAPERS.[1] 1671–1714. (MSS. Locke)

John Locke (1632–1704), the philosopher, was secretary to the Lords Proprietors for Carolina 1669–72.

MS. Locke. b. 5, no. 9. Appointment of Locke as a Landgrave of Carolina, 1671.

c. 4, f. 8. Letters, 20 Jan. 1698 and 8 Feb. 1699, of James Blair, of Virginia, to Locke.

c. 16, f. 157. Letters, 30 Mar. 1697, 26 May 1698, 4 Feb. 1699, of Governor Francis Nicholson to Locke.

c. 30, f. 1. Minutes by Locke of meetings of the Lords Proprietors of Carolina, 1671–5.

f. 38. Notes by Locke on trade in Sweden, Denmark, and New England, 1696.

---

[1] This collection of his papers is that bequeathed by Locke to Peter King. It remained with his descendants until acquired by the Bodleian in 1941. P. Long, *A Summary Catalogue of the Lovelace Collection in the Bodleian Library* (Oxford, 1959) (Oxford Bibliographical Society Publications, N.S. viii).

f. 40. Notes by Locke on New England [1696].[1]

f. 55. Notes by Locke concerning the claim of the Duke of Hamilton to lands in Connecticut [1698].

f. 59. 'Queries to be put to Coll. Henry Hartwell or any other discreet person that knows the constitution of Virginia, August 30 1697.'

f. 134. Two copies of a commission of Nicholas Trott as Chief Justice in South Carolina, granted 8 Mar. 1707 and confirmed 8 Sept. 1714 (presumably added to Locke's papers by Peter King).

c. 39, f. 3. Copy of a note by Locke for the constitution of Carolina.

d. 7. 'Of the American plantations', 18 Oct. 1714, a copy of a report by James Stanhope to the Council for Trade and Plantations.[2]

e. 9. Papers on Virginia, [1697]. i, 71 leaves:[3]

f. 1. 'Some of the chief greivances of the present constitution, of Virginia with an essay towards the remedies thereof.'

f. 39. 'Queries' about the land, people, constitution, and revenue of Virginia.

f. 43. A paper on public administration in Virginia.

NORTH PAPERS. 1702–78, 1861.

Papers of the North family including a very few of Lord North (1732–92). A catalogue is available in the library.

a. 6, ff. 57–68v. Pages 266–89 of a booklet of instructions for the Governors of the Leeward Islands, Maryland, New Jersey, and New York, 1702–14.

f. 172. Petition to the King from Glasgow merchants trading in tobacco with the British colonies in America, c. 1756. They fear slave risings and attacks by French and Indians, and ask for at least as good a defence system for Virginia and Maryland as is enjoyed by the Northern colonies.[4]

f. 187. A comparison of military expenditure in the American plantations and Gibraltar, 1758, 1759.[4]

ff. 201–14. Copy of an unsigned letter, London, 15 Jan. 1760 (to the Duke of Newcastle?) suggesting the boundaries necessary for the defence of North America, and other points to be raised in peace negotiations with France.

ff. 237–40. Observations on North America made by Captain J. Innis, of the Royal American Regiment, during his residence there, 1756–60. Includes remarks on situation, soil, climate, &c., of Louisiana.[4]

ff. 274–80. Copy of a letter, Edinburgh, 15 June 1761, by the writer of the letter in f. 201, advocating a policy of exclusion of the French from North America.

[1] Cf. *Calendar of State Papers, Colonial Series, America and the West Indies, 1696–7*, nos. 250 and 1120 (London, 1904).

[2] Cf. *Calendar of State Papers, Colonial Series, America and the West Indies, 1714–1715*, no. 236 (London, 1928).

[3] Cf. *Calendar of State Papers, Colonial Series, America and the West Indies, 1696–7*, nos. 1320, 1396 (London, 1904).

[4] Typed transcript at Rhodes House, Oxford, in a bound volume, 'MSS. Brit. Emp. s. 1'.

a. 12. A complete list of ships engaged in American trade, 5 Jan. 1772–5 Jan. 1773, with kind, tonnage, and details of voyages, and a list of imports and exports of the colonies (with quantities) for the same period.

b. 6, ff. 47–50. Letter, 1762, from Peter Collinson to the Earl of Bute, stating that the British should take possession of St. Augustine, Fla., as it is a 'thorn in the side' of the American colonies, a harbour for runaway slaves and criminals, and a base for Spanish depredations.[1]

f. 168. Memorial, 3 July 1762, to the Earl of Bute from William Franklin of Pennsylvania, requesting the office of Secretary to South Carolina.

f. 178. Petition, Nov. 1762, of Henry Woodward, late Captain of H.M. Provincial Regiment of Virginia, to the King, praying to be appointed 'Commander of Lakes Erie, Huron, etc.' (See also ff. 207, 209, 210: letters of recommendation of Woodward by Governor Francis Fauquier of Virginia.)

f. 181. Extract from a letter, Annapolis, Md., 6 Dec. 1762, from Horatio Sharpe, Governor of Maryland, to his brother William, concerning an office in the colony.[1]

ff. 186–93. 'Short observations upon North America and the Sugar Islands', 1762. Chiefly comments on what should be done with Canada and Louisiana at the coming peace.[1]

f. 219. Note on quit-rents in Georgia.

f. 238. Request to the Earl of Bute from Mr. Ware for removal to a better office from that of Comptroller of Customs in New England.

f. 241. Memorial to the Earl of Bute from Benjamin Barons, late Collector of Customs at Boston, concerning his suspension from that office.

ff. 260–78. Recommendations, 8 June 1763, from the Board of Trade to George III relating to the future administration of newly acquired territories in Canada, Florida, and the West Indies.[1]

ff. 297–303. 'Explanation of the several branches of H.M. revenues arising in the plantations at the King's free disposal.' c. 1762.[1]

f. 327. Petition to the Earl of Bute of Lieutenant Timberlake for expenses ncurred in bringing three Cherokee chiefs to London, c. 1762–3.

ff. 333–4. Statement of account of Lieut.-Col. James Robertson, Deputy Quartermaster-General of H.M. Forces in North America, 1757–65. Includes amounts paid for provisions, &c.[1]

f. 339. Extract from a letter, 13 Jan. 1771, from Thomas Bishop of Boston to 'J. T.', stating that the Bostonians desire peace and concord.[1]

ff. 380–2. Extracts from an unsigned letter, New York, 25 Jan. 1778, complaining of Howe's dilatoriness in carrying on the war. The general tenor is that, with more energy, it could have been won already.[1]

b. 27, ff. 96–98, 107–9, 149, 182–6. Papers relating to ships in which Francis North, 2nd Baron Guilford, had an interest; several are about the *Billinghurst* engaged in the slave trade, including (f. 184) a reinsurance policy for a voyage from Jamaica to America and London, 1719.

b. 69. 'Copies of all entries of goods and merchandise outwards for North

---

[1] Typed transcript at Rhodes House, Oxford. See note 4, (p. 371).

America, which have been made at the port of London, or any other port within . . . England (except such ships as have entered outwards by virtue of licences granted by the Lords Commissioners of the Admiralty for shipping of goods into any ships taken into His Majesty's service bound to North America) since passing an Act to prohibit all trade and intercourse with the colonies . . . during the continuance of the present rebellion (from 22 Dec. 1775 to 13 May 1776) . . .' In every case the ships were bound for Canada or Florida.

b. 78, ff. 9–17. Rated and unrated East India goods (tea excepted), exported from England between Christmas 1760 and Christmas 1776 to Africa, foreign parts, West India islands, and North American colonies.

c. 83. Alphabetical list of goods imported into North America from Great Britain and Ireland, 5 Jan. 1769–5 Jan. 1770.

  f. 3v. British goods imported into North America, &c.
  f. 17v. Foreign goods imported into North America, &c.
  f. 25v. Articles subject to duty.

d. 35, ff. 56–65. Letter, 9 Nov. 1861, from General Hastings Doyle to (his brother) Colonel S. North,[1] describing the military weakness of New Brunswick, and the possibility of an American attack.[2]

BRYCE PAPERS. American papers: 33 volumes. 1870–1922.

James Bryce, 1st Viscount Bryce (1838–1922), jurist, historian, and politician; M.P. 1880–1906, and a member of three Cabinets. He first visited the United States in 1871 and last in 1921. Author of *The American Commonwealth* (1888); British Ambassador to the United States 1907–13.

The American papers are arranged as follows:

  Bryce–Eliot Correspondence. 2 volumes.
  Major American Correspondents. 8 volumes.
  Miscellaneous American Correspondents. 11 volumes.
  Bryce Letters to Americans. 2 volumes.
  Letters relating to *The American Commonwealth*. 3 volumes.
  Embassy Papers. 7 volumes.

Many letters are accompanied by clippings from United States newspapers, pamphlets, &c. It is probable that the volumes of 'English Correspondents' —especially the correspondence of Goldwin Smith and Bryce—and others concerning Bryce's literary and political career will be found to contain some relevant material.

A catalogue of the collection is available in the Library.

(*a*) BRYCE–ELIOT CORRESPONDENCE. 2 volumes. (*Arranged chronologically.*)

Charles William Eliot (1834–1926), President of Harvard University, 1868–1909.

---

[1] Colonel J. S. Doyle, son of Sir C. W. Doyle, took the name of North on his marriage to Susan, Baroness North, in 1835.

[2] Typed transcript at Rhodes House, Oxford. See note 4, (p. 371).

96 letters, 1871–1922, to Bryce, with one photostat copy (1907) and 9 later letters, 1922–6, to Lady Bryce.[1]

136 letters (37 in photostat and 99 in typed copy), 1879–1921, from Bryce to Eliot.[2]

The letters of 1879–1908 from Bryce to Eliot (all in photostat here) are mainly of minor interest, e.g. on lectures to be given by both Bryce and Eliot. Those in typed copy (1909–21) range through all Bryce's American interests, with the notable addition of a considerable amount on labour problems in the United States. Eliot's letters are also noteworthy as expounding the views of one who was convinced that American neutrality in the First World War was the best policy both for the United States and the Allies.

(*b*) MAJOR AND MISCELLANEOUS AMERICAN CORRESPONDENTS. 8 and 11 volumes respectively. (*Arranged alphabetically*.)

Main topics discussed include: various presidential campaigns and elections, 1884–1920; tariff; Negro problem; civil service reform; Canadian–American relations; international copyright legislation; the government of American cities, especially New York; the Armenian question; the Irish question and American opinion; women's suffrage; the Venezuela crisis; the Spanish–American War, Cuba, the Philippines, and imperialism generally; repercussions of the Boer War in the United States; Mexico question; the Panama tolls question; the United States and the First World War, notably the organization of support for the Allies, German propaganda activities; division of feeling between the East and West (isolationism being stronger in the West), and maritime disputes with both Britain and Germany; the American League to Enforce Peace; arguments in United States for and against the League of Nations; anti-Wilson sentiment; the struggle over the ratification of the Peace Treaty, 1919–20, and America's retreat from collective security. There is also considerable discussion of academic matters.

Major correspondents are:

Adams, Charles Francis, the younger. 23 letters. 1898–1915.

Barton, J. L., Secretary of the American Board of Commissioners for Foreign Missions (Congregational). 17 letters. 1913–21.

Butler, Nicholas Murray, President of Columbia University. 52 letters (including typed copies). 1891–1921.

Carnegie, Andrew. 39 letters, mostly slight notes. 1891–1917.

Choate, Joseph. 15 letters. 1899–1916.

Garrison, Wendell P., of the *Nation*. 134 letters. 1881–1905.

Godkin, E. L., editor of the *Nation*. 54 letters. 1882–1902, and 2 from Mrs. Godkin, 1904.

Godkin, Lawrence, son of E. L. Godkin. 11 letters. 1882, 1903–18.

Henry, Bayard, lawyer of Philadelphia. 76 letters. 1915–21.

[1] Nineteen to Bryce and 3 to Lady Bryce are printed, in whole or in part, in Henry James, *Charles W. Eliot, President of Harvard University, 1869–1909.* 2 vols., (Boston and New York, 1930; London, 1931).

[2] Twenty-one of these are printed in H. A. L. Fisher, *James Bryce, Viscount Bryce of Dechmont*, 2 vols. (London and New York, 1927).

Jameson, J. F., historian. 19 letters. 1891, 1910–22.[1]

Johnson, Robert Underwood, secretary of the American Copyright League. 40 letters. 1884–1921.

Lodge, Henry Cabot. 34 letters. 1893–1922.

Low, Seth, New York municipal reformer, President of Columbia University. 40 letters. 1887–1916.

Lowell, A. Lawrence, President of Harvard University. 44 letters. 1899–1921.

Macy, Jesse, Professor of Political Science at Grinnel College, Iowa. 18 letters and 3 from Mrs. Macy. 1887–1919.

Marburg, Theodore, member of the executive committee of the American League to Enforce Peace. 31 letters. 1915–20.[2]

Rhodes, James Ford, historian. 31 letters. 1895–1921.

Roosevelt, Theodore. 53 letters.[3] 1886–1918.

Root, Elihu. 11 letters. 1905–20.

Sedgwick, Ellery, editor of the *Atlantic Monthly*. 12 letters. 1914–21.

Storey, Moorfield, business man. 40 letters. 1906–21.

Taft, William Howard. 19 letters. 1911–21.

Villard, Henry, journalist, railroad promoter, and financier. 16 letters. 1883–1900.

Among the Miscellaneous Correspondents are:

Adams, Herbert B. 4 letters. 1882–96.

Addams, Jane, superintendent of Hull House, Chicago. 1 letter. 1915.

Atkinson, Edward, economist. 1 letter. 1901.

Bancroft, George. 1 letter. 1881.

Beveridge, Albert J., United States Senator. 1 letter. 1915.

Bingham, Hiram, Professor of Latin American History at Yale University. 10 letters. 1911–21.

Bishop, Joseph B., of the New York *Evening Post*. 4 letters. 1895–1921.

Bowker, R. R., publisher and author. 3 letters (one a copy). 1888–1918.

Bradford, Gamaliel, author. 8 letters. 1884–1911.

Burton, Theodore E., United States Senator. 3 letters. 1911–19.

Clemens, Samuel L. ('Mark Twain'). 1 postcard. 1900.

Croly, Herbert. 1 letter. 1917.

Davis, John W., United States Ambassador to Britain 1919–21. 1 letter. 1920.

Edmunds, George F., United States Senator. 1 letter. 1885.

Eggleston, Edward, historian and novelist. 3 letters. 1889–96.

[1] Six of these are printed in Elizabeth Donnan and Leo F. Stock, eds., 'An historian's world, selections from the correspondence of John Franklin Jameson', *Memoirs of the American Philosophical Society*, vol. xlii, 1956; and a further five in Leo F. Stock, ed., 'Some Bryce–Jameson Correspondence', *American Historical Review*, vol. 50, pp. 261–98, 1945.

[2] Eleven of these are printed in *Development of the League of Nations Idea; Documents and Correspondence of Theodore Marburg*, 2 vols., ed. by John H. Latané (New York, 1932).

[3] Only some of these letters have been printed in *Letters of Theodore Roosevelt*, selected and edited by E. E. Morison and others. 8 vols. (Cambridge, Mass., 1951–4).

Garrison, Francis J., publisher. 1 letter. 1893.

George, Henry. 1 letter. 1884.

Gilder, Richard W., editor. 17 letters. 1880–1906.

Goodnow, Frank J., political scientist. 2 letters. 1889, 1896.

Gregory, Charles Noble, university dean. 16 letters. 1913–21.

Hart, Albert Bushnell, historian. 1 letter. 1903.

Hay, John. 4 letters. 1887–98.

Higginson, Thomas Wentworth, author. 8 letters. 1881–1904.

Hoar, George Frisbie, United States Senator. 1 letter. 1897.

Holmes, Oliver Wendell, Sen. 2 letters. 1886.

Holmes, Oliver Wendell, Jr. 15 letters. 1871–94, 1914–21; and 1 to Lady Bryce. 1926.

Hopkins, Archibald, lawyer. 17 letters. 1916–21.

House, Edward M. 10 letters. 1915–19.

Hughes, Charles Evans. 2 letters. 1910, 1921.

Keen, W. W., surgeon. 3 letters (one printed). 1915–21.

Lansing, Robert. 3 letters. 1915–21.

Laughlin, James L., political economist. 3 letters. 1919.

Lea, Henry C., historian and Philadelphia municipal reformer. 3 letters. 1870–1904.

Longfellow, Henry W. 1 letter. 1871.

Lowell, James Russell. 2 letters. 1884, 1886.

MacVeagh, Wayne, lawyer, diplomat and reformer. 1 letter. 1897.

Marshall, Thomas R., Vice-President of the United States 1913–21. 2 letters. 1917.

Norton, Charles D., banker. 2 letters. 1914, 1921.

Norton, Charles E. 4 letters. 1903–7.

Page, Walter Hines. 7 letters. 1914–17.

Putnam, George Haven, publisher. 6 letters. 1891–1917.

Reed, Thomas B., Speaker of the House of Representatives 1889–91, 1895–9. Letter. 1891.

Schurz, Carl. 2 letters. 1884, 1899.

Shaw, Albert, editor. 6 letters. 1885–1904.

Stimson, Henry L., Secretary of War 1911–13. 6 letters. 1913–20.

Straight, Willard, financier and 'dollar diplomatist' in Far East. 4 letters. 1916–17.

Thayer, W. R., historian. 14 letters. 1903–20.

Villard, Oswald Garrison, editor of the *Nation*. 3 letters. 1900, 1920.

Washington, Booker T. 2 letters. 1908.

White, Andrew D. 3 letters. 1883–98.

White, Henry, American plenipotentiary to the Peace Conference. 7 letters. 1914, 1919–20.

Wicksham, George, Attorney-General 1909–13. 12 letters. 1914–21.

Wilson, William L., Representative from West Virginia, sponsor of 1893 Tariff. 6 letters. 1892–6.

Wilson, Woodrow. 13 letters. 1888–1918. There is also a draft reply by Bryce on the back of an envelope from Wilson (dated 1919) but Wilson's letter is missing.

(c) BRYCE LETTERS TO AMERICANS. 1881–1921. 2 volumes. *(Arranged chronologically.)* Typescript copies—with a few drafts handwritten by Bryce, 1881–1921.

Most of the letters are to the following:

Bingham, Hiram. 34 letters. 1910–21.
Butler, Nicholas Murray. 31 letters. 1893–1919.
House, Edward M. 5 letters. 1915–17.
Low, Seth. 28 letters. 1892–1915.
Lowell, A. Lawrence. 55 letters. 1900–21.
Macy, Jesse. 25 letters, and 1 to Mrs. Macy. 1891–1921.
Rhodes, James Ford. 25 letters. 1900–21.
White, Henry. 8 letters. 1913–19.

Others are to George P. Brett, J. A. Chambliss, R. H. Dana, S. Edelman, Bayard Henry, Thomas W. Higginson, Oliver Wendell Holmes, Jnr., Henry Holt, Henry C. Lea, Henry Cabot Lodge, William Loeb, Jnr., Denys P. Myers, Charles E. Norton, A. E. Pillsbury, G. H. Putnam, Theodore Roosevelt, Elihu Root, Theodore Stanton, F. J. Stimson, William H. Taft, Everett P. Wheeler, and Sarah Whitman.

Most of the subjects mentioned under 'Major and Miscellaneous American Correspondents (p. 374) are again represented, with—in addition to comments on British politics and matters relating to *The American Commonwealth* —also the following: Cleveland's civil service policy; municipal politics in Philadelphia; immigration; American and British railroad rates; an elective judiciary; the Iowa primary system; the American Labor Party; Wilson's domestic policy. In a letter, 1920, to J. F. Rhodes, Bryce is severely critical of Wilson's handling of the ratification question.

(d) *The American Commonwealth.* 3 volumes. *(Arranged alphabetically.)*

Letters to Bryce about the book from many and diverse Americans and Britons; some before the publication of the first edition in 1888 in reply to queries put by him, but most after publication criticizing, or suggesting amendments or further reading. There is a letter from Denis Kearney castigating the chapter on 'Kearneyism in California', and another of the same year setting forth what he (Kearney) claims to be the true position— annotated by Bryce. There are also many replies to questions put by Bryce before revision of the book, 1905–11, e.g. about women's suffrage, boss rule in the cities, the Referendum and Recall, and the Negro problem. Many correspondents enclose printed material which they think will be useful in future editions. There are also a number of letters relating to the libel action brought against Bryce by Oakey Hall, Mayor of New York under Tweed, over Frank J. Goodnow's chapter on the Tweed Ring in the first edition—suppressed in the second edition (1889)—including some from Goodnow himself.

(*e*) EMBASSY PAPERS. 1907–13. 7 volumes. (*Arranged chrono-logically.*)

Include miscellaneous papers—notes, draft letters, aide-memoires by Bryce, copies of telegrams, &c.—and letters from American Cabinet members, notably Root and Knox, Senators and Representatives, other Ambassadors in Washington, and newspaper men. Also letters of thanks for addresses, invitations to lecture, &c.

The collection includes Bryce's commission and credentials as Ambassador; and also letters and papers on: Canadian–American relations (with printed copies of treaties affecting Canada signed during Bryce's tenure of office); Canadian Boundary Waters question; and Passamaquoddy Bay (1908); conservation; proposed transformation of International Prize Court into Arbitration Tribunal (1908); Newfoundland fisheries (1909–12), especially the Hague Award (1910); situation in Central America in 1910; fur seals negotiation (1911) with a draft of the proposed treaty; Canadian Recipro-city Treaty (1911); American armed vessels on the Great Lakes; Panama tolls. There is also a memo (? by George Young) of conversations with Senator Borah on arbitration.

Writers of letters include the following:

Edward VII on Theodore Roosevelt.

Grey, Sir Edward, on the North Atlantic Fisheries Agreement (1912), the faked interview with Bryce on the Oklahoma Constitution (1907), possible action against the British Imperial Tobacco Company under the Anti-Trust Law, a proposed arbitration treaty with the United States, Anglo-American policy in the Far East, Panama tolls, Bryce's retirement and Spring-Rice's appointment—also some short replies by Bryce.

Hardinge, Sir Charles, of the Foreign Office on foreign affairs generally, and American–Canadian and American–Japanese relations in particular.

Howard, Esme, Chargé while Bryce was on vacation in Britain 1908, on Boundary Waters negotiations, and also copies of dispatches from Howard to Sir Edward Grey.

Innes, A. Mitchell, who was in charge of the embassy while Bryce was in summer quarters in 1909 and 1910, on Boundary Waters, American–German relations, Canadian reciprocity, Far Eastern affairs; and later, in 1912, on Panama tolls, the Republican platform and the 'rottenness' of Congress.

Young, George, Attaché at Washington and secretary of the North Atlantic Fisheries Arbitration at The Hague, 1909–10, chiefly on the latter.

Various members of the embassy staff—notes of minor importance: C. C. Bayley, British Consul at New York—mostly about Irish agitation there; various other Consular letters from Bayley's successors C. W. Bennett and R. Walsh, and from the Consuls in San Francisco and Chicago.

British Ministers in other countries, notably Brazil, Mexico, Guatemala, and Nicaragua, on events in those places.

Johnston, Sir H. H., in Liberia on the Negro problem.

Taft, President. Six letters, 1908–12, with one of which is enclosed a copy of the Senate's resolutions limiting the proposed Arbitration Treaty between Britain and the United States.

Knox, Philander C., Secretary of State, on fisheries (with replies by Bryce).

Laurier, Sir Wilfred, Sir Robert Borden, and various Canadian Cabinet members, officials, &c., as well as Sir William Macgregor and Sir Ralph Williams, Governors of Newfoundland 1908–9 and 1911–12 respectively, and Sir Robert Bond and Sir Edward Morris, Prime Ministers of same, 1909, 1909–12, mostly on Canadian–American relations and fisheries.

MISCELLANEOUS COLLECTIONS. (*Arranged chronologically.*)

MS. Hatton 51 (S.C. 4099).

Some seventeenth-century notes about methods of making fire, and manufacturing glue in Virginia, written in the margins of an earlier work.

MS. Eng. hist. c. 4 (S.C. 29724). f. 3.

Copy of a newsletter, 18 Nov. 1610, from George Yardly about affairs in Virginia.

MS. Malone 16 (S.C. 20564).

A common-place book of poems, &c., 1620–30, including a description of a voyage to America.

MS. Add. C. 244 (S.C. 28087). p. 495.

A contemporary copy of the charter granted to the Company of Massachusetts Bay, 4 Mar. 1629.

MS. Add. C. 267 (S.C. 29563).

Copies of letters, invoices, business memoranda, &c., 1655–9, of Thomas Pengelly, cloth and general merchant of London, chiefly relating to his foreign ventures in Virginia, &c.[1]

MS. Add. A. 95 (S.C. 28961).

Diary (29 pages), kept by a Quaker companion of George Fox during his visit to New England, June 1671–Apr. 1673. Endorsed on the flyleaf, 'said to be the autograph of Ellwood, the friend of Milton'.[2]

MS. Aubrey 13 (S.C. 25287). f. 98.

Letter, Philadelphia, 13 Apr. 1683, from William Penn to Aubrey, describing the favourable condition of Pennsylvania.

Rawlinson Letters 94 (S.C. 14982). f. 188.

Copy of a letter, Boston, 3 Oct. 1683, from Increase Mather to an unnamed friend in Amsterdam, chiefly on affairs in England, and that he expects a large number of believers from there shortly to come to New England.

Rawlinson Letters 108 (S.C. 14996). f. 87.

Letter, Boston, 27 Nov. 1683, from Cotton Mather to Richard Chiswell about books.

[1] H.M.C. vii, p. 691. (Listed as in possession of the Rev. Thomas William Webb, Hardwick Vicarage, Herefordshire.)

[2] Printed in the *Journal of the Friends' Historical Society*, vol. ix, pp. 5–52, 1912.

MS. Aubrey 4 (S.C. 25279). f. 1.

An almost complete draft of an indenture, 1684, between two merchants, William Paggen [place of residence cut away] and John Hardmian, of James River, Va., by which Hardmian agrees to be Paggen's exclusive agent in Virginia.

MS. Carte 81 (S.C. 10527). ff. 742–51, 754–65, 779, 803–8.

Papers of Philip Wharton, 4th Baron Wharton (1613–96), and Thomas Wharton, 1st Marquis of Wharton (1648–1716), relating to New England and Virginia, 1689–90. Includes statements of settlers' grievances; patent for the appointment of Sir Edmund Andros as governor of New England; two petitions from Connecticut for fair treatment in the levying of the militia quota; and the 'case' (scarcely legible) of New England in a dispute with New York.

Rawlinson Letters 51 (S.C. 14933). f. 329.

Letter, Boston, 11 Sept. 1689, from Increase Mather to Lord Wharton, asking him to speak to the King in order to counteract malicious 'informations' laid against the church in New England.

MS. Eng. th. c. 50. f. 72.

A letter beginning 'Worthie Mr. Doctor: concerning our plantation in the American world'. The letter is undated, but late seventeenth century, lacking both address and signature, and concerns the conversion of the natives, of which the writer has little hope.

MS. Gough Somersetshire 7 (S.C. 18217).

Copies of papers relating to schemes and calculations addressed to, or connected with, James Brydges, 1st Duke of Chandos (1673–1744). Includes proposals for raising naval stores in Ste.-Croix, Que. 1716 (pp. 122–6). Letter, 14 Aug. 1718, from Col. Alexander Spottiswood [or Spotswood], Lieut.-Governor of Virginia, pointing out the danger from the French in the Lake Erie region, and proposing that the British should occupy the region in strength (pp. 127–35). Paper by Francis Harrison (pp. 231–9), 1724, setting forth the advantages which the Royal African Company may derive by establishing an agency at New York for the supply of Negroes to the Jerseys and New England.

MS. Eng. misc. c. 311. ff. 4–21.

Register of the patentees for the growth of cochineal and medicinal drugs in the American plantations, including copies of letters patent to George Sinclair, articles of agreement with his partners and minutes of the meetings of the patentees, in the hand of Daniel Campbell, secretary, 1722–8.

MSS. Add. A. 289–300 (S.C. 29404–15)

Letters, notices, and notes of all kinds received by William Henry Turner, who was largely employed in historical and genealogical research at the Bodleian Library by English and American men of letters, c. 1860–80. They include a list of papers and an abstract relating to South Carolina in the State Paper Office, London, 1728–40, notes taken from collections of the South Carolina Historical Society, volumes 1 and 2, sent to Turner to check in London by G. B. Chase from Boston, 27 Apr. 1875. (MS. Add. A. 295, f. 162.)

MS. Top. Oxon. d. 224.

Record of the campaigns of the 52nd (Oxfordshire) Light Infantry, 1755–1822, giving a summary description of its movements, with casualties and promotions, and extracts from dispatches and field orders. The regiment served in Canada, 1765–74, and in America from 1774 to 1778. Its troops were concerned in the skirmish at Lexington, in the battles of Bunker Hill, Brooklyn, Pelham Manor, and Brandywine, in operations on Staten Island and Long Island, and the capture of Forts Montgomery and Clinton.

MS. Montagu d. 18 (S.C. 25448). ff. 132, 134.

Two letters from George Washington from Mount Vernon. One, 30 Sept. 1762, is presumably to a firm of merchants, and is chiefly about the shipment by him of tobacco;[1] the other, 22 Feb. 1788, is to an unnamed correspondent, asking for red clover seed.[2]

MS. Gough Surrey 8 (S.C. 18247).

Calendars of papers in 'the Lambeth Library', 'Digested by Dr. Ducarel', 1767, including (ff. 3–27) papers concerning the American colonies, and the work there of the Society for the Propagation of the Gospel, 1641–1762.

MS. Gough Gen. Top. 40. f. 66.

Letter, Enfield, 31 Dec. 1756, from Rev. W. Bush to R. Gough says that reports from America are depressing. Indians have hoisted French colours on a fort built as a bastion against the French. An authoritative source in New England is of the opinion that if the mouth of the St. Lawrence were blockaded the French would surrender within three months.

f. 134. Letter, 5 Jan. 1768, from the same asking Gough's advice about supporting an appeal by Mr. Edwards, a Rhode Island Baptist minister, for funds to enlarge a school there. Gough's reply (f. 135), 11 Jan. 1768, is unfavourable.

MS. Eng. hist. a. 5 (S.C. 32934).

Letter, Mount Vernon, 6 Oct. 1773, from George Washington, ordering goods for himself and 'books for Mr. Custis' from Robert Cary & Co., London merchants.[3]

MS. Eng. hist. c. 306, f. 5. Le Fleming Papers.

Letter, 17 Dec. 1774, from Sir Michael Le Fleming to — Moore, on the rebellion in America, and Lord North's attitude thereto.[4]

---

[1] See *Writings of George Washington*, ed. by John C. Fitzpatrick, vol. ii, pp. 383–4 (Washington, D.C., 1931).

[2] Ibid., vol. xxix, pp. 421–2, quotes a letter from Mount Vernon of the same date to Clement Biddle asking for red clover seed.

[3] Ibid., vol. iii, pp. 154–5.

[4] Transcript, H.M.C. xii (vii), p. 359. (Listed as in possession of S. H. Le Fleming, Esq., of Rydal Hall.)

MSS. Eng. misc. c. 132, ff. 42–43, 44–45, 53–56.

Letters from Lord Shelburne to Dr. Richard Price, two n.d., third, Bowood Park, 24 Sept. 1777. First says that the American cause is gaining ground in the country, assisted by a recent speech by Lord Mansfield. By next spring, he estimates, the Americans will have thirty frigates and sloops well manned and armed. Second apparently implies that if Britain were to make certain concessions to the colonists they would make faithful subjects. Third contains various comments on military operations in America, the numbers in Washington's army, and the administration's displeasure with General Carleton for not employing the Indians sooner.

MS. Bor. 48 (S.C. 20689).

'Dissertationem de America ab Islandis ante Columbum detecta . . . submittet Geir Vidalinus Hafniae anno MDCCLXXXVII', followed by the dissertation (B.D., 1787).

MS. Fairfax 35 (S.C. 31069). f. 283.

An anecdote of Washington's last words (reputed to have been 'I die hard'), also comments on his state of health towards the close of his life (in a letter written from Mount Eagle, near Alexandria, Va., 18 Jan. 1800, by Bryan, Lord Fairfax of Cameron, to an unidentified kinsman.

MS. Maps. misc. a. 2 (S.C. 33091). f. 8.

'Plan of the operations of the British and American forces before New Orleans between 23 December 1814 and 8 January 1815.'

MS. Eng. misc. d. 164. ff. 84, 119.

Letters, Boston, 4 June and 10 Sept. 1817, from Rev. Charles Lowell to Mark Noble, concerning the newly-incorporated American Antiquarian Society, with an account of his family history and his own career.

MS. Eng. misc. c. 29 (S.C. 32396).

This is similar to the typescript travel journal of Sir Henry Singer Keating in the Cambridge University Library (p. 17), but the relevant pages are 222–353.

MS. Autogr. d. 10 (S.C. 36017). f. 23.

Autograph letter, Montgomery, Ala., 18 May 1861, from Jefferson Davis to Professor A. T. Bledsoe, thanking him for his sympathy with 'the great cause' and saying that he cannot leave Montgomery while Congress is in session.

MS. Don. e. 47. Thomson Papers.

Diary of business done by James Thomson (1834–82), the poet, for the Champion Gold and Silver Company in Colorado, 16 May–31 Dec. 1872 (iii+205 pages, pp. 109–202 blank). Mentions investments in the Company, proposed division of profits, legal proceedings by injunction, visits to Idaho, defects in the mine.

MSS. Eng. hist. d. 181–4.

Notes on Columbus's first voyage to America, by Edmund Palmer. Largely a discussion of which islands Columbus discovered first, with charts of islands and anchorages. Two letters, 19 Nov. 1898 and 4 Apr. 1899, enclosed in d. 181 about his 'research' on this subject.

MS. Autogr. d. 15.

Letters, 1916–19, from eminent Americans, including (ff. 14, 15) two from Elihu Root, to Professor Walter E. Peck. Personal and academic only.

NALSON PAPERS. (The property of the Duke of Portland.)

Vol. xviii, item 90. (Dep. c. 171, ff. 233–5.) June 1651. Draft treaty between the United Provinces and England proposed by the Commissioners of the States-General includes provisions 'for settling . . . the boundaries of the possessions of either in North America'; and a clause providing that subjects of either power may thereafter trade freely with 'the Caribee Islands and other places of Virginia'.[1]

Vol. xxii, item 157. (Dep. c. 175, f. 427.) 1651. Petition of Dirck Janson of Middelburgh to the Parliament praying for restoration of the cargo of a ship seized for violating the Act prohibiting trade with Virginia. Had sailed from Europe before passage of the Act, and had left Virginia before news of the prohibition arrived.[2]

DASHWOOD PAPERS.

See Betty Kemp, 'Some letters of Sir Francis Dashwood, Baron le Despencer, a joint Postmaster General, 1766–81', *Bulletin of the John Rylands Library*, vol. xxxvii. 204–48, 1954.

D. D. Dashwood (Bucks.) b. 5.

There is one printed piece, *Narrative of Facts relative to American Affairs* (15 pages). It is a resumé based on official documents and on letters, principally from Governor Francis Bernard of Massachusetts. The latest letters are 1 and 3 Oct. 1768, received on 4 Nov. On the first is the note: 'This paper is given to you in great confidence of your secrecy, with a request that you will not communicate it to any person whatever.'

CLARENDON PAPERS (UNITED STATES).[3] 14 volumes manuscripts. 1853–8, 1865–70. 6 volumes papers printed for Cabinet use, &c., 1848–57. 5 boxes letters, papers. 1868–70. (MSS. Clar. Dep.)

George William Frederick Villiers, 4th Earl of Clarendon and 4th Baron Hyde (1800–70), was Foreign Secretary 1853–8, 1865–6, and 1868–70.

I. 1853–8.
MS. Clar. Dep. c. 11, 24, 25, 43, 44, 63, 64, 65, 81, 83 are from the series of bound 'in letters'.

---

[1] H.M.C. xiii (i), pp. 605-7.   [2] Ibid., p. 617.
[3] These papers have been deposited by Lord Clarendon on condition that no quotations are made from them without his consent.

c. 11. 'United States: [letters from] Mr. Crampton and miscellaneous, 1853.'

Deals with fisheries; reciprocity; prospects, especially regarding the tariff, for Anglo-American relations during the Pierce administration; filibustering; Honduras; conclusion of international copyright convention; abatement of anti-British sentiment in United States; to Britain's advantage not to interfere in the slavery issue; Cuba; Pierce's Inaugural address; isthmian canal; speeches in Congress on the Clayton–Bulwer Treaty; the dispute between the 'Hards' and 'Softs' in New York; division of spoils under Pierce; landing of the Americans at Greytown, Nicaragua; appointment of Pierre Soulé to Madrid; the character of Buchanan; conversations with Marcy about the Clayton–Bulwer Treaty; Central American affairs generally; adverse effects in some quarters of American opinion of Mrs. H. B. Stowe's warm reception in Britain; the Mosquito Coast; the fugitive slave problem; United States attitude on Anglo-Russian relations; navigation of the St. Lawrence; the affair of Koszta, a Hungarian refugee; United States suspicions about British intentions concerning Cuba. (See also c. 225, p. 386.)

c. 24. 'United States, January–June 1854.' Mostly from Crampton, with some copy enclosures from American statesmen, and some letters from Consuls, &c.

Deals with South Carolina's action on coloured seamen; Senator Sumner and arbitration; further discussion of the Clayton–Bulwer Treaty; United States alarm over the Mosquito protectorate; the Nebraska question; alleged fitting out of Russian privateers in United States ports; fisheries; Central America; the belief that United States was planning the seizure of Cuba; the *Black Warrior* incident.

c. 25. 'United States, July–December 1854.' Mostly as c. 24 above.

Deals with the Quebec meeting on fisheries; offer of mediation by United States in Crimean War; the Reciprocity Treaty (Crampton says that this is popular in the United States, but there may be delay in its ratification); bombardment of Greytown, Nicaragua; rumours of Hawaiian annexation; Soulé's activities at Madrid; United States designs on Samaná Bay, Dominican Republic; the 'aggressive' activities of a United States naval officer at the Falkland Islands; the Ostend meeting and manifesto; Nicaragua, the state of which prevents settlement of the Central American question; recruitment in the United States for the Crimean War.

c. 43. 'United States, January–August 1855.' Mostly as c. 24 above; and including some letters to Clarendon from Buchanan as United States Minister in London.

Mainly about enlistment for the Crimean War, which was finally stopped in this period; steamers for sale in the United States; dropping of treaty with Santo Domingo by the United States; difficulties between the United States and Spain; the United States squadron going to Cuba; hostility towards Britain in the United States; negotiations between Britain and United States over the detention of coloured seamen in Southern ports.

c. 44. 'United States, September–December 1855.' Mostly as c. 24 above.

Deals with Irish anti-British agitation in United States; indictment of Consuls over Crimean recruiting; unpopularity of the Pierce administration; United States government's desire for Crampton's recall; aversion of mercantile classes to the quarrel with Britain over recruiting; election of Speaker of the House of Representatives.

c. 63. 'United States, January–April 1856.' Mostly as c. 24 above, with several from Sir Henry Bulwer.

Crampton mentions rumours of his recall; the appointment of Dallas to London; William Walker's activities in Nicaragua; effect of the Peace of Paris in the United States; improvement of feeling towards Britain.

c. 64. 'United States, May–July 1856.' Mainly from Crampton until his dismissal in 1856, then from the Chargé and various others, including Bulwer.

Deals with Costa Rica and Walker; Brooks's attack on Sumner; Crampton's dismissal by Pierce; Frémont's nomination for President; aftermath of Crampton's dismissal; the presidential campaign of 1856 (conflicting reports as to the probable outcome from various correspondents).

c. 65. 'United States, August–December 1856' (with letters of May and June), from various persons, but notably John S. Lumley, British Chargé.

Deals with dismissal of Consuls; the presidential election; the Kansas question; United States designs on British North America; the transatlantic telegraph; the Oregon Boundary Commission; desire in United States to renew diplomatic relations with Britain; slavery agitation; appointment of Lord Napier as British Minister to the United States; Cass to be the new Secretary of State.

c. 81. 'United States 1857.' Principally from Napier.

Chiefly concerned with events in Central America; probable policy of the new administration; negotiations on steamers on the Great Lakes; Cuba; Kansas; the President (Buchanan) on the Clayton–Bulwer Treaty; Stephen A. Douglas; filibustering; Walker's arrest.

c. 83. 'Belgium, Netherlands, Denmark, Sweden, Italian States, Greece, United States, 1858.' Letters are from Jan.–Mar. 30 only, mostly from Napier and Sir William Gore Ouseley.

Deal with filibustering; the debate on Kansas; the threatened break-up of the Union; further discussion of the Clayton–Bulwer Treaty.

MS. Clar. dep. c. 125–41 are from the series of bound copies of out-letters. All volumes are indexed.

c. 125–36 cover the period Feb. 1853–Oct. 1856. They contain a few letters to Crampton and James Buchanan.

c. 137–41 cover the period Oct. 1856–Feb. 1858. They contain a few letters to Napier.

MS. Clar. dep. c. 224. Register of letters to the U.S., 25 Feb. 1853–28 Dec. 1855.

On same subjects as above for same period, and such as frauds practised on British emigrants to Australia passing through the United States; extradition efforts to secure reduction of duties on various British products; Canada.

c. 225. 'Register of letters from U.S., 1 Feb. 1853–26 Dec. 1853.' (*See* c. 11 above.)

Printed Cabinet Papers. c. 246–75.

c. 246 and c. 247. Correspondence relative to the Mosquito territory, 1848–54.

c. 260. Correspondence concerning the British North American fisheries, and a commercial convention with the United States, 9 June 1852–28 Apr. 1854.

c. 263. Papers concerning recruiting in the United States for the British Army in the Crimea, parts I and II, 1854–5.

c. 264. Another copy of c. 263 containing also Part III, 1855–6, and miscellaneous correspondence.

c. 275. Contains correspondence on the boundary between British Guiana and Venezuela, Nov. 1857. Also correspondence, proposals, &c., between British and American governments on maritime law.

II. 1865–6.
c. 90. 'America, 1865–1866.' Chiefly from Sir Frederick Bruce, British Minister to the United States 1864–7.

Deal with relations with Seward; Reconstruction; much comment on Fenian activities; reciprocity; Mexico and France; disputes between President Johnson and Congress; fisheries; the Negro problem; arbitration; the tariff; the *Alabama* case.

c. 142. Letter-book 'America, 1865–1866', copies of out letters.
Deal with Maximilian in Mexico; Fenians; neutrality laws; reciprocity; St. Thomas island; Negroes; *Alabama* and *Shenandoah*.

III. 1868–70.[1]

c. 476. Box marked 'F.O. Letters to British Embassies III'.
Forty-five letters and one memo, 12 Dec. 1868–4 June 1870, chiefly from Clarendon (but two from Edmund Hammond) to Edward Thornton, British Minister to the United States.

For subjects *see* c. 480 below.

c. 480. Box marked 'F.O. Letters from British Embassies [*sic*]: Washington, 1868–1869'. Forty-nine letters, 22 Dec. 1868–21 Dec. 1869, to Clarendon from Edward Thornton, British Minister to the United States. One from Edmund Hammond, 1 Aug. 1869. Also miscellaneous press cuttings enclosed by Thornton.

Deal with the *Alabama* claims—and especially the Johnson–Clarendon

---

[1] All these papers are unbound and have no indexes.

Convention; Sumner, and especially his Claims speech; the Cuban insurrection; Congressional legislation, 1868–9; the San Juan boundary; the United States and Santo Domingo; the Tenure of Office Act—especially its partial repeal under Grant in 1869; the characters of Grant and Fish; Motley's appointment to London and Sickles's to Madrid; Fenians; John Rose's mission to Washington; Canadian public opinion on claims, boundary, &c.

c. 481. Box marked as above but for 1870. Thirty-one letters, 4 Jan.– 7 June 1870 from Thornton, to Clarendon (also press cuttings).

Deal with desire in some quarters in the United States for annexation of Canada; coolness between Fish and Sumner; visit of Prince Arthur to the United States; rejection of St. Thomas treaty, 1867, with Denmark on the purchase of the island.

c. 492. Box marked 'Clarendon Papers F.O. Misc. Papers & Correspondence. U.S.A., *Alabama*, etc.'

Twenty-nine manuscript letters, memos, &c., 4 June 1869–22 Apr. 1870, to Clarendon from John Laird, William Harcourt, L. Oliphant, Montague Bernard, A. Helps, Edmund Hammond, Lord John Russell, and Edward Thornton—also a copy, 18 June 1870, Clarendon to Bernard—all concerning the *Alabama* claims.

Letter, 3 Nov. 1859, from President James Buchanan to Clarendon on various questions in Anglo-American relations; and one, Paris, 20 May 1868, from Benjamin Rush to Clarendon, on various manifestations of Anglo-American cordiality, e.g. singing patriotic songs in theatres, &c. (*see also* 'Printed Cabinet Papers' below).

c. 493. Box marked 'F.O. Misc. Papers and Correspondence—U.S.A. Embassy, London'. Fifteen letters from Reverdy Johnson, 18 Dec. 1868– 22 July 1869, and nine from J. L. Motley, 8 June 1869–13 Jan. 1870.

Several slight notes; also touch upon the Johnson–Clarendon Convention, Sumner's speech on the claims, San Juan, and incidents involving individual Americans.

Printed Cabinet Papers. MS. Clar. dep. c. 492 also contains various printed Cabinet memoranda and dispatches, 1869, on the *Alabama* claims, and one on possible British and French mediation in the Civil War in 1862.

Also the following: convention on naturalization signed by Clarendon and Motley (n.d. but ? 1869).

Printed *Correspondence . . . on the questions of the 'Alabama' and British Claims, Naturalization and San Juan Water Boundary*, 1869.

Printed *Correspondence respecting British and American Claims arising out of the late Civil War in the United States*, 1867.

The above are the major sources of Americana in this collection, but the following volumes will be found to contain scattered items:

1853–65.
MSS. Clar. dep. c. 3, c. 4, c. 14, c. 15, c. 29, c. 30, c. 31, c. 48, c. 49, c. 50,

c. 69, c. 70, all of which are volumes of letters to other cabinet ministers, &c., especially Palmerston, 1853–7. Also c. 104, to Russell, 1847, 1854, 1858–65. (All these volumes have indexes.)

1868–70.

MSS. Clar. dep. c. 497, 498. Letters from Gladstone, 1868–70. Some allusions to American affairs, notably the *Alabama* claims.

c. 501. Letters of Clarendon to Gladstone, 1868–70.

Rhodes House Library, OXFORD

NORTH PAPERS. 1756–1861.

Most of the manuscripts in the North Papers in the Bodleian Library (pp. 371–3) relating to the British possessions in North America and the West Indies have been transcribed, and typed copies of them have been bound into a single volume (MSS. Brit. Emp. s. 1) in Rhodes House.

DIARY OF THE SIEGE OF QUEBEC, 1775–6, kept by an English soldier. 1 volume (120 pages). (MSS. Can. r. 2)

'Journal of the most remarkable occurrences in the province of Quebec from the appearance of the rebels [the Americans under Montgomery and Arnold] in September 1775 until their retreat on 6 May 1776.'

CALE & CHUTER. Letter-book: containing some 1,030 letters. 1783–96. (MSS. Brit. Emp. s. 3)

London merchants and brokers who had a considerable trade with the United States. They dealt in various commodities including tobacco, cordage, firearms, potash, pearls, and timber, and also effected insurances on ships and cargoes. Most of these letters are addressed to American firms.

CLARKSON, THOMAS (1760–1846). Letter (photostat).[1] 1817. (MSS. Brit. Emp. r. 1*)

From Thomas Clarkson to James Monroe, chiefly about colonization of free Negroes in Africa.

ANTI-SLAVERY PAPERS.[2] 1823–1941.

The Anti-Slavery Committee was founded in 1823. The Aborigines Protection Society (1837) and the British and Foreign Anti-Slavery Society

---

[1] Photographed by the New York Public Library. Location of original not known.

[2] For microfilms of manuscripts relating to the United States and the suppression of slave trade see Louis B. Frewer, *Rhodes House Library, its Function and Resources*, p. 16 (1956). (Reprinted from the *Bodleian Library Record*, vol. v, no. 6, Oct. 1956.)

(1839) amalgamated in 1909 to form the Anti-Slavery and Aborigines Protection Society (recently its 'working' title was changed to 'Anti-Slavery Society').

The papers of this Society contain considerable American material. There is a convenient handlist and a detailed card index of letters in the collection. It is clear from the card index that the known losses which these Papers have suffered—ravages of damp in a cellar over many years—have destroyed correspondence, &c., from American abolitionists such as William Lloyd Garrison, Wendell Phillips, Lucretia Mott, James Gillespie Birney, who should be well represented in this collection, when their epistolary habits are borne in mind. Some such material, which has apparently been destroyed since 1927 by bad storage conditions before the papers were taken over by Rhodes House Library, appears in A. H. Abel and F. J. Klingberg, eds., *A Side-Light on Anglo-American Relations, 1839–58; Furnished by the Correspondence of Lewis Tappan and others with the British and Foreign Anti-Slavery Society* (Lancaster, Pa., 1927). Among particular items of American interest which may be noted are:

MSS. Brit. Emp. s. 18. C 1–121—main series of nineteenth-century correspondence with the secretaries of the British and Foreign Anti-Slavery Society which contains many American letters from United States abolitionists particularly from Lewis Tappan of the American Anti-Slavery Society.

MSS. Brit. Emp. s. 19. D. 5/5—letters and papers relating to the United States lecture tour of Sir John Harris, secretary of the Anti-Slavery and Aborigines Protection Society in 1917.

MSS. Brit. Emp. s. 20. E. 2/11–20—three volumes of minute-books of the General Anti-Slavery Convention held in London in 1840, at which several American representatives were present.

MSS. Brit. Emp. s. 22 is a section of the papers arranged by territory and it contains substantial American materials. Here, files which may be noted particularly are: G. 84–85, correspondence, 1833–97, with various American bodies. G. 86, materials relating to Texas and anti-slavery controversies of the 1840's. G. 87–88, correspondence, 1866–8, with America of the British National Freedman's Aid Association. G. 298, American correspondence, 1930–7, especially the correspondence with Sherwood Eddy on American co-operative experiments. G. 432, materials on the 1921 London Pan-African Congress with letters, &c., from Professor W. E. B. DuBois. G. 492, correspondence on the proposed visit in 1914 of Booker T. Washington to Europe.

The collections also include volumes of press cuttings, newspapers, and photographs for 1906–36 which contain materials on the American Negro and his interest in and influence on Europe and Africa. (MSS. Brit. Emp. s. 24. J 1–49.)

In 1961 the records of the present Anti-Slavery Society for 1941–51 will be added to Rhodes House Library, and this addition will continue at intervals of ten years. As the Society's correspondence is still world-wide and it continues to take an interest in general Negro affairs, it may be expected that this new material will contain fresh items of American interest.

QUINAN, W. R. (1848–1910). Box of papers; and autobiography (1 volume). 1877–99. (MSS. Afr. s. 123–8)

The papers relate to the period 1877–99, during which period Quinan was employed in turn by the Vigorit Powder Works; and the California Powder Works, 1883–99; and consist mainly of business correspondence with mining firms and the military authorities, with a number of references to lawsuits over the manufacture of gunpowder.

DOYLE, JOHN ANDREW (1844–1907). Correspondence: 60 letters. 1882–1904. (MSS. Amer. s. 2)

Sixty letters, 1882–1904, to Doyle about his work *The English in America*, 5 vols. (London, 1882)[1] from American historians, authors, &c., including Justin Winsor, C. F. Adams, Herbert Adams, Moses Coit Tyler, and others.

TREVELYAN, SIR GEORGE OTTO (1838–1928). Manuscript of one volume of *The American Revolution*. 215 leaves. (MSS. Amer. s. 1)

WHITE, MONTAGU (1875–1916). Letter-book and volume of press cuttings, 1899–1900. (MSS. Afr. s. 116, 117)

White was sent to the United States in 1899 as a representative of President Kruger of the South African republic, to arouse sympathy, and if possible gain support, for the Boers against Britain. He mentions interviews with John Hay, and other leading Americans, but gained little more than formal expressions of sympathy, except from the militant anti-British sections of the press and the Irish. Some letters are in Afrikaans.

The Library, All Souls College, Oxford

VAUGHAN, SIR CHARLES RICHARD (1774–1849). Papers.[2]

Diplomatist. Private secretary, 1809–20, to the Earl of Bathurst while Foreign Secretary. British Minister to the United States 1825–35 (on leave of absence 1831–3). Knighted 1833.

---

[1] Reprinted as *English Colonies in America* (New York, 1882–1907).

[2] See also Paullin & Paxson, pp. 58–64. Twenty-five of the letters and two memoranda have been printed in 'Papers of Sir Charles R. Vaughan, 1825–1835', ed. by John A. Doyle, *American Historical Review*, vol. vii, pp. 304–29 and pp. 500–33, 1901–2.

A typescript 'Calendar of the Vaughan Papers', prepared by J. A. Doyle, is available in the library, and the following description is taken from it.

The papers are arranged in alphabetically labelled packets, and within the packets are arranged either by writer or date, as indicated below. The packets containing most of the American material are A, B, C, and H.

A. 'General Correspondence' (arranged by writer).

The most important American letters, either because of writer or subject, are from the following:

Adams, John Quincy. Two slight notes, 1830 and n.d.

Archer, William Segar. Two letters, 1840. 1840 election and 'financial difficulties'.

Beckett, Henry. Letter, 1836. Philadelphia has chartered new United States Bank; Washington, D.C., news.

Crampton, Sir John F. T. Two letters, 1848. Discussion in the United States of European revolutions of 1848; Cass and Taylor as candidates for the presidency.

Everett, Edward. Three letters, 1833, 1835, 1837. Personal; American foreign relations; Mexico and Texas; abolition.

Grosvenor, Robert, 2nd Earl Grosvenor. Letter, 1828. His estates in Florida.

Hamilton, James Alexander (son of Alexander Hamilton). Three letters, 1830, 1844, 1847. Annexation of Texas and Northern opposition to it; predicts civil war.

Jackson, Andrew. Two slight notes, 1829 and 1832.

Peters, Richard. Letter, 1840. Progress of American affairs since Vaughan left.

Rush, Richard. Several slight notes, 1825-35.

Southard, Samuel Lewis. Three letters, 1829 and 1834. The one of 1834 is on the New Jersey Poor Laws.

B. 'Dispatches and Official Correspondence in Chronological Order.'

(a) Correspondence:

Forty-nine letters (draft or copy), chiefly from Vaughan but some to him, relate to the American period, 1825-35, and deal with such matters as Anglo-American mails, British claims to land in Florida, banking in the United States, the American Navy, state boundaries, cases of individual British subjects in the United States (e.g. of a deserting British seaman), consular fees, slave trade conventions. Some are simply covering letters enclosing official papers.

(b) Dispatches (listed from the typescript calendar):

'Vaughan's lists of his Official Correspondence.

Book 1. Précis of Dispatches sent to the Foreign Office, (includes) Washington, 1825-7.

Book 2. Dispatches sent home from America, 1828–35.

Book 3. Inventory of correspondence with Canning and others, 1825–9.

Book 4. (At one end) Correspondence with the Government of the U.S., 1825–34; (at other end) Dispatches from Foreign Office during the same period.

Book 5. (At one end) Dispatches received from the Foreign Office in 1834; (at other end) Correspondence with the American Department of State.'

C. 'Correspondence of Political or General Interest' (arranged by writer).

Addington, Henry Unwin. Thirty-one letters, 1826–30. Chiefly on matters connected with the North-East and North-West boundary controversies. Also four copies, 1826–7, Vaughan to Addington, on the same.

Backhouse, John, Under Secretary of State for Foreign Affairs. Twenty-eight letters, 1829–37. Mainly North-East and North-West boundaries. Also thirty-seven drafts, 1827–38, Vaughan to Backhouse, on the boundaries, tariffs, and individual British subjects in America.

Bankhead, C., and Mrs. Bankhead. Seventeen letters, written chiefly from Washington, D.C., or Mexico, 1831–47. Boundaries, slavery, Mexican affairs (especially the Mexican war).

Bartlett, Dr. John Sherren, editor of the *Albion*, New York. Three letters, 1847–8. Anglo-American hostility, Mexican affairs, trouble over Anglo-American postal rates. Also one copy, 1847, Vaughan to Bartlett, expressing surprise at American ill feeling towards Britain.

Canning, George. Letter, 1826. North-West boundary. Also seven copies, 1825–6, Vaughan to Canning, on legation matters, Rufus King, slave trade.

Clay, Henry. Eight slight notes, 1828–35.

Douglas, Sir Howard, Governor of New Brunswick. Thirty-seven letters, 1825–32. North-East boundary. Also eleven copies, 1825–9, Vaughan to Douglas, on same.

Doyle, Percy W. Three letters, 1843–8. The latter two, 1845–8, are on United States–Mexico affairs, and the settlement of Oregon.

Featherstonhaugh, G. W. Seven letters, 1839–46. Chiefly on North-East and North-West boundaries; in 1846 gives an evaluation of Calhoun.

Hall, Captain Basil and Mrs. Hall. Nineteen letters, 1827–9. Chiefly on their travels in the United States and Hall's book on these. Comments on the incompatibility of slavery and democracy. Also two copies, 1827, Vaughan to Hall, on intercourse of American vessels with British colonies.

Hay, R. W. Four letters, 1829 and 1833, on boundaries and Andrew Jackson; and, 1833, refutation of charges against British officers at New Orleans in 1815.

Kempt, Sir James. Five letters, Quebec, 1829–30. Jackson's Inaugural, boundaries, American trade with the West Indies. Also two copies, 1826–7, Vaughan to Kempt, on the closing of American ports to British vessels.

Ryder, Dudley, 2nd Earl of Harrowby. Three letters, 1824–7. Those of 1826 and 1827 are inquiries about the American banking system. Also one draft, 1824, Vaughan to Harrowby, on banking in America.

Story, Joseph. Thirteen notes, mainly slight, 1828–37, but a letter, 7 Nov. 1837, discusses the effects of currency experiments in the United States, recent elections and whether Webster would stand for the presidency.

Stuart, Sir Charles, Baron Stuart de Rothesay. Two letters, 1835. His land in Florida. Also one copy, 1835, Vaughan to Lord Stuart de Rothesay on the same, and one letter, 1835, from a Colonel White to Vaughan on the same.

Sumner, Charles. Eight letters, 1839–48. Election campaign of 1840, Harrison, Webster, Everett, Motley (just appointed to St. Petersburg), Tyler. Appointments under the Whig administration of 1840; debasing effects of the Mexican War on American politics.

Temple, Henry John, 3rd Viscount Palmerston. Nine letters, 1827–43. Franco-American relations, boundaries, naturalization in the United States. Also eleven drafts, 1831–40, Vaughan to Palmerston, on similar topics.

Van Buren, Martin. Six slight notes, 1830–8. Also one copy, 1830, Vaughan to Van Buren.

Vaughan, Sir Charles Richard. Copy, 1825, to H. T. Kilbee, on British and American Cuban policy, and his (Vaughan's) impressions of America. Nineteen copies, 1827–9, to Joseph Planta of the Foreign Office, mostly slight (enclosing United States State Papers, &c.). Also see copies and drafts of letters from Vaughan to correspondents in this group.

Ward, H. G. Twenty-seven letters, 1825–6, written from Mexico. Deal *inter alia* with Anglo-American relations over Mexico. Also four copies, 1826, Vaughan to Ward, partly on same.

Wellesley, Henry, 1st Baron Cowley. Letter, 1828. Commercial relations of Britain and the United States.

H. 'Papers Relating to America, 1825–37.'
Classified as follows:

(*a*) 'Drafts of Dispatches from Vaughan as British Minister in U.S., 1825–31.'

Contains dispatches successively to Canning, Dudley, Aberdeen, and Palmerston. The numbers of dispatches for each year are as follows: 30—1825, 102—1826, 69—1827, 86—1828, 70—1829, 73—1830, 32—1831.

Subjects dealt with include slavery and the slave trade, fisheries, West Indian trade, Canadian frontier incidents, Latin-American relations with the United States, tariffs (especially that of 1828), Indian affairs, impressment of American sailors, arrests of British subjects in the United States, the Congress of Panama, North-West and North-East boundaries, foundation of a company to cut an isthmian canal, proceedings in Congress, reciprocity, the election of 1828, Jackson's inauguration, efforts of the Southern states to secure repeal of the 1828 Tariff, appointments (especially diplomatic) under Jackson, possible acquisition of Texas by the United States, the Bank of the United States, Bills for internal improvements vetoed by Jackson, arrests of free coloured British subjects in the South.

(*b*) 'Drafts of Dispatches from Vaughan as British Minister in U.S., 1833–5 (and Slave Trade, 1833).'

Contains dispatches successively to Palmerston and Wellington: 50—1833, 109—1834, 56—1835, and thirteen to Palmerston on the slave trade, 1833–4.

Subjects include settlement of the dissension between the federal government and South Carolina (i.e., over nullification), boundaries, removal of public funds from the Bank of the United States, New York elections of 1834, extradition. The slave-trade dispatches are about the possible accession of the United States to the Anglo-French Slave Trade Convention, and its final refusal to accede.

(c) 'America: Dated and Undated Papers.'

Dated, 1824–46. Some sixty or seventy miscellaneous items on suppression of the slave trade, boundaries, interviews with American statesmen, Anglo-American trade, United States tariffs, West Indian trade, probable effects of an Anglo-American war, 1827; invoices of tea shipped at Boston, observations on democracy and vote by ballot in the United States in 1831, the Bank of the United States, the Southern states and the tariff, the Webster–Ashburton Treaty of 1842, Oregon.

Undated. Some thirty miscellaneous items on the American Constitution, political parties in the United States, American geography, tours in the United States, various treaties—especially that of Ghent, an isthmian canal, trade, fisheries, impressment, tariff, slave labour.

(d) 'America: Papers Relating to the Boundary Question.'

Dated, 1824–39. Some fifty miscellaneous items on the North-East boundary, including précis of British and American arguments. Undated. Some thirty miscellaneous items, including an atlas.

I. 'Papers Relating to South America.'
This packet contains a few items relating to Texas and Florida.

K. 'Journals and Commonplace Books.'
The commonplace books do not refer at all to the period of his American sojourn.

(a) 'Portsmouth to Annapolis, United States of America, 11 June to 12 August 1825.' Simply a diary of part of his trip out.

(b) 'Washington to Niagara . . . 1826.' Describes an extensive tour through the North East, including a description of the New York navy yard, a visit to Van Buren, descriptions of the locks on the Erie Canal, of the New York State Prison, and of the Philadelphia penitentiary. Lists his expenses.

(c) '1829'. A short journal describing a journey into Canada. En route he meets Philip Hone and Chancellor Kent in New York.

(d) 'From New York to London, 1831' and 'From Liverpool to New York, 24 February 1833.' Both journals are simply accounts of the respective voyages.

The Library, Christ Church, OXFORD

SALISBURY PAPERS.[1]

Papers of Robert Arthur Talbot Gascoyne-Cecil, 3rd Marquess of Salisbury (1830–1903). These are in course of arrangement, but in general it may be said that the major American items will be found in six bound volumes and scattered in small groups throughout the unbound material. A brief description of the contents of the volumes is given below.

The unbound letters, 'Special Correspondence', are alphabetically arranged under writers in several series. The most useful of these is 'Special Correspondence: Main Series', in which the most important name is Julian Pauncefote, 1st Baron Pauncefote; but Americana will also be found for Sir Edward Thornton; Sir George Smyth Baden-Powell; Sir Frederick Stanley, 16th Earl of Derby; Col. George Denison (of Toronto); Goldwin Smith; Lionel Sackville-West, 2nd Baron Sackville; Henry C. K. Petty-Fitzmaurice, 5th Marquess of Lansdowne; Sir James Fergusson; George Nathaniel Curzon, 1st Marquess Curzon; and William St. J. F. Brodrick, 1st Earl of Midleton, during the periods in which they were Under-Secretaries of State for Foreign Affairs; and George Earle Buckle. In the 'Special Correspondence: Foreign Series' will be found a few letters from Edward John Phelps, Edwards Pierrepont, Joseph Hodges Choate, Charles Richard Williams, Senator Edward Oliver Wolcott, and John Milton Hay; in the main the subjects dealt with are akin to those dealt with in the six bound volumes, a description of which follows:

(a) Vol. A/19: 'F.O. (Private Correspondence): United States [Dispatches], 1878–1880.'

(i) Sir E. Thornton to Salisbury. Forty-eight letters and one telegram, 30 Apr. 1878–24 Feb. 1880, on Russian efforts to buy steamers in United States for conversion to cruisers, United States politics (State elections and presidential ambitions), Indian and labour unrest, Fenians, Ontario Boundary Commission, fisheries question, Halifax award, United States relations with Japan, China, Russia, Canada, and Mexico; Chinese immigration, isthmian canal projects, and C. S. Parnell's visit.

(ii) Four American press cuttings.

(iii) J. Welsh to Salisbury, 18 Apr. 1878, on position of three British deserters in 22nd New York Regiment.

(iv) Colonel Stanley (later Lord Derby) to Salisbury, 24 Apr. 1878, on same.

(b) Vol. A/21: 'Miscellaneous, 1878–1880.'

(i) Salisbury to Thornton. Three letters, 13 Apr. and 23 Nov. 1878 and 26 Apr. 1880. The first and last are formal; the other deals with the fisheries question.

[1] We are grateful to the Marquess of Salisbury for permission to make this report. A calendar of the contents of all 140 volumes will in due course be available in selected libraries. No photographic reproductions of the papers are allowed.

(*c*) Vol. A/77. 'United States (From) 1887–1890.'

(i) H. G. Edwardes to Barrington. Five letters, 22 Mar.–20 Sept. 1889, on Harrison and Blaine, Bering Sea sealing and seizures of Canadian sealing vessels, and Robert Todd Lincoln.

(ii) M. H. Herbert to Barrington. Five letters, 2 Nov. 1888–8 Feb. 1889, on the 'Murchison letter' affair and its impact on Anglo-American relations and American opinion; Blaine; Samoa.

(iii) Pauncefote to Salisbury (and two to Stanley). Thirty letters and seven telegrams, 3 May 1889–26 Dec. 1890, chiefly about Bering Sea controversy, but also on his reception in Washington; Blaine, extradition, Alaska boundary, International Marine Conference of 1889, Canadian-American relations, international copyright, Samoa. There are also four memos, 1890, by Pauncefote: the first on Haiti, Hawaii, and a merchant shipping convention; the other three (marked 'secret') on movements of American cruisers and the Bering Sea.

(iv) Sackville to Salisbury. Fourteen letters and two telegrams, 30 Jan. 1887–14 Dec. 1888, on fisheries, Blaine's visit to Europe, the Samoan Conference, rejection of the fisheries treaty, the 'Murchison letter' episode. Also a statement by Sackville, 8 Nov. 1888, on this last.

(v) There are also supporting papers on the Bering Sea controversy and a number of American press cuttings sent by Sackville, Herbert, and Pauncefote.

(*d*) Vol. A/78: 'United States (from), 1891–2; United States (to), 1887–92; U.S. Legation, 1887–92; Canada; Fisheries Commission, 1887; Sir G. Baden-Powell, 1891–2.'

(i) 'United States (from), 1891–2': Pauncefote, chiefly to Salisbury, some to Barrington. Thirty letters and four telegrams, 8 Jan. 1891–26 May 1892, on Bering Sea, press attacks on Pauncefote, fisheries, Newfoundland, Tonga, Canadian reciprocity conference, United States relations with Chile, Hawaii, presidential election prospects for 1892, anti-British feeling in the United States. Also included are further correspondence and supporting papers on the Bering Sea controversy and arbitration; a draft maritime convention; and a draft Anglo-American treaty by Pauncefote for recovery of deserters from merchantmen.

(ii) 'United States (to), 1887–92': Similar material.

(iii) 'U.S. Legation, 1887–92': Phelps to Salisbury, 13 Apr. 1887 and 16 Nov. 1888, on the case of Thomas Gallagher and the Sackville incident. Salisbury to Phelps, 16 Apr. 1888, on the Gallagher case; and to Robert Todd Lincoln, 2 Jan. 1892. Henry White to Barrington, 24 May 1888, on Bering Sea.

(iv) 'Canada.' Twenty-six telegrams, 2 July 1888–10 Oct. 1891, between Salisbury and Lord Stanley, Governor-General of Canada, and a letter from Baden-Powell to Stanley; almost entirely about the Bering Sea controversy.

(v) 'Fisheries Commission, 1887': Seven letters, 18 Nov. 1887–16 Feb. 1888, between Joseph Chamberlain and Salisbury, chiefly on the work of the Commission.

(vi) 'Sir G. Baden-Powell, 1891–2': Exclusively concerned with the Bering Sea controversy. Fourteen letters, 5 Aug. 1891–4 May 1892, Baden-Powell to Salisbury; copy, 15 July 1891, of a proclamation by Harrison; minute, 13 Jan. 1892, by Salisbury; copy of a letter, 9 Nov. 1892, from Baden-Powell to Sir John Abbott.

(e) Vol. A/139: 'U.S.A. 1895–1898.'
(i) Charles Adams to Salisbury, 23 Oct. 1897, on the Bering Sea conference.
(ii) C. E. Akers. Two letters to Pauncefote, 13 May and 14 Nov. 1896, on Cuba, especially Cuban sugar and the United States and Weyler; and one, 13 May 1896, to Richard Olney on Cuba, especially Spanish bitterness against the United States and absence of atrocities in the islands.
(iii) Count Cassini to Pauncefote. Letter, 15 Nov. 1898, on Nicaraguan canal, &c.
(iv) Lord Gough to Salisbury. Letter, 12 Sept. 1896, repealing 'a message from J. Chamberlain on Major Willoughby's defence'.
(v) Pauncefote to Salisbury. Forty letters and nine telegrams, 25 Oct. 1895–23 Dec. 1898. Bering Sea and, especially, the Venezuela crisis, are the two most important topics; Cuba, the Philippines, McKinley, and the Nicaraguan canal project all enter into the correspondence.
Pauncefote to Olney and Olney to Pauncefote, two copies, both 12 Jan. 1896, on the John Hays Hammond case (in Transvaal). Letter, 27 Mar. 1896, Olney to Pauncefote on the Venezuelan dispute, and copies, 11 and 12 Dec. 1896, Olney to Pauncefote and Pauncefote to Olney, respectively urging and deprecating the appointment of a Venezuelan arbitrator.
Draft by Pauncefote entitled 'Scheme of arbitration for the settlement of the Venezuela Boundary Question'.
Pauncefote to Barrington. Two letters, 31 Jan. and 17 Apr. 1896, both dealing with the Venezuelan dispute; in addition, the former comments on the low standard of the United States Senate, and the latter on the Pacific cable, embassy staff, and the desirability of Pauncefote's absence from the United States during the 1896 presidential campaign.
Pauncefote to Villiers. Letter, 25 July 1897, enclosing one from J. D. Campbell to Pauncefote, 25 July 1897, on the Jubilee.
(vi) R. Tower to Barrington. Two letters, 11 June 1897 and 19 Nov. 1898, the first on American reactions to the Jubilee.
(vii) The volume also contains, besides several press cuttings, a memorandum, Dec. 1895, by H. O. Bax-Ironside on the origin of the President's Venezuela message.

(f) Vol. A/140: 'U.S.A. (from) 1899–1900; (to) 1896–1900.'
(i) 'U.S.A. (from) 1899–1900': Farrer Herschell, 1st Baron Herschell, to Salisbury, letter, 25 Nov. 1898, and telegram, 6 Feb. 1899, on the fishery question and the tariff. Pauncefote to Salisbury, ten letters and eight telegrams, 16 Jan. 1899–6 Nov. 1900, on the Nicaraguan canal, Herschell, 'open door' in China, Canadian-United States relations, the United States and the Hague Peace Conference, Alaska boundary, presidential campaign of 1900, arrangements for Pauncefote's retirement. Pauncefote to Barrington,

letter, 31 Oct. 1899, on equal commercial treatment in Samoa of Britain, the United States, and Germany. Tower to Barrington, 29 May 1899, dealing with Canadian-United States negotiations. Also a letter from Barrington to Salisbury, and several minor letters to Barrington.

(ii) 'United States (to) 1896–1900': Salisbury to Pauncefote. Three letters, fourteen telegrams, and three printed drafts, 7 Feb. 1896–27 Mar. 1900, dealing with Venezuela, general arbitration, and the Alaska boundary. Also three letters from Barrington, two from Salisbury to Barrington, and one from Salisbury to Gough on similar topics.

(iii) The concluding section of this volume is entitled 'U.S. Embassy in London'. It contains: Barrington to Salisbury, letter, 6 Apr. 1900, on the Alaska boundary; Barrington to Henry White, letter, 2 Feb. 1899 (and a copy of this) on the Clayton–Bulwer Treaty. 'E. W. P.' to Crane, St. Louis, Mo., Mar. 1900, on Anglo-American relations, especially as regards the presidential campaign, the anti-canal lobby, the Philippines, &c. Salisbury to Barrington, letter, 28 Feb. 1896, on Venezuela. Six letters, 29 Feb. 1896–25 Jan. 1900, James R. Roosevelt, Henry White, and J. H. Choate to Salisbury or Barrington, on Venezuela, Spanish-American peace negotiations, Nicaraguan canal, and the case of Mrs. Maybrick (an American woman sentenced to imprisonment in Britain for murder). Document, 6 Apr. 1900, entitled 'List of cases in which executive clemency has been requested of other governments by the diplomatic representatives of the United States or Great Britain' (presumably connected with the Maybrick case). Americana will also be found in other volumes, e.g. concerning Samoa in correspondence with Berlin.

The Library, Nuffield College, OXFORD

COBBETT, WILLIAM (1762–1835).[1]

Manuscripts of the *Political Register*, vol. xxxiv, nos. 2 and 8, written from North Hampstead, Long Island, 15 May and 28 July 1818.

Also part of an article in the *Political Register*, vol. lxix, no. 20, 15 May 1830, to Mr. Haywood . . . of Sheffield, written from Wolverhampton, 11 May 1830, about emigration to America. The manuscript is not complete.

MILTON AGRICULTURAL LABOURERS UNION (later the Oxford District of the National Agricultural Labourers Union). Minute-book. 1872–9.

Contains resolutions concerning the establishment of, contributions to, and grants from, an emigration fund; also notes of a number of votes to make grants to certain individuals to assist them to emigrate. There is no mention of the destination of the emigrants, although an entry of 2 Sept. 1873

---

[1] Since the compilation of this report the Library has received a large deposit of Cobbett manuscripts including many dating from his American sojourns.

records a proposal that 'in consequence of Mr. Arch [*sic*] visit to America, the emigration fund be left open until further notice'.

G. D. H. COLE COLLECTION. Printed material.

Includes fifty volumes by and about Robert Owen including material on New Harmony, Ind.; fifty-seven volumes by or about Thomas Paine; eighteen volumes on communitarianism, especially in the United States and particularly about Oneida and Icaria, N.Y.; and over three hundred volumes by or about William Cobbett.

The Library, Manchester College, OXFORD

SHEPHERD MANUSCRIPTS. Papers, letters. 1760–76.

Papers of the Rev. William Shepherd (1768–1847), Unitarian minister.

Vol. V contains an entry in Shepherd's diary for 6 Sept. 1838 (pp. 63–65), where he relates meeting 'an American barrister at law, of the name of Sumner' at the house of Lord Brougham, and showing him one of the stamps, prepared for the administration of the Stamp Act, which had recently been discovered in Somerset House.

Vol. XVIII contains copies of letters,[1] 1760–76, from Henry Hulton to Robert Nicholson, a Liverpool merchant and the father of Mrs. Shepherd. The earlier letters deal with Hulton's experiences as a British official in Germany and in the Treasury in London; but the bulk of the correspondence dates from 1769 to 1776, when he was employed as a revenue officer in Boston. The letters give an eyewitness account of the beginnings of the War of Independence. As early as 1769 Hulton comments on the perils faced by the revenue officers from the colonists. In 1770 he speaks of and suffers from the growth of discontent and mob violence stirred up by demagogues and the press in Boston; he is, however, of the opinion that Boston will find itself unable to manage without British manufactures. He says, in 1774, that since the Tea Party all authority has been in the people's hands, and those who do not 'conform in all things to the will of the people' are persecuted. He describes the battle of Bunker Hill, the flight of many Loyalists to Britain, and the scarcity and high prices of food in Boston in 1776. In Jan. 1776 he says that the aim of the rebels is obviously to establish 'one or more independent republics'. The last letter is written in May 1776 from Halifax, N.S., just before Hulton embarked for Britain.

AMERICAN UNITARIANS. 91 autograph letters (scattered in 2 boxes and 1 volume). 1822–1908.

Writers of these letters, who are mainly Unitarians, include: Elihu Burritt, W. E. and W. H. Channing, James Freeman Clarke, Ralph Waldo Emerson,

---

[1] The copies are thought to have been made *c.* 1805; it is not known whether the originals are still in existence. Copies are also held by the Unitarian College, Manchester.

William Lloyd Garrison, Thomas Wentworth Higginson, Oliver Wendell Holmes, Sen., Julia Ward Howe, A. A. Livermore, James Russell Lowell, Susan Martineau, Samuel J. May, Theodore Parker, and A. P. Putnam. There is also a facsimile of a letter, 2 July 1756, from Benjamin Franklin to George Whitefield, about the possibilities of colonization on the Ohio.[1]

Most of the letters are of personal or theological interest only; however, some include discussion of other matters, as follows:

Burritt, *c.* 1848, comments on the League of Universal Brotherhood and ocean penny post.

Holmes, 1879, on Motley as Minister to Britain, with reasons for his failure in that capacity (including a reference to the Grant-Sumner feud).

Livermore on the success of *Uncle Tom's Cabin*, 1853, the non-smoking aspect of the temperance movement, 1882, and the presidential campaign of 1884.

Martineau, Susan, writes three letters, 1861 and 1864, about a Mrs. Whitaker, who had emigrated to the United States from Britain, and after her husband's death and a period of poverty, had taken a job with the Western Sanitary Commission at St. Louis, Mo., and was working on behalf of the freed Negroes.

And among forty-five letters, 1822–39, to Lant Carpenter, from various correspondents, the slavery question and temperance are touched upon.

Oxfordshire County Record Office, County Hall, OXFORD

DILLON COLLECTION. 1872–92.

Bundle of letters, pamphlets, pedigrees, notes, and newspaper clippings, also a volume of pedigrees, 1872–92, relating to a discussion, mainly between C. F. Lee, Jr., of Virginia, and Capt. Harold Dillon, of London, about the descent of the Lees of Virginia, and, in particular, of General Robert E. Lee.

Charles Early & Co. Ltd., Witney Mills, WITNEY

BUSINESS RECORDS.[2] 1815–24.

Blanket manufacturers.

(*a*) Letter, London, 3 Apr. 1815, from J. H. & C. Lean to Early's requesting a list of articles made by Early's for the United States, with prices, terms of

[1] Original in the Autograph Collection, John Rylands Library, Manchester (p. 98). See *Complete Works of Benjamin Franklin*, ed. by John Bigelow, vol. ii, pp. 466–8 (London and New York, 1887).

[2] A number of these documents are printed in Alfred Plummer, *The Witney Blanket Industry*, chap. iv, Letters and orders, pp. 231–55 (London, 1934).

credit and discounts. Copy of the reply, Witney, 4 Apr. 1815, giving the required information; and a letter of thanks from Lean's, London, 5 Apr. 1815. There are other letters about shipments to the West Indies and Canada.

(b) Numerous copies of orders for blankets from the Hudson's Bay Company, and from Wistar, Siter & Price of Philadelphia. An order book for 1823–8 includes an order from the latter firm, 10 Dec. 1824, for 'mock mackimaw', a thick blanket at one time distributed to the Indians of the Northwest by the American government; also another from the same firm, 14 Sept. 1824, containing a footnote that 'the new tariff much reduces their profits'.

RUTLAND

Lieutenant-Colonel James Hanbury, BURLEY-ON-THE-HILL

FINCH PAPERS.

Correspondence of Daniel Finch, 2nd Earl of Nottingham (1647–1730) while Secretary of State 1688–93. (*Letters unless otherwise stated.*)

(a) Minute for 17 June 1690 has the following entries: 'Lord Chief Justice about Governor of Maryland, Capt. Copley, to attend Committee of Plantations.—Lord Howard to be Governor of Virginia.'[1]

(b) Deposition of Edmund Everard 'of Grays' Inne', 1691, relative to a Jacobite conspiracy mentions piratical activities off America, and the imprisonment 'at Virginia' of one Captain Davis for piracy.[2]

(c) 17 July 1691, from Abraham Stock to Nottingham, concerning the protection of the Virginia fleet from the French.[3]

(d) 31 July 1691, from Nottingham to the King giving His Majesty 'some account of a paper relating to the charter of New England which my Lord Sydney will lay before' him. Describes how the Committee [of Plantations] has drawn up a charter as far as possible in accordance with the wishes of the agents of New England, but says that they still desire further concessions.[4]

[1] H.M.C. Finch MSS. iii [71], p. 380. (Formerly owned by Allan George Finch, Esq.)   [2] Ibid., p. 357.
[3] Transcript, ibid., p. 163. *See also* pp. 237, 254, 255, 260, 287, 290, 297, 302, 303, 406, 408, other letters and minutes, all 1691, containing brief references to the convoying of the Virginia fleet from Kinsale, County Cork.
[4] Transcript, ibid., pp. 187–8.

(*e*) 10 Aug. 1691, from Sidney [or Sydney] to Nottingham, conveying the King's approval of what has been done in the matter of the Massachusetts Charter.[1]

(*f*) 11 Aug. 1691, from Nottingham to Sydney, sending 'papers relating to the charter of New England'. Says that the colonial agents are now willing to accept the Committee's terms.[2]

(*g*) 18 Aug. 1691, from Nottingham to Sydney, says he will have the charter 'speedily despatched'.[3]

(*h*) 20 Aug. 1691, from Sydney to Nottingham, communicating news of the King's pleasure at the New England agents' acceptance of the charter.[4]

(*i*) 'Memorial of Committee of Plantations about a 5th rate to New England and 6th rate to New York: to be sent to Admiralty with directions.' Extract from Minute for 29 Sept. 1691 of the Committee appointed to advise the Queen during the King's absences from England, 1690 and 1691.[5]

Earl of Gainsborough, EXTON PARK, Oakham

BARHAM PAPERS.[6] Miscellaneous naval papers. 1773–93.

Charles Middleton, 1st Baron Barham (1726–1813), admiral, was Comptroller of the Navy 1778–90, and First Lord of the Admiralty in 1805.

(*a*) Letters, 1780–2, concerning the West Indian and American Stations from Parker, Rodney, Graves, Prescott, Spry, Rowley, Hunt, Hood, and Thompson.

(*b*) Nineteen miscellaneous papers, 1773–93, on the War of Independence (one signed by Hood).

(*c*) Books A and B, 1779–83, 290 letters, drafts, lists, and notes on victualling and convoys for America and Gibraltar (including victuals for the Army) with 26 letters and drafts by Sir Charles Middleton.

N.R.A. 0315.

---

[1] Transcript, H.M.C. Finch MSS. iii [71], p. 199.
[2] Transcript, ibid., p. 201.   [3] Transcript, ibid., p. 217.
[4] Transcript, ibid., p. 220.   [5] Ibid., p. 410.
[6] Some of these have been published in *Letters and Papers of Charles, Lord Barham, Admiral of the Red Squadron 1758–1813* . . . 3 vols. (London, 1907–11) (Publications of the Navy Records Society, vols. xxxii, xxxviii, xxxix).

SHROPSHIRE

Corporation of Shrewsbury, Guildhall, SHREWSBURY

MUNICIPAL RECORDS. Petition.[1] 1775.
Unanimous petition to the King against the rebellion in America by the Mayor, Aldermen, and Burgesses of Shrewsbury, 6 Oct. 1775.

Salop Record Office, Shire Hall, SHREWSBURY

SHIREHALL COLLECTION. Papers. 1733–74.
Relating to the Shrewsbury property of Thomas Bowers of Maryland.

SANDFORD HALL COLLECTION.[2] Letters. 1776–7.
Relating to the appointment of Hugh Alexander Kennedy to the forces in America.

MARRINGTON COLLECTION. Papers of Lewis R. Price.[3] c. 1833–70.
Lewis R. Price (1817–82) and his brother Daniel spent many years in Mexico engaged in trading ventures. The papers include:

(a) Lewis Price's account of his life: his first journey to Mexico in 1833 when he entered the house of Marshall & Manning; his life in Mexico; reference to a journey to New Orleans to buy cotton.

(b) Description of a journey to California, 1849, including a description of San Francisco.

(c) Letters between Lewis Price and Commodore Dunlop, in which Dunlop asks for advice on the political situation in Mexico during the revolutions of 1860 and 1861. There are references to the effects of the blockade of American ports during the Civil War.

(d) Diary of Lewis Price's wife, 1865, describing their life in Mexico City and their return to England via New York.

---

[1] H.M.C. xv (x), p. 24. Taken from the original minutes of a meeting of the Council held on 6 Oct. 1775.

[2] We thank Mrs. H. Sandford for permission to make this report.

[3] One of these diaries has been used by W. Turrentine Jackson in 'Mazatlan to the Estanislao; the Narrative of Lewis Richard Price's Journey to California in 1849', *California Historical Society Quarterly*, vol. xxxix, pp. 35–51, 1960; and his article on 'Lewis Richard Price, British Mining Entrepreneur, and Traveler in California', *Pacific Historical Review*. vol. xxix, pp. 331–48, 1960.

(e) Letters concerning Lewis Price's business, c. 1868 onwards, as a director of the North Star Mining Company, which failed, and in connexion with the Sierra Buttes Mines. There are also letters from Mr. Coulter, promoter of the London and California Mining Company, in which Price lost money. The account of his life gives a narrative of this incident.

SOMERSET

The Records Office, C. & J. Clark Ltd., STREET

BUSINESS RECORDS.[1] 1825–1900.

Quaker boot and shoe manufacturers, and, up to 1870, makers of sheepskin rugs; a partnership business, 1825–1903.

Extracts from the partners' letter-books, made by L. H. Barber, Esq., Archivist to C. & J. Clark Ltd., show that the firm was exporting a few small consignments of sheepskin rugs, wool-lined boots and slippers, and chamois to the United States through a New York agent, Wild & Julian (later Joseph Wild), during the 1850's and 1860's. As Joseph Wild was a personal as well as a business friend, some of the letters contain comments on the political situation, particularly during the Crimean and Civil Wars.

After the 1860's little attempt was made to export footwear to the United States in the face of a growing American manufacture, and the rug business, which had formed the chief contact, was transferred to the firm of Clark, Son & Morland. But C. & J. Clark remained deeply interested in American inventions in shoe-making machinery, from the 1850's onwards, and were informed through friends in the States, usually fellow Quakers, of developments in sewing machines, sole-cutting machines, &c. A letter of 1881 makes it clear that by then they were importing American machinery and that their manager had learned the trade there.

The following are some volumes in this very large collection which are likely to contain American material, though not all of them have yet been examined in detail:

Partners' copy letter-books: 1853–6, 1858–62, 1862–7, 1867–77, 1877–83, 1881–1900, 1892–6, 1896–1900.
Ledgers: 1825–30, 1825–45.
Order book: 1834–6.
Weekly trade account book: 1857–1900.
Stock accounts: 1852–65, 1872–90, 1879–1900.
Summary of stock: 1850–1900.
'Fur' book: 1871–8.

[1] See also the history of the firm, *Clarks of Street 1825–1950* (London, priv. print., 1951).

Lord Strachie, SUTTON COURT

STRACHEY PAPERS. 1774–82.

Large collection of papers relating to the War of Independence and the Treaty of Paris, of Sir Henry Strachey (1736–1810), secretary to H.M. Commissioners during their mission 'to restore peace in the colonies and plantations of North America', 1774–82.[1]

Includes a series of letters, 3 Jan. 1774–3 Jan. 1776, from Governor Tryon of New York to Dartmouth. These describe the progress of the rebellion in the province of New York. The last letters, Oct. 1775–Jan. 1776, are written from various ships in the harbour of New York, to which the Governor fled to escape the mob.[2] Also included is a memorial of the Loyalists of New York, to Richard, Earl Howe (and General Sir William Howe), n.d.—a conventional expression of loyalty and hope for the speedy restoration of the union between Britain and the colonies.[3]

Somerset Record Office, Obridge Road, TAUNTON

PRANKARD AND DICKINSON PAPERS.[4] 1730–94. (DD/DN)

Graffin Prankard (d. 1756) was a Quaker merchant of Bristol, mainly in the iron trade. His American and West Indian ventures appear to have been but a small part of his activities, most of which were centred on the Baltic. Caleb Dickinson, the son of a West Indian merchant, was apprenticed to Prankard in 1733 and married his daughter; he was the father of William Dickinson, M.P.

Prankard's correspondence is well preserved; some 'in' and 'out' letters covering every detail of some of his complicated ventures survive, such as the voyage of his ship the *Parham* to South Carolina in December 1730, from where it took rice and logwood to Hamburg, then to Stockholm in ballast, then to Bristol in Sept. 1731 with iron, deal, and tar. There is as yet no list of the sixty-eight boxes, but the contents are in good order. Many of the boxes are nineteenth-century Dickinson estate papers (letter-books of the Prankard Baltic and domestic trade begin from 1695, the Caleb Dickinson boxes being mainly domestic and estate). It was not possible to examine every box, but the principal American bundles appear to be (as at present arranged):

Box 5:

Trading and account book of the ship *Baltic Merchant*, 1732–9, between Charleston, S.C., Holland, and Hamburg, prefaced by instructions from Prankard to his Charleston agents, Jennys & Baker. The trade was mainly in rice.

---

[1] Fuller description and extracts in H.M.C. vi, pp. xiv, xv, 399–404.
[2] Extracts, ibid., pp. 399–400. [3] Transcript, ibid., p. 401.
[4] See W. E. Minchinton, ed., *The Trade of Bristol in the Eighteenth Century*, pp. 101–22 (Bristol, 1957) (Bristol Record Society's Publications, vol. xx.)

Correspondence, 1737–42, from various agents in Charleston, S.C. (Watson & McKenzie, Paul and Thomas Jennys, and Benjamin Savage); invoices and bills of lading. Trade in bar iron, chains, nails, steel, and plough-shares from England; mainly rice and logwood from South Carolina. One letter, 24 Apr. 1738, from Thomas Jennys, refers to a journey to Georgia and the 'risk of engaging the Spaniards'. Another, 18 Sept. 1742, from Benjamin Savage, speaks of alarms in South Carolina 'occasioned by the Spaniards invading Georgia'.

Account book, 1742, recording trade in cotton and logwood with New York.

Bill of insurance for ship *Parham Pink*, 1742, bound for Carolina, together with correspondence with the master, Captain Alloway.

Account book, 1743–8: detailed trading and shipping lists, giving date and cost of cargo, including sailings to the Carolinas, Virginia, Jamaica, and, less frequently, New York and Boston, mainly from Bristol.

Correspondence, 1750–5, from Lawrence Growden, George Pennington, and Susana Dilwin, Quakers, concerning debts in Philadelphia.

Letter, 1759, from Stephen Fuller to W. H. Lyttleton, Governor of South Carolina, recommending to him the merchant Thomas Young.

Correspondence, 1792–4, to Stephen Fuller from Simon Taylor, Jamaica agent. Letters of 1794 contain detailed references to West Indian trade suffering from England's war with France, with protests at England's folly in provoking an American embargo on English goods. Some similar letters from another Jamaica agent, John King, culminating in a petition to Parliament on the 'drawback of sugar bounty'.

Box 14:
Letter, Charleston, S.C., 16 Apr. 1740, from Nathaniel Alloway to Caleb Dickinson, about a shipment of clothes—what can and cannot be worn in Georgia.

Two letters, Williamsburg, Va., 30 June and 5 Nov. 1750, from Thomas Dickinson to Caleb Dickinson, about trying to procure and ship to Bristol some wild turkeys, grey and also flying squirrels—also a hogshead of tobacco.

Box 25:
Ledger III: Accounts of ships trading with, *inter alia*, Boston, Phila-delphia, the Carolinas, together with dealings with Jennys & Baker, Watson & McKenzie of South Carolina, William Hare of Providence, R.I., and John King of Williamsburg, Va. Iron figures prominently. *c.* 1740's.

Ledger XXXXI: Accounts of voyage of *Brogden* and *Parham* to the Carolinas; trade in lead and sugar. *c.* 1740's.[1]

Fox Bros. & Co. Ltd., Tonedale Mills, WELLINGTON

BUSINESS RECORDS. 1783–1807.

This Quaker woollen firm, known as Were & Company until 1796, at which

[1] See Minchinton, op. cit., p. 105.

date Thomas Fox became sole partner, possesses Common Letter-books and Foreign Letter-books covering at least the years 1770–1821, and containing extensive references to trade with America, particularly in the years 1783–1807. This trade is mentioned by Hubert Fox in his book *Quaker Homespun* (London, 1958). Chapter 9, headed 'North American Markets', quotes detailed and interesting letters about the difficulties of trade with America during the early years of the Republic. Often, it appears, Thomas Fox had to accept payment in kind for his rough serge and other woollen goods—wheat, indigo, tobacco, turpentine, and rice were all consigned to Were & Company at various times. His cousins, George Croker Fox and Robert Were Fox (G. C. Fox & Co. of Falmouth, Cornwall (p. 28), acted as agents for these mixed cargoes. There is correspondence to William Anderson, a merchant of Virginia; and relating to the visit in 1787 of Samuel Gardner, a South Carolina merchant, who discussed the requirements of the American market and who subsequently defaulted on his obligations to Thomas Fox.

STAFFORDSHIRE

Wedgwood Museum, Josiah Wedgwood & Sons Ltd., BARLASTON, Stoke-on-Trent

WEDGWOOD FAMILY. Business and personal papers. 1765–.

From time to time permission has been granted to students to inspect documents held by the firm. Such permission can, however, only cover a period of one or two days, since facilities for carrying out written work are limited.

The following relevant material is held among the archives of the firm:

(*a*) Letters, 1762–95, of Josiah Wedgwood. Besides the originals, the Museum has typewritten copies of the letters and a subject index to these. A large number of Wedgwood's letters to Thomas Bentley include comment on the obtaining and use of American clay, and on Anglo-American political relations; these, and a 1765 letter to Sir William Meredith about possible competition from South Carolina, are printed in K. E. Farrer, ed., *Letters of Josiah Wedgwood, 1762–80* (London, 1903). A draft letter, 1789, to Sir John Dalrymple including comment on the use of Cherokee clay, is printed in K. E. Farrer, ed., *Correspondence of Josiah Wedgwood, 1781–94*, pp. 104–6 (London, 1906). The collection also includes a draft letter, 1768, to William Logan of Philadelphia, recommending Wedgwood's nephew, Thomas Byerley.

(*b*) Thomas Griffith's journal,[1] 1767–8. Journal of a trip to Ayoree, in the Cherokee country of South Carolina, in search of clay for Wedgwood.

[1] The Museum holds a photostat of the manuscript as well as the original. Part of the journal was published in *Ceramic Age*, pp. 165–9, Nov. 1929.

(c) Miscellaneous business papers. An alphabetical index by author is available for the mass of miscellaneous manuscripts up to about the middle of the nineteenth century. Included are letters about trade with the United States from James Rivington, New York, 1769; Mr. Clark, Boston, 1772; William Gilchrist, Liverpool, 1783; William Knox, Boston, 1784; William Sing of the New York firm of Gailbraith & Sing, 1791; A. Humphrys, Philadelphia, 1801; Richard Shaw, 1809; and Jacob Thomas Waldon of New York, 1810.

(d) Ledgers, order books, &c.[1] The Museum holds a large number of volumes of various kinds of business records, dating from the late eighteenth century onwards. An experiment book, 'J.W.'s Experiments Nos. 1–4832', begun in 1759, includes records of some experiments using Cherokee clay; an order book for 1849–52 contains orders for ornamental ware from American customers; a letter-book for 1898–1906 includes copies of a few letters to firms in Boston and New York; discussion of the setting up of the firm's American agency occurs in early volumes of the directors' minute-books and the shareholders' minute-books, both available from 1895.

The Library, University College of North Staffordshire, KEELE

RAYMOND RICHARDS COLLECTION.[2]

(a) William Davenport & Co. Business records. 1746–82. Liverpool merchants. Most of the collection relates to the West Indies as the third stage in the triangular trade, but some of the material relates to the mainland.

(i) A sales book refers to sales, charges, and net proceeds of five elephant teeth received from Virginia, 13 Sept. 1746.

(ii) The ship's book for the brig *William* and other vessels includes a copy of a letter, 11 Nov. 1764, from the company to Captain William Patten of the *William*, containing instructions for his voyage: for the purchase, in Africa, of 120 Negroes suitable for the Carolina market; for application to Messrs. Brewton & Smith for management of the sale of the cargo on arrival at Charleston, S.C.; for the purchase of rice as a return cargo. The volume also includes the accounts, 10 Dec. 1765, for the sale of the slaves, and the invoice, 13 Feb. 1766, for the rice purchases at Charleston, as well as the accounts for the later sale of the rice.

(iii) A bill-of-exchange book includes a number drawn in Virginia, Charleston, S.C., and New York, 1769–75, and one drawn in New York, 1782.

---

[1] Some of this material was used by R. M. Hower, 'The Wedgwoods: Ten Generations of Potters', *Journal of Economic and Business History*, vol. iv, pp. 281–313 and pp. 665–90, 1931–2.

[2] This collection was, until 1958, deposited in the John Rylands Library, Manchester.

(*b*) Sneyd Manuscripts. Letter. 1816.

Washington, D.C., 12 Aug. 1816, from Mary Bagot, wife of the British Minister, to Ralph Sneyd. It consists mainly of scathing descriptions of the odd customs of the Americans, and concludes with the warning 'don't *let out* my fondness for Yankees and admiration of them'.

Earl of Harrowby, SANDON HALL, Stafford

HARROWBY PAPERS.[1]

The collection of 105 volumes contains some American items.

(*a*) Volume IX: General Correspondence, 1803–9.

Nos. 83–86. Lord Bathurst to Lord Harrowby, 30 July 1808, giving, *inter alia*, a detailed account of the causes of the quarrel with the United States over the right of search.

(*b*) Volume X: General Correspondence, 1803–9.

Nos. 55–56. George III to Lord Harrowby, 2 Oct. 1804, on Spain, America, Russia, France.

(*c*) Volume XI: General Correspondence, 1803–9.

Nos. 120–1. Lord Melville to Lord Harrowby, 17 Sept. 1804: 'The power of France has laid hold of the ruler of America.'

(*d*) Volume XII: General Correspondence, 1803–9.

Nos. 39–40. William Pitt to Lord Harrowby, 18 Sept. 1804. No likelihood of a rupture between Spain and America.

Nos. 173–8. Earl of Warwick to Lord Harrowby, 27 June 1804. Covering two letters to the writer from Charles Vancouver: the first, 23 June 1804, concerns Vancouver's position in Kentucky, his knowledge of the United States, his acquaintance with Mme Jerome Bonaparte, his fears of French designs in the United States, an offer of his services to the British government; the second, 18 July 1804, is on his secret mission to Holland.

Nos. 223–4. James Wormeley to Lord Harrowby, 27 Nov. 1804. Prospect of war with Spain, due to the latter's regret at loss of Louisiana, and fears for South American colonies; offering his services in Virginia.

(*e*) Volume XXXII.

pp. 1–10. Lord Bathurst, President of the Board of Trade, presumably to William R. Hamilton, Under Secretary for Foreign Affairs, 28 July 1811. Discusses the United States opposition to the British Orders in Council and the American refusal to let British men-of-war use their ports. It ends, 'I think some advantage might be derived from thus making an unpopular measure of their own government (the Non-Intercourse Act) the ground upon which a rupture takes place, if this question is so to end?' (Copy.)

[1] See Bradford Perkins, 'George Canning, Great Britain and the United States', *American Historical Review*, vol. lxiii, pp. 1–22, 1957.

(*f*) Volume XXXIV: Miscellaneous Papers.

pp. 175–243. Report on Newfoundland, by John Reeves, Chief Justice. 1791–2.

pp. 244–64. Newfoundland fishery.

(*g*) Volume XCIV: Third series: Letters and Papers of Rt. Hon. Richard Ryder, Home Secretary 1809–12.

ff. 5–16. Memoranda on responsibility for government of the plantations; the first being an extract from a representation of the Board of Trade, 1721.

ff. 215–16. William Pinkney to R. Ryder, 4 Jan. 1810.

ff. 219–20. R. Ryder to William Pinkney, 4 Jan. 1810.

N.R.A. 1561.

Chance Brothers Ltd., Spon Lane, SMETHWICK, Birmingham 40

W. & G. CHANCE. Account books. 1815–26.

American merchants, Birmingham. The firm was founded in 1815, with William Chance handling the business in Birmingham and his brother George in New York.

CHANCE BROTHERS & CO. Business records. *c.* 1824–.

Glass and alkali manufacturers. (Robert) Lucas Chance began manufacturing glass at Smethwick in 1824; the firm's first agent in New York was his brother George. Records of various kinds covering much of the history of the firm were used by J. F. Chance, *History of the Firm of Chance Brothers & Co., Glass and Alkali Manufacturers* (London, priv. print., 1919),[1] and these are still in existence.[2] It appears from Chance's book that at least the following relevant material is available:

(*a*) Report by John Reynell on his 1833 journey through Europe for the firm, including notes on American glass output.

(*b*) Memoranda by Lucas Chance, Dec. 1846, referring to the demand for thick glass in the United States.

(*c*) Orders for optical glass, 1860, from Alvan Clark & Sons, Boston.

(*d*) Alexander Chance's report of his 1866 trip to the United States, giving information about the character and status of American firms engaged in glass manufacture.

[1] There is some information also in J. F. Chance, *Chance of Bromsgrove and Birmingham* (London, priv. print., 1892).

[2] We are grateful to Sir Hugh Chance for confirming this.

Staffordshire County Record Office, County Buildings, Martin Street, STAFFORD

HATHERTON MANUSCRIPTS.

Edward John Littleton, 1st Baron Hatherton (1791–1863), statesman. The forty-eight volumes of his correspondence were indexed by W. Littleton in 1882, in two manuscript volumes under names of correspondents. Among Americans with whom Lord Hatherton corresponded were:

Bassett, F. Five letters, 1849–55, on the state of American politics, American opinion on the Crimean War, agriculture, &c.

Everett, Edward. Letters. 1842–53, include comments on the effects of emigration on Britain, fishery disputes, &c.

Glynn, Captain James, of the United States Navy. Seven letters, 1855–60, with political comments and details of currency problems.

Sumner, Charles. Seven letters, 1855–9, including details of Massachusetts constitutional provisions and the American constitution.

There are also letters from James Buchanan, Henry Colman, William Seward, &c.

Lord Hatherton's journals consist of ninety-one volumes, 1817–62, except for gaps between Mar. 1825–Jan. 1828, Feb. 1828–June 1831, and Aug. 1833–Mar. 1835; they include almost daily entries.[1]

QUARTER SESSIONS RECORDS.

One bundle of c. fifty bonds, 1720–40, for transporting felons to colonies and plantations in America. One bundle which contains accounts for the transport of prisoners to Liverpool for transportation to America, and a certificate for prisoners consigned to Port York, Va., 1720.

William Salt Library, Eastgate Street, STAFFORD

DARTMOUTH PAPERS.[2] 1676–1802. (*Letters unless otherwise stated.*)

William Legge, 2nd Earl of Dartmouth (1731–1801), was President of the Board of Trade and Foreign Plantations 1765–66; Secretary of State for the American Department and President of the Board of Trade 1772–5; and Lord Privy Seal 1775–82.

H.M.C. xiv (x) is devoted entirely to his American papers. Pp. 1–494 are concerned with what is now the United States; pp. 494–544 with the

---

[1] See Arthur Aspinall, ed., *Three Early Nineteenth Century Diaries* (London, 1952). One of these is Lord Hatherton's.

[2] Listed in H.M.C. reports as in possession of the Earl of Dartmouth, Patshull House, Wolverhampton.

West Indies; and pp. 545–606 with Canada, Labrador, Newfoundland, Nova Scotia, and the Island of St. John. Pp. iii–xxi give a useful introduction to the collection by B. F. Stevens. The bulk of the manuscripts in this volume fall within Dartmouth's term of office as Secretary of State for the American Department, although the dates actually range from 1676 to 1839. The Canadiana has now gone to Canada, but otherwise, with a few small exceptions, the collection is intact.

The papers are thus of the greatest importance for the study of the beginning of the War of Independence; those for 1765–6 also deal largely with the Stamp Act and its repeal. The collection contains a number of draft schemes for the conciliation of the colonies; correspondence with Franklin and other American agents; papers relating to schemes for settlement in Florida and beyond the Alleghenies; copies of intercepted letters from the American mails; and dispatches from the Colonial Governors 'each with its own tale of the anarchy and strife amongst the people, the acts of the provincial Assemblies, the subversion of the Royal authority, and the final departure of the Royal governors'.[1] There are also some records of the part played by Dartmouth in parliamentary debates on American affairs; and letters in connexion with the foundation of what later became Dartmouth College. *The papers covered by H.M.C. xiv (x), then, are not separately treated here.* However, there are several reports on the other Dartmouth Papers in other H.M.C. reports—principally xi (v) and xv (i), but also ii and xiii (iv), which contain some additional American items;[2] those of some apparent importance being:

18 Mar. 1683, from Thomas, Lord Colepeper, in Virginia, to George Legge, 1st Baron Dartmouth (1648–91), gives favourable account of the progress of the colony.[3]

Boston, 31 Aug. 1687, from Sir Edmund Andros, Governor of New England, to Lord Dartmouth, 'On the fortifications, etc., at Boston. . . .'[4]

New York, 15 Oct. 1688, from Col. Thomas Dongan, Governor of New York, to Lord Dartmouth, stating that the Six Nations of Indians have been annexed to the Crown.[5]

Boston, 17 Feb. and 23 Apr. 1714, from Francis Nicholson to William Legge, 1st Earl of Dartmouth (1672–1750) on seditious propaganda being spread among the people of Boston and other places.[6]

'A long and interesting letter, four folio pages, in 1765, from Wm. Smith of New York, to the Rev. Mr. Whitfield on the discontents of America, specially regarding the Stamp Act.'[7]

---

[1] H.M.C. xiv (x), p. xi.

[2] Since the compilation of this report two supplementary N.R.A. Reports, both 5197, have been made, which list certain papers not described by the H.M.C. reports.

[3] Transcript, H.M.C. xi (v), pp. 80–81.

[4] Ibid., p. 134.

[5] Synopsis, ibid., p. 162.

[6] Synopsis, ibid., p. 320.

[7] H.M.C. ii, p. 12. See also H.M.C. xi (v), pp. 331–2, for synopsis of another letter on the same subject from same to same, 6 Dec. 1765.

Sept. 1765, from the Earl of Hillsborough to Dartmouth, stating that the latter's powers with regard to trade and the colonies should be increased to equal those of the First Lords of the Treasury and Admiralty.[1]

16 Dec. 1765, from Samuel Garbett of Birmingham to Dartmouth on American complaints as to the quality of English nails and prospects of American competition in this field.[2]

24 May 1766, from the Earl of Chesterfield to Dartmouth relative to the latter's appointment as Secretary of State for America and Dartmouth's reply, 25 May.[3]

21 Mar. 1767, from Richard Stockton to Samuel Smith on American affairs, contains 'Stockton's scheme for the pacification of Great Britain and her colonies'.[4]

'1771, Oct. 4—Remarks on some parts of Nova Scotia, New England, and Rhode Island respecting navigation etc. by Commodore Gambier.'[5]

Letters, between 1773 and 1776, chiefly 1774 and 1775, from George III to Dartmouth, on American affairs.[6]

Various letters from George III to Dartmouth in 1774 and 1775, touching upon British determination that the colony of Massachusetts must be reduced to obedience, the measures taken by General Gage, and the skirmish at Concord; that of 28 Feb. 1775 expresses pleasure at 'the very comfortable appearance of temper in the Assembly of New York'.[7]

Several letters from George III to Dartmouth, including one of 28 Jan. 1775, in which he does not approve of Gage as Commander-in-Chief, America; and one, of 10 June 1775, in which he says that America must be a colony or be treated as an enemy.[8]

Letters from Judith Reed, at Philadelphia, 1773-5, some of which touch on the rebellion.[9]

A number of letters from Joseph Reed of Philadelphia to Dartmouth and one from Dartmouth to Reed, 23 July 1773-14 Feb. 1775. They discuss the purchase of Indian lands; the history of the American revolt; the non-importation of tea; the bad postal system; the proceedings against Franklin; and the intention of the colonies to hold a General Congress; the prime importance of the question of parliamentary taxation, the actions of the first Congress, and the completeness of non-importation.[10]

A number of letters, 1773-4, from Governor Hutchinson to Dartmouth, describing the deterioration of the political situation in Massachusetts and especially Boston.[11]

Various papers concerning the riots directed against consignees of tea in Boston in 1773.[12]

[1] Synopsis, H.M.C. xv (i), p. 179.   [2] Transcript, ibid., p. 180.
[3] Transcript, ibid., p. 182.   [4] H.M.C. xi (v), p. 332.
[5] Ibid., p. 334.   [6] Transcripts, H.M.C. xiii (iv), pp. 499–502.
[7] Transcripts, H.M.C. xi (v), pp. 439–40.
[8] H.M.C. ii, p. 12.   [9] Ibid., p. 12.
[10] Synopses, ibid., pp. 337, 345, 351, 353, 354, 358, 362-3, 366, 367-8, 371, 372, 373-4.
[11] Synopsis, H.M.C. xi (v), p. 338, 339, 341-4, 346-8, 350.
[12] Synopses, ibid., pp. 341-2.

Letters, 1773, from Mr. Pownall concerning the recall of Governor Hutchinson, and 'the French plot for stealing away our gum trade'.[1]

'Report by the Lords of Trade . . . upon a proposed formation of a colony on the banks of the River Mississippi.' 22 Jan. 1773.[2]

19 Apr. 1773, Boston, from Governor Hutchinson to Mr. Pownall on the spread of disaffection from New England to Virginia. Advises that if Parliament is to deal with the situation it must deal with all the colonies together, not singly.[3]

21 Apr. 1773, from John Gray to Dartmouth, enclosing a pamphlet, being a refutation of the answer of the Bostonians to Governor Hutchinson's speech.[4]

5 May and 2 June 1773, from Governor Tryon of New York to Dartmouth; in the former he says that 'His Majesty's instructions and His Majesty's interests are not at all times one and the same thing', and that he (Tryon) has put his own interpretation upon the instructions; in the latter he refers to purchase of lands from the Indians.[5]

(Copy), 7 July 1773, from Franklin, possibly to the Provincial Congress; setting forth the situation in England and advising how the colonists might best obtain redress of their grievances.[6]

23–29 Nov. 1773. Boston. Report of debates in the Council between these dates. Debates show strong opposition to the Governor.[7]

28 Dec. 1773, from Maj.-Gen. Haldimand at New York to Dartmouth, concerning reaction in New York and Philadelphia to the Boston Tea Party.[8]

No date. [1774?] 'Paper, unsigned, as to the advantages and disadvantages of the proposal for a new colony on the banks of the Ohio.'[9]

2 Feb. 1774, from Maj.-Gen. Haldimand to Dartmouth says that New York is quiet, but that 'little matters . . . might give new vigour to the spirit of opposition'.[10]

'1774, 25 March. South Carolina. Copy of message from the Commons House of Assembly to the Lieut.-Governor, respecting the rejection of bills passed by them by the Council. Copy of Lieut.-Governor Bull's answer adjourning the House till May. Copy of resolutions of the House of Assembly relative to the distress under which of public creditors labour.'[11]

Boston, 30 Mar. 1774, from Governor Hutchinson to Dartmouth enclosing copy of a letter from Mr. Lee, agent of the House of Representatives, of Boston, in England in the absence of Dr. Franklin.[12]

Series of letters[13] from Dartmouth to Governor Gage in 1774, and one from Gage to Dartmouth:

9 Apr. On Gage's appointment. To carry closure of port of Boston into effect; to remove seat of government to Salem; to prosecute at his discretion

---

[1] Synopses, H.M.C. xi (v), p. 338.   [2] Ibid., p. 334.
[3] Synopsis, ibid., pp. 335–6.   [4] Ibid., p. 336.
[5] Synopsis, ibid., p. 336.   [6] Synopsis, ibid., p. 337.
[7] Synopsis, ibid., pp. 342–3.   [8] Synopsis, ibid., p. 346.
[9] Ibid., p. 372.   [10] Extract, ibid., p. 348.
[11] Ibid., p. 350.   [12] Extracts, ibid., p. 350.
[13] Synopses, ibid., pp. 351, 352, 353–4, 355, 361–2, 365.

(i.e. only if impartial verdicts can be obtained) ringleaders in riots; to veto election to Council of persons opposed to the King's Government.

11 Apr. Notifying him of general pardon.

3 June. Requesting him to procure copies of two supposedly treasonable letters from Franklin and Arthur Lee; and two other letters of same date enclosing Acts concerning Massachusetts (including one abolishing elective Council).

6 July. Promising that Boston Port Bill will be rescinded when compensation has been paid to East India Company.

2 Sept. Copy of a long letter from Boston from Governor Gage to Dartmouth about violence offered to members of the Council by colonists and the spread of disaffection to other colonies (especially Connecticut and Rhode Island).

8 Sept. Regrets that colonists have summoned a Congress of Deputies from the several colonies.

17 Oct. On dangerous state of affairs in Massachusetts; more troops being sent.

Extracts from a letter, 9 Aug. 1774, from Major McDonald of the Virginia Militia to Major Connolly at Pittsburgh, describing operations against the Indians.[1]

Extract from a letter, Pittsburgh, 10 Aug. 1774, from Col. George Croghan to Dartmouth on Indian affairs. He has been maintaining the peace with the Six Nations and the Delawares, but cannot do so much longer, unless supplies are sent, and the Virginians stop attacking the Shawnesse Indians.[2]

Cambridge, Mass., 13 Aug. 1774, from Mr. Brattle to Governor Hutchinson 'mentioning alterations in the constitution of the province which he should rejoice to see effected'.[3]

31 Aug. 1774, from Nathaniel Colver to Dartmouth enclosing a petition from New York Indians complaining of ill usage by New York government, &c.[4]

Various letters to Dartmouth on the rebellion, including one of 27 Sept. 1774 from Mr. Fraser concerning secret intelligence about America.[5]

Two letters, 13 Oct. 1774, from J. Temple to Mr. Pownall and Dartmouth respectively 'expressive of his mortification at being superseded in the Lieut.-Governorship of New Hampshire'.[6]

27 Oct. 1774, from the Hon. Thomas Walpole to Dartmouth, 'enclosing papers received from America relating to the rupture with the Indians on the River Ohio'.[7]

12 Nov. 1774, 'Viscount Barrington to Dartmouth offering suggestions for the reduction of the rebellion in the colony of Massachusetts.'[8]

22 Nov. 1774, from the Earl of Suffolk to Dartmouth recommending the supersession of Gage.[9]

Minutes of Cabinet meetings on 1 Dec. 1774 and 21 Jan. 1775, to consider

[1] Ibid., p. 359.   [2] Ibid., p. 360.   [3] Synopsis, ibid., p. 360.
[4] Synopsis, ibid., p. 361.   [5] Synopses, ibid., pp. 363, 364.
[6] Ibid., p. 365.   [7] Ibid., p. 366.
[8] Ibid., p. 368.   [9] Transcript, ibid., p. 370.

what measures shall be taken to restore order in the colonies, especially Massachusetts, and (on the second occasion) agreeing that Britain should desist from taxing colonies (except for commercial purposes) if they could make adequate provision for their defence, &c., and contribute extraordinary supplies in war-time.[1]

20 Dec. 1774. Note endorsed 'Mr. Pownall', about the American petition recently received by Franklin, which is either to be presented to the King by as many Americans as can be persuaded to take part, or delivered to Dartmouth to be presented.[2]

'N.D. (1775). Two drafts of an address from the House of Commons to the King on the subject of the late riots in Massachusetts Bay, Rhode Island and Connecticut.'[3]

N.D. [? 1775]. 'Thoughts on the state of the colonies' by the Rev. Mr. Vardill.[4]

Minutes of letters from and to Lord Dartmouth and the Agents for Indian affairs in America of the year 1775.[5]

Bundle of minutes of dispatches from and to Dartmouth, 1775. The majority are from the Governors and Deputy Governors of the various North American colonies. Many of them are undated, but they all deal with the commencement of the war, and are mostly concerned with stating the general temper of the colonies. Included are dispatches from Connecticut, Georgia, Massachusetts Bay, Maryland, New Hampshire, New Jersey, New York, North Carolina, Pennsylvania, Quebec, Rhode Island, South Carolina, and Virginia.[6]

16 Feb. 1775, from James Meyrick to Governor Legge, says that the Ministry and Parliament are determined to force the Americans to submission. Then details the troops ordered to embark or be ready to embark for America under Howe, Clinton, and Burgoyne.[7]

17 Feb. 1775, New York, from the Rev. John Rodgers to J. T., Esq., describes loyalty of Americans to the Crown, but also their unanimous intention of opposing the claims of Parliament. The Assembly of New York 'is the only one . . . that has met and not approved the measures of the Continental Congress'. This is because they differ from other Assemblies on means not ends.[8]

A long letter, 18 Feb. 1775, unsigned and unaddressed, endorsed 'Thoughts upon American commerce and resistance.'[9]

Two letters, 3 Mar. 1775. Dartmouth to Deputy Governor of Maryland enclosing (enclosure not now with the letter) a resolution of the Commons 'declaratory of the nature of the indulgence they are ready to show to any of the Colonies' that return to their allegiance—this is not to be communicated officially to the Assemblies, but explained by the Governors 'to such persons as may be able by position and connexion to facilitate the measures it points to'.[10]

[1] H.M.C. xi (v), pp. 371, 372–3.   [2] Transcript, ibid., p. 372.
[3] Transcript, ibid., p. 396.   [4] Ibid., p. 397.
[5] Ibid., p. 396.   [6] Synopses, ibid., pp. 390–6.
[7] Extract, ibid., p. 374.   [8] Transcript, ibid., p. 374.
[9] Ibid., p. 374.   [10] Synopses, ibid., pp. 374–5.

A series of letters, 23 Apr.–3 Oct. 1775, from General Gage to Governor Legge, chiefly concerning the raising of troops and obtaining of supplies from Nova Scotia; rebel plans to foment trouble there and to attack the province, and counter-plans for its defence by sea; general news of the rebellion (including Washington's assumption of command); and Gage's impending departure for England, and dispositions made before that event.[1]

(Copy), Cambridge, Mass., 13 May 1775, from Dr. Joseph Warren to the select men of Boston, a defence of the colonists' action in taking up arms, and argument against exchanging prisoners with Gage.[2]

London, 11 June 1775. 'Long paper upon the rise and progress of the disputes between Great Britain and America, with suggestions for an accommodation. Unsigned, but marked on the back "Ld. D——d".'[3]

14 June 1775, from John Wesley to Dartmouth protesting against coercion in America.[4]

Two letters (copies), both 21 June 1775, from British soldiers about the battle of Bunker Hill.[5]

Boston, 25 June 1775, from E. Le Cras to Mr. Le Cras, London. Sends a resolution of the Continental Congress to starve the navy and army.[6]

Two letters, 5 July 1775. One from William Strahan to Franklin urging him to use his influence to settle the dispute; and one from H. Cruger to his brother John Harris Cruger anticipating utter ruin to America.[7]

25, 26, and 27 July 1775, describing the distress of the beleaguered city of Boston.[8]

(Copy), Philadelphia, 4 Aug. 1775, from Thomas Wharton to Samuel Wharton, says that the Canadians and Indians have refused to fight against the colonists. Possibility that General Schuyler will invade Canada.[9]

Paper of 21 Aug. 1775, stated to be by a Mr. Morris, and entitled 'The present state and condition of the colonies with respect to their governors and government.'[10]

A number of letters, written at intervals between Sept. 1775 and Jan. 1778, on military matters and of minor significance, from General Sir William Howe to Governor Legge.[11]

29 Sept. 1775, from Lord Lewisham to his father, the Earl of Dartmouth, about French sympathy for the Americans and shipment of troops to Santo Domingo since the outbreak of the rebellion.[12]

On American plans to attack Nova Scotia. 13 Dec. 1775.[13]

17 Mar. 1776, from General Howe to Governor Legge, informing him that he has evacuated Boston and is proceeding to Halifax.[14]

A long letter, 13 July 1778, from J. Galloway of New York to Ambrose Serle, describing the French blockade of New York and the disposition of

[1] Synopses, ibid., pp. 375–87 passim.
[2] Synopsis, ibid., pp. 377–8.
[3] Ibid., p. 378.
[4] Extracts, ibid., p. 378.
[5] Transcripts, ibid., pp. 379–81.
[6] Ibid., p. 381.
[7] Ibid., p. 381.
[8] Extracts, ibid., p. 382.
[9] Synopsis, ibid., p. 383.
[10] Transcript, ibid., p. 384.
[11] Synopses, ibid., pp. 386–9 passim, 399, 417.
[12] Transcript, H.M.C. xv (i), pp. 221–2.
[13] Synopses, H.M.C. xi (v), p. 389.
[14] Transcript, ibid., p. 402.

the French and British fleets. Says that the British lost more men on the march from Philadelphia than they would have done had they gone out to Valley Forge and there attacked Washington's camp. News of Washington's latest movements, and opinion that even after a junction with Gates he will have only 10,000 men to the British 20,000.[1]

N.D. [? 1778]. 'A Squib—"To be sold, the British rights in America. Consisting, among other articles of:—The thirteen Provinces in rebellion. . . . The British West Indies will be included in the sale if agreeable. Apply to George Johnston Esquire. . . . To make it easy to the purchasers, a seat in Congress will be taken as part payment, the rest in Continental currency. . . ." '[2]

27 Mar. 1779, from Alexander Macaulay to Lord Lewisham mentions that success in Georgia has elated the friends of Britain [in Holland] and depressed those of France, more than it deserved to do.[3]

23 Sept. 1781, from Granville Sharp to Dartmouth discussing the prospects and desirability of peace with America, regretting that it had not been made earlier, and enclosing an anonymous letter to same effect.[4]

1802. Correspondence between George Legge, 3rd Earl of Dartmouth (1755–1810), and John Wheelock, Ll.D., President of Dartmouth College.[5]

SIR THOMAS SALT COLLECTION. Plan. 1683.

Plan of the estate of Thomas, Lord Colepeper, on the James River, Virginia, 1683.

HAND MORGAN MANUSCRIPTS: Drakeford naval papers. 1 document. 1729.

Description of Georgia in 1729: the condition of the plantation and an attempt on the life of Governor Oglethorpe by mutinous soldiers.[6]

AQUALATE HALL COLLECTION. 1 document. Early mid-18th century. (D. 1788/24/6)

Account of the inhabitants, militia, &c., in the several plantations of America (giving the numbers only of the inhabitants and of the militia in the various plantations, in some cases distinguishing between taxables and untaxables, and between whites and Negroes). N.d., but early mid-eighteenth century.

WASHINGTON, GEORGE. Will (printed copy); several loose papers.

Printed copy of Washington's will. Observations on the will by the Earl of Buchan, with several other loose papers relating to Washington's bequest to Buchan, &c.

[1] Transcript, H.M.C. xi (v), pp. 417–20.   [2] Transcript, ibid., pp. 419–20.
[3] Transcript, H.M.C. xv (i), p. 245.
[4] Transcript, ibid., pp. 254–6.   [5] H.M.C. xi (v), p. 437.
[6] See S. Burne, *Some Notes on . . . Recent Manuscript Additions to the William Salt Library*, p. 7 (Stafford, 1950).

Horace Barks Reference Library, Pall Mall, Hanley, STOKE-ON-TRENT

POTTERS' EXAMINER AND WORKMAN'S ADVOCATE.[1] 1 volume. 1843–5.

The library holds vol. 1, no. 1, 2 Dec. 1843–vol. 3, no. 26, 24 May 1845, of this weekly newspaper edited by William Evans for the United Branches of Operative Potters. Much space was taken up by the subject of emigration to the United States. In an early issue Evans urged the formation of an emigration scheme to help solve the problem of surplus pottery labour, and later issues contained articles and letters discussing emigration as a solution, and the particular plan proposed of raising £5,000 to purchase farm land in the United States.

In addition, Evans printed in the *Examiner* a series of forty-two letters from emigrants from 'the Potteries' area to relatives and friends; mainly from Illinois, Ohio, and Wisconsin; these give information about farming and pottery-making methods and prospects, and, urging the correspondents to emigrate, give details of the best routes.

SUFFOLK

Bury St. Edmunds and West Suffolk Record Office, 8 Angel Hill, BURY ST. EDMUNDS

BARNARDISTON FAMILY PAPERS. 5 letters, documents. 1637–1823.

(*a*) Typed copies of letters from Sir Nathaniel Barnardiston (1588–1653):[2] those of 4 Apr. 1637,[3] 15 Mar. 1640[4] and 19 Mar. 1647[5] to John Winthrop, Governor of Massachusetts; and that of 5 Apr. 1636[6] to his son, John Winthrop, first Governor of Connecticut. (613/909)

---

[1] Used by W. H. Warburton, *The History of Trade Union Organisation in the North Staffordshire Potteries* (London, 1931). See also Harold Owen, *The Staffordshire Potter* (London, 1901); Grant Foreman, 'The Settlement of English Potters in Wisconsin', *Wisconsin Magazine of History*, vol. xxi, pp. 375–96, 1938.

[2] See 'Letters of Sir Nathaniel Barnardiston' in the 'Winthrop Papers', *Collections of the Massachusetts Historical Society*, 4th ser., vol. vi, pp. 545–50 (Boston, 1863).

[3] *Winthrop Papers*, vol. iii, p. 384 (Boston, Massachusetts Historical Society 1943).

[4] Ibid., vol. iv, pp. 217–18.

[5] Ibid., vol. v, pp. 144–5.

[6] Ibid., vol. iii, p. 245.

(*b*) Letter, 15 Mar. 1640, from Sir Nathaniel Barnardiston to John Winthrop, Governor of Massachusetts. (Original of letter of this date in (*a*).) (613/870)

(*c*) Notice, 12 Mar. 1823, to attend a special general court of the Society for the Propagation of the Gospel in New England, with reports on the state of the Society's affairs, sent to Nathaniel Barnardiston (1755–1837). (613/65)

N.R.A. 1015.

THOMAS FAMILY CORRESPONDENCE. 2 letters. 1709, 1743. (E 19/421)

Correspondence between the Thomas family of Lavenham and Carolina include:

London, 10 Nov. 1709, from Edward Brookby to Elizabeth Thomas, concerning the departure of her son Edward, aged 14, to Carolina, and giving a list of all the items purchased for his journey.

South Carolina, 12 May 1743, from Elizabeth Brown, daughter of Edward Thomas, to her uncle Samuel Thomas of Lavenham. Gives some account of the misfortunes which overtook the family. Her father talked of a trip to New York for his health, but she hoped to dissuade him because of the Spanish privateers.

BURWELL, LEWIS. Letter (or copy). 1734. (E 1/29/22)

Letter (or possibly contemporary copy), 8 July 1734, from Lewis Burwell, a student of law in Virginia, to his friend James Burrough of Gonville and Caius College, Cambridge. Concerns his matrimonial prospects, his law studies, and his Cambridge friends.

WATSON, HENRY. Case-book. *c*. 1745–74. (E 2/41/7)

Concerning tithes in estate of Henry Watson of Maryland and London, &c.

GRAFTON PAPERS.[1] 1768–9.

Papers of Augustus Henry Fitzroy, 3rd Duke of Grafton (1735–1811).

(*a*) Five letters, 30 July–10 Aug. 1768, from Jeffrey Amherst to the Duke of Grafton (nos. 696, 695, 692, 693, 689).

(*b*) Letter, 13 May 1769, from the Earl of Hillsborough to all the Governors upon the continent of North America and the Islands (no. 43).

(*c*) Loose papers made into a miscellaneous bundle—William Pitt, Thomas Walpole—matters of American interest (nos. 819–37).

BUNBURY FAMILY RECORDS. Diary (copy). *c*. 1814. (E 18)

Copy of a diary of events to 1814, possibly copy of one kept by Sir Charles James Napier (1782–1853), relating to expeditions against Washington, D.C., and New Orleans.

[1] Now listed (summer 1960) in N.R.A. 2567, showing considerably more Americana.

Napier commanded a brigade which took part in the expedition under General Sir Thomas Sydney Beckwith in operations against the United States, 1813; he commanded an attack on the town of Little Hampton, and was later detached to the coast of Carolina where minor operations took place.

Miss T. Chevallier, 3 Sidegate Avenue, IPSWICH

JOHNSON, SIR WILLIAM (1715–74) and SIR JOHN JOHNSON (1742–1830). Scrapbook. 1784–1885.

Sir William and his son Sir John both held office as Superintendent of Indian Affairs in North America. Sir John commanded the Queen's Own American Regiment—'Johnson's Greens'—during the War of Independence. The scrapbook contains letters, copies of letters, and notes on family history.

JOHNSON, LADY. 'Narrative of Lady Johnson.' Bound volume, n.d.

Relates her adventures during the War of Independence.

JOHNSON FAMILY HISTORY. Notebook. n.d.

Copied by Mrs. A. E. O. Chevallier from a collection of old letters made by her father, Vice-Admiral John Ormsby Johnson and including notes by Sir John Johnson. Refers to North America.

N.R.A. 0616.

Ipswich and East Suffolk Record Office, County Hall, IPSWICH

IPSWICH CORPORATION GENERAL COURT BOOK, 1572–1636. Document.[1] [1611.]

Order, 4 Mar. [1611], for 'adventuring out of the towne treasure one hundred pounds in the name of the bayliffes burgesses and commonaltie of the said towne . . . in the voyage to Virginia'; the order being made in compliance with letters from Henry Reynolds.

BERNERS FAMILY ARCHIVES. Deeds. 1622–37. (S1/10/11. 1, 2)

Title deeds, 1622–37, of the estates of Timothy Dalton, rector of Woolverstone, Suffolk, 1616–36, and of New England.

[1] H.M.C. ix (i), p. 256. (Listed as in possession of the Corporation of Ipswich.) It is possible that the Court Books contain other relevant references, but they have not been checked in detail.

READ COLLECTION. Will (copy). 1663. (T4/19/3)

Copy of will of Thomas Ives, mercer of Ipswich, including bequests to John Ives, his brother, in Virginia.

TOLLEMACHE COLLECTION. Document. 1705. (In private ownership.) (B1/2 Folder 25a/12)

'Warrant from George, Prince of Denmark, Lord High Admiral of England, to the Earl of Dysart, Vice-Admiral of Suffolk, to lift embargo on ships bound for Virginia and Maryland. 17 March 1704/5.'

NORTH (LITTLE GLEMHAM) FAMILY ARCHIVES. Document. 1706. (331)

Marriage settlement, Dudley North (1684–1729), son and heir of Sir Dudley North, and Katherine Yale, daughter of Elihu Yale, endorsed with account of jewels bought by Yale for his daughter, 1706.

ALBEMARLE PAPERS. Letter-book, documents, letter. 1754–66.

(a) Naval letter-book, 1754–61, of Admiral Viscount Keppel. Indexed. Keppel commanded the ships of the North American Station 1754–5. The letter-book covers the command at Virginia and all the coast of North America, Dec. 1754–Oct. 1755. (461/235)

(b) Naval and military documents relating to North America, 1757–8. Two folded sheets ('2nd' and '3rd' recording), being an account of an engagement with the French in which Brig. Wolfe and Col. Hawke were involved, mentioning 'Green Hill', an island. Louisbourg, N.S. 1757–8. (461/12)

(c) Letter, 22 Apr. 1766, from General Amherst to Viscount Barrington concerning action to be taken in America. (461/16)

HENNIKER, JOHN (1724–1803), later 1st Baron Henniker. London day-book. 1765–89. (S1/2/102)

Includes business transactions as a merchant for provisioning ships—army and American contracts, adventures to New England, Riga, and the like; purchase and sale of ships and freights.

STANSBURY, GEORGE. Document. 1784. (435) (T108/25)

Testimony, London, 4 Mar. 1784, of Stansbury concerning the activities of Benedict Arnold in supplying information to Sir Henry Clinton. (Stansbury was employed in decoding the correspondence which passed between them.)

HALESWORTH PARISH RECORDS. Log book. 1825–7. (FC 184/N1/8)

Log book of the ship *Merope* during a voyage from India to China, thence to the Sandwich Islands and so to California, and back again to India, 1825–7.

FISHER COLLECTION. 16 letters. 1831–62. (2815/1–4)

(a) John Fisher. Nine letters,[1] 1831–8, from the United States, to his mother, Mrs. Lydia Fisher of Brooke, Norfolk. They deal with his travels through Canada and New York state, to Michigan Territory; his acquisition of a farm in a new settlement there and its development; his marriage; prices of agricultural produce and wages; a little on farming methods; reflections on the advantages of life in America—no paupers, no poor rates, cheap land for all, an expanding nation, friendship among Methodists, Presbyterians, and Baptists; experiences when caught up in a Methodist revival; advice to a brother contemplating emigration.

(b) William Scolten. Letter, Arcade, N.Y., 1837, from Scolten to a friend in England about his purchase of a saw-mill, and about various friends.

(c) Robert Fisher Smith. Letter, Franklin, 1848, from Robert Fisher Smith, a carpenter (son of Robert Smith, an emigrant), to Francis Fisher at Brooke, Norfolk, executor of Francis Fisher, deceased, who was apparently Smith's maternal grandfather.

(d) Robert Smith. Three letters, Michigan, 1851–60, to Francis Fisher about family matters and sums due to Fisher's children with their receipts.

(e) Nathan Pooley. Two letters, Indiana, 1860 and 1862, to Francis Fisher about money due to members of the Pooley family, the history and wanderings of the various members of which, since they moved to America and multiplied there, he outlines.

MACNAB, SIR ALLAN NAPIER (1798–1862). Personal papers.[2] 1837–49. (In private ownership of the Earl of Albemarle.)

Canadian soldier and politician. Bundles 3, 4, and 5 concern the rebellion in Upper Canada, 1837–8 (one of 1849); the *Caroline* affair, 1840–1; and miscellaneous Canadian matters, 1838–40.

WEBBER, CHARLES. Letter. 1847. (50/23/7.6)

Letter from Webber, a ship's surgeon, to George Mingay, Orford, Suffolk; written from Southampton *en route* for the West Indies. Includes description of the American steamer *Washington*, first of the Ocean Steam Navigation Company, New York.

RAVEN, CANON JOHN JAMES (1833–1906). Correspondence and papers. 1888–98. (S2/4/5.13)

Deal with Massachusetts church bells.

EMIGRANT RECORDS.

Information in parish records, government circulars, shipping advertisements, papers, and correspondence about raising the necessary money. Includes Canada and Australia, as well as the United States.

[1] Photostats in the Collection of Letters of Emigrants to America in the British Library of Political and Economic Science, London School of Economics.
[2] Microfilmed by the Public Archives of Canada.

Parish Church, PEASENHALL, Saxmundham

EMIGRANT RECORDS.

Overseers' Account Book contains an entry for 3 May 1833 giving a detailed account of the cost of a family's migration to America.

SURREY

Colonel E. H. Goulburn, BETCHWORTH HOUSE, Betchworth

TOWER, HARVEY. Californian diary (bound volume). 1858.

On back: 'July 1856 to July 1861. Mexico, California 1858.' On front: 'from July 1858 to July 1861' (some photographs).

N.R.A. 0777.

Colonel A. C. Barnes, Foxholm, Redhill Road, COBHAM

HAMMOND PAPERS. Miscellaneous family papers. 1763–1877.

George Hammond (1763–1853), diplomat, first British Minister to the United States; married in 1793 to Margaret Allen of Philadelphia. American material includes:

(a) De Lancey and Allen Families. Claims. (1 bundle.) 1787–nineteenth century. Loyalists. Included are legal papers, estate accounts, a few deeds, and an abstract of title to lands in New York from the seventeenth century.

(b) Estate accounts: bundles relating to De Lancey estate, including accounts and sales of property, 1763–72; bundles relating to De Lancey finances, 1763–1814; papers relative to the death of Mrs. Chetwynd-Stapleton, 1838; bundle relative to the will of George Hammond, 1853.

(c) Account book of household expenses of Margaret Allen De Lancey, 1783–96, including notes on American families. Genealogical notes on the Allen family of Philadelphia, on the Penn family, on the Marquand family (printed).

(d) Wills of James De Lancey, 1789; William Hammond, 1832; Anthony Merry, 1835 (codicil); George Hammond (copy), 1877.

(*e*) Certificate of membership of George Hammond to the 'Society of the Sons of St. George', Philadelphia, 25 Jan. 1792.

(*f*) Letter, 1 Jan. 1793, from Hammond to Grenville on his marriage in Philadelphia; 5 Feb. 1793, from Phineas Bond to William Hammond on George Hammond's marriage.

(*g*) 'Original [Biographical] Sketches, Nos. 6 and 7.' June 1809. Addressed from Philadelphia to Mrs. George Hammond. No. 6 is chiefly on Thomas Paine; No. 7 on Mrs. [James] Madison.

N.R.A. 0566.

Guildford Museum and Muniment Room, Castle Arch, GUILDFORD

ONSLOW COLLECTION. Document. 1718.

Deed, 31 July 1718, bearing the signature of Elihu Yale.

LOSELEY MANUSCRIPTS. Documents. *c.* 1760.

A few deeds of *c.* 1760 to which General J. E. Oglethorpe, the founder of Georgia, was a party. (At Loseley Park, Surrey, three are, in an uncatalogued bundle of eighteenth-century correspondence, several letters signed by Oglethorpe. These bundles are very damp, and it would be difficult, if not impossible, to consult them as they stand. These letters probably relate to business matters.)

The Library, Royal Botanic Gardens, KEW, Richmond

HOOKER CORRESPONDENCE. 1823–65.

The library holds an extensive collection of letters on botanical matters written to Sir William Jackson Hooker (1785–1865), Director of the Gardens, together with two index volumes to these. Volumes lxi–lxv are devoted to letters from American correspondents or from America, 1832–65, while volume xliv includes some earlier relevant letters.

Among Hooker's many correspondents in the United States the following are represented by fifteen or more letters each: Daniel C. Eaton, George Engelmann, Jno. Evans, Asa Gray, Benjamin D. Greene, Thomas P. James, Thomas Nuttall, Charles W. Short, and John Torrey. There are also twenty-four letters from Thomas Drummond, written from the United States, 1831–5, while on a plant-collecting trip; and letters from the Northwest from David Douglas, 1825–30, and from D. Lyall of the North American Boundary Commission, 1859–61.

GRAY, ASA (1810–88). Letters (2 volumes). 1839–88.

Botanist; Professor of Natural History at Harvard University. Two volumes, labelled 'Kew Correspondence: Asa Gray', consist of letters from Gray to the British botanists George Bentham and Sir Joseph Hooker.

MISCELLANEOUS LETTERS. 1865–1914.

Among the bound volumes of letters to Kew—mainly to the director of the time—are volumes as follows (an alphabetical index to the writers of the letters is given at the beginning of each volume or section):

'United States Letters. North. 1865–1900': three volumes of letters from correspondents in the Northern states.

'United States Letters. South and West. 1865–1900' (1 volume).

'Supplementary Foreign Letters. 1865–1900': one volume, including a considerable number of letters from America or Americans, including some from D. Lyall of the North American Boundary Commission to Joseph Hooker, 1858–61.

'United States Letters. 1901–1914. Nat. Museum, Harvard, Dep. Agric.': one volume, containing letters from the Smithsonian Institution, the Botanic Garden of Harvard University, and the Bureau of Plant Industry of the United States Department of Agriculture.

'United States Letters. 1901–1914. Britton, Missouri B.G., Sargent, S. United States, etc.': one volume, containing letters from the New York Botanical Gardens—mainly from Elizabeth G. Britton; from the Missouri Botanical Garden in St. Louis; from the Arnold Arboretum at Harvard University—mainly from C. S. Sargent; and miscellaneous letters from the Southern and Western states.

'Brit. N. America, S. United States, and Bermuda Letters. 1901–1914': this volume includes letters from the Northern (not the Southern) states.

HILL, ARTHUR W. (1875–1941). Diary (1 volume). 1926.

Botanist; Director of the Gardens. The diary of his trip to the United States in 1926 consists of brief comments on plants seen, people met, &c., in his journey across to California and back by way of Canada.

Public Library, Fairfield Road,
KINGSTON-UPON-THAMES

MUYBRIDGE COLLECTION.

Eadweard Muybridge (1830–1904), the pioneer of animal-motion photography, was born in and died in Kingston; he migrated to the United States and became director of the photographic surveys of the United States government. He left most of his original plates and apparatus, including the zoopraxiscope, to the Kingston Public Library, which preserves them (in the adjacent Museum) together with scrapbooks of press articles about his career kept by Muybridge during his lifetime and subsequently added to—1860–1930. There is also a microfilm (but no reader) of his notebooks, the originals of which are in the Eastman Museum, Rochester, N.Y.

Surrey Record Office, County Hall,
KINGSTON-UPON-THAMES

GOULBURN PAPERS.

Henry Goulburn (1784–1856),[1] statesman, was one of the Peace Commissioners who negotiated with the Americans at Ghent in 1814. A good handlist revealed no titles of papers likely to be connected with this mission; a brief search merely revealed some personal letters to his wife in 1814 and 1815 that contain some trivial references to the course of the negotiations. Also, among the many letters from Robert Peel, a few in 1817 discuss Irish emigration to America in relation to possible government support of emigration schemes. However, a few pages of a manuscript autobiography deal with the War and the peace negotiations.[2]

PAUNCEFOTE PAPERS. 18 letters (photostats).[3] 1889–1902.

Sir Julian Pauncefote, 1st Baron Pauncefote (1828–1902), was British Minister, and then first British Ambassador to the United States 1889–1902. Most of his correspondence was destroyed by his widow. These few surviving letters are all of a congratulatory kind; they contain only a few incidental scraps of politics or diplomacy: two letters from the Marquis of Salisbury in 1889 touch briefly on the Bering Sea question; one from the Marquess of Lansdowne in 1900 gives the views of the Cabinet on the Davis Amendment renouncing the Clayton–Bulwer Treaty. John Hay's congratulatory letter, 11 Nov. 1900, when Pauncefote entered the Lords, is some measure of Pauncefote's popularity in Washington.

POOR LAW UNION RECORDS.

The Record Office contains the official minute-books of all the eleven Poor Law Unions in Surrey except Croydon. A search of three of these unions yielded merely a single reference to assisted emigration to the United States: eleven paupers from the Guildford Union in June 1844.

C. S. Marris, Esq., 7 The Fairway, NEW MALDEN

CROWTHER FAMILY. Business and private papers: *c.* 100 letters; some miscellaneous papers.[4] 1769–1825.

---

[1] His main American papers are in the William L. Clements Library, Ann Arbor, Mich.

[2] See 'A British View of the War of 1812 and the Peace Negotiations', ed. by Wilbur Devereux Jones, *Mississippi Valley Historical Review*, vol. xlv, pp. 481–7, 1958.   [3] The originals are in the possession of Lady Bromley.

[4] See H. Heaton, 'Yorkshire Cloth Traders in the United States, 1770–1840', *The Thoresby Miscellany*, vol. xi, pp. 225–87, 1945 (Thoresby Society Publications, vol. xxxvii).

Woollen manufacturers and merchants, Gomersal, Churwell, and Leeds, Yorkshire. The correspondence relates both to family and to business affairs.

The earliest item of American interest appears to be a letter, 30 Aug. 1769, from Buchanan Hastie & Co., Glasgow, to George Crowther & Co., concerning a bill remitted from Virginia for payment in Whitehaven; the latest, a letter, 8 and 9 Oct. 1825, from David Crowther, Liverpool, to George Crowther & Co., including comment on the probable demand for woollen goods in the New York market. The two major blocks of relevant material, however, consist of correspondence relating to the American journeys, 1772–5, of Benjamin Crowther, and to the stay in the United States, 1811–24, of his nephew, David Crowther.

(*a*) The first of these two includes letters from Burntisland, Scotland, and Boston, written by George Parker of Glasgow and Wilmington, N.C., as whose apprentice Benjamin Crowther went to America; and letters written by Crowther from Burntisland, from New Brunswick, and from Boston. The letters are addressed to George Crowther or to Crowther & Porrit; they deal with Parker's shipbuilding and merchanting affairs, Crowther's impressions of Boston, &c.

(*b*) The second group consists mainly of letters written from New York by David Crowther:

(i) Letters to his brothers George and Thomas, 1819–24, usually concern business matters—demand for various types of woollens; news of other Yorkshire merchants; trade with Havana ('we endeavour to keep our Havana business as much a *secret* as possible & pray you do the same'); suggested revision of their partnership agreement in order to lessen cost of United States customs duties.

(ii) Letters to his sister, Mrs. Ann Barrett, 1811–15, to her son George, 1817–24, and to her daughter Mary, 1817–24, concern family affairs, political and religious conditions and customs, &c.

(iii) There is also some correspondence relating to the death and settlement of the affairs of George Crumbleholme, the Charleston, S.C., agent of the Crowthers, 1820; a printed letter, Philadelphia, 1 Mar. 1818, *To the Merchants of Great Britain Trading to the United States of America* (4 pages), by John Cook; and a copy of a document, 9 Feb. 1824, giving David Crowther power of attorney to dispose of the South Carolina Bank shares held by Sarah Nussey of Batley, Yorks.

See also Crowther Family letters in the Brotherton Library, University of Leeds (p. 455).

Corporation of Reigate, Town Hall, Castlefield Road, REIGATE

SOMERS PAPERS. Letters, documents. 1693–1709.

John Somers, Baron Somers (1651–1716), was Lord Chancellor of England 1697–1700.

(*a*) Penn, William. Petition, *c.* 1693, and correspondence, 1694–1709.

Petition for the restitution of the province of New York (not in Penn's hand); and letters written by Penn to Lord Somers. Letters, 17 Apr. 1694 (sent with a paper), 23 Nov. 1696 and 22 Nov. 1698, request interviews—that of 1696 about the case of J. Phillips. Letter, 31 Mar. 1707, includes a petition for settling the boundaries between his (Penn's) and Lord Baltimore's territories.

(*b*) Two letters from Richard Coote, 1st Earl of Bellamont (1636–1701), Governor of New York 1697–1701, to Lord Somers:

16 Oct. 1697, requests permission to pardon pirates; refers to Captain Kidd; mentions peculation of troops' allowances at New York, and Blathwayt's patent for collecting revenues.

16 May 1699, discusses proroguing the Assembly and the opposition of Attorney-General Graham and others.

(*c*) Census of population of New York province, 1698. Account, arranged by counties, from Richard Coote, 1st Earl of Bellamont.

(*d*) Abstract of revenue of New York, 8 June–29 Sept. 1698. Collected and signed by Commissioners and Receivers of the Revenue: Stephanus Van Cortlandt and Ducie Hungerford.

(*e*) Settlement of Palatines (Pfälzer) in North Carolina. Copy of agreement, 10 Oct. 1709 (and copy of bond for execution of agreement, *c.* 1709), between Commissioners of the Palatines and Christopher de Graffenried and Lewis Michel for settling 600 Palatines on their land in North Carolina.

Four letters, all in 1709, from Col. Robert Hunter from London to Lord Somers. The first, 19 Oct., discusses the transporting of Palatines to New York, and the proposal that they be armed and enlisted in a regiment for defence of frontiers, &c. The second gives an estimate of the cost of manufacture of tar by Palatines in New York (with copy). The third gives the scheme of an estimate for naval stores if made by Palatines. The fourth contains a statement for sending 3,000 Palatines to New York (unsigned).

N.R.A. 3018.

SUSSEX

Duke of Norfolk, ARUNDEL CASTLE

NORFOLK PAPERS. 1633–7 (or 1639?).

(*a*) '1633, 7 Aug. Appointment by Leonard Calvert . . . [Governor of Maryland] of Sir Richard Lechford, of Shellwood, Surrey . . . as his attorney to receive and dispose of all such merchandizes and commodities as he shall at any time send out of the province of Maryland.'[1]

[1] H.M.C. Various Collections, ii [55], p. 343.

(b) Short letter from London, 6 May 1637 [or 1639?] to Calvert from Sir Richard Lechford, complains that small profits have come from their adventure in Maryland, from which they expected much. He desires that the stock remaining with Calvert may be employed to the best advantage, but will invest no more until better results are seen.[1]

LYONS PAPERS.[2] 1857–65.

Correspondence of Richard Bickerton Pemell Lyons, 2nd Baron and 1st Earl Lyons (1817–87), British Minister to the United States 1858–64. Include:

(a) Private letter-books (13 volumes), 1857–65. Copies of letters from Lyons to Consuls, United States officials, the Foreign Office, &c.

(b) Letters to Lyons (71 packets), 1858–65. Much of the correspondence is from the Consuls in New York, Charleston, S.C., Boston, Philadelphia, St. Louis, Mo., and other cities. There are also letters from Lord John Russell, and drafts of letters from Lyons to the Foreign Office; from British representatives in Canada, Mexico, and Central America; from Admiral Milne; from Americans, including a number of letters from C. C. Felton, president of Harvard University. Many of the letters concern, of course, various aspects of the Civil War and resulting Anglo-American relations; there is also a considerable group of letters concerning the visit to the United States of the Prince of Wales. A list of (some of ?) the letters, with brief summary of contents, is available for 1862–5 in a small volume marked on the fly-leaf 'Private letters of Lord Lyons in my keeping. Ernest Clay. Washington, 1862.'

(c) Foreign Office Confidential Print: *Correspondence relative to the Occupation of the Island of San Juan by United States Troops*, 29 Oct. 1859.

(d) Dispatch books (8 vols.), 1859–64. Summaries and copies of letters from Lyons to the Foreign Office.

(e) Letters from Lyons to his sister Minna, Duchess of Norfolk (2 packets), 1860–4. The letters mainly concern personal and family matters, with only a few scattered references to American affairs.

Parish Church, BURWASH, Etchingham

EMIGRANT RECORDS.[3]

(a) Overseers' Account Books, or Disbursements. 6 vols. 1815–36.

(b) Poor Law Account Books, or Paupers' Ledgers. 5 vols. 1816–35.

---

[1] Synopsis, H.M.C. Various Collections, ii [55], p. 344.
[2] Some of the letters were published in Lord Newton, *Lord Lyons, a Record of British Diplomacy*, 2 vols. (London, 1913).
[3] These were used by M. D. Wainwright, 'Agencies for the promotion or facilitation of emigration from England to the U.S.A., 1815–1861', M.A. thesis, University of London, 1951.

(*c*) Select Vestry Minute-book. 1819–35.

(*d*) Request Books. 4 vols. 1820–31. Include requests to the Select Vestry for assistance to emigrate, with name of applicant, nature of request, and what was granted.

(*e*) Burwash Parish letters. 1 bundle, *c*. 1820–35. Mostly requests for relief.

Marquess of Abergavenny, ERIDGE CASTLE, [Tunbridge Wells, Kent]

ABERGAVENNY PAPERS. Letters. 1774–84.

(*a*) 19 Nov. 1774, from Lord North to John Robinson, '. . . The state of America is neither better nor worse than when you were in London. . . .'[1]

(*b*) 14 June 1775, Boston, from General Burgoyne to Lord North, proposing that he be relieved from military responsibilities and be allowed to travel through New York and Pennsylvania in the cause of conciliation, prior to a return home.[2]

(*c*) Three letters, 1775, concerning the rebellion:—July, from A. Wedderburn to Lord North, criticizing adversely the conduct of the war. 31 July, Lord North to General Burgoyne, promising reinforcements and expressing optimism about the war. 8 Nov., from Captain Pearson, commander of the *Speedwell*, to Mr. Stephens, recounting 'his proceedings with regard to the *Patriote*, a snow of Altona, supposed to be laden with arms and saddles for the rebels in America'.[3]

(*d*) Letters listed for 1777: 17 May, 'Declaration by Count Floridablanca to Mr. [Arthur] Lee as to the intentions of the King of Spain relative to the United States of America.' 18 May, 'Reply of Mr. Arthur Lee to [the above]. 17 July, John Robinson to P. Stephens 'concerning the ship *Richard Penn* starting for America' (copy).—July, Extracts from a letter from a spy (?) at Paris concerning the relations between England, France, and America. 7 Aug., 'Memorial delivered to France and Spain by the three Commissioners of America' (copy). 25 Aug., William Eden to Lord North on the French attitude, and on ships for America. 18 and 19 Dec., letters from the three American Commissioners to Samuel Adams (copy). 19 Dec., Arthur Lee to the Secret Committee at Congress (copy.)[4]

(*e*) 6 June 1777, from New York, Sir William Howe to John Robinson in which he says that the war will not be terminated during that campaign but that he hopes to 'strike deep towards concluding it in the next.'[5]

(*f*) 'Memorial, presented to the States of Holland by B. Franklin and A. Lee, Plenipotentiaries for the United States of America' (copy) [1778].[6]

[1] H.M.C. x (vi), p. 7.
[2] Transcript, ibid., p. 8.
[3] Extracts, ibid., pp. 9, 12.
[4] Ibid., pp. 16–17, 19.
[5] Ibid., p. 16.
[6] Ibid., p. 21.

(g) 11 Jan. 1778, from John Robinson to Lord North concerning, *inter alia*, 'the policy to be adopted towards America'.[1]

(h) 15 Jan. 1778, from 'the three American Commissioners to Captain Paul Jones of the *Amphitrite*'.[1]

(i) 18 Jan. 1778, Minute of Lord Amherst's opinion that it would not be possible to reduce the colonies without an extra 30,000 men and that, therefore, future operations must be principally naval.[1]

(j) 14 Feb. 1778, from 'the three American Commissioners to the Secret Committee at Congress'. Also 'secret intelligence from France' mentioning Lord North's plan of reconciliation.[2]

(k) New York, 19 and 20 July 1778, from William Eden to Lord North describing the French blockade of New York.[3]

(l) 1 Jan. 1779, Downing Street, from William Eden to Lord North: 'Lord Carlisle and I cannot make any claim to a continuance of the emoluments annexed to the American commission. As to the great object we have been quite unsuccessful. Yet our commission had its uses. We have been the means of transmitting above a million sterling of British property to this country and into mercantile circulation. By accepting that temporary situation, I quitted a profitable office in England.'[4]

(m) 6 Jan. 1784, from John Robinson to Lord North, sending him, *inter alia*, a packet of papers relative to 'transactions with [the] American Army ... 5 October 1781'.[5]

Muniment Room, Public Museum and Art Gallery, John's Place, HASTINGS

PRIVATEERING. Document. 1779.

Commission for a privateer, the *Roebuck* of Hastings, 1779, to 'cruise against the French and Spanish kings and their subjects and to take any ships, goods, wares or merchandise belonging to them ... or to any of the rebellious colonies or any trading with them'.

East Sussex Record Office, Pelham House, LEWES

RYE MANUSCRIPTS. 2 letters (copies). 1634, 1637.

(a) Copy of a letter, 31 Dec. 1634, from the Commissioners of Trade and Plantations to the Lord Warden of the Cinque Ports on restriction of emigration to America.[6]

[1] H.M.C. x (vi), p. 19.   [2] Ibid., p. 20.   [3] Ibid., p. 22.
[4] Ibid., pp. 23–24.   [5] Ibid., p. 65.
[6] Transcript, H.M.C. xiii (iv), pp. 195–6. (Listed as in possession of the Corporation of Rye, which deposited them in 1955.)

(*b*) Copy of a circular letter, 7 June 1637, from Sir John Manwood, a gentleman of the King's Privy Council, of Dover Castle, to officials of the Cinque Ports and other places, passing on orders of the Lord Warden to obtain lists of emigrants to America.[1]

SHIFFNER MANUSCRIPTS.[2] American material: 306 documents, 2 miscellaneous bundles, and 1 volume. 1677–1816.

Relates to estates in West Jersey and Pennsylvania which came into the family when Sir John Bridger (knighted 1760) married Rebecca Eliot, heiress of a mercantile family and descendant of Giles Fettiplace of Coln St. Aldwyn, Glos., and John Bellers, through whom the properties came into the family. The properties, passing into the Shiffner family through the marriage of Sir John Bridger's daughter, were disposed of in 1806. The collection includes seventeenth-century leases and releases—to several of which William Penn is a party; correspondence concerning the estates—especially during and after the War of Independence, and in 1794–5 when the owners sent out an agent to report—and their disposal; and Rebecca Eliot's ledger covering 1749–63.

Sussex Archaeological Society, Barbican House, Lewes

GAGE PAPERS.[3] (375 items.) 1740–1874.

Major-General Henry Gage (1761–1808), the son of General Thomas Gage, inherited through his wife a share in the substantial American estate of Sir Peter Warren (1703–52), Admiral, Governor of Louisbourg, N.S., M.P. for Westminster. This collection is, together with some other papers of Sir Peter Warren's, the record of the administration of these properties, and of other American investments in the nineteenth century, by American agents who were relations of the heirs. The middle and later sections of the collection, then, contain full and candid accounts of the economic and political situation of the time. There is a full calendar (duplicated) of the papers. They are best briefly described under the following heads.

(*a*) Sir Peter Warren's Papers. 1729–51. (G/Am 1–66)
    Concerning the administration of his affairs mainly in America—in South Carolina, New England, and New York. They include cash books and account books—the cash book for 1740–7 shows, *inter alia*, a small purchase from Oliver De Lancey, his brother-in-law, of lots in 'Broad Way' for £41. 8s. 7d.

[1] Extracts, ibid., p. 203.
[2] F. W. Steer, ed., *The Shiffner Archives: a Catalogue* (Lewes, 1959).
[3] The papers are on loan from the present Lord Gage and were previously at Firle Place, as were the papers of General Gage that were sold to the William Clements Library, Ann Arbor, Mich., in 1930. We are grateful to Lord Gage for permission to examine the papers and make this report.

(*b*) Sir Peter Warren's 'Private Letters': letter-book with 37 letters. 1746–7. (G/Am 6)

Written by Warren while Governor of Louisbourg, they concern the war against France in North America, particularly naval affairs; intrigue for the job of Governor of New Jersey—letters to the Duke of Newcastle; instructions to Messrs. Saml. & W. Baker to invest his moneys, and to use their good offices towards the governorship; and a long and far-seeing letter to Lord Sandwich on the military position of the colonies in America.

(*c*) Lady (Susannah) Warren's Papers. 1752–72. (G/Am 67–94)

Many from her brother, Oliver De Lancey, concerning the settlement of her husband's estate. Her bank-books and some household accounts are included.

(*d*) Papers relating to the Settlement of Sir Peter Warren's Estate. 1756–72. (G/Am 95–113)

Detailed accounts of his American holdings (particularly in New York), also of his Irish property. His 'personal estate' amounts to some £31,000 to each of his three daughters (who married Willoughby Bertie, Earl of Abingdon; Charles Fitzroy, Baron Southampton; and Lieut.-General William Skinner. Major-General Henry Gage married the daughter and heiress of the latter.)

(*e*) American Estate Affairs, from Agents and Relatives there. 1768–90. (G/Am 114–203)

Correspondence mainly between Oliver De Lancey in New York and the three above-mentioned heirs, for whom he managed the property. The beginnings of the correspondence between the Kembles and Henry Gage—initially with Peter Kemble, his uncle (Thomas Gage married Margaret Kemble, daughter of Peter Kemble, who was President of the Council of New Jersey and a cousin of De Lancey).

(*f*) American Estate Affairs, between the Gage and the Kemble Family. 1791–1870. (G/Am 204–338)

These letters (and accounts) between two generations of the Kemble and Gage families mingle personal affairs with detailed discussions of financial prospects in the American market (and some good letters on contemporary politics throughout the period). Land sales and speculation figure largely in the 1790's, American banking stock and Consols in the 1810's, and by the 1850's, railway investments—with highly informative letters from William Kemble about the standing of various lines (and some letters from his brother, Gouverneur Kemble). In 1870 Henry Hall Gage, 4th Viscount Gage, had American securities valued at $70,000. William Kemble wrote on into his eighty-eighth year and discussed in his letters, *inter alia*, Jackson's election and the Bank of the United States controversy, the Kansas question, the panic of 1857, American resentment at British attempts to recruit soldiers for the Crimean War, Lincoln's election, the Civil War, war-time finance, and reconstruction.

(*g*) Wills and Settlements relating to many of the above figures which would reveal actual holdings of American property. (G/Am 1305–16)

Major John Wyndham, PETWORTH HOUSE, Petworth

NORTHUMBERLAND PAPERS. 1612–1763.

(a) Map of Virginia by Captain John Smith (early 17th century).[1]

(b) 'A trew relation of the proceedinge and occurrents of momente which have hapened in Virginia . . .' (1609).[2]

(c) 'The first [and second books] of the first decade, containing the historie of travel into Virginia' describing topography, products, Indians, other settlements, by William Strachey [1612].[3]

(d) Letters, 12 Dec. 1761–20 July 1762, to and from Sir Jeffrey Amherst, C. Colden, Governor of New York, the Governors of North Carolina, Connecticut, South Carolina, Fort Pitt, Georgia, Maryland, Nova Scotia, New Jersey, New York, New England, New Hampshire, Placentia, Quebec, Virginia, and papers about Montreal and Canada (289 pages).[4]

(e) 1 July 1763, the Earl of Egremont chosen Chancellor of the College of William and Mary in Virginia (choice made on 21 Dec. 1762).[4]

Brigadier J. R. C. Andre, Church House, SIDLESHAM, Chichester

ANDRE, MAJOR JOHN (1751–80). Letters from North America. 1775–80.

Soldier and spy. The letters to his mother, sisters, and uncle tell of his personal experiences and of the progress of the war, including the operations on Delaware River and his appointment as Adjutant-General to Sir Henry Clinton. Letter, 29 Sept. 1780, to Sir Henry Clinton after his arrest and before trial, reports considerate treatment by General Washington and others, and includes copy of the report of the proceedings of the Board of General Officers held by order of General Washington for his trial as a spy on 29 Sept. 1780, with extract of letter from General Washington to the President of Congress (8 double sheets).[5] Letter, 1 Oct. 1780 to General Washington asking not to be executed by hanging. Also packet of very capable maps and sketches. Other documents.

N.R.A. 4721.

[1] H.M.C. vi, p. 308. (Listed as in possession of Lord Leconfield.)
[2] Ibid., pp. 307–8.
[3] Ibid., p. 308. Printed as *The Historie of Travaile into Virginia Britannia* . . . ed. R. H. Major (London, 1849).   [4] Ibid., p. 316.
[5] See *Writings of George Washington*, ed. by John C. Fitzpatrick, vol. xx, pp. 130–4. (Letter dated 7 Oct. 1780.) (Washington, D.C., 1937.)

WARWICKSHIRE

Mrs. Alston-Roberts West, ALSCOT PARK, Stratford-on-Avon

WEST, JAMES (1704?–72). Letters from correspondents in America. 1754–5.

Politician and antiquary. Joint Secretary to the Treasury 1741–62.

(a) Private correspondence addressed to James West includes three letters, 1754–5, from Peter Rayer, customs officer in Philadelphia, giving interesting particulars about Pennsylvania.

(b) Williamsburg, Va., 1755, from Robert Dinwiddie, concerning the government of that colony, and warfare with the French and Indians.

N.R.A. 4349.

Assay Office, Newhall Street, BIRMINGHAM 3

MATTHEW BOULTON COLLECTION.[1] c. 100 boxes of letters, 1750–1810; c. 50 letter-books, ledgers, account books and journals of the firms with which Boulton was connected, c. 1750–1850.

Matthew Boulton (1728–1809), engineer, corresponded with most of the leading men of the day on topics of considerable scientific and technological interest. The letters are filed alphabetically in boxes, and there is an eleven-volume typescript index under names of correspondents which gives the general contents of each letter. Some names under which letters of American interest can be found are: Dr. J. Baader, Sir F. Baring, S. Bayard, Elias Boudinot, A. Buchanan, T. Cockran, Lord Dartmouth, Benjamin Franklin, J. Gilpin, Peter P. Goelet, Sir G. Jackson, Thomas Jefferson, Rufus King, W. Knox, J. Lacy, Ralph Mather, J. H. Mitchell, S. Moore, I. Ogden, R. N. Patterson, Joseph Priestley, D. Rittenhouse, Nicholas Roosevelt, Turnbull, Forbes & Company, J. Tustin, John Warder, George Watson.

Subjects include supplying copper blanchette to the United States Mint;

---

[1] See John Hinckley Mitchell, *The Mitchell-Boulton Correspondence 1787–1792* (New York, priv. print., 1931); J. P. Muirhead, ed., *The Origin and Progress of the Mechanical Inventions of James Watt, Illustrated by His Correspondence with his Friends and Specifications of his Patents*, 3 vols. (London, 1854); A. and N. Clow, *The Chemical Revolution* (London, 1952); B. D. Bargar, 'Matthew Boulton and the Birmingham Petition of 1775', *William and Mary Quarterly*, vol. xiii, pp. 26–39, 1956; and R. E. Schofield, 'Membership of the Lunar Society of Birmingham', *Annals of Science*, vol. xii, pp. 118–36, 1956.

building a new mint; the state of markets; trade in hardware, buttons, nails, guns, &c.; inventions.

In addition there are boxes containing single subjects, some of which are indexed separately. One labelled 'America' containing a wrapper endorsed 'American disputes 1775' includes notes, drafts of letters, and newspapers concerned with the Birmingham petitions of 1775; one box labelled '(Various) Mints' contains a bundle labelled 'United States Mint, estimates and proposals 1830'; one box containing correspondence of Boulton and Watt with Dr. William Small, physician and natural philosopher, mostly concerning inventions; a manuscript entitled 'An estimate of iron supposed to be manufactured into nails annually, America 1775'.[1]

Letter-books, ledgers, &c., include: Cash books 1752–1814, and letter-books 1757–80, for Boulton & Fothergill. Letter-books 1784, for Boulton & Scale. Boulton's private letter-books c. 1760–94. Letter-books 1796–1801, 1815–19, for Boulton Plate Company. Mint and Coinage day book 1834–49, &c.

Public Libraries, Ratcliff Place, BIRMINGHAM 1

ZACHARY LLOYD PAPERS. Letters. 18th century.

'Among the letters of the 18th century there are several from Thomas Owen, Sarah Middleton, and others, in South Carolina.'[2]

RUSSELL FAMILY PAPERS.[3] 1731.

(a) Copy of the will, 28 Jan. 1731, of William Russell, the younger, iron-master, of Birmingham. Devises all his properties in Britain and America to his father, William Russell. (418824)

See also Russell Diaries below (p. 438).

(b) Indenture between William Russell the elder, ironmaster, of Birmingham, Thomas Russell the elder, his eldest son, and William Russell the younger, another son of the said William Russell, the elder, concerning the Principio Works in the province of Maryland, and a furnace called 'Potomack' in the colony of Virginia in America. 19 Aug. 1731 (418822). (And also a similar indenture of 3 Dec. 1735 (418827).

LYTTELTON PAPERS (Hagley Hall Collection). 2 documents. 1755.

(a) Letters patent of George II appointing William Henry Lyttelton Captain-General and Governor-in-Chief of the Province of South Carolina. 1 Mar. [1755]. (390025)

---

[1] See W. H. B. Court, *The Rise of the Midland Industries, 1600–1838*, p. 196 (London, 1938), for use of this manuscript.

[2] H.M.C. x (iv), p. 450. (Listed as in possession of S. Zachary Lloyd, Esq., Areley Hall, Stourport, Worcs.)

[3] These papers are mentioned in R. A. Pelham, 'The West Midland Iron Industry and the American Market in the Eighteenth Century', *University of Birmingham Historical Journal*, vol. ii, p. 154, 1950.

(*b*) Commission from George II to Lyttelton to be Vice-Admiral Commissary and Deputy in the office of Vice-Admiralty in the Province of South Carolina in the room of James Glen. Given at London in the High Court of Admiralty of England, 6 Mar. 1755. (352031)

BOULTON AND WATT COLLECTION. Letters. 1794–1812.

(*a*) 4 Nov. 1794–23 Feb. 1805 from Robert Fulton, civil engineer and inventor, concerning the purchase of a suitable steam engine for boat propulsion. Letter, New York, 15 Sept. 1810, mentioning that the engine made for him in 1804 has for four years been used to drive a boat on the Hudson River, and asking for a further engine as he wishes to provide boats on other rivers. Letter, New York, 4 Jan. 1812, dealing with the violation of his patent for steam-boats.[1]

(*b*) Clermont, N.Y., 4 Nov. 1798, from Robert R. Livingston to James Watt, in which he sets forth his ideas on steam-boats.

(*c*) 24 Aug. 1793–7 May 1812, from Joseph Priestley, Jr., to James Watt, Jr., the first written just before Priestley left for Northumberland, Pa., four from Northumberland, and four from Philadelphia. Priestley urges Watt to emigrate, and describes his own situation in Northumberland. For the rest the letters cover mainly personal matters. Priestley left for England in Jan. 1812.

RUSSELL DIARIES.[2] 3 journals (and typescript copies), paper. 1794–1801.

Include the journals kept by Misses Martha and Mary Russell, and Thomas Pougher Russell, of their tour to America, 1794–5, travels in America and return voyage, 1796–1801. They were captured by the French during their voyage to America and taken to France. Joseph Bryan secured their release. There is also a manuscript article composed for or by William Russell and addressed to the editor of the *Monthly Magazine*, 1801. (12 pages.)

See also the Russell Family Papers, above (p. 437); and the Russell of Birmingham Papers, Add MSS. 44992–45022 in British Museum (p. 173).

LADIES' SOCIETY FOR THE RELIEF OF NEGRO SLAVES. Minute-book. 1825–52. (302206)

Chiefly directed towards slaves in British territories, but there are references to talks given to the Society on slavery in the United States and letters read from correspondents in the Southern states.

KING, WILSON (1846–1930). Autograph letters collected by King: 2 volumes. (569342)

United States Consul in Birmingham 1879–85. The letters are very miscellaneous. A brief inspection showed two notes signed by Lincoln on one

---

[1] See H. W. Dickinson, *Robert Fulton: Engineer and Artist, his Life and Works* (London, 1913).

[2] See S. H. Jeyes, *The Russells of Birmingham in the French Revolution and in America, 1791–1814* (London, 1911).

of which is written 'Allow Francis T. King of Baltimore to pass with the English Friends through our lines to North Carolina. Oct. 25, 1864';[1] and two letters, 1880, 1882, from Bret Harte from Glasgow, where he was Consul 1880–5, concerning an invitation to speak in Birmingham and asking for an address, &c.

BIRMINGHAM COLLECTION. Printed pamphlet (4 pages).[2] 1865. (359807)

A copy of the correspondence between the American Secretary of State, W. H. Seward, and J. M. G. Underhill, concerning the latter's dismissal from the post of United States consular agent in Birmingham in favour of Elihu Burritt.

AUTOGRAPH LETTERS.

There are a few letters of American interest, including one, 18 Nov. 1885, from Andrew Carnegie to Joseph Chamberlain, enclosing a copy of the *Statistical Atlas of the U.S.*, inscribed 'To Joseph Chamberlain. The leader of the masses and future premier of Britain I send this record of the reign of the people under institutions based upon the only true doctrine "the political equality of the citizen".' (This Atlas became worn out and discarded, but the Library possesses another copy with a similar inscription to the men of Birmingham.) (67419)

CADDICK, HELEN (1843–1927). Travel diary (typescript with photographs): vol. 6. 1900. (336856)

Miss Caddick visited the principal American cities, often staying with American friends. She describes social customs, scenery, and institutions. (Also visited the Philippines, 1913–14, vol. 12. 336862.)

Rev. Charles E. Surman, 4 Holly Lane, Erdington, BIRMINGHAM 24

CONGREGATIONAL BIOGRAPHIES.[3]

Private collection of biographical materials relating to the Congregational Ministry in England from 1640 onwards.

Among these are various fugitive references to ministers who emigrated to or came from the United States.

---

[1] See *Collected Works of Abraham Lincoln*, ed. by R. P. Basler, vol. viii, p. 76 (New Brunswick, N.J., 1953).

[2] From City of Birmingham Public Libraries, Reference Department, *A Catalogue of the Birmingham Collection, Supplement, 1918–1931* (Birmingham, 1931).

[3] This is now in Dr. Williams's Library, London, the Rev. Surman retaining a copy.

The Library, University of Birmingham, Edgbaston, BIRMINGHAM 15

CORBETT COLLECTION. Letter. 1777.

In Autograph Letters, vol. 1, there is a Paris letter, 29 May 1777, from George Chalmers, to George Carlting, London. In code but deciphered. Chalmers was an English spy during the War of Independence. He speaks of an indiscretion by Lord George Germain; he suggests that France and Spain wish to place themselves again where they were before the last war, that France would be glad of the offer of Canada, that Pensacola and both Floridas might be offered to Spain. Negotiations with Baron Schulenburg are mentioned and a visit by Beaumarchais to Dunkirk about artillery. Franklin and Dean are also mentioned.

CHAMBERLAIN, JOSEPH (1836–1914). Papers.

These papers were not available for inspection at the time of compilation. But a temporary list showed them to include the following Americana:

(a) Box two: American correspondence (non-official). 1881–97.

file 1: Social engagements and introductions, 1887–8.
    2:     „   „   „   „   1890.
    3: 'Murchison correspondence', 1888 (American presidential election).
    4: Alaska boundary, 1888.
    5: Canadian invitations, 1887–90.
    6: Visit to the United States, 1890.
    7: Plot to assassinate Chamberlain in the United States, 1897.
    8: Miscellaneous correspondence with or about the United States, 1881–92.

(b) Box two: Washington Fisheries Conference, 1887–8.

file 1: Principal correspondence relating to the Conference, including letters from Lord Salisbury, bound in guard-book.
    2: Printed papers.
    3: Letters relating to the Conference from the following: George Baden-Powell, T. F. Bayard, J. H. G. Bergne, H. G. Edwardes, W. H. Hurlbert, Lord Lansdowne, Willoughby Maycock, Sir Julian Pauncefote, Sir Lionel Sackville-West, Cecil Spring-Rice, Sir Charles Tupper, and 'various correspondents'; also some press cuttings.

(c) Box seven: Foreign affairs, 1880–99.

file 9: United States: miscellaneous correspondence, 1890–9; F.O. Confidential Prints, 1898; manuscripts of magazine articles on 'Anglo-American Alliance' and 'Municipal Institutions in Britain and the United States'.

Woodbrooke College, Bristol Road, BIRMINGHAM 29

BEVAN-NAISH COLLECTION.[1]

This collection of Quaker Manuscripts, which consists of twenty bound volumes (some of which are indexed) and three boxes, is not catalogued. A brief inspection revealed the following items of American interest:

(*a*) Bevan-Naish Library, vol. 4, includes a deed with William Penn's signature; a list of the names of Friends who visited America from Great Britain, 1656–1775; and of Friends who visited Britain from Pennsylvania and New Jersey, 1693–1773.

(*b*) 'Some account of the forepart of the life of Eliz. Ashridge . . .', 1713–55. Mainly an account by Elizabeth Ashridge of her life and conversion to the Quaker faith in America, including some account of travels in New England and Rhode Island, her experiences as a bonded servant and as a teacher.

(*c*) 'Letter-book 1770.' Contains a copy of an epistle from some squaw Indians to women Friends, 1797.

(*d*) 'John Pemberton and other letters.' This volume contains extracts from two letters from Philadelphia: one concerns the adventures of Mary Prior, shipwrecked on her way to America, with some details of conditions on board and her fellow passengers, 1798; the other, n.d., gives an account of the conversion of Nicholas Waln, a lawyer of Philadelphia.

(*e*) An envelope inscribed 'Hicksites' contains an extract from a letter, Philadelphia, 11 July 1832, from Samuel Bettle to T. Robson, giving the verdict of a chancery suit in Jersey in favour of the Friends—'the Hicksites are seceders'.

(*f*) Minutes of the North Warwickshire Monthly Meetings of the Society of Friends, 1862–71. Contains introductions to the Friends Monthly Meetings in Pennsylvania on behalf of Warwickshire Friends settling in Pennsylvania, 1863; a list of Friends who have left Birmingham for America with addresses and circumstances; report of Friends appointed to correspond with members abroad, 1864.

Sir Robert George Maxwell Throckmorton, COUGHTON COURT, Alcester

THROCKMORTON PAPERS. 1681.

In a group of papers connected with the Popish Plot there is one of 24 Oct. 1681, which says that Shaftesbury has asked to be allowed to go to Carolina, but has been refused.[2]

---

[1] Used by Arnold Lloyd, *Quaker Social History, 1669–1738* (London, 1950).

[2] H.M.C. x (iv), p. 173.

City Record Office, Council Offices, Earl Street (South Side), Coventry

CITY ARCHIVES. Letter. 1615.

Covering letter, 22 Mar. 1615, from the Privy Council to the Mayor and Aldermen of Coventry, to a declaration (not found) of the state of the colony in Virginia with a project to help it by a lottery, which the Mayor and Alderman are asked to support.[1]

TRANSPORTATION RECORDS.

There is a little correspondence, 1741–52, with shipping merchants engaged in the transport of convicts to Maryland and Virginia, together with a few bonds, vouchers, receipts, and copies of orders to 1766.[2]

Earl of Denbigh, Pailton House, Rugby

DENBIGH PAPERS. 4 letters. 1691–1775.

(a) 1691, includes a reference to the Spaniards in America. (In French.)[3]

(b) 1693, refering to a convoy for merchants of America. (In French.)[4]

(c) 6 Oct. 1775, from Earl of Sandwich to Denbigh, in which he urges Denbigh to attend Parliament in order to support the Government's measures against America.[5]

(d) Draft, 19 Oct. 1775, from Denbigh to Dr. Rochford. Denbigh writes that loyal addresses in support of the Government are coming in slowly.[6]

Oscott College, Sutton Coldfield, Birmingham

PAPERS. 2 volumes.

'Noticia de la California, y de su conquista espiritual y temporal hasta el año 1768', 2 vols., c. 1768. Relates to the Jesuit missions in California.[7]

---

[1] Mentioned in Benjamin Poole, *Coventry: its History and Antiquities*, p. 382 (London, 1870).

[2] Two of the letters are quoted in Frederick Smith, *Coventry. Six Hundred Years of Municipal Life*, pp. 103–4 (Coventry, 1945).

[3] Transcript, H.M.C. vii, p. 200.

[4] Transcript, ibid., p. 220.

[5] Transcript, H.M.C. Denbigh MSS. [68], pp. 297–8.

[6] Transcript, ibid., p. 298.   [7] H.M.C. i, p. 90.

Warwick County Record Office, Shire Hall, WARWICK

HOLBECH OF FARNBOROUGH COLLECTION.[1] Document. 1641. (L1/242)

Bill of lading by Henry Hazard, master of the ship *Sampson* of Bristol for George 'Willys' of Fenny Compton, Warwickshire, of goods for Boston to be delivered to Captain C[oll?]ins, Boston; dated at Bristol, 5 May 1641. (As many of the deeds in this collection are concerned with the Willis family of Fenny Compton, the George Willis mentioned is doubtless the one of that name who settled in Hartford, Conn., where he became governor 1642, and died in 1645.)

PHILIPS OF WESTON HOUSE COLLECTION. George Philips and Co.: Business records (9 vols.). 1801–30.

Insurance and general commission business. Founded 1801 as London branch of the Manchester firm. The letter-books, nine volumes, 1801–30, include one for America, 1801–3, which contains correspondence with merchants in Philadelphia, New York, Baltimore, Charleston, S.C., &c., giving details of cargoes, ports of shipment, prices, and conditions of markets. One volume 'Correspondence' 1802, contains day-to-day notes of letters received and written, some of which are from America and from the shipping firm of G. C. Fox & Co., Falmouth, Cornwall (p. 28). Mr. George Philips's 'Private letter-book 1820–1830' includes letters concerning property in America and difficulties encountered with American agents.

SEYMOUR OF RAGLEY COLLECTION (catalogue in progress).

In this collection of more than forty large boxes, Box 39 contains letters, 1851–61, from Francis Hugh George Seymour, 8th Marquis of Hertford, (1812–84), to his father Admiral Sir George Francis Seymour, from America during the Civil War. Also letters to Sir George from various other American correspondents at about the time of the Civil War, and a bundle in an envelope marked 'The Marquis of Hertford—Letters, &c., of Admiral Sir George Seymour on the Fishery Question in North America'. About forty of these letters, 1849–58, seem to relate to the Labrador–Newfoundland dispute between England and France.

BOUGHTON-LEIGH OF BROWNSOVER COLLECTION.

This collection, which is unsorted and uncatalogued, may contain material relating to Peter Leigh (d. 1759), Lord Chief Justice of South Carolina; and to his son Sir Egerton Leigh (d. 1781), Attorney-General of South Carolina.

[1] There is also a later deposit of the same collection not yet catalogued (CR 457).

WESTMORLAND

Earl of Lonsdale, ASKHAM HALL, [Penrith, Cumberland]

LONSDALE PAPERS. 1690–1763.

(a) 'Memoranda on trade and plantations 1690, September 11th. Affrican Companie. They cannot return in time:—the Plantations ill supplied with Negroes the last year:—they therefore desire convoy:—the castles and plantations will be in danger:—betwixt 30 & 40 ships to be employed, and about 40 men a peece:—they would send before the end of October 16 sail:—12 are the fewest they ought to send in October. . . .'[1]

(b) Letter, 16 June 1701, from William Penn to Sir John Lowther, describing the situation and trade of Pennsylvania.[2]

(c) Letter, 3 Feb. 1763, from the Earl of Bute to Sir James Lowther, mentioning the French abandonment of Louisiana to the Spaniards.[3]

O. R. Bagot, Esq., LEVENS HALL, Kendal

BAGOT PAPERS. 1814–19, c. 1841–3.

In this large collection of family papers the papers of Sir Charles Bagot (1781–1843), Minister to the United States 1815–20, Governor-General of Canada 1841–3, contain American material.

(a) One volume 'Negotiations at Ghent', 1814, concerning North America, Canada, West Florida, &c.

(b) From two boxes containing bound volumes entitled 'Letters and Papers of Sir Charles Bagot, G.C.B.': Series II, vols. 1–7, 1815–19.[4]
Volume 1: Official, to Secretary of State for Foreign Affairs.
Volume 2: Official and private, to Secretary of State for Foreign Affairs.
Volume 3: Official, from Secretary of State for Foreign Affairs.
Volumes 4 and 5: Correspondence with Secretary of State of United States.
Volume 6: Canada.
Volume 7: Consuls—Appendix.

(c) Red leather official box containing letters and papers of Sir Charles Bagot, c. 1841–3. Included are a Cabinet printed paper on fortifications and defences of Canada, 1840–1; letters of recommendation, arranged alphabetically under names of persons recommended; some executorship papers.

N.R.A. 6234.

[1] Transcript, H.M.C. xiii (vii), p. 102.
[2] Transcript, ibid., p. 246.   [3] Transcript, ibid., p. 132.
[4] See Bradford Perkins, 'George Canning, Great Britain and the United States', *American Historical Review*, vol. lxiii, pp. 1–22, 1957.

WILTSHIRE

Wiltshire Archaeological and Natural History Society, The Museum, Long Street, Devizes

WYNDHAM, HENRY (1709–88). 25 draft letters to his son. 1765–7.

The Wyndham family had great influence in Salisbury. The son, Henry Penruddocke Wyndham (1736–1819), was a topographer and M.P. for Wiltshire 1795–1812, in the main supporting Pitt's administration. The draft letters from Henry Wyndham were in reply to letters written by the son while on a European tour. They are a complete set, and contain social and political news, including proceedings in Parliament concerning the American rebellion.

See also his Account books in the Hampshire Record Office, Winchester (p. 76).

Marquess of Bath, Longleat, Warminster

BATH PAPERS. 1607–97.

(*a*) ' . . . bundle of letters and papers relating to . . . Newfoundland . . . Carolina . . . New York and New England.'[1] n.d.

(*b*) Various papers relating to the plantations during the seventeenth and early eighteenth centuries.[2]

(*c*) Two parcels labelled 'Virginia and Surinam' and 'Virginia and Barbadoes'. The former contains address, 1674, by Virginians against royal grant of all lands between 'Pottamock and Rapahamock' to Lord Hopton and others in 1662. The latter contains the patent to Sir Thomas Gates, and various letters, charters, and commissions (to Sir Francis Wyatt and Sir W. Berkeley and others) at various times between 1607 and 1663.[3]

(*d*) '(1628, March ?) Instructions to shipwrights sent to Virginia to procure masts and ships, timber out of the woods of that country. Instructions to Captain John Harvey, Governor there;—and proposed additions; for him to carry on war against the natives.'[4]

(*e*) Letters, 1674–7, from Henry Coventry, Secretary of State, to Major Andros, Governor of New York, and Sir William Berkeley, Governor of Virginia. [No indication of contents.][4]

[1] H.M.C., iv, p. 237.
[2] H.M.C. iii, p. 193.
[3] H.M.C. iv, pp. 236–7.
[4] H.M.C. iii, p. 190.

(*f*) 'An interesting account by Edward Randolph of the State of New England, he being sent from England by the King, and letters by him.' (14 pages.) 1676.[1]

(*g*) The correspondence of Matthew Prior while he was engaged in various diplomatic missions in the Low Countries and France includes a number of letters mentioning the American aspect of the negotiations leading up to the Peace of Ryswick, 1697, but nothing of any length or importance.[2]

(*h*) Letter, 10 Aug. 1697, from the 'Traders and inhabitants of Virginia and Maryland' to William Blathwayt, asking him to support an enclosed petition to the King which asks His Majesty to use his influence with the Czar to procure the removal of the prohibition on the importation of tobacco into his Empire.[3]

Wiltshire Record Office, County Hall,
TROWBRIDGE

SUFFOLK AND BERKSHIRE ARCHIVES. Bundle of papers including letters, maps, copies of deeds, &c. 1773–1808.

Among the papers of the Howard family, Earls of Suffolk and Berkshire, are some relating to the purchase of lands in the province of New York by Colonel Thomas Howard from General Bradstreet.

WILLES AND LOVELL FAMILIES' PAPERS (of Cole Park, Malmesbury). Letter. 1838.

1838, from J. G. Shawe to his mother, Mrs. Lovell, about travel along the Great Lakes, affairs in Quebec, &c.

Earl of Pembroke, WILTON HOUSE, Salisbury

PEMBROKE PAPERS. Letter. 1780.

New York, 26 Oct. 1780, from Augustus Reebkomp to Lord Herbert, on the fleets of Rodney and Arbuthnot; the impending final defeat of the rebellion; Gates's defeat in Carolina; and Arnold's defection from the American side; the latter has been made a Brigadier-General and appointed 'to raise a regiment of as great scoundrels as himself if he can find them'.[4]

---

[1] H.M.C. iv, p. 237.
[2] H.M.C. iii, p. 193.
[3] H.M.C. Bath MSS. iii [58], p. 149.
[4] Transcript, H.M.C. ix (ii), p. 383.

WORCESTERSHIRE

Viscount Cobham, HAGLEY HALL, Stourbridge

LYTTELTON PAPERS. 1755–62.
'A large collection of papers and letters, including those from Secretaries of State to Wm. H. Lyttelton while Governor of South Carolina . . .' [1755–1762].[1]

Mrs. Fulwar Coventry, Holy Well House, MALVERN WELLS

COVENTRY, F. C. A. Report on a visit to America, 1902. (Typescript.)
Includes an account of engineering and railway works.
    N.R.A. 0598.

The Library, The Cathedral, WORCESTER

MUNIMENTS. Letter. 1777. (D 725)
28 Aug. 1777, from W. Digby, Dean of Worcester, says, 'It was rumored at Court that Philadelphia was seized by the Quakers for government. Some believed, some not.'[2]

Worcestershire Record Office, Shirehall, WORCESTER

WESTERN QUARTERLY MEETING OF THE SOCIETY OF FRIENDS. Records: bundle of copies of American epistles. 1783–94. (Bulk accession no. 1948, parcel no. 4, class 898. 2.)
Copies of annual letters from the Yearly Meeting of Friends or Women Friends held at Philadelphia for Pennsylvania, New Jersey, and the western parts of Maryland and Virginia, to the Yearly Meetings of Friends or Women Friends held in London.

[1] H.M.C. ii, p. 38.   [2] H.M.C. xiv (viii), p. 190.

YORKSHIRE

East Riding County Record Office, County Hall, BEVERLEY

HOTHAM COLLECTION. 1771–1815.

(a) Thompson, Sir Charles Hotham (1738–92). c. 100 letters from America. 1771–9. (DDHO 4/16–21)
Adjutant-General to the Forces in the Seven Years War. Some hundred letters in his correspondence are from persons serving with the British forces in America and others, referring to American affairs.

(b) Hotham, William, 1st Baron Hotham (1736–1813). 23 letters. 1776–80. Admiral. Commodore on North American Station during War of Independence.
 (i) 29 Apr. 1776–13 July 1780 from Lord Howe. Eighteen from New York, Philadelphia, or H.M.S. *Eagle*, off America, four from London, dealing with the movement of ships, the state of anchorages, &c., off the American coast; with a few references to rebel activities ashore. (DDHO 5/1)
 (ii) 9 Nov. 1776, from General Howe, Camp at Dobbs Ferry, N.Y., asking if the artillery ships can be got up more quickly, as the stores in them are needed. (DDHO 5/2)

(c) Copy of a loyal motion passed by the Beverley Corporation relating to the War of Independence. (DDHO 4/272)

(d) Hotham, Vice-Admiral Sir Henry (1777–1833). Letters, 5 letter-books, orders, two journals, miscellaneous documents. 1811–15.
Captain of the Fleet on the North American Station during the earlier stages of the War of 1812.
 (i) Standing Orders on North American Station, July 1811–July 1814; Halifax, N.S., Port Orders, Oct. 1813; 'Public Orders of the Commander-in-Chief' of the North American Station, Apr.–Nov. 1814; 'Public Orders issued by Commodore Hotham', Aug. 1814–Mar. 1815. (DDHO 7/45–48)
 (ii) Copy of a report, 15 Nov. 1812, of Captain James Stirling, *Brazen* sloop, on Florida. (DDHO 7/99)
 (iii) About 350 letters, Mar. 1813–May 1815, to Sir Henry while First Captain and second-in-command of the fleet on the North American Station, relating, *inter alia*, to the war with America; Sir Henry's orders and instructions; safe-conducts and passports for neutrals and others; United States Navy; the coastline blockade; and the neutrality of the island of Nantucket, Mass. (DDHO 7/2)
 (iv) Five letter-books (four are partly order books), Apr. 1813–July 1814. Letters, all from Bermuda, are mainly about routine naval matters, but include references to American weakness, prisoner of war exchanges,

employment of refugee American Negroes in the West Indies, impressed seamen claiming to be American citizens, &c. (DDHO 7/30–34)

(v) Book of 'remarks', 1813, suggesting ways and means of attacks on America in the prosecution of a war. (DDHO 7/99)

(vi) Proceedings of a court martial, 28–31 May 1813, of the captain and crew of the *Macedonia*, captured by American ships. (DDHO 7/97)

(vii) Proceedings, 7 June 1813, of a court martial of the captain and crew of H.M.S. *Peacock* captured by U.S.S. *Hornet*. (DDHO 7/98)

(viii) Twelve documents, 1814–15, giving information about the American forces in the area of the North American Station. (DDHO 7/70)

(ix) Four documents of secret instructions, 1814–15, from the Admiralty in the event of the American fleet putting to sea. (DDHO 7/71)

(x) Twenty-nine letters, July 1814–Apr. 1815, being instructions from Admiral Sir Alexander Cochrane, Commander-in-Chief of the North American and West Indian Station. (DDHO 7/4)

(xi) Journals, two volumes (the second unbound), Apr.–Dec. 1814. Chiefly records of ships arriving and departing, but mentions also the shipping of American prisoners to Halifax, N.S., and the blockade. (DDHO 7/52–53)

(xii) Twelve letters, Oct.–Nov. 1814, 'delivered to me by Captain Hayes the senior officer off New London [Conn.] on the 14th Dec. 1814, being a correspondence held between Colonel Barclay (late British Consul General for the Eastern States of America) and the Commanding Officer on it, in my absence, respecting his leaving the United States, and from the Dutch and Swedish Ministers on other subjects'. (DDHO 7/5)

Major George Howard, CASTLE HOWARD, Malton

CARLISLE PAPERS. 1754–83. (*Letters unless otherwise stated.*)

Mainly the papers of Frederick Howard, 5th Earl of Carlisle (1748–1825), who was the head of the Commissioners sent out in 1778 to treat with the American colonists.

(a) 7 Dec. 1754, from Sir Thomas Robinson (ex-Governor of Barbados) to Lord Carlisle, complaining that the former Governor of Massachusetts Bay, Mr. Shute, and Lieut.-Governor of New York, Mr. Clarke, had both received more money from the Duke of Newcastle than had he.[1]

(b) 24 Aug. 1758, from General Sir Charles Howard to Lord Carlisle on the taking of Louisbourg and drafts for America.[2]

(c) 14, 28, and 29 Dec. 1775, from Anthony Storer to Lord Carlisle on events in America.[3]

(d) Numerous letters from Carlisle, chiefly to his wife; papers by him, and letters to him, written while he was head of the Peace Commissioners in

---

[1] Transcript, H.M.C. xv (vi), p. 208.
[2] Transcript, ibid., p. 212. [3] Transcripts, ibid., pp. 311, 314–15.

1778. The contents of the letter-book of the Commissioners are also enumerated.[1]

(e) 'Instructions by King George III to his Commissioners to treat with the North American Colonies', 12 Apr. 1778.[2]

(f) Paper headed 'News from Connecticut' 13 Jan. 1779, purporting to be by Elihu Hall, 'who left New Haven the 5th inst.' Describes unrest in the Continental army, desertions, reluctance to serve, &c., scarcity and high price of foodstuffs, decline in trade, &c. (In Chief Justice William Smith's hand.)[3]

(g) Paper headed 'Intelligence by Mr. Thomas Fanning', 19 Jan. 1779. Concerns up-state New York, shortage of food, depreciation of paper money, defections from and discount in the American Army, loyalty of the 'King's Friends'. (In Chief Justice William Smith's hand.)[4]

(h) Savannah, Ga., 18 Jan. 1779, from Lieut.-Colonel Archibald Campbell to Carlisle, describing the success of the expedition to Georgia.[5]

(i) Four newsletters, 1 and 14 Feb., 4 and 19 May 1779, from Andrew Elliot at New York. Chiefly concerned with what he considers the parlous state of the American forces, British successes in Georgia, dissensions in Congress; and giving advice such as that all offers of pardon should be accompanied by promises of restoration of property, and that Britain should reject all offers but submission from Congress.[6]

(j) 2 Feb., 3 May, 10 June, 24 Oct., and 10 Dec. 1779, from William Smith, Chief Justice of New York, to Carlisle. Touch upon such matters as Congressional taxation of the colonies; the inability of New York to bear such taxation; the auspicious opening of Clinton's 1779 campaign and then his lapse into inactivity, when, as Smith thinks, only determined blows are needed to end the rebellion. There is also information about supposed dissensions in the rebel camp, Washington's inability to keep an army together, and Cornwallis's embarkation for the south.[7]

(k) New York, 21 May 1779, from Sir Henry Clinton to Carlisle, saying that the Chesapeake expedition has accomplished all he expected of it, and that he is taking the field immediately to prevent Washington detaching part of his force, but has little hope of success.[8]

(l) Paper, 8 June 1779, entitled 'Information from the Highlands' [of North America], speaks of the unpopularity of the Congress and its French treaty; depreciation of the Continental currency, rapacity of the American troops; and the general scarcity of food.[9]

---

[1] Transcripts, H.M.C. xv (vi), pp. 334–410.
[2] Transcript, ibid., pp. 322–33.   [3] Transcript, ibid., pp. 412–13.
[4] Synopsis, ibid., pp. 414–15.   [5] Transcript, ibid., pp. 413–14.
[6] Transcripts, ibid., pp. 415–17, 419–20, 425–8.
[7] Transcripts, ibid., pp. 417–19, 424–5, 430–1, 431–5.
[8] Transcript, ibid., p. 428.   [9] Transcript, ibid., pp. 429–30.

(*m*) Paper, 7 Dec. 1779, headed 'Intelligence from Mr. Hunter'. Hunter, who came in under a flag of truce at King's Bridge, from Dutchess Country in the province of New York, to procure the exchange of certain families, told of the general depression on the American side consequent upon the failure of the Georgia expedition; scarcity of food, much of which is being given to the French; the prospect of bankruptcy and the dissatisfaction with the terms of service in Washington's force; exultation of the Loyalists, who, however, wish for more vigour in the campaign.[1]

(*n*) 11 Oct. 1780, from Carlisle to Lord —— praising Cornwallis's vindication of Saratoga, and saying that he has no fears for New York.[2]

(*o*) 12 Dec. 1781, from Sir Henry Clinton at New York to Carlisle on the surrender of Cornwallis's army. He attributes this to the lack of a covering fleet. Is also concerned to vindicate his own course of action.[3]

(*p*) 25 Mar. 1782, from Cornwallis to Carlisle, says that Cornwallis is sending to the latter all the correspondence between himself and Clinton from the time of his marching into Virginia.[4]

(*q*) 12 June 1783, from Lord Cathcart to Carlisle, on the situation in New York, and especially the harsh treatment of the Loyalists.[5]

G. E. Buckley, Esq., Brookfield, DELPH, [Oldham, Lancs.]

BUCKLEY FAMILY. Business papers. 1805–22.

John Buckley, of Broadhead, Saddleworth, Yorkshire, was a woollen manufacturer whose son Henry was a merchant in New York and whose son Hugh was a merchant in Lisbon. The family traded with America throughout the nineteenth century. The papers of American interest in the small collection are:

(*a*) A folder containing four business letters to Henry Buckley in New York. Two of these are from 'John Withington, for Richard Milne', Philadelphia, referring to Brooks & Potter of Charleston, S.C., 1805 and 1806; one is from Richard Milne, Philadelphia, 1806; one is from John Buckley in Broadhead, 1807. Two of the Philadelphia letters are directed to Henry Buckley, c/o Messrs. Lawrence, Van Sinderen. It appears from the correspondence that Henry Buckley sold his father's woollen goods, and bought cotton.

(*b*) Three loose letters, as follows: John Buckley & Sons, Broadhead, 11 July 1817, to John McAdam & Co., Liverpool, asking that insurance be obtained for woollens which are being shipped to Charleston, S.C.; H. Schofield & Co., Liverpool, 30 Nov. 1821, to Hugh Buckley in Lisbon,

---

[1] Transcript, ibid., pp. 433–4.
[2] Transcript, ibid., p. 445.
[3] Transcript, ibid., pp. 550–1.
[4] Transcript, ibid., p. 605.
[5] Transcript, ibid., pp. 636–7.

including comment on demand for 'course wool' in the American market; Abram Buckley, Broadhead, 28 Dec. 1821, to his brother Hugh in Lisbon, including comment on American demand for 'cotton warp goods such as Satanets and Cassinets'.

(c) Copy of a letter from Hugh Buckley, Lisbon, 20 Feb. 1822, to H. Schofield & Co., Liverpool, noting that 'the Americans are the principle purchasers here in the low sorts of wool'.

There may possibly be other items in the papers relating to the family's American trade.

Bankfield Museum, Ackroyd Park, HALIFAX

CLAY, J. T., & CO. Business records. 1899–1931.

Woollen manufacturers, Rastrick, Yorkshire. Most of the extensive records held by the Museum are volumes of samples; in none of the volumes examined did the occasional correspondence attached to these appear to refer to the United States. However, 'after the year 1868 [woollens] were extensively sold . . . through commission houses to customers in the United States', according to the firm's submission before the New York Southern District Circuit Court in 1899 in its case charging Marks Arnheim with misrepresentation of goods as made by Clay; this document, and several other papers concerning the case, are included in an envelope labelled 'New York Trade Mark'.

Other miscellaneous relevant materials in the collection include a packet of eleven letters, 1905–20, from E. H. Van Ingen of New York and London, on business and personal matters; and a few letters of the 1930's.

Shibden Hall, Folk Museum of West Yorkshire, HALIFAX

LISTER FAMILY. Papers. 1733–75.

The Shibden Hall collection includes manuscripts relating to various connexions of the Lister family with America in the eighteenth century—the trading careers in Virginia in the 1730's of several Lister brothers, the service in the War of Independence by one of their sons, and miscellaneous other contacts.

(a) Lister Letters.

The earliest relevant documents concern the visits to or settlement in Virginia in the 1730's of the brothers Thomas (1708–40), William (1712–43), and Jeremy (1713–88):

    (i) Letters to their brother Samuel (1706–66) in Halifax about their reasons for going to Virginia and the trade in tobacco and skins which they hope to carry on there; news in 1735 of their varied activities—purchase of wheat and a share in a ship in which to transport it to Madeira or Lisbon, the pickling of pork to trade for rum and sugar in the West Indies, &c.

(ii) Reports, 1736–40, of Thomas's mismanagement, illness, and death.

(iii) Correspondence, 1743–7, of Samuel with William's widow, Susannah, of New Bern, Neuse River, N.C., and her father, John Lewis of Virginia, concerning difficulties impeding the settlement of William's debts to Samuel.

Also included is a letter of 1769 to Thomas's son William (1734–80) in London from his mother Ann in Virginia, containing news of her marriage to James Sturdivant, since dead.

(b) Fawcett Letters.

(i) 1744, from William Fawcett (1728–1804; later General Sir William Fawcett) to his uncle, Rev. John Lister (1703–59), concerning his imminent departure for Georgia with Oglethorpe and the hardships to be expected there.[1]

(ii) 1750, from Fawcett to his uncle, Samuel Lister, concerning a proposed woollen business in London and noting that Mr. Caygill of Halifax has just sent £700 worth of Yorkshire goods to New England.

(iii) Correspondence during the War of Independence between Fawcett and the Lister family, concerning the British army service of his cousin Jeremy Lister (1752–1836) in North America; and a letter to Fawcett from Henry Basset, Boston, 23 Apr. 1775, giving a brief account of the battle of Lexington.

(c) Rev. John Lister Papers. Correspondence, 1757, between William Lister (1734–80) and his uncle, Rev. John Lister, concerning the former's intention of returning to Virginia from London, and the latter's objections.

(d) Lister Manuscripts. Certificate, 1765, respecting the disposal of woollen goods shipped from England by Japhet Lister (1715–82), signed by Thomas Claiborne of Virginia as attorney for William Middleton.

(e) Jeremy Lister Letters. The papers of Jeremy Lister (1752–1836) include letters written to his family in London and Halifax during his army service in Quebec and Niagara, 1771–4, and while stationed in Boston, 1774–5; although mainly concerned with promotion possibilities, these contain occasional reports of battles, comments on officers, &c. Also included is his journal for 1770–83.[2]

Earl of Harewood, HAREWOOD HOUSE, Leeds

CANNING PAPERS. 5 letters. 1817–23.

Papers of George Canning (1770–1827), statesman.

(a) Washington, D.C., 1 Nov. 1817, 2 and 3 Dec. 1818, from Charles Bagot, British Minister to the United States, to George Canning.

---

[1] Printed in full in John Lister, 'John Lister, Master of Bury Grammar School, and his Correspondents', *Transactions of the Lancashire and Cheshire Antiquarian Society*, vol. xxviii, pp. 153–4, 1911.

[2] Part of this journal, together with three of the letters written from Boston and a fragment by Lieut.-Col. Val Jones describing the battle at Charlestown, Mass., has been published as Jeremy Lister, *Concord Fight* (Cambridge, Mass., 1931).

(b) Private and confidential, Washington, D.C., 12 Mar. 1823, from Stratford Canning, British Minister to the United States, to George Canning.

(c) Précis, Washington, D.C., 10 July 1823, from Stratford Canning to George Canning.

Public Library, Victoria Avenue, HARROGATE

GREEVES, CHARLES. (1795?–1847). Diary (1 volume). 1842–5.

Land agent and surveyor, Harrogate. His very miscellaneous diary includes reports of visits from friends emigrating to the United States—mainly to the Illinois area; items of news concerning local people living in the United States; and extracts from letters to relatives in Harrogate from T. Ellinsworth, a tailor of Elgin, Ill., from Mr. Brydone of Rock Hall on the Des Plaines River, Ill., and from Mrs. Mary Birch of Kentucky and Missouri. The extracts deal mainly with the quality of the soil, the yield of various crops, &c.

H.M. Customs and Excise, HULL

See H.M. Customs and Excise, London (p. 206).

Archives Department, Public Libraries, LEEDS 1

GASCOIGNE COLLECTION. Letters patent. 1635. (GC/F3/1)

Letters patent creating John Gascoigne (1556?–1637) of Parlington a Baron of Nova Scotia, and granting him estates between the rivers Magin, Grand Sohiboyin, and Pargendo for plantation and settlement (never taken up). 1635.

CARR MANUSCRIPTS. 1771–83. (CA)

The copies of deeds and other legal papers in these six volumes appear to have been made for use as precedents in the office of an attorney, probably James Carr of Birstall, Yorkshire. Included in volume 1 are articles of agreement, 2 Sept. 1771, between Wigglesworth, Kent & Co. of Leeds, woollen merchants, and Thomas Gumersall, who is to go to America as their agent. Vol. 4 includes articles of agreement ('special form'), 25 Aug. 1783, between the 'assignees of Ellis' and Cornelius Buck, the agent going on their behalf to the United States to deal with debts owed the estate, &c.

HOLROYD, JOHN & JOSEPH, *later* JOSEPH HOLROYD & SON. Business records. 1788–1821.

Wool dyers and merchants, Leeds. The firm appears to have carried on a considerable trade with the United States: a book listing bills of exchange, 1788–1807, includes a number shown as due in Savannah, Ga., New York, and other places in America; an account book, covering 1812–21, includes notes of transactions with Marx & Linsley of New York, charges for insurance on woollens sent from Liverpool to New Orleans, details of accounts relating to shipment of cotton from New Orleans by Maunsel White & Co., &c.

PRIESTLEY BROTHERS. Business records. 1890–6. (P 4/1, 2)

L. E. and G. F. Priestley, hardware, &c., manufacturers, Halifax, Yorkshire. Most of the collection relates to their business, which seems to have had no American connexions. However, during the latter part of the 1890's they began investing abroad, and letter-books contain copies of letters from G. F. Priestley to George Murray in London and R. Bridger in New York concerning the Febroline Company; there may also be other American investments involved.

Brotherton Library, University of Leeds, LEEDS 2

CROWTHER FAMILY. 6 letters. 1774–1822.

Family of woollen manufacturers and merchants, Gomersal, Churwell, and Leeds, Yorkshire. The Library holds six letters, one, 1774, from Benjamin Crowther, on his departure for North Carolina; and five from David Crowther, Montreal, 1811 and 1812, and New York, 1813 and 1822. In a letter of 12 Jan. 1813 David Crowther discusses the war and its effects on Yorkshire trade; his letter of 15 Dec. 1822 includes comment on American concern about piracy in the West Indies, and the case of Lieut. Allen.

See also Crowther Family Papers in the possession of C. S. Marris, Esq., New Malden, Surrey (pp. 427–8).

GOTT, BENJAMIN (1762–1840). Business records. 1797–1867.

Woollen manufacturer and merchant, Leeds. This large collection includes documents, 1770–1860's, many of them relating to the firm's extensive American trade. The earlier papers are those of Wormald & Fountaine, woollen merchants, the firm to which Benjamin Gott was apprenticed in 1780, of which he became a partner in 1785 and gained control in 1790; in 1792 he began cloth manufacture as an added activity of the firm; both manufacturing and merchanting were continued by two of Gott's sons who took over the firm when he died; the firm ended with the death of the second of the sons in 1867. For a description of the collection, and extracts from some relevant letters, see 'The papers of Benjamin Gott in the Library of the University of Leeds', in W. B. Crump, ed., *The Leeds Woollen Industry, 1780–1820* (Leeds, 1931) (Thoresby Society Publications, vol. xxxii). Also H. Heaton, 'Benjamin Gott and the Anglo-American Cloth Trade', *Journal of Economic and Business History*, vol. ii, pp. 146–62, 1929.

WOOLLEN INDUSTRY. Business archives.

The records of a considerable number of West Riding woollen and worsted industry firms—merchants, weavers, spinners, &c.—are deposited in the Brotherton Library. These records include ledgers, letter-books, invoice books, &c.; they refer to periods between the late eighteenth and the early twentieth centuries. The set relating most extensively to trade with the United States is that of John Foster & Son Ltd. of Queensbury; the profits of this firm's American sales of woollen goods were usually invested in American railroads, &c.[1] Other firms whose records include relevant material are W. Lupton & Co., Wormald & Walker Ltd., and Robert Jowitt & Sons Ltd. It is possible that there is occasional American material in the records of some of the other firms.

BROTHERTON COLLECTION.

(*a*) Alfred Mattison Collection.
The collection includes the following papers relating to John Francis Bray (1809–97), American-born social reformer:

(i) Correspondence, 1802–56, among members of the Bray family. Forty-six letters (of which eleven are transcripts of originals not in the Collection) include five from Bray written in 1822–56—to his mother (2); to his aunt, Mrs. Gauler (1); to his uncle, Joseph Bray (2). Most of the letters, however, are from Boston, from Sarah Bray, mother of John Francis, 1824; from Sarah Barnes ('Barney', a friend of the family), 1827–34; from Charles Frederick Bray, 1828–55; from Edgar W. Bray, 1828–40; and from Edwin Bray Nichols, 1836–40.[2]

(ii) Twentieth-century letters on Bray to John Passmore Edwards, and to Mattison, including letters (copies) from Philip Snowden, 1923, and Ramsay MacDonald, 1925; pamphlets; offprints of articles, &c.

(*b*) Canon Leigh Collection. 3 letters.
Irving, Washington. Ashford, 5 Dec. 1831, to Rev. Reastor Rodes, concerning a prospective tour of England with Van Buren.

James, Henry. Undated portion of a letter.

Longfellow, Henry Wadsworth. Cambridge, Mass., 25 May 1845, to Lady Sitwell, enclosing autographs of Washington and Franklin.

---

[1] See E. M. Sigsworth, *Black Dyke Mills* (Liverpool, 1958).
[2] Many of the letters and transcripts are quoted in John Edwards, 'John Francis Bray', *Socialist Review*, vol. xiii, pp. 329–41, 1916; a typescript of the article is in the collection. There are also Bray papers in the British Library of Political and Economic Science, London School of Economics (pp. 322–3).

(c) Dickens, Charles. 7 letters. 1841–67.
Letters to various correspondents, 11 Dec. 1841–10 Nov. 1867, from Britain or on board ship, relating to his visits to America, to George Dolby going there, to his opinion of the American press, and to his *American Notes*.

(d) Swinburne, Algernon Charles and Paul Hamilton Hayne. Correspondence (1 volume). 1875–1911.
Letters, 1875–84, between Hayne, of Augusta, Ga. (five letters) and Swinburne (copies of eight letters, mainly from London). They deal with Edgar Allan Poe—his monument and memorial volume—and with American political and literary matters. The volume also contains three letters to W. T. Watts-Dunton, Swinburne's literary executor, concerning possible publication of the correspondence; of these, one, 1910, is from the editor of *Harper's Magazine*, and two, 1910 and 1911, from Hayne's son.

(e) Gosse, Edmund William. Correspondence. 1882–1923.
Writer. The published catalogue[1] lists the correspondents and the dates of their letters, most of which are to Gosse or members of his family.
Included are letters from Henry Mills Alden, Thomas Bailey Aldrich, George Bancroft, Edwin Booth, John Burroughs, Nicholas Murray Butler (one of the two letters, 27 June 1917, concerns Balfour's reception in the United States), Ralph Waldo Emerson, Edward Everett Hale, Oliver Wendell Holmes, Sen., William Dean Howells, Henry Cabot Lodge, James Russell Lowell, John Singer Sargent, Mrs. Fanny (R. L.) Stevenson, and Owen Wister. There are over 250 letters from Henry James, and a few letters from other members of the James family; letters from many of Gosse's other correspondents include comment on James.
In addition, there are letters, 1914, on receiving a copy of the White Paper on the European crisis, from Arthur T. Hadley, John G. Hibben, Seth Low, Abbot L. Lowell, and William Howard Taft; letters while on visits to the United States from George Rathbone Benson, 1st Baron Charnwood, Rupert Brooke (including comments on Edwin Arlington Robinson), John Drinkwater, and Alfred Noyes; and various other relevant letters—Marie A. Brown on the difficulty of arranging an American edition of her work, Gosse on his meeting with Mark Twain, George Frederic Watts on the American exhibition of his work.

(f) Bram Stoker Correspondence. 20 letters, 3 cards. 1882–1907.
The collection includes letters to Stoker, or to Henry Irving, whose agent he was, from Edwin A. Abbey, Henry Mills Alden, T. B. Aldrich, James Archer, Luigi Arditi, Edwin Booth, William Dean Howells, and Elihu Root.

(g) Clement King Shorter Correspondence. 23 letters. 1896–c. 1922.
Shorter (1857–1926) was the editor of the London *Sphere* from 1900. The collection includes three letters from William Dean Howells, 1904 and 1910; nineteen letters from Henry James, 1896–1907—mainly covering letters for work sent for inclusion in the Sphere; and a letter [c. 1922] from Katherine Osbourne, Monterey, Calif., concerning Robert Louis Stevenson.

---

[1] *A Catalogue of the Gosse Correspondence in the Brotherton Collection* (Leeds, 1950) (University of Leeds, Library Publications No. 3).

(*h*) Edward Clodd Collection. Letter. 1904.

William Dean Howells, London, 25 Apr. 1904, to Clodd: 'It would be adding pleasure to pleasure if I could meet Hardy at your house.'

(*i*) H. A. Jones Correspondence. 2 letters. 1906, 1912.

William Dean Howells, New York, 1906, concerning the use of stage directions in play-writing, and 1912, both to Jones.

(*j*) Romany Collection. Letter. 1911.

Albert T. Sinclair, Boston, 18 Jan. 1911, to Rev. F. W. Galpin. A covering letter sent with his *Gypsy and Oriental Musical Instruments* (Boston, 1908).

(*k*) Osbourne Manuscripts. 3 letters (2 copies). 1922–3.

Three letters (bound in two volumes) from Katherine Osbourne concerning Robert Louis Stevenson, Fanny Stevenson, and Sir Sidney Colvin. The letters are:

> Palo Alto, Calif., 16 Aug. 1922, to Edmund Gosse; 18 pages.
> New York, 22 July 1923, to Clement K. Shorter; 9 pages (copy).
> New York, 5 Sept. 1923, to an unknown correspondent; 17 pages (copy).

MISCELLANEOUS LETTERS. 11 letters. 1883–1930.

Mainly on literary matters, as follows:

(*a*) Letters from the United States, 1883–1901, to C. T. Whitmell, from William A. Bell, James M. Hutchings, Benjamin J. Jeffries, Nathaniel P. Langford (two letters), and Charles A. Young (four letters).

(*b*) Arthur Dickson to Paul Barbier. New York, 17 Nov. 1930.

(*c*) Clark S. Northup to Mr. Stokes. Ithaca, N.Y., 4 Oct. 1926.

MARSHALLS. Business records.

Leeds was the foremost flax-spinning town in Europe during the early nineteenth century, and records relating to the firm of Marshalls, 1788–1886, are deposited in the Brotherton Library.[1]

C. K. C. Andrew, Esq., F.S.A., Hill Brow, Brompton, NORTHALLERTON

SEVEN YEARS WAR: BRITISH NAVAL AND MILITARY ACTIONS. 1 sheet. 1758.

The manuscript includes a list of the names of French ships burnt, taken, sunk, &c., on various dates in June and July 1758; the numbers of killed and wounded 'the day the troops landed'; the number taken prisoner in the 'garrison of Louisbourgh', &c. The manuscript is thought to be in the hand of, and is endorsed by and found in the family archive of, Philip Rashleigh (1729–1811), antiquary and M.P.

[1] W. G. Rimmer, *Marshalls of Leeds*, chap. 3 (London, 1960), deals with John Marshall's investments in the Second Bank of the United States and in state funds, 1820–40.

North Riding County Record Office, County Hall, NORTHALLERTON

BERESFORD-PEIRSE ARCHIVE. 2 papers. *c.* 1806, 1812. (ZBA)

(*a*) Beresford, Sir John Poo (1766–1844). Memorandum (1 sheet). *c.* 1806. Admiral; commanded on North American Station 1806. The memorandum, believed to be written by Beresford, is dated 13 Dec., no year. It concerns negotiations for an attack on Mexico between Mr. [Aaron] Burr and Mr. M[erry, British Minister to the United States], and news of preparations in New Orleans for 'some expedition'.[1]

(*b*) War of 1812: Directions for the taking of Philadelphia (1 sheet). *c.* 1812.

This manuscript was found among the documents of Admiral Sir John Poo Beresford, who was a senior officer on the American coast 1812–14. It is a detailed plan for an attack on Philadelphia.

QUARTER SESSIONS RECORDS.

Bonds, memoranda of contracts, justices' certificates, and orders for payment of fees occasionally relate to the transportation of convicted persons, mainly 1736–73.

Public Library, Howard Street, ROTHERHAM

PAINE, THOMAS (1737–1809). Letter. 1789.

London, 16 Jan. 1789, from Paine to Thomas Walker of Rotherham, deals with current British political and constitutional issues—'. . . as a republican I think the British Constitution a hodge-podge'.

Corporation of Scarborough, Town Hall, SCARBOROUGH

MUNICIPAL RECORDS. Letter and copy of petition.[2] 1813. (Bundle C4)

22 Apr. 1813, from A. W. Morgan, written from London, to B. Fowler, Trinity House, Scarborough, transmits the (manuscript) form of a petition to Parliament against the admission into the United Kingdom of articles

[1] The memorandum appears to add no further details to the story as told in T. P. Abernethy, *The Burr Conspiracy* (London and New York, 1954).

[2] Noted in *Catalogue of Ancient Documents Belonging to the Corporation of Scarborough* (Scarborough, 1915), [pages not numbered].

from the United States in neutral shipping, urging that the shipowners of Scarborough consider action on this without delay; Morgan adds that the shipowners and merchants of Liverpool have already petitioned, and those of London are in the course of signing.

Edgar Allen & Co. Ltd., Imperial Steel Works, SHEFFIELD 9

BUSINESS RECORDS: Letter-books (3 volumes). 1883–1900.

Steel manufacturers, Sheffield. Copies of outgoing letters; a few for 1883–9, but the vast majority for 1890–1900. Include a few references to the beginnings of the firm's interest in the American market (it finally became incorporated in New York in 1909, and in Illinois in 1911); and to the introduction of the Tropenas process of steel-making, of which the Company was the British licensee, into the United States. References also to American tariffs, the quality of American steel, and the cheapness of raw material. Letter, 10 Oct. 1899, compares the production per day of United States and British steel firms, and gives the reasons for American superiority as the greater mechanization of the industry in the United States and the American workman's willingness to do an 'honest day's work'. (At the time of examination in 1958 the papers were temporarily in the care of E. N. Simons, Esq., Pond Cottage, Pevensey Park, Pevensey, Sussex.)

James Dixon & Sons Ltd., Cornish Place, SHEFFIELD 6

BUSINESS RECORDS:[1] Letter-books (1 volume, 1 folder). 1811, 1835–9.

Manufacturing silversmiths and cutlers. The firm still holds a few nineteenth century records.

One of these is a letter- and pattern-book for 1813 inserted in which are some pages containing copies of earlier letters; one of these, 22 Feb. 1811, from the firm (at that time Dixon & Smith) to Mr. A. Willis, notes that 'We are now executing an order for . . . spoons . . . for America.'

The firms also has James Willis Dixon's copies of the letters he wrote, 1835–9, while acting as American agent for the family business. Most of these letters are addressed to his father and brothers, and concern business affairs— comment on the American firms with which he has dealings, discussion of types of goods in demand, copies of orders from particular firms in Brooklyn, N.Y., Baltimore, &c.; the letters also contain news of Sheffield business men in America, and give Dixon's impressions of Boston, New York, and other cities.

[1] See P. C. Garlick, 'The Sheffield Cutlery and Allied Trades', M.A. thesis, University of Sheffield, 1951. A microfilm of the 1835–9 letter-book is held by the Sheffield City Libraries.

Marsh Bros. & Co. Ltd., Ponds Steel Works, P.O. Box 82, SHEFFIELD 1

BUSINESS RECORDS.[1] 1819–76.

Steel, tool, and cutlery manufacturers. The firm maintained agents in the United States from 1817 onwards, but the earliest relevant figures appear to be the £2,600 due from American firms noted for 31 Dec. 1819 in a stock book covering 1810–34.

Much information about the American connexion is available in two letter-books; one of these, labelled 'Extracts of letters from the United States', consists of copies by the Sheffield partners of parts of letters, 1833–42, from James Marsh the younger in Philadelphia, Charles Wreaks in New Orleans, and Joseph Cam and Edward Mullins in New York. As well as details of orders, these contain information about prices and positions of competitors, and comment on American financial and political affairs.

The other is the letter-book used by John Marsh, Jr., in 1841–2 while he was in Philadelphia dealing with the inefficient organization of the office there; the copies are of letters sent to East Coast firms concerning their accounts with Marshes & Shepherd (as the firm was called then), to the New York agent Joseph Cam, and to the Sheffield office. It was also used for letters written, 1842–3, by W. N. Woodcock, whom Marsh left in charge of the American branch, now moved to New York.

In addition, a volume containing extracts from and summaries of letters received by the Sheffield firm, 1845–76, includes references to the credit position and general standing of various American firms, including some in Chicago and Indianapolis, Ind., as well as in Philadelphia, &c.

See also the Letters of this firm in the Sheffield City Libraries (p. 468).

Department of Local History and Archives, Sheffield City Libraries, Surrey Street, SHEFFIELD

Most of the following collections are noted or described in *Guide to the Manuscript Collections in the Sheffield City Libraries* (Sheffield, 1956).

WHARNCLIFFE MUNIMENTS. 1749–1893.

This large collection of family papers includes the following:
(*a*) Edward Wortley Montagu (1678–1761), M.P. Montagu was an opponent of the Bill to reduce duty on American iron, and his papers include a

---

[1] S. Pollard, *Three Centuries of Sheffield Steel: the Story of a Family Business* (Sheffield, priv. print., 1954), is a history of the firm.

bundle containing printed leaflets and pamphlets on the subject, answers in manuscript to some of these, and a few letters and copies of letters about the Bill from Joseph Broadbent of the Wortley Wire Works. 1749–50. (Wh. M. 118)

(*b*) Ainslie and Young Families. (Wh. M. 445)

(i) Letters, 1794–5, from J. A. Stuart, later Stuart-Wortley, when a young naval officer, to Miss C. Ainslie (afterwards Mrs. Young) of Quebec.

(ii) Letters, copies of memorials, &c., from John Young and Mrs. C. Young, 1817–18. John Young was a member of the Executive Council of Lower Canada and was considered entitled to some recompense from the government.

(iii) Several bundles of letters, memorials, &c., from Mrs. C. Young and her son Gilbert, and from Lord Bathurst and others, concerning recompense for the services of John Young, now deceased; 1819–30. The letters are addressed from Quebec and London.

(*c*) Bundle of about a dozen letters, 1805–44, from Col. Thomas Talbot, pioneer colonist in Upper Canada.[1] (Wh. M. 444)

(*d*) A few letters, Quebec, 1820–7, from George Ryland, concerning the office of Receiver General of Lower Canada. (Wh. M. 447)

(*e*) John Stuart-Wortley, 2nd Baron Wharncliffe (1801–55). The diary kept while he travelled in America in 1824–5 is so faded as to be virtually illegible. (Wh. M. 450–2)

(*f*) Edward Stuart-Wortley-Mackenzie, 1st Earl of Wharncliffe (1827–99):

(i) Three letters, 1840 and 1852, from Charles Sumner, concerning, *inter alia*, Pierce's nomination, Daniel Webster, the Fugitive Slave Bill, and the publication of 'the Cuban correspondence'. A letter, 1846, from W. W. Storey of Boston asks for material to be used in the biography of his father. (Wh. M. 503)

(ii) Printed matter and letters, 1863–5, mostly relating to the Southern Independence Association, of which Wharncliffe was president. The printed material consists of leaflets issued by various organizations urging the necessity of peace, giving details of fund-raising for relief of Southern prisoners, &c. The letters include two from Charles Francis Adams, a number from James Spence in Liverpool, and Alexander Collie in London, and a large group so faded as to be illegible. (Wh. M. 460)

(iii) Over 100 letters, 1864–72, dealing with various aspects of the Civil War; many are very faded. There are a large number of letters from Spence and Collie relating to cotton shipments and other business affairs; letters from Americans now living in Europe, asking for aid, giving first-hand accounts of treatment of prisoners, &c.; letters from correspondents in England concerning disposal of the funds collected for relief, and attitudes towards the war. (Wh. M. 461)

---

[1] Edited by W. H. G. Armytage, 'Thomas Talbot and Lord Wharncliffe: some new letters hitherto unpublished', *Ontario History*, vol. xlv, pp. 177–97, 1953.

(iv) Powder River Cattle Company. Two bundles contain letters, letter copies, printed reports, and other papers of this British-financed Wyoming cattle ranch. Many of the letters are from or about Moreton Frewen, who was the owner of the land and became manager for the company on its formation in 1882. Most of the material relates to the management and mismanagement of the ranch until the winding-up of the company in the 1890's. (Wh. M. 477)

There may also be American letters in the bundle of general correspondence (as yet unindexed) of the 1st Earl. (Wh. M. 418)

BAGSHAWE COLLECTION.

(a) Barker, John. Letter-book. 1753–60. (493)
Consists of copies of letters from him, John Gardom, and James Crosbie, from Liverpool, Manchester, and various places in Derbyshire, to correspondents in America. Most of the letters deal with the partners' potash business in Philadelphia and elsewhere ('. . . we have a patent for the sole making of pott:ash or pearl:ashes in all America for fourteen years, which is dated in 1751'). The letters are addressed mainly to the managers in Philadelphia—William Ashe, James Palmer, and Humphrey Robinson—and to the agent in Fredericksburg, Va., Charles Dick; they contain instructions about methods of manufacture and accounting, and about the winding up of the venture after the death of Crosbie. There are also a few letters to Edward Salter, merchant 'near Bath Town', N.C., concerning the export of deer skins and indigo.

(b) B. & W. Wyatt, lead-mine owners, Derbyshire. One folder of their business papers contains documents, 1773 and 1785, relating to the duty on exported lead, including several manuscript copies of an undated three-page article entitled 'Observations on the tax or duty laid upon lead exported by an Act passed the last session of Parliament'; one paragraph of this deals with the possibility of competition from England. (587/66)

(c) Frost, John, and Benjamin Bagshawe, Jr. 2 letters. 1871. (776)
Frost's letter, from Tideswell, Derbyshire, 2 Mar. 1871, asks for advice concerning the legality of disposing of his father's estate in order to invest the money in the United States, where he and several members of his family plan to emigrate; his cousin's reply is dated the following day.

FITZWILLIAM (WENTWORTH WOODHOUSE) MUNIMENTS.

(a) Rockingham (2nd Marquis) Letters and Papers.[1]
Charles Watson-Wentworth, 2nd Marquis of Rockingham (1730–82), was Prime Minister 1765–6 and 1782, and led the opposition from the House of Lords 1768–81. The collection of his papers is of prime importance for the English side of the War of Independence. There is a mimeographed list in the Library, 'Letters and papers of the 2nd Marquis of Rockingham', to

---

[1] See *Guide to the Manuscript Collections in the Sheffield City Libraries* (Sheffield, 1956), Appendix II, pp. 87–96, for an index of correspondents. This is now being revised and corrected.

which the reference numbers below refer. Among the more important items are:

R 1: Over 2,000 letters,[1] including letters from America from Thomas Combe, Philadelphia, 14 May and 5 Nov. 1774; James De Lancey, 4 Feb. and 22 Apr. 1769, 26 Oct. 1773, another letter of 1773, and one 22 Oct., no year; Thomas Dowdeswell, Raritan Landing, N.J., 16 Jan 1777; Benjamin Franklin, 3 Oct. 1776 and 13 Apr. 1782 (both copies); Joseph Harrison, 3 Nov. 1768; James Rivington, New York, 9 May 1782; James Thompson, New York, 12 May 1782; Samuel Wentworth, Boston, 29 July 1759; and anonymous letters. 'A list of persons gone into North America within the last eighteen months or thereabouts [from the Sheffield area]', enclosed in a letter of 16 Jan. 1769. (R 1/1149)

R 19–32: Matters connected with Stamp duties in America, 1763–6. Included in R 24 are letters, 1764–6, of Thomas Hutchinson to W. Bollan, and of Andrew Oliver, John Hughes, and Barlow Trecothick (from New York).

R 33–50: Various matters concerning colonial trade, 1761–6. R 44 contains Major Robert Rogers's proposals, 1765, for finding the Northwest Passage, with a letter, New York, 15 Jan. 1766, to Rockingham. (Another letter from Rogers is in R 75/67.) R 48 contains the papers[2] of Col. George Mercer of the Virginia Regiment, 1763–6, including Virginia committee of correspondence to Edward Montagu, 17 June 1763, and George Mercer to Rockingham, 11 Apr. 1766.

R 51–55: Papers concerning the repeal of the Stamp Act. R 55 contains letters from America about the reception of the news of repeal, including a letter, New York, 6 May 1766, to Barlow Trecothick and the merchants trading to North America; Samuel Carey, Boston, 21 May 1766, to Rockingham; House of Representatives of Massachusetts to Rockingham, 21 June 1766, with a vote of thanks.

R 61: Statistical tables of various aspects of American and British trade, including N. Tucker to Rockingham, 25 Apr. 1779, 'Hints relative to the cultivation of tobacco in Virginia'. (R 61/11/7)

R 62: Quebec papers, 1766–7, including letters from Francis Maseres, 20 Nov. 1766, and William Hey, 31 Jan. 1767.

R 63: Miscellaneous letters from America, 1767–75. Included are letters, 1767–9, from Joseph Harrison, collector of customs at Boston; this is perhaps the most important American correspondence in the whole collection. Also included are letters to Rockingham, 22 Jan. 1768 from Thomas Cushing and 23 Mar. 1770 from James Bowdoin, Samuel Pemberton, and Joseph Warren. (Other Cushing letters are in R 55 and R 152.)

R 64: Case of Governor John Wentworth of New Hampshire, 1772–3: charges brought by Peter Livius about land declared forfeit, with correspondence, briefs, &c.; and R 65. Miscellaneous writings on American problems, including Governor Wentworth's long considerations on American affairs, 1 Sept. 1765. (There is also a separate collection of Wentworth family records within the Fitzwilliam Muniments in the Library.)

---

[1] There is now a full list of these letters in N.R.A. 1083.

[2] Printed in J. E. Tyler, 'Colonel George Mercer's Papers', *Virginia Magazine of History and Biography*, vol. lx, pp. 405–20, 1952.

R 111: Petitions from American refugees and others, and Sir George Collier's claims for expenses for helping American refugees. *c.* 1782–3.

R 127: A small packet of letters from North America addressed to the Marquis or to Hugh Wentworth, 1767–9, including three letters, 1767–8, from John Clapham from Maryland, and one letter, 1769, from Governor John Wentworth.

R 129: Copies of Captain Keppel's American papers, captured with Henry Laurens in 1780.

R 150: Letters, extracts, copies from America, 1775. Included are letters to Rockingham from Arthur Lee, 2 Sept. 1775, and from James Murray, [1775] and 18 July 1775. There are also copies of two letters of 23 Apr. 1775 from Boston to Dr. Rogers, giving 'truths that the Admiral may rely on' of the expedition to Concord on 18 Apr.

There are also letters from various American governors, including Sir Francis Bernard, Thomas Boone, Thomas Fitch, Stephen Hopkins, Sir Henry Moore, and Samuel Ward; and many copies of official papers.

(*b*) Letters and papers of the 2nd (4th) Earl Fitzwilliam.

William Wentworth Fitzwilliam (1748–1833), statesman. No complete examination of these papers was made. They include, however, some correspondence with Governor John Wentworth, and 'Copy of Mr. Champion's account of the state of America', 1785. (F 125)

(*c*) Edmund Burke (1729–97). Letters and papers.[1]

There is a complete list of Burke's correspondence in print,[2] and this includes the letters in the Fitzwilliam Muniments so an extended report on these well-known papers has not been thought necessary. In addition, the collection includes many drafts of Burke's speeches on American affairs. And in Bk. 4 may be found several American letters: 4 Jan. 1775, Oliver De Lancey to Moses Franks; 13 Dec. 1774, John Harris Cruger to Moses Franks; 16 Jan. 1775, Samuel Tufts to Joseph Walds; 19 July 1791, George Washington to Richard Champion.[3]

VASSALL, WILLIAM. 2 letter-books. 1769–99. (MD 2047)

Owner of Jamaican sugar plantations, resident of Boston and London. Vassall, born in Jamaica, lived in Boston from childhood until 1775. His business was the export to England of sugar and rum from his Jamaican estates. The letter-books consist of copies of letters from Boston, 1769–75; from Nantucket, Mass., in 1775; and from London, 1775–99, except for a

---

[1] A complete microfilm is held by the University of Kentucky.

[2] T. W. Copeland and M. S. Smith, *A Check list of the Correspondence of Edmund Burke, Arranged in Chronological Order and Indexed under the Names of 1,200 Correspondents* (Cambridge, printed at the University Press for the Index Society, New York, 1955). All the letters from Burke and some to him are being edited and will be published in 10 vols. as *Correspondence of Edmund Burke*, general editor, T. W. Copeland (Cambridge and Chicago); vol. 1, Apr. 1744–June 1768, ed. by T. W. Copeland (1958); vol. 2, July 1768–June 1774, ed. by Lucy S. Sutherland (1960); vol. 3, July 1774–June 1778, ed. by George H. Guttridge (1961)

[3] See *Writings of George Washington*, ed. by John C. Fitzpatrick, vol. xxxi, pp. 314–15 (Washington, D.C., 1939).

H h

brief period in 1786 when Vassall was in Bristol, R.I. Most of the pre-war letters concern his business, and are addressed to merchants in England and to his agent and others in Jamaica; the letters to England frequently include requests for goods to be sent to Boston for his personal use—shoes, the works of Cicero, &c. After the war there are many letters to Boston and to Bristol, R.I., to a large number of correspondents, concerning the confiscation and sale of Vassall's farm in Bristol, R.I.; he felt this to be a great injustice, since his sympathies had been, if anything, with the Americans, and his removal to Britain had occurred solely because his livelihood depended on the trade between his Jamaican estates and that country.

SPENCER STANHOPE OF CANNON HALL (CANNON HALL MUNIMENTS).

Include:

(a) Papers of Benjamin Spencer, a London merchant in a rather small way, consisting of correspondence, bills of lading, seamen's wages, &c., in connexion with his shipping business. A small number relate to the American trade, especially to the port of Charleston, S.C., 1750–9. (60549–52)

(b) Fourteen letters, 1774–6, from John and Ashton Shuttleworth, from America, giving accounts of the War of Independence (60542), and five further letters, 1777–81. (60578)[1]

(c) Correspondence, accounts, and receipt books of Captain John Shuttleworth, British army officer and apparently paymaster of the 7th Regiment, the Royal Fusileers. Most of the papers concern regimental pay and accounts, the period 1791–4 being at Quebec; three letter-books include copies of a few letters, 1793, dealing with the claim of Isaac Ogden of Quebec for payment for services as counsel for Shuttleworth's late brother in the latter's New York court martial. (60595–8)

(d) Prospectus, letters, accounts, &c., concerning the Big Horn Cattle Company, Powder River, Mont. 1883. (60721)

BRADBURY, THOMAS, & SONS. Business records.[2] 1805–46.

Silver platers, Sheffield. The earliest references to trade with the United States in the large collection of this firm's records held by the Library appears to be an undated—apparently pre-1806—order for candlesticks and other goods for John & Lawrence Brickwood of Baltimore, but it was after 1816 that extensive relations developed. From 1817 onwards there are many letters from George H. Newbould, the firm's New York agent; these contain discussion of demand, &c., and give details of orders for particular firms. The correspondence folders also include letters from G. & W. Simmons of Liverpool, who shipped the goods to America, and insurance forms for

[1] Part published in A. M. W. Stirling, *Annals of a Yorkshire House from the Papers of a Macaroni (Walter Spencer-Stanhope) and his Kindred*, vol. i (London, 1911).

[2] See P. C. Garlick, 'The Sheffield Cutlery and Allied Trades', M.A. thesis, University of Sheffield, 1951.

such goods. Other relevant material includes, e.g., a notebook containing details of shipments in 1844 to particular American firms (Br. Coll. 202), and a 'stock and order book' for 1825-7 showing details of orders (in Apr. 1825, six New York firms are represented). (Br. Coll. 3)

NOWILL, THOMAS, & CO. Ledger,[1] 1812-25. (LD 196)

Spring-knife cutlers, Sheffield. The ledger for 1812-25 contains entries of transactions with Davis, Brown & Co. of Boston between 1817 and 1821.

LEADER COLLECTION. Letter.[2] 1844. (196)

In this large antiquarian collection there is a single emigrant letter, 9 Mar. 1844, from W. C. Beardsall, near Niagara in Upper Canada, to a Mrs. Foster of Sheffield. A lively, very detailed and sensible description of Canadian life; includes a sketch of the farm; some of the letter is written in doggerel verse.

TIBBITTS COLLECTION. Shaw & Fisher: Business records. 1849-54.

Britannia metal and plated wares manufacturers, Sheffield. The business papers of this firm show extensive dealings with the United States, 1850-4, during which period the firm maintained an agent in New York who covered the Eastern seaboard. A bundle of correspondence contains a large number of letters from this agent, Charles Congreve, with discussion of financial arrangements, comment on demand, copies of orders from various American firms, &c.; there are also a few letters in 1849 from Sansom Cariss of Baltimore and Andrew Love of the New Orleans firm of Love, Hogg & Co. Both in this bundle and in another marked 'vouchers' there are records of shipment of goods to particular American firms through the Liverpool house of Cowie, Roxburgh & Co., with financial arrangements being made by Brown, Shipley & Co. of Liverpool. A folder containing bills of exchange includes a few from Charleston, S.C., and from New York. (1056-8)

ROBERTS, JAMES, and THOMAS J. BRADLEY. 11 letters (photostats).[3] 1849-70. (MD 2027)

James Roberts was a Sheffield cutlery worker who emigrated to the United States in 1849. Five letters from Waterville, Conn., 1849-50, to his relatives in Sheffield deal with family news, local customs, and working conditions

[1] See P. C. Garlick, 'The Sheffield Cutlery and Allied Trades', M.A. thesis, University of Sheffield, 1951.
[2] Photostat in the Collection of Letters of Emigrants to America in the British Library of Political and Economic Science, London School of Economics.
[3] Used by J. B. Himsworth, *The Story of Cutlery, from Flint to Stainless Steel* (London, 1953), and C. Erickson, *American Industry and the European Immigrant* (London and Cambridge, Mass., 1957). Photostats also in the Collection of Letters of Emigrants to America in the British Library of Political and Economic Science, London School of Economics.

at the Waterville Company. His last letter tells of the company informing its employees that they must start providing their own tools, and the resulting decision of Roberts and fifteen others to set up their own factory—'we are dermind [*sic*] to have nobody but working men so you can see we are determined to have no capitulists'.

Thomas J. Bradley was the president of this venture (the 'New York Knife Company, of Walden, Orange county, New York and of Wallkill River Works', according to its letter-head) at the time he wrote the letters to Sheffield included in the collection. One of these, 1867, is to his brother and sister; and five, 1869–70, are to James Roberts, who was on a visit to England. The letters mainly concern the obtaining of Sheffield craftsmen for employment by the firm.

MARSH BROS. & CO. Two folders containing 212 letters, &c.[1] 1863–7. (MD 1485)

Steel, tool, and cutlery manufacturers, Sheffield. Most of the letters, which deal with details of orders, are from the Sheffield firm to their New York office, addressed to W. N. Woodcock and Theophilus Marsh in 1863–5, and to J. W. Cockayne in 1866–7. There are also a few letters to New York from B. & S. H. Thompson, Birmingham, concerning the sale of their guns and chains.

See also entry for the Business Records still held by the firm (p. 461).

WILSON, HENRY JOSEPH (1833–1914). Correspondence, notebook. 1876–7.

Social reformer, M.P. In 1876 Wilson and Rev. J. P. Gledstone went to the United States on behalf of the British, Continental, and General Federation for the Abolition of Government Regulation of Prostitution. The collection of Wilson's papers held by the Library includes the following material relating to this journey:

(*a*) Fourteen letters to his family, written from New York, Washington, D.C., &c. Most of these are to his children and contain comment on American customs and attitudes; in a letter to his wife he notes that 'there is no *demand* for us anywhere—people make the best of us when they can't help it'. (MD 2478)

(*b*) Letters to Wilson about his mission—arrangements for meetings, attitudes towards government regulation of prostitution, reasons for American apathy, &c.—from F. A. P. Barnard, James Freeman Clarke, Neal Dow, William Lloyd Garrison, Elizabeth Gay, C. G. Hussey, Enoch Lewis, A. M. Powell, and I. L. Townsend. (MD 2542)

(*c*) A notebook containing names and addresses of possible American contacts, with comment on their positions, outlooks, and probable influence; notes added during the American trip concern help given by some of them. (MD 2543)

[1] See the history of the firm, S. Pollard, *Three Centuries of Sheffield Steel, the Story of a Family Business* (Sheffield, priv. print., 1954).

JOHNSON, CHRISTOPHER, & CO. Business records. 1882-90.

Cutlers, Sheffield. The earliest item relating to the United States appears to be a copy of a letter to Jackson & Co., Brooklyn, N.Y., on 14 Mar. 1882, noting that they have no agent in New York but are interested in marketing prospects there (MD 2368). A letter-book for 1888-90 (MD 2369) includes copies of more than twenty letters to Lewis G. Weatherley and to the San Francisco firms with which he was associated, Huntingdon, Hopkins & Co. and Weatherley, Jardine & Co.; these letters deal with orders for razors, knives, scissors, &c. The volume also includes copies of letters written in 1890 to L. A. Jones of Springfield, Mass., and to C. A. Winan of New York.

CARPENTER COLLECTION.[1]

Edward Carpenter (1844-1929), social reformer. The collection of his papers includes:

(*a*) 'Across the Atlantic.' Manuscript notes for a lecture, 1884.

(*b*) A folder containing letters from Carpenter's friends. Included are five long letters, 1894-6, from Robert A. Nicol, Weimar, Calif., about his philosophy and way of life; three letters, 1907, from Edgar Ira Oford, Brooklyn, N.Y., on Carpenter's books and relations between the sexes; and one letter each from Daniel G. Mason, 1902, Anne F. Miller, 1906, and Mrs. L. S. K. Crouse, 1925.

(*c*) A bundle of 142 letters from eight American publishers. These deal mainly with the publication of Carpenter's books in the United States; the letters from A. B. Stockham, Chicago—100 items, 1900-11—and John Huschler, San Francisco—nineteen items, 1909-12—also contain information concerning attitudes towards Carpenter's books, and discussion of some of the subjects raised in these.

(*d*) 'Primitive life in the Maine woods: a modern experiment', [1924]. Manuscript and three typescript copies; also a letter to Curtis Brown, London, asking to arrange for publication.

The collection also includes the original manuscripts, various dates, of Carpenter's articles and books on Walt Whitman.

ALLEN, EDGAR, & CO. LTD. Business records. 1924-34.

Steel manufacturers, Sheffield. One of the thirty-eight order-books held by the Library is for the firm's Chicago and New York agencies; as well as brief notes of orders, it includes occasional extracts from letters referring to orders. A volume marked 'Journal of Accounts' (MD 2336) includes some figures of dealings—steel purchases, freight charges, &c.—with the Chicago agency and American firms.

See also the Letter-books held by the firm (p. 460).

[1] See *A Bibliography of Edward Carpenter* (Sheffield City Libraries, 1949).

W. & G. Sissons Ltd., 75–77 St. Mary's Road,
SHEFFIELD 2

BUSINESS RECORDS. 1859–61.

Metal-working firm. During 1859–61 the firm attempted to enter the American market, engaging Henry B. Jackson as agent in New York for the sale of candlesticks and other plated ware. The letters in which he reported in great detail the progress of his efforts are pasted in an old account book. They concern demand, selling methods, financial arrangements, the effect of the Civil War on business, &c.; the customer most frequently mentioned is Tiffany & Co. of New York. There are also two letters from the United States now kept separate from the others; one of these consists of the accounts with Sissons of New York and Philadelphia firms. A letter containing comment on the Civil War has been lost but a typescript copy of part of this is available.

Spear & Jackson Ltd., Aetna Works,
Savile Street, SHEFFIELD 4

BUSINESS RECORDS. 1825–1903.

Founded in 1760. Makers of special steels and edge tools, particularly saws. A black trunk contains letter-books and bundles of correspondence and accounts, both of the firm and the family, mostly for 1865–1903, but some invoices and bills of lading of 1825 show exports of files and saws to New York, as well as to many European countries. A brief examination showed the following items:

(*a*) Diaries of J. B. Jackson for 1865, 1869–72, 1874, 1877, 1880, 1889, and 1893. While these diaries are mainly a list of appointments, though some detailed comments on incidents at the Works, the entries examined for 1872 show monthly notations of earnings from 'New York store', and general bank balance, e.g. '30 March. Sales N.Y. Store $1,250.60 gold. Bank bal £9,723. 3. 4. . . . 20 July. Sales N.Y. Store for June $889.68 gold.'

(*b*) Letter-books of J. F. Jackson include one covering June 1887–July 1889 when he was in New York, which has correspondence with American, Canadian, French, and Australian firms, and notations of tool handles ordered from American firms.

(*c*) Among the firm's letter-books there is a copy of a letter, 26 Apr. 1892, inquiring from an Irish firm about the reliability of American saw-sharpening machines.

The firm thus appears to have had sizeable American interests, and materials clearly exist for a fairly precise study of its exports from about 1865 to 1903. In the 1920's a factory was built in Oregon and recently one in Vancouver.

The Library, University of Sheffield, Western Bank, SHEFFIELD 10

MUNDELLA, ANTHONY JOHN (1825–97). Correspondence.[1] 1870–1904.

Statesman. The collection of Mundella's letters to Robert Leader, editor of the *Sheffield Independent*, includes one written from New York during Mundella's visit to the United States in 1870; there are also occasional references to American affairs in other of the letters. In the letters written to Mundella there are thirteen from American correspondents, as follows:

Dana, Richard Henry. Rome, 20 Mar. 1881, concerning Mundella's 1870 New York speech.

Eaton, John. Washington, D.C., 30 Jan. 1871.

Holmes, Oliver Wendell. London, 18 May, no year.

Lowell, James Russell. London, 1880–4, eight letters, including a few concerning Texas fever and trichinosis.

Phelps, T. London, 15 Dec. 1890.

Wells, David A. Norwich, Conn., 13 Jan. [1871].

Also in the Library are three boxes of Miss Mundella's correspondence. Included in one of these are seventeen letters from Henry James, mainly written in London, addressed to Miss Mundella, Mrs. Mundella, or Miss Noble; these concern social engagements. The dated letters are 1882–1904.

George Wostenholm & Son Ltd., Washington Works, Wellington Street, SHEFFIELD 1

BUSINESS RECORDS.[2] 1833–1957.

Cutlery manufacturers. The following records relating to the firm's very extensive American trade are still in existence:

(a) A scrap-book which includes the following: an invoice dated 17 Aug. 1833 for goods sent to Charles Dilworth, the firm's New York agent; a printed letter, 22 Feb. 1848, announcing the taking over of the New York agency by Charles Congreve; an invoice for goods bought by W. P. Walker, Philadelphia, 3 Oct. 1849; an undated leaflet addressed to American customers containing a caution about methods of whetting cutlery; two letters from Joseph S. Fisher, the Philadelphia agent, both dated 14 Aug. 1885 and addressed to the chairman of the board of Wostenholm's, one concerning Fisher's financial difficulties and the other giving a detailed history of his business career in the United States; some correspondence, 1939–57, on whether the firm supplied knives to James Bowie (1799–1836).

---

[1] See W. H. G. Armytage, *A. J. Mundella, 1825–97: the Liberal Background to the Labour Movement* (London, 1951).

[2] Some of this material has been used by H. Bexfield, *A Short History of Sheffield Cutlery and the House of Wostenholm* (Sheffield, priv. print., 1945).

(*b*) A packet labelled 'Asline Ward's agreement with George Wostenholm' contains the memorandum of agreement, 22 Feb. 1850, confirming Ward's appointment as New York agent, and fifteen letters written by Ward from New York, 1858–63, containing comment on competition, demand, &c., as well as on personal matters and, in a few cases, the Civil War.

(*c*) Letter-books for 1875–1917 contain copies of a few letters to the United States or about American trade.

(*d*) A large group of ledgers contains at least eight with accounts of trade with American firms; these cover the period 1889–1932. The fullest details of transactions are given in the 'New York Agency Ledger' for 1907–16; firms all over the country are included.

(*e*) Three folders contain material relating to the firm's trade mark registration and protection in the United States, 1905–7.

H.M. Customs and Excise, Whitby

See H.M. Customs and Excise, London (p. 205).

Borthwick Institute of Historical Research, St. Anthony's Hall, Peasholme Garden, York

The Institute houses the archives of the Province and Archdiocese of York.

VIRGINIA TOBACCO TRADE PAPERS.[1] 1675–7.

A number of documents relate to the Virginia tobacco trade in 1675–7, these apparently coming from cases before the Archbishops' Court of Admiralty. The papers consist of evidence, accusations, &c., in the damaged cargo case of Abel Grant *v.* John Bothomley and Andrew Perrott (R. As. 17B/12, 23B/23, and 25B/15; R. VII. H. 4850 and 4852), and in the breach of charter case of Thomas Cox *v.* George Pattison (R. As. 17B/17, 19/10, 21B/52, and 23A/118; R. VII. P.D. 12, 52, 276–8). Some are written in Latin and French.

WRIGHT, JOHN. Letter.[2] 1774. (Included in papers R. VII. I. 1987.)

The letter, which is much damaged, was written, 12 May 1774, from New York to Wright's wife Jane at Paper-mill-beck, near Tadcaster, Yorks. It concerns his plans for buying a well-wooded farm 260 miles from New York and for shipping the wood to Hull.

---

[1] The Library of the University of Virginia holds typescripts of much of this material. Also microfilms made by the Virginia Colonial Records Project.

[2] A photograph of the letter is held by the Long Island Historical Society, N.Y.

WALES
AND
MONMOUTHSHIRE

ANGLESEY

Marquess of Anglesey, PLÂS NEWYDD, Llanfairpwll

SHIRLEY, GENERAL WILLIAM (1694–1771). 2 dispatches (copies). 1756.
On the arrival of British troops in America, 1756.
N.R.A. 0010.

CAERNARVONSHIRE

The Library, University College of North Wales, BANGOR

EMIGRANT LETTERS. 1795–1878.
Letters from Welsh emigrants to America, mostly in Ohio—members of Bebb and Howell families, Llanbrynmair, Montgomeryshire, mostly in Welsh.

H.M. Customs and Excise, CAERNARVON

See H.M. Customs and Excise, London (p. 201).

CARDIGANSHIRE

National Library of Wales, ABERYSTWYTH

The National Library of Wales is rich in Americana, particularly records relating to Welsh emigration to America in the nineteenth century: both emigrant letters and extensive correspondence between Baptist, Congregational, and Methodist ministers in the United States and Wales. There are also voluminous papers relating to the legend of Prince Madoc's discovery of America and the subsequent debate about, and search for, the Padoucas or Welsh Indians. These three types of papers are well listed in the special number of the *National Library of Wales Journal*, vol. ii, nos. 3 and 4, 1942, which was wholly devoted to *Wales and the United States of America*.[1] It has therefore seemed unnecessary to reproduce fully the manuscript list contained therein. The following list does not purport to be a full list: it omits these papers, covered by the *National Library of Wales Journal*, which chiefly relate to Prince Madoc and the Welsh Indians, and gives details of only a few representative or especially important collections of emigrant letters or ministers' letters. But it includes subsequent accessions under all three heads.

ACCESSIONS TO 1942.

The following report is in archival order, except that the papers relating to Samuel Roberts have been drawn together as one note here at the head.

Papers of and relating to Samuel Roberts. 1834–85. Manuscripts 590C, 3265D, 9522B, 9523A, 9529B, 13195D, 13196D, 13197C, 13199D, 14046–50A, 14091D, 14092C, 14093C.

Samuel Roberts (1800–85), known as 'S.R.', prominent social and political reformer, Welsh poet and journalist. In 1857 he tried to establish a large Welsh settlement called Brynffynon in Scott county, Tenn., together with William Bebb (of Welsh descent), former Governor of Ohio, and others. It failed, largely due to the Civil War and to the vendor having had no clear title. The situation was complicated by Roberts's denunciation of the North for using force to restore the Union. He returned to Wales in 1867, revisiting America in 1870 to dispose of his property.

All his life he kept closely in touch with Welshmen in America, so there is much correspondence describing American life and institutions generally (of which he held exaggerated hopes), Welsh culture and religion in America, as well as letters relating specifically to the conception of the Tennessee venture and its winding up. Among the very many correspondents, there are some letters from William Henry Channing and more from William Bebb. Roberts's letter-books and diaries survive for most of his American sojourn. And, *inter alia*, there is correspondence relating to his claims against the United States government for his losses in Tennessee.

See also Tennessee Papers in Deposited Collections (p. 482).

474E. Letters of Goronwy Owen (1723–69?), the Welsh poet who emigrated to Virginia in Dec. 1757. Of the last three letters, one, 1757, is addressed to the Cymmrodorion Society in London, soliciting aid to emigrate; and two are to Richard Morris—the first, on board ship, 1757, and the second, Brunswick, Va., 1767, giving his opinion of his neighbours. (*In Welsh*.)

986C. Letters to Jonathan Reynolds ('Nathan Dyfed'). The correspondents include (*in Welsh and English*):

Aneurin Jones, New York, 1884–8, on family news, his life in America, eisteddfodic interests, American politics, his dismissal in 1885 from the post

---

[1] See also Alan Conway, 'Welsh Emigration to the United States', *Bulletin of the British Association for American Studies*, no. 8, pp. 11–18, 1959, and the bibliography therein.

of superintendent of public parks on the defeat of the Democrats, his appointment in 1889 as chief inspector of Brooklyn parks.
J. T. Lewis, New York, 1888, on Stradling inheritance.

987c. Letters of David Howell ('Llawdden'), including a letter addressed to him by Thomas W. Price ('Cuhelyn'), Sacramento, Calif., 1866, on his employment as enrolling clerk to the Senate, the state library, American Grand National Eisteddfod, his proposed biographical dictionary of distinguished Welshmen. (*In English.*)

2163E. Miscellanea relating to Robert Owen, the social reformer, including a typewritten letter, Washington, D.C., 1893, from Henry Hunter to William Beck, Saxondale, on the disappearance of the model of the 'ideal community' and on changes in the furnishings of the Executive Mansion. (*In English.*)

2381B. A 'book of anecdotes or of records' begun by David Stephen Davies when he was a student at the Theological Seminary, Alleghany City, Pa., 1861. (*In English.*)

2600E. Letters sent home by Humphrey and Sarah Roberts, emigrants from the Brymbo district, North Wales. The letters, Madison, Ohio, 1856–64, concern family news, Calvinist emigrants from Llangeitho and Trefecca and their character, Mormons, Catholics, climate and crops, economic depression, American politics, the Kansas question, Civil War news, their three sons in the Northern Army, General Morgan's visit to their settlement, the 'treachery' of Samuel Roberts and his defence of the South. (*In Welsh.*)

2704F. Letter, Marcy, Utica, N.Y., 1848, from Rowland Owen to Morgan Davis ('Clochydd Llanelltud'), giving an account of his own family and of other Merioneth settlers in the United States, and discussing the proposal to start a Welsh church for the benefit of Welsh members of the Established Church in the district. (*In Welsh.*)

2719B. Miscellanea from the collection of Edward Griffith, Dolgelley, including a letter, n.d., from an assembly of Congregational ministers in Monmouthshire to ministers of Welsh denominations in the United States on the Oregon dispute. (*In Welsh.*)

2722D. Transcripts of letters addressed to relatives in Merioneth by the following emigrants (*in Welsh and English*):
Hugh and Catherine Thomas, Trenton, Oneida, N.Y., 1816: description of their holding and neighbourhood near Steuben; religion, wages and prices, success of Welsh settlers, livestock, children.
John Richards, Johnsburgh, N.Y., 1817, encouraging his friends to emigrate; climate, soil, and produce; prices, work on canals, &c.; advice to emigrants; all royalists should go to Upper Canada; Welsh preaching at Steuben.
William Thomas, Utica, N.Y., 1818: his work in a canal cut; his disappointment (John Richards's account was misleading) and intention of returning—the district a wilderness, with no market or fair and no dealers buying around Utica; craftsmen no better off than labourers.
David Richard, Utica, N.Y., 1818: his family; his work constructing

arches under the canal; prices, rent, taxes, and wages; lack of demand for sawyers in Utica; low state of religion.

David Jones, Albany, N.Y., 1817: his voyage; good prospects for all craftsmen except weavers; great demand for joiners; Welsh settlers in Steuben; regrets at not having settled in Canada; relatives in America and Wales; the Indians; arranging to have his two older sons over; the superiority of American ships for emigrants; cautions against slate ships from Caernarvon; labour conditions, &c.; scarcity of homes.

4616B. Letters to David Stephen Davies. The correspondents include (*in Welsh and English*):

G. James Jones, Findlay, Ohio, 1888-9, on American degrees and giving autobiographical details.

R. Gwesyn Jones, Utica, N.Y., 1894, on theology, baptism, American politics, the decline of Welsh churches in America.

William S. Jones, Scranton, Pa., 1872, on *Baner America* and *Y Drych* and the Welsh colony in Patagonia, and England's fears lest American Welshmen should emigrate to Patagonia.

R. Roberts, Pittsburgh, Pa., 1875, on D. S. Davies's departure from New York.

David Lodwick, Mystic, Iowa, 1911, on the death of J. J. Davies.

A few papers relate to the Welsh Colonizing and General Trading Co. Ltd., including a list of American subscribers.

4620E. Register of shareholders of the American branch of the Welsh Colonizing and General Trading Company Ltd., 1871. The aim of the American branch was the same as that of the Welsh parent company founded in 1866 to purchase land and buildings and to buy or charter ships to carry on a regular trade with South America, and, more particularly, with the Welsh colony in the Chubut valley, Patagonia. (*In English.*)

5503C. Letters to Henry Richard, M.P., including three from Elihu Burritt, the American internationalist, New Britain, Conn., 1856, 1874, 1876, on the Peace Movement, the Paris conference, the proposed abolition of war on commerce, ill health, Miles and Beckwith, the Geneva Congress, his semi-theological work in an assumed style and name, his simplified grammars of Oriental languages, James Long and the Russian question, his Hebrew handbook, severe haemorrhage, and the secret of his theological work.

6174E. Letters to Griffith Owen, Vaner, Dolgelley, and others, from the following (*in Welsh and English*):

John and Margred Owen, Baraboo, Wis., 1857: regret that they did not emigrate earlier; were the first Welsh family to cross the Wisconsin river; had only a pound left to start life; good land; prices and prospects; no religious meetings; need for missionaries; agriculture and implements.

William and Margaret and William G. Bebb, Van Wert, Ohio, 1850: agriculture; few Welsh settlers (only twelve families); religion.

Edward —, Miliken's Bend, La., 1863: campaign around Vicksburg.

J. F. Williams, St. Paul, Minn., 1877: seeking information about the family of Howell Roberts.

T. Ll. Williams, Racine, Wis., 1907: a family reunion at Caledonia, Wis.
John Gwylym Owen, Portage, Wis., 1907: the Owen family.

Also two incomplete letters, and photographs of Caledonia Welsh church and Caledonia home-coming, 1907.

7163–6, 7176–7, and 7779E. Correspondence addressed to William Roberts ('Nefydd'), including the following (*in Welsh and English*):

William David, New York, 1843: 'Yankee clocks' and customs duties.

John Gould, Minersville, Pa., 1846: voyage to America; Baptist church at Minersville.

J. Edred Jones, New York, 1871: Utica, N.Y., eisteddfod essay adjudication.

Theophilus Jones, New York, Pughtown, and Philadelphia, 1846–57: the fate of the ship *Virginia*; Welsh Baptist ministers in America; qualifications for successful ministerial careers in America; his church at Nantmeal; Welsh Baptist Assembly; economic depression; children's education; family news.

William B. Jones ('ap P.A. Mon'), New York and Kansas, 1858–71: dreams; Wisconsin eisteddfod; Welsh Baptist ministers in America; 'Gohebydd's' impressions of North Missouri; Samuel Roberts's apology for the South; the need for a Welsh Baptist magazine in America; the Neosho and Emporia, Kan., land schemes; the failure of democracy in America; the degree of LL.D. conferred upon 'Nefydd' [William Roberts].

R. Littler, New York, 1848: American Home Mission.

Phillip D. Phillips, Utica, N.Y., 1871: eisteddfod adjudication.

Also an incomplete letter written on notepaper of the office of Aetna Iron and Nail Co., Cleveland, Ohio, containing an inquiry whether William Roberts would accept the pastorate of a church at Newburgh.

8827c. Correspondence relating to a tour of North America made in 1879 by W. J. Parry, mostly letters of introduction. (*In Welsh and English.*)

9108–9D. A photostat facsimile of the 'Ilston Book' made for the National Library of Wales by permission of the members of the First Baptist Church of Swansea, Mass., at the John Carter Brown Library. The 'Ilston Book', 1649–1855, is a register belonging to the Baptist Church founded in Gower, South Wales, by John Miles, which followed him to Massachusetts in 1662. It contains lists of members of the original church in South Wales and of the First Baptist Church of Swansea, Mass., church decrees and covenants, and transcripts of letters and of the general laws and liberties of New Plymouth. (*In English.*)

9521A. Miscellaneous notes on the United States and on Welsh settlements and settlers there, written by R. D. Thomas ('Iorthryn Gwynedd') during his tours in New York, Ohio, and Pennsylvania, 1851–2. (*In Welsh and English.*)

10297A. An essay by John Robert Pryse ('Golyddan') on the Civil War and its causes. (*In Welsh.*)

10982F. Papers, 1868–9, relating to Harry H. Davis, United States Consul at Cardiff. (*In English.*)

13191D. Letters to Evan Roberts, Dolgadfan Mills, Llanbrynmair, from his children: George Roberts, [Ebensburg, Pa.], 1804–11—a religious revival originating in Kentucky, news of emigrants from Llanbrynmair, the Louisiana purchase, 1803; and Grace Morgan, 1811—her family, livestock, and crops. (*In Welsh.*)

13202D. Letters to David Howell, Machynlleth. The correspondents include William Bebb, Hamilton, Ohio, 1848: thanks for gifts of plate by his cousins, Lewis and John Howell in America, the 'unjust war' in Mexico, his 'great faith in the permanency of the American Union'. (*In English.*)

13203D. Letters, mainly to William Bebb, from politicians, lawyers, and members of Congress. The letters relate to public appointments, politics, and public functions during Bebb's governorship of Ohio 1847–9; the correspondents include John W. Allen, ex-Governor M. Bartley, James A. Briggs, Joseph H. Crane, D. T. Disney, N. Evans, T. Ewing, S. Ford, Horace Greeley, J. R. Grindings, J. Mason, John M. Millikin, O. M. Mitchell, J. W. Scott, C. B. Smith, Governor William Smith of Virginia, B. Storer, Charles L. Telford, Governor Philip F. Thomas of Maryland, S. F. Vinton, T. Walker, and John Woods. (*In English.*)

13204D. (*See also* 13189D, 13190D, and 14094E.) Miscellaneous correspondence including letters from (*in Welsh and English*):

George and Jane Roberts, Ebensburg, Pa., 1805–53—family news, details of husbandry and livestock, offices of constable and assessor, opinion on emigration from Wales, religious life of the community, temperance, transport facilities and their effects on the prosperity of Ebensburg, neighbours and emigrants from the Llanbrynmair district.

Evan R. Bebb, New York, 1835, introducing Dr. Gardiner Spring to Samuel Roberts.

D. Howell, Toledo, Ohio, 1890, on the death of his brother.

Evan R. Morgan, Ebensburg, 1857, giving family news.

13713D. Letters and miscellanea relating to Dr. George Lewis, of Llanuwchllyn, Merioneth, including a letter from the Rev. Jedidiah Morse, Charlestown, Mass., 1793, on a Boston society for the information and advice of foreign settlers, with a list of members, and on vacancies for ministers in the state of Vermont, a very thriving country of good land. (*In English.*)

14110B–14111D. Letters to their relatives in Llanbrynmair from Ann Peat, on board the *France*, 1868; Edward Peat, Liverpool, Ebensburg, Pa., and Gomer, Ohio, 1868–78; Edward Peate, Gomer, 1878–83; and Morris Peat, Ebensburg and Iowa City, Iowa, 1865–87. The letters of Edward Peat are particularly important on account of their detailed descriptions of American customs and the life of the Welsh communities in Ohio. (*In Welsh.*)

14348D. Correspondence and papers of Dr. John Ryland (1753–1825), including the diploma of the degree of Doctor in Theology conferred upon him by Rhode Island College, Providence, 1792, signed by David Howell, Jonathan Mazey, Peres Fobes, Benjamin West, and George Benson. (*In Latin.*)

14352C. Typescript copies of correspondence mainly addressed to Robert Owen, from the William Galpin collection. An imperfect letter to William Allen relates to the acquisition of New Harmony, Ind., 1825, and two letters, 1828, from Alexander Campbell and P. O. Skene refer to America, the latter to the Texas scheme. There is also one letter, 1846, by Robert Dale Owen, on Webster's manifesto on the Oregon question, and another fragment by him, 1844, on family accounts in connexion with New Harmony. (*In English.*)

CWRTMAWR MANUSCRIPTS.

818–819E. Letters addressed to Ellis Evans, Baptist Minister, Cefnmawr, Denbighshire. The correspondents include (*in Welsh and English*):

William Davies, Deerfield, Utica, N.Y., 1821–2: account of Owen Owens and his children, his emigration in 1794, the Welsh settlement at Steuben, N.Y.; religion, Baptists in Steuben and Utica, Welsh Baptist ministers, Utica a village of six hundred dwellings, the construction of a canal from Lake Erie to the Hudson river, economic depression, low prices, Welsh people doing very well, the best government in the world.

Jesse Jones, Steuben, N.Y., 1844, on religious disputes, the secession of the Welsh Baptist church at Steuben and its stand for the traditional articles of faith.

Owen Owens, Trenton, Oneida, N.Y., 1821, giving news of members of his family and of Welsh settlers, with a note by his niece Lily Maurice.

1044E. Miscellaneous correspondence including letters by the following (*in Welsh and English*):

Hugh Evans, Utica, N.Y., 1843—a proposal to revisit Wales, pressing his wife and children to join him on his farm near the Black river in New York state.

John H. Evans, Remsen, 1842, on differing opinions about America, the nature of lands in New York, Pennsylvania, and Ohio, on Wisconsin as the ideal state for Welsh settlers, excellent laws but execution falling short, with slight penalty for murdering a 'Gwyddel' (? Irishman or tramp), scarcity of currency, unsatisfactory state of the banking system, bad roads, good prospects for good craftsmen and for farmers with large families, religious sects (Mormonism a disgrace to humanity).

John Owen Jones, Green Hall, Jackson, Ill., 1848, on his family, his son in the Mexican campaign, his farm and timber, the reasons for his removal from Columbus, Ohio.

DEPOSITED COLLECTIONS.

(*a*) Llanfair and Brynodol Documents.

Among correspondence of the Griffith family in this collection is a letter to Hugh Griffith, Caernarvon, from Evan Thomas, Chester river, Md., 1708: his good and beneficial office with fees settled by Act of Assembly of the province amounting to 30,000 lb. of tobacco; great writing business; inquiring for a clerk assistant; Herbert Griffith's business and death near

Annapolis; his building of a house in expectation of his wife's emigration, and to comply with the law that all clerks should reside at the towns where the courts are kept. (*In English.*)

(*b*) Tennessee Papers (Luther Thomas Deposit).

Correspondence and memoranda, 1856–64, relating to the purchase of lands and the Welsh settlement in East Tennessee projected by William Bebb of Illinois, and G. Williams, William and John Roberts Jones, and Samuel and Richard Roberts, all of Llanbrynmair, Montgomeryshire. The correspondents include Edward Bebb, Fountaindale, &c.; James E. Goll, New York; L. D. Howell, Utica, N.Y.; E. B. Jones, Monticello; William Jones and Richard Roberts, of Brynffynon; E. D. Saxton and Benjamin J. Timms, of New York; John G. Vaughan, Salem, Ill.; and Mary Vaughan, Paddy's Run. William Bebb's letters relate also to American politics and the Civil War. There are, in addition, a large number of draft letters by Samuel Roberts and memoranda by him on the difficulties which the settlers experienced over the title to their purchases, and on the unsatisfactory arrangements made for them by Saxton, Jones, and Bebb. (*In Welsh and English.*)

(*c*) Dillwyn Diaries and Papers.

The collection includes minutes of William Dillwyn's voyage from Philadelphia to Bristol, 1774; diaries of his tour in Great Britain, his return to America, 1775, and his voyage to England, 1777; and genealogical memoranda of the Dillwyn family. (*In English.*)

(*d*) National Eisteddfod Manuscripts.

Subjects relating to the history and activities of Welshmen abroad have been set for competition from time to time at the National Eisteddfod of Wales. The original manuscripts deposited in the National Library include three entries in a competition for a handbook on emigration for Welsh farmers and workers at the London Eisteddfod, 1887, and the manuscript of 'An enquiry as to the extent to which Welshmen from home retain their peculiar characteristics in the lands of their adoption', submitted to the Mountain Ash Eisteddfod, 1905, by D. Jones, of Scranton, Pa.

ACCESSIONS SINCE 1942.

This list is drawn from the annual *Reports* of the National Library of Wales. Each item below is headed by the year and page number of the *Report* in which it is noted.

1941–2, p. 17. Dr. Erie Evans Deposit.

Manuscript and printed materials for a biography of Griffith Evans (1835–1935), a pioneer in research into parasitology. Included are a note concerning purchase of land, 3 Jan. 1777 (?), on Lady's Island, Carolina, given to Evans on the battlefield in Virginia in 1864; portions of his Canadian journal, 1864; correspondence, 1921, with John Drinkwater about the latter's play, *Abraham Lincoln*.

1942–3, pp. 25, 34. Luther Thomas Deposit.
Additional material relating to Samuel Roberts and the Roberts family of Llanbrynmair, including letters, 1825–82, from the United States from E. R. Bebb, William Bebb, B. Williams Chidlaw, Ezekiel Hughes, and George Roberts; correspondence, 1859–82, concerning the Welsh settlement in Tennessee founded by Samuel Roberts, and notebooks containing entries relating to the land purchased by Roberts; correspondence and circulars, 1871–83, concerning Roberts's claims against the United States government.

——, p. 34. Sir Charles L. Dillwyn Venables-Llewelyn Deposit.
Passports issued to William Dillwyn to pass through combat areas and to visit England during the War of Independence; and certificates of membership of American institutions, 1777–1802.

1944–5, p. 17. Mrs. John Davies Deposit.
Journal, 1887, kept by Mrs. John Evans during a tour of the United States with her husband.

——, p. 21. Sir Henry Haydn Jones Deposit.
Letters to Richard Jones, including one from James Owen, Remsen, 28 Oct. 1831, and one from Morris and Margred Roberts, Utica, N.Y., 30 Aug. 1832. (*In Welsh.*)

1945–6, p. 20. Mr. H. M. Cleaver Deposit.
Letter, St. Louis, Mo., 1867, from George R. Rowland, giving an account of members of the Cleaver family settled in Missouri.

——, p. 28. Luther Thomas Deposit.
Additional material concerning Samuel Roberts's American claims.

1946–7, p. 26. 6710B. Seventeenth-century manuscript containing a critical account of some Congregational churches in New England, said to have been compiled by Richard Sadler, lecturer at Ludlow, Salop.

1947–8, p. 43 (also mentioned 1948–9, p. 61). Mrs. E. Yale Deposit.
Journals of a tour in America by Thomas Lewis, M.P. for Bangor, 1874.

1948–9, p. 31. 15505D. Seven letters, 1799–1834, from Thomas Picton, minister at Woodbury, N.J., and West Point, N.Y.

1949–50, p. 43. Tredegar 1500. Notebook containing orders issued by General James Wolfe, 30 Apr.–12 Sept. 1759, in the campaign leading up to the taking of Quebec.

1950–1, p. 23. 15267B. Minutes, 1888–1905, of the Welsh Prairie Presbyterian Church district meetings, United States.

——, p. 28. 17239C. Rev. Gomer M. Roberts Deposit.
J. G. Davies: diary of a voyage to the United States, and letters relating to the voyage, 1893.

1953–4, p. 23. Professor T. A. Levi Deposit.
Three manuscript notebooks containing accounts of visits to America by Rev. Thomas Levi, 1867, 1873, and 1874.

1953–4, p. 26. 15532B. Diaries of Rev. David Davies, Oshkosh, Wis., for 1880, 1882–4, 1887–8, 1893, 1895–6, and 1899. Also a bound typescript volume of addresses delivered, 1947, at the centenary celebrations of the Welsh settlement at Oshkosh.

——, p. 28. 15506D. Typewritten copies of letters, 1862–4, written by John G. Jones to his family during the Civil War.

1954–5, p. 49. Admiral Herbert W. Hope Deposit.
Volume containing copies of four letters, 1771–2, from 'J. W.', Philadelphia, announcing and acknowledging shipments of goods, and accounts of the receipt and payment of bills of exchange, &c.

——, pp. 54–55. Miss F. N. Norman Deposit.
Notes on trade relations with the American colonies, 1769; and a petition, 1778, from merchants, traders, and other inhabitants of New York to the commissioners appointed to quieten the disorders in the American colonies.

CYFARTHFA PAPERS.

Letter-books, ledgers and correspondence of the Crawshay family, 1786–1877. The Crawshay ironworks, Cyfarthfa, Merthyr Tydfil, founded by Anthony Bacon, a Maryland settler who returned in 1745,[1] became one of the greatest iron firms of the nineteenth century. The papers were not examined. However, John P. Addis, *The Crawshay Dynasty: a Study in Industrial Organisation and Development, 1765–1867* (Cardiff, 1957), based mainly on these papers, includes references to letters in the 1850's and 1860's concerning the firm's monetary arrangements with American buyers; pricing policies on, for example, rails to the 'Mobile and Ohio pattern'; orders for American rods; the effects of the Civil War; American tariff changes. (*See also* Monmouthshire Record Office, p. 488.)

HARPTON COURT COLLECTION.

Among this large collection, now being listed, are papers of Sir George Cornewall Lewis (1806–63), who was Secretary for War 1861–3.
Some forty letters, 1849–62, from his close personal friend Sir Edmund Head, contain, while Head was Governor-General of Canada 1854–61, discussion of the threat of war with the United States and the defence of Canada. There are also twelve or so letters from Edward Twisleton relating to his visit to the United States, 1850–2, and to the Civil War and British neutrality, 1861. There is also, among the papers so far sorted, an incomplete draft of a Cabinet memorandum, 1862, on relations with the United States, including the questions of recognition of the Confederacy and possible intervention.

[1] See L. B. Namier, 'Anthony Bacon, an Eighteenth Century Merchant', *Journal of Economic and Business History*, vol. ii, pp. 20–70, 1929.

FLINTSHIRE

Lord Kenyon, GREDINGTON HALL, [Whitchurch, Shropshire]

KENYON PAPERS. Letter. 1771.

15 May 1771, from Edward Thurlow to Lloyd Kenyon concerning 'the legality of granting a ministerial office in the Court of Justice in America, for more than one life, and I remember two cases upon that head . . .'.[1]

GLAMORGAN

Central Library, The Hayes, CARDIFF

MS. 3. 173 (*formerly* PHILLIPPS MS. 16056).

(*a*) Manuscript copy in brief of the Dutch records of New York, 1629–45.

(*b*) Memoranda copied from American State Papers, Nov. 1760–Mar. 1766, under Governor Bernard: Ratification of land grants. Measures against New Orleans smuggling. Colonial policy. Boston customs disputes. Propagation of Christian knowledge among the Indians. Forgery of treasury notes.

BUTE CORRESPONDENCE.

The correspondence, 1752–90, of John Stuart, 3rd Earl of Bute (1713–92), consists mainly of letters written to the Earl, with some written by him. The greatest concentration is in the early 1760's.

A good list revealed the following relevant material:

Amherst, Jeffrey, and Admiral Edward Boscawen. Signed plan of military affairs in North America after the siege of Louisbourg, 8 Aug. 1758.

Anon. Copy of abstracts of resolves of Providence, R.I., Maryland, Essex county, N.J., and Philadelphia, loyally asserting rights of local assemblies to levy taxes, and objecting to the new stamp duties. Sept. 1765.

Boone, Daniel. Letter, 20 Oct. 1760, soliciting a life pension for his wife.

Boscawen, Admiral Edward. Unsigned statement, 1758, of the disposition of his fleet at Louisbourg.

[1] Transcript, H.M.C. xiv (iv), p. 502.

Johnstone, George, Governor of West Florida. Letters, 12 June, 25 July, and 18 Sept. 1765 from Pensacola, Fla. Gossip of Indians, tobacco, plants for Kew. The letter of 12 June contains details of advice on administering the Pensacola area.

Davers, Sir Robert. Memorial, 3 Mar. 1763, requesting a land grant in North America lying in the mouth of the river Detroit.

George III. *c.* 400 personal letters and notes, mostly undated, include sporadic and slight comments on American affairs. Appended to these is his 'Thoughts on the British Constitution', *c.* 1760.

Montagu, Edward Wortley. Letter of 27 June 1763 enclosing a map of the Mississippi mouth from Bayagoulas to the sea.

Philadelphia College, Academy and Charitable Trust. Loyal address of the trustees to Lord Bute, 27 May 1763.

H.M. Customs and Excise, CARDIFF

See H.M. Customs and Excise, London (p. 200).

Glamorgan Record Office, County Hall, CARDIFF

DOWLAIS IRON COMPANY. Letters.[1] 1782–1900.

The Dowlais Iron Company was one of the leading iron companies of South Wales in the nineteenth century and, like many of the other great iron companies of that region, concentrated on the production of rolled merchant bars and rails. The letter files which have been deposited include about 563,000 letters, 1782–1900. These are the files of incoming letters formerly kept at the Dowlais works of the Company. Incoming letters to the various sales offices—Cardiff, Liverpool, and London—are not included, nor are copies of any outgoing letters. The incoming records of the London house, and of the Liverpool and Cardiff houses, appear to have been destroyed. The Company now forms part of the Guest Keen and Nettlefolds group of companies, whose head office is in Birmingham.

The letters are divided into two series. The first, 'Dowlais Iron Company', is indexed alphabetically by years, 1782–1900; it covers such topics as labour relations, relations with other iron companies, technical questions concerning the production of iron, transport of iron, purchase of supplies, general financial matters and business of the Merthyr Tydfil Bank. The second series, 'London house', begins in 1837 with the establishment of that house and is arranged chronologically; the letters deal almost exclusively with instructions to the Dowlais works about orders taken by the London

---

[1] Some of the letters are reproduced in *Iron in the Making: Dowlais Iron Company Letters, 1782–1860*, ed. by Madeleine Elsas (Cardiff, 1960).

house, and are extremely full and informative for certain periods, especially the late 1840's and early 1850's, when every inquiry for iron was discussed in detail. However, for anyone not fully conversant with early American railway history, the usefulness of these letters is impaired by the difficulty of identifying the various orders—even the manager of the works was not always informed for whom he was rolling.

The Company had extensive dealings with American railroad companies, but as the material is so vast, only specimen volumes up to 1854 were examined. American references found in these are as follows:

(a) 'D.I.C., 1837, A–Y': Orders for Camden & Amboy Railroad Co. Purchase of New Orleans City Bonds. Preliminary inquiries from Liverpool agent for iron edging for granite paving in New Orleans (catalogued under Ogden). Payment from Grand Junction Railroad, through Glyn, Mills, Hallifax & Co.

(b) 'D.I.C., 1838, A–Y': Correspondence on an order of rails through James Maury & Sons for Maury, Latham & Co. of New York and Philadelphia.

(c) 'London house, 1841–1842': Transactions with T. & P. George, Philadelphia. Letters from the London agent to Messrs. Baring urging shipment of rails 'to America'. Discussion of rail order from Messrs. Ralston of Philadelphia.

(d) 'D.I.C., 1845, E–W': Draft via the Pottsville, Pa., agent from P. R. McMurray, New York. Appeal from Jane Head, Philadelphia, to Sir John Guest to represent her legal interests.

(e) 'London house, 1850–1852': Orders of rails by Boorman, Johnston & Co. of New Orleans, Camden & Amboy Railroad Co. (with difficulties encountered in manufacture and delivery), Michigan Central Railroad Co., and Messrs. Souther of New York. Order of axle iron by T. & P. George, Philadelphia.

(f) 'D.I.C., 1854': Importation of timber from Quebec (catalogued under Batchelor).

H.M. Customs and Excise, SWANSEA

See H.M. Customs and Excise, London (p. 201).

MERIONETHSHIRE

Bob Owen, Esq., M.A., O.B.E., Ael y Bryn, CROESOR, Llanfrothen

WELSH EMIGRANT LETTERS.

Mr. Owen, a private scholar and antiquarian, has many emigrant letters from America, mainly in Welsh but some in English, among his large

private collection of books and manuscripts. He also has completed in typescript a history of Welsh emigration to America with statistical tables drawn
from his own examination of scores of parish registers and possibly hundreds
of shipping lists; he is willing to let serious scholars who visit him consult
this huge compilation.[1]

MONMOUTHSHIRE

Monmouthshire County Record Office, County Hall, NEWPORT

CRAWSHAY, RICHARD (1739–1810). Letter-book. 1789–90.

Ironmaster and merchant. The letter-book contains copies of business and
personal letters from Crawshay, in chronological order, 1788–97. Among
these are letters of 3 Feb. 1789, regretting the shortage of Baltimore iron;
and of 25 May 1790, to H. Charles of Lynn, Mass., arranging to dispatch
a shipload of grain to return with a cargo of iron, followed by letters from
Crawshay's Cyfarthfa agent James Cockshutt urging the dispatch.

For the bulk of the Crawshay papers *see* National Library of Wales,
Aberystwyth (p. 484).

---

[1] Mr. Owen has contributed many articles on Wales and the United States to
Welsh language publications, especially on emigration. See especially, 'Yr Ymfudo
o sir Gaernarfon i'r Unol Daleithiau', *Transactions of the Caernarvonshire Historical
Society*, vol. xiii, pp. 42–67, vol. xiv, pp. 35–50, and vol. xv, pp. 51–65, 1952–4;
'Ymfudo o sir Aberteifi i Unol Daleithiau America, o 1654 hyd 1860' (with English
summaries), *Ceredigion*, Journal of the Cardiganshire Antiquarian Society, vol. ii,
no. 3, pp. 160–9, and no. 4, pp. 225–40, 1954 and 1955; and *Lleufer*, vol. xiii,
pp. 25–28, 73–76, 137–42, 173–8, 1957; vol. xiv, pp. 29–34, 69–74, 1958.

SCOTLAND

ABERDEENSHIRE

Aberdeen-Angus Cattle Society, 17 Bon-Accord Square, ABERDEEN

PEDIGREE EXPORTATION CERTIFICATES (manuscript).[1]
7 volumes. 1887– to date.

These volumes contain a complete record of all exports of pedigreed Aberdeen-Angus cattle from Great Britain, Northern Ireland and Eire, and include many references to American buyers. Exports prior to 1887 can be found in the first ten volumes of the Society's *Herd Book*, dating back to *c*. 1850.

Aberdeen Comb Works Co. Ltd., Hutcheon Street, ABERDEEN

BUSINESS RECORDS. Ledgers. *c*. 1880–1920's.

Record the export of combs to numerous destinations in the United States. The earliest reference is *c*. 1880, and the export is said to have continued into the 1920's.

Machinery was imported from New England in the nineteenth century; it is possible that this is also recorded in these ledgers.

Aberdeen Town Council, Town House, ABERDEEN

COUNCIL REGISTERS OF THE CITY OF ABERDEEN.

Vol. lxiv of this series of ninety-five volumes (manuscript), fourteenth century–1883, contains various items of interest on the War of Independence, including a loyal address to George III on the breaking out of the war, the offer by Aberdeen Town Council to raise a regiment for service in the war (the offer was refused); and an order to the citizens of Aberdeen to be armed for the defence of the town in case of invasion.

---

[1] See Alvin H. Sanders, *History of Aberdeen-Angus Cattle, with Particular Reference to . . . North America* (Chicago, 1928).

Aberdeen Typographical Society, Trades Hall, Adelphi, ABERDEEN

MINUTE-BOOKS (printed). 1853–to date.

Branch of the Scottish Typographical Association. The minute-books contain occasional references to the emigration of members, and to such public questions as the American copyright controversy.

The Society also holds the *Annual Reports* of the Scottish Typographical Association, Glasgow. From 1890 the accounts of the Association contain a figure for emigration grants paid to members, but no indication is given of the destination of recipients. However, some clues on this subject may be found in the reports from branches, also reprinted in the *Annual Reports*.

Amalgamated Union of Building Trade Workers of Great Britain and Ireland, Aberdeen Branch, 21 Adelphi, ABERDEEN

OPERATIVE MASONS' AND GRANITECUTTERS' JOURNAL. May 1901–Apr. 1909.

This monthly journal dealt with news of interest to members of the Operative Masons' and Granitecutters' Union of Aberdeen. Various, and fairly frequent, references are made to letters received from union members who had left Aberdeen district for the United States, particularly Barre, Vt.

J. & J. Crombie Ltd., Grandholm Works, ABERDEEN

BUSINESS RECORDS.

Woollen manufacturers. Two large entry books record information about business done with customers *c.* 1869–1919. Several American firms are included. In many cases notes are added about the standing, connexions, and prospects of these firms; sometimes these were supplied by the Bradstreet Company and others were from private sources. A few loose items of correspondence are inserted in these volumes.

The Company has other records concerning later trade with America. From 1880 to 1890 it maintained a New York office, but these particular records do not appear to have been preserved.

H.M. Customs and Excise, ABERDEEN

See H.M. Customs and Excise, London (p. 204).

Christie Memorial Library, Diocese of Aberdeen and Orkney, Church House, 2 Bon-Accord Crescent, ABERDEEN

SEABURY CONSECRATION. 23 letters (1 volume). 1784.

These letters, written by Dean John Skinner (1744–1816) of Aberdeen to A. Petrie of Old Meldrum, Aberdeenshire, contain reference to a scheme of Seabury for drawing up a concordat, and other matters. Samuel Seabury (1729–96) was the first bishop of the Episcopal Church in America. After the War of Independence he proceeded to England for consecration, but was refused by the Church of England. He then took himself to the Episcopal Church in Scotland where he was consecrated.

The Library, University of Aberdeen, ABERDEEN

ATHOLL PAPERS.[1]

(*a*) Copy letter, 9/19 Dec. 1673, from the States General of the United Provinces to Charles II. Their desire for peace; offer to restore the New Netherlands and other places taken by the Dutch in the late war.[2] (29.I(12)3)

(*b*) Copy of a letter from Lieut. Thomas Campbell, R.M., on board the *Dragon* at Portsmouth, to Lord Adam Gordon, 'being a faithful narrative of every thing remarkable he observed among the Creek Nations from November 1764 to June 1765'. Campbell was sent by Governor Johnstone from Pensacola, Fla., on 20 Nov. 1764 to interview leaders of the Creek Indians. (49(6)99)

(*c*) Letters, 1767, concerning an emigration scheme in which the Duke of Atholl had some interest. The plan was to send a number of Lincolnshire people to an estate in New York state owned by Lord Adam Gordon, a relative of the Duke. A complete list of the proposed emigrants' names is given.[3] (49(6)96–98)

[1] On temporary deposit from the Duke of Atholl, Blair Castle, Blair Atholl. A very thorough and detailed inventory of this collection is at present in process, and should be completed in the near future. This will be held at the University Library, the original papers returning to Blair Castle.

[2] Synopsis in H.M.C. xii (viii), p. 32.

[3] See *Chronicles of the Atholl and Tullibardine Families*, collected and arranged by John J. H. S. Murray, 7th Duke of Atholl, 5 vols. (Edinburgh, priv. print., 1908).

(*d*) Two letters, St. Augustine, Fla., 1768, from James Grant, Governor of East Florida. (49(7) 15 and 157)

BELL, PATRICK (1799–1869). Journal of travels between Great Britain and Upper Canada, 1833–4.

This contains many references to the north-eastern parts of the United States.

ABERDEEN TRADES COUNCIL.

Eighteen minute-books, 1876–1939, contain occasional general references to emigration questions.[1]

Anderson and Woodman Memorial Library, STRICHEN

SEDERUNT BOOK OF THE EXECUTORS OF MRS. GEORGE WATT. 1841.

Dr. George Watt was an uncle of George Smith (1806–99), the Chicago millionaire, and, by marriage, of Alexander Copland of Hinchinbrook, Montreal (and ? Waterton, Ohio?). These records deal largely with a bequest to Copland's daughter, Georgina Watt, and her marriage contract, in 1856, with Dr. Stephen de Wolfe of New York.

ANGUS

Alliance Trust Co. Ltd., Meadow House, 64 Reform Street, DUNDEE

BUSINESS RECORDS.[2]

Records consisting of 22 minute-books, 26 balance sheets, 2 scrap-books, company reports, &c., concerning investment in the United States,

---

[1] See K. D. Buckley, *Trade Unionism in Aberdeen, 1878 to 1900* (Edinburgh, 1955) (Aberdeen University Studies no. 135).

[2] See J. C. Gilbert, *A History of Investment Trusts in Dundee, 1873–1938* (London, 1939), *passim*; W. Turrentine Jackson, 'The Chavez Land Grant: A Scottish Investment in New Mexico, 1881–1940', *Pacific Historical Review*, vol. xxi, pp. 349–66, 1952. See also *When Grass was King* (Boulder, Colo., University of Colorado Press, 1956) particularly a monograph on 'British Interests in the Range Cattle Industry'. Professor Jackson was able to examine certain records of other investment trusts which we were not able to; some of them figure in the above works, others in a study on which he is working, 'The Enterprising Scot'.

especially farm mortgages, land speculation, and railroads, 1873–1914. The operations of the company covered a wide area, including Oregon, Washington, New Mexico, Wisconsin, and Hawaii.

H.M. Customs and Excise, DUNDEE

See H.M. Customs and Excise, London (p. 204).

Northern American Trust Co. Ltd., Friarfield House, DUNDEE

BUSINESS RECORDS.[1] *c.* 100 volumes. 1873–1900.

Records of a group of investment trust companies with extensive interests in the United States, including investment in railroads.

Donald B. Stewart, Esq., 26 Shamrock Street, DUNDEE

AMERICAN RAILWAY INVESTMENT. 2 volumes. 1865.

These volumes, compiled by the Hon. Arthur Fitzgerald Kinnaird (later 10th Baron Kinnaird) (1814–87), contain press clippings and letters of introduction from leading Americans relating to the visit to the United States of a group of twenty-six British business men, led by Sir Samuel Morton Peto, M.P.,[2] who were concerned mainly with railroad investment, especially the Atlantic and Great Western Railroad Company.

H.M. Customs and Excise, MONTROSE

See H.M. Customs and Excise, London (p. 204).

ARGYLLSHIRE

H.M. Customs and Excise, CAMPBELTOWN

See H.M. Customs and Excise, London (p. 203).

[1] See J. C. Gilbert, op. cit., *passim.*
[2] See his *Resources and Prospects of America, ascertained during a visit to the States in the autumn of 1865* (London and New York, 1866).

AYRSHIRE

H.M. Customs and Excise, AYR

See H.M. Customs and Excise, London (p. 202).

BERWICKSHIRE

J. W. Home-Robertson, Esq., PAXTON HOUSE, Berwick-on-Tweed

HOME OF WEDDERBURN PAPERS.

These contain a small but interesting collection of letters from Captain, afterwards Admiral, Sir David Milne, to George Home of Wedderburn, 1811–18. Milne fought in the War of 1812, when he conducted the blockade of Boston, and was afterwards employed in the task of rounding up American vessels engaged in fishing in Canadian waters. His letters contain comments on the War, on American designs on the Spanish colonies—especially Cuba—the potential naval challenge to Britain, the American threat to Canada, fishery disputes, and the need for friendly Anglo-American relations.[1]

CLACKMANNANSHIRE

H.M. Customs and Excise, ALLOA

See H.M. Customs and Excise, London (p. 204).

DUMFRIESSHIRE

Duke of Buccleuch, DRUMLANRIG CASTLE, Thornhill

BUCCLEUCH AND QUEENSBERRY MUNIMENTS. Letters. 1682, 1796?

(a) 13 July and 10 Oct. 1682, and 4 Aug. 1683, from James, Duke of

---

[1] Transcripts, H.M.C. Milne Home of Wedderburn MSS. [57] pp. 145–75 *passim*. (Listed as in possession of Colonel David Milne Home of Wedderburn.)

Albany to Lord Queensberry, concerning Sir John Cochrane's proposed expedition to Carolina. In the second letter James states he told Cochrane that he was glad that he and others of his persuasion [? Presbyterian] were going, because that would get rid of disaffected people. In the third he is of the opinion 'that Carolina was only a pretence to carry on their damnable designs' [? the Rye House plot].[1]

(*b*) n.d. from George Washington to James W. Jamison, stating that some time ago he had received a letter from the Duke of Buccleuch asking his assistance for a Donald Dewar who had left for America in 1796 and asking Mr. Jamison to call on the said Donald and inform him of this.

N.R.A. (Scotland).

H.M. Customs and Excise, Dumfries

See H.M. Customs and Excise, London (p. 202).

E. W. Hope-Johnstone, Esq., Raehills House, Lockerbie

JOHNSTONE PAPERS. Letter. 1700.

11 Jan. 1700, from James Ogilvy, Viscount Seafield, to the Earl of Annandale, stating that the King has promised that Scots shall be accorded equal freedom of trade with the plantations.[2]

FIFESHIRE

Andrew Carnegie Birthplace Memorial, Moodie Street, Dunfermline

CARNEGIE, ANDREW (1835–1919). Papers.

The caretaker at the Museum will make the papers available to any interested student. The papers themselves are collected in various parcels. There is no index or inventory of the holdings, which include the following items of interest:

(*a*) Manuscript essay by Thomas Morrison entitled 'Rights of Land'.

[1] Transcripts, H.M.C. xv (viii), pp. 242, 174, 195.
[2] Extract, H.M.C. xv (ix), p. 115.

Morrison was Carnegie's maternal grandfather and a noted Chartist Radical in the early decades of the nineteenth century. There is a note on the fly-leaf in Carnegie's handwriting.

(*b*) A privately prepared genealogy of the Morrison family (typescript).

(*c*) Notebooks Carnegie used for his tour around the world 1878–9, which later appeared in book form as *Round the World* (London, 1884).

(*d*) Notebooks Carnegie used for his coaching trip from Brighton to Inverness, 1881, later appearing in book form as *An American Four-in-Hand in Britain* (London, 1883).

(*e*) Original manuscript of Carnegie's *Triumphant Democracy* (New York, 1886).

(*f*) Various pamphlets of speeches given and accounts of Carnegie's travels in Scotland.

(*g*) A packet of correspondence, 1904, between Carnegie and W. H. Ellis in regard to the Emperor of Ethiopia, Menelik, concerning a proposal of Ellis to establish a colonization programme for Negroes (American freed slaves) in Ethiopia, and a letter of tribute to Carnegie from the Emperor.

(*h*) Various drafts for Carnegie's rectorial address, St. Andrews University, 1905.

(*i*) Manuscript (in part) of Carnegie's autobiography[1] with various marginal corrections.

(*j*) List of 212 books in Carnegie's personal library which have been dedicated or inscribed to him.

Ross & Connell, Solicitors, Guildhall Chambers, DUNFERMLINE

CARNEGIE, ANDREW (1835–1919). Papers.

John D. Ross (later Sir John D. Ross), handled Carnegie's legal and Scottish business affairs from 1876 until Carnegie's death in 1919. Ross also was on the Board of Trustees of the Carnegie Dunfermline Trust and the Carnegie Hero Fund Trust from the creation of the trusts in 1903 and 1908 until he resigned as chairman in 1923.

The papers are in two large strong boxes, labelled 'Andrew Carnegie'. There is no particular order to the collection, nor is there an inventory of contents. These papers are not available to the public and permission to see them will be granted only with the authorization of the Carnegie Dunfermline Trust, and Carnegie's daughter, Mrs. Margaret Carnegie Miller.

[1] *Autobiography of Andrew Carnegie*, ed. by J. C. Van Dyke (London, 1920).

Much of the collection is simply on personal affairs, but some items of wider interest were found:

(*a*) The negotiations for the purchase of Pittencrieff Glen from the Hunt family which was the first step in the creation of the Dunfermline Trust.

(*b*) Numerous letters concerning and reports on the various individuals in Dunfermline, mostly relatives, to whom Carnegie granted an annuity.

(*c*) Correspondence about and negotiations for the purchase of Skibo Castle, Sutherland.

(*d*) Correspondence with Thomas Graham, a member of the Carnegie–Storey newspaper syndicate, regarding Carnegie's withdrawal from the syndicate and his financial involvement with it.

(*e*) Three or four letters from Mrs. Carnegie, 1903–39.

INVERNESS-SHIRE

H.M. Customs and Excise, INVERNESS

See H.M. Customs and Excise, London (p. 203).

KINCARDINESHIRE

J. M. Burnett, Esq., MONBODDO HOUSE, Fordoun

MONBODDO PAPERS.

Papers of James Burnett, Lord Monboddo (1714–99), Scottish judge.

(*a*) Letter, 18 Mar. 1789, from Philip Thicknesse who had served in the West Indies and Georgia, and was the author of a number of travel books, &c., to Monboddo, says, 'I . . . was one of the first fools who went over with Oglethorpe to . . . Georgia', and goes on to speak of the language of the Indians.[1]

(*b*) Various treatises on North America (especially Indians) listed in a 'Catalogue of MSS' of 1794; but it is not clear whether these treatises are in the collection or not.[2]

---

[1] Transcript, H.M.C. iv, p. 519.   [2] H.M.C. vi, pp. 679–80.

KIRKCUDBRIGHTSHIRE

Major Richard Alex. Oswald, CAVENS, Kirkbean

OSWALD, RICHARD (1705–84) of Auchencruive. 3 letter-books.[1] 1764–84.

Merchant and shipowner. Inherited estates from wife's father in West Indies and in the southern colonies.

Book I, 1761–3, contains the correspondence of Richard Oswald with his wife, Mary Ramsay Oswald.

Book II, 1764–84, contains miscellaneous letters to Richard Oswald; some reporting on military affairs in America, 1776–81.

Book III, 1765–84, contains John Maxwell's letters to Richard Oswald, mainly of business interest.

LANARKSHIRE

H.M. Customs and Excise, GLASGOW

See H.M. Customs and Excise, London (p. 203).

Public Libraries, Mitchell Library, North Street, GLASGOW C. 3

BOGLE PAPERS.[2] Letter-book, *c.* 100 letters. 1725–31, 1759–61.

Merchants of the firm of Bogle & Scott. The Bogle family lived at Daldowie, Lanarkshire. The letter-book, 1725, of George Bogle contains many references to the tobacco trade; most of the letters are written from Leyden or Rotterdam. Also commercial letters, some of 1729–31 and some of 1759–61, from agents and members of the family, from the Rappahannock river, Va., Glasgow and London. By the later period the firm had a London office and was freighting in London ships outward bound to America.

---

[1] Microfilm of these held in the National Library of Scotland, Edinburgh.
[2] Microfilms made by the Virginia Colonial Records Project.

WILLIAM SMEAL COLLECTION.[1] Manuscripts and printed material. *c.* 1833–76.

William Smeal (? 1792–1877) was a Glasgow Quaker grocer who took a leading part in reform—especially anti-slavery—movements in nineteenth-century Glasgow. He was secretary of the Glasgow Emancipation Society throughout its history, 1833–75, and was a leading supporter of the William Lloyd Garrison wing of the Scottish anti-slavery movement.

Includes the following important anti-slavery materials:

(*a*) Glasgow Emancipation Society minute-books, 1833–76: 4 volumes, bound in one. There is a great deal of correspondence with George Thompson on his anti-slavery campaign in the United States in 1834. An entry for 1861 refers to the memorial to Palmerston calling on the British government not to recognize the Confederacy; another for 1863 deplores the aid given by some M.P.s and British capitalists to the Confederacy.

(*b*) Glasgow Emancipation Society cash book, 1833–76.

(*c*) Over a hundred volumes of anti-slavery pamphlets, tracts, and books, which include annual reports of the Glasgow Emancipation Society, and a wide range of American anti-slavery writings. 1833–61.

(*d*) Glasgow Emancipation Society subscription book, 1833.

(*e*) Sundry papers relating to the anti-slavery movement in Glasgow. Included are various broadsides on American slavery, press cuttings, and two letters from George Thompson. 1834–5.

(*f*) Miscellaneous collection of letters, posters, and papers on the anti-slavery activities of the Glasgow Emancipation Society. 1841–76.

(*g*) Glasgow Freedmen's Aid Society minute-book, 1864–7. (William Smeal was its secretary.)

GLASGOW FEMALE ANTI-SLAVERY SOCIETY. 4 annual reports (printed pamphlets). 1843–51.

Second, fourth, fifth, and sixth reports for 1843, 1845, 1846, and 1851 respectively. Contain extracts from letters of Mrs. Maria Weston Chapman, secretary of the Boston Female Anti-Slavery Society, to this Glasgow society. The fourth report contains the copy of a letter from William Lloyd Garrison concerning his attitude towards Christianity.

MORTON, ALFRED (1854–1941?). Diaries: volume 48. (Autobiography covering 1854–82.)

Birmingham bricklayer. Morton went to the United States in 1871 and returned to England in 1882. The first forty-seven volumes of his diaries

---

[1] This collection has been used in Robert Botsford, 'Scotland and the American Civil War', Ph.D. thesis, University of Edinburgh, 1955. See also George Shepperson, 'Harriet Beecher Stowe and Scotland, 1852–53', *Scottish Historical Review*, vol. xxxii, pp. 40–46, 1953.

contain little of American interest; the last, Morton's autobiography, describes his American experiences. He travelled quite extensively in the United States—New York, Pittsburgh., Pa., Cleveland, Ohio, and through the Southwest—mainly in search of employment. On his return to England he continued to correspond with various people in the United States, mainly in the Pittsburgh area.

MIDLOTHIAN

Lady Elphinstone, CARBERRY TOWER, Musselburgh

ELPHINSTONE PAPERS. Letter (copy). 1756.

Among the papers of Field-Marshal James Keith there is a 'Copy of a letter to the King of Prussia dated Paris, 5 April 1756, probably by Baron Knyphausen, in which he informs the King that the French Court had opened the trade to French America to neutral ships, and that the French merchants were meaning to prefer the Prussian Flag during the war. . . .'[1]

Duke of Buccleuch, Dalkeith House, DALKEITH

BUCCLEUCH AND QUEENSBERRY MUNIMENTS. Townshend Papers.

Box VIII of this collection includes the papers of Charles Townshend (1725–67), mainly correspondence on American affairs, 1751–85. They include:

Bundle 2. War Office papers, mainly financial, regarding North America, including establishment list for Northern Department of Indian Affairs, 1766.

Bundle 4. Papers in Townshend's holograph relating to America, both military and political. Includes state of the Newfoundland fishery, 12 May 1761. 1745–c. 1766.

Bundle 17. Papers relating to excise duties on linen, paper, leather, and beer. Includes proposals for regulating trade to North America, 1766–7.

Bundle 22. Papers relating to America, on agriculture, manufactures, army, imports and exports. Includes list and extracts of papers laid before Parliament relative to disturbances in America on account of the Stamp Act. 1691–1766.

Bundle 25. American papers, 1765–7.

Bundle 27. Papers from the Board of Trade, including draft Bill for recruiting in North America, 1766.

[1] H.M.C. ix (ii), p. 228.

Bundle 28. Estimates of army expenses in North America, and other American papers, 1765–7.

Bundle 31. American papers, 1765–7.

Bundle 34. Papers mainly relating to America, including report of examinations before the Parliamentary committee for American affairs, 1766.

Bundle 39. American papers, including copy Journal of the General Assembly of New York (10 Nov.–19 Dec. 1766). 1766.

Bundle 45. Miscellaneous papers, including copies of papers of General Wolfe regarding the attack on Quebec, 1759; thoughts concerning Florida; and a general scheme of the inhabitants and fishery of Newfoundland, 1759. 1759–64.

Bundle 52, notebook 7. Representations, mainly from the American and West Indian colonies. 1735–46.

N.R.A. (Scotland).[1]

General Assembly Library, Church of Scotland, 352 Castlehill, EDINBURGH 1

RECORDS OF GENERAL ASSEMBLY.[2]

The records, 1720–1957 (printed since 1929), contain several references, particularly in the eighteenth century, to the Scottish Presbyterian Congregation of New York, usually dealing with financial matters.

SOCIETY IN SCOTLAND FOR PROPAGATING CHRISTIAN KNOWLEDGE. Document.[3]

'Inventory of Letters, Memorials, Minutes, &c.' relating to the Society, one volume, 1707–32, contains a paper, n.d., proposing the establishment of a colony in Florida.

National Library of Scotland, EDINBURGH 1

Every Manuscript with a number lower than 1801 is described in the Library's *Catalogue of MSS. acquired since 1925* (Edinburgh, 1938–). Uncatalogued collections are referred to by accession numbers.

YESTER PAPERS. 1662–1815.

Box II (Acc. 1630). Four papers, including one referring to John Brown's licence for trading in the Caribbee islands, 1662–5.

---

[1] A full list of the Townshend Papers is with the N.R.A., London.

[2] These records are now in the Scottish Record Office.

[3] This document is now in New College Library, Edinburgh, to which the bulk of the old General Assembly Library has been dispersed.

Box III (Acc. 1853). Twenty-seven letters and papers, 1698-9, concerning the Darien scheme.

Box VII (Acc. 1611). Thirty-one letters, 1757-9, mostly to Lord Charles Hay while on service in Halifax, N.S. Also twenty letters, 1757-81, from John McColme and others, the first seventeen refer to the Seven Years War, the last two to the War of Independence.

Box VIII (Acc. 1611). Journals of Lord Charles Hay, 21 Apr.–23 June 1758, 3-24 June 1758, and 25 June-31 July 1758. Major Rodolphe's journal, and his detachment of the militia of Lunenburg, N.S., on the western side of the River Lahave, 1757. Narrative account by Lieutenant Shomberg, of Major General Hopson's regiment, 1756.

Box IX (Acc. 1611). Forty-two letters, 1807-15, to George Hay, 8th Marquess of Tweeddale, mainly on military affairs in Canada; also thirty-nine documents of a military nature, mostly monthly returns of regiments in Canada 1813-14.

JOHNSTONE, JAMES, Chevalier de Johnstone (1719-1800?). 'Memoirs.' (MS. 1028.) (Microfilm; the original with the owner.)

The originals are the manuscripts for two published works by Chevalier de Johnstone, *Memoirs of the Rebellion* (London, 1820), and *Memoirs of the Chevalier de Johnstone*, 3 vols. (Aberdeen, 1870-1), which include descriptions of the war in Canada in 1758 and 1759.

MICMAC RELIGIOUS WORK. (MS. 1900)

Catechism, including prayers, doctrinal instructions, the order of the administration of the sacraments, &c., in French and in Micmac, by Antoine Simon Maillard (d. 1768).[1]

STEUART PAPERS.

(a) Microfilm[2] of the letter-books, 1751-63, of Charles Steuart, Receiver-General, American Board of Customs, containing copies of his business correspondence as a merchant in Norfolk, Va. (Acc. 2444)

(b) Correspondence and papers of Steuart, 1758-97. The official correspondence is mainly with customs officials, and especially with Nathaniel Coffin, Steuart's deputy in Boston. There are also letters from Loyalists, mainly from Norfolk, Va. Steuart's 'Account books for the years 1776-1796' are also contained in this collection. (MSS. 5025-46)

---

[1] For an account of Maillard see his *Account of the Customs and Manners of the Micmakis and Maricheets Savage Nations, Now Dependent on the Government of Cape-Breton* (London, 1758) (published anonymously).

[2] Presented by Colonial Williamsburg, Williamsburg, Va.

STRACHAN, CHARLES (later Fullarton). Letter-book. 1763–70. (MS. 119)

Trader in Mobile, Ala., 1763–70. The letters are almost exclusively concerned with business affairs. Strachan retired to Scotland in 1770, on the death of his grandfather, to manage the Kinnaber estates.

ROBERTSON-MACDONALD PAPERS. 1765–1805. (MSS. 3942–88)

Family papers of the Robertsons, a branch of the Robertsons of Strowan, and the MacDonalds of Kinlochmoidart. The chief correspondents are William Robertson (1721–93), Principal of Edinburgh University, and his son William, of the College of Justice. Included are the materials collected by Principal Robertson for his work on America; the manuscript, in his hand, of a portion of his *History of America* (London, 1777), published by his son William in 1796; Colonel George Croghan's journal of his journey down the Ohio in 1765.

Also included in the collection are letters on the military experiences of successive Chiefs of the MacDonalds and Robertson-MacDonalds: of Alexander MacDonald in America, 1775–80, and of Donald MacDonald in the West Indies, where he became Governor of Tobago, 1800–5 (both MacDonalds of Kinlochmoidart).

CUNINGHAME, WILLIAM & CO. 3 letter-books.[1] 1767–74. (Microfilm.) (Acc. 2461)

Glasgow merchants with agents in North America. The letter-books—the last is only a fragment—were written by agents in Falmouth and Williamsburg, Va., and are concerned with business matters.

STUART STEVENSON PAPERS. (MSS. 5320–404)

Papers of the family of Stuart of Castlemilk and of Andrew Stuart, W.S., mainly eighteenth century.

(a) Letters, 1776–7, of Major Hon. Charles Cochrane concerning progress of the war in America.

(b) Correspondence of Hon. John Cochrane, Deputy Commissary to Forces in America, mainly concerning a Canadian lawsuit, 1777, 1782–4, 1788.

Also papers relating to the family's West Indian affairs.

ELLICE PAPERS.[2] 1770–1867. (Accs. 1993 and 2072)

Include letters, accounts, deeds, bonds, and mortgages relating to family property in New York and Canada.

---

[1] Originals in the possession of the Marchioness of Ailsa.

[2] All portions relating to Canada are on microfilm in the Public Archives of Canada. Permission of the family is necessary for the making of a copy of any material in this collection.

HOUSTON, ALEXANDER, & CO. 3 letter-books.[1] 1776–81.

Houston & Co. were general merchants and shipowners, Glasgow, trading principally with the West Indies. Most of the letters are to the Company's agents in Great Britain and in the West Indies, and to the captains of the Company's ships, relative to American trade.

COCHRANE PAPERS. (MSS. 2264–505 and 2568–608 and 3022)

Correspondence and papers, private and official, 1779–1856, of Admiral Sir Alexander Forrester Inglis Cochrane (1758–1831), who served as Commander-in-Chief of the Leeward Islands 1805–14, and of the North American Station 1814–15; and of his son Admiral Sir Thomas John Cochrane (1789–1872), Governor of Newfoundland 1825–34. The papers contain much information about operations and conditions in those regions.

MISCELLANEOUS LETTERS AND DOCUMENTS.

(a) List of sailings from Scottish and northern English ports, giving cargoes, destination, and master's name, 1781. (4 folios.) (MS. 1801)

(b) Letters of Samuel L. Clemens to F. H. Skrine (making fun of Kipling's 'absent-minded beggar'), 1902; of Oliver Wendell Holmes, Sen., 1883; of James Hourse, 1784; and of Thomas Jefferson to M. Thouin, 1813. (Adv. MS. 7. 1. 19)

MELVILLE PAPERS. 1787–1819.

Papers of Henry Dundas, 1st Viscount Melville (1742–1811), and of Robert Saunders Dundas, 2nd Viscount Melville (1771–1851).

(a) Memorandum, 1787, on financial affairs in Canada by John Cochrane, Deputy Commissary to Forces in America, addressed to Thomas Harley, Lord Mayor of London, and Henry Drummond, banker. (MS. 3849)

(b) Miscellaneous letters, 1787–1815, mostly relating to Canadian affairs. Correspondents include John Graves Simcoe, first Governor of Upper Canada, Sir George Buchan Hepburn, Sir Archibald MacDonald, and Canadian officials. (MS. 3847)

(c) Papers on the West Indies, 1791–1819, dealing with estate-owners, slaves, and campaigns. Also papers, 1789, 1800–1, n.d., on Russia and the Northern Confederation, with information supplied by Joseph Billings about his voyage to northeast Asia and the American coast. (MS. 1075)

(d) Canada and Newfoundland, 1793–1813: papers relating to Canadian convoys, timber, and fishing rights of Newfoundlanders. (MS. 3848)

(e) Memorandum, 1800, by General Sir David Dundas, relating to 1762 expedition against Havana. (MS. 3850)

---

[1] Microfilm in the Library of Congress, Washington, D.C.

(*f*) Letters, 1815, of General Sir George Murray to the 2nd Viscount Melville, relating to the former's arrival in Canada as Governor, and to Canadian affairs in general. (MS. 3851)

HUGH SHARP COLLECTION. Letters, document. 1791–1864.

In the collection of first editions there are 230 books and nine newspapers of American and Canadian interest. Also the following manuscripts:

(*a*) Letters of General Philip Schuyler to Stephen van Rensselaer, 1791, and to Alexander Hamilton, 1796; letter, 1814, from Andrew Jackson to David Holmes, Governor of Mississippi Territory; and a note, 1864, to Abraham Lincoln requesting the discharge of a soldier, endorsed with a note of Lincoln's ordering this. (MS. 3310)

(*b*) Deed of sale of a slave woman and child, Edgecombe county, N.C., 1831. (MS. 3316)

LISTON, SIR ROBERT (1742–1836). Papers (3 boxes, less than 1,000 items).[1] 1796–1800. (Acc. 720)

These papers cover the period of Liston's service as the second British Minister to the United States 1796–1800. They are a file of his personal correspondence, and still more of his wife's (Henrietta Marchant),[2] mainly with her uncle in Glasgow. Comments on social life in Philadelphia; yellow fever; visits to South Carolina, Boston, Albany, N.Y., &c.; personality of Washington and Adams. Correspondence with Coutts, the bankers; George Hammond, Liston's predecessor; Lord Bute, Timothy Pickering, Lord Grenville.

ANDERSON, ROBERT (1750–1830). Correspondence: 26 letters. 1805–29. (Adv. MSS. 22. 4. 16, vol. vii)

'Original letters' addressed to Robert Anderson, editor of the *Edinburgh Magazine*: six letters, Boston, 1817–26, from Rev. Andrew Bigelow; two letters, Boston, 1807, from Rev. J. W. B. Buckmaster; fourteen letters, Boston, 1805–29, from Rev. Charles Lowell; three letters, Harvard University, 1814–17, from Rev. Dr. Joseph McKean; and one letter, Philadelphia, 1822, from George Ticknor.

MURRAY PAPERS. 1814–15. (Adv. MSS. 46. 1. 1 to 47. 7. 4)

General Sir George Murray (1772–1846) served in Canada 1814–15, where he commanded the troops and also the civil government of Upper Canada. The papers give information about the conditions of settlement in Canada, relations with the Americans, and operations before New Orleans.

---

[1] Microfilm of all these papers are in the University of Virginia Library.
[2] These edited by Bradford Perkins, 'A Diplomat's Wife in Philadelphia . . . 1796–1800', *William and Mary Quarterly*, 3rd ser., vol. xi, pp. 592–632, 1954.

WATSON AUTOGRAPHS. (MSS. 577–600)

William Finlay Watson (1831–74), bookseller. The collection covers the period from the sixteenth to the nineteenth century.

(*a*) The volume 'Literary and Scientific' contains a letter, Granada, 9 May 1829, from Washington Irving to his brother Peter at Rouen.

(*b*) The volume 'American and Foreign' contains forty-five items, mainly letters, from various noted Americans to a variety of people. Among the writers are John Quincy Adams, George Bancroft, W. C. Bryant, Elihu Burritt, William Ellery Channing, Benjamin Franklin, Horatio Gates, John Hancock, Oliver Wendell Holmes, Sen., Andrew Jackson, John Jay, Thomas Jefferson, Henry Wadsworth Longfellow, James Monroe, W. H. Prescott, Harriet Beecher Stowe, George Washington, and Daniel Webster.

LOCKHART, JOHN GIBSON (1794–1854). Correspondence: 4 letters. 1831–6. (MS. 930, nos. 64–67)

Biographer of Sir Walter Scott. Volume viii of this collection of letters to Lockhart contains four letters, 1831–6, from Washington Irving; one of these is written from New York introducing 'Professor Longfellow'.

COMBE PAPERS. (ACC. 2102)

George Combe (1788–1858),[1] Writer to the Signet, phrenologist. Besides his phrenological interests Combe was caught up in the general reforming ferment of the first half of the nineteenth century and had some influence on educational reforms. He visited the United States in 1838–40, and met, among others, Van Buren, John Quincy Adams, Nicholas Biddle, H. Mann, L. Mott, W. E. Channing, and W. C. Bryant. He kept a journal of his tour (three volumes) which he later amended and published.[2] His American correspondence is fairly extensive and includes letters from some of the above as well as a good number of others.

PATON COLLECTION. Letter. 1847. (MS. 3218)

Contains a letter, 1847, from Elihu Burritt, and an envelope designed for Ocean Penny Postage, suggested by him, bearing an 1861 postmark.

CARLYLE, THOMAS (1795–1881). Letter. [1869] (MS. 518, no. 46)

A volume of letters from Carlyle to his family, from 1865, contains an unsigned letter [1869] from Carlyle to Emerson.

---

[1] A. C. Grant, a postgraduate student of the University of Edinburgh, whom we thank for this information, is working on a life of Combe.

[2] *Notes on the United States of North America, During a Phrenological Visit in 1838–9–40.* 3 vols. (Edinburgh and Philadelphia, 1841).

HALDANE PAPERS.[1] (MSS. 5901–6108)

Richard Burdon Haldane, Viscount Haldane of Cloan (1856–1928), Secretary of State for War 1905–12. This collection includes letters from Andrew Carnegie, Colonel House, Sir Wilfrid Laurier, and Woodrow Wilson.

MATHIESON, WILLIAM LAW (1868–1928). 'Governor Eyre.' c. 1938. (MS. 2616)

An account of the Negro rising of 1865 in Jamaica, being the final draft of part of an uncompleted work on Governor Edward John Eyre by William Law Mathieson, c. 1938.

The Library, New College, Mound, EDINBURGH I

This library holds, as well as the manuscripts noted below, an extensive collection of pamphlets (estimated at 30,000) which includes a number of pamphlets of American and Canadian interest, mainly dealing with church affairs but some on slavery.[2]

CHALMERS, THOMAS (1780–1847). Papers: mainly letters.

Scottish theologian and political economist. First Principal of New College, college of the Free Church of Scotland. Leader of the disruption of the Scottish churches in 1843. The papers consist mainly of correspondence to Chalmers, though there are some letters in his private shorthand. Chalmers's writings were influential among American Presbyterians and he received many letters from Americans of Scottish descent, nostalgic for the old country. His correspondents include Elihu Burritt, James Lenox of New York, Dr. Thomas Smyth of Charleston, S.C., and a number of lesser-known Americans. The collection contains materials which are relevant to Scottish-American anti-slavery and ecclesiastical controversies of the mid-nineteenth century.

NEW COLLEGE MISSIONARY ASSOCIATION. Letters and records. 1843– .

Organization of students for the ministry of the Free Church of Scotland, formed in 1843, at the time of the Scottish disruption, by breaking away from Edinburgh University Missionary Association. Some correspondence with like-minded American students, particularly at Princeton Theological Seminary, which touches on, among other matters of common interest, anti-slavery questions.

---

[1] Permission of the family is necessary for consultation of these papers. (At the time of inspection these papers were unsorted and uncatalogued.)

[2] American elements in this collection have been surveyed by George Shepperson, in 'Thomas Chalmers, the Free Church of Scotland and the South', *Journal of Southern History*, vol. xvii, pp. 517–37, 1951; and in 'The Free Church and American Slavery', *Scottish Historical Review*, vol. xxx, pp. 126–43, 1951.

Scottish American Investment Co. Ltd., 45 Charlotte Square, EDINBURGH 2

BUSINESS RECORDS.[1]

Formed in 1873 with investment in various United States holdings as its main purpose. American railroads in particular attracted a good proportion of the Company's funds. It holds the following:

(a) Minute-books (15 vols.) (manuscript), 1873–to date.

(b) Annual reports (2 vols.) (printed), 1874–to date.

(c) Investment ledgers (5 vols.) 1874–1917. (After 1917 kept in loose-leaf form.)

(d) Investment valuation lists for 1884, 1885, and 1900 onwards.

Scottish American Mortgage Co. Ltd., 30 Charlotte Square, EDINBURGH 2

BUSINESS RECORDS.

Formed in 1873. Originally all the funds were invested in mortgage loans on real estate alone, but later general investment, particularly railroads.

(a) Annual reports (3 vols.) (printed), 1875–to date.

(b) Reports of proceedings at annual general meetings (4 vols.) (printed), 1876–to date.

Scottish Record Office, H.M. General Register House, EDINBURGH 2

BARCLAY-ALLARDICE PAPERS.

Notes of various members of the family Barclay (some of them American), 1659–1774.[2]

MARCHMONT PAPERS. 3 letters. n.d. and 1682.

Two undated and one dated 2 Aug. 1682: one from Sir John Cochrane of Ochiltree to 'Mr. Mortoune [Joseph Morton], Governour at Ashley River',

---

[1] See John Clay, *My Life on the Range* (Chicago, priv. print., 1924).

[2] H.M.C. v, p. 632. (Listed as in possession of Mrs. Barclay-Allardice, Loyal House, Perthshire).

S.C.; one from Charles Charteris to Sir George Campbell of Cessnock; and one from Sir Patrick Hume of Polwarth to Sir John Cochrane. All three letters are on the subject of an expedition to Carolina (or two separate expeditions?) and settlement there.[1]

ABERCAIRNY COLLECTION. Letters. 1685–1797.

(a) Perth Amboy, N.J., 17 Mar. 1685, from D. Toshach to the Earl of Perth, Lord High Chancellor of Scotland, complaining that he is unable to use the writs he has had from Perth entitling him to land in New Jersey, because all the accessible land is taken up by Quakers and other 'off scourings off hell'.[2]

(b) Twenty-three letters, 1760–97, to Sir William Stirling of Ardoch from his brother Thomas Stirling during his career in the army and relating to the campaigns in America.

(c) Twelve letters and copies, 1760–75, to Lord Kames from Benjamin Franklin.[3]

CUNINGHAME OF THORNTON PAPERS. 1746–82, 1876–83.

(a) Notebook, 1746–9, containing garrison orders of Louisbourg, N.S.

(b) Thirteen notebooks, covering 1776–82, being the journal of Captain John Peebles during the War of Independence.[4]

(c) Copy proceedings of a treaty held at Easton, Pa., between American Commissioners and the Six Nations, 6 Feb. 1777.

(d) Letter, Brunswick, N.J., 7 May 1777, from John Peebles to his father, John Peebles at Irvine, Ayrshire, informing him of an expedition into New England under General Tryon and Sir William Erskine.

(e) Letter, Long Island, 26 Oct. 1778, from John Peebles to Dr. Charles Fleeming in Irvine, giving news of the American war.

(f) Letter, New York, 30 Aug. 1780, from John Peebles to his father, 'the Admiral is still watching the French fleet ... Mr. Washington is on the other side of the North River within a few miles and has a stronger army in the field than he has had these two years'.

(g) Letter, Newtown, Long Island, 27 Jan. 1781, from Peebles to his father, telling of sailing of expedition under Brigadier Arnold, and of mutinies in the rebel army.

(h) Diary, 1876, of hunting trip in the Rocky Mountains.

[1] Extracts, H.M.C. xiv (iii), p. 114. (Listed as in possession of Sir Hugh Hume Campbell, Marchmont House, Berwickshire.)
[2] Transcript, H.M.C. x (i), p. 137. (Listed as in possession of Charles Stirling-Home-Drummond Moray, Esq., Blair-Drummond and Ardoch, Perthshire.)
[3] Eight published in Jared Sparks, ed., *Works of Benjamin Franklin*, 10 vols. (Boston, 1836–40).
[4] Microfilm held by the Library of Congress, Washington, D.C.

(i) Letters, 1880–3, from George Wrey to his aunt, Mrs. C. E. Stuart, describing his hunting trips in the Western part of America, his orange groves in Florida, and plans to cultivate vines in California.

SOCIETY IN SCOTLAND FOR PROPAGATING CHRISTIAN KNOWLEDGE. Papers. 1760, 1839.

In the eighty-five boxes of letters and papers, the following relate to America:

(a) An account of some attempts of the Society to christianize the North American Indians, n.d.

(b) A commission to correspondents in New England, 1760, from the Society in Edinburgh.

(c) Letter, Lebanon, Conn., 1 Dec. 1760, by Eleazar Wheelock to William Hyslop, concerning 'perishing state of the pagans of this land', presumably the Delawares; also mentions Rev. John Brainerd.

(d) Report on a visit of investigation to America in 1839, in connexion with the fund under the Society's charge for the education of Indians.

MURTHLY CASTLE AND GRANDTULLY MUNIMENTS. Letters.[1] 1841–5.

One of the thirty-four deed boxes, labelled 'Grandtully Correspondence, 1841–1845' (c. 1,450 letters), contains a number of letters from Americans to Captain William Steuart, later Sir William Drummond Steuart of Grandtully. The writers include William Sublette, fur-trader, and Washington Hancock, and refer to trans-Mississippi affairs. There are also letters from the artist A. J. Miller who accompanied Steuart on his travels in the United States.

The Library, University of Edinburgh, EDINBURGH 8

LAING MANUSCRIPTS. 1635–1832.

These are part of the collection formed by David Laing (1793–1878), antiquary and librarian to the Signet Library. Since these have been covered by an H.M.C. report only the more important items are noted. (*Letters unless otherwise stated.*)

(a) Edward Gorges, Baron Gorges, President of the Council of New England. Copy of a petition to the King on behalf of the members of the Council for the drawing of the patents to their lands in terms of an arrangement made, 1 May 1635. Officially certified copy used in the Chancery suit between John Penn and Lord Baltimore, signed by Sir Edward Northey.[2] (La. II. 637/14)

---

[1] See Bernard A. De Voto, *Across the Wide Missouri* (Boston, 1947), and Sir William Fraser, *The Red Book of Grandtully*, 2 vols. (Edinburgh, limited ed., 1868).

[2] H.M.C. Laing MSS. i [72], p. 194.

(*b*) 8 Nov. 1676, from Edward Sherburne to George Wharton, treasurer and paymaster of H.M. Ordnance, desiring him to pay certain sums to some gunners 'appointed to attend the expedition to Virginia'.[1] (La. II. 639/19)

(*c*) 'Coppie of a letter from . . . Carolina, Charleston, 18 May 1680', from N. Matthew, giving a description of Charleston (4 pages). (La. II. 718/1)

(*d*) Diary, 1661–1722, of the Rev. Francis Borland, clergyman at Glassford, Lanarkshire. He spent some time at Boston, 1682–5, 1690–1, 1700–1.[2] (La. III. 262)

(*e*) Brief memorandum, 8 Oct. 1700, sent by R. Wodrow to R. Birnie. Queries about Virginia.[3] (La. III. 355, f. 81)

(*f*) Treasury order, 8 July 1719, for payment to Jonathan Forward, a London merchant, for the transportation of malefactors to Maryland.[4] (La. II. 640/26)

(*g*) 28 May 1735, from Samuel Mather, Boston, to an unknown correspondent, touching on the state of education and religion in New England.[5] (La. II. 184)

(*h*) List, 25 Aug. 1740, of military stores sent to General James Oglethorpe for the defence of South Carolina and Georgia.[6] (La. II. 640/30)

(*i*) 22 July 1741, from Rev. Alexander Malcolm, Marblehead, Mass., to Prof. Charles Mackie, about Rev. Hooper and Rev. Charles Chauncey of Boston, opponents of George Whitefield.[7] (La. II. 90)

(*j*) 13 Aug. and 1 Sept. 1742, from Arthur Robertson, Glasgow, to Thomas Crawford of Cartsburn about George Whitefield.[8] (La. II. 480/5)

(*k*) Letters, 3 Dec. 1743, from Governor Gabriel Johnston, Edenton, N.C., to the Bishop of . . . and to Adair, about Lord Carteret's 'prodigious bargain' in the Carolinas and elsewhere, and a statement of Johnston's financial condition.[9] (La. II. 647/5)

(*l*) Suggestions by Duncan Forbes of Culloden after the Rebellion of 1745 include the possibility of transporting some of the Highlanders to America. *c.* 1746–7.[10] (La. II. 123)

(*m*) Report on Arthur Dobbs's petition to the Privy Council on the subject of the Northwest Passage. 10 Aug. 1748.[11] (La. II. 641/24)

(*n*) 'Statement of the relative numbers belonging to the Church of England and to the Dissenters in the province of Nova Scotia.' *c.* 1762.[12] (La. II. 678)

[1] Ibid., p. 410.　　　　　　　　　　　　　　[2] Ibid., p. 331.
[3] Printed in *Early Letters of Robert Wodrow, 1698–1709*, ed. by L. W. Sharp, p. 115 (Edinburgh, 1937).　　　[4] H.M.C. Laing MSS. ii [72], p. 204.
[5] Extract, ibid., pp. 240–1.　　　　　　　[6] Ibid., p. 324.
[7] Extract, ibid., pp. 327–8.　　　　　　　[8] Extracts, ibid., pp. 329–30 and 335.
[9] Extracts, ibid., pp. 336–40.　　　　　　[10] Transcript, ibid., p. 382.
[10] Transcript, ibid., pp. 395–9.　　　　　[12] Transcript, ibid., pp. 434–7.

(*o*) Instructions, 7 Dec. 1763, from George III to George Johnstone, Governor of West Florida.[1] (La. II. 76)

(*p*) A bundle of correspondence, 1775–6, about General Simon Fraser's raising of the 71st Regiment to engage in the war in America.[2] (La. II. 506)

(*q*) 2 Aug. 1775, from William H. Zuylestein, 4th Earl of Rochford, to the Lords Commissioners of the Treasury, about Major Roche's plan for raising recruits in Ireland to serve in America.[3] (La. II. 640/40)

(*r*) 10 June 1776, from George Warrington, collector of customs, White-haven, to Sir James Johnstone about the arrival of the ship *Kings Fisher* from Cape Ann, Mass.[4] (La. II. 502)

(*s*) 14 July 1776, from N. Ferguson, Ayr, to Archibald Crawford, Carts-burn, giving 'an account of the state of Pennsylvania and the other provinces at the time of my leaving it'.[5] (La. II. 480/9)

(*t*) Three letters, 1777–8, from Lieut.-Col. Patrick Ferguson, about the beginning of the War of Independence.[6] Also a copy of a letter from T. Butler to Captain Douglas describing the naval battle on Lake Champlain, 1777. (La. II. 456)

(*u*) 8 Jan. and 24 Feb. 1777, from Alexander Cochrane, Rhode Island, to his brother Archibald, Lord Cochrane, about the engagement with the Americans at White Plains, N.Y.[7] (La. II. 98/5)

(*v*) 'Address to His Excellency the President and other members of Congress etc.' Apparently drawn up by Professor Adam Ferguson (2 pages, incomplete). *c.* 1778. On peace between Britain and America. (La. II. 73)

(*w*) Headquarters, 9 June 1778, from George Washington to Dr. Adam Ferguson of Edinburgh University, regretting that the passport requested cannot be issued to Sir Henry Clinton 'without the previous direction of Congress'. Signed by Washington, but in the hand of his secretary, Robert Hanson Harrison.[8] (La. II. 163)

(*x*) 19 Dec. 1780 and 23 Apr. 1781, from Francis Dundas to his brother Robert, from Charleston, S.C. and from Wilmington, N.C., about various campaigns.[9] (La. II. 500)

(*y*) Philadelphia, 11 Sept. 1786, from Dr. Walter Minto to David Steuart Erskine, 11th Earl of Buchan, about the probability of his accepting the chair of mathematics at Washington College in Maryland, and other matters.[10] (La. II. 588)

---

[1] H.M.C. Laing. MSS. ii [72], p. 440.   [2] Brief extracts, ibid., pp. 486–7.
[3] Ibid., pp. 470–1.   [4] Extract, ibid., pp. 488–9.
[5] Extract, ibid., pp. 491–3.   [6] Ibid., p. 494.
[7] Extract and transcript, ibid., pp. 495–7.
[8] See *Writings of George Washington*, ed. by John C. Fitzpatrick, vol. xii, p. 39 (Washington, D.C., 1934).
[9] Transcript, H.M.C. Laing MSS. ii [72], pp. 503 and 509–11.
[10] Transcript, ibid., p. 524.

(z) New York, 28 Oct. 1787, from W. Minto to the Earl of Buchan about New Jersey College, the American Constitution, &c. (La. II. 588)

(aa) 26 Apr. 1793, from James Fraser, Edinburgh, to Sir Henry Moncreiff about his problems as a Loyalist.[1] (La. II. 500)

(bb) 25 May 1794, from Washington's secretary, Tobias Lear, to the Earl of Buchan, on opportunities for emigrants from Great Britain to America. (La. II. 588)

(cc) Philadelphia, 20 Feb. 1796, from George Washington to the Earl of Buchan, about his preference for farmers from Britain rather than 'the slovenly farmers of this country'.[2] (La. II. 588)

(dd) Paris, 28 Feb. 1806, from James Bowdoin, American Minister to Spain, to Sir Robert Barclay about Anglo-American political and economic relations; and a covering letter from Barclay to C. J. Fox.[3] (La. II. 504)

(ee) St. Marys, Ga., 20 July 1807, from George Ker to General Walter Ker about his loyalty to Great Britain and about American anger over the *Chesapeake* affair.[4] (La. II. 118)

(ff) A collection of forty-four letters, 1811–19, to and from Thomas Douglas, 5th Earl of Selkirk: chiefly correspondence with Alexander McDonald, Writer to the Signet, on the obtaining of settlers from the Scottish Highlands for Hudson Bay, Assiniboia, the Red River area, &c.[5] (La. II. 202)

(gg) In addition to the above, the Laing Manuscripts are also noted as containing letters from: William Ellery Channing to R. Ainslie, 9 November 1832[6] (La. II. 369); George Johnstone[7] (La. II. 73); Tobias Lear, secretary to George Washington[8] (La. II. 588); Walter Minto[9] (La. II. 588); John and Charles Wesley[10] (La. II. 125); and George Whitefield.[11] (La. II. 125 and La. II. 283). The Lear and Minto letters are to David Steuart Erskine, 11th Earl of Buchan.

COLDEN, CADWALLADER (1688–1776). Papers.

Lieutenant-Governor of New York 1761–76. Early American scientist.

(a) Notebook of 'Notes from the lectures of Wm. Law, Regent at Edinburgh, 1705'. (Df. 9. 84)

(b) Materials for a new edition of Colden's *The Principles of Action in Matter* (London, 1751). Printed, with manuscript notes and corrections. (Dc. 1. 25–26)

---

[1] Extract, ibid., pp. 558–9.

[2] Transcript, ibid., pp. 587–8. See *Writings of George Washington*, ed. by John C. Fitzpatrick, vol. xxxiv, pp. 471–2 (Washington, D.C., 1940).

[3] Transcript, ibid., pp. 697–8.   [4] Extract, ibid., pp. 710–12.

[5] Selection, ibid., pp. 716–56.   [6] Ibid., p. 801.

[7] Ibid., p. 144.   [8] Ibid., p. 530.   [9] Ibid., p. 530.

[10] Ibid., i, p. 379.   [11] Ibid., i, p. 379 and ii, p. 804.

(c) Supplement to *The Principles of Action in Matter*, 1757, by Cadwallader's son David. Printed, with manuscript notes and corrections. (*In* Dc. 1. 26)

BRAINERD, DAVID (1718–47). Journal. 1745–6. (Dc. 7. 68)

Missionary. From 1742 until his death Brainerd, commissioned by the correspondents of the Society in Scotland for Propagating Christian Knowledge, was a missionary among the American Indians. The journal appears to be the same as that printed in Jonathan Edwards, *Life . . . of David Brainerd*, pp. 375–437 (Edinburgh, 1765), and covers the Crossweeksung, New Jersey, Indians.

BROWN, ANDREW (1763–1834). 'History of North America during the War of Independence and afterwards.' (SRA 1–6)

Scottish Presbyterian minister. Ordained in 1787 to pastoral charge of the Scottish church, Halifax, N.S. Returned to Scotland in 1795. In 1801 he was appointed Professor of Rhetoric and Belles Lettres in Edinburgh University, and in 1813 elected moderator of the General Assembly of the Church of Scotland. He left an unfinished history of America, interesting for the accounts of the curious conferences and harangues of the Indian chiefs in good classical style.

JARDINE, SIR WILLIAM (1800–74). Correspondence: 6 letters. 1830–40. (Dk. 6. 20)

Naturalist. Six letters to Jardine from: R. Parnell, New Orleans, 30 Jan. 1840, with his impressions of that town; R. MacDowall, New York, 23 Apr. 1840, about the ornithology of West Africa; W. MacMillan, Librarian and Collector of Natural History to the University of Alabama (four letters), 1830–1, mostly about ornithology.

HALLIWELL-PHILLIPPS, JAMES ORCHARD (1820–89). Correspondence: 157 letters. 1851–85. (H.-P. Coll. L.O.A.)

Shakespearian scholar. One hundred and fifty-seven letters to Halliwell-Phillipps mainly on literary and personal topics, six on Shakespeare. Correspondents include: Hiram Corson of Cornell University (11); Joseph Crosby of Zanesville, Ohio (6); Horace H. Furness (55); W. G. Medlicott of Massachusetts (6); Henry Stevens, bookseller, of Vermont and London (70); Genevieve Ward, actress (3); Justin Winsor, librarian of Harvard University (6). There is one letter from Halliwell-Phillipps to Horace H. Furness.

AGASSIZ, ALEXANDER (1835–1910). 288 letters. 1867–1910.

Seventy-one letters to Sir C. Wyville Thomson and 217 to Sir J. Murray. Mainly about coral reefs.

MUIRHEAD, ROLAND EUGENE (1868–   ). Papers.[1] 1900.

In 1900 Mr. Muirhead (in 1957 the president of the Scottish Congress and a well-known Scottish nationalist) visited the Co-operative Brotherhood Colony of Burley, Washington (one of the last communitarian attempts of the Social Democracy of America), and the Mutual Home Association, an anarchist colony at Home, Henderson Bay, Washington. The papers relating to this visit are:

(a) His diary for 1900, which also contains material on his visit to British Columbia.

(b) A few letters between Mr. Muirhead and the anarchists Jay Fox and Oliver Verity, leading members of the Mutual Home Association.

(c) Copies of the anarchist journals *Agitator* and *Discontent*.

(d) Fifteen photographs of the two colonies.

The collection is a small but interesting record of a vanishing form of American social experiment. (The final disposition of the papers is at present uncertain, but at least a microfilm of them will be deposited in the University Library.)

MISCELLANEOUS AMERICAN MATERIALS

(a) Letter, Charleston, S.C., 17 (rest of date torn off), from Lionel Chalmers to Robert Whytt, Professor of the Theory of Medicine, Edinburgh University 1747–66, mentioning an outbreak of smallpox. (Dc. 4. 98/1)

(b) Letter, 11 Dec. 1777, from David Murray, 7th Viscount Stormont, from America, to William Eden, Baron Auckland, on the War of Independence. (Dc. 4. 101–3)

(c) List of American students in Professor John Walker's classes in natural history and mineralogy at Edinburgh University, 1783–1800. (From the original records in Walker's own hand.) (Dc. 1. 18/9)

(d) Nova Scotia: defence in the event of war with America. 49 letters. 1791–1813.

Forty-nine letters, the authors of which include Henry Dundas, Sir John Wentworth, and others concerned with North American defence. (Dc. 1. 15)

(e) American Physical Society. Dissertations, 1794–7. (SRX)

This was a society of American medical students at Edinburgh University.

(f) Jefferson, Thomas. Letter (copy). 1803. (Dc. 6. 111, ff. 83–84)

Copy of a letter, Washington, D.C., 10 July 1803, to the Earl of Buchan. The copy is in the Earl's hand, and was sent by him as a gift to Dugald Stewart on 21 Dec. 1803. Jefferson thanks the Earl 'for a volume on the life and writings of Fletcher of Saltoun'; praises his states-rights sentiments; and discusses the war between Britain and France.

[1] See 'Private papers: an unexpected Scottish Nationalist source', *Bulletin of the British Association for American Studies*, no. 5, p. 32, 1957.

(g) 'Universities of France MSS.' 1 volume. The volume relates to l'Université Imperiale, and contains documents dated 1808–13. (Dc. 6. 82)

An undated six-page memorandum in the volume is entitled 'Idées sur l'établissment d'une maison d'éducation française et d'une maison de commerce aux États Unis d'Amérique'. There is no indication of the author.

William Younger & Co. Ltd., Abbey and Hollyrood Breweries, EDINBURGH 8

BRUCE, ALEXANDER LOW (1839–93).[1] Diary of American journey. 1873.

Scottish partner in the Younger's brewery business. Married Agnes, daughter of David Livingstone, the African explorer. Keenly interested in the promotion of British interests in Africa and a founder of the Royal Scottish Geographical Society. Did much to advance the Younger business, travelling to the United States in 1873. His journal of this visit consists of fifty-seven pages which cover the period 15 Sept.–8 Dec. 1873. It consists mainly of observations on the American beer and brewing trade with reference to Younger's interests; but there are some comments on the financial crisis of 1873, and other general topics. The journal also contains copies of business letters written home to Younger's; a 'bill of fare' from Gleason's Restaurant, Little Rock, Ark.; and two specimens of labels from American bottled beer.

L. A. Hogg, Esq., 17 Coillesdene Crescent, JOPPA

SIMPSON, ROBERT (1772–1844). '. . . Narrative of a Scottish Adventurer: from the Memoirs of Robert Simpson, Esqr., Edinburgh (1827).'

This narrative has been reprinted in the *Journal of the Presbyterian Historical Society* (Philadelphia), vol. xxvii, pp. 41–67, 1949. It describes the experiences of a young man who emigrated at the age of sixteen from Scotland to America and settled in Philadelphia for nine years, 1788–97. He was apprenticed to the proprietor of the *Philadelphia Gazette*, and subsequently became a bookseller and publisher. The narrative gives much information about conditions of life in America.

H.M. Customs and Excise, LEITH

See H.M. Customs and Excise, London (p. 205).

[1] See David Edwin Keir, *The Younger Centuries: the Story of William Younger & Co. Ltd., 1749 to 1949* (Edinburgh, priv. print., 1951).

MORAYSHIRE

Sir William Gordon-Cumming, Blairs House, ALTYRE, Forres

GORDON PAPERS. 2 letters. 1684.

(a) 4 Jan. 1684, from Robert Barclay, the Quaker apologist, to Sir John Gordon, on emigration to East Jersey.[1]

(b) 26 Mar. 1684, from Gawen Laurie [Lawrie], Deputy Governor of East Jersey, to a correspondent whose address has been lost, in which he gives a detailed description of East Jersey, especially its agriculture.[2]

Mrs. Wharton-Duff,[3] Darnethills, ORTON

DUFF OF BRACO PAPERS (per J. and F. Anderson, 48 Castle Street, Edinburgh).

Among the 'Correspondence, 1713–1853', of this collection, mainly family and social, is a letter, July 1775, Charles Town Heights, Boston, from William Braco Gordon, describing military life during the War of Independence.

N.R.A. (Scotland).

RENFREWSHIRE

H.M. Customs and Excise, GREENOCK

See H.M. Customs and Excise, London (p. 202).

Public Library, High Street, PAISLEY

ANTI-SLAVERY PRESS CUTTINGS. 1846. In *Paisley Pamphlets. 1845–1846*.

Mainly from the *Paisley Herald and Renfrewshire Advertiser*, entitled 'Anti-Slavery meetings in Paisley by Messrs. Douglass, Buffum, Thompson and Wright, during the months of March, April & May, 1846'. The collection

---

[1] Transcript, H.M.C. vi, p. 684. [2] Ibid., pp. 684–5.
[3] The owner is now deceased and the papers have been offered to the Scottish Record Office.

describes the Paisley activities of Frederick Douglass, Arnold Buffum, George Thompson, and Henry C. Wright in their campaign throughout Scotland in 1846 against the new Free Church of Scotland's acceptance of contributions from Presbyterian and other Scots in America who had interests in slavery.

ROSS AND CROMARTY

H.M. Customs House, STORNOWAY

See H.M. Customs and Excise, London (p. 203).

SELKIRKSHIRE

Duke of Buccleuch, BOWHILL HOUSE, Selkirk

BUCCLEUCH AND QUEENSBERRY MUNIMENTS. Townshend Papers. (1 bundle.) 1751–85.
Miscellaneous papers include a stray bundle of Townshend Papers, 1751–85, mainly correspondence on American affairs.

N.R.A. (Scotland).

SHETLAND ISLANDS

H.M. Customs House, LERWICK

See H.M. Customs and Excise, London (p. 203).

SUTHERLAND

Duke of Sutherland, DUNROBIN CASTLE, Golspie

SUTHERLAND PAPERS. Letter. 1658.
13 July 1658, from Rachell Newport to her brother, Sir R. Leveson, mentions her grandson who has just returned after four years in Virginia, and says 'there is no profit to be had there, trading is so poor'.[1]

[1] H.M.C. v, p. 145.

NORTHERN IRELAND

ANTRIM

Public Record Office of Northern Ireland, Law Courts Buildings, May Street, BELFAST

There is no county archive system in Ulster, but the Public Record Office acts as a repository of private papers as well as of public documents. Indeed, the Office seems extremely energetic in searching out materials relevant to the six counties of Northern Ireland and, when it cannot obtain the originals, in making photographic reproductions, or occasionally typescripts.

Public documents have only been deposited in Belfast since the establishment of the separate government of Northern Ireland in 1921, although some papers of the period prior to partition have been transferred from Dublin.

There is a card index of names mentioned in the records; otherwise the researcher must rely on the list of accessions and the descriptions of the principal collections to be found in the series of Deputy Keeper's *Reports*.

The references to the materials examined were all supplied by the Deputy Keeper and his staff. 'D.O.D.' refers to deposited original documents, 'T.' to transcripts.

DOBBS PAPERS. 1683–1775. (D.O.D. 162)

Arthur Dobbs (1689–1765),[1] Irish author and statesman, Governor of North Carolina 1754–65. Even before he was appointed governor, he was greatly interested in North American affairs, particularly Canada; and he became a vigorous critic of the activities of the Hudson's Bay Company. So the collection includes important manuscripts relating to Canada that he collected, as well as his own papers. Among the latter there are few official papers of his governorship, but more concerning his efforts to stimulate American trade; including the journal of the ship *California* (N. 44) which he dispatched in 1746 to Hudson Bay to find a Northwest Passage. Of particular interest are the following:

(*a*) Journal of Henry Kelsey, 1683–1722.[2] It covers the life of a Hudson's Bay Company official, and gives an account of Kelsey's explorations, north of Churchill, N. Man., in 1689 and two years later among the Indians, actually reaching the Prairies.

(*b*) Twelve or more letters or copies of letters, 1749–52, from Dobbs, or sponsored by Dobbs, concerning conditions and prospects for settlement in North Carolina, also some references to the Ohio region. (Nos. 45–48, 52, 57, 60–61, 69.)

---

[1] See Desmond Clarke, *Arthur Dobbs Esquire, 1689–1765* (London, 1957).

[2] Published as *The Kelsey Papers*, with an introduction by A. G. Doughty and Chester Martin (Ottawa, 1929).

(c) Letter, London, 10 Mar. 1750, from P. Collinson to Dobbs concerning trees and fruits imported from America.

(d) Statement of reasons for high price and scarcity of beaver fur in London. n.d. (c. 1751).

(e) Paper attacking the management of the affairs of the Hudson's Bay Company. n.d. (c. 1752).

(f) Letter, 17 Mar. 1755, from Dobbs to Alex McAulay, on his work in North Carolina and his efforts for direct trade with Ireland.

(g) Anonymous diary, 27 June to 19 Sept. 1759 (about 8,000 words), apparently kept by an officer of Wolfe's staff and relating to the Quebec campaign.

(h) Letters and legal documents relating to the disposal of Dobbs's estates in North Carolina, 1764–75.

FLOYD PAPERS. (T. 1095)

Journal of Capt. Alexander Chesney (1755–1815).[1] The 'journal' is really an autobiography, written at various times and with some additions, concerning previous and subsequent family history, probably by his son, Charles Francis. Alexander Chesney's parents settled in South Carolina about 1768 and prospered; he served under Cornwallis and Hastings, raising companies of Loyalists. The descriptions of Loyalist sentiment and action are detailed and interesting. He then returned to press claims for compensation in London, and became a customs officer in County Down.

MACARTNEY PAPERS. 1770–89. (D.O.D. 572)

George Macartney (1737–1806), 1st Earl Macartney; statesman, Secretary for Ireland 1769–72. Many of the letters come from Thomas Allan, an M.P. in the Irish Parliament, who appears to have acted as a kind of agent for the Irish government in London.[2] Macartney was not directly involved in American affairs. A typed calendar has the following American entries:

(a) Discussion of Burke's motion on America. 1770. (Vol. 3, no. 67.)

(b) Lord North and the repeal of the American Acts. 1770. (Vol. 3, no. 40.)

(c) Commons debate on American taxes. 1770. (Vol. 3, no. 43.)

(d) Repeal of American duties. 1770. (Vol. 3, no. 39.)

(e) A justification of the War of Independence. 1789. (Vol. 9, no. 49.)

[1] Published as *The Journal of Alexander Chesney, a South Carolina Loyalist in the Revolution and after*, ed. by E. Alfred Jones and others (Columbus, 1921). (Ohio State University Studies. Contributions in history and political science, no. 7.)

[2] See Edith M. Johnston, 'The Career and Correspondence of Thomas Allan, c. 1725–1798', *Irish Historical Studies*, vol. x, pp. 298–324, 1957.

PERCEVAL-MAXWELL PAPERS. 1774–8. (Transcripts and photostats.) (T.1023)

The American section of these papers mainly concern Richard Montgomery, (1736–75), a distinguished general in the Continental Army, who was born in Donegal (his father was M.P. for Lifford), and served at the taking of Quebec in 1759. In 1772 he settled in America, at Rhinebeck, N.Y., and in 1775 was appointed brigadier-general by Congress, and the attack on Canada fell into his hands; he was killed in the assault on Quebec. Some of the later documents may have passed through the hands of Hugh Maxwell, born in Ireland, emigrated to New England, also a distinguished American officer. There is a typed Calendar.

(a) Loyal address, Sept. 1774, of Canadian citizens of Quebec to George III dissociating themselves from 'murmures du tres petit nombre'. (No. 112)

(b) Letter, 21 Feb. 1775, of Samuel Adams, W. Mackay, and Joseph Warren on behalf of the Boston Committee of Correspondence to certain 'friends of liberty' at Quebec (Zachary McCawley, John Aitkin, John Lee, John Patterson, John Wells, and Randal Meredith) arguing the American cause. (No. 113)

(c) Draft of a reply, 12 Apr. 1775, to the above, criticizing 'the mode the Congress at Philadelphia thought proper to pursue'. Ignorance and the power of the priests make any concurrence with the rebels unlikely in Quebec, and besides they expect speedy redress of grievances from the next Parliament. (No. 114)

(d) Letter, 18 May 1775 (endorsed 'a true and exact copy') from Ethan Allen to James Morrison and 'the merchants that are friendly to the cause of liberty in Montreal', demanding provisions for the Continental Army. (No. 115)

(e) 'Resolutions of His Majesty's loyal subjects and inhabitants of the city of Quebec' to secure property, peace and order (the leading signatures are all of English officers!), 20 July 1775. (No. 116)

(f) Various letters, 22 Oct. 1775–19 Jan. 1776, from Richard Montgomery to Governor Carleton and others demanding the surrender of Montreal and then Quebec, and concerning treatment of prisoners of war. The letter, 19 Jan. 1776, is from Donald Campbell to Clinton, thanking him for General Montgomery's watch, and referring to treatment of prisoners, &c. (Nos. 117–21)

(g) Monthly return, 1 Apr. 1776, of H.M. forces in the garrison at Quebec. (No. 22)

(h) General Schuyler at Saratoga to Col. John Paterson giving detailed orders for his regiment to go to Quebec, 29 Apr. 1776. (No. 123A)

(i) Contemporary copy of a letter, 24 May 1776, from Moses Hazen, La Prairie, Que., to the Commissioners of Congress at Montreal describing a visit to Benedict Arnold's camp and discussing policy towards the Indians. (No. 124) (*j*) Printed circular (in French), 31 Jan. 1778, from H. T. Cramahé to the officers of the militia asking for continued vigilance, and announcing the rates of compensation for those who took part in the campaigns of 1776 and 1777. (No. 125)

(*k*) Letter (in French), 18 Sept. 1778 [or 1779?] from Jas. Livingston, to the officers of the militia, asking them to bring their men to La Pointe Olivie, Que., and conveying the thanks of General 'Bastonay'. (No. 126)

DOWNSHIRE   PAPERS   (HILLSBOROUGH   COLLECTION).
Letters. 1778–9. (D.O.D. 607)

The large collection of papers relating to Wills Hill, 1st Earl of Hillsborough, and 1st Marquis of Downshire (1718–93) is, from an inspection of a typescript calendar in the Record Office, mainly estate papers having almost no reference to his service as Lord North's Secretary of State for the Northern Department of Europe during the later part of the War of Independence, 1779–82. However, it includes the following:

(*a*) Belfast, 28 Nov. 1778, from Thomas Greg to Lord Downshire expressing anxiety for his property at New York and Dominica. He has sent his son to New York and asks for letters of recommendation for him.

(*b*) 6 May 1779, from Haddon Smith, formerly rector of Savannah, Ga., to Downshire, thanking him for the vicarage of Kilmud (or Kilmood), County Down, but asks for a compensation or pension as well.

(*c*) Memoranda, 21 June 1779, from Robert Hodgson setting out a plan for the military and economic domination of North and South America by the utilization of the British West Indies and Nicaragua as military and naval bases.

DUNLAP, JOHN (1747–1812). Letters. 1780's. (T. 1136)

Immigrant to Philadelphia from Strabane, County Tyrone, printer of the *Pennsylvania Packet*, printer to the Convention of 1774, to the First Continental Congress, and of the Declaration of Independence. An incomplete examination showed about a dozen letters, mostly in the 1780's, mostly on family affairs, but some account of his role as a captain of the militia in putting down the rebellion of 1794 in Western Pennsylvania.

MASSEREENE-FOSTER PAPERS. (D.O.D. 562)

Among this huge collection, 1625–1845, a basic source for Irish eighteenth-century history, the papers of John Foster, Baron Oriel (1740–1828) and of his father Antony, contain many important references to trade with America. John Foster was Chief Baron of the Exchequer 1766–77; both John and Antony were closely connected with the Linen Board. For further details of the general nature of the collection see Deputy Keeper's *Report* for 1949–50, pp. 13–17. Time allowed only a quick inspection of the following papers in which the typescript calendar specifically mentions America, but obviously many general headings under 'Linen' would also refer to such exports.

(*a*) Bundle of about two dozen long letters and highly detailed statistical reports, 1763–97, on Irish-American trade, some on London's exports to America, American Loyalists, abstracts of American laws, including that setting up a bank of the United States. (No. cviii)

(*b*) Six manuscript and annotated printed drafts of different states of a Bill on American trade, 1783–5. (No. cl)

(*c*) Bundle of miscellaneous papers: two land sale circulars from New Hampshire, 1785. Printed pamphlet, *Facts and calculations respecting the population and territory of the United States of America, c.* 1797. Some notes on a Bill or Act headed 'Alterations for American Trade Bill, n.d. Copy of His Majesty's Advocate's opinions given to cases referred to him from the Treasury on various problems arising from the Peace Treaty concerning American trade, 1785'. (No. ci)

(*d*) Bundle of papers concerning the Irish Linen Board and exports, and petition to Parliament in 1804 for the removal of export duties; includes a table giving the quantity and type of linen exported to twenty-three different markets in America, Canada, and the West Indies, 1795–1805; also a table of the total quantities and value of all linen exports to America, 1798–1807. (No. ccxcviii)

DAWSON, LIEUT. A. C. Diary. 1818–21. (D.O.D. 618)

This diary of a voyage to the West Indies contains a rather slight account (pp. 168–9) of a short visit to New York. He visits a penitentiary, the dockyards, and generalizes rapidly and tritely about the relative beauty of English and American women and American national expansion.

GLASGOW. Journal of a voyage on board from Liverpool to New York, Oct. to Dec. 1833. (D.O.D. 280)

Journal [a fifth of which is missing] addressed by an unknown writer to his mother, giving full and detailed account of the voyage—usual brutality of crew and apparent fecklessness of passengers in not bringing enough food with them.

DAWSON, LIEUT. ROBERT PEEL. Extracts of letters from the United States. 1838–9. (T. 850)

Dawson, a nephew of Robert Peel, was a young officer with the 2nd Grenadier Guards. He was involved in the operations to crush the rebellion of 1838 in Canada, and the following year toured in the United States, through the north-east to Maryland and Virginia. He was much impressed by both New York and Virginian society. All this he describes in rather simple letters home to his parents.

MITCHEL, JOHN (1815–75). 3 letters. 1854–5. (T. 413)

Irish journalist and Fenian leader who was transported to Van Diemen's Land in 1848, then in 1853 escaped to the United States where he edited the *Citizen* in New York, then the *Southern Citizen* at Knoxville, Tenn., and the *Richmond Enquirer* during the Civil War—he consistently supported the slave power; two of his sons were killed in the Confederate Army. Three letters to a Miss Thompson are from America.

(*a*) New York, 24 Apr. 1854, upholding his defence of slavery against charges of being inconsistent with his work for Irish emancipation.

(*b*) Stonington, Conn., 26 Aug. 1854, describing the puritanical 'dreariness' of Connecticut, professing to prefer Virginia, and arguing that justice can never be expected from England 'until the whole structure of society . . . shall have been destroyed by a revolution'.

(*c*) Tucaleechee Cove, Tenn., 1 Nov. 1855, vividly describing the primitiveness of the mountain people, the beauty of the landscape, the prospects of Tennessee, also criticizing the attitude of the Catholic clergy in Ireland to nationalism and hoping for a war between England and America as the best possible thing for Ireland.

STEPHENS, JAMES (1825–1901). American diary, 13 Oct. 1858 to 25 Mar. 1860. (About 22,000 words.) (D.O.D. 518)

Stephens, the well-known Fenian leader, wrote an account of his trip to secure control of the funds in the hands of the 'Directory' formed in 1848 when revolution seemed imminent in Ireland. He apparently intended to deposit the diary with John O'Mahony as a defence of his own actions. He visits John Mitchel himself at Knoxville, Tenn., who gives him letters to the leaders of the Directory asking them to accede to his wishes as regards available funds. The five recipients were: T. F. Meagher, Judge Robert Emmet, Judge O'Connor, Richard O'Gorman, and Horace Greeley. The diary is a vivid and detailed account of Ireland-in-exile, and of the very beginnings of the Fenian movement.

EMIGRANT LETTERS AND RECORDS. 18th and 19th century (in various collections).

(*a*) Some notes on emigration from Ulster to North Carolina, 1736–7. (T. 342)

(*b*) Letters, 1774–96, written by members of the family in New York and later as merchants in the East Indies to relatives in Newry, County Down. (Blair Family Papers.) (D.O.D. 717)

(*c*) Book of letters, 1786–92, written by Hamilton Young, New York, to his sister Martha Young at Belfast. Include many references to current events. (Duffin Family Papers.) (D.O.D. 729)

(*d*) Some notes on emigration from Newry and district, 1783. (Drennan-Bruce Letters.) (D.O.D. 553, no. 14)

(*e*) Three letters, 1794–6, between William Wade and Joseph Bralston, a prominent freemason, of Philadelphia. (T. 1269, nos. 1–3) (*f*) Some occasional references to emigration in 1796. (Rentals of the McCartney Estate, e.g. D.O.D. 572/21/98/13)

(*g*) Over 100 nineteenth-century letters of the O'Hanlon family in various states in America and at home near Downpatrick, County Down. (D.O.D. 882)

(*h*) Letters, 1810 and 1814, from William Heazleton, Pittsburgh, to John Greeves, County Tyrone, describing conditions in America (Heazleton had opened a store in Pittsburgh); and correspondence settling Heazleton's estate, post-1815. (D.O.D. 592, nos. 10, 13, 16, 17, 18, 26, 29, 30, 32)

(*i*) Thirty letters, 1819–37, to McLurg of Templemoyle from his son Robert, mainly from Philadelphia and New York; the folder also encloses three letters, *c.* 1787, from one David Potlock addressed to Anne McLurg as 'my sister' from Greensburg, Pa., and then Chambersburg, Pa. (T. 1227, nos. 1–33)

(*j*) Two letters, from San Francisco, ? 1851, and Marysville, Calif., 1851, from Thomas Vogan, who had originally emigrated to Australia, but had left there for California in 1849. (D.O.D. 268, nos. 7, 8)

(*k*) Two emigrant letters, one of 1853 from Missouri, and the other, 1865, from Pennsylvania. (D.O.D. 556, nos. 517, 621)

(*l*) There are some references to the emigration of Protestants in 1728 among the 'Groves notes', which are mainly genealogical. (T. 808, no. 15261)

(*m*) Emigrant letters, 1826–61, Doake family, from Kinallen, County Down, and friends and relations in various states in America. (D.O.D. 682, nos. 38, 55, 57, 62)

(*n*) Collection of sixteen letters, 1872–1915, from the Gass family in Indiana and California to the family at home in County Armagh. (T. 1396)

EMIGRANT PASSENGER LISTS: 1792–1870 (incomplete).

The Office contains various transcripts and photostats of lists of emigrants sailing to America, culled from newspapers and other sources: of 1792 (T. 711), of 1802–4 and 1833–5 (T. 1011), of 1804–5 (T. 521), of 1836 (T. 671), and of 1860–70 (T. 1428).

LONDONDERRY

Sir Henry MacDonald-Tyler, The Umbra, MAGILLIGAN, Limavady

TYLER PAPERS. 1828–67.

(*a*) Long letter, New York, 22 Apr. 1828, from William Sampson (the exiled revolutionary of 1798) to Dr. Henry H. Tyler, concerning Tyler's claim for a legacy in America.

(*b*) 'Journal of a Voyage to America',[1] 1836, by Thomas Cather. Cather and Henry Tyler, son of the above Dr. Tyler, made a ten-week tour of the United States, covering most of the inhabited country, meeting many celebrities, including President Jackson, Martin Van Buren, and Henry Clay.

(*c*) Six letters, from Liverpool, New York, Baltimore, Charleston, S.C., Havana, and New Orleans, 2 Feb.–7 July 1836, from Henry Tyler while on the above tour to relatives at home. Mainly descriptive; one of 7 May quite interesting on Southern habits of violence.

(*d*) Seven letters, 19 Mar.–3 Aug. 1836, from Thomas Cather. These are fuller letters than Tyler's; they include references to visits to meet President Jackson, and then Senators Clay and Crittenden in Kentucky; the widow of Wolfe Tone; to a Shaker settlement at Pleasant Hill; and some ordinary but spontaneous comments on the fine prospects for the emigrant from Ireland.

(*e*) Two letters, 1 Aug. 1853 and 17 Mar. 1867 (?), from one D. S. Cooper, a family friend, to Henry H. Tyler, describing briefly his investments on the New York stock exchange; and, very fully, his fishing trips in Maine and New Brunswick. Some inevitable and salty comments on American character.

---

[1] Published in part as Thomas Cather's *Journal of a Voyage to America in 1836* (London and Emmaus, Pa. [Rodale Press], 1955).

REPUBLIC OF IRELAND

DUBLIN

Genealogical Office, The Castle, DUBLIN

Since there has been so much emigration from Ireland to America it is but to be expected that the records of the Genealogical Office would have some relevance to American history. While there is no corpus of material relating exclusively to America, the series of Registered Pedigrees would naturally contain references to families or individuals who had settled in the New World. Again, in the Registers of Grants and Confirmations of Arms occasional entries relating to Americans may be found. To these major series must be added the many other collections—will abstracts, unofficial pedigrees, funeral entries, &c.—which might prove to be of assistance in any effort to ascertain the ancestry or immediate background of people of Irish descent who achieved prominence in American history.

Irish Folklore Commission, 82 St. Stephen's Green, DUBLIN

EMIGRATION TO AMERICA. Questionnaires: 5 volumes. 1955. (Vols. 1407–1411.)

In 1955 Dr. Arnold Schrier, in conjunction with the Commission, prepared a questionnaire to collect oral tradition relating to emigration to America in particular, and former attitudes to America in general. Twenty-one interviewers of the Commission returned twenty-six notebooks of about 100 pages each from all over Ireland. The material was used by Dr. Schrier for his doctoral dissertation submitted to Northwestern University in 1956, 'Ireland and the American emigration, 1850–1900',[1] of which a microfilm is in the offices of the Commission.

Irish Manuscripts Commission, 73 Merrion Square, DUBLIN

The Commission, unlike its English equivalent, does not itself keep lists and indexes of material in archives and private possession throughout the country. But there is little need to do this in the Republic of Ireland, since there are virtually no local archives and the National Library of Ireland

---

[1] See Arnold Schrier, *Ireland and the American Emigration, 1850–1900* (Minneapolis, 1958).

collects vigorously and microfilms whatever records are still in private hands. (The actual work of inspecting such records has, indeed, been temporarily transferred from the Manuscripts Commission to the National Library.)

The Commission, rather, sponsors the publication of manuscripts relating to Ireland, more than a hundred volumes having already been issued. It publishes also the *Analecta Hibernica*, which calendars or prints manuscripts and includes the reports of the Commission:

No. 4, pp. 139–286, Oct. 1932, reprints many documents concerning the Irish in the West Indies in the seventeenth and eighteenth centuries. Some of these documents also relate to Virginia, and include extracts on Irish prisoners transported to Virginia, *c.* 1620. Daniel Gookin (1612?–87), writer on American Indians, in Virginia, *c.* 1621–3. Edmund and Simon Tuchin in Virginia, *c.* 1623–4, two brothers expelled from Ireland for adherence to the Catholic religion who went to Virginia as adventurers in 1623. Two specimens of indentures of Irish servants, *c.* 1677–9, one of which was to serve in Maryland 'or any part within the Cape of Virginia'.

No. 15, pp. 126–7, Nov. 1944 (from the Longford Papers, property of the Earl of Longford, Pakenham Hall, Castlepollard, Co. Westmeath) reprints calendar entries including twenty-one letters, 1776–8, from Richard Pakenham, an officer in the British Army, to his brother Thomas Pakenham, from various places in America during the War of Independence, dealing with current affairs, chiefly the progress of the campaign. Copy of a report dated Port aux Basques, Newf., 20 Sept. [17]86, by Edward Pakenham to a correspondent unknown on Labrador and other parts of the North American continent, dealing with fishing, native customs, French officers, &c. Description, 1815 (with five diagrams), of musket alleged to have been used by the Americans, 1814–15, at Plattsburg, N.Y., and elsewhere, showing a primitive machine gun.

No. 22, pp. 329–94, June 1960, contains papers from the Quit Rent Office in the Public Record Office of Ireland relating to a state-aided emigration scheme in the 1850's (see pp. 544–5).

The Commission has also published:
The Correspondence of Emily, Duchess of Leinster, 1731–1814, ed. by Brian Fitzgerald, vol. ii, pp. 36–38 and 57–60 (Dublin, 1953), contains letters from Lord Edward Fitzgerald written from America in 1782 and 1788.

National Library of Ireland, Kildare Street, DUBLIN

The National Library of Ireland contains probably the largest collection of historical manuscripts in Ireland, and is pursuing a vigorous policy of acquisition, both by microfilming and by the searches throughout the Republic of Ireland by an Inspector of Manuscripts, attached to the Irish Manuscripts Commission.

There is a card index of names of principal families in the collection, and also a card index to a special Autograph Collection. The manuscripts will eventually be indexed as part of a huge undertaking that is under way, to index all materials, printed and manuscript, relating to Irish history—materials abroad are being filmed and will also be included.

It will be seen that the principal American relevance is in the American side of the records relating to the nineteenth-century nationalist movements. Since they are so interrelated they have been grouped together, and are placed first; the other papers follow in chronological order. There may be some other letters of less obvious importance in other collections of post-1848 nationalists.

HICKEY COLLECTION. (MSS. 3225–6)

(a) 'Young Ireland', Volume 1: Typescript copies of two manuscript biographies, each of about 10,000 words, by Michael Cavanagh, of:

(i) Joseph Brenan (1828–57), the poet and Irish Nationalist who fled to America in 1849; describes his life there, first in New York and then in New Orleans.

(ii) John Mitchel (1834–64), the son of John Mitchel (1815–75); joined his father in America in 1853; killed in action while commanding Fort Sumter for the Confederates.

(b) 'Young Ireland', Volume 2: 6 letters (typescript copies). 1854–67. Collection illustrating the 'Young Ireland' movement. Items of American interest are:

(i) Letters from John Mitchel. New York, 18 Feb. 1854, to one Reid, a friend in Tasmania. Describes life in New York and the hostility to his new journal, the *Citizen*. Three letters to Mrs. Williams, a friend in Tasmania. Tucaleechee Cove, Tenn., 24 July 1855, describing at length his rustication and the primitive habits of his neighbours who, he asserts, still believe that they are voting for General Jackson. Knoxville, Tenn., 16 Feb. 1858, announcing his founding of a newspaper 'intended to advocate ... a revival of the slave-trade from Africa'. Washington, D.C., 1 May 1859, mostly describing the success of O'Brien's American tour, and more praise for the Southern cause.

(ii) Two letters from Thomas Francis Meagher to his father. New York, 17 July 1865, mentions that he is joining an emigrant train to Indian Territory, with letter of introduction from the Rev. Father Provincial of the Province of Missouri; Virginia City, Mont., 15 June 1867, mentions that he has been in charge in Governor Smith's absence, and has been inspecting defences against the Indians.

O'BRIEN, WILLIAM SMITH (1803–64). Letters and papers. (MSS. 426–62)

William Smith O'Brien, M.P., 1828–31 and 1835–49, was transported to Tasmania for his part in the rising of 1848. He returned to Ireland in 1856. He visited the United States in 1859. His letters show that he kept in touch with the prominent Irishmen of his time and provide a commentary on the political scene.

There are 3,434 letters, covering O'Brien's lifetime. They are bound into twenty-four volumes and there is a name index with hundreds of entries. In addition there are thirteen unindexed books containing speeches and notes on many subjects. Among the correspondents in America are John Mitchel, Thomas Francis Meagher, Richard O'Gorman, James Gibbons of Philadelphia, Lucius O'Brien of Toronto, the Albany Repeal Association, the Repealers of Newfoundland, Halifax N.S. Repeal Association, and the Emmett Club of New Orleans.

MEAGHER, THOMAS FRANCIS (1823–67). 2 letters. 1858, 1866. (Autograph Collection.)

Young Irelander and American soldier. Two letters to James Roche: 5 Mar. 1858, announces his departure to Central America, and asks Roche to take over the editorship of the *Irish News* in his absence. 28 Mar. 1866, from the Executive Office of the Territory of Montana, urging Roche to come to Montana and to bring John Duffy with him to found an Irish newspaper.

LARCOM, SIR THOMAS AISKEW (1801–79). Papers. 1851–72. (MSS. 7453–7792)

Papers as Under Secretary for Ireland 1853–68. The handlist to the 191 volumes of these papers showed these obvious items of American interest:

(*a*) List of the total emigration from Ireland for each year 1851–9; and some press cuttings on Irish and Scottish emigration from Liverpool, 1860. (MS. 7603)

(*b*) Letters on American Fenianism. 1855–67. (MS. 7517)

    (i) Copies of letters, 1855–67, to Larcom giving reports on Fenianism and the Nationalist movement in America, including a short history of Fenianism.

    (ii) Copies of letters, 1867, from Pierrepont Edwards, Acting Consul in New York, reporting on Fenianism.

(*c*) Letter, 1863, on recruitment in Ireland for the Federal Army in the Civil War (MS. 7585), and another, 1864, on recruitment for American ships. (MS. 7587)

(*d*) Volume of newspaper cuttings of 1865 on Canadian Confederation and the reunion of the United States. (MS. 7470)

(*e*) References to the Fenian raid on Canada and the Canadian trials; to President Johnson's message and to General Meade's report on the raid into Canada, 1866. (MS. 7680)

(*f*) Six volumes of newspaper cuttings, 12 Aug. 1871–23 Sept. 1872, mainly concerned with the *Alabama* incident. (MSS. 7464–7469)

FENIAN ORGANIZATION IN AMERICA. Paper. *c.* 1860. (MS. 5771)

Undated, anonymous—signed 'Cato'—manuscript, *c.* 1860, of about 1200 words describing the Fenian organization in the United States and comparing it with the Irish Fenians, rather to the discredit of the latter; speculates on the possibility of war between Britain and America, but thinks, even then, an American invasion of Ireland unlikely.

'AN ACCOUNT OF FENIANISM FROM APRIL 1865 TILL APRIL 1866 BY ONE OF THE HEAD CENTRES FOR IRELAND: NEW YORK 1866.' (143 folios) 1866. (MS. 5963)

This anonymous manuscript contains considerable information on the activities and membership of the Fenian Brotherhood of America, as well as in Ireland. O'Mahony and Stephens figure prominently; there are some pages on the Fenian raids in Canada.

KEARNEY, FREDERICK. 'Memoir of Major-General Thomas Francis Meagher' (400 pages). 1869. (In Hickey Papers.)

This memoir is a manuscript for a book—never published—by Frederick Kearney, written in New York. Meagher was transported to Tasmania after the unsuccessful rebellion of 1848, but escaped to America in 1852. He served with distinction in the Irish Brigade of the Federal Army, becoming a brigadier-general and commanding the Brigade in their famous stand at Fredericksburg, Va. In 1865 he was appointed Secretary (or Acting Governor) of the Territory of Montana. Over half of the 400-page manuscript is concerned with Meagher's career in America.

DEVOY, JOHN (1842–1928). Letters.[1] 1871–1928. (Devoy Papers.)

Fenian leader. He joined the Irish Revolutionary Brotherhood in 1860, was imprisoned in 1866 and released on condition that he left Ireland, thereafter spending most of his life in America. Devoy apparently preserved nearly every letter sent to him, as well as a very large number of press cuttings, conference reports and Clan na Gael documents. This is a fundamental source for the study of the American aspects of the Fenian movement.

IRISH NATIONAL LAND LEAGUE. American correspondence: 121 letters. 1880–1. (MS. 8291)

Among the records of the Irish National Land League is this file of letters, 1880–1, enclosing donations for relief from individuals and Irish organizations in America, e.g. from Irish famine relief funds in California, Boston,

---

[1] About half the letters have been published as *Devoys Post Bag*, ed. by William O'Brien and Desmond Ryan, 2 vols. (Dublin, 1948–53). Permission to see the letters must be obtained from the representatives of the donor.

New York, Milwaukee, Wis., New Orleans, Georgia, &c.; the Shoemakers Union of New York city contributes; the editor of the *Irish World*, New York, organized appeals, as did J. J. W. Donoghue of the *Chronicle*—among the moneys he forwards is $4,000 from the Democratic Committee of Tammany Hall. Several of the letters are addressed personally to Parnell. A list of such American donations shows about £13,000 contributed between 9 Jan. and 6 Mar. 1880.

IRISH NATIONAL LEAGUE OF AMERICA. 7 letters. 1890. (MS. 8582/2)

From the Rev. Dr. Charles O'Reilley, of Detroit, treasurer of the Irish National League of America, to Dr. Joseph E. Kenney, of Dublin, treasurer of the National League of Ireland. The letters discuss fund-raising in America, the abuse coming from 'the Chicago press', and American-Irish sentiment generally.

HARRINGTON, TIMOTHY CHARLES (1851–1910). American travel diary. 1890. (MS. 2195)

M.P., Hon. Secretary of the Irish National League, prominent in the Land League movement. Harrington was on tour in America with his colleagues Dillon and O'Brien in 1890, raising funds for the Home Rule agitation, when the Parnell–O'Shea scandal broke. The first part of the diary concerns the well-attended fund-raising meetings, but the main part concerns Harrington's disputes with his colleagues over Parnell's leadership of the Irish Parliamentary Party. However, the diary throws some light on the reaction of American Catholics to Parnell's disgrace, both before and after the Irish bishops denounced him.

LUBY, THOMAS CLARKE (1821–1901). 'Brief synopsis of early Fenian events in Ireland and America.' (346 pages.) 1890–1. (MS. 331)

Written as a series of letters by Thomas Luby at Newark, N.J., beginning 27 July 1890, to John O'Leary. Much of the American interest of the diary appears, on a partial inspection, to centre on James Stephens's fund-raising visit to America in 1863; but there are constant references throughout to the American Fenian Brotherhood—detailed and very lively. O'Leary drew on these letters for his *Recollections of Fenians and Fenianism*, 2 vols. (London, 1896).

ANCIENT ORDER OF HIBERNIANS IN AMERICA. Membership ledger. 1911. (MS. 3278)

Gives members names, dues paid, occasional comments, and subscriptions to *Irish News*. The names include most, if not all, of the prominent Irish-American politicians of the day.

CASEMENT, SIR ROGER (1864–1916). Letters. 1915–16. (MS. 8605)

Fourteen letters, 1 Apr. 1915–13 Mar. 1916, to St. John Gaffney. Gaffney was United States Consul in Munich in 1915 until he was dismissed, allegedly for his friendship to Casement. Casement, from Berlin and then Munich, discusses Gaffney's dismissal in a ten-page letter, 1 Nov. 1915; and comments on the American attitude to the British 'fabrications' about himself. Other letters allude slightly to Casement's contacts with Irish nationalist groups in the United States.

ORMONDE PAPERS. 1678–1710.

(a) 'The importation of tobacco', four papers:[1] (In MS. 2382)

(i) Deposition by Col. John Custis of Virginia that he has satisfied the King's Collector in Virginia about duty.

(ii) An invoice for the amount of tobacco shipped for Custis on board the *Providence*.

(iii) Affidavit of one of the crew of the ship that Custis had paid the duty.

(iv) Statement concerning the case, especially on the state of the tobacco when it arrived in England.

All the papers are dated 1678; the shipment took place in Nov. 1678.

(b) In a 'catalogue of letters and papers from 1665 to 1679 inclusive' is mentioned one, 16 Sept. 1678, from James Butler of Boston to Ormonde.[2] (In MS. 2377.)

(c) Letter, Dublin, 26 Nov. 1684, from Israel Feilding to the Earl of Arran, mentions the King's 'rebellious subjects in New England'; and that of 2 Dec. 1684 says that military service there is likely 'to be hot'.[3] (In MSS. 2440 and 2441.)

(d) Letter, Dublin, 5 June 1686, from Primate Boyle to Ormonde speaks of French Protestants, driven from France, desiring now to leave England and Ireland for Pennsylvania.[4] (In MS. 2449.)

(e) Brigadier John Corbet petitions the Earl of Oxford and Mortimer, Lord High Treasurer, 'for a moiety of the matters in the hands of the President and Council of Maryland to be paid to him'.[5] n.d., c. 1710. (In MS. 2495.)

BALFOUR PAPERS. 3 letters. 1764–5.

These letters were written by James Pillson of New York to Harry Brabazon of Drogheda, County Louth, merchant, about the marketing of flax-seed and butter.

[1] H.M.C. Ormonde MSS. n.s. iv [36], pp. 304–5. (Listed as in possession of the Marquis of Ormonde, Kilkenny Castle.)
[2] H.M.C. vi, p. 763.
[3] H.M.C. Ormonde MSS. n.s. vii [36], pp. 289, 291.
[4] Ibid., pp. 423–4.   [5] H.M.C. vii, p. 828.

ISLE ST. JOHN (Prince Edward Island). Account. *c.* 1770. (MS. 246)

A table of the proprietors, giving the size and quality of their holdings, extracts from a report of the Board of Trade, and a copy of the 'Articles of agreement between proprietor and settlers'.

MANSFIELD PAPERS. Letters. 1782, 1874–85.

(*a*) 13 May and 18 June 1782, written by William Snow to his brother Robert of Waterford city, Ireland. He describes his plight as a prisoner in New York though he was offered the post of aide-de-camp to General O'Hara when he would be exchanged. New York is an 'extravagant place' where a dollar has only as much value as sixpence in Waterford.

(*b*) Six letters, 1874–85, to George Patrick Lattin Mansfield (1820–89), of Morristown Lattin, County Kildare, by his first cousin, Owen Mansfield, appealing for aid when the crops of maize failed for two successive seasons in Iroquois county, Ill. The first letter was written after a silence of twenty-five years and a cheque for £20 was dispatched immediately. Money gifts were sent on at least four occasions on the strength of 'hard-times' in Illinois.

OSBORNE, RICHARD BOYSE (1808–*c.* 1897). Diary. (MSS. 7888–95)

Railway engineer. Volume 1 of his seven-volume diary is an account of the life of his grandfather, Richard Boyse of Graige, of his own early life in Ireland, and the financial overthrow of his eccentric father. Volumes 2 and 3 concern life in Upper Canada, whence they emigrated, and then in 1835 a journey to Reading, Pa., stopping at Centerville, Mich., Chicago, St. Louis, Mo., and Baltimore. By 1842 Osborne was chief engineer to the Philadelphia and Reading Railroad, and was the first to make use of the 'iron Howe bridge'. He resigned in 1845 and worked in Ireland for Vignoles on the Waterford and Limerick Railway; met Robert Stephenson, and then worked a short while in Darien as engineer for Graves & Sons of Liverpool. Returning to America he was, successively, 1851–61, chief engineer to the following railroads: the Catawissa, the Camden and Atlantic, the Dauphin and Susquehanna, the Cornwall, and the Lebanon Valley Railroad.

MONTEAGLE PAPERS.

Time did not allow examination of the 105 volumes and the several thousand loose documents that are the papers of Thomas Spring Rice, 1st Baron Monteagle of Brandon (1790–1866), Secretary to the Treasury in Grey's administration 1830–4, Chancellor of the Exchequer in Melbourne's second ministry 1835–9. These papers are largely unexplored and there is no list of them, but there are certainly documents relating to Irish emigration, colonial affairs (including Canadian dispatches), and the slave trade.

ALL HALLOWS COLLEGE, DUBLIN. Letters (microfilms). 1843–77. (P. 2782 and P. 3849–51)

This is a collection of letters the originals of which are in All Hallows College, Drumcondra, Dublin, a college founded in 1842 for the education of missionary priests for foreign countries, especially the countries of Irish emigration. By 1843, bishops from American dioceses were seeking Irish priests. On P. 2782 is a selection of letters from over twenty of the American bishops. Accounts are given of conditions and diocesan organization, with references to contemporary events. At least fourteen are in French.

P. 3849 consists of part of a thesis submitted by Patrick F. Murray for an M.A. degree, University College, Dublin, Autumn 1956. This is 'A Calendar of the Overseas Missionary Correspondence of All Hallows College, Dublin, 1842–1877', which has an introduction and index, a chronological list of documents and a calendar of correspondence from the United States and elsewhere. Only 1,583 letters of the calendar are as yet microfilmed; of these, 1,196 are from the United States, 251 from Canada and Newfoundland, and 136 from the West Indies and Central America. P. 3849–50 give those American and Canadian letters not included on P. 2782.

LALOR CORRESPONDENCE. 1843–84. (MS. 8567)

About thirty family letters, with a few exceptions written to Richard Lalor (1823–93), Tenakill, Mountrath, King's County (Leix); brother of the Irish nationalist James Finton Lalor, M.P. 1880–92. Nine were written by his brother William, a farmer in Wisconsin, who describes the ups and downs of farming. Three were written from the Convent of the Visitation, St. Louis, Mo.—two by a cousin, Mary Anne Murphy—seeking information about Alice Lalor, founder of the Visitation Order in the United States, who emigrated from Ireland in 1784. Other cousins who wrote, mostly about family affairs, were A. M. Darcy, Mary Darcy, Maria Dillon (*née* O'Brien), George Dillon; and H. T. Lalor from New Orleans, seeking some hard-working emigrants.

PAKENHAM-MAHON PAPERS. Letters. 1846–7.

These estate papers contain letters written mainly by Major Denis Mahon (1787–1847) to his agent in Ireland arranging for the emigration of his tenants in County Roscommon to Canada and the United States in May–June 1847. The names and sailing dates of the emigrant ships are given, but no lists of names were found nor is it possible to say from the letters how many emigrated, though an estimate of 1,600 families is mentioned at an early date. Major Mahon was shot, it was alleged, by some of his tenants for his insistence on the emigration scheme.

COOLATTIN EMIGRATION RECORD. List. 1847. (MS. 4974)

A list of the members of three hundred and twelve families from Coolattin, with their ages, who were emigrating to America in 1847, evidently due to distress and evictions on the FitzWilliam estates, County Wicklow.

H.M.S. *PLOVER*. Journal of the voyage (2 volumes). 1852-4. (MSS. 267-8)

Journal of the *Plover*'s Arctic explorations, touching on Alaska and Bering Strait.

LOCKE FAMILY PAPERS. 12 letters, 1858-63; and *c.* 25, 1880-90.

The earlier letters were written by Charles H. Locke to his brother John an official of the Incumbered Estates Court, Dublin, and a writer on Irish economic problems. They describe his wanderings and his efforts to get work from Canada to New Orleans; his adventures in the Confederate Army, his subsequent desertion and surrender. He used money sent to him by John to buy clothes to replace his 'rebel' uniform. He had two married daughters living in Detroit who had given him up for dead. The remainder were written by Richard, son of John Locke, his wife Lelia and children, to Miss Jeannette Locke, Dublin. Richard Locke kept a store in Bonafacio, Fla.; the letters deal mainly with family affairs, and refer to his economic prospects.

KEOGH, MYLES WALTER (1840-76). 32 letters. 1861-9. (MS. 3885)

Letters from or concerning Keogh to his brother Thomas of Carlow. Myles Keogh fought in the Army of the Potomac as a captain of cavalry, later as a colonel. He served in the Mississippi campaign, where he was taken prisoner but soon exchanged; joined General Sheridan's staff and was in the Tennessee campaign. The letters contain graphic descriptions of the fighting and of the Army's morale. (Keogh served in the United States Cavalry in the Indian Wars after the Civil War, and died with Custer at Little Bighorn, Mont.; no papers from this period survive, but there are several mementoes in the National Museum of Ireland.)

O'CAHILL, JOHN M. (1840-1928). Irish verse (3 volumes). *c.* 1863-1926. (MSS. G. 510, G. 529, and G. 543)

Accounts in prose and verse in the Irish language by John M. O'Cahill of Peatwater, Mich., of his experiences in America, notably the Indian Wars, including his captivity. He was born in Templeglantine, County Limerick, and emigrated in 1863.

BUCHANAN, SAMUEL (1837-post 1905). 32 letters (typed copies). 1870-1903. (Buchanan Papers.)

Letters written by Samuel Buchanan to various relatives in Dublin, from Cincinnati, Ohio; Haysville, Ala.; Nashville, Tenn.; and Branchville, Summerton, Silver, and St. Pauls, S.C. They describe the life of a 'rolling stone' who worked as a train collector from Toronto to Niagara Falls; a cotton plantation overseer; cotton grower and mechanical engineer. He described the changed economic conditions on the plantations since the Civil War.

FITZPATRICK OF OSSORY PAPERS. Letter. 1878. (In Autograph Collection.)

Charles E. Starr, of the United States Army, was stationed at Fort Lincoln, Dakota Territory; the letter, 1 Apr. 1878, is written to Bernard Fitzpatrick, Granston Manor, Abbeyleix, Ireland, in reply to a query on hunting trips in the Mid-Western states. Among the guides he suggests are Frank Gruard, Chief of Scouts for General Crook, 'Texas Jack', and 'Buffalo Bill' (W. F. Cody). The letter also records his vicissitudes in the Civil War. Some autobiographical details follow. Starr left Ireland, from Roscrea, County Tipperary, at the age of ten with an uncle who was returning to near Gainesville, Fla., and whose name he adopted.

CLARKE, WAD. c. 120 letters. 1880-95. (MS. 8746)

Emigrated to Canada. Letters written to his mother at Liverpool describing his life in Manitoba.

Basil O'Connell, K.M., 76 Palmerston Road, Rathmines, DUBLIN

O'CONOR PAPERS. 1799-1840.

Collection of thirty-six letters addressed from Philadelphia to Sir Patrick O'Conor, merchant of Cork, and to his son Rear-Admiral Sir Richard O'Conor, about a property acquired by Johannes (John) O'Conor, brother of Sir Patrick in America.

John O'Conor (1750-99) died in Philadelphia, leaving over £6,000 of which Sir Patrick was executor. From an indenture of 16 August 1791 it appears that one Carter Braxton of the state of Virginia by deed of 4 May 1785 signed a bond for £629. 14s. 4d. Arising out of this debt it appears that John O'Conor (or Connor) acquired at least a third part of a tract of 5,400 acres in Luzerne county in Pennsylvania and land in Susquehanna. This land was overrun by squatters and pretensions to the ownership by the O'Conor family were finally abandoned in about 1840. The letters which also deal with trading accounts and with Johannes O'Conor's estate are signed by General Stephen Moylan (a friend of the family) and Sir Patrick's agent.

Public Record Office of Ireland, Four Courts, DUBLIN

The Record Treasury Room of the Public Record Office was blown up during the Civil War of 1922; practically the only records that survived were those that happened to be out of the Treasury Room at the time.

The records before then are described in Herbert Henry Wood, *A Guide to the Records Deposited in the Public Record Office of Ireland* (Dublin, 1919). A statement of what survived appears in the appendices to the 55th and 56th *Reports of the Deputy Keeper of the Public Records of Ireland* (Dublin, 1928, 1931). The situation today is briefly and clearly described in Margaret Griffith, *A Short Guide to the Public Record Office of Ireland*, reprinted by the Stationery Office, Dublin, 1952, from *Irish Historical Studies*, vol. viii, no. 29, Mar. 1952. Subsequent acquisitions are listed in the 57th and 58th *Reports of the Deputy Keeper of the Public Records of Ireland* (Dublin, 1936, 1951).

It should be remembered, however, that the papers of the former Chief Secretaries of Ireland were kept in the State Paper Office, Dublin Castle (see pp. 547–8) some of these, including all the seventeenth-century and most of the eighteenth-century material, had been transferred to the P.R.O. before 1922, but the rest survives.

ABSTRACTS OF EXPORTS AND IMPORTS OF IRELAND.
4 volumes. 1764–73; 1784–8; years ending 25 Mar. 1790 and 25 Mar. 1800. (M 2482–3, 2489–90)

These would appear to be complete returns of the trade of Ireland for the years mentioned. There are tabulated entries giving the names of the ports, countries of consignment, names of the goods, amount and value. Among the goods exported were 'acqua vita', beef, pork, books, bread, butter, candles, drapery, glass, glue, linen, tallow, tongues, fish, salmon, &c. Imports included apples, juniper berries, cider, corn, dyestuffs, furs, nuts, pitch, tobacco, whalebone, &c. Goods were sent to Carolina, New England, New Providence, Pennsylvania, Quebec, Virginia, West Indies.

PROCLAMATIONS.

Among the proclamations, 1701–1875, are the following:

3 Mar. 1795: The embargo was removed on ships sailing for Newfoundland.

10 Apr. 1795: One ordinary seaman was allowed on ships bound for Newfoundland.

31 Oct. 1817: Ships from Charleston, S.C., were to be quarantined due to the prevalence of a 'malignant fever' there.

7 Nov. 1817: Similar. Ships from Savannah, Ga.

TITHE APPLOTMENT BOOKS.[1] 1830's.

These, of possible interest to emigration studies, arise from the Tithe Commutation Acts. There is a typed index by parishes in the Search Room.

QUIT RENT OFFICE: Documents relating to Crown Estates. *c.* 1850's.

This Office was absorbed in the Land Commission in 1943; it had dealt with the quit rents and other land revenues of the Crown, the management

---

[1] Note on these in *Analecta Hibernica*, no. 10, pp. 295–8, 1941.

of Crown property and related matters from the seventeenth century on-wards. There are lists of emigrants from Crown lands to the United States and Canada under a State-subsidized emigration scheme in the 1850's, and also miscellaneous letters and documents relating to the whole scheme. The estates were those at Kingwilliamstown, County Cork; Ballykilcline, County Roscommon; Boughill and Irvilloughter, County Galway; and Kilcon-couse, Offaly.[1]

VALUATION OFFICE COLLECTION.

Of possible interest as sources of emigration studies are:

Reports on the General Valuation of Rateable Property in Ireland (printed), in the 1850's, together with some of the manuscript note-books or 'house-books' used by the inspectors in compiling these reports—these latter will occasionally note that a householder has emigrated.

PARISH RECORDS OF THE CHURCH OF IRELAND.

These are also a possible source for emigration studies. Church of Ireland parish records were made public records in 1875, following the disestablishment of 1869. But a further Act, in 1876, allowed local retention where suitable storage existed. Many registers transferred to the Record Office in Dublin were lost in the fire of 1922; those surviving in the Record Office came in after that date. However, the Record Office can supply information as to which registers survive and whether copies exist of those that have perished.

Royal Irish Academy, 19 Dawson Street, DUBLIN

CHARLEMONT MANUSCRIPTS. 1776–96.

Papers of James Caulfeild, 4th Viscount and 1st Earl of Charlemont (1728–99), Irish statesman. There are nineteen bound volumes of correspondence with a calendar of contents at beginning of each volume. (*Letters unless otherwise stated.*)

(*a*) Memoirs by the Earl of Charlemont briefly mentioning the war in America, and chiefly its effect upon Ireland. 1776–82.[2]

(*b*) New York, 15 Dec. 1777, from C. Lee at New York to Charlemont on personal affairs.[3]

---

[1] *Analecta Hibernica*, no. 22, pp. 329–94, June 1960, prints many of these documents, including the lists of names; the accounts for the voyage; interdepart-mental correspondence between the Commissioners of Woods, the Quit Rent Office and the Treasury; letters and memorials from tenants, local landlords, and agents; and four letters from emigrants shortly after their arrival in the United States.

[2] H.M.C. xii (x), pp. 32, 42, 45, 49, 50, 59.

[3] Transcript, ibid., p. 173.

(c) London, 20 Apr. 1782, from Annesley Shee to Charlemont, suggesting that Ireland might mediate between Britain and America.[1]

(d) 2 June 1782, from Alexander Henry Haliday, a Belfast physician, to Charlemont, describing the conduct and misfortunes of his brother, formerly collector of Charlestown, S.C.—the only collector, he says, 'who had the firmness to get the obnoxious teas stored, instead of being sent back or destroyed'.[2]

(e) St. Petersburg, 10 Sept. 1784, from Lord Carysfort to Charlemont mentions America as an example for Ireland.[3]

(f) Bandon, County Cork, 16 Nov. 1784, from George Wood to Charlemont, commends the non-establishment of any church in the United States.[4]

(g) 31 Dec. 1789, from Sir Edward Newenham, M.P., to Charlemont, in which he quotes extensively from a letter he has just received from Benjamin Franklin, in which the latter describes the formation of the Union, the reluctance of Carolina and Rhode Island to accede, the greatness of George Washington as a statesman, and the desirability of a commercial treaty between the United States and Ireland.[5]

(h) Dublin, 15 Dec. 1791, from Charlemont to A. H. Haliday, in which he states that the American constitution will last only until 'that immense region . . . shall be divided into various states, republics, and kingdoms'.[6]

(i) Belfast, 13 and 20 Nov. 1793, from A. H. Haliday to Charlemont; the former advising quarantine for all ships from Philadelphia, where a plague is raging, the latter expressing satisfaction that this has been imposed.[7]

(j) 19 and 23 June 1794, between Charlemont and A. H. Haliday refer to the 'wisdom and firmness' of George Washington, especially over non-importation.[8]

(k) 29 Oct. 1794, from Charlemont to Edmund Malone deprecating the advisability of war with America; and Malone's reply, 7 Nov., that no such war is contemplated in England.[9]

(l) 26 June 1796, from A. H. Haliday to Charlemont, mentions emigration of thousands of Irish Catholics to America, under pressure of Orange persecution.[10]

ORDNANCE SURVEY OF IRELAND, MANUSCRIPT MEMOIRS. 52 boxes. 1833–9.

Arranged under counties, subdivided into parishes. The Survey, made during the 1830's, provides historical, archaeological, social and other information for most of the counties of Ireland, as well as maps, sketches

---

[1] Transcript, H.M.C. xii(x), p. 401.
[2] Transcript, ibid., pp. 404–5.
[3] Transcript, H.M.C. xiii (viii), p. 6.
[4] Transcript, ibid., pp. 8–9.
[5] Transcript, ibid., p. 113.
[6] Transcript, ibid., pp. 181–3.
[7] Transcripts, ibid., pp. 220, 223.
[8] Transcript, ibid., pp. 242–3.
[9] Transcripts, ibid., pp. 251–2.
[10] Transcript, ibid., pp. 274–5.

and statistics, the last mentioned including 'lists of emigrants, 1833–1839'. These lists are very detailed for Antrim and Londonderry. Short notes on emigration, of a very general nature, occur for Counties of Armagh, Cavan, Donegal, Down, Fermanagh, Leitrim, Longford, Mayo, Sligo, Tyrone. There is a typed calendar.

State Paper Office, Dublin Castle, DUBLIN

The Office was established in 1702 though records date from 1697. Under an Act passed in 1867, papers of more than fifty years standing when fully catalogued and indexed were to be transferred to the Public Record Office of Ireland. By 1922 the State Papers down to 1790 had been so transferred, and as they did not survive the explosion and fire of 1922, the State Papers now mainly date from 1790 to 1924, although there are a few earlier documents. The office is in charge of the Keeper of State Papers to whom queries should be addressed, but permission to inspect State Papers must be obtained from the Secretary, Department of An Taoiseach,[1] Government Buildings, Dublin. At present all documents from 1790 to 1874 are open to inspection.

The main record groups in the State Paper Office containing Americana are the Records of the Chief Secretary's Office, of the Chief Crown Solicitor's Office, and those relating to the Fenian movement. In addition, the records of the period to 1831 include relevant material in the Rebellion Papers; Fane Correspondence; Official Papers, series II. They are arranged in that order (and not chronologically) below.

CHIEF SECRETARY'S OFFICE (C.S.O.). Records.

(a) Series of Registered Papers.

This, the largest and most important series in the Office, covers the period 1818 through 1874 to 1924, and contains the letters inward to the Office of the Chief Secretary to the Lord Lieutenant, the centre of the administration. (Each letter has a notation on it, or in a corresponding file, about action to be taken.) They deal with innumerable aspects of internal government and cover a large variety of subjects. The letters and papers are in files in cartons. Indexes and registers are available. Among items of American interest are the following:

(i) American agents are appointed at the principal Irish ports, 1861–2 (2090, 2128, 2147, 3023, 6847, 10926, &c.).

(ii) Extradition problems are considered at great length during the discussion on the extradition of Michael Hayes, who was suspected of having shot a landlord's agent, from the United States, 1861–2 (14992).

(iii) There were reports that both sides in America were enlisting men for the army from Mitchelstown, County Cork (4372); Cahir, County Tipperary (4608); Charleville, County Cork (4704); &c. 1863–4.

[1] Prime Minister.

(iv) A group of about a hundred men were recruited in Dublin, ostensibly to work on the railways. On arrival in America they were forced to enlist, 1864 (16765). A letter from John Connor to his brother Thomas in Dublin gives some details (14056). It was reported that at least 1,278 enlisted men sailed from Cork (5606).

A list of British subjects who landed in Cork was also noted, 1859 (4817), and there are several references to those whose passage was paid in return for 'information' (3909), &c.

For the years 1845-52 there are separate registers and indexes for Outrage Reports and Crown Witnesses. (For other years see the general registers and indexes to the C.S.O. collection under the heading 'outrage', &c.) There are a few references under appropriate headings, e.g. emigration.

(b) Series of Unregistered Papers. Passenger lists of immigrants to the United Kingdom, 1858-67.

These references are indexed under both 'Emigration' and 'Immigration'. They are lists of passengers supplied by the ship's master giving names, ages, sex, whether married or single, profession or occupation, nationality (English, Scottish, Irish or alien), and the port at which passengers contracted to land. The name of the ship, date of arrival, and ports of departure and arrival are also given. Lists are mostly from Liverpool and Glasgow but there are some from London, Southampton, Greenock, Derry, Cork, and Galway. Ports of embarkation were New York, Portland, Me., Philadelphia, Boston, New Orleans, Dorchester, Mass., St. John's, Newf., Montreal, and Quebec. These lists were supplied to the Lord Lieutenant of Ireland by order of the Commissioners of Customs of 11 Dec. 1858. Some lists are also to be found in the C.S.O. Registered Papers.

(c) Prisoners' Petitions and Cases, 1778-1836. These are petitions from prisoners awaiting trial for criminal offences; some seek to be allowed to emigrate to America. This series was continued after 1836 as 'Convict and Criminal Files'. The petitions are arranged alphabetically.

(d) Country Letter-Books, 1827-51; then Letter-Books, 1st Division, to 1876. These are mostly communications from the Office of the Chief Secretary to other government departments, private individuals, sheriffs, &c. on general matters of administration. Letter-books were sometimes named after the Lord Lieutenant of the period, e.g. Lord Bessborough's Letter-book. They are indexed. American references are comparatively rare.

CHIEF CROWN SOLICITOR'S OFFICE. Records.

Among the records of this Office are a series of miscellaneous papers, in six cartons, c. 1860 onwards. These papers, which are not indexed, deal with many aspects of Fenianism:

Carton 22 contains the official history of Fenianism by Samuel Lee Anderson (son of Matthew Anderson, the Crown Solicitor, and a brother of Sir Robert, Home Office adviser on political crime from 1868—much of the history appears in fact to be Sir Robert's work) and references to American officers who were in the rising of 1867.

Carton 24 has newspaper cuttings from the *Irish American* and the *Irish People*.

FENIAN MOVEMENT. Records.

This large collection consists of letters, reports, printed documents and briefs, newspaper cuttings, photographs, &c., connected with the Fenian movement from *c.* 1856 onwards, in Ireland and in Great Britain and America. Together with the collections in the National Library of Ireland, it is obviously a major source for any study of the growth of the Irish-American influence on American domestic politics and in Anglo-American relations.

(*a*) Fenian files.

The nature of the contents, *c.* 1860 onwards, is noted on the outside of each of the ninety-two cartons and those which seemed relevant were examined. A descriptive list of the contents, of a general nature, is also available.

The following items were noted:

Cartons 62–64 contain dispatches from the British Minister in Washington and the Consul in New York on the strength of the Fenian organization there, *c.* 1867.

Cartons 66–67 contain photographs of suspected persons with their description. The 'former residence' in some cases was America.

Carton 92 has the following inscription on the outside: 'Ireland: Newspaper cuttings &c. received with Sub-Inspector Doyle's reports from America 1859–1861.' These are the reports and press cuttings sent by Doyle during a period of almost two years which he spent in New York observing Irish activities. They include accounts of the Phoenix Society.

(*b*) Fenian Conspiracy Book: the Crown case against Luby, O'Leary, &c. n.d. (title-page torn. 304 pages).

The trial took place in 1865. This book gives the list of prisoners charged with conspiracy; extracts from the newspaper the *Irish People*; the indictments, names of witnesses and copies of documents produced at the trial. There are several references to letters and money alleged to have been received from the Fenians in America. Among the twenty-nine defendants were James Stephens, John O'Leary, Thomas Clarke Luby, Charles J. Kickham, James O'Connor, and Jeremiah O'Donovan Rossa. (Much of the Crown case subsequently appeared in print as *Report of the Special Commission for the trial of Thomas Clarke Luby and Others for Treason Felony* (Dublin, 1866).)

(*c*) Abstracts of cases under Habeas Corpus Suspension Acts.

Three volumes, 1866–74, give names and personal details of persons suspected of being connected with the Fenian movement, and, in many cases, references are given to files with relevant information. There are references to prisoners who had returned from America, or who had been in the army there. In many cases prisoners got their discharge on promising to emigrate to England or America. Addresses and occupations of the prisoners are given.

(d) Fenian papers.

These papers, in 22 cartons, 1867–74, also deal with the activities of suspects and other aspects of Fenianism. The indexes are in calendar form. The Abstracts of cases, above, serve as indexes to these papers.

Note: the indexes to the Chief Secretary's Office Series of Registered Papers (pp. 547–8) must also be consulted.

REBELLION PAPERS.

These sixty-six cartons cover the period before and after the 1798 rebellion, 1796–1803. There is a calendar of them to which a slip index has been made. Items of American interest were sought under the appropriate headings, and the following were noted:[1]

(a) 'The transported felon's sorrowful account of 14 years transportation at Virginia in America' by James Ruel, 'the unhappy sufferer'. (8 pages) n.d.

(b) Portion of a letter, 1 Aug. 1797, written from New York to George Ivie, Dublin, describing a voyage from Europe, the boarding of a vessel by French privateers, scenes on board ship, suspected vessels, boarding houses, wages, &c.

(c) Papers of Thomas Russell (1767–1803), United Irishman. Among these is a letter from Wolfe Tone describing his life in Philadelphia, Washington's aristocratic leanings in politics, &c. n.d.

(d) Colonel Durham of the Fife Fencibles to Rev. C. Soden, 29 May 1796: 'Powder comes from America in flax seed casks.'

(e) Captain Alex. Chesney, Prospect, nr. Kilkeel, County Down, 3 June 1797, to Thomas Pelham, Chief Secretary for Ireland, describing the behaviour of the people of Charleston, S.C., during the War of Independence.

FANE CORRESPONDENCE.

John Fane, 10th Earl of Westmorland (1759–1841), was Lord Lieutenant of Ireland 1790–5. A calendar of the two cartons of documents, which is indexed, is available. Among the few items of American interest are five printed documents on the American and West Indian Intercourse Bill, 1806, giving the case for the petitioners against the Bill, the proceedings of the committee of the port of London, and the position regarding the remaining British colonies in America.

---

[1] Rebellion Papers now include material mentioned in the following printed reports of the Deputy Keeper of the Public Records of Ireland, Dublin: 8th *Report*, Appendix viii, p. 23 (Dublin, 1876); 9th *Report*, Appendix ii, p. 17 (1877); 16th *Report*, Appendix, i, p. 14 (1884); 22nd *Report*, Appendix v, p. 34 (1890).

OFFICIAL PAPERS, SERIES II.

These are calendared partly in two volumes, 1790–1831, and partly in a special calendar entitled 'Calendar of Situation and Relief Papers, 1790–1831'. An index to both sets of calendars is in progress.

(a) The following items were noted in the two-volume calendar: An American vessel in Cork harbour sought permission to sail, 1811. The American brig-of-war *Angus* was at the Pigeon House quay in Dublin Bay, 1813. Distress was reported on British ships due to the regulations on taking passengers to American ports, 1816–19.

(b) Situation and Relief Papers comprise petitions to the Lord Lieutenant, Chief Secretary, and other officials in Dublin Castle from persons seeking employment and assistance, monetary and otherwise. There are petitions from George Breading, 30 May 1810, who wants to go to Baltimore (carton 543); from Thomas Logan, 25 June 1816, and John Franklin, land surveyor, 12 Nov. 1818, to go to America (cartons 584 and 577); and from Michael O'Kelly, 1817, to go to Canada (carton 569). (Similar applications for situations or relief are to be found, of course, among C.S.O. Registered Papers right up until the end of the Dublin Castle administration.)

The Library, Trinity College,[1] DUBLIN

SPANISH AMERICA. 603 folios (*c.* 100 are now missing). First half of seventeenth century. (MS. K. 3. 20)

Papers relating to proceedings—ecclesiastical, civil, and military—in Spanish America in the first half of the seventeenth century. At the beginning of the collection it is stated that they are 'originals'. Spanish (and some Portuguese) is used, and there is a table of contents.

CARIBBEES AND BARBADOS. Papers. (187 pages). Mid-seventeenth century. (MS. G. 4. 15)

Consists of copies of grants, inquiries, &c., in connexion with the grant of the Caribbee islands and Barbados to the Earl of Carlisle; reports of the connexion of the 2nd Earl with the islands, and an account of the island of Barbados. There is also a copy of the charter of the Company of Massachusetts, 1628.[2]

NEW ENGLAND LAWS.[3] 15 folios [n.d. but before 1670]. (MS. G. 4. 8., ff. 118–32)

KING PAPERS. 1704–5.

Correspondence of William King, Archbishop of Dublin, contains items in 1704–5 touching upon the Protestant Church in South Carolina and the plantations.[4]

---

[1] T. K. Abbott, *Catalogue of the Manuscripts in the Library of Trinity College, Dublin* (Dublin, 1900).   [2] H.M.C. viii (i), p. 585.   [3] Ibid., p. 585.
[4] H.M.C. ii, p. 234.

NEW MEXICO AND CALIFORNIA VOYAGES. Bound volume (33 leaves). [late 18th century]. (MS. K. 3. 21)

Written in Spanish, giving an account of missionary voyages and discoveries in New Mexico and California. There is also a diary, pp. 47–63, written by a Jesuit, Father G. Fernando Corsa. (The paper and binding suggest that the manuscript was written in the Philippines.)

R. R. MADDEN PAPERS.

A collection of the papers of R. R. Madden, the historian of the United Irishmen, contains correspondence about exiles in America. (These are entered in Abbott's *Catalogue* under nos. 873, 1469, 1470, and 1472. This information came too late for a search to be arranged.)

LONGFORD

Earl of Granard, CASTLE FORBES, Newtownforbes

GRANARD PAPERS. Letters. 1776–81.

Letters of Francis, Lord Rawdon, including details connected with civil and military affairs in America, 1776–81.[1]

Mrs. B. Walsh, White Hill, EDGEWORTHSTOWN

WEBB, R. D. 3 letters. 1861–2.

Written by Webb, who belonged to one of the New York Militia regiments, to his cousin, G. W. Wilson-Slator, dealing with the American Civil War.

ROSCOMMON

Rev. Charles O'Conor, S.J.,[2] c/o CLONALIS, Castlerea

O'CONOR PAPERS.[3] 1 document. 1766.

A statement of the Irish Catholic case by Charles O'Conor (1710–91), written for Viscount Taaffe, contains, *inter alia*, favourable account of religious liberty in America.

[1] H.M.C. iii, pp. 430–1. An extract from one of the letters is given—a description of the battle of Camden, dated 19 Sept. 1780.

[2] The O'Conor Don is the owner. The present holder of the title is Rev. Charles O'Conor, S.J., Gonzaga College, Ranelagh, Dublin.

[3] Extracts, H.M.C. viii (i), p. 453. Printed in Nicholas Taaffe, *Observations on Affairs in Ireland, from the Settlement in 1691 to the Present Time* (Dublin, 1766).

TIPPERARY

Earl of Donoughmore, KNOCKLOFTY, Clonmel

DONOUGHMORE PAPERS. 3 letters. 1774–6.

16 Mar. 1774, from Lord Townshend to John Hely Hutchinson, on the blockade of Boston and the pending alteration of the Boston Charter. Criticisms of Chatham and 'Rockingham's faction' for alleged support of American independence.[1]

25 Oct. 1775 and 6 Mar. 1776, from Charles Jenkinson to John Hely Hutchinson concerning the rebellion, and debates in Parliament thereon.[2]

[1] Transcript, H.M.C. xii (ix), p. 279.
[2] Transcripts, ibid., pp. 284–5.

INDEX

ALL SUBJECTS, unless otherwise qualified, relate to the United States, e.g. Agriculture is Agriculture in U.S.

NOBLEMEN appear under their family names, with references from their titles. Owners of manuscripts are entered under their titles only. Life dates of persons have been given only when readily available.

Alphabetical arrangement is 'word by word'.

Holders and location of manuscripts are printed in capitals.

Cities and towns are listed under States.

Under States (U.S.), provinces (Canada), islands (West Indies), the arrangement is:

    (i) History (divided by periods).

    (ii) Subject subdivisions. (Please note that DESCRIPTION includes travel; MERCHANTS includes individual merchants and groups of merchants, whilst TRADE covers trade and commodities; IMMIGRANTS covers individual immigrants and groups of immigrants, whilst SETTLEMENT covers also exploration.)

    (iii) Geographical subdivisions.

Abbe, Cleveland (1838–1916), 301.

Abbey, Edwin Austin (1852–1911), 457.

Abbott, Andrew (1743–1819), 43.

Abbott, Charles, 2nd Baron Colchester (1798–1867), 276.

Abbott, Charles Stuart Aubrey, 3rd Baron Tenterden (1834–82), 162, 168, 170, 274, 278.

Abbott, John, 43.

Abbott, Sir John Joseph Caldwell (1821–93), 397.

Abbott, T. K., *Catalogue of the MSS. in the Library of Trinity College, Dublin*, 551 fn.

Abbott Collection, 43.

Abduction, 268.

Abdy, Nicholas, 50.

Abdy Papers, 50.

Abel, A. H., and F. J. Klingberg, eds., *A Side-Light on Anglo-American Relations*, 389.

Abercairny Collection, 511.

Abercromby, James (1706–81), 154.

Aberdeen, 4th Earl of, *see* Gordon, George Hamilton (1784–1860).

ABERDEEN, 491–4; Customs records, 204.

Aberdeen and Orkney, Diocese of, 493.

ABERDEEN-ANGUS CATTLE SOCIETY, 491.

ABERDEEN COMB WORKS CO. LTD., 491.

Aberdeen Papers, 127, 158–9.

ABERDEEN TOWN COUNCIL, 491.

Aberdeen Trades Council, 494.

ABERDEEN TYPOGRAPHICAL SOCIETY, 492.

ABERDEEN UNIVERSITY LIBRARY, 493–4.

ABERGAVENNY, MARQUESS OF, 431–2.

Abergavenny Papers, 431–2.

Abernethy, T. P., *The Burr Conspiracy*, 459 fn.

ABERYSTWYTH, CARDIGANSHIRE, 475–84.

Abolition of slavery, *see* Slavery: Antislavery movements.

Aborigines Friend and Colonial Intelligencer, 122.

Aborigines Protection Society, 121, 388.

Abraham, Judah I., 361.

Académie des Sciences, 343.

Acadia, Settlement, 182.

Acadians, 346.

Acheson, David, 86.

Acton, Sir John Emerich Edward Dalberg, 1st Baron (1834–1902), 17, 169.

Adair, James (c. 1709–c. 1783), 513.

Adair, W. A., 286.

Adam, Charles Fox Frederick (1852–1913), 397.

Coutts, Thomas, 182.
COUTTS & Co., 187–8; 507.
Coventry, F. C. A., 447.
COVENTRY, MRS. FULWAR, 447.
Coventry, Henry (1619–86), 445.
Coventry, Thomas, 1st Baron (1578–1640), 23.
COVENTRY, WARWICKSHIRE, 442.
COVENTRY CITY RECORD OFFICE, 442.
Cowell, John W., 68, 123.
COWES, ISLE OF WIGHT, 74; Customs records, 198.
Cowie, L. W., *Henry Newman*, 312 fn.
Cowie Roxburgh & Co., 467.
Cowley, 1st Baron, *see* Wellesley, Henry (1773–1847).
Cowley, 1st Earl, *see* Wellesley, Henry Richard Charles (1804–84).
Cowley Papers, 274.
Cowper, William (1731–1800), 120.
Cowper Collection, 78.
Cowper-Temple, William Francis, Baron Mount-Temple (1811–88), 92.
Cox, Thomas, 472.
Cracroft, Francis, 118.
Cracroft, Robert Weston, 118.
Cracroft, Sophia, 21.
Cradock, Matthew (d. 1641), 368.
Crafer, I., 264.
Cramahé, Hector Theophilus, 526.
Crampton, Sir John Fiennes Twisleton (1805–86), 92, 93, 177, 178, 247, 274, 287, 384, 385, 391.
Crane, Joseph H., 48.
Crane, Robert Newton (1848–1927), 398.
Cranfield Papers, 80.
Crawford, Archibald, 514.
Crawford, Thomas, 513.
Crawley, George, 105.
Crawshay, Richard (1739–1810), 488.
Crawshay family, 484.
Creole, ship, 151, 159.
Cresson, Caleb, 89.
Creswell, W., 90.
Crevet, John, 303.
Crick, B. R., 'A Survey of Library Resources for the Teaching of American History and Literature in the Universities', *Journal of Documentation* (1958), vii; and A. Daltrop, 'Union List of American Newspapers in Great Britain and Ireland',

Bulletin of the British Association for American Studies (Supplement 1958), vii.
Crick, W. F., and J. E. Wadsworth, *A Hundred Years of Joint Stock Banking*, 245 fn.
Crime, 270; *see also* Capital punishment; Prisons; Probation system; Transportation of criminals.
Crimean War, 1853–6, American opinion, 70, 384, 404, 411, 478; Recruiting in U.S., 70, 92, 156, 171, 178, 384, 385, 386, 434.
Criminal law, 337.
Cripps Papers, 81.
Crittenden, John Jordan (1787–1863), 530.
CROESOR, MERIONETHSHIRE, 487–8.
Croft, John, 92.
Croghan, George (d. 1782), 242, 415, 505.
Croly, Herbert David (1869–1930), 375.
CROMBIE, J. & J., LTD., 492.
Crook, George (1829–90), 543.
Crosbie, James, 463.
Crosby, Joseph, 516.
Crosfield, J. D., 'Richard Smith and his Journal', *J.F.H.S.* (1916 and 1917), 217 fn.
Crosfield, Joseph (1821–79), 217.
Crosfield family, 217.
Crouse, Mrs. L. S. K., 469.
Crowther, Benjamin, 428, 455.
Crowther, David, 428, 455.
Crowther, George, 428.
Crowther, George, & Co., 428.
Crowther, Thomas, 428.
Crowther & Porrit, 428.
Crowther family, 427–8, 455.
Cruden, John, 277.
Cruger, Henry (1739–1827), 417.
Cruger, John Harris (1738–1807), 417, 465.
Crumbleholme, George, 428.
Crump, W., ed., *The Leeds Woollen Industry, 1780–1820*, 456.
Cwrbmawr MSS., 481.
Cyfarthfa Papers, 484.
Cymmrodorion Society, London, 476.
Cuba: 1810–99, 97, 149, 269, 359, 384; Insurrection, 1849–51, 70, 92, 177; Insurrection, 1868–78, 141, 143, 144, 166, 269, 387; Revolution,

Declaration of Independence, 526.

Deer skins, *see* Hides and skins.

Defence: Colonial period, 7, 13, 34; *see also* Army.

Defoe, Daniel (1661?–1731), 182.

Delane, John Thadeus (1817–79), 142.

Delaplaine, John, 90.

Delaware, 17th century, 6, 130.
    Land, 100; Religious history, 244.

Delaware Bay, 148.

Delbridge, John, 40.

Delemare, J., 303.

DELPH, YORKSHIRE, 451–2.

Democracy, 377, 392, 394, 479.

Democratic Party, 141, 146, 149, 320, 325, 394; *see also* Elections.

DENBIGH, EARL OF, 442.

Denbigh, 6th Earl of, *see* Feilding, Basil (1719–1800).

Denbigh Papers, 442.

Denham, J. D., 3.

Denison, George Taylor (1839–1925), 395.

Denison, William, 165.

Denman, Thomas, 1st Baron (1779–1854), 340.

Denmark, Relations with U.S., *see* Relations with Denmark.

Denny, William, 218.

Dent, Robert, 101.

Denton, William (1605–91), 13.

Derby, 14th Earl of, *see* Stanley, Edward George Geoffrey Smith (1799–1869; 15th Earl of, *see* Stanley, Edward Henry (1826–93) *styled* Lord Stanley, 1851–69; 16th Earl of, *see* Stanley, Frederick Arthur (1841–1908).

DERBYSHIRE, ENGLAND, 33–36; *see also* Business records: Derbyshire.

DERBYSHIRE COUNTY RECORD OFFICE, 33.

Description (and travel), *see* Travel diaries; *and subdivision* Description *under place names.*

Deserters, Military and naval, 74, 268, 294, 295, 296, 301.

Despatch, ship, 207.

DEVIZES, WILTSHIRE, 445.

DEVON RECORD OFFICE, 38–39.

DEVONSHIRE, DUKE OF, 33.

DEVONSHIRE, ENGLAND, 36–42; *see also* Immigrants from Devon.

Devonshire Association, 38.

Devonshire Papers, 33.

Devoy, John (1842–1928), 537; *Devoys Post Bag*, 537 fn.

Dewar, Donald, 497.

Dewey, Davis Rich (1858–1942), 325.

Dewey, Orville (1794–1882), 107.

Diaries, *see* Travel diaries.

Dick, Charles, 303, 463.

Dickens, Charles (1812–70), 14–15, 247, 457; *American Notes*, 14, 457.

Dickenson, Capt., 254.

Dickins, Asbury, 4.

Dickinson, Anna Elizabeth (1842–1932), 210.

Dickinson, Caleb, 59, 405, 406.

Dickinson, H. W., *Robert Fulton*, 438 fn.

Dickinson, Thomas, 406.

Dickinson, William (1771–1837), 405.

Dickinson, Prankard and, Papers, 405–6.

Dickson, Arthur, 458.

Digby, Henry, 7th Baron and 1st Earl (1731–93), 44.

Digby, Sir John, 1st Earl of Bristol (1580–1653), 6, 44.

Digby, M., *Horace Plunkett*, 255.

DIGBY, S. WINGFIELD, ESQ., 44.

Digby, Wm., 447.

Digby Papers, 44.

Diligence, armed schooner, 11.

Dilke, Sir Charles Wentworth (1843–1911), 165; *Greater Britain: a Record of Travel in English-Speaking Countries . . . 1866–7*, 165.

Dilke Papers, 127, 165.

Dillon, Harold Arthur Lee, 17th Viscount (1844–1932), 400.

Dillon, John (1851–1927), 538.

Dillwyn, William (1743–1824), 120, 482, 483.

Dillwyn Diaries and Papers, 482.

Dilwin, Susana, 406.

Dilworth, Charles, 471.

Dinwiddie, Robert (1693–1770), 436.

DIOCESE OF ABERDEEN AND ORKNEY, 493.

Diplomacy, *see* Relations with (Country) *and names of individual ministers and ambassadors.*

Diplomatic service, 24, 393; Immunities, 154; *see also* Consuls; *and names of individual ambassadors, ministers and consuls.*